The Student Edition of
dBASE IV™

Programmer's Version

Limited Warranty

Addison-Wesley warrants that the magnetic media on which the program is distributed and the documentation are free from defects in materials and workmanship during the period of 90 days from the date of original purchase. Addison-Wesley will replace defective media or documentation or correct substantial program errors at no charge, provided you return the item with dated proof of purchase to Addison-Wesley within 90 days of the date of original purchase. If Addison-Wesley is unable to replace defective media or documentation or correct substantial program errors, your license fee will be refunded. These are your sole remedies for any breach of warranty.

Except as specifically provided above, neither Addison-Wesley nor Ashton-Tate makes any warranty or representation, either express or implied, with respect to this program, documentation, or media, including their quality, performance, merchantability, or fitness for a particular purpose.

Because programs are inherently complex and may not be completely free of errors, you are advised to verify your work. In no event will Addison-Wesley or Ashton-Tate be liable for direct, indirect, special, incidental, or consequential damages arising out of the use of or inability to use the program, documentation, or media, even if advised of the possibility of such damages. Specifically, neither Addison-Wesley nor Ashton-Tate is responsible for any costs including, but not limited to, those incurred as a result of lost profits or revenue (in any case, the program must be used only for educational purposes, as required by your license), loss of use of the computer program, loss of data, the costs of recovering such programs or data, the cost of any substitute program, claims by third parties, or for other similar costs. In no case shall the liability of Addison-Wesley or Ashton-Tate exceed the amount of the license fee.

The warranty and remedies set forth above are exclusive and in lieu of all others, oral or written, express or implied. No Addison-Wesley or Ashton-Tate dealer, distributor, agent, or employee is authorized to make any modification or addition to this warranty.

Some statutes do not allow the exclusion of implied warranties; if any implied warranties are found to exist, they are hereby limited in duration to the 90-day life of the express warranties given above. Some states do not allow the exclusion or limitation of incidental or consequential damages, nor any limitation on how long implied warranties last, so these limitations may not apply to you. This warranty gives you specific legal rights and you may also have other rights which vary from state to state.

To obtain performance of this warranty, return the item with dated proof of purchase within 90 days of the purchase date to: Addison-Wesley Publishing Company, Inc., Educational Software Department, Jacob Way, Reading, MA 01867.

The Student Edition of dBASE IV™
Programmer's Version

Setting the new database standard...*adapted for education*

Robert Krumm

Founder, microComputer Schools, Inc.

Addison-Wesley Publishing Company, Inc.
Benjamin/Cummings Publishing Company, Inc.

Reading, Massachusetts • Menlo Park, California • New York
Don Mills, Ontario • Wokingham, England • Amsterdam • Bonn
Sydney • Singapore • Tokyo • Madrid • San Juan

The Student Edition of dBASE IV, Programmer's Version is published by Addison-Wesley Publishing Company, Inc. and Benjamin/Cummings Publishing Company, Inc. Contributors included:

Alan Jacobs, Executive Editor
Dana Degenhardt, Senior Product Development Manager
Mike Vose and Michelle Neil, Development Editors
Mary Coffey, Senior Software Production Supervisor
Peter Holm, Project Manager
Ann DeLacey, Director of Manufacturing and Inventory Control
Lu Anne Piskadlo, Manufacturing Media Supervisor
Marshall Henrichs, Corporate Art Director
Jean Seal, Cover Designer
Jean Hammond, Text Designer
Modern Graphics, Inc., Compositor

Ashton-Tate, the Ashton-Tate logo, dBASE, dBASE II, dBASE III, and CHART-MASTER are registered trademarks of Ashton-Tate Corporation. dBASE III PLUS, dBASE IV, Framework II, and RapidFile are trademarks of Ashton-Tate Corporation.

Additional trademarks/owner: IBM, PC XT, Personal Computer AT, Personal System/2, PC-DOS/International Business Machines Corporation; Compaq, DESKPRO/Compaq Computer Corporation; Novell, NetWare/Novel, Inc.; 3Com, 3+/3Com Corporation; Lotus, 1-2-3/Lotus Development Corporation; MS-DOS/Microsoft Corporation; Net/One/Ungermann-Bass, Inc.

General notice: Some of the product names used herein have been used for identification purposes only and may be trademarks of their respective companies.

The Student Edition of dBASE IV, Programmer's Version User's Manual
Copyright © 1990, Addison-Wesley Publishing Company, Inc.

It is a violation of copyright law to make a copy of the accompanying software except for backup purposes to guard against accidental loss or damage. Addison-Wesley assumes no responsibility for errors arising from duplication of the original programs.

All rights reserved. No part of this publication may be reproduced, stored in a retrieval system, or transmitted, in any form or by any means, electronic, mechanical, photocopying, recording, or otherwise, without the prior written permission of the publisher. Printed in the United States of America. Published simultaneously in Canada.

0-201-90707-0 (User's Manual)
0-201-50561-4 (Programmer's Manual/bundle version)
0-201-50701-3 (5 1/4" disk format package)
0-201-50702-1 (3 1/2" disk format package)

ABCDEFGHIJK-MU-89

Introduction: The Goal of This Book

Welcome to The Student Edition of dBASE IV, Programmer's Manual.

This book was designed and written for two similar, but not identical, purposes:

1. To teach students how to write computer programs using dBASE IV.
2. To teach students how to write dBASE IV programs.

The difference between the two goals is subtle but significant. The first goal stresses the fundamental skills necessary to develop, write and perfect computer programs. Since a program, like a book, must be written in a specific language, the programs discussed in this book use the dBASE IV programming language as a means of teaching important programming concepts.

The second goal hints at the reason there are many different programming languages in the first place: namely that there are specific features and procedures that make dBASE IV programming different from programming in BASIC, Pascal or even C. This book will help students exploit the richness of the dBASE IV language, which allows even new programming students to create sophisticated looking applications.

The book seeks to teach the concepts and features that dBASE IV has in common with all programming languages as well as the unique flavor of the dBASE IV language. In addition, the last two chapters of this book cover the IBM SAA-compatible Structured Query Language (SQL).

This combination of goals is designed to stimulate the student's imagination about what is possible using a state-of-the-art tool like dBASE IV, while grounding the student in the fundamentals of good programming style.

Do You Need Experience with dBASE?

This book is not a complete guide to dBASE IV. dBASE IV is a computer application and a database manager—used by thousands of people who know nothing about programming—and a computer language used by professional programmers in businesses around the world. This book skips the application side of dBASE IV and concentrates on the programming aspect.

While knowledge about the database management side of dBASE IV (or an earlier dBASE version) is helpful, it is not necessary to use this book. This book contains all of the commands and procedures you will need to write the programs discussed.

Put another way, although this book will not teach you everything about dBASE IV, it is not necessary to know everything about dBASE IV in order to write programs in the dBASE IV language.

Features of this Book

This book includes a variety of features designed to enhance understanding of dBASE IV while minimizing the time it takes to master the material. It is designed to be both a learning aid and a dBASE IV reference. The manual includes the following:

- Detailed installation and loading instructions
- Ten chapters, which include
    - In-depth coverage of a fundamental programming concept, including hands-on, step-by-step instructions for applying that concept to dBASE IV
    - A summary
    - A list of key terms
    - Review questions and practice problems

How the Book Is Organized

This book is organized in a learning sequence. This means that the first chapter begins with the most basic information, procedures, and exercises. Subsequent chapters enlarge and expand upon the concepts presented in the previous chapters. It is not necessary to complete the entire book in order to write dBASE IV programs. Each chapter amplifies and supplements the ideas already presented to illustrate other approaches to solving programming problems and tasks.

Often the same program is written and rewritten several times. Good programs do not spring to life full blown, they evolve from simple programs. Watching a program evolve and take shape, students will begin to develop their own style of programming, based on their own personal preferences but rooted in good programming structure and style.

This book is divided into two parts: the Getting Started section and ten chapters that provide instruction and hands-on application in programming and using dBASE IV.

Getting Started
The Getting Started section provides a list of the contents of this package, installation instructions, and starting and ending instructions for the Student Edition of dBASE IV.

Chapters 1 through 10
Chapter 1 introduces the data management side of dBASE IV. It explains how data files are created and data entered, and how the data manager functions as a stand-alone database program to be used by itself or as a support for programmed applications.

Chapter 2 introduces the most basic level at which programming can be implemented. The programs in this chapter are called linear programs because they are simply lists of dBASE IV commands strung together to create command sequences.

Chapter 3 discusses the idea of creating customized screen displays. The ability to control and manipulate information on the screen is crucial to creating specific applications.

Chapter 4 explains in detail the use of @/SAY/GET commands to create interactive programs. Interactive programs are different from the linear programs students have created so far in that they will pause to allow the user to enter data.

Chapter 5 introduces structured programming techniques. It explains how commands can be grouped together to form a program structure.

Chapter 6 teaches the student how to create and use menus as part of their programs. It also introduces special dBASE IV menu techniques, such as pop-up and bar-type menus.

Chapter 7 discusses how to operate with multiple database files and how to create applications that relate data stored in more than one database. The programs created in this section explore the concepts of workareas, relationships between databases, and the creation of a unified display that draws information from more than one database file.

Chapter 8 explains how dBASE IV programming techniques can be applied to the creation of printed reports. In Chapter 8, the student will create a series of reports, each illustrating a different type of report. Each report type reflects a different type of information processing and require a unique approach.

Chapter 9 teaches the student about database operations under dBASE IV SQL. The concepts developed in earlier chapters are used to explore a different approach to database management—the SQL system.

Chapter 10 describes how to use the SQL database in programs that perform major database operations, such as editing data, retrieving data, and creating reports. It shows how SQL commands can be integrated into programs that display full user interfaces just as the dBASE IV programs did.

Differences Between *The Student Edition* and dBASE IV

The Student Edition of dBASE IV program is identical to dBASE IV release 1.0, including all features and functions. One difference is that the number of records that can be stored in a single database is limited to 120 (and you can have up to 10 files open at one time). A second is that only two printer drivers, a generic that works with most printers and an ASCII, are available with the student version.

The Ultimate Goal of This Book

This book is not meant to be an end in itself. Rather, it is intended to be a starting point from which a student can continue to learn, even if he or she does not intend to become a professional computer programmer or a computer professional. The logical thinking process necessary to understand and construct the applications discussed in this book is a valuable tool in any field of learning.

Rob Krumm
Martinez, CA

Contents

1 Elements of dBASE IV   1

An Application and a Language   2
   Application   2
   Program Language   2
   Why dBASE IV?   3
The Modes of dBASE IV   4
   Assist Mode   4
   Command Mode   5
   Program Mode   5
   Exiting the Assist Mode   5
Database Files   6
   Fields   7
   Records   7
Creating an Example Database File   8
   Field Name   9
   Field Type   10
Building the Database Structure   11
   Date-Type Fields   11
   Numeric Fields   12

Numeric Fields with Decimals   14
Logical Fields   15
Memo Fields   15
Saving the Structure   17
Entering Decimal Numbers   19
Making Logical Field Entries   19
Creating Memo Fields   20
Form and Table Display   22
Filling Out the File   23
   The Extra Record   28
   Removing Records   29
Housekeeping   30
   Clearing the Screen   30
   Listing Information   31
   Expressions   32
   Replacing Data   35
   Printing   35
   Opening and Closing Files   36
   The Record Pointer   37

End of File   39
Listing Memo Fields   39
Copying Files   40

Summary   42
Review Problems for Chapter 1   44
Answers to Exercise Questions   45

2 Linear Programming   47

Deferred Execution   47
  How Instructions Are Deferred   48
  Command Sequence Types   49
  Setup   50
Writing a Simple Program   51
  Modifying a Program   54
  Printer vs. Screen   55
The Parts of dBASE IV Commands   57
  Expressions   58
  Scope   58
  Selecting by Logical Expression   60
  Selecting by Logical Fields   61
  Selecting by Dates   62
  The $ Operator   64
  Case Sensitivity   65
  Multiple Criteria   66

Programs That Use Selection   67
  Filters   68
  Global Field Selection   70
Modular Programming   72
  Subroutines   76
Indexing Records   78
  Descending Index Order   81
  Expressions as Index Keys   82
  Mixing Data Types in Indexes   83
  Selecting Index Tags   84
  Adding Indexes to Programs   86
Summary   87
Review Problems for Chapter 2   90
Answers to Exercises   91

3 Programming Screen Displays   92

Setup   93
Structured vs. Unstructured Displays   93
  Using ? for Output   94
  Unstructured Displays   97
  ? Command Clauses   102
Screen Display Presentations   107
  Repeating a Character   108
  Centering an Item   109
  A Formal Screen Display   110
  Time and Date Functions   112

Placing Items on the Same Line   112
  Literals and Variables   113
Statistical Programs   117
  The CALCULATE Command   118
  Statistics in Progress   119
  Program Editing Techniques   125
Summary   134
Review Problems for Chapter 3   136
Answers to Exercises   136

4 Interactive Programming — 138

Fully Structured Screen Displays   138
   Input Areas   140
   Calculation Programs   143
   Range Limits   144
   Positioning the Cursor   145
   Special Screen Features   148
   Passing Control Parameters   150
   Selecting Defaults   152
   Validity Checks   153
Customized Screen Displays   154
   Format Files   155
   Nonrecord Information   156
   Displaying Fields   157
   PICTURE Clauses   159
   Using a Format File   161
   Logical Fields   163
   Memo Fields   164
   The IIF() Function   165
   Multiple Pages   167
Searching for Records   170
   Searching   173
   Rapid Searches   176
   The SEEK Command   179
Summary   184
Review Problems for Chapter 4   185
Answers to Exercises   186

5 Loops and Branches — 187

Branching Structures   188
   Indenting Commands   190
   Looping the Program   194
   The End of the Loop   198
Adding Records   201
   Transactions and Rollbacks   205
   Batch Processing   210
Implicit Conditions   213
   Exit and Automatic Loops   214
Frequency Distributions   218
   Scanning the Database   219
   A Display Frame   220
   End of File Loop   221
   Moving the Pointer   222
   The SCAN Command   225
Categories with Cases   229
   The DO CASE Structure   231
   Accumulators   234
   Limiting the Display   237
   Counters   241
   Arrays   244
Summary   251
Review Problems for Chapter 5   254
Answers to Exercises   255

6 Menus and Debugging   257

The Standard Menu   258
   Implicit Exit   263
   Menu Modification   264
   A Menu That Runs Menus   265
Debugging a Program   268
   Displaying Values in Debug   270
   Breakpoints   272
   Dot Command Access   275
Private Variables   278
Popup Menus   281

Event Management Commands   286
Non-Option Text in Popup Menus   290
Popups in Programs   293
Special Item Lists   298
A Field Popup   301
Error Trapping   305
Summary   306
Review Problems for Chapter 6   310
Answers to Exercises   310

7 Using Multiple Databases   314

One-to-Many Relationships   314
   New Databases   316
   Opening Multiple Databases   318
   Pointer Independence   322
   Using Data from Open Files   323
   Programming Multiple Databases   326
Procedures and Bar Menus   332
   Using a Menu Bar   334
   Procedures   338
   Executing a Procedure File   339
   Menu Bars and Multi-Database Applications   340

Running a Procedure   348
Retrieving Data from Multiple Databases   349
Programming with Multiple Databases   356
   Programming One-to-Many Relationships   363
   Unique Indexes   363
   Paging the Screen   369
Summary   372
Review Problems for Chapter 7   373
Answers to Exercises   375

8 Reports and Printing   377

Turning the Printer On   378
Printing with @/SAY   381
   Printing Forms   382
   Selecting a Printer   385
   Printing Using @/SAY Commands   387
   Relative Addressing   390
   Preprinted Forms   390

Column Reports   391
   Pagination   395
Programs That Paginate   396
   Reports with Totals   401
   Programs with Subtotals   405
Block Format Reports   418

Setting Page Length 419
Multiple Column Blocks 423
Report from Multiple Databases 428

Summary 438
Review Problems for Chapter 8 440
Answers to Exercises 441

9 SQL 442

Personal vs. Shared Computing 442
   SQL Databases 444
   Object Orientation 444
   Why Use SQL? 445
   Why Use SQL with dBASE IV? 446
Starting an SQL Session 447
   Creating a Database 448
   Tables 449
   Adding Columns to Databases 450
   Data Entry 450
   Loading Information Into a Table 452
   Adding Complete .dbf Files 460
Selecting Information 462
   Select Clauses 465

The WHERE Clause 466
The DISTINCT Clause 470
Grouping Data 470
Updating Information 473
The HAVING Clause 475
Sequencing Output 476
Multiple Table Selections 478
   Subqueries 483
   Ending an SQL Session 485
   Starting an SQL Database 485
Summary 485
Review Problems for Chapter 9 487
Answers to Exercises 488

10 Programming in SQL 489

How dBASE SQL Works 489
   dBASE SQL Files 490
Programs That Use SQL Commands 495
Interactive Programs with SQL
Databases 498
   The INTO Clause 501
   Temporary Tables 505
   SQL Cursors 508

Editing an SQL Row 513
   SQL Codes 521
Reports 527
   Multi-Table Reports 535
Summary 543
Review Problems for Chapter 10 545
Answers to Exercises 545

Index I-1

Getting Started

This chapter will get you started using dBASE IV. First, read Checking Your Package to be sure that you have all the components of the dBASE IV Student Edition. Before you run dBASE IV for the first time, follow the instructions in Installing dBASE IV to store the program on your computer's hard disk. Each time you use dBASE IV, follow the instructions in Starting dBASE IV to run the program. Read the section about Conventions in This Manual to learn about the terms and typefaces used in this book.

Checking Your Package

Your dBASE IV Student Edition should contain the following:

- The User's Manual (this book)
- Nine 5¼-inch or five 3½-inch disks
- Registration Card

Fill out the registration card and return it to Addison-Wesley. The registration information ensures that you will receive any information about updates and enhancements to the Student Edition of dBASE IV.

Product Support

Addison-Wesley provides telephone assistance to instructors who are registered adopters of dBASE IV. To keep the cost of the software as reasonable as possible, neither Addison-Wesley nor Ashton-Tate provides telephone assistance to students. If you have questions, talk to your instructor.

However, a great deal of assistance is built into the dBASE IV package. To help you use dBASE IV, refer to:

Table of Contents. The Table of Contents or the Index will help you find information in the User's Manual. The User's Manual contains chapters about designing a database, maintaining a database, writing queries, creating and using forms, reporting, indexing, creating applications, and writing programs. It also contains a Reference section that includes every command in the dBASE programming language.

Help Screens. The Help screens will assist you on the specific activity you wish to perform. You can call Help by pressing F1 from any part of the program.

If you do ask your instructor for assistance, describe your question or problem in detail. If you tried something that didn't work correctly, write down which steps or procedures you followed, and the error message (if any) you received.

Installing dBASE IV

The Student Edition of dBASE IV includes nine diskettes in 5¼-inch format (or five diskettes in 3½-inch format) that store the software program with all the database files you will use in the tutorials and exercises. Each diskette is numbered on the label. It is a good idea to make back-up copies of your disks before beginning the installation process. In addition, if you need a data disk to store your files, format one now.

The installation procedure creates a subdirectory on the hard disk (C drive) named DBSAMPLE. You must be in this subdirectory to start dBASE IV.

To install dBASE IV on your hard disk, follow these steps.

1 Insert the disk labeled Disk 1 in Drive A.

2 At the C> prompt, type A: and press ⏎. This changes the default drive to A. The A> prompt appears on the screen.

3 At the A> prompt, type INSTALL *Drive: Monitor* (C for color; M for monochrome) and press ⏎. For example, if you are installing dBASE to your C drive and you have a color monitor, you would type

INSTALL C: C ⏎

After a few seconds, the dBASE IV copyright screen appears. Press ⏎ to continue.

4 Follow the directions displayed on the screen to complete the installation.

5 At the end of the installation, **INSTALLATION COMPLETE** will be displayed on the screen.

6 If the A> prompt appears, type C: and press the ⏎ key. This changes the default drive back to C. The C> prompt will appear on the screen.

7 Now copy the data files that you will use in this manual onto your hard disk. **If you have 3½-inch disks,** re-insert Disk 1 into drive A. **If you have 5¼-inch disks,** re-insert Disk 2 into drive A and close the drive door.

8 At the C> prompt, type copy a:*.dbf c:\dbsample⏎. File files will be copied.

9 Now type copy a:*.txt c:\dbsample⏎. One file will be copied.

A generic printer driver, which works with most printers, has been automatically selected as the default printer during installation. If you wish to change the default driver to the ASCII printer driver, see "Changing to the ASCII driver" in the Reference section.

Starting dBASE IV

Follow these steps to start dBASE IV.

1 Turn on your microcomputer if it isn't already on, or reset (reboot) the microcomputer by holding down the Ctrl and Alt keys and pressing the Del key. This resets your microcomputer so it reads the new Config.Sys file created in the installation.

2 At the C> prompt, type `CD DBSAMPLE` and press ⏎. This changes the current directory to the DBSAMPLE subdirectory. This subdirectory holds all the database files you need to use for the tutorials and exercises. You must be in this subdirectory to start dBASE IV.

3 At the prompt, type `DBASE` and press ⏎ to start dBASE IV.

4 The dBASE IV copyright notice will appear on the screen.

The copyright information and the License Agreement describe the ways in which you may use the Student Edition of dBASE IV.

5 To accept the License Agreement, press ⏎. After a moment, dBASE IV will display the Control Center.

The Cursor

The cursor indicates your position on the screen. Sometimes the cursor is a blinking underline, usually when dBASE IV is waiting for you to type characters. Sometimes the cursor is a small rectangle, one character wide. Other times, the cursor marks a larger rectangle on the screen. This wide cursor is sometimes called the highlight.

When dBASE IV first displays the Control Center, the cursor rests on the word <**create**>.

Leaving dBASE IV

To exit from dBASE IV:

1. Press F10.

2. Press → twice, until the cursor rests on the word **Exit** and the **Exit** menu appears.

3. Press ↓, so that the cursor rests on the words **Quit to DOS**.

4. Press ⏎.

Conventions in this Manual

This manual uses the following typographical conventions:

Menu titles, menu options, and references to any other text on the screen appear in boldface type, as in the following example.

■ Getting Started

Choose the **Mark record for deletion option** from the **Records** menu. Near the right corner of the status bar **Del** will appear, indicating that the current record is marked for deletion.

dBASE commands appear in capital letters, as in the following example.

You can use the APPEND, INSERT, BROWSE, EDIT, or CHANGE commands to enter new records in a database.

References to keyboard keys appear in a key cap, as in the following example.

[F6] allows you to select a rectangular area of the screen.

dBASE IV uses some key combinations: two keys pressed together to perform a single function. To press a key combination, you will hold down the first key while pressing the second key, then release both keys. In this manual, key combinations appear as key caps with a hyphen between them, as in the following example.

[Shift]-[F8] allows you to enter data that is identical from one record to the next.

Instructions to type text or enter program lines appear in a different typeface as in the following example.

Type MODIFY COMMAND Admit

When you are asked to *enter* a command, you should press [↵] at the end of the line although the Enter key will not appear at the end of each line. For example, to enter the previous command, you would actually type

MODIFY COMMAND Admit[↵]

Note: The directory shown in the screen illustrations is C:\DB4. You directory will actually be C:\DBSAMPLE.

Command lines that are too long to print on one line are broken by putting a semicolon at the end of the line. The semicolon does not substitute for necessary spaces, however. If a space is necessary, it will be shown by an indent at the beginning of the next line. A long command line might look like this:

? "Total",Alldays PICTURE "999" AT 40, "100.0";
 AT 60

Be sure to press the spacebar at the beginning of the line following a semicolon if one is necessary.

Getting Started ■ xix

Conclusions and Review

In this chapter, you learned how to start dBASE IV, how to get help with dBASE IV, how to use the conventions in this manual, and how to finish a session with dBASE IV and return to DOS. In the next chapter, you will explore several of dBASE IV's features and get your first hands-on experience using dBASE IV.

1 Elements of dBASE IV

This book will teach you how to create programs using the dBASE IV programming language. Many of the concepts and techniques discussed here apply to any programming text, but this book's exact implementation of those techniques applies only to dBASE IV.

The skills and ideas that make a good programmer do not limit you to any one programming language. You can learn those skills by studying programming in general. However, you must eventually select a specific programming environment in which to master those skills.

dBASE IV differs from the traditional programming languages Cobol, Fortran, or even BASIC in many respects. dBASE IV is a computer application as well as a programming language. There are hundreds of thousands of people who use dBASE products every day who have no idea how to write a computer program. Your objective here is to learn how to write computer programs; therefore, there are many everyday dBASE IV operations that you will not learn because they are not related to programming concepts.

Before you begin to create dBASE IV files and programs, let's define some of the terms associated with programming and computer applications.

If you have not already loaded dBASE IV, do so now by typing DBASE and pressing ⏎ at the DBSAMPLE> prompt.

An Application and a Language

dBASE IV has a dual character: it can function both as a computer application and as a programming language.

Application

The term *application* refers to a computer program that solves a specific problem. For example, a computer program designed to help a pharmacist keep track of prescriptions is considered an application because it focuses on problems that are specific to that profession. Someone who knows little about computers or programming can use an application. The application presents the user with lists of options. All the user has to do is pick the desired option or operation.

Program Language

A programming language is used to create computer applications. A language is not dedicated to any one specific use but can be used to create an almost unlimited number of specific applications. Programming languages require an understanding of programming concepts and a working knowledge of the specific commands available in that language.

Where does dBASE IV, as both an application and a language, fit? As an application, dBASE IV is a database manager. A database management program stores and retrieves information. Typical database management tasks include data entry, updating, searching, selecting groups, sequencing by numeric or alphabetical order, and producing summary reports. You can perform all of these activities with dBASE IV without creating any programs. A system of menus called the Control Center makes these operations available.

But dBASE IV can also be used as a programming language. As a programming language, dBASE IV can perform specific tasks by letting a programmer create custom-designed menus and operations not originally supplied within the dBASE IV system.

Programming requires an understanding of concepts that cannot be gathered by simply selecting options from a menu. Writing programs requires the creation of logic structures and the use of variables, loops, and conditionals. These concepts form the core subject matter of this book.

You may wonder why it is necessary to program dBASE IV when it can be used without programming. dBASE IV programming, and programming in general, lets people apply the power of the computer to specific tasks to increase productivity and eliminate mistakes and tedium. While dBASE IV can be used without programming, its features are often too generalized to help people who have not had the time or opportunity to learn about database management. Experience shows that when a computer application is tailored to the very specific needs of the individuals who use it, those users can often operate the computer with much less instruction.

For example, dBASE IV menus address database ideas in terms of records, fields, and files. If you were working in a hospital emergency room, it would make more sense if the menus used familiar phrases like "patients," "doctors," and "treatment." Programmers can shape the basic building blocks provided by dBASE IV into specific applications like an emergency room program.

Why dBASE IV?

Why would you want to program in dBASE IV rather than in a traditional programming language like BASIC or Pascal? Because dBASE IV is a language designed to support database applications using many built-in database functions.

dBASE IV provides the programmer with a tool kit of database management operations that can easily be used for a wide variety of specific applications. Experienced programmers know that while an emergency room and an auto repair shop are very different businesses, record keeping for both is essentially a matter of storing and retrieving data. The dBASE IV tool kit can be applied to almost any record keeping task. Because you begin with the tool kit, you can complete an application in less time than would be required if you had to build all of the tools yourself, as with a traditional programming language.

If dBASE IV is so well-suited to database programming, why are there so many other programming languages? dBASE IV assumes that the programmer wants to create a database management application. While these applications are very common in the business world, there are many other applications that require graphics and other functions not supported by dBASE IV.

dBASE IV creates a special type of program. dBASE IV programs require the computer running the program to have a copy of dBASE IV to interpret the program, similar to the way that the BASIC programming language operates. In contrast, languages like Pascal create programs that operate independently of any interpreter. These applications are referred to as compiled applications.

Note: dBASE IV uses the term *compiled* in a very different sense from that is traditionally used. When dBASE IV compiles a program, it creates a file that is still dependent on dBASE IV.

This book will explain how to use the dBASE IV tool kit to create computer applications that run under the dBASE IV interpreter.

The Modes of dBASE IV

When dBASE IV loads, it automatically displays a series of labeled boxes called the Control Center (see Figure 1.1). This display represents one of the three basic modes of operation in dBASE IV. Those three modes are Assist, Command, and Program.

Assist Mode

Assist mode is the default mode of dBASE IV. It is designed to help users carry out dBASE IV operations by displaying a series of menus from which to select various verbs and objects. dBASE IV refers to the display as the Control Center because you can control a variety of

Figure 1.1

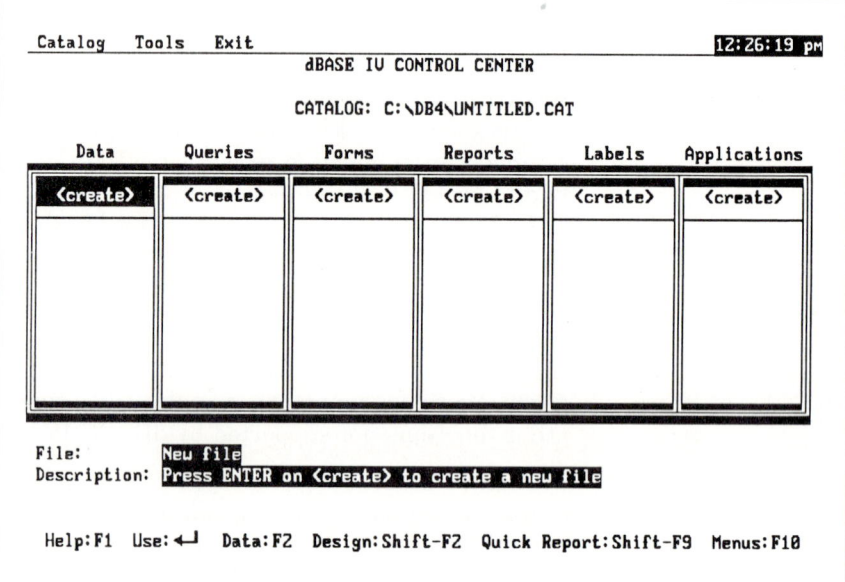

4 ■ Elements of dBASE IV

activities from this master display. While the Assist mode is helpful in carrying out dBASE IV operations, it is not directly related to the task of writing programs with dBASE IV; this book ignores Assist mode operations.

Command Mode

When you exit the Assist mode, dBASE IV changes to the Command mode. When the Command mode is active, menus disappear from the screen, leaving only a time display in the upper right corner. The bottom of the screen displays a single line called the status line. Just above the status line, on the left side of the screen, is a period. This period is called the *dot prompt*. The dot prompt indicates that dBASE IV is ready to receive a command. The commands you can enter are dBASE IV command statements terminated with ⏎. The command mode executes each statement immediately after it has been entered. When execution is complete, dBASE IV returns to the command mode.

Program Mode

When dBASE IV is in the Program mode, the screen display and all other aspects of dBASE IV are controlled by the dBASE IV command statements in the program that is running.

This book requires that you begin all your work at the dot prompt. Since dBASE IV normally enters the Assist mode when it is loaded, you will need to exit the Assist mode to begin working.

Exiting the Assist Mode

If you have just loaded dBASE IV, the initial screen displays the Control Center of the Assist mode. To change to the Command mode, press (Esc).

dBASE IV will display a box in the center of the screen with the message: **Are you sure you want to abandon operation?** This message is a bit confusing because it may not be clear that dBASE IV sees the entire Assist mode as a single operation. The message is really asking you whether you are sure that you want to exit the Assist mode. Type y to clear the screen and display the dot prompt. Should you desire to return to the Assist mode, you can do so in two ways:

1. **Press** (F2). The (F2) function key is programmed, by default, to activate the Assist mode.

2. **Enter ASSIST.** The word "assist" functions as a dBASE IV command verb at the dot prompt. Entering ASSIST and pressing ⏎ will change the mode back to Assist.

The Modes of dBASE IV ■ **5**

Activate the Assist mode by pressing F2.

The Assist mode reappears on the screen. Exit to the dot prompt mode. Try this on your own. If you need help, you can find the correct command at the end of the chapter in the Answers to Exercises section as exercise 1.

Database Files

Most dBASE IV programs work with information stored in database files. Database files contain the raw information that the programs you create will process.

Note: It is possible to write dBASE IV programs that create new database files when you run the program. However, most programs are designed to hide files and their file structure from the person using the program. Later sections of this book illustrate methods for programs to permit users to modify file structures.

In more traditional programming environments such as Pascal and BASIC, programmers must be concerned with the details of creating and maintaining the data in files. dBASE IV automatically handles the many detailed tasks involved in creating, editing, and expanding data files.

In order to create a database file, you must first enter a description of the data that you intend to store. This description is called the structure of the database. dBASE IV files organize data into structures called *fields* and *records*.

Database files store information in an *organized* form. The word organized is emphasized because not all computer programs organize the data they store. Word processing programs store data in blocks of text; the content of a text block is irrelevant.

For a database to operate properly, the data must be stored in such a way that each data item is classified as a specific type of information. For example, you can recognize that Rebecca is a person's name while New York is the name of a place. Your ability to make that distinction is based on your experience. A computer does not have the ability to draw on experience to recognize the meaning of items. Instead, data is not simply entered but entered into a structure that contains information about the classification of each item.

dBASE IV uses a table-like layout to identify the meaning of data. Each column is assigned a field name and each field represents one data item such as a name, a phone number, or a date of birth. Below the field names, each row in the table contains specific information that describes a specific person, place, object, or event. Taken together, all of the fields in the same row, which describe the same person, place, object, or event, make up a record.

Each new addition of data to the fields of the database creates a new record (see Figure 1.2). All of the fields and records together constitute a database file.

Fields

A field stores information about one of the items in your database. A database must have one or more fields. dBASE IV allows you to define up to 255 fields in a single record.

Records

A record consists of one complete set of fields that represent the information stored about a single person, place, object, or event. As you add new records, the size of the database file expands. The Student Edition of dBASE IV allows 120 records in a database file.

The table-like structure of dBASE IV files means that database files have certain properties.

All Fields in All Records

Because dBASE IV files are organized like a large table, all records must contain all fields. For example, if some records require the entry of a middle initial, then all of the records must contain that field whether you enter any data into the field or not. If you do not fill a field with data, dBASE IV will store the field as a series of blank spaces. An empty field and a full field take up the same amount of space in a file stored on a disk.

Figure 1.2

First	Last	City	State	Sex
Rebecca	LaFish	New York	New York	Female
Walter	Morgan	Chicago	Illinois	Male
Rebecca	LaFish	Chicago	Illinois	Female
Morgan	Smith	New York	New York	Female
Walter	Smith	New York	New York	Male
Rebecca	Mathews	Chicago	Illinois	Female
Robert	LaFish	New York	New York	Male

Fixed-Length Fields The table structure of dBASE IV files also implies that the amount of information that can be entered into each field is fixed when the structure of the table is created. This means that when you create a field, you must determine the size of the largest entry that the field will hold. This is not always easy to decide. If you select too small a size, you will not be able to enter all of the data that you want. If you make the size too large, very few entries will fill the field and you will end up storing a large number of blanks, which can slow down the processing of the file. Experience with the data that you will be storing is the best guide to determining the correct field size.

The term *fixed length* does not imply that the field size cannot be changed after it has been created, only that within a given structure all records contain the same amount of space for each field whether it is full or empty. dBASE IV allows you to modify the structure of a file after it has been created.

Creating an Example Database File

dBASE IV can be used to create applications of many different types. In order to tie together all of the techniques, procedures, and programs discussed in this book, you will use a single example database throughout the text. The example describes a record-keeping program for the emergency room of a hospital. In the remaining chapters of this book, you will construct a series of programs that transform the general nature of dBASE IV into a specific hospital emergency room application.

The first step in this project is to create a database file for our hospital system. This file records data about the patients who are admitted to the emergency room, with one record for each patient admitted. The records will contain information about the patient. The file will be called Admit.

In dBASE IV, you create database files with the CREATE command. The command is followed by the name of the file you want to create, in this case Admit. Enter

```
CREATE Admit ↵
```

This command prompts dBASE IV to change the screen display. This new display is used for creating or changing a file's structure (see Figure 1.3).

■ **Elements of dBASE IV**

Figure 1.3

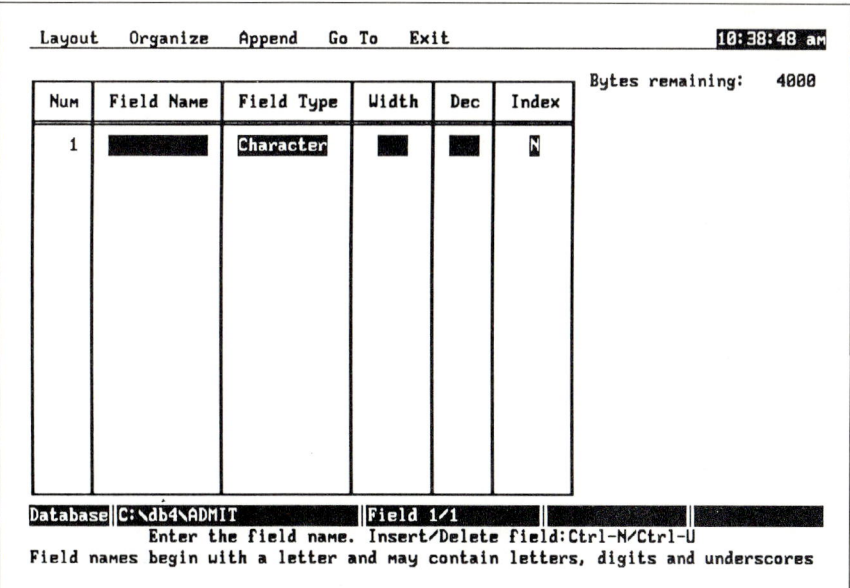

This display allows you to define the fields in the example database. You can enter up to 255 fields. To create a field you must enter the field name and the field type.

Field Name

Field names assign a label, or name, to every data item entered into a field. For example, Address and Zip_Code can be used as field names. Field names are important because they are the labels you use to identify the data items in your database. Field names are limited to 10 characters, including the letters A–Z (upper- and lower-case) and numerals 0–9. You cannot use a space as part of a field name.

Since traditional programming languages allow much longer names for data items, at least 40 characters in some versions of BASIC, the 10-character limit in dBASE IV means that you need to think carefully about the labels you select since you will need to remember what they represent.

To create field names that give the appearance of consisting of more than one word, use an underscore character (_) instead of a space. Suppose you want to create a field to hold information about a CT scan. You could create a field called Ctscan or Ct_scan. The advantage of the name Ct_scan is that it is a bit more readable than

Creating an Example Database File ■ 9

Ctscan. The disadvantage is that typing an underscore requires a shift key on most keyboards.

Field Type

dBASE IV uses five different types of fields in database files: character, number, date, logical, and memo.

1. **Character.** Character fields hold normal text information. They are limited to 255 characters per field.

2. **Number.** dBASE IV uses two types of number fields, one for fixed decimal numbers and one for floating-point decimal numbers.

3. **Date.** Date fields are specialized fields that hold chronological date information.

4. **Logical.** A logical field is one that can contain either a true or false value. This type of field is useful for recording yes/no or true/false information. Logical fields hold a single character.

5. **Memo.** A memo field allows you to enter large amounts of text in paragraph format. Memo fields are different from other field types in that the information entered into the memo is not stored in the same file as the other fields. All the other field information is stored in a file with a .dbf MS-DOS file-extension suffix. Memo information is stored in a .dbt file. dBASE IV automatically links the text in the .dbt file with records and fields in the .dbf file.

    Note: If you want to copy files to a different directory or drive, you must remember that MS-DOS will not automatically copy the .dbt file when you copy the .dbf file. You must make sure that if a .dbt file is associated with a .dbf file, you copy both to the new location. If you forget the .dbt file, dBASE IV will refuse to open the .dbf file.

Width

When you create Character or Number fields, you must enter a value for the width of the field. The field width limits the total number of characters that can be entered into that field. Logical, date, and memo fields are automatically assigned widths of 1, 8, and 10 characters, respectively.

Decimals (shown as DEC on the Create screen)

The Decimals option applies only to number fields and selects the number of decimal places that will be displayed when the field is used for input or output. The number of decimal places, plus one place for the decimal point, must be added to the whole numbers in the field to calculate its total width. For example, if you want to enter numbers

■ Elements of dBASE IV

as large as 99,999.99, the field width should be set at eight: 5 whole numbers + 2 decimals + 1 decimal point = 8.

Index

The Index option is not part of the database file structure but relates to the creation of separate file indexes, stored in files with a .mdx or .ndx extension. An index file stores keys used to sort database files. The purpose of the Index option is to allow you to select index fields when you create the database structure, a convenience but not a necessity. Index files can be created at any time following the creation of the file. Because this book focuses on dBASE IV programming, you will learn how to create indexes later.

Building the Database Structure

The first three fields of our example database record the name of the patient. Let's start building this database's structure. Type

Last ⏎⏎

20 ⏎⏎

Because you specified a character field, dBASE IV skipped the decimal column. You may have found it interesting to observe that dBASE IV automatically set the field type to character. The width is always set to match the width of a previous field, if any.

Now enter the fields for first name and middle initial.

First ⏎⏎

20 ⏎⏎

Middle ⏎⏎

1 ⏎⏎

Your screen should look like Figure 1.4.

Date-Type Fields

Up to this point, the fields in our example have all been character fields. The next two items are date fields and will record the admission and discharge dates for the patient. Type admit and press ⏎.

To make this field a date field, you must change the field type from character to date. This can be done in two ways.

1. **Space bar.** If you press the space bar while the cursor is in the Field Type column, dBASE IV will change the field type. Each press of

Figure 1.4

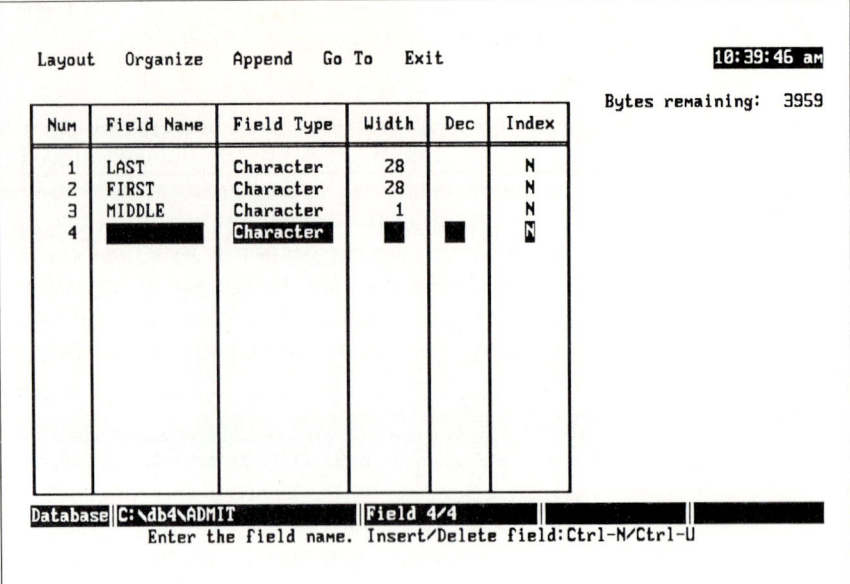

the space bar scrolls the cursor through the types from character, to numeric, to floating-point, to date, to logical, to memo, and then back to character.

2. **Type letter.** You can also obtain the exact type of field you desire by entering the first letter of the type: c for character, n for numeric, f for floating-point, d for date, l for logical, and m for memo.

Next, type d and press ⏎.

dBASE IV will automatically set the width of date fields to eight characters. Dates in dBASE IV are entered in a month, day, year (mm/dd/yy) format.

Create the Discharge date field. Type

Discharge ⏎ d ⏎

Numeric Fields

Numeric fields contain values that can be used in calculations. Items referred to as phone numbers and social security numbers are really character sequences that are composed of number characters. It would not be correct to enter 999-9999 into a numeric field. In fact, if you enter 999-9999 into a numeric field, dBASE IV will display "−9000," the result of subtracting 9,999 from 999.

12 ■ Elements of dBASE IV

dBASE IV uses two kinds of numeric-type fields, numeric and floating point.

Numeric

Numeric values in dBASE IV are those that always have a fixed number of decimal places. In most business applications, you would use numbers with two decimal places to represent monetary values.

Floating-Point

Floating-point numbers are used for applications that use numbers in calculations involving complex mathematical operations. These operations, which usually require more precision than calculations involving dollar values, are typically used in scientific and engineering applications.

The difference between the two types of values is not easy to grasp because, from the user's point of view, they appear to be the same. The difference between the types involves the internal method by which dBASE IV stores the numbers.

> *Note:* The difference between fixed decimal and floating-point decimal numbers can be understood when you consider that all computers must convert decimal numbers into binary representation when they are stored. (Decimal notation uses a base of 10 for number representation, and binary notation uses a base of 2.) The numbers are then converted back to decimal when they are retrieved. This process of binary-to-decimal and decimal-to-binary conversion can create small changes in the value of numbers, particularly the very large or very small numbers used in scientific calculations. These small errors are usually not individually significant. However, they can add up and create aggregate errors. Typically, two numbers that appear to have the same value on the screen will be viewed internally as not equal by the computer. This is due to a rounding problem not visible on the screen display. To avoid this problem, you should usually select numeric-type fields for numbers in business applications where addition or subtraction is the most common kind of calculation. However, if you are doing scientific-type applications, floating-point numbers will provide greater precision when working with numbers with several decimal places.

The first numeric field in our example database is the age of the patient. This numeric field will not require decimal places because age is always recorded as a whole number value.

Building the Database Structure

Type

Age ⏎

n

3 ⏎

⏎⏎

The next two fields are Phone, a character field that is nine characters wide, and Sex, a one-character field. Set these up on your own. If you need help, the correct commands can be found at the end of the chapter in the Answers to Exercises section as exercise 2.

Numeric Fields with Decimals

The next two fields store information about the length of a patient's stay in the hospital. You will need to record the number of days the patients were in the hospital as well as the number of days, if any, they were in the intensive care unit (the ICU, in hospital jargon). In this case, two decimal places are required in order to record quarter, half, and three-quarter days. When you instruct dBASE IV to add decimal places to a numeric field, you must consider that the overall width of the field should be at least one character larger (for the decimal point) than the number of decimal places. Here, you will assume that no patient will stay more than 999 days. Thus, the largest number that could be entered is 999.99. The total width of the field is six: 3 whole numbers + 2 decimal places + the decimal point = 6. Type

Days_stay ⏎

n

6 ⏎

2 ⏎

⏎

Now, enter the ICU stay field.

Days_icu ⏎

n

6 ⏎

2 ⏎⏎

14 ■ **Elements of dBASE IV**

Logical Fields

The next field in the example database records whether or not the patient has medical insurance. Because the answer to this question requires either Yes or No, use a logical field for this information. You can also use a one-character field for this purpose. However, logical fields have three advantages over single-character fields. First, a logical field will not accept any value other than t, f, y, or n. This means you cannot accidentally enter some other character. Second, the logical field will process faster than a character field of the same size. Last, testing the veracity of a logical field is simpler than testing a character field, an operation that requires a compare-and-match function.

Create a logical field called Insured, by entering

```
insured ⏎
l (the letter ell)
```

Because the size of a logical field is automatically set at one character, dBASE IV skips the cursor to the next line after you enter l.

The table below shows the next five fields that you need to enter into the example's file structure. Try this on your own. If you need help, the correct commands can be found at the end of the chapter in the Answers to Exercises section as exercise 3.

Name	Type	Width
Payor	character	25
Anesthesia	logical	
Truma_team	logical	
Ct_scan	logical	
Charges	numeric	10, 2 decimals

The screen shown in Figure 1.5 lists the 16 fields defined so far.

Memo Fields

The last field in the Admit database, a memo field, stores large text entries in paragraph form. Memo fields are special because they are treated very differently from other field types.

The information stored in a memo field is not stored in the same database file as the other information, but in a file with a .dbt (database text) extension. Since the memo field is not a fixed-length field, its very nature makes this separate storage necessary. The number of characters entered in a memo field vary with each memo entered.

Building the Database Structure ■ 15

Figure 1.5

Num	Field Name	Field Type	Width	Dec	Index
2	FIRST	Character	20		N
3	MIDDLE	Character	1		N
4	ADMIT	Date	8		N
5	DISCHARGE	Date	8		N
6	AGE	Numeric	3	0	N
7	PHONE	Character	9		N
8	SEX	Character	1		N
9	DAYS_STAY	Numeric	6	2	N
10	DAYS_ICU	Numeric	6	2	N
11	INSURED	Logical	1		N
12	PAYOR	Character	25		N
13	ANESTHESIA	Logical	1		N
14	TRUMA_TEAM	Logical	1		N
15	CT_SCAN	Logical	1		N
16	CHARGES	Numeric	10	2	N
17		Character	10	2	N

Database C:\db4\ADMIT Field 17/17
Enter the field name. Insert/Delete field:Ctrl-N/Ctrl-U
Field names begin with a letter and may contain letters, digits and underscores

Bytes remaining: 3879

Therefore, the fixed-length method normally used by dBASE IV is not applicable to memo information. Instead, dBASE IV creates a separate file to hold these variable-length memos.

The memo file and the database file are linked by a key. It is this key that is stored in the database file. dBASE IV reserves 10 characters for the memo field key.

The memo field appears in dBASE IV screen displays as a four-character item that reads "memo." In order to enter data into a memo field, you must enter the command sequence Ctrl-Home while in the memo field. This instruction prompts dBASE IV to load the dBASE IV text editor. This full screen display places you in a word processing mode where you can enter up to 65,536 characters of text. Entering Ctrl-End saves the text in a .dbt file.

dBASE IV provides a way to allow data entered into a memo field to be extracted by a dBASE IV program.

Note: This is a change from dBASE III, where data stored in memo fields is not accessible to programs.

Elements of dBASE IV

To create the memo field, enter

Remarks [↵]

m

Once again, dBASE IV will automatically enter the field length and move on to the next field.

Saving the Structure

Once you have entered the fields that make up the structure of the file, you are ready to save the structure. If you look in the upper right corner of the screen, just below the clock display, you will see **Bytes Remaining: 3869.**

> *Note:* A byte is the unit of computer storage needed to hold one character.

dBASE IV limits the total number of characters in a single database file to 4,000. As you enter fields, their length is subtracted from 4,000 and the remainder posted to remind you of the file structure limit. Our current structure uses 131—or 4,000 – 3,869—characters.

To save the file, press [Ctrl]-[End].

dBASE IV will display the message **Input data records now? (Y/N)** in the message area just below the status line. Let's put some real data into this database. Enter some sample records into the file.

First, type

y

dBASE IV will automatically enter the Append/Edit/Browse mode (see Figure 1.6).

dBASE IV displays a screen layout with the names of the fields listed down the left side of the display. Next to each field name, a highlighted area called the input area is displayed. The size of each area corresponds to the width specified in the file structure. The cursor is positioned in the first field.

You will also notice that the specialized fields—numeric, date, logical, and memo—have characters already inserted in them. The numeric fields show the location of the decimal point. The date fields have slash (/) characters to mark off the month, day, and year. The memo field displays the word "memo."

Building the Database Structure ■ 17

Figure 1.6

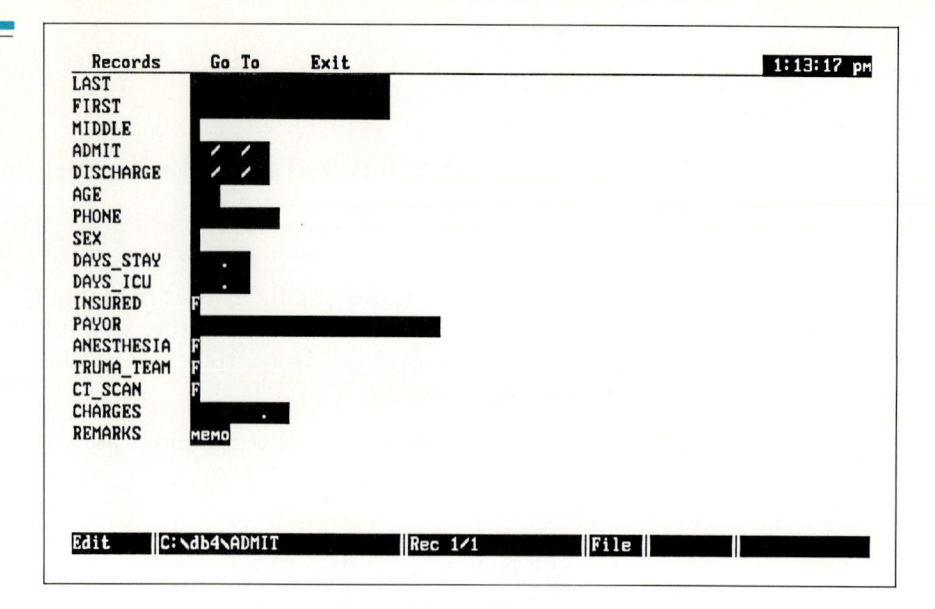

```
   Records    Go To      Exit                              1:13:17 pm
LAST
FIRST
MIDDLE
ADMIT           / /
DISCHARGE       / /
AGE
PHONE
SEX
DAYS_STAY          .
DAYS_ICU           .
INSURED       F
PAYOR
ANESTHESIA    F
TRUMA_TEAM    F
CT_SCAN       F
CHARGES            .
REMARKS       MEMO


 Edit    C:\db4\ADMIT         Rec 1/1       File
```

Enter the name of the first patient.

LaFish ⏎

Walter ⏎

Q ⏎

Notice that the cursor automatically advances when you fill a single-character field. dBASE IV always advances the cursor to the next field when you fill up an entire field. In the case of date entries, dBASE IV jumps over the slash (/) marks. You must enter two digits for the month and the day and the year. Enter an admit date:

110188

dBASE IV checks for date validity. Enter a discharge date:

130188

The program will beep and displays the message **Invalid date, (press SPACE)** at the bottom of the screen. This date checking is automatic whenever you enter data into a date field. Press (Spacebar) and enter a valid date:

110588

The next field is a numeric entry for age. Type 36 then press ⏎.

■ **Elements of dBASE IV**

Because age is a numeric field, dBASE IV aligns the value, 36, on the right side of the field. Now, enter the phone number and gender data:

`943-1200` ⏎

`m`

Entering Decimal Numbers

The next item is a decimal number. Enter

`5.` ⏎ (note the period after the number)

dBASE IV automatically positions the cursor when you enter the decimal point in a numeric field. Complete the number by typing 5 and pressing ⏎.

Skip the next field by pressing ⏎.

Making Logical Field Entries

The next field, Insured, is a logical type field. This field only allows the letters t or y for a true (yes) value or f or n for a false (no) value. Type

`x`

The program beeps as a warning that the letter "x " is not a valid entry. Type

`y`

The program will convert the y to a T.

> *Note:* If you want to display the value in a logical field as Y or N, you must create a customized screen display. This type of programming is discussed in Chapter 3.

Type the name of the insurer.

`Blue Cross` ⏎

The next three items can be left as false. Type f (three times).

Enter the amount of the charges for this patient. Enter

`95` ⏎

The program assumes that 95 is a whole number and automatically adds two zeros for the unused decimal places.

Building the Database Structure

Creating Memo Fields

The memo field records text information in a free-form, word-processing environment. When the cursor is positioned in a memo field, you can enter the text entry mode by entering Ctrl-Home.

Enter Ctrl-Home.

dBASE IV changes to a full-screen, text-editing display (see Figure 1.7). As mentioned earlier, you can enter up to 65,536 characters. Keep in mind that blank spaces and ⏎ also take up character space.

Enter the following text as a memo:

Injury: ⏎ Laceration of the lower right arm. ⏎

To save this memo, press Ctrl-End.

The first record in the example database is now complete (see Figure 1.8).

The following table displays a summary of the editing keys available during the data entry process.

Key	Action
← or →	Move cursor to next field
PgUp	Display previous record
PgDn	Display next record
Home	Move cursor to beginning of field
End	Move cursor to end of field
Backspace	Delete previous character
Tab	Move cursor to next field
Shift-Tab	Move cursor to previous field
⏎	Move cursor to next field
Esc	Terminate without saving
Del	Delete current selection
Ins	Toggle between Insert/Typeover
Ctrl-→	Move one word to right
Ctrl-←	Move one word to left
Ctrl-PgDn	Move to last record
Ctrl-PgUp	Move to first record
Ctrl-Home	Open a memo field
Ctrl-End	Exit memo field or save records
Ctrl-t	Delete word right
Ctrl-y	Delete to end of field
F1	Display Help

■ **Elements of dBASE IV**

Figure 1.7

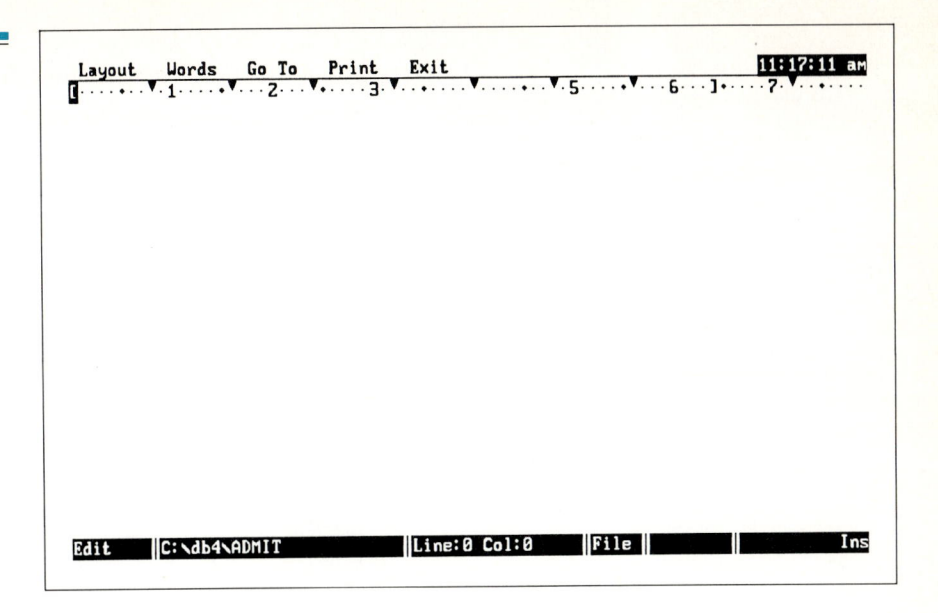

Figure 1.8

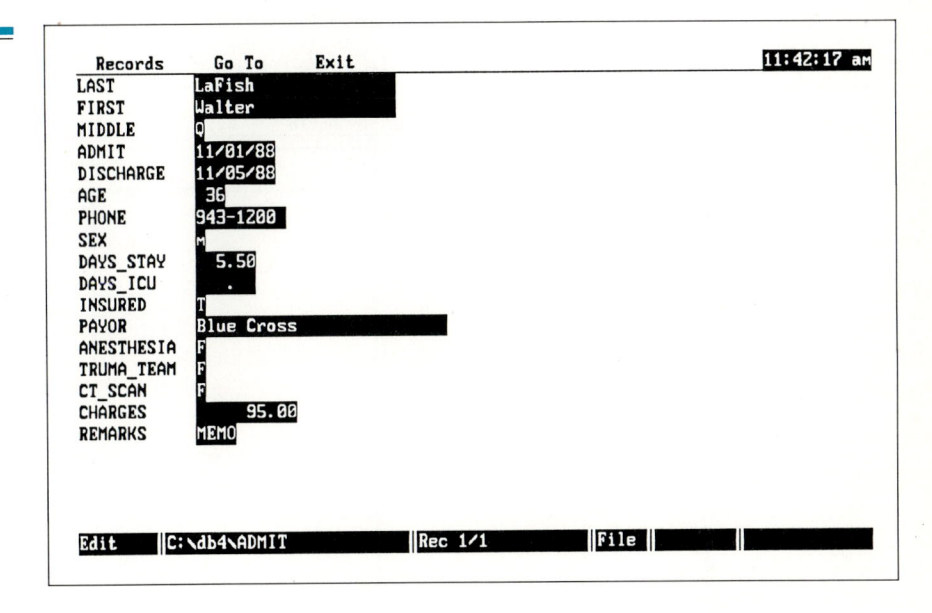

Building the Database Structure ■ 21

Key	Action
F2	Toggle between Browse/Edit
F3	Move to previous field; open a memo field
F4	Move to next field; open a memo field
F9	Open a memo field
F10	Access menu bar
Shift-F8	Copy corresponding field in previous record

Form and Table Display

dBASE IV can display records two ways. The current display is the forms view of the first record. You can change the display to a table view (see Figure 1.9) by pressing F2.

In this view, each record becomes a row in the display and each field becomes a column. The advantage of this display is that you can view more than one record at a time. The disadvantage is that not all of the fields can fit onto the screen at one time. To move to the end of the record, press End.

dBASE IV will scroll the screen display horizontally to display the remaining fields in the record.

To return to the forms view, press F2.

Figure 1.9

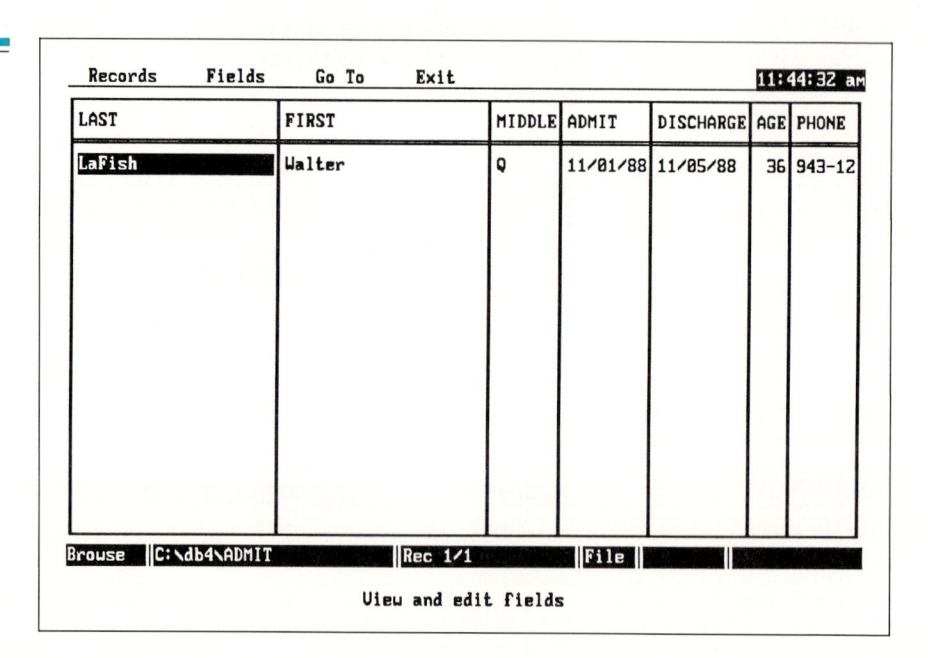

```
 Records     Fields     Go To     Exit                    11:44:32 am
┌──────────────┬──────────────┬──────┬──────┬─────────┬───┬──────┐
│LAST          │FIRST         │MIDDLE│ADMIT │DISCHARGE│AGE│PHONE │
├──────────────┼──────────────┼──────┼──────┼─────────┼───┼──────┤
│LaFish        │Walter        │Q     │11/01/88│11/05/88│ 36│943-12│
│              │              │      │      │         │   │      │
└──────────────┴──────────────┴──────┴──────┴─────────┴───┴──────┘
 Browse  C:\db4\ADMIT              Rec 1/1         File
                        View and edit fields
```

■ Elements of dBASE IV

Filling Out the File

The data entry mode is an automatic function of the built-in database manager provided with dBASE IV. For user-written programs, you will take advantage of the commands provided in the dBASE IV language to create your own version of the Append/Edit/Browse display. For now, use the built-in dBASE IV facility to enter a series of records. These records will form the core of the Admit database.

It is always a tedious task to enter data, but it is necessary before you can begin to create dBASE IV programs. While data entry is a mundane task, it is this data that allows you to test your programs and watch how they operate. Never forget that good test data is essential to writing and debugging programs. In this book, the amount of data entry is kept to the minimum required to teach the concepts of dBASE IV programming.

Add the following nine records to the Admit database file. When you are finished, you can save the records with (Ctrl)-(End). dBASE IV will then redisplay the dot prompt.

When the record appending mode is active, dBASE IV automatically displays a new record when you press (↵) in the last field, or if you press (PgDn). However, there is a small difference in how dBASE IV's built-in Append/Edit/Browse function operates when you move back to look at a previous record. For example, suppose you are in record 2 and you want to look at something in record 1. Pressing (PgUp) will display the previous record. Pressing (PgDn) will return you to record 2. But because you have moved backwards, dBASE IV will change to the edit mode. The edit mode is different from the append mode in one subtle detail. If you were to move to the next record, a new record 3, by pressing (PgDn), dBASE IV would not automatically display a new blank record. Rather, it would display the message

= = = > **Add new records? (Y/N)**

at the bottom of the screen. If you enter Y, then you reenter the append mode and can enter new records.

Enter the data:

Record #2
LAST   Tate
FIRST   Harold
MIDDLE
ADMIT   11/09/88
DISCHARGE   11/09/88

AGE	42
PHONE	945-9383
SEX	m
DAYS_STAY	0.00
DAYS_ICU	0.00
INSURED	F
PAYOR	
ANESTHESIA	T
TRUMA_TEAM	T
CT_SCAN	T
CHARGES	18,294.00
REMARKS:	Injury:
	Burns on hands and arms

Record #3

LAST	Ivanovic
FIRST	Frank
MIDDLE	
ADMIT	11/12/88
DISCHARGE	11/13/88
AGE	27
PHONE	345-9823
SEX	m
DAYS_STAY	0.00
DAYS_ICU	0.00
INSURED	F
PAYOR	
ANESTHESIA	F
TRUMA_TEAM	T
CT_SCAN	F
CHARGES	27,445.00
REMARKS:	Injury
	Broken Leg

Record #4

LAST	Lutz
FIRST	Carol

MIDDLE	L
ADMIT	11/10/88
DISCHARGE	11/13/88
AGE	43
PHONE	432-5555
SEX	f
DAYS_STAY	0.00
DAYS_ICU	0.00
INSURED	T
PAYOR	Mutual of Omaha
ANESTHESIA	F
TRUMA_TEAM	F
CT_SCAN	F
CHARGES	11,103.00
REMARKS:	none

Record #5

LAST	Anderson
FIRST	Ken
MIDDLE	
ADMIT	11/13/88
DISCHARGE	11/17/88
AGE	0
PHONE	444-5555
SEX	m
DAYS_STAY	0.00
DAYS_ICU	0.00
INSURED	T
PAYOR	Glaziers & Glass
ANESTHESIA	T
TRUMA_TEAM	F
CT_SCAN	T
CHARGES	7,324.00
REMARKS:	none

Record #6
LAST	Westrup
FIRST	Milton
MIDDLE	
ADMIT	11/14/88
DISCHARGE	11/15/88
AGE	20
PHONE	555-6666
SEX	m
DAYS_STAY	0.00
DAYS_ICU	0.00
INSURED	T
PAYOR	National
ANESTHESIA	F
TRUMA_TEAM	T
CT_SCAN	F
CHARGES	3,325.00
REMARKS:	none

Record #7
LAST	Jones
FIRST	Timothy
MIDDLE	R
ADMIT	11/20/88
DISCHARGE	11/22/88
AGE	22
PHONE	666-7777
SEX	m
DAYS_STAY	0.00
DAYS_ICU	0.00
INSURED	F
PAYOR	Progressive Casualty
ANESTHESIA	F
TRUMA_TEAM	F
CT_SCAN	F
CHARGES	2,842.00
REMARKS:	none

Record #8

LAST	Morgan
FIRST	Robert
MIDDLE	
ADMIT	11/21/88
DISCHARGE	11/24/88
AGE	17
PHONE	777-8888
SEX	m
DAYS_STAY	0.00
DAYS_ICU	0.00
INSURED	T
PAYOR	Blue Shield
ANESTHESIA	T
TRUMA_TEAM	T
CT_SCAN	T
CHARGES	5,875.00
REMARKS:	none

Record #9

LAST	Mcdowell
FIRST	Angelia
MIDDLE	M
ADMIT	11/14/88
DISCHARGE	11/20/88
AGE	20
PHONE	999-0000
SEX	f
DAYS_STAY	0.00
DAYS_ICU	0.00
INSURED	F
PAYOR	
ANESTHESIA	T
TRUMA_TEAM	T
CT_SCAN	F

CHARGES	3,093.00
REMARKS:	none

Record #10

LAST	Eckardt
FIRST	Lois
MIDDLE	
ADMIT	11/24/88
DISCHARGE	12/03/88
AGE	49
PHONE	100-2222
SEX	f
DAYS_STAY	0.00
DAYS_ICU	0.00
INSURED	T
PAYOR	Blue Cross
ANESTHESIA	T
TRUMA_TEAM	F
CT_SCAN	T
CHARGES	3,929.00
REMARKS:	none

Remember to enter Ctrl-End after completing the 10th record to save the database file and return to the dot prompt.

The Extra Record

When you enter records in the dBASE IV Append/Edit/Browse mode, it is very easy to enter an extra blank record accidentally. This will happen if you have a blank record displayed on the screen when you enter Ctrl-End. In the the data entry exercise you just finished, for example, it is easy to complete the last record, 10, and then go on to display the blank screen for record 11. If this happens and you enter Ctrl-End with record 11 displayed, you will have saved a blank record at the end of the file.

You can check the number of records in three ways.

The status bar at the bottom of the screen shows the number of records. If your status bar shows **EOF/10**, you have the correct number, 10 records. If the bar shows **EOF/11**, then you have accidentally added a blank record. (EOF means "end of file"; more on this later.)

The second way to count the number of records in a database is to have dBASE IV calculate them. The COUNT command performs this operation. Enter

COUNT

dBASE IV displays either 10 records or 11 records, depending upon how you saved your file.

The third method of counting numbers of records is to display the value of a special system function, RECCOUNT()—record count. This function displays the total number of records in the active file. Enter

? RECCOUNT( )

(? is the dBASE IV print command.)

This time, dBASE IV displays a number, 10 or 11, corresponding to the number of records in the current file. If you have 11 records, you will want to remove the empty record from your file.

Removing Records

dBASE IV divides the process of removing data from a file into two parts.

Mark Records

The first step is to mark the record or records that you want to delete. This process does not actually remove or destroy any data. Rather it places a special mark at the beginning of each record selected for deletion. dBASE IV automatically adds an extra character to each record for this mark. You can turn on the mark with the DELETE command or remove the mark with the RECALL command. Neither command actually changes the data in the file.

If you look at the total number of characters in the file, you see that dBASE IV now lists 132. But if you add up the actual width values, you arrive at 131. What is the extra character for? The answer is that the 132nd character is automatically added by dBASE IV. This character contains the delete mark if you select to delete a record. For that reason dBASE IV always lists a file structure size that is one character larger than the total of all the field widths.

Pack File

The data in the file changes when you use the PACK command. PACK rewrites the contents of the file. While the file is being rewritten, any records marked as deleted will be eliminated. The packed file contains only the undeleted records. Once a pack has been performed, you cannot recover the deleted records.

Filling Out the File ■ 29

If you have entered an extra record, you can delete it by entering

```
DELETE RECORD 11
```

This command marks that record for deletion. To actually remove the record, enter

```
PACK
```

dBASE IV confirms the packing process by displaying **10 records copied.**

The two-step deletion process has several advantages. First, it provides you with a chance to change your mind about deletions before they become final. This process also means that dBASE IV does not spend time compressing the file each time a record is marked for deletion. You can make a number of deletions without having to wait each time for the file to be compressed.

You can infer from the message **10 records copied** that dBASE IV views packing as a special form of copying, in which deleted records are removed.

The packing process affects the numbers of individual records. For example, if you had deleted record 5, all of the records in the file after record 5 would be moved up one. You can conclude that using the actual record number as a reference point in the file is not a good idea since those numbers may be altered when records are deleted.

Housekeeping

Now that you have created a database, you have the sample data to test your dBASE IV programs. However, you will probably want to perform some basic operations in the dBASE IV database manager like listing information, printing lists, opening files, closing files, and copying files. These tasks are referred to as housekeeping tasks.

Clearing the Screeen

As you enter various dBASE IV commands, the screen will begin to get cluttered with information. You can clear the screen display by entering

```
CLEAR
```

Listing Information

dBASE IV is capable of printing formal reports with headers, footers, and summary data. However, in the course of developing applications with the dBASE IV programming language, you will find a need to display or print lists of information. These lists are not highly formatted reports but information dumps. The term "dumps" implies that the information is not formatted into pages or columns but is displayed more or less as it is stored in the database file.

The simplest example of this type of list is a full listing of the database. Enter

LIST

dBASE IV will dump all of the information contained in the database onto the screen. You will notice that because each record contains more information than can fit across the screen, the records are wrapped into three lines (see Figure 1.10).

The logical fields display special symbols: .T. and .F. This is done to help you tell the difference between a logical true or false and the letters T and F in a character field. The memo fields do not display their contents, only the word memo.

Figure 1.10

```
      432-5555  f                          .T.    Mutual of Omaha              .F.         .
 F.         .F.       11103.00 memo
        5  Anderson                Ken                    11/13/88 11/17/88    0
      444-5555  m                          .T.    Glaziers & Glass             .T.         .
 F.         .T.        7324.00 memo
        6  Westrup                 Milton                 11/14/88 11/15/88   20
      555-6666  m                          .T.    National                     .F.         .
 T.         .F.        3325.00 memo
        7  Jones                   Timothy        R       11/20/88 11/20/88   22
      666-7777  m                          .F.    Progressive Casualty         .F.         .
 F.         .F.        2842.00 memo
        8  Morgan                  Robert                 11/21/88 11/24/88   17
      777-8888  m                          .T.    Blue Shield                  .T.         .
 T.         .T.        5875.00 memo
        9  Mcdowell                Angelia        M       11/14/88 11/20/88   20
      999-0000  f                          .F.                                 .T.         .
 T.         .F.        3093.00 memo
       10  Eckardt                 Lois                   11/24/88 12/03/88   49
      100-2222  f                          .T.    Blue Cross                   .T.         .
 F.         .T.        3929.00 memo
.
 Command  C:\db4\ADMIT              Rec EOF/10       File
```

Housekeeping ∎ 31

You can limit the number of fields displayed by following the list command with a list of fields. For example, suppose you want to list first name, last name, and phone numbers only. Enter

LIST First,Last,Phone

Because you have limited the amount of output from each record, the list appears more organized (see Figure 1.11).

In addition to listing the contents of the file, you might want to list the details of the file structure. Enter

LIST STRUCTURE

dBASE IV displays a summary of the information entered into the file structure (see Figure 1.12).

Suppose you want to list the last name, the days spent in the hospital, and the charges. You would need a LIST command that selects just those fields. Try this on your own. If you need help, the correct commands can be found at the end of the chapter in the Answers to Exercises section as exercise 4.

Expressions

You may have noticed that only the first record contains a value for numbers of days in the hospital. You were not asked to enter that

Figure 1.11

```
T.         .T.        5875.00 memo
      9 Mcdowell              Angelia              M      11/14/88 11/20/88   20
999-0000  f                      .F.                                    .T.      .
T.         .F.        3093.00 memo
     10 Eckardt               Lois                        11/24/88 12/03/88   49
100-2222  f                      .T.       Blue Cross                   .T.      .
F.         .T.        3929.00 memo

. list first,last,phone
Record#  first              last                 phone
     1   Walter             LaFish               943-1200
     2   Harold             Tate                 945-9383
     3   Frank              Ivanovic             345-9823
     4   Carol              Lutz                 432-5555
     5   Ken                Anderson             444-5555
     6   Milton             Westrup              555-6666
     7   Timothy            Jones                666-7777
     8   Robert             Morgan               777-8888
     9   Angelia            Mcdowell             999-0000
    10   Lois               Eckardt              100-2222

.
Command  C:\db4\ADMIT                 Rec EOF/10        File
```

32 ■ Elements of dBASE IV

Figure 1.12

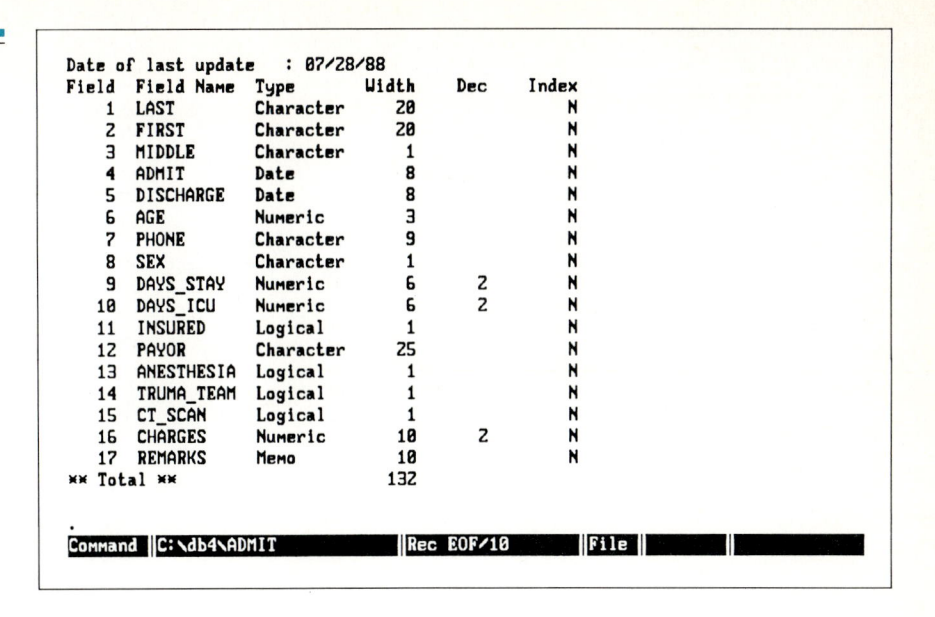

```
Date of last update   : 07/28/88
Field  Field Name  Type        Width   Dec   Index
    1  LAST        Character      20                N
    2  FIRST       Character      20                N
    3  MIDDLE      Character       1                N
    4  ADMIT       Date            8                N
    5  DISCHARGE   Date            8                N
    6  AGE         Numeric         3                N
    7  PHONE       Character       9                N
    8  SEX         Character       1                N
    9  DAYS_STAY   Numeric         6      2         N
   10  DAYS_ICU    Numeric         6      2         N
   11  INSURED     Logical         1                N
   12  PAYOR       Character      25                N
   13  ANESTHESIA  Logical         1                N
   14  TRUMA_TEAM  Logical         1                N
   15  CT_SCAN     Logical         1                N
   16  CHARGES     Numeric        10      2         N
   17  REMARKS     Memo           10                N
** Total **                      132

Command  C:\db4\ADMIT         Rec EOF/10      File
```

value when you entered record data because you can calculate the number of days in the hospital using the Admit and Discharge dates.

dBASE IV performs arithmetic operations, such as addition and subtraction, with date fields. The LIST command can display the number of days difference between the Admit date and the Discharge date. Enter

`LIST Admit,Discharge,Discharge-Admit`

dBASE IV will list the difference in days between the two dates (see Figure 1.13).

The LIST command can accept two types of instructions:

Field name. When you enter a field name after the LIST command, dBASE IV lists all of the data entered into that field. Fields retrieve the actual data stored in the database file.

Expression. An expression is a statement that expresses a logical relationship between fields. In the example above, dBASE IV recognizes the minus sign as a calculation using two dates. The program calculates the difference and then lists the results for each record in the database.

Expressions play an extremely important part in the dBASE IV command structure because they allow you to generate new information

Housekeeping ■ 33

Figure 1.13

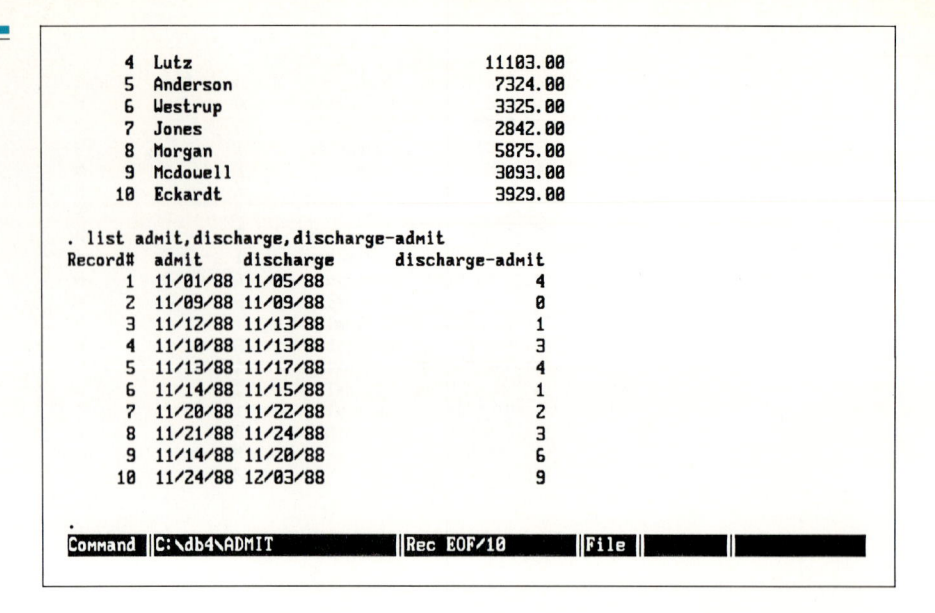

```
     4  Lutz                      11103.00
     5  Anderson                   7324.00
     6  Westrup                    3325.00
     7  Jones                      2842.00
     8  Morgan                     5875.00
     9  Mcdowell                   3093.00
    10  Eckardt                    3929.00

. list admit,discharge,discharge-admit
Record#  admit    discharge   discharge-admit
     1  11/01/88 11/05/88            4
     2  11/09/88 11/09/88            0
     3  11/12/88 11/13/88            1
     4  11/10/88 11/13/88            3
     5  11/13/88 11/17/88            4
     6  11/14/88 11/15/88            1
     7  11/20/88 11/22/88            2
     8  11/21/88 11/24/88            3
     9  11/14/88 11/20/88            6
    10  11/24/88 12/03/88            9
.
Command  |C:\db4\ADMIT         |Rec EOF/10    |File|
```

not entered into the database. As you learn more about the dBASE IV command language, you will be able to construct more sophisticated and complex expressions.

In the command above, dBASE IV calculated the difference between the dates, namely, the difference between 11/01/88 and 11/05/88 = 4 days. However, in practical terms you want to include the beginning date as one of the days in the hospital. Thus, the total number of days in the hospital is Discharge − Admit + 1.

dBASE IV allows you to revise a command previously entered and then run the revised command. Although you cannot see it on the screen, dBASE IV retains the last 20 commands entered in a buffer in the computer's memory. You can display these commands by pressing the ↑ key at the dot prompt. Press ↑.

dBASE IV will display the last command entered. Press ↑.

The second-to-last command appears. You can move down the list as well. Press ↓.

The cursor is on the right end of the last program line. To add +1 to the expression, type

+1 and press ↵.

Elements of dBASE IV

Adding +1 changes the command and reruns it. This time the list reflects the proper count of hospital days.

An expression cannot stand alone. It must be used in conjunction with some other dBASE IV command, like LIST.

Replacing Data

The LIST command displays information from fields, and expressions involving fields, on the screen. Some of the information, such as the number of hospital days, may be useful to store as part of the database. dBASE IV allows you to insert information into fields based on an expression. The REPLACE command lets you place the results of an expression into an existing field. In this case, you want to replace the Days_stay field with the value calculated for Discharge-Admit+1. Enter

```
REPLACE all Days_stay with Discharge-Admit+1
```

dBASE IV confirms the operation by displaying the message **10 records replaced.** This message refers to the fact that the specified field, Days_stay, was changed in 10 records. To actually see the results of this change, you must request a list of the field. Enter

```
LIST Days_stay
```

to see the now modified records.

The REPLACE command is one of the most powerful operations in dBASE IV because it can take the place of manual entry. Not only is the REPLACE command faster than manual entry, but it is more accurate because the computer generates the data based on a logical relationship between existing data items.

Printing

You can direct the information displayed on the screen to the printer by adding TO PRINT to the LIST command. To print the file structure, enter

```
LIST STRUCTURE TO PRINT
```

dBASE IV does not create page breaks or eject the rest of the page when you print with commands like LIST. If you want to eject the remainder of the page, you can enter the EJECT command. EJECT causes the printer to issue a form feed. This is the same operation the printer performs when you manually use the form feed button to advance the page. Enter

```
EJECT
```

Housekeeping

List the entire Admit database file to the printer. Try this on your own. If you need help, the correct command can be found at the end of the chapter in the Answers to Exercises section as exercise 5.

When the printing is complete, eject the page by entering

```
eject
```

Opening and Closing Files

The last step in creating and working with a database file is to close the file. Closing files is important because of the way computer programs actually store data. When you enter a new record into a database, the information is entered into the memory of the computer, which acts as a temporary storage area. In order for the information to be available the next time you want to use the computer, this temporarily stored data must be copied into a disk file. In theory, all of the data you input is placed into a disk file. But in practice, dBASE IV delays the actual transfer of data until you have entered more information than it can hold in temporary memory at one time. The reason for this delay is to improve the performance of the program. Disk transfers slow down the operation of the application program. dBASE IV attempts to minimize the number of transfers it makes in order to process the data as quickly as possible. When you close a file, dBASE IV makes sure that all records entered into the file are transferred to the disk. dBASE IV performs the transfers when you exit the program. However, if a power failure should occur before you quit, it is possible to lose data.

To close the file without quitting dBASE IV, enter

```
CLOSE DATABASE
```

Closing the database does not clear the screen. The data generated by previous commands remains on the screen even though the file is closed. However, the status bar reflects the change. The second section of the bar from the left shows the name of the active database file. That section is blank, indicating that no file is active. Without an active database file, dBASE IV cannot perform database operations such as listing. Enter

```
LIST
```

dBASE IV displays a box in the center of the screen that tells you there is no database in use (see Figure 1.14).

Cancel the command by pressing (Esc).

Figure 1.14

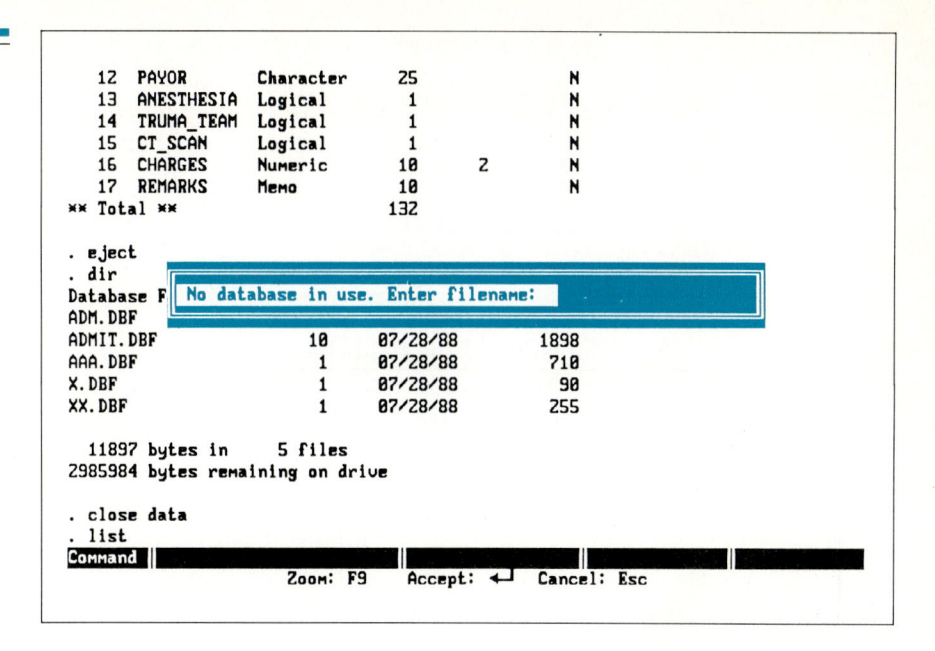

```
  12  PAYOR        Character    25              N
  13  ANESTHESIA   Logical       1              N
  14  TRUMA_TEAM   Logical       1              N
  15  CT_SCAN      Logical       1              N
  16  CHARGES      Numeric      10      2       N
  17  REMARKS      Memo         10              N
** Total **                    132

. eject
. dir
Database F│ No database in use. Enter filename:         │
ADM.DBF
ADMIT.DBF               10      07/28/88        1898
AAA.DBF                  1      07/28/88         710
X.DBF                    1      07/28/88          90
XX.DBF                   1      07/28/88         255

   11897 bytes in    5 files
 2985984 bytes remaining on drive

. close data
. list
Command
                  Zoom: F9    Accept: ↵    Cancel: Esc
```

Before you can perform operations like append, edit, or list, you must place a database file in use. The dBASE IV command to open a database file is the USE command. The USE command is followed by the name of the database file that you want to work with. Open the Admit database file by entering

`USE Admit` ↵

When you place the database in use, the status line reflects the change by displaying the name of the file, C:\DBSAMPLE\ADMIT, the file size, 1/10, and the word "file," indicating database file activity.

Note: The drive and directory may be different on your computer.

The Record Pointer

One of the most important concepts in processing dBASE IV database files is that of the record pointer. When a database file is open, dBASE IV always selects a single record as the active record. dBASE IV always points to a particular record and the internal device it uses to select an active record is called the *record pointer*.

When a database file is first opened, the pointer is always set to the first record in the file. For example, the value of the first field is Walter when the first record is active. You can ask dBASE IV to display information from the current record using the DISPLAY command. Enter

DISPLAY First

The program displays the record number, 1, and the contents of that record's first field, Walter.

The value of the field changes if you move the pointer to another record. You can move the pointer down one record by entering the SKIP command. Enter

SKIP

dBASE IV confirms the movement of the record pointer in two ways. First, the message "Admit: Record No 2" appears in the display area. The center section of the status bar shows 2/10. This means that the pointer is positioned at record 2 in a file of 10 records.

Now that you have moved the pointer, the value of the fields changes to reflect the data stored in the second record in the file. Repeat the DISPLAY command.

DISPLAY FIRST

This time, the value of that field is Harold. The DISPLAY command is a pointer-dependent command because its value changes as the pointer moves through the database file.

You can move the pointer to any specific record by simply entering the number of that record. For example, to position the pointer to record 7, enter

7

The status line shows 7/10, indicating the 7th record is active. Display the current value of the first field. Enter

DISPLAY FIRST

This time, the command returns the name Timothy. You can position the pointer to the top or bottom of the database by using the command GO TOP or GO BOTTOM. Enter

GO BOTTOM

The status line displays 10/10 indicating the 10th of 10 records. Enter

```
GO TOP
```

The pointer moves back to record 1.

End of File

When you use commands like LIST that dump all of the information in all of the records in the database file, what happens to the pointer? Enter the following command and watch the pointer position indicator on the status line. Enter

```
LIST
```

The indicator changes to EOF/10. The letters EOF stand for end of file and indicate that the pointer is at the end of the file. What is the difference between the beginning and the end of the file, and using GO TOP or GO BOTTOM?

EOF

When the pointer is positioned at EOF, it is positioned past the last record in the database. The value of any character field is blank, numerics are zero, logicals are .F. and dates are empty except for the two slashes. You can think of a pointer to EOF as pointing to a blank record.

Bottom

The bottom of the file means that the pointer is positioned at the last record. The fields draw their value from the last record in the database.

The LIST command scans the entire database. A scan automatically starts the pointer at the top of the database and leaves the pointer at the EOF. Because the database scan is part of the LIST command, it is not pointer dependent. In order to use pointer-dependent commands, you must first position the pointer to a valid record in the database.

Listing Memo Fields

In all of the commands you have issued so far, you may have noticed that the contents of the memo field have simply been ignored. Because of the nature of memo fields—variable-length text stored in a separate but linked file—dBASE IV does not normally include that data in a dump command like LIST. But dBASE IV will display the contents of the memo fields if you specifically request that field. You must include the field name Remarks in order to list the memo information in the Admit database. Enter

```
LIST Remarks
```

The program displays the contents of the memo field (see Figure 1.15).

Since the memo fields are variable length, you may wonder how the width of the memo fields is determined when they are listed. The answer is that dBASE IV has a special setting called "memo width" that controls the width of memos when they are listed. The default setting is 50 characters. This means that memo fields will behave like a series of character fields 50 characters wide when the memos are listed or displayed.

Note: The memo width can be altered by using the SET MEMOWIDTH TO command.

Copying Files

In addition to the other housekeeping operations, you need to know how to make copies of dBASE IV database files. Copies are important for several reasons. First, it is always a good idea to have a backup copy of your data when you are testing a program. If the program should delete or alter the wrong records, you have a copy of the original file. Making a copy of a database also means that you can transfer it to another computer via a computer network or to another disk within the same computer.

Figure 1.15

```
F.         .T.        3929.00 memo
. list remarks
Record#  remarks
      1  Injury:
         Laceration of the lower right arm.

      2  Injury:
         Burns on hands and arms.

      3  Injury:
         Broken Leg
      4
      5
      6
      7
      8
      9
     10
.
Command  C:\db4\ADMIT         Rec EOF/10    File
```

Elements of dBASE IV

You can copy dBASE IV files with the MS-DOS COPY command. But the advantage of copying from within dBASE IV is that dBASE IV will automatically copy the memo file (.dbt extension), if any, when the database file (.dbf extension) is copied. To create a copy of the Admit database, enter

```
COPY TO Patients
```

dBASE IV creates a duplicate file with the name Patients. On the disk, two files are created: Patients.dbf and Patients.dbt. How did dBASE IV know that you wanted to make a copy of Admit and not some other database file? The answer is that dBASE IV takes its cue from the active database file. Since Admit was the active file when the COPY command was given, Admit was the source file for the copying process.

To place a copy of the Admit file onto another disk or into a different directory, you simply specify that location along with the name of the new file. Suppose you want to place a copy of the Admit file on a floppy disk. You need a floppy disk with sufficient space for both files, about 20K, in the A drive. If you do not have a disk for this purpose, skip this command. Enter

```
COPY TO A:Patients
```

Another useful variation on the COPY command is the COPY STRUCTURE command. COPY STRUCTURE is useful when you want to copy the file structure but not the records. Enter

```
COPY STRUCTURE TO Admitfrm
```

To get a list of the .dbf files in the current directory, you can use the DIR command. The DIR command in dBASE IV does not perform like the DIR command in MS-DOS. In dBASE IV, only the .dbf files are listed, as if you entered the MS-DOS command DIR *.dbf. Enter

```
DIR
```

The database files are listed. dBASE IV displays the number of records in each file.

Complete this chapter by closing the example database file and clearing the display. Enter

```
CLOSE DATABASE
CLEAR
```

Summary

This chapter discussed the basic operations required to create and enter data into a dBASE IV database file. Understanding the following concepts is required before you can begin to write dBASE IV programs.

Database manager. dBASE IV functions on the applications level as a database management program. This means that dBASE IV has a built-in method of creating data files, organizing their structure, entering, deleting, saving, and retrieving information. Without the database management section of dBASE IV, you would have to write programs to perform these operations. The database manager in dBASE IV simplifies programming tasks and allows the programmer to concentrate on shaping the program to the user's needs.

Database files. dBASE IV creates database files using fixed-length records. The file is divided into data fields and records. A file's records can contain up to 255 different fields.

Fields. Each database file classifies data in terms of fields. Each field is designed to contain a distinct item of information. Fields can be one of five types: character, numeric (floating-point or decimal), date, logical, or memo. Each field is assigned a unique, 10-character name, a width in characters (maximum 255 for character fields, 20 for numeric fields), and an indication of whether or not they are index keys.

Records. A record is one complete set of related fields. Each person, place, thing, or event added to the database is a record. All records contain space for all the fields, even if you do not choose to fill in all the fields.

Date fields. A date field is a special type of field used for handling chronological dates. All dates are entered in mm/dd/yy format. dBASE IV automatically checks date fields for date validity.

Logical fields. A logical field can contain only a true or false value. True values are entered as T or Y, while false values are entered with F or N. No other characters are accepted.

Memo fields. Memo fields can contain up to 65,536 characters of paragraph-oriented text. A memo field is different from other fields in that it is stored in a separate disk file because it is variable in length. dBASE IV links the records to the text stored in the memo file.

Delete records. dBASE IV uses a two-stage operation to remove records from a database file. First, the DELETE command marks records for deletion. The PACK command rewrites the database and eliminates any records marked as deleted. Following a pack, records cannot be recovered. Prior to a pack, you can recover records by using the RECALL command.

CLEAR. The CLEAR command clears the screen display of output.

LIST. The LIST command scans the entire database and dumps all of its information to the screen. You can limit the output by supplying the command with a specific list of fields to display.

TO PRINT. You can direct the output of a LIST command to the printer by adding TO PRINT, as in LIST TO PRINT.

EJECT. dBASE IV does not automatically feed the remainder of the form when a print operation is complete. In order to execute a form feed, you must enter an EJECT command.

The pointer. dBASE IV makes one record active at a time while a database file is open. The program is said to point to that record. Many dBASE IV commands are pointer dependent, which means that they use only the data stored in the record being pointed to when they execute. The pointer can be moved by commands such as SKIP, GO TOP, and GO BOTTOM.

DISPLAY. The DISPLAY command displays only the information in the current record.

Expression. dBASE IV can generate information from stored data by evaluating logical expressions. Expressions are statements used by dBASE IV to calculate a value.

CLOSE DATABASE. The CLOSE command closes the active database file.

USE. The USE command opens and activates a database file. When the file is opened, the pointer is automatically positioned to the first record in the database. You cannot perform data-oriented operations, such as display or list, unless a database file has been opened with the USE command.

COPY. You can create duplicates of the file or its structure with the COPY and COPY STRUCTURE commands. The dBASE IV COPY command automatically copies the memo file.

Review Problems for Chapter 1

1. Create a database file called Sales with the following structure:

Field	Field Name	Type	Width	Decimal
1	COMPANY	Character	30	
2	DATE_SOLD	Date	8	
3	INV_NUM	Character	10	
4	PROD_CODE	Character	10	
5	ITEM_NAME	Character	30	
6	PRICE	Numeric	6	2
7	QUANTITY	Numeric	4	
8	TOTAL_AMT	Numeric	8	2
9	TAXABLE	Logical	1	
10	TAXRATE	Numeric	5	3
11	TAX	Numeric	8	2

2. Enter the following record into the Sales database.

   ```
   COMPANY      NORTH ENTERPRISES
   DATE_SOLD    07/06/88
   INV_NUM      2707
   PROD_CODE    837
   ITEM_NAME    SCOTT NAPKINS
   PRICE        22.30
   QUANTITY     150
   TOTAL_AMT    0
   TAXABLE      .F.
   TAXRATE      0
   TAX          0
   ```

3. In order to save time, you can copy the rest of the data for this file from the file Sales.txt, which you copied to the DBSAMPLE directory when you installed dBASE. Type the following commands:

   USE Sales
   APPEND FROM C:\DBSAMPLE\Sales TYPE DELIMITED

4. Enter a command that lists all of the companies and item names.

5. Suppose payment is due 45 days after the sales. Enter a command that lists the date 45 days after the sale date.

6. The file does not contain any values for the tax or the total amount of the sale. You can calculate these values and place the results into the currently empty field. Enter a command that will fill in the tax field.
   (Hint: Use the REPLACE ALL command to multiply the price by the quantity by the tax rate. The * indicates multiplication.)

7. List the price, quantity, tax rate, and tax fields.

8. Fill in the total amount field by multiplying the price by the quantity and adding the tax.

9. List the price, quantity, tax, and total amount field.

10. Print a copy of the file's structure.

11. Print a list of the companies and the dates of the sales.

12. Print a list of the total amount and tax.

13. The taxable field can be related to the value in the tax rate field. Enter a command that sets the taxable field to true when the tax rate is greater than zero. Then enter a command that sets the taxable field to false when the tax rate is zero.

Answers to Exercise Questions

1. Exit Assist mode.

    [Esc]

    y

2. Enter two fields.

    Phone [↵] [↵]

    9 [↵] [↵]

    Sex [↵] [↵]

    1 [↵] [↵]

3. Create five fields.

   Payor ⏎ ⏎
   25 ⏎ ⏎
   Anesthesia ⏎
   1
   Truma_team ⏎
   1
   Ct_scan ⏎
   1
   Charges ⏎
   n
   10 ⏎
   2 ⏎ ⏎

4. List name, days, and charges.

   LIST Last,Days_stay,Charges

5. List database to the printer.

   LIST to print

2 Linear Programming

This chapter explores the creation of the simplest type of program, a linear program. However, before moving into the details of programming, we'll explore the use and meaning of some important programming terms.

Deferred Execution

The previous chapter described how you can create and use database files in dBASE IV. The Command mode lets you enter commands and carry out operations such as file creation, data entry, and data retrieval. All of these operations took place in the immediate execution mode. Immediate execution means that as soon as you enter a command, like LIST TO PRINT, dBASE IV immediately carries out that instruction.

Most computer applications, even spreadsheets and word processors, operate in the immediate mode; many also have built-in programming languages called macro languages. The concept of programming in dBASE IV and in application macro languages is to defer the execution of commands until some later point in time. There are three basic advantages to deferring the execution of commands.

1. **Automatic sequence.** In the immediate execution mode, you must wait until a command finishes executing before you can enter another command. If the task you are carrying out requires a specific sequence of commands, it is more efficient to enter all of the commands first, and then have the program execute them one after another.

2. **Replay.** The very nature of deferred execution requires that you store the commands in some permanent form, called a program, usually as a text file on a disk. Once stored, there is no limit to the number of times you can access this same sequence of commands, and you can repeat the program as many times as you need.

3. **Logical structures.** The two just-mentioned advantages of programming provide increased speed, convenience, and accuracy. However, by deferring the execution of commands, your program also can perform logical operations, called conditional branches and loops. These operations allow your program to react in different ways to conditions that develop as the program runs. These structures enable the program to operate differently each time it is used by building in a level of flexibility that is not possible when you execute individual commands.

How Instructions Are Deferred

How can a program like dBASE IV, that is automatically set for immediate execution of commands, be switched to a deferred execution mode? How can you create command sequences designed for deferred execution?

dBASE IV normally expects to receive instructions directly from the keyboard. When you enter a command at the dot prompt, such as USE ADMIT, dBASE IV waits until you press ⏎. It then takes the text you entered and attempts to carry out that command. This is the immediate execution mode.

But suppose that instead of looking for information entered from the keyboard, dBASE IV looked to another source for instructions, namely, a text file on disk. That text file contains characters just like the characters you enter from the keyboard. The only difference is that the characters in the text file are stored on the disk, while each command entered from the keyboard must be typed manually.

Writing programs is simply the task of creating text files that consist of a series of the same commands you could enter at the dot prompt.

Note: This is not true of all programming languages. One of the major advantages of dBASE IV as a programming language is that many of its programming operations use the same commands as the dBASE IV database manager. The only difference is that their execution is deferred.

dBASE IV programs are actually text files. This means that they can be created by any text editor or word processor that can store text in a standard text format. WordPerfect, Microsoft Word, WordStar, and the Norton Editor are some popular programs that can be used to create dBASE IV programs.

dBASE IV also supplies a text editor as part of the database manager. The editor is automatically used when you edit a memo field. This text editor can also be used to create dBASE IV programs.

Once you have created a text file that contains a sequence of commands, the program will execute when you tell dBASE IV to begin reading commands from that file instead of the keyboard. A special command transfers control of dBASE IV from the keyboard to the commands stored in the file. When dBASE IV reaches the end of the list of commands in the file, it returns control to the keyboard.

Command Sequence Types

You can classify the command sequences of every dBASE IV program into three categories according to the nature of the logic used in the sequence (see Figure 2.1).

1. **Linear.** A linear program is the simplest type of program. A list of commands executes in a straight line from first to last. Following the last command, the program terminates and control returns to the keyboard.

2. **Branched.** Branched command sequences contain a testing instruction. This instruction tests to see if some condition is true or false. The program then splits into two threads based on whether the condition is true or false.

3. **Looped.** A loop is a construction that causes the program to move backwards in the list of instructions and repeat a section of the program over and over again. Loops allow a small program to process a large number of operations by repeating groups of commands. Of course, if the repetition goes on forever, the program never returns

Figure 2.1

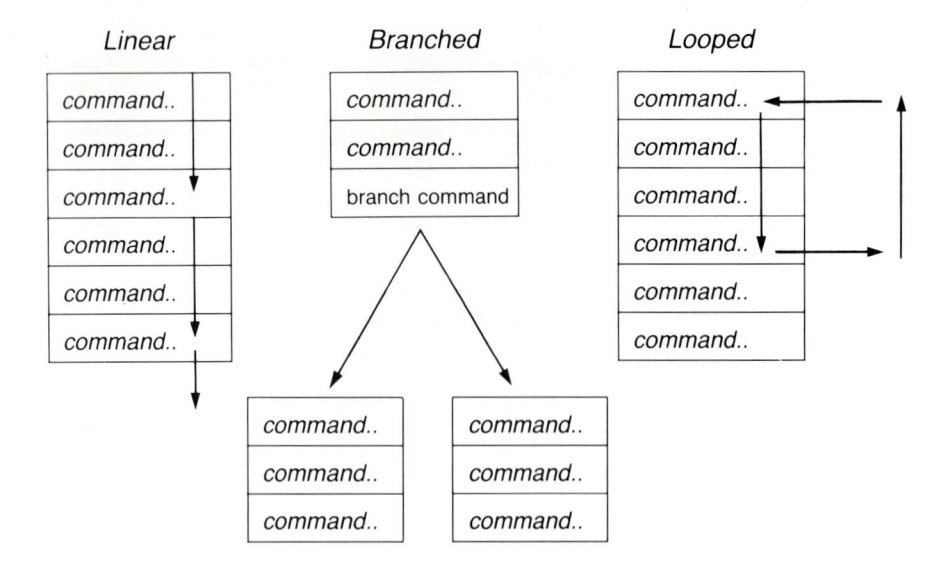

Program Structures

Linear	Branched	Looped
command..	command..	command..
command..	command..	command..
command..	branch command	command..
command..		command..
command..		command..
command..		command..

Branched (sub-branches):
- command.. / command.. / command..
- command.. / command.. / command..

execution to the keyboard. Therefore, it is always necessary to combine a loop with a branch of some kind that will tell the program when to stop looping and go on to the next instruction.

In this chapter, you will begin programming by creating linear programs. Although these programs have a simple structure, they can perform a variety of useful tasks. This chapter describes methods for using sequences of existing dBASE IV commands to form simple programs.

Setup

To begin this chapter, you must have the following:

- dBASE IV should be loaded into the memory of the computer and running. Then exit the dBASE IV menus to the dot prompt by pressing (Esc) and typing y.

- The default drive and directory should be set to the directory that holds the files you have been using with this book. Remember that these chapters are predicated on the use of a hard disk labeled drive C. If your computer system is different, please make the correct adjustments for drive and directory.

- The cursor should be next to the dot prompt. Now you are ready to begin.

50 ■ Linear Programming

Writing a Simple Program

Suppose you want to create a program that lists the name, address, and phone number of all the patients in the previous chapter's Admit file. The complete process requires three steps.

1. Use the database file
2. List the information
3. Close the database file

You can create a simple program to accomplish this task. Because a program is a text file, you must call up the dBASE IV editor in order to create that file. dBASE IV uses the command MODIFY COMMAND to create a text file and automatically adds a .prg (for program) extension to the file.

> *Note:* The dBASE IV text editor can create files with any extension you specify. When you use MODIFY COMMAND, the default extension is .prg.

Call this program Names. Enter

```
MODIFY COMMAND Names
```

The screen will show the dBASE IV editor.

The top line of the display shows five pull-down menus: **Layout, Words, Go To, Print,** and **Exit.** The second line is a ruler line on which tab locations are marked with triangles. At the bottom of the screen, the status bar shows the name of the file you are editing and the line and column in the file where the cursor is positioned.

To create a program, you simply type in the sequence of commands that you would normally enter at the dot prompt. Enter

```
USE Admit
```

Because you are editing a text file, not entering commands at the dot prompt, dBASE IV does not react to the entry of this command. The effect of this command is being deferred until the program has been completed, stored in a disk file, and then run.

The next command in the program will remove all currently displayed data from the screen. Enter

```
CLEAR
```

Next, enter a command to list the required information.

```
LIST First,Last,Phone
```

Finally, enter a command to close the database file.

```
CLOSE DATABASE
```

There is one final command you should enter. This command, RETURN, is placed at the end of all dBASE IV programs to tell dBASE IV to terminate the execution of the current program and return to previous activity. The previous activity can refer to the dot prompt mode or another program. Later, you will see how RETURN functions when programs are nested inside one another.

In this example, the RETURN command is not strictly necessary. dBASE IV will return to the dot prompt mode when it reaches the end of the program, anyway. But it is a good habit always to place the RETURN command in the program at the point at which it should terminate. Enter

```
RETURN
```

The program now looks like Figure 2.2.

Figure 2.2

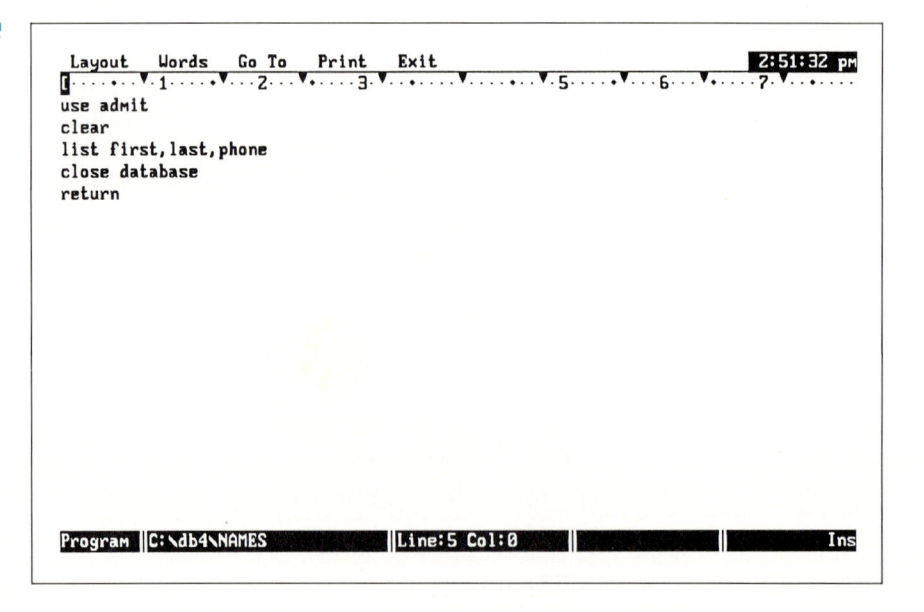

```
 Layout  Words  Go To  Print  Exit                    2:51:32 pm
 ....V..1....V...2...V....3.V.......V....5....V...6..V....7.V....
use admit
clear
list first,last,phone
close database
return




                                                              
                                                              




 Program  C:\db4\NAMES        Line:5 Col:0                  Ins
```

52 ■ Linear Programming

In dBASE IV there are two ways to save the text and exit the editor: by pressing Ctrl-End or Alt-e. Since Ctrl-End is shorter, enter Ctrl-End.

You can confirm that you have created the file by using the DIR command. Enter

```
DIR *.prg
```

The file Names.prg appears in the directory listing. You now have a simple program that you can execute.

Compiling a Program

Once you have created a text file that contains the commands you want to execute, you can tell dBASE IV to transfer control to that program file. dBASE IV will then read each command in your text file and execute it. But first, a step is added between the creation of the text file for the program and the execution of the program.

The reason for this step, called compiling, is to speed up the execution of the program. The compiling process converts your text program files (files with the .prg extension) into a more compressed, nontext format called an object file (with a .dbo extension).

> *Note:* Use of the term *compile* in dBASE IV should not be confused with the more standard compiling process performed by language compilers for BASIC or Pascal. In those environments, the result of the compiling process is a program file that can be directly executed by MS-DOS. In dBASE IV, a complied program still requires the presence of dBASE IV to execute.

The compiling process has two advantages.

1. **Error Checking.** When a program is complied, it is checked for syntax errors such as typing mistakes. This allows you to catch errors before you begin the execution of the program.

2. **Speed.** The compressed format of the .dbo file allows dBASE IV to execute its commands faster.

dBASE IV will automatically compile a program file before executing the program. It will also recompile the program if the program file has been updated.

> *Note:* dBASE IV depends on the time and date stamp entered by MS-DOS to determine when it is necessary to recompile a program. If you use a computer that does not maintain the correct time and date, the automatic recompile feature may not work

Writing a Simple Program

properly. If that is the case, you may need to manually compile programs with the compile command. A program is compiled right before its first execution. The next time it is run, dBASE IV will execute the compiled object file unless a modification has been made to the program.

The command that tells dBASE IV to execute a program is the DO command. DO is always followed by the name of the program to execute. Enter

```
DO Names
```

The program will first compile and then execute. The resulting output of the program is a listing of the names and phone numbers from the Admit file.

Modifying a Program

Suppose you want to display several lists of information as part of this program. You can return to the program and add to or modify its commands. Enter

```
MODIFY COMMAND Names
```

Move the cursor down to line 2 using the ↓ key. You can add a blank line at this point in the file by using the **Add line** option from the **Words** menu. Editing commands like this one can be found on the pull-down menus at the top of the screen. Display the **Words** menu by pressing (Alt) and typing W.

To select **add line,** type

a

Move the cursor down to the blank line by pressing ↓.

Enter a command to list the admittance date, discharge date, days in the hospital, and charges. Enter

```
LIST Admit,Discharge,Days_stay,Charges
```

Save and execute the program by entering

(Ctrl)–(End) DO Names

This time, the program will display several lists (see Figure 2.3).

But there is a problem. The two lists require more lines than can be displayed on the screen at one time. When the second LIST command executes, it forces part of the first list off the screen.

Figure 2.3

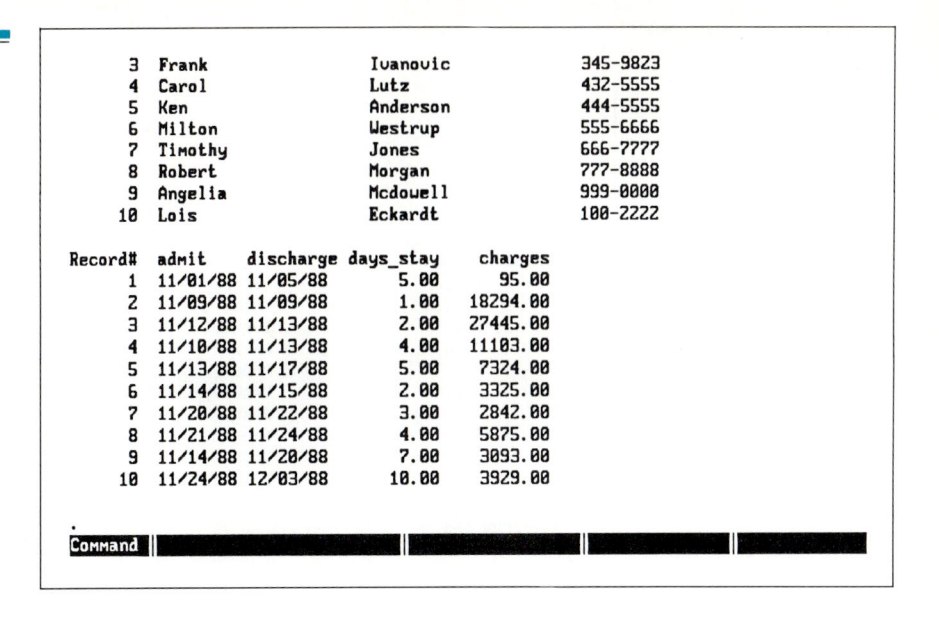

```
    3  Frank           Ivanovic         345-9823
    4  Carol           Lutz             432-5555
    5  Ken             Anderson         444-5555
    6  Milton          Westrup          555-6666
    7  Timothy         Jones            666-7777
    8  Robert          Morgan           777-8888
    9  Angelia         Mcdowell         999-0000
   10  Lois            Eckardt          100-2222

Record#  admit     discharge  days_stay    charges
    1    11/01/88  11/05/88       5.00       95.00
    2    11/09/88  11/09/88       1.00    18294.00
    3    11/12/88  11/13/88       2.00    27445.00
    4    11/10/88  11/13/88       4.00    11103.00
    5    11/13/88  11/17/88       5.00     7324.00
    6    11/14/88  11/15/88       2.00     3325.00
    7    11/20/88  11/22/88       3.00     2842.00
    8    11/21/88  11/24/88       4.00     5875.00
    9    11/14/88  11/20/88       7.00     3093.00
   10    11/24/88  12/03/88      10.00     3929.00

Command
```

You can create a pause between the two LIST commands so you can read the first list before you go on to the second list. dBASE IV provides a command, WAIT, that will pause the program's execution until any key is pressed. Modify the program by inserting a WAIT command between the two LIST commands. Try this on your own. If you need help, you can find the correct command at the end of the chapter in the Answers to Exercises section as exercise 1.

The dBASE IV editor has a special command that will both save and execute the program. Display the **Exit** menu by pressing (Alt) and typing e.

Select **Run program** by typing

r

dBASE IV saves, compiles, and executes the program. The program now pauses following the first list and displays the message **Press any key to continue** . . . (see Figure 2.4).

To allow the program to continue, press any key. Press ⏎.

Printer vs. Screen

Suppose you want to create a program that sends this list to the printer. In that case, you would not be concerned with screen-oriented commands like CLEAR and WAIT. Instead, you would want to make

Writing a Simple Program ■ 55

Figure 2.4

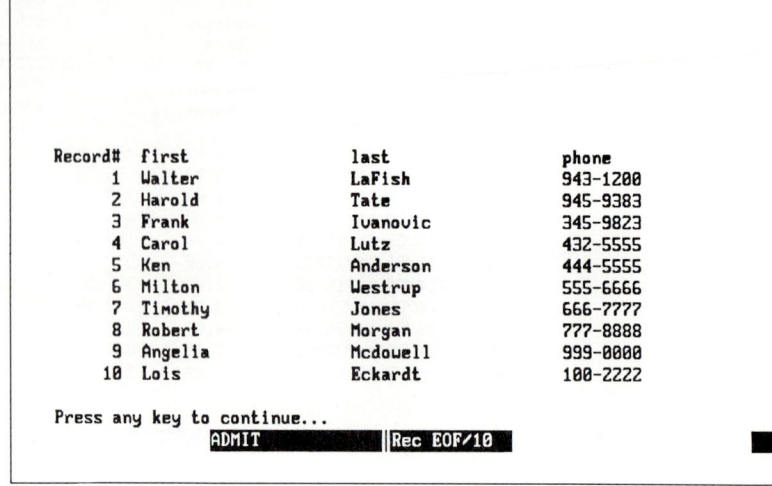

```
Record#  first        last         phone
     1   Walter       LaFish       943-1200
     2   Harold       Tate         945-9383
     3   Frank        Ivanovic     345-9823
     4   Carol        Lutz         432-5555
     5   Ken          Anderson     444-5555
     6   Milton       Westrup      555-6666
     7   Timothy      Jones        666-7777
     8   Robert       Morgan       777-8888
     9   Angelia      Mcdowell     999-0000
    10   Lois         Eckardt      100-2222

Press any key to continue...
          ADMIT              Rec EOF/10
```

sure that each list begins at the top of the page. The command that ensures that the form is fed properly is EJECT. Create a new program called Namespr (for names printing) by entering

MODIFY COMMAND Namespr

Enter the program shown below:

EJECT

USE Admit

LIST First,Last,Phone TO PRINT

EJECT

LIST Admit,Discharge,Days_stay,Charges TO PRINT

EJECT

CLOSE DATABASE

Why does the program begin with an EJECT? This command appears first because you cannot be sure that the current page in the printer is positioned at the top of the form. The EJECT command makes sure that printing begins at the top of the form. Of course, if the paper is properly set when the program executes, it will eject an entire sheet of blank paper.

Note: This initial use of the command EJECT is standard procedure in programs that follow traditional style. However, you may choose to eliminate it from your programs.

You have now created two simple linear programs. However, you have not reached the useful limit of simple, straight-line programs. To increase the power of these programs, you will need to learn more about the structure of dBASE IV commands.

The Parts of dBASE IV Commands

In Chapter 1, you entered a number of dBASE IV commands to perform basic file creation and maintenance operations. The most basic command in the database manager is the USE command, which places a database file (with a .dbf extension) into use. From the dot prompt, place the Admit file into use by entering

```
USE Admit
```

The command you have just entered consists of two parts, a command verb and a database object.

Command verb. The command verb, in this case USE, is the part of the command that tells dBASE IV what operation you want to perform. In dBASE IV, all commands begin with a verb. dBASE IV expects the first word in a command line to match one of the commands built into the dBASE IV program. If the first word is not one of those commands, dBASE IV rejects the command with the message **Unrecognized command verb.**

Database object. As in the English language, verbs require an object upon which to act. In dBASE IV, those objects are the database items you create. The nature of the command verb dictates the type of object that should be used with it. For example, the USE command opens files; therefore, the object following a USE verb should always be the name of a database file.

On the other hand, the LIST verb operates on data fields. The objects following a LIST command should be field names.

Many verbs operate without specified objects. The LIST verb can be used by itself. When a verb is used without a specific object, dBASE IV automatically assumes an object or objects. This assumption is called the default object. For example, the LIST command used without an object automatically assumes that you want to list all the fields of the database currently in memory.

Verbs and objects are not the only parts of a dBASE IV command. In Chapter 1 you learned that adding TO PRINT to a list command could direct the output to the printer instead of the screen. TO PRINT is called a *clause*. A clause modifies the way a verb operates, similar to the way an adverb modifies the meaning of an English-language verb.

Expressions

The most common objects used by dBASE IV commands are fields. Suppose you want to list the first and last names of the patients in the Admit file. You would specify those fields following the LIST command. Enter

```
LIST First,Last
```

You learned in Chapter 1 that dBASE IV also accepts an expression as an object for listing. An expression can perform calculations on numeric or date fields. The table below shows the calculations dBASE IV permits.

Operation	Field Type
Addition(+)	dates, numeric, floating
Subtraction(-)	dates, numeric, floating
Multiplication(*)	numeric, floating
Division(/)	numeric, floating
Exponentiation(^)	numeric, floating

Suppose payment is due 45 days after the discharge of a patient. You could tell dBASE IV to list the discharge date and the date 45 days later. Enter

```
LIST Discharge,Discharge+45
```

You can also create expressions with numeric values. For example, you can calculate the Admit file's average cost per day by dividing the total charges by Days_stay (see Figure 2.5). Enter

```
LIST Charges/Days_stay
```

Scope

dBASE IV commands can also have a range, or a scope. The scope specifies the number of records affected by a command's operation. dBASE IV uses the following scopes:

Figure 2.5

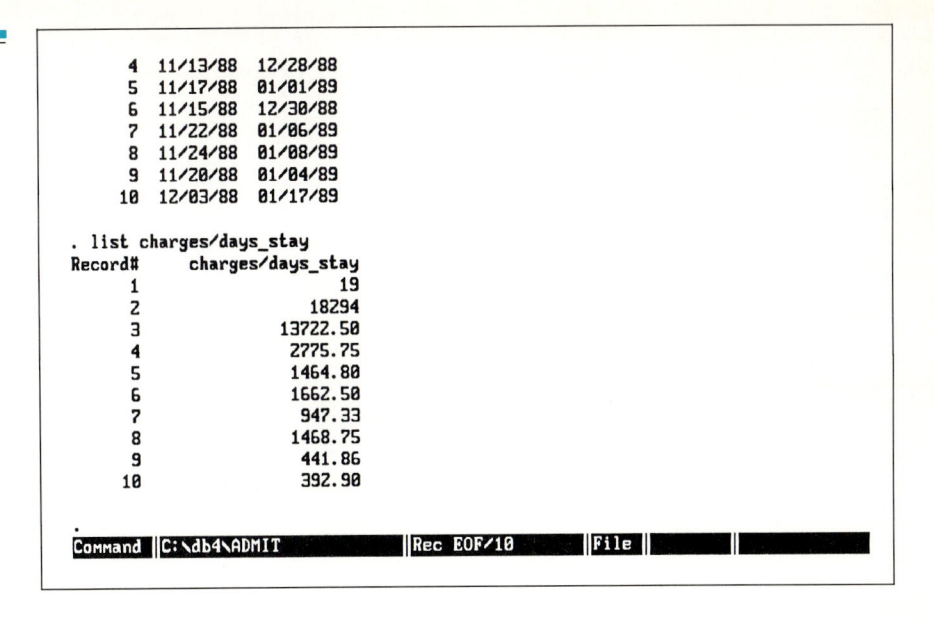

```
     4  11/13/88  12/28/88
     5  11/17/88  01/01/89
     6  11/15/88  12/30/88
     7  11/22/88  01/06/89
     8  11/24/88  01/08/89
     9  11/20/88  01/04/89
    10  12/03/88  01/17/89

. list charges/days_stay
Record#     charges/days_stay
     1                    19
     2                 18294
     3              13722.50
     4               2775.75
     5               1464.80
     6               1662.50
     7                947.33
     8               1468.75
     9                441.86
    10                392.90
.
```
`Command` `C:\db4\ADMIT`   `Rec EOF/10`   `File`

Scope	Records
ALL	first to last records
RECORD *n*	record # *n*
NEXT *n*	the next *n* records
REST	from pointer onward

Note: The scope NEXT always begins with the record the pointer is currently positioned on. This means that the scope NEXT 1 would actually affect the current record.

For example, by adding the scope RECORD to the LIST command, you can list one particular record. Enter

```
LIST Record 5
```

The program lists only record 5. If you want to list the rest of the database, from the current record 5 onward, you would use the REST scope. Enter

```
LIST Rest
```

The program will list records 5 through 10.

As with command objects, all verbs have a default scope. For example, the LIST command defaults to the ALL scope. This means that LIST used alone will act as if you had entered LIST ALL. The RE-

The Parts of dBASE IV Commands ■ 59

PLACE command defaults to NEXT 1, which means only the current record would be affected. Scopes are used, therefore, to select blocks of records to be affected by a command.

Selecting by Logical Expression

Modifying commands with clauses lets your program select groups of records based on a logical expression. A logical expression evaluates as either true or false. Logical expressions can compare two items for the following relationships:

Symbol	Meaning
=	equal to
#	not equal to
>	greater than
<	less than
>=	greater than or equal to
<=	less than or equal to
$	is part of

These comparison operators can be used with character, numeric, or date fields. The $ symbol is the only exception; it can be used only with character fields.

A logical expression can be combined with LIST to list values corresponding to the conditions found in each record. Suppose you want to see which records contain charges over $5,000.00. The expression that tests that condition reads "Charges>5000." Combine that expression with the LIST command verb. Enter

```
LIST Charges,Charges>5000
```

The output of this command might surprise you when it is first displayed. The logical expression displays .T. (true) or .F. (false), depending on the whether the condition, Charges>5000, is true or false.

While the listing of true and false values is interesting, logical expressions are usually used only to select records. This selection is accomplished by using a FOR clause. A FOR clause is always followed by a logical expression. The clause limits the display to records that test true for the logical expression. For example, if the expression Charges>5000 was used with a FOR clause, it would select only those records for which the expression was true. Enter

```
LIST Charges FOR Charges>5000
```

The command now lists those records for which the condition is true.

FOR clauses are very powerful because they perform one of the most important activities in database management: the selection of groups of records with common qualities.

Suppose you want to list the names of all the Admit file's female patients. You could accomplish this by testing the contents of the Sex field. This test expression takes on a different form because Sex is a character field. The expression compares the Sex field to a *text literal*. The term literal refers to an actual character or group of characters enclosed in quotation marks. To select all female patients, you use an expression, Sex = "f", that compares the contents of the Sex field to the letter f. Adding such an expression to a LIST FOR command sequence creates the command below that lists the names of the female patients. Enter

```
LIST First,Last FOR Sex="f"
```

The program now lists the three female patients.

You can apply a clause that scans the database for records to any dBASE IV command. In Chapter 1, you used the COPY command to copy the records from the active database to a new file. This operation requires a scan of the database records and can therefore be controlled with a FOR clause. Suppose you want to copy only the records of the Admit file's male patients. You would attach a FOR clause to the COPY command to select just the records you want to copy. Enter

```
COPY TO Males FOR Sex="m"
```

Here, the COPY command selects the seven male records and transfers only those records to the new database file, Males.

Selecting by Logical Fields

Logical fields are designed for use as selection criteria. The contents of a logical field can be tested rapidly because the program knows in advance that the contents of the field are either true or false. This known field type also allows you to use a simple logical expression using a logical field. For example, the clause FOR INSURED simply means "for insured is true." It is not necessary to write an explicit statement such as FOR INSURED = .T.

To test for a false value, you use the special logical connective .NOT. to invert the logic of the expression. Therefore, FOR .NOT.INSURED selects records for which the value of INSURED is false. This simplified expression makes it easy to select records using logical fields. Enter

```
LIST First,Last FOR Insured
```

dBASE IV selects the six out of ten patients who are insured. To select by a false value, enter

```
LIST First,Last FOR .NOT.INSURED
```

The other four records are selected.

Selecting by Dates   When you use date fields to select records, it is necessary to use special date conversion functions. Dates are entered in the format, mm/dd/yy. Suppose you want to select any records with an admission date of exactly 11/14/88. Enter

```
LIST First,Last FOR Admit=11/14/88
```

dBASE IV will respond with an error message box in the center of the screen indicating that something is wrong with the command (see Figure 2.6).

The error indicates that dBASE IV does not see 11/14/88 as a date. When dBASE IV attempts to translate the items on the line, the 11/14/88 is read as the numeric expression "11 divided by 15 divided by 88." The correct way to tell dBASE IV that you want to specify a date value is to use a special function that converts the characters into a valid dBASE IV date.

Figure 2.6

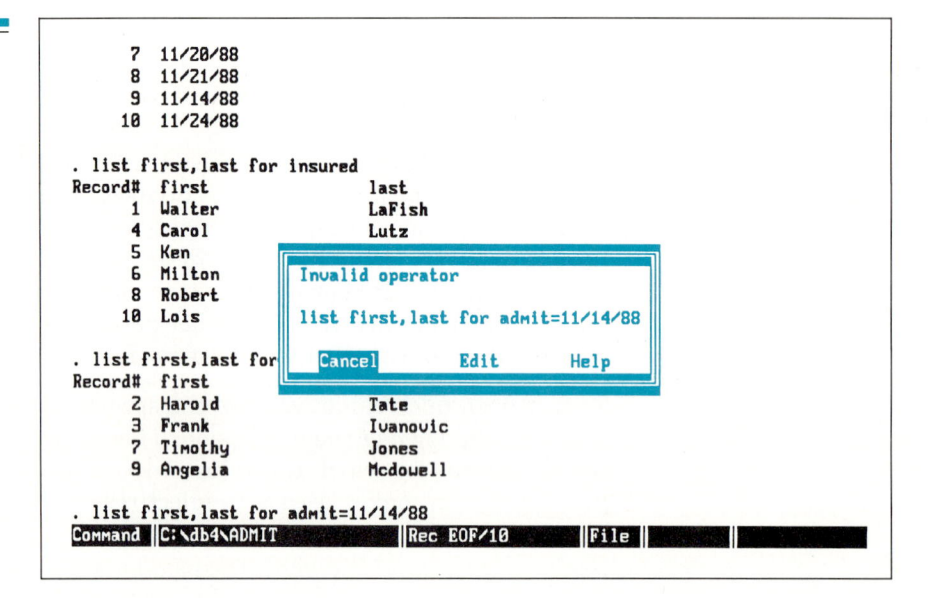

```
         7  11/20/88
         8  11/21/88
         9  11/14/88
        10  11/24/88
. list first,last for insured
Record#  first              last
      1  Walter             LaFish
      4  Carol              Lutz
      5  Ken
      6  Milton     ┌─────────────────────────────────────┐
      8  Robert     │ Invalid operator                    │
     10  Lois       │                                     │
                    │ list first,last for admit=11/14/88  │
. list first,last for
Record#  first      │  Cancel         Edit        Help    │
      2  Harold     └─────────────────────────────────────┘
      3  Frank              Ivanovic
      7  Timothy            Jones
      9  Angelia            Mcdowell
. list first,last for admit=11/14/88
Command  C:\db4\ADMIT              Rec EOF/10       File
```

A function, another element in the dBASE IV vocabulary, modifies or transforms data objects. It is roughly equivalent to an adjective in English that modifies or transforms the meaning of a noun.

Functions in dBASE IV have a strict syntax. The function is always followed by an argument enclosed in parentheses. The argument is the name of the field or literal that will be modified by the function.

In this case, there are two functions that could solve our problem.

DTOC() The DTOC(), Date to Character, function converts a date value into an 8-character item. This function can convert the dates in the Admit field into character-type data, which allows you to compare it to a character-type literal like "11/14/88."

CTOD() The CTOD(), Character to Date, function converts a text item such as "11/14/88" into a dBASE IV date. The converted data can then be compared to a date field.

Let's try both functions. First, cancel the present command by pressing ⏎.

The following command uses the DTOC() function to change the contents of the Admit field to characters so they can be compared to the text literal "11/14/88." Enter

```
LIST First,Last FOR DTOC(Admit)="11/14/88"
```

With the function properly employed, dBASE IV can locate the two records, 6 and 9, that match that admission date. You can achieve the same result by converting the literal "11/14/88" to a date. Enter

```
LIST First,Last FOR Admit=CTOD("11/14/88")
```

The program lists the same two records. Both commands have the same result because the logic behind the commands is the same.

Other Date Functions dBASE IV has a number of special functions to convert date information into more specific items. The table below shows the date functions in dBASE IV.

Function	Use
CDOW()	day of the week, e.g., Sunday
CMONTH()	month, e.g., January
CTOD()	character to date conversion
DAY()	number value of day of the month
DOW()	number day of week, e.g., 1 for Sunday

The Parts of dBASE IV Commands

DTOC()   date to character conversion
MONTH()   number value of month, e.g., 1 for January
YEAR()   number value of year, e.g., 1988 for 88

Suppose you want to list all the patients discharged in December. You would convert the date into the numeric value of the month with the MONTH() function and compare it to the number 12. Enter

```
LIST First,Last FOR MONTH(Discharge)=12
```

The program displays record 10, the only discharge date in December.

The $ Operator

The logical operations used in dBASE IV are quite similar to those used in standard programming languages like BASIC and Pascal. There is one unusual, and useful, operator that is peculiar to dBASE IV, the $ operator. The $ operator works only with text fields, literals, or functions that produce text. The $ is inserted between two text items. The $ operator asks the question "Is the text on the left contained within the text on the right?"

Suppose you were trying to locate a patient whose name might have been Mcdowell, Macdowell, or Dowell. You could search three times for LAST = "Mcdowell", LAST = "Macdowell", and LAST = "Dowell". Another solution would be to list all the last names that contain the characters "owel" in any part of the last name. The characters "owel" are called a substring. The term *substring* refers to a series of characters within a larger text item, such as a character field. The $ operator can test for the presence of a substring within a larger field. In this case, you would use an expression that reads: "owel"$Last. This expression reads "are the characters 'owel' some part of the last name field?" The following command uses that expression to select records. Enter

```
LIST First,Last FOR "owel"$Last
```

The command selects Angela Mcdowell because the last name contains the four-character sequence you specified. The $ operator is so flexible that it can solve a number of selection problems in a simpler manner than in the conventional programming languages. The following sections demonstrate how this works.

Case Sensitivity   Mismatched upper- and lower-case characters are a frequent cause of errors in selecting records. For example, the Admit file's Sex field contains either an m or an f character. But suppose someone had entered an upper-case character, F or M, instead.

You can use the REPLACE command to alter the Sex entry in these records. Enter

```
REPLACE Sex WITH "M" RECORD 6
REPLACE Sex WITH "F" RECORD 9
```

Now list the first and last names of the female patients. Try this on your own. If you need help, the correct command can be found at the end of the chapter in the Answers to Exercises section as exercise 2.

This time, only two patients were listed. The third, record 9, is omitted because it contains an F, not an f. dBASE IV is sensitive to differences in case in character fields. How can you get dBASE IV to select records without case sensitivity? There are two ways.

1. **UPPER().** dBASE IV contains a function, UPPER(), that converts all characters in the argument, the characters within parentheses, to upper-case. The expression UPPER(SEX) = F will be true for fields that contain both F and f. The literal F must be upper-case for this to work properly. The expression UPPER(SEX) = "f" would never evaluate as true.

2. **$.** You can also use a substring search to overcome problems with case sensitivity by comparing the single character in the Sex field to either an F or an f: sex$"Ff", for example. This expression tests to see if the contents of Sex matches either of the characters in "Ff".

Try both types of solutions. Enter

```
LIST First,Last FOR UPPER(Sex)="F"
```

The three female records are correctly listed. Enter a command that uses the $ operator to achieve the same results. Enter

```
LIST First,Last FOR Sex$"Ff"
```

The same three records are located. You can see that two very different expressions can yield the same results. Which is correct? The answer is that both are equally correct. In a programming language, there are usually several ways to achieve a desired result. Because it is a language, you can often find a variety of ways to express the same idea. There is often no one right answer but a variety of ways to attack a problem.

Multiple Criteria

Suppose you want to select from the Admit file any patients who were admitted on a weekend. dBASE IV provides a means of determining the day of the week by using either the DOW() or CDOW() functions. The DOW() function returns a numeric value for each weekday: 1 for Sunday, 2 for Monday, and so on. The CDOW() function returns the actual name of a day: Sunday, Monday, etc.

To list the day of the week for each patient, enter the following command (see Figure 2.7).

```
LIST CDOW(Admit),DOW(Admit)
```

How would you use this information to select those patients who were admitted on a Saturday or Sunday? This problem is simple if you only want to select a single day. To select the records with a Saturday admission date, you can select for DOW(ADMIT)=7. Enter

```
LIST First,Last FOR DOW(Admit)=7
```

But how can you get the program to select for either Saturday or Sunday? There are two methods.

1. **Logical connectives.** You can use logical connectives to create compound expressions. A compound expression contains more than one logical expression. The expressions are joined by a logical connective that expresses a relationship between the criteria. The .AND. con-

Figure 2.7

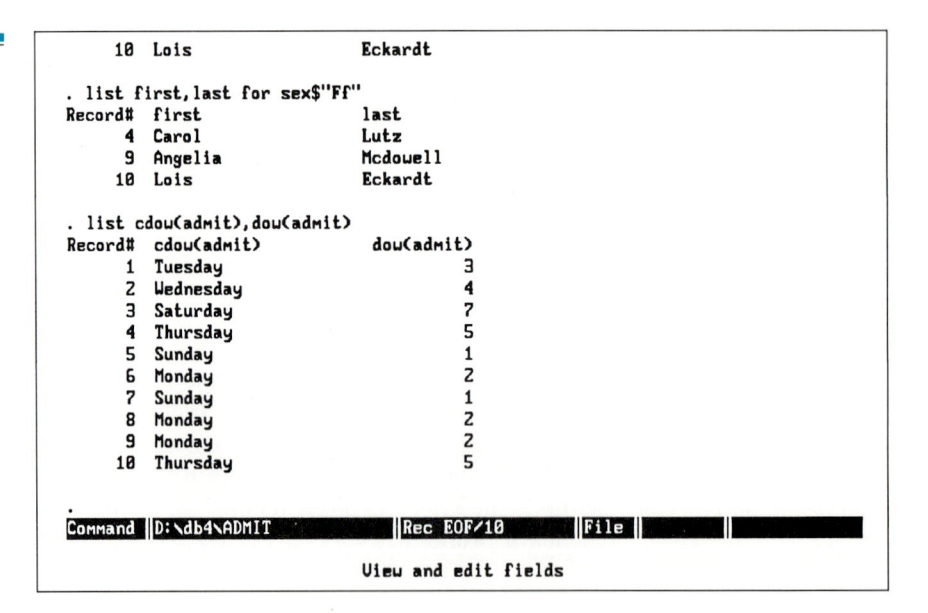

```
         10  Lois             Eckardt

. list first,last for sex$"Ff"
Record#  first            last
      4  Carol            Lutz
      9  Angelia          Mcdowell
     10  Lois             Eckardt

. list cdow(admit),dow(admit)
Record#  cdow(admit)      dow(admit)
      1  Tuesday                   3
      2  Wednesday                 4
      3  Saturday                  7
      4  Thursday                  5
      5  Sunday                    1
      6  Monday                    2
      7  Sunday                    1
      8  Monday                    2
      9  Monday                    2
     10  Thursday                  5

.
Command ||D:\db4\ADMIT            ||Rec EOF/10      ||File||
                        View and edit fields
```

66 ■ Linear Programming

nective creates a compound expression that is true only if both of the individual expressions are true. An .OR.-connected compound expression is true if either of its subexpressions is true.

2. $. The $ operator can be used if the target expression both involves character or character-converted-type data and you are seeking an OR type of relationship. You can test the contents of a field by comparing it to a list of items. If the field's contents match any of the listed items, the expression will be true.

You can apply both of these methods to the problem of picking days of the week because dBASE IV provides both a numeric and a character value for each day of the week. Begin with the logical connective method. To select both Saturday and Sunday admissions, you need to connect two expressions, DOW(ADMIT)=1 and DOW(ADMIT)=7 with the .OR. connective. An or relationship is correct because the record should be included if the admission date is either a Saturday or a Sunday. Enter

```
LIST First,Last FOR DOW(Admit)=1 .OR. DOW(Admit)=7
```

Here, the program correctly locates three weekend admissions. When you create a compound expression, it is necessary to enter two complete expressions, each of which is valid on its own. It is a common mistake to try to take a shortcut when both expressions use the same field. The following command will not execute properly because the second expression is not complete:

```
LIST First,Last FOR DOW(Admit)=1 .OR. =7
```

How can the $ operator solve this problem? The answer is that you need to compare the text value of the day of the week, CDOW(), to the actual names of the days, Saturday and Sunday. Enter

```
LIST First,Last FOR CDOW(Admit)$"SaturdaySunday"
```

This command locates the same records as the previous command. You must enter the text "SaturdaySunday" with the capitalization exactly as shown because that is the way dBASE IV generates the days of the week. If you entered "saturdaysunday" or "SATURDAYSUNDAY", the command would fail to locate the correct records because those capitalizations do not match the ones generated by the CDOW() function.

Programs That Use Selection

You can use the FOR clause with commands in a dBASE IV program to execute commands selectively. For example, suppose you want to list male and female patients separately. Write a simple program that first selects the male patients and then the female patients for listing. Create a program called By_sex by entering

```
MODIFY COMMAND By_sex
```

Begin the program by opening the Admit database and clearing the screen. Enter

```
USE Admit
CLEAR
```

The first list will be the names and phones numbers of the males. Enter

```
LIST First,Last,Phone FOR UPPER(Sex)="M"
```

The next command should list the same data for the females. Try this on your own. If you need help, the correct command can be found at the end of the chapter in the Answers to Exercises section as exercise 3.

Conclude the program by closing the database. Enter

```
CLOSE DATABASE
RETURN
```

Execute the program by pressing (Alt)-e then typing r.

The program will use the FOR clauses to create separate male and female patient lists (see Figure 2.8).

Filters

Selection of records with the FOR clause is command specific. This means that the selection criterion applies only to the command to which it is attached. Any subsequent commands are unaffected by the selection criterion used with previous commands.

In some cases, you might want to apply the same criterion to a number of commands. One method is simply to enter the same FOR clause following each command. dBASE IV provides a method to apply a selection criterion to all subsequent commands. This type of global criterion is called a *filter*. A filter can be created at any time after you have opened a database. The filter will automatically select records for all subsequent commands that scan the database until a new filter is selected or the database is closed. The filter is automatically removed when a database is closed.

Reopen the Admit database by entering

```
USE Admit
```

Figure 2.8

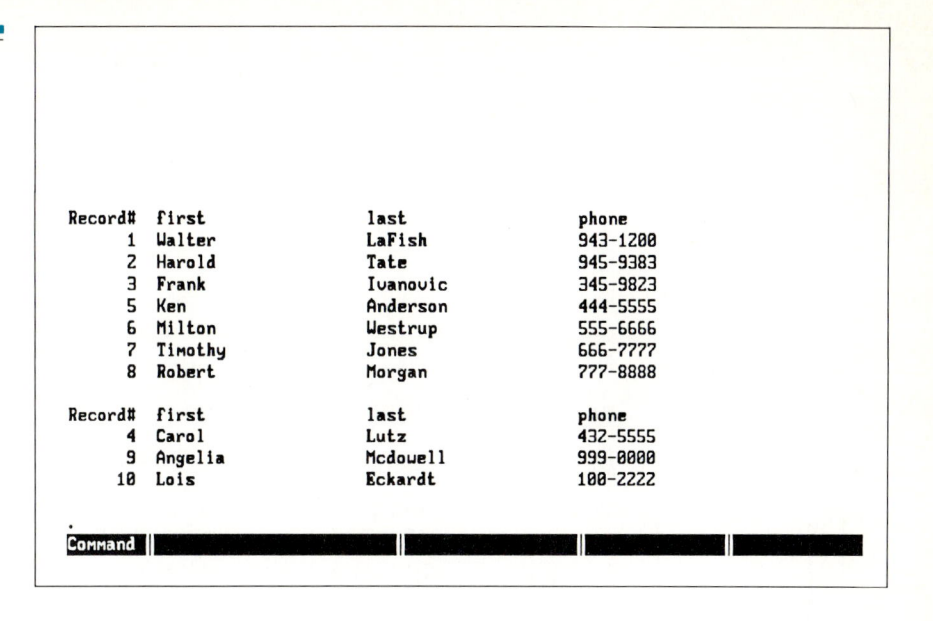

```
Record#  first          last              phone
     1   Walter         LaFish            943-1200
     2   Harold         Tate              945-9383
     3   Frank          Ivanovic          345-9823
     5   Ken            Anderson          444-5555
     6   Milton         Westrup           555-6666
     7   Timothy        Jones             666-7777
     8   Robert         Morgan            777-8888

Record#  first          last              phone
     4   Carol          Lutz              432-5555
     9   Angelia        Mcdowell          999-0000
    10   Lois           Eckardt           100-2222
```

`Command`

The command that creates a filter is SET FILTER TO. This command requires a logical expression like the one used with the FOR clause. The database filter sets up the database so that it functions as if the selected records were the only ones in the database. For example, suppose you want to work only with patients who have not had anesthesia. The expression to select those records would be .NOT.Anesthesia. Recall that logical fields like Anesthesia use the simplified form of expression. Enter

`SET FILTER TO .NOT.Anesthesia`

All subsequent commands now automatically use this filter criterion. Enter

`LIST First,Last`

The LIST command shows only selected records even though you did not add a FOR clause to the command.

When a filter is active, you can use FOR clauses to further select records from within the group. For example, to list only the female patients in the nonanesthesia group, you would enter a command with a FOR clause. Enter

`LIST First,Last FOR UPPER(Sex)="F"`

This command narrows down the list of patients to one, Carol Lutz.

The Parts of dBASE IV Commands ■ **69**

Filters allow you to easily modify a program by setting a filter at its beginning. All subsequent commands automatically conform to the filter criterion. Thus, it is not necessary to modify all the commands in a program to change the selection criterion. For example, let's change the Names program to work only with patients discharged on or before 11/15/88. Load the program into the editor by entering

```
MODIFY COMMAND Names
```

Insert a blank line at line 2 by pressing (Alt)-w and typing a, and enter the following command on that blank line. This command uses the DTOC() function to compare the date to "11/15/88".

```
SET FILTER TO DTOC(Discharge)<="11/15/88"
```

Execute the program by pressing (Alt)-e and typing r.

When the program pauses, press any key to allow it to complete. The program limits the output to the records that qualify under the selection filter. The filter applies the criterion equally to both of the LIST commands in the file (see Figure 2.9).

Global Field Selection

In the previous section, you learned how a selection criterion in the form of a logical dBASE IV expression can be globally applied to establish a database filter. dBASE IV also supplies a global setting to

Figure 2.9

```
Record#  first           last              phone
      1  Walter          LaFish            943-1200
      2  Harold          Tate              945-9383
      3  Frank           Ivanovic          345-9823
      4  Carol           Lutz              432-5555
      6  Milton          Westrup           555-6666

Press any key to continue...
Record#  admit     discharge  days_stay    charges
      1  11/01/88  11/05/88        5.00      95.00
      2  11/09/88  11/09/88        1.00   18294.00
      3  11/12/88  11/13/88        2.00   27445.00
      4  11/10/88  11/13/88        4.00   11103.00
      6  11/14/88  11/15/88        2.00    3325.00
.
Command
```

70 ■ **Linear Programming**

automatically generate a list of fields to be used with each command. For example, in this chapter most of the commands list the fields First and Last several times. dBASE IV allows you to specify a group of fields that are automatically selected. Open the Admit database file.

```
USE Admit
```

You can specify fields by using SET FIELDS TO, followed by a list of the fields that should be used. The order of the fields is significant since that is the order in which they will be displayed. In this case, select the following fields: First, Last, and Phone. Enter

```
SET FIELDS TO First,Last,Phone
```

The SET FIELDS TO command will permit only those fields selected to be listed. Those fields will be automatically selected if no field list is used with a command. For example, if you enter a LIST command with no field list, the SET FIELDS TO setting will supply those three fields automatically. Enter

```
LIST
```

The output contains only the three selected fields. With SET FIELDS TO in effect, you cannot enter commands that refer to fields in the structure that are not included in the set fields to list. Enter

```
LIST Admit
```

dBASE IV responds with a **variable not found** error message. Press ⏎.

In addition, you cannot use references to unselected fields. Enter

```
LIST FOR UPPER(Sex)="M"
```

Once again, a **variable not found** error message is displayed because of the reference to an unselected field. Press ⏎.

The advantage of a fields setting is similar to the advantage of the SET FILTER TO command: you can execute several commands that automatically select the same group of fields. For example, suppose after listing the data from the currently selected fields, you wish to copy only those fields to another database. Enter

```
COPY TO Phonelst
```

Place the new file, Phonelst (phone list), in use by entering

```
USE Phonelst
```

List the structure of this file by entering

LIST STRUCTURE

The new file contains only three fields, those that were selected by the SET FIELDS TO command when the COPY command, which created this file, was issued (see Figure 2.10).

Modular Programming

The SET FIELDS TO and the SET FILTER TO commands make it possible to treat a large database with a sizable structure as if it contained only selected records and/or fields. This allows you to write a program that handles data in a more generalized way. A generalized approach to writing programs suggests dividing programs into small sections, each of which can be combined with other small sections to carry out a complete task. The advantage of this approach is that programs can share code already written. This approach eliminates the entry of commands that duplicate the commands already in another program.

This approach would change the strategy you would use to create a program. Programs can be created in a modular fashion in which each program file accomplishes one phase of the task. The entire task

Figure 2.10

```
        6  Milton          Westrup             555-6666
        7  Timothy         Jones               666-7777
        8  Robert          Morgan              777-8888
        9  Angelia         Mcdowell            999-0000
       10  Lois            Eckardt             100-2222
. list admit
. list for sex="F"
. copy to phonelst
       10 records copied
. use phonelst
. list structure
Structure for database: D:\DB4\PHONELST.DBF
Number of data records:        10
Date of last update   : 07/31/88
Field  Field Name  Type       Width    Dec   Index
    1  FIRST       Character     20                N
    2  LAST        Character     20                N
    3  PHONE       Character      9                N
** Total **                      50
.
Command  D:\db4\PHONELST      Rec 1/10      File
```

72 ■ Linear Programming

would require the execution of several of these program modules. The advantage is that one useful module could be used in combination with a variety of other modules to eliminate redundant commands.

In the case of the simple programs you are experimenting with, the practical advantage of modular program design is negligible. But these simple programs provide an opportunity to learn about modular concepts, without which writing large, complicated programs can be impossible.

For example, you can use the By_sex program previously created as a module. The program is listed below.

```
USE Admit
CLEAR
LIST First,Last,Phone FOR UPPER(Sex)="F"
LIST First,Last,Phone FOR UPPER(Sex)="M"
CLOSE DATABASE
RETURN
```

This program lists a specific set of fields, first for male, then for female. You might generalize this program in a variety of ways. Suppose you want to create the male-female list for field groups other than First,Last,Phone. The modular approach requires that you separate the commands that control the screen display, LIST and CLEAR, from the ones that select the data. A modular approach uses one program to open the database and select the fields, and a second program to actually perform the listing.

The commands SET FILTER TO and SET FIELDS TO lend themselves to this type of modular approach. To see how this works, you can create a program called Lstbysex (List by sex) that contains only the commands needed to list records by male and female groups. The program will not contain the USE command or a field list. Enter

```
MODIFY COMMAND Lstbysex
```

Enter the following program

```
CLEAR
LIST FOR UPPER(Sex)="F"
LIST FOR UPPER(Sex)="M"
RETURN
```

Save but do not execute the program by pressing (Alt)-e and typing s.

Modular Programming ■ 73

The Lstbysex program is an example of a program module. Alone, the module does not contain a complete set of instructions. It does not contain an instruction that selects the database file to work with. In order to use this module, you must make sure, either by manually entering commands at the dot prompt or by running another program module, that the prerequisite conditions for this module are in place.

Suppose that in this case you want to run the Lstbysex module for the Admit database and the fields Last, Days_stay, and Charges. Enter the USE and SET FIELDS TO commands manually.

```
USE Admit
SET FIELDS TO Last,Days_stay,Charges,Sex
```

Why does the SET FIELDS TO command include the Sex field? It is necessary because the FOR clauses in the Lstbysex program require that the Sex field be active. Execute the Lstbysex program by entering

```
DO Lstbysex
```

The Lstbysex program is in part controlled by the commands entered at the dot prompt. Because Lstbysex is not a complete description of the task, it will use the current database and database settings when it executes (see Figure 2.11).

Figure 2.11

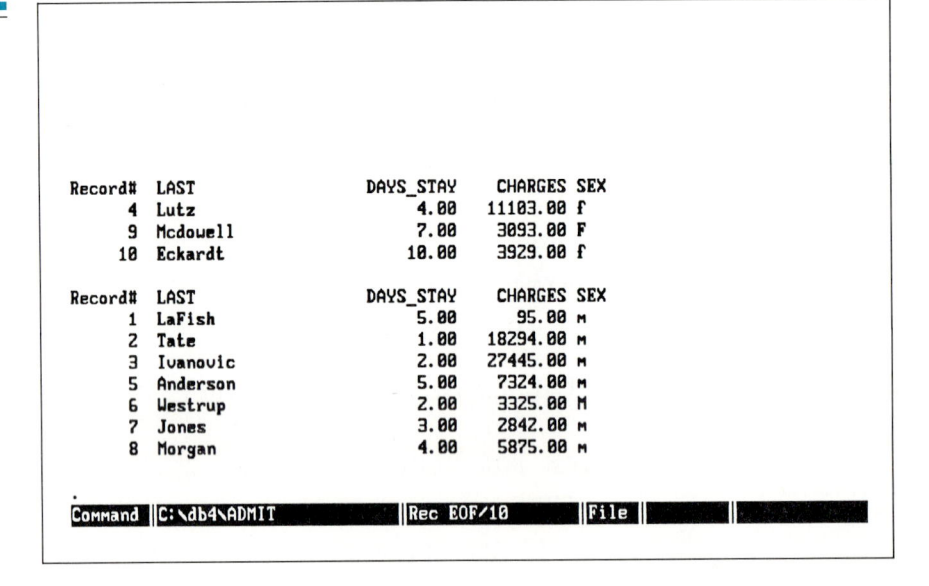

```
Record#  LAST              DAYS_STAY    CHARGES SEX
     4   Lutz                   4.00   11103.00 f
     9   Mcdowell               7.00    3093.00 F
    10   Eckardt               10.00    3929.00 f

Record#  LAST              DAYS_STAY    CHARGES SEX
     1   LaFish                 5.00      95.00 M
     2   Tate                   1.00   18294.00 M
     3   Ivanovic               2.00   27445.00 M
     5   Anderson               5.00    7324.00 M
     6   Westrup                2.00    3325.00 M
     7   Jones                  3.00    2842.00 M
     8   Morgan                 4.00    5875.00 M
.
Command  C:\db4\ADMIT         Rec EOF/10    File
```

74 ■ Linear Programming

You can modify the results of the Lstbysex program by changing the current environment. For example, you could add the Anesthesia field to the list of active fields. Enter

SET FIELDS TO Anesthesia

The effect of the SET FIELDS TO command is cumulative. The previous command simply adds Anesthesia to the other active fields. To create a new fields list, you must first enter SET FIELDS TO with no fields listed, then enter a new SET FIELDS TO list.

Execute the program again by entering

DO Lstbysex

The Lstbysex program demonstrates how modular programs use the current environmental settings.

When you use a modular program, each module has a specific relationship to the other modules you create. The Lstbysex program can operate properly only if a database has been opened and records and fields selected. In the example used in the previous section, the other necessary commands were entered manually at the dot prompt. But those commands could be placed into a program module of their own.

Suppose you want to create an environment in which the records from the Admit database are limited to those with a discharge date in November along with the Last, Days_stay, and Charges fields. Create the program Novcharg (November charges) by entering

MODIFY COMMAND Novcharg

Begin by placing the Admit database in use. This command serves two functions: it places the correct database in use, and it turns off any SET FILTER TO or SET FIELDS TO commands currently set. Following a USE command, you can be sure that all records and all fields are available. Enter

USE Admit

The next two commands select the records with a discharge date in November and the fields, Last, Days_stay, Charges, and Sex. The SET FILTER TO command must precede the SET FIELDS TO command. Why?

The filter will be selecting records based on an expression, Month(discharge) = 11, that uses a field not part of the SET FIELDS TO field list. By placing the filter before the field list, you can select

Modular Programming ■ 75

the records without having to include the discharge date as part of the field list. Enter

```
SET FILTER TO MONTH(Discharge)=11
SET FIELDS TO Last,Days_stay,Charges,Sex
RETURN
```

Save, but do not execute, the program by pressing Ctrl-End.

You now have two programs, Novcharg and Lstbysex, that are designed to perform two aspects of a single task. You can accomplish the task by executing the two programs sequentially. Enter

```
DO Novcharg
DO Lstbysex
```

The resulting output shows last name, charges, and days spent in the hospital for the patients discharged in November. The nine records in the display show that record 10, which has a December discharge date, was filtered from the display (see Figure 2.12).

Subroutines

The advantage of a modular program is that it can be used in conjunction with other modular programs to produce a variety of results. In this example, the Novcharg program selects the fields and records, and the Lstbysex program creates the data display.

Figure 2.12

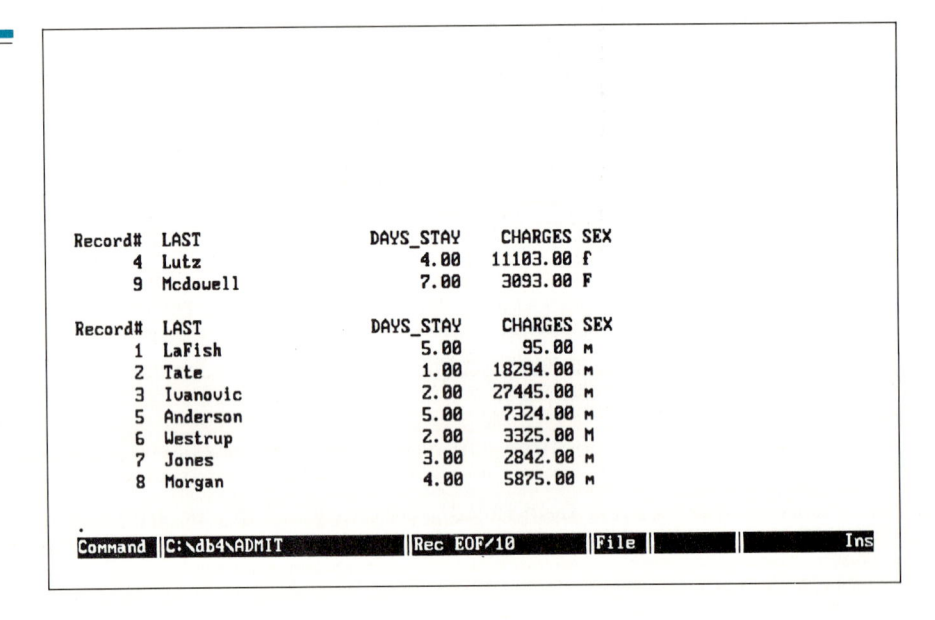

```
Record#  LAST              DAYS_STAY    CHARGES SEX
     4   Lutz                   4.00   11103.00 f
     9   Mcdowell               7.00    3093.00 F

Record#  LAST              DAYS_STAY    CHARGES SEX
     1   LaFish                 5.00      95.00 M
     2   Tate                   1.00   18294.00 M
     3   Ivanovic               2.00   27445.00 M
     5   Anderson               5.00    7324.00 M
     6   Westrup                2.00    3325.00 M
     7   Jones                  3.00    2842.00 M
     8   Morgan                 4.00    5875.00 M

Command  C:\db4\ADMIT          Rec EOF/10    File              Ins
```

■ Linear Programming

It would be convenient if you could combine the execution of the programs, in the proper order, without having to enter the DO commands one at a time.

The solution is to treat the modules as subroutines. A subroutine is a program that is executed as part of another program. You can place a DO command into a dBASE IV program. When the DO command is encountered, dBASE IV pauses the execution of the current program so that it can load and execute the program specified by the DO command. Control passes to that subroutine, and dBASE IV processes the commands in that file until encountering the RETURN command. dBASE IV then returns to the program that was paused and continues executing commands from that program (see Figure 2.13).

Create a program called Novdata (November data) by entering

`MODIFY COMMAND Novdata`

This program will use two DO commands to execute the two subroutines, Novcharg and Lstbysex. Enter

Figure 2.13

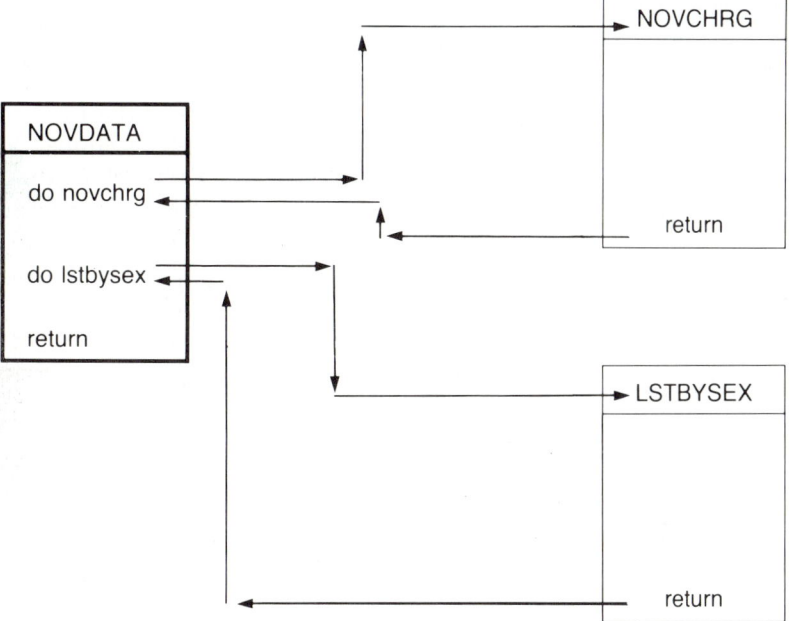

Program calling subroutines

Modular Programming ■ 77

```
DO Novcharg
DO Lstbysex
SET FIELDS OFF
RETURN
```

Save and execute this program by pressing (Alt)-e and typing r.

The program will execute, performing all the commands that are stored in the two subroutines, Novcharg and Lstbysex, and produce the same result as that achieved by consecutive manual execution of the modules.

Modular programming divides programs into two basic types: subroutines that carry out one part of a task, and controlling routines that combine and sequence the execution of the subroutines. Modular programming makes it possible to create large, complicated programs out of simpler subroutines that are easier to write.

When a subroutine is executed by a program, it is said to be called by the program. In the previous example, the calling program is Novdata and the subroutines are Novcharg and Lstbtsex.

Indexing Records

Along with selecting records, one of the most important operations performed by a database manager is sequencing, or sorting, records. dBASE IV sequences records in alphabetic, numeric, or chronological order. There are two methods of sequencing records.

1. **Sort.** Sorting in dBASE IV is a form of copying in which the records in the current database are copied into a new file in a specific alphabetic, numeric, or chronological order.

2. **Index.** Indexing is a more sophisticated method that avoids the need to copy the data into a new file. Instead, dBASE IV creates an index file that changes the order in which the records in databases are listed. The index file is not part of the database, but is a related file.

Indexing is generally a superior method of sequencing databases. Because indexing does not actually affect the database file, you can create indexes for a number of different orders for the same database. For example, you might want to have index orders for patient name, admit or discharge dates, days stayed, or any of the other items.

An index is created with the SET INDEX TO command. This command requires you to enter a field name or an expression as the index key.

Suppose you want to list the Admit database alphabetically by the last names of the patients. The first step is to place the database in use, without any filters or fields set. Enter

`USE Admit`

dBASE IV uses two types of index files.

1. **Single.** A single-index file specifies a single order for sequencing records. Each single-index file can hold one order, like last name or admission date. Since each index order is stored in a separate file, the index file names are limited to the usual MS-DOS eight-character filenames. Single-index files carry an .ndx extension. dBASE IV allows you to open up to seven individual index files at one time.

2. **Multiple.** A multiple-index file records a variety of index orders in a single file. The multiple-index files are assigned an .mdx file extension. A multiple-index file can hold up to 47 different index orders as part of the same file. Each index order is called a tag. While the name of the multiple-index file is limited to eight characters, each of its 47 possible tags can have a 10-character tag name.

If you intend to maintain more than one index order for a file, the multiple-index method has several advantages. With a multiple-index file you can gain access to several different index orders by opening a single file. With single indexes you must remember to open and close each index file. In addition, you can use slightly longer names, with 10 as compared to eight characters, for each index tag name.

You create a multiple index by indexing the database using one to 47 tags. A multiple-index command has four parts.

1. **Key.** The key is the name of a field or an expression that indicates how the records should be ranked.

2. **Tag name.** The tag name is a 1- to 10-character name that represents the name of that particular order. If a field is used as the key, you will usually use the field name as the tag, although you could use any 1- to 10-character name.

3. **Index file.** The third component of the index entry is the name of the index file that will hold all the index order tags, up to 47, that you create.

4. **Type.** Type indicates either an ascending or descending ordering preference. dBASE IV normally assumes that you want to index the records in ascending order. You can specify descending order if desired.

The index command has the following general form:

INDEX ON *key* TAG *tagname* OF *index filename*

In this case the name of the index file is the same as the database, Admit. The tag name is last. The key is the contents of the last field. Enter

INDEX ON Last TAG LAST OF Admit

dBASE IV displays the message **100% indexed 10 Records index** to indicate that all the records in the file have been recorded in the index file. Immediately following the creation of an index tag, the file assumes that you want the records listed in order of the index tag, that is, alphabetically by last name. Enter

LIST First,Last

This time the records are not listed 1 through 10 but are arranged in a different order according to the last names of the patients. This places record 5, Ken Anderson, at the top and record 6, Milton Westrup, at the bottom (see Figure 2.14). The records retain their original numbers because they have not been physically rearranged. The index file simply tells dBASE IV to scan and display the database in alphabetical order rather than in record-number order.

Figure 2.14

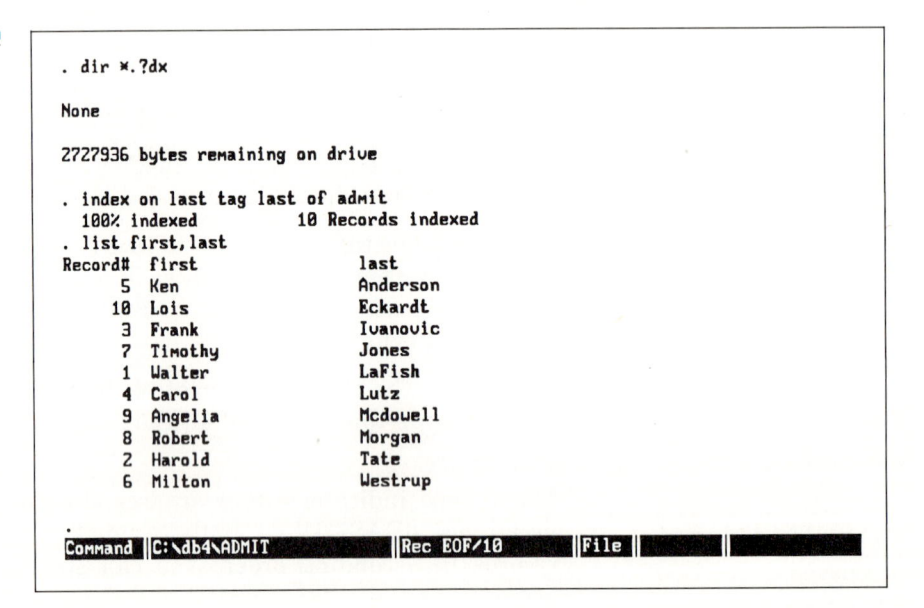

```
. dir *.?dx

None

2727936 bytes remaining on drive

. index on last tag last of admit
   100% indexed        10 Records indexed
. list first,last
Record#   first              last
     5    Ken                Anderson
    10    Lois               Eckardt
     3    Frank              Ivanovic
     7    Timothy            Jones
     1    Walter             LaFish
     4    Carol              Lutz
     9    Angelia            Mcdowell
     8    Robert             Morgan
     2    Harold             Tate
     6    Milton             Westrup
.
Command  C:\db4\ADMIT              Rec EOF/10       File
```

80 ■ Linear Programming

You can create up to 46 more tags for the same index file. For example, you might want to arrange the records in order of discharge date. Enter

INDEX ON Discharge TAG Discharge OF Admit

List the records again. Enter

LIST First,Last,Discharge

With this index order, only record 9 is placed out of record-number order.

Descending Index Order

Most sequences are ascending, beginning with the lowest value and moving toward the highest. However, in some cases you may want a list in descending order. You can select a descending index order by adding the clause DESCENDING to an INDEX command. Enter

INDEX ON Charges TAG Charges OF Admit DESCENDING

List the records by entering

LIST First,Last,Charges

The records are now listed in descending order according to the total amount of the charges (see Figure 2.15).

Figure 2.15

```
        5   Ken                 Anderson            11/17/88
        9   Angelia             Mcdowell            11/20/88
        7   Timothy             Jones               11/22/88
        8   Robert              Morgan              11/24/88
       10   Lois                Eckardt             12/03/88
. index on charges tag charges of admit descending
   100% indexed        10 Records indexed
. list first,last,charges
Record#  first              last                    charges
     3   Frank              Ivanovic              27445.00
     2   Harold             Tate                  18294.00
     4   Carol              Lutz                  11103.00
     5   Ken                Anderson               7324.00
     8   Robert             Morgan                 5875.00
    10   Lois               Eckardt                3929.00
     6   Milton             Westrup                3325.00
     9   Angelia            Mcdowell               3093.00
     7   Timothy            Jones                  2842.00
     1   Walter             LaFish                   95.00
.
Command  C:\db4\ADMIT              Rec EOF/10     File
```

Indexing Records ■ 81

Expressions as Index Keys

One of the most powerful of dBASE IV's indexing features is the ability to use any valid dBASE IV expression as an index key. This allows flexibility in creating index keys, which means that you can compensate for the vagaries of data entry during the index process. For example, suppose you want to index the database by gender. Create an index tag by entering

    INDEX ON Sex TAG Sex OF Admit

List the records.

    LIST First,Last,Sex

Examining this list reveals a problem. Indexing, like the other dBASE IV commands, is sensitive to the difference between upper- and lower-case text in a field. In this case, indexing on the field content does not produce the desired result.

The problem can be corrected by using an expression, like UPPER(Sex), that removes the case distinction. Revise the tag by entering

    INDEX ON UPPER(Sex) TAG Sex OF Admit

dBASE IV displays a box that contains the message **Index TAG already exists: SEX.** This message warns you that you already have an index tag defined, called Sex. In this case, you will want to overwrite the old tag with the new tag. Press ⏎.

List the sequence created by the new tag by entering

    LIST First,Last,Sex

This time, all males and females, both upper- and lower-case, are grouped together correctly.

Suppose you want to have the names of the patients listed alphabetically within the gender groups. No one field contains all the information needed to indicate the correct order for the index. The solution is to combine the contents of several fields into a single key expression. This is done by using the plus symbol (+), the concatenation operator, to link several character fields together.

> *Note:* The term concatenation is derived from the Latin word for chaining. It refers to the process by which character items are linked together to form larger character items.

You can create the key to sequence the records in the order you desire by linking the fields in the order of their priority.

In this case, the major sort criterion is gender. However, a number of records will have the same value for the Sex field. Within each gender, you want to have the patients listed by last name. In order to sort records that may have the same gender and last name, you can include the First name field. You might want to go even further and add the middle initial, just in case the first three fields are exactly the same. Is there any limit to the number of relationships you can specify? The answer is that the total size of the index key cannot exceed 100 characters. This does not refer to the key expression used in the command, but to the text it generates. In this example, you want to use the Sex, Last name, and First name fields. Since the number of characters included in each of those fields is specified in the structure of the database file, you can find the total number of characters for the index key by adding the field widths together: Sex (1) + Last (20) + First (20) = 41 characters, well within the 100-character limit.

Enter the command that will create an index tag called Names.

```
INDEX ON UPPER(Sex)+Last+First TAG Names OF Admit
```

You can examine the effect this index has by listing the patients' names. Enter

```
LIST Last,First,Sex
```

The females are grouped at the beginning of the list and the males at the end. Further, within each gender group, the names are alphabetized.

Mixing Data Types in Indexes

When you combine data from several fields to create an index-key expression, you need to make sure that all the items are character-type fields. If you attempt to combine a numeric or date field with a character field, you must convert the date or numeric field to a character field.

Numeric fields can be converted to text by using the STR() function. Suppose you want to sequence the database by Sex, a character field, and within that category by Days_stayed, a numeric field. Enter

```
INDEX ON UPPER(Sex)+STR(Days_stay) TAG Days OF;
    Admit
```

Display the results by entering

```
LIST Last,Days_stay,Sex
```

Indexing Records ■ 83

The list shows females and males grouped, with each group ordered by the number of days in the hospital (see Figure 2.16).

If you want to combine text with dates, you must use a special function, DTOS(), date to string. The DTOS() function is different from the DTOC() function in that it creates a string in which the year, month, and day values are displayed in that order, rather than month, day, and year. This is necessary because indexing requires that the characters be in the proper logical sequence. Enter

```
INDEX ON UPPER(Sex)+DTOS(Admit) TAG Admit OF Admit
```

To see the result of this indexing strategy, enter

```
LIST First,Last,Sex,Admit
```

Selecting Index Tags

Once you have created a multiple-index file with more than one index tag, special techniques are required to access a previously created index order tag.

When you close the database file, the index file currently open will close. Enter

```
CLOSE DATABASE
```

Figure 2.16

```
        7  Jones          Timothy
        1  LaFish         Walter
        8  Morgan         Robert
        2  Tate           Harold
        6  Westrup        Milton

. index on upper(sex)+str(days_stay) tag days of admit
   100% indexed       10 Records indexed
. list last,days_stay,sex
Record#  last                  days_stay sex
      4  Lutz                       4.00 f
      9  Mcdowell                   7.00 F
     10  Eckardt                   10.00 f
      2  Tate                       1.00 M
      3  Ivanovic                   2.00 M
      6  Westrup                    2.00 M
      7  Jones                      3.00 M
      8  Morgan                     4.00 M
      1  LaFish                     5.00 M
      5  Anderson                   5.00 M
.
Command  D:\db4\ADMIT            Rec EOF/10    File              Ins
```

When you open the database file, you need to consider whether or not you want to open the multiple-index file also. If you do, dBASE IV provides two methods by which this can be done.

1. **Index clause.** You can attach an INDEX clause to the USE command so that dBASE IV will open both the database and the index file.
2. **SET INDEX TO.** The SET INDEX TO command is used to access an index file after you have opened the database file.

Use the INDEX clause with the USE command by entering

```
USE Admit INDEX Admit
```

dBASE IV will display the message **Database is in natural order.** This message indicates that the index file has been opened but none of the index tags has been activated. dBASE IV will list your records in the same order in which they were entered, referred to as the natural order, until you select one of the index tags.

You can display a list of the available index tags by using the DISPLAY STATUS command. Enter

```
DISPLAY STATUS
```

DISPLAY STATUS lists the name of the database and index file and all of the tags created in the multiple index along with the key expression used by each tag. This is a very valuable display because it is the only way to find out what key expression was used to create an index tag (see Figure 2.17).

Return to the dot prompt by pressing (Esc).

To select one of the tags as the active index, you can use the SET ORDER TO command. The SET ORDER TO command indicates which of the multiple index tags should control the listing of the file's records. This index is referred to as the master index tag. Enter

```
SET ORDER TO Tag Names
```

The file will now be sequenced according to the key expression used to create the names index tag—Sex, Last, and First.

The USE/INDEX, SET INDEX TO, and SET ORDER TO commands can be used in a number of ways to accomplish the same task. The USE command accepts an ORDER clause. This allows you to open a database file, open an index file, and select the master tag in a single command. Below is an example of a command that will open the Ad-

Figure 2.17

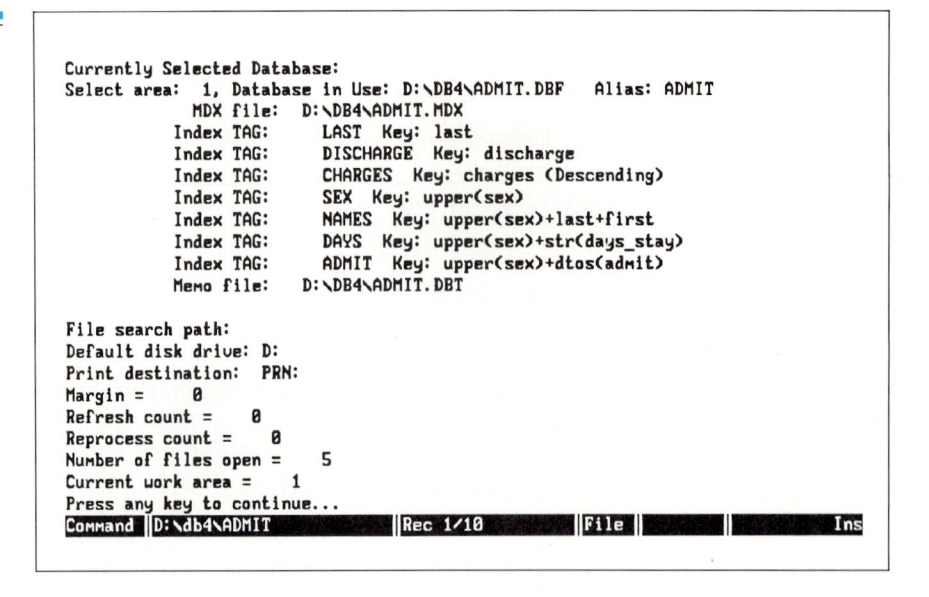

```
Currently Selected Database:
Select area:  1, Database in Use: D:\DB4\ADMIT.DBF   Alias: ADMIT
         MDX file:   D:\DB4\ADMIT.MDX
        Index TAG:     LAST  Key: last
        Index TAG:     DISCHARGE  Key: discharge
        Index TAG:     CHARGES  Key: charges (Descending)
        Index TAG:     SEX  Key: upper(sex)
        Index TAG:     NAMES  Key: upper(sex)+last+first
        Index TAG:     DAYS  Key: upper(sex)+str(days_stay)
        Index TAG:     ADMIT  Key: upper(sex)+dtos(admit)
        Memo file:   D:\DB4\ADMIT.DBT

File search path:
Default disk drive: D:
Print destination: PRN:
Margin =      0
Refresh count =    0
Reprocess count =   0
Number of files open =    5
Current work area =   1
Press any key to continue...
Command  D:\db4\ADMIT         Rec 1/10      File                Ins
```

mit database, open the Admit multiple-index file, and select Charges as the master index. Enter

`USE Admit INDEX Admit ORDER Charges`

dBASE IV displays the message **Master index: CHARGES** to confirm that the index and order clauses have done their job.

Adding Indexes to Programs

You can use an existing index order within a program by including the index-related commands in your program. For example, it might make sense to use the Charges index order in the Novdata program. The best place for the INDEX command is inside the Novcharg subroutine because that is the one that contains the USE command. Enter

`MODIFY COMMAND Novcharg`

Remove the current USE command by entering (Ctrl)-t (2 times).

Enter a command that will open the Admit database, the Admit index file, and select the Charges index tag. Try this on your own. If you need help, the correct commands can be found at the end of the chapter in the Answers to Exercises section as exercise 4.

Following the entry of that command, save, but do not execute, the program by entering (Ctrl)-(End).

The addition of the INDEX clause in the subroutine affects the sequences of records listed by the Novdata program. Run that program by entering

DO Novdata

This time, the display shows the database contents in descending order of charges within gender groups.

Close the files by entering

CLOSE DATABASE

Summary

dBASE IV is part database management application and part programming language. In this chapter, you have seen how the database manager can be transformed into a programmable environment by deferring the execution of commands that would normally be typed in one at a time.

The programs you created are called linear programs because the commands contained within the program files are executed in sequence from first to last. This is the simplest type of dBASE IV program to create. In these programs, most of the complicated processing tasks, such as selecting or indexing records, are performed automatically by dBASE IV. Your programs consist of an outline of database management tasks that need to be carried out to achieve a specific result. The linear programs you create organize and automate database functions that normally require the entry of a number of consecutive database commands.

Linear programs can be built in a modular fashion so that each program carries out one phase of a task. You can then create a master program that calls the smaller modules, called subroutines, in a specific order. The advantage of modular programming is that you can create new applications by mixing and matching the subroutines in different combinations and orders. This avoids writing duplicate commands in programs that have similar structures.

dBASE IV also provides environmental commands that begin with the verb SET and establish a condition that continues until a new condition is set. Environmental commands make it possible to write generalized programs that adapt to the current environment when they execute. Writing generalized programs that conform to previous environments is another way of getting the most performance out of the smallest number of program files.

The key concepts in this chapter include:

Language Concept. A computer language is a collection of written commands. The commands are composed of definite parts. Commands begin with a verb that refers to one of the operations that dBASE IV can perform, such as index, list, or copy. The command can also require an object or list of objects. An object in dBASE IV is a data item such as a field, or an expression that can be calculated from field information. Commands also can have clauses that modify the way that the verb operates, as when the FOR clause selects records for the verb to operate on. The key to writing programs is to be able to combine, not memorize, dBASE IV commands.

Strategy Concept. The structure of a programming language makes possible several coding options to accomplish the same end. The best option depends on the program's goal. Modular programs are more difficult to write but more efficient in the long run. Effective programming requires a plan or a strategic approach to solving a problem. There is no one right way to write a program that solves a problem. There are many correct paths, each with its own strengths and weaknesses.

MODIFY COMMAND. dBASE IV programs are text files. These files are created by invoking the dBASE IV editor with the MODIFY COMMAND command. You can use any standard text editor or many of the popular word processing programs, like WordPerfect or Microsoft Word, to write programs.

Compiling. To speed up the execution of programs, dBASE IV converts text files with a .prg extension into a compressed format called an object file with a .dbo extension. dBASE IV can read and execute commands in a .dbo file faster than it can by reading an original text file. Compiling in standard programming languages like Pascal has a different meaning than does compiling in dBASE IV.

DO. The DO command executes a dBASE IV program. The command can be included in a program to call up a subroutine.

Expressions. An expression is a statement that tells dBASE IV how to calculate a value. Expressions can use numeric or character data. A numeric expression uses arithmetic to arrive at the expressed value. A character expression may join, or concatenate, several character fields.

FOR Clause. The FOR clause selects records to be used with a command verb. When a FOR clause is added to a verb, dBASE IV tests each record in the database to see if it qualifies for inclusion in the verb's operation. The FOR clause requires a logical expression.

Logical Expressions. Logical expressions perform true/false tests. They usually compare the contents of a field to some literal value. The expression can test for equal to, not equal to, greater than, less than, greater or equal to, or less than or equal to relationships. Logical expressions always evaluate as either true or false.

Scope. Scope limits the operation of a command to a specific physical area of the database. Scope does not require an expression because it does not perform a test. dBASE IV allows you to select the following scopes: ALL, NEXT *n*, RECORD *n*, or REST.

Functions. A function is a built-in dBASE IV feature that modifies the contents of a data item in a special way. It plays the same role in a programming language that an adjective in the English language does. The function transforms the data into a variation on the original data. For example, dBASE IV provides a number of functions that transform dates into specific types of chronological data: for example, CDOW() yields the name of the day of the week of the specified date field.

Filters. A filter functions like a global application of a FOR clause. When a filter is set, all commands that follow will automatically select certain records. Filters allow you to write generalized programs that will adapt to differing environments.

Indexing. Indexes sequence databases in a logical order. dBASE IV can create individual indexes or multiple indexes. The multiple-index file can hold up to 47 different index orders called tags. The index tags are related to a field or expression that tells dBASE IV the order records should be sequenced in. The SET ORDER command allows you to select from among the available index tags. Index expressions allow you to create complex multi-level sequences when fields contain duplicate data.

Review Problems for Chapter 2

Chapter 2 covered skills that allow you to retrieve and manipulate data stored in dBASE IV database files. The following problems will help you review those skills. The problems assume you are working with the Sales database created in the Review Problems section of chapter 1.

1. Enter a command to list the companies and total amounts for taxable sales.

2. Enter a command to list the companies and total sales amounts that are not taxable.

3. List the sales date and item name for all items sold in July.

4. List the price and quantity from records 12 through 20.

5. List the company and item for any sales on 7/14/88.

6. List the dates of any sales that were recorded for a Saturday or Sunday.

7. Enter a command that lists the price and item name of all items that contain the word "mask."

8. Enter a command that lists all the company names and the total amount for sales between 7/14/88 and 7/21/88.

9. Create a program that lists all the taxable sales and then the non-taxable sales.

10. Create an index tag called Dates for the Sales database in a multiple-index file called Sales ordered by sales date.

11. Create two more index tags called Company ordered by company name and Item ordered by item name.

12. Create a program that lists the company, total amount, and tax for only the taxable records. The list should be in company name order.

13. Modify the previous program to print the list.

14. Create a program that lists the date, company, total amount, and quantity for all products that contain the word "bag." The list should be ordered by sales date.

Answers to Exercises

1. Add the WAIT command to a program.

   ```
   MODIFY COMMAND Names
   ```
   ⬇ (2 times)

   Alt–W a

   ⬇
   ```
   WAIT
   ```

2. List the female patients.

   ```
   LIST First,Last FOR Sex="f"
   ```

3. List the female patients.

   ```
   LIST First,Last,Phone FOR UPPER(Sex)="F"
   ```

4. Open the database and use the Admit index.

   ```
   USE Admit INDEX Admit ORDER Charges
   ```

3
Programming Screen Displays

In chapter 2, you learned how the dBASE IV data manager handles data stored in .dbf files. You used commands that constitute the basic dBASE IV database tool box that you would otherwise have to create. The advantage of programming with dBASE IV—compared to standard programming languages—is that these programming tools and operations already exist.

dBASE IV also provides basic tools for the entry and display of data using commands like APPEND, EDIT, ?, LIST, and DISPLAY.

To create customized applications, you will have to go beyond those basic commands and learn to create input and output displays of your own design. This chapter introduces you to the tools and techniques that allow dBASE IV programs to control the information displayed on the screen.

Interactive programs directly address the user. Interactive programs contrast with the linear programs you have already created in two important ways. First, interactive programs pause to allow a user to enter information or respond to a question. Second, the processing that takes place during the program's operation is hidden from users. The program presents only the information you want a user to see.

Setup

To begin this chapter, you need the following:

- dBASE IV should be loaded into the memory of the computer and running. Exit the dBASE IV Control Center menus by entering [Esc]-y, as discussed in chapter 1.

- The default drive and directory should be set to the directory holding the files that you have been using with this book. Remember that these chapters are predicated on the use of a hard disk labeled drive C. If your computer system is different, please make the correct drive and directory adjustments.

The cursor should be beside the dot prompt. You are ready to begin.

Structured vs. Unstructured Displays

dBASE IV allows you to display information on the screen in two different ways: unstructured and structured. Unstructured output is the simplest kind of output you can generate with dBASE IV.

The commands that create this output, ?, LIST, and DISPLAY, are called unstructured because they display information at the next available line on the screen, based on the current cursor location.

Structured output allows you to select the screen location where data will be displayed. Structured output uses an imaginary screen grid of rows and columns (see Figure 3.1). The standard IBM PC or compatible display adapter offers a grid that is 80 columns wide and 25 lines long.

Note: If you are working with an EGA or VGA monitor and adapter system, dBASE IV has special display modes to increase the number of screen lines to 43.

Row and column numbers begin in the upper-left corner of the screen. The first row is 0 and the last is 24, while the first column is 0 and the last is 79. Every character position on the screen can be specifically addressed by a row/column pair of values.

The following sections explore the differences between the two types of output and the appropriate use for each.

Figure 3.1

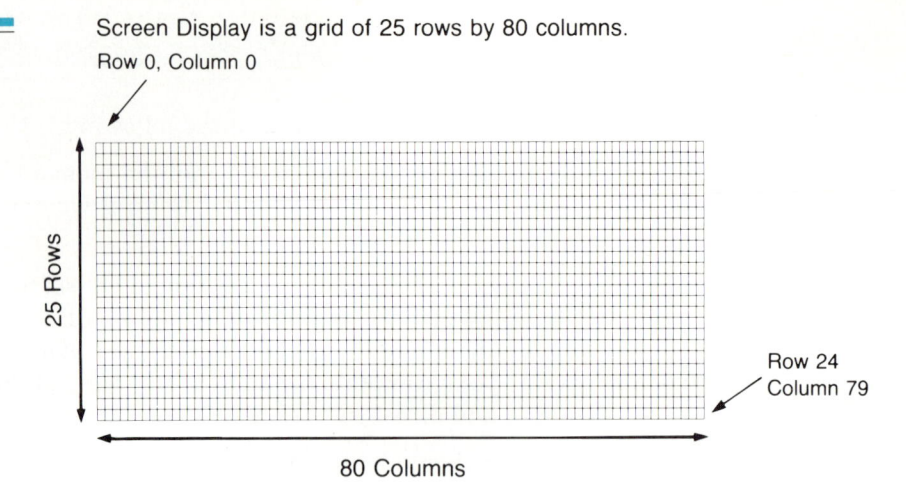

Screen Display is a grid of 25 rows by 80 columns.
Row 0, Column 0

Row 24
Column 79

25 Rows

80 Columns

Using ? for Output

The basic difference between unstructured and structured output is the selection of screen lines. Unstructured output always places new information at the next available line on the screen. As an example, we'll create three memory variables called Name, Amount, and Date.

The concept of memory variables is very important in programming languages. A memory variable temporarily stores a single piece of information—a number, character string, or date—for use during the program. Memory variables are different from the data stored in database files because they are held in memory and not transferred to a disk file. When you quit dBASE IV, the values of the variables in memory are lost. dBASE IV allows you to create up to 500 memory variables at one time. As you will learn later, memory variables are essential to writing programs. Memory variables also have the advantage of being independent of any particular database file since they are held in memory rather than database files. Variables can be treated much like field names when it comes to entering them into commands.

You will now create three memory variables to act as data for experimenting with dBASE IV output commands. Enter

```
NAME="Walter LaFish"
AMOUNT=10000
```

The third item raises an interesting point about dates as memory variables. Your goal is to create a memory variable that is a date-type variable for the date 10/15/88. Enter

```
DATE=10/15/88
```

94 ■ **Programming Screen Displays**

dBASE IV will respond by displaying 0.01, indicating that the value stored is not a date but a numeric decimal value. Why?

dBASE IV does not view the entry as a date but as a numeric expression meaning "10 divided by 15 divided by 88." The slashes were read as mathematical operators indicating division. Since you do not want the entry to be stored as a numeric variable but as a date variable, this is not what you had in mind. Try enclosing the date in quotation marks. Enter

```
DATE="10/15/88"
```

The program displays 10/15/88. The results this time look more promising. But is this really a date-type variable? You can list all the memory variables currently defined by using the DISPLAY MEMORY command. Enter

```
DISPLAY MEMORY
```

dBASE IV lists the three memory variables currently defined (see Figure 3.2). The display shows that the date variable is not a D (date-type) but a C (character-type) variable. The quotation marks changed the data from numeric to character but not to date.

To get dBASE IV to create a date-type variable, you must use a conversion function to change a character item to a date item. dBASE IV

Figure 3.2

```
. amount=10000
          10000
. date="10/15/88"
10/15/88
. disp memo
          User Memory Variables

DATE       pub   C   "10/15/88"
AMOUNT     pub   N           10000  (10000.00000000000000)
NAME       pub   C   "Walter LaFish"

   3 out of 500 memvars defined (and 0 array elements)


          User MEMVAR/RTSYM Memory Usage

   2800 bytes used for 1 memvar blocks (max=10)
    850 bytes used for 1 rtsym blocks (max=10)
      0 bytes used for 0 array element memvars
     21 bytes used for 2 memvar character strings

Press any key to continue...
Command
```

Structured vs. Unstructured Displays

supplies a character-to-date conversion function called CTOD(). Return to the dot prompt by pressing (Esc).

Use the CTOD() function to create a date variable from a character string. Enter

```
DATE=CTOD("10/15/88")
```

Display the memory variables again by entering

```
DISPLAY MEMORY
```

In this situation, use the conversion function CTOD() to create a date variable. In the previous chapter, you entered dates into database fields that were defined as dates in the database structure. When you define individual variables, the type of variable is implied by the type of data assigned to it. If you use numeric data in the assignment, the variable is defined as a numeric type. Character data—data delimited with quotation marks—creates a character-type variable. Dates are a special case; there is no direct way to type literal information in date format because "10/15/88" is considered character data while 10/15/88 is considered numeric.

With three variables now defined, let's move on to the task of creating a screen display. Terminate the DISPLAY MEMORY listing by pressing (Esc).

You can now enter commands to display the information in memory.

> *Note:* Unlike most dBASE IV commands, a space is not required following ?. The ? command is borrowed from the BASIC language where ? is shorthand for the full command verb PRINT. To be consistent with other dBASE IV commands, this book uses a space following the ? command.

Enter

```
? NAME
```

dBASE IV displays "Walter LaFish" on the next available line on the screen. ? also allows list processing, meaning that you can enter a list of items, separated by commas, for the command to display. Enter

```
? NAME,Amount,Date
```

dBASE IV displays:

```
Walter LaFish                              10000 10/15/88
```

■ **Programming Screen Displays**

What caused the gap between Walter LaFish and 10,000? The answer again relates to the difference between the way a memory variable and a field in a database are defined.

In a database, the size of a field is fixed at the time the file is created. However, when you create a memory variable, there is no way to specify the length of the variable. That length is inferred from the assigned data. Character variables are defined to the exact length of the text that is assigned. Date variables are always defined as eight characters, just as date-type fields are automatically set to eight characters.

Numeric variables are treated differently. dBASE IV automatically assumes a length of 20 characters for each numeric value stored as a variable. This is true no matter what the size of the value stored.

The length of variables is an important factor to remember when printing values stored as variables. For example, you might use the SUM TO command to add up the values in a field. The variable that holds the total will be set to a width of 20 characters even though the values used to accumulate the total were restricted by their field size.

> *Note:* Decimals numbers are treated differently in dBASE IV. If a number has two significant decimal places, like .02, it is stored as a normal number. But if the number exceeds two decimal places, dBASE IV will store the number in a 20-character scientific notation format: .002 would be stored as .200000000000000E−2. If you want to avoid scientific notation for decimal numbers of a specific size, you can use the SET DECIMALS TO command to allow larger decimal numbers without causing the switch to scientific notation. The default value for SET DECIMALS TO is 2.

Unstructured Displays

To better understand unstructured screen displays, let's create a series of programs that use the ? command. The first program will be called Scr1.

All screen display programs have three basic parts:

1. **Set Screen Attributes.** dBASE IV has a number of special items and lines that programs automatically display. You can suppress these lines so that only the data you want to display appears when your program runs.

2. **Create/Locate Data.** Before you can display information, you must create or locate the data you will need for the display. The most common source of data is a database (.dbf) file. However, display data can be created with memory variables or system functions such as DATE() and TIME(). Another source of display data, direct user input, is covered in the next chapter.

3. **Output Commands.** These commands place the data on the screen.

An optional fourth screen-display program component resets the dBASE IV screen back to its default values. This component has no effect on your program. However, it is usually a good idea to return dBASE IV to its normal settings after you run a program. This optional command set is the opposite of the commands used in the Set Screen Attributes section. All programs that display data have these elements in common.

To create a program, you must first invoke the dBASE IV editor. Enter

```
MODIFY COMMAND Scr1
```

Setting Up the Environment

The first step in writing a screen display program is to set the screen environment. The environment consists of the following components:

Talk
Many dBASE IV commands echo messages to the screen during or following their execution. These responses, called talk, provide information to a user about the operation of the command just entered. In most cases you do not want this information to appear when you construct a screen display. Setting talk to off suppresses this display so that only a command that outputs information will place data on the screen.

Status Bar
The highlighted bar that runs across the bottom of the screen is called the status bar. It contains information about the current status of the dBASE IV system, such as the names of open files and the position of the record pointer. You can hide the display of this bar by setting status to off.

Scoreboard
The scoreboard is a part of the dBASE IV display that monitors the status of four aspects of the dBASE IV system: the status of the Caps Lock key, the Ins key, the Num Lock key, and the delete attribute of the current record, if any; set scoreboard to off to suppress their display.

The items covered by the scoreboard are also covered by the status bar display. This means that if status is on, the status bar is displayed and the scoreboard setting has no effect. However, when status is turned off, the scoreboard, which is set on by default, appears on line 1 of the screen display.

In order to suppress all text except that output by your program, the scoreboard should also be set to off.

CLEAR

The CLEAR command wipes the screen clear of all characters. The cursor is repositioned to the bottom-left corner of the screen. That corner is on line 23 when the status bar is displayed and on line 24, the last line on the screen, when the status bar is not displayed.

If you want your program to control all aspects of the information displayed on the screen, you should begin a program by setting talk, status, and scoreboard to off and using CLEAR to remove any characters on the screen.

Below are the first four commands of the Scr1 program. They are accompanied by a note, or comment, signified by an *. Notes are added to programs to explain their functions in plain English. Creating notes in your programs is strongly recommended. However, for our purposes here, you can save time entering these sample programs by skipping the notes.

> *Note:* Program line numbers referred to in this text are based on a program's length, including comment lines. If you omit the notes, you might want to leave blank lines to keep the total number of lines in the program the same as the listings in this book.

Enter

```
* create clear screen
SET TALK OFF
SET STATUS OFF
SET SCOREBOARD OFF
CLEAR
```

The next part of the program is the Create/Locate data section. The information for the display is created or located here. The procedures needed to gather data can be simple, like opening a .dbf file, or quite complex. You can create a few simple data items by defining memory variables just as you did earlier at the dot prompt. The following lines define three memory variables, Name, Amount, and Date. Enter

Structured vs. Unstructured Displays ■ 99

```
* define memory variables
NAME="Walter Lafish"
AMOUNT=10000
DATE=CTOD("10/15/88")
```

The next series of commands will place information on your screen. To explore how the ? command operates, enter several variations of the same command. Begin by entering a note and a ? command that displays a list of variables. Enter

```
* displays commands
? NAME,Amount,Date
```

The ? command and the items after it are automatically followed by a carriage return/linefeed combination. If the ? command is used without any data items, it creates a blank line on the screen. Enter

```
?
```

You can print a series of data items on separate lines by using a series of ? commands. Enter

```
? NAME
? Amount
? Date
```

The final step in a screen display program is to pause the program before you reset the screen display. The WAIT command pauses the program until a user strikes a key. Enter

```
WAIT
```

The final section of the Scr1 program sets the screen display attributes back to their original condition. Enter

```
* reset screen
SET SCOREBOARD ON
SET STATUS ON
SET TALK ON
CLEAR
RETURN
```

The entire program should look like this:

```
* create clear screen
SET TALK OFF
```

```
SET STATUS OFF
SET SCOREBOARD OFF
CLEAR
* define memory variables
NAME="Walter Lafish"
AMOUNT=10000
DATE=CTOD("10/15/88")
* displays commands
? NAME,Amount,Date
?
? NAME
? AMOUNT
? DATE
WAIT
* reset screen
SET SCOREBOARD ON
SET STATUS ON
SET TALK ON
CLEAR
RETURN
```

Save the program by pressing Ctrl-End.

Execute the program by entering

```
DO Scr1
```

dBASE IV compiles the program and then executes its instructions. The screen will look like Figure 3.3.

There are several points of interest concerning this display.

- **Vertical location.** When the ? command displays information, the first line of text is written at the top of the screen. Each subsequent line of text scrolls the screen display down one line.

- **Horizontal location.** The horizontal location of each line of displayed data is the flush left edge of the screen.

- **Format.** The values appear exactly the way they are stored in memory. The numeric variable Amount is preceded by blank spaces both times that it prints, creating an odd alignment that differs from the other two items.

Structured vs. Unstructured Displays ■ 101

Figure 3.3

```
Walter Lafish            10000 10/15/88

Walter Lafish
                10000
10/15/88
Press any key to continue...
```

You can improve the look of this program by taking advantage of some of the optional clauses that dBASE IV allows with the ? command.

Terminate the program by pressing ⏎.

Display the Scr1 program for editing by entering

MODIFY COMMAND Scr1

? Command Clauses

dBASE IV provides flexibility for the ? command with the addition of four kinds of optional clauses: function, picture, at, and style.

FUNCTION
A FUNCTION clause is similar in purpose to a PICTURE clause. Both control some aspect of the displayed data. The difference is that a function affects the entire data item. If you want to convert some, but not all, of the characters to upper-case, choose a PICTURE clause. If you want the entire item converted to upper-case, use a FUNCTION clause.

PICTURE
A PICTURE clause controls the way the data is displayed by using a template. A PICTURE template is a model that tells dBASE IV how to display data. PICTURE templates are most frequently used with

numeric values to add formatting characters, such as dollar signs, commas, and extra decimal places. There are also templates that apply to text data, like conversion to upper-case characters.

AT

The AT clause permits you to specify a horizontal column location to align the data. Use this option to place items at locations other than the default—flush at the left side of the screen.

STYLE

STYLE adds special attributes to text to yield bold, italic, or underlined characters. The effect of a STYLE clause is device-dependent; not all screen displays (or printers) can produce all the special styles available. If a STYLE is selected, dBASE IV uses normal text if the screen or printer driver does not support that attribute.

Move the cursor to the beginning of line 11. Delete the current list of ? commands by entering Ctrl-y five times.

Make sure that the dBASE IV editor is in the Insert mode.

> *Note:* Ins will appear on the right edge of the Status line to indicate the Insert mode is active. If this is not the case, press Ins to change to the Insert mode.

Using a FUNCTION Clause

First, let's look at an example use of a FUNCTION clause. Suppose you want to print the Name variable in all upper-case characters. The ! symbol indicates case conversion and is entered as a text string following the word function. dBASE IV recognizes the following characters as special symbols for the FUNCTION clause:

> *Note:* Letters can be entered as either upper or lower case.

Symbol	Use
!	Characters, convert to upper-case characters
^	Numeric, scientific notation
$	Numeric, fills leading blanks with $
(	Numeric, negative numbers with parentheses
A	Character, alpha only
B	All, left align within field width
C	Numeric, display CR for positive (credit)
D	Date, American date
E	Date, European date

H	All, set horizontal width
I	All, center within field width
J	All, right align within field width
L	Numeric, display leading zeros
R	All, add nonstored characters
T	All, trim leading and trailing blanks
X	Numeric, display DB for negative (debit)
Z	Numeric, display zero values as blanks

To convert the name to upper-case characters, enter

`? NAME FUNCTION "!"`

You can use the $ function to fill the leading blanks in the Amount variable with $ signs instead of blank characters. Enter

`? AMOUNT FUNCTION "$"`

Picture Clauses

PICTURE clauses differ from FUNCTION clauses by requiring the creation of a template. A template is a series of symbols written as a string of text. Each symbol controls the display of a single character in the output. If you use fewer characters in the template than in the data item, dBASE IV truncates the display of the data item so as not to exceed the total number of symbols in the template. The individual character control provided by PICTURE templates allows you to control more precisely the display of each character. Templates use the following symbols:

Symbol	Use
!	Characters, convert character to upper-case
$	Numeric, displays $ in place of blank
*	Numeric, displays * in place of blank
,	Numeric, displays a comma if sufficient digits
.	Numeric, decimal point location
9	Numeric, displays any number
A	Character, alpha only
L	Logical values only
N	Alpha and numeric only
X	Any character or number
Y	Logical, Y or N only

Suppose you want to display the Amount variable as 10,000.00. You would have to build a template that shows dBASE IV how you want the value formatted. The template should be large enough to accommodate the value you want to display. Enter

```
? AMOUNT PICTURE "999,999.99"
```

This template has two effects. First, it inserts a comma between the thousands and hundreds places. Second, it inserts a decimal point and two zeros following the value. There is a third effect: the template's size restricts the number of characters displayed to six-digit numbers.

You can also use templates to control individual characters. For example, you can use the ! symbol to convert individual characters to upper-case. In the command shown below, the first six characters are set for upper-case conversion, while the remaining characters display as they are stored. Keep in mind that if the text is longer than the number of character symbols entered into the template, the item display is truncated.

```
? NAME PICTURE "!!!!!!XXXXXXX"
```

Horizontal Location

dBASE IV places the output of the ? command at the left edge of the screen. The AT clause allows you to select a specific column at which to print the item. This is useful when you want to line up text in columns or space data across a line. The AT keyword is followed by a numeric value, 0 to 79, to indicate a screen column location. The commands shown below are examples of commands that use the AT clause to control horizontal placement. All three items will print at column 35. Enter

```
? NAME AT 35
? DATE AT 35
? AMOUNT AT 35 FUNCTION "B"
```

The last item in this list, Amount, requires a more elaborate command. Remember that numeric variables are defined as 20-character values. Numeric values display unused characters to the left of the first character. To make sure that the first character in the number, rather than a blank space, is placed at column 35, you need to use the FUNCTION clause to prompt the number value to be left-aligned. The B function clause performs this operation.

STYLE Clauses

The STYLE clause allows you to add special screen or printer attributes to the items that you display. The STYLE clause produces device-dependent effects. This means that the actual effect of a STYLE clause depends upon the exact type of screen display and adapter or printer used. It also assumes that if you have a device with special features, you have installed the proper device drivers for dBASE IV.

Note: It is not necessary to use the device drivers and STYLE settings to implement printer functions. You can use dBASE IV programming commands to send special printer codes to the printer as part of your program, creating or expanding printer functionality not provided by the dBASE IV device drivers. dBASE IV supplies printer drivers for users unfamiliar with printer-code programming.

The STYLE clause recognizes the following parameters:

Symbol	Use
B	Bold text
I	Italicized text
U	Underlined text
R	Raised, superscript printing
L	Lowered, subscript printing

The underline attribute is the one that is most likely to apply to most screen displays and printers. Enter

```
? NAME STYLE "u"
```

You can combine FUNCTION, PICTURE, AT, and STYLE clauses to produce the type of display you desire. For example, the command below produces a bold numeric value formatted with a PICTURE template and positioned at column 25. Enter

```
? AMOUNT AT 25 PICTURE "999,999.99" STYLE "b"
```

Create a command that will display the Name variable, underlined, beginning at column 35, and in upper-case characters. Try this on your own. If you need help, the correct commands can be found at the end of the chapter in the Answers to Exercises section under exercise 1.

Save and execute the program by entering (Ctrl)-(End),

```
DO Scr1
```

When the program runs, you will see the variables displayed using the various clauses (see Figure 3.4).

Figure 3.4

```
WALTER LAFISH
$10000
10,000.00

WALTER Lafish
                              Walter Lafish
                              10/15/88
                              10000
Walter Lafish
                        10,000.00
                              WALTER LAFISH
Press any key to continue...
```

The three displayed lines show the use of FUNCTION clauses. The $ FUNCTION clause fills the 20-character numeric variable with 15 $ signs.

The fourth and fifth lines show the use of PICTURE clauses to affect individual characters. The next display shows the use of the AT function to position text to a different horizontal column.

Finally, the last three lines use the STYLE clause, in combination with other clauses, to add text attributes to displayed items.

Complete the program by pressing ⏎.

Screen Display Presentations

The previous program displayed a series of unrelated examples of screen display items that make use of the ? command and its FUNCTION, PICTURE, AT, and STYLE clauses. The real goal of using these screen display functions is to create useful screen displays.

To show how this is done, our next step is to modify the Scr1 program to create a more standard screen display. For simplicity, you will use the three variables Name, Amount, and Date as the raw data for the display.

The program you have been working with had three data items defined as memory variables. The goal of this revision to the program is to present this information as a coherent screen display using the ? command with dBASE IV functions and clauses. This exercise will teach you some of the fundamental techniques used to present data on the computer screen.

Before you modify the program, use the dot prompt mode to explore some of the functions you will use in the revised program.

Repeating a Character

One way to make the screen display of data more pleasing to the eye is to add lines, boxes, and patterns to the display. One easy way to do this is to repeat a character a number of times. dBASE IV provides a function called REPLICATE() that repeats a character a specified number of times. For example, to display 25 asterisks, enter

```
? REPLICATE("*",25)
```

If you enter more than one character, dBASE IV repeats the entire string the specified number of times. Enter

```
? REPLICATE("*-",25)
```

Repeating two characters 25 times creates a 50-character output.

To make your displays more interesting, you can add characters to the display that do not appear on the keyboard. These characters are referred to as the extended IBM character set. The lines and boxes that appear as part of the dBASE IV screen display are composed of these characters. You can access these characters from your dBASE IV programs and make use of them to enhance your screen displays.

These characters use character code values 128 through 254.

There are two ways to enter a special character.

1. **Text string.** You can insert an extended character into a text string by using a hardware function available on most PC-compatible computers. Hold down the (Alt) key and type the number of an extended character on the numeric keypad. Type the numbers on the numeric keypad; the number keys on the top row of the keyboard will not work.

2. **CHR() function.** dBASE IV provides a special function, CHR(), that displays the character that corresponds to an extended character number used as an argument for the function. For example, ? CHR(128) will display ç.

The advantage of the CHR() function is that you can use numbers to control how often the character is displayed.

In this example, character #196 is a single horizontal line. You can draw a line all the way across the display by repeating that character 79 times.

> *Note:* Even though the screen display is 80 columns wide, replicating a character 80 times causes dBASE IV to insert a second linefeed, causing a blank line to follow the output. To avoid this problem, use 79 repetitions to draw across the screen display. Enter

```
? REPLICATE(CHR(196),79)
```

You can draw a double line by using character #205. Enter a command that will display the double line. Try this on your own. If you need help, the correct command can be found at the end of the chapter in the Answers to Exercises section under exercise 2.

Centering an Item

Suppose you want to display a text item centered between the edges of the screen. dBASE IV has no explicit command or function that will center text on the screen. Centering is just a matter of inserting the proper number of spaces in front of an item so that it appears to be in the center of the screen.

Here are the steps for calculating how to center data:

1. Count the total number of characters in the item to be displayed. For this example, let's use 20 characters.
2. Subtract that number from the total width of the screen. Since the screen is 80 characters wide, that would be 80 minus 20, leaving 60 spaces.
3. Divide this number of spaces in half, 60/2 = 30.
4. Insert that number of spaces before the text item.

At first, this may seem very complicated to express in a computer program. But by using some of dBASE IV's functions you can include the entire calculation in a single ? command.

To learn how this works, define a new variable called Title by entering.

```
TITLE="Sample Title"
```

The first step in centering text is to figure out the number of characters in the text string. This can be done by using the LEN() function. This function returns a value equal to the total number of characters in a field, variable, or literal. Enter

    ? LEN(Title)

dBASE IV displays the value of 12, the exact number of characters in the title. You can use the LEN() function to calculate the number of spaces that need to be inserted in front of the title to make sure that it is centered. This is done by subtracting the length from 80 and dividing the answer by 2. Enter

    ? (80-LEN(Title))/2

The result is 34. Because of the order of operations used by dBASE IV, use a set of parentheses to ensure that the subtraction from 80 takes place before the division by 2.

But how can you turn the value of 34 into 34 spaces? One way is to use the SPACE() function. The SPACE() function creates a text string equal to a specified number of spaces. For example, SPACE(5) creates a string of five spaces. Instead of entering a literal value such as 5, you can place the calculation (80-LEN(Title))/2 inside the SPACE() function to create the number of spaces required to center the text. Enter

    ? SPACE((80-LEN(Title))/2)+Title

The text is displayed in the center of the screen (see Figure 3.5).

This general command form will center text of any length stored in the variable Title. Change the text of the title by entering

    TITLE="This is a larger title"

You can reenter the centered title command by moving back through the command history. Press ↑ (2 times) and ↵.

The command adjusts the number of spaces for the revised text and produces a centered title.

A Formal Screen Display

The next step is to produce a screen display that makes a formal presentation of our three sample variables. Load the Scr1 program into the dBASE IV editor by entering

    MODIFY COMMAND Scr1

Move the cursor to line 11.

Figure 3.5

```
. ? replicate("*",25)
*************************
. ? replicate("*-",25)
*-*-*-*-*-*-*-*-*-*-*-*-*-*-*-*-*-*-*-*-*-*-*-*-*-
. ? replicate(chr(196),80)
─────────────────────────────────────────────────

. ? replicate(chr(205),80)
═════════════════════════════════════════════════

. title="Sample Title"
Sample Title
. ? len(title)
                12
. ? (80-len(title))/2
                34
. ? space((80-len(title))/2)+title
                                  Sample Title
.
Command
```

Remove the ? commands by pressing Ctrl-y 10 times.

Insert a blank line by pressing

Ctrl-n

Note: Make sure that the Insert mode is ON.

The first three lines of our new screen display will consist of a banner made up of a straight line, a row of asterisks, and another straight line. Enter

? REPLICATE(Chr(196),79)

? REPLICATE("*",79)

? REPLICATE(Chr(196),79)

Then enter two blank lines. A blank line is created by using a ? command by itself. Enter

?

?

Screen Display Presentations ■ 111

The next line will contain a centered heading for the display. Use the centering method previously discussed. The STYLE and FUNCTION clauses will create bold and upper-case text. Enter

```
TITLE="patient information screen display"
? SPACE((80-LEN(Title))/2)+Title FUNCTION "!";
  STYLE "b"
```

Add two more blank lines.

```
?
?
```

Time and Date Functions

Suppose you want to display the current system date and time as part of the screen display. dBASE IV provides both DATE() and TIME() functions to return the current system's date and time. The DATE() function returns a date-type value while TIME() returns a character-type item.

You can use these functions just as you would fields or variables with ? commands. Enter

```
? DATE() AT 10
```

Placing Items on the Same Line

Suppose you now want to print the TIME() function on the right side of the same line. dBASE IV displays the output of a command on the same line by using the ?? command, a variation of the ? command. ?? operates exactly the same as ? except that it places its output at the next column on the same line instead of at the beginning of the next line.

If you use an AT clause with the ?? command, the column location is counted from the left edge of the screen. To place the time at column 70 on the same line as the date, enter

```
?? TIME() AT 70
```

Add two more blank lines.

```
?
?
```

Draw a double line across the screen. Remember that a double horizontal line uses the extended character #205. Try this on your own. The correct command can be found at the end of the chapter in the Answers to Exercises section under exercise 3.

Literals and Variables

The most common way to print information on the screen is to combine literal text with a variable or field. The literal text identifies or labels the variable or field. You might want to print the words "Name of Patient" before displaying the contents of the Name variable.

There are three ways to display a label.

1. **Consecutive placement.** The individual commands ? and ?? can print data at specific horizontal locations using the AT clause. Using consecutive ? commands is the simplest way to display variables and their labels because you avoid the problems that arise when you print data of a numeric or date type along with the a text literal label. The disadvantage of this method is that it usually takes longer to write an individual command for each item than the other two methods shown below, which require only one or two commands.

2. **Concatenation.** Concatenation uses dBASE IV operators and functions to assemble the literal text and any variable information into a single print item. This method is usually the most direct means of outputting information, but it requires the correct use of dBASE IV functions.

3. **New variable.** The concatenation technique can also be used to create a new variable that contains the assembled information. You then print the new variable. This method is useful if you need to print the same item more than once in the same program.

Since you have three variables to output, you can explore all three methods. Begin with the Name variable. Since Name is a character variable, it is a simple matter to concatenate the label's text and the Name variable. The concatenation operator in dBASE IV is the + sign. dBASE IV also uses this symbol for addition. dBASE IV first determines what activity is taking place. When numeric data is involved, then dBASE IV performs an addition. When the items are characters, then concatenation is performed. The rule is that all items jointed by + signs must be of the same type. If not, a **Type mismatch** error will result. The command shown below prints the phrase "Name of Patient," five blank spaces, and the contents of the Name variable. Enter

```
? "Name of Patient:"+Space(5)+Name
```

This command prints all three elements, the label, the spaces, and the variable, as a concatenated unit. You can achieve a similar result using separated ? and ?? commands to display the data on the same line.

Next, you'll display the date. The method you'll use here requires two commands to do the job done by a single command previously, but there are some advantages. First, you do not have to convert noncharacter data like date and numeric values. You can also use ? command functions to add special attributes to the text. Let's use the AT function to determine its horizontal placement and the STYLE function to boldface the date. Enter

```
? "Date Admitted"
?? DATE AT 21 STYLE "b"
```

The last method to display data items on the same line creates a new variable and is useful if you intend to display the same data item more than once. In this case, you need to combine the literal text, "Total Charges," with the numeric value stored in the variable Amount.

You accomplish this by converting the numeric value into a text value using the TRANSFORM() function. TRANSFORM() allows you to accomplish two things at once:

1. It converts the specified numeric value to a character string.
2. It lets you include a formatting template similar to the PICTURE clause.

The command below uses the SPACE and TRANSFORM functions to create a new variable, Charges. That variable can then be printed. Enter

```
CHARGES="Total;
 Charges"+Space(8)+Transform(Amount,"99,999.99)
? CHARGES
```

The primary advantage of this method is that you can repeat the same text again later in the document. Enter

```
?
?
? REPLICATE(Chr(205),79)
? CHARGES STYLE "b"
```

Add three blank lines at the bottom of the display.

? (3 times)

114   ■ Programming Screen Displays

Here is a listing of the Scr1 program up to this point:

```
* create clear screen
SET TALK OFF
SET STATUS OFF
SET SCOREBOARD OFF
CLEAR
* define memory variables
NAME="Walter Lafish"
AMOUNT=10000
DATE=CTOD("10/15/88")
* displays commands
? REPLICATE(Chr(196),79)
? REPLICATE("*",79)
? REPLICATE(Chr(196),79)
?
?
TITLE="patient information screen display"
? SPACE((80-LEN(Title))/2)+Title FUNCTION "!";
 STYLE "b"
?
?
? DATE() AT 10
?? TIME() AT 70
?
?
? "Name of Patient:"+Space(5)+Name
? "Date Admitted"
?? DATE AT 21 STYLE "b"
CHARGES="Total Charges"+Space(8)+Transform;
(Amount,"99,999.99")
? CHARGES
?
?
? REPLICATE(Chr(205),79)
```

Screen Display Presentations ■ 115

```
? CHARGES STYLE "b"
?
?
?
WAIT
* reset screen
SET SCOREBOARD ON
SET STATUS ON
SET TALK ON
CLEAR
RETURN
```

Save and execute the program by entering Ctrl-End,

```
DO Scr1
```

The program displays the formal output screen created by the ? commands in your program (see Figure 3.6).

Terminate the program by pressing ⏎.

You have now learned the basic techniques for creating formal screen displays using the unstructured display commands ? and ??. But there are some vital elements missing from this screen display. First, once

Figure 3.6

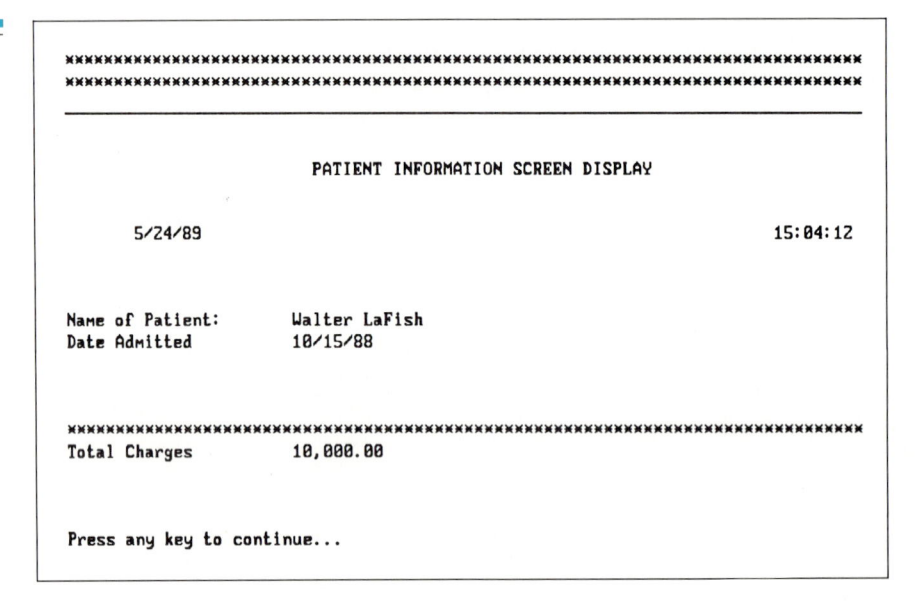

```
xxxxxxxxxxxxxxxxxxxxxxxxxxxxxxxxxxxxxxxxxxxxxxxxxxxxxxxxxxxxxxxxxxxxxxxx
xxxxxxxxxxxxxxxxxxxxxxxxxxxxxxxxxxxxxxxxxxxxxxxxxxxxxxxxxxxxxxxxxxxxxxxx
_____

                        PATIENT INFORMATION SCREEN DISPLAY

        5/24/89                                                  15:04:12



    Name of Patient:      Walter LaFish
    Date Admitted         10/15/88



    xxxxxxxxxxxxxxxxxxxxxxxxxxxxxxxxxxxxxxxxxxxxxxxxxxxxxxxxxxxxxxxxxxxx
    Total Charges         10,000.00


    Press any key to continue...
```

■ **Programming Screen Displays**

the screen is full, the data always scrolls from the bottom of the display toward the top. You also have no direct control over the vertical placement of the text. All of the screen display operations have performed output only. In order to have effective interaction with a user, you must be able to allow input as well as output operations on a given screen display.

We'll address both of these problems in the next chapter with explanations and illustrations of structured output commands.

Statistical Programs

The screen display techniques discussed in this chapter provide the basis for a very useful class of programs called statistical programs. The purpose of these programs is to display a screen that summarizes the activity in a database file. These programs combine the selection techniques discussed in chapter 2 with the screen presentation techniques discussed in this chapter.

Before you create any statistical programs, you will need to become familar with another group of dBASE IV commands that can produce summary statistics. For example, the Admit database contains a field to hold the amount of charges each patient incurs. How can you determine the total amount for all the patients?

The SUM command calculates the total value of a field or list of fields. To find the total value of the charges in the Admit database, enter

```
USE Admit
SUM Charges
```

The program calculates and displays the total amount of all the charges—83325. The SUM command scans the entire database and produces totals. You can sum more than one field at a time by using a list of field names. Enter

```
SUM Days_stay,Charges
```

This time the command produces two totals, 43 for the number of days, and 83,325 for the total value of the charges.

The AVERAGE command calculates the arithmetic mean of the specified fields. Enter

```
AVERAGE Days_stay,Charges
```

The command shows the average days stayed as 4.30 and the average charges as $8,333.50.

In Chapter 2, you learned how a FOR clause can select records for processing as the database is scanned. You can use FOR clauses with the SUM and AVERAGE commands, too. Suppose you want to determine the average charges for male patients. You would use a FOR clause to select only the records for which the Sex field is M. Enter

```
AVERAGE Charges FOR Upper(Sex)="M"
```

The program selects the seven male records in the database and calculates their average charges as $9,314.29, slightly higher than the overall average. How would you calculate the average for the female patients? Try this on your own. If you need help, the correct command can be found at the end of the chapter in the Answers to Exercises section under exercise 4.

That average is $6,045.

The CALCULATE Command

The CALCULATE command allows you to perform a number of calculations with a single command. With the CALCULATE command, you specify both the name of the field or variable and the type of calculation you want to perform. Suppose you want to calculate the sum and average of both the Charges and Day_stay fields. Using SUM and AVERAGE, execute two commands. With CALCULATE you can get all four values with a single command. Enter

```
CALCULATE SUM(Charges),AVG(Charges),SUM(Days_;
  stay),AVG(Days_stay)
```

This single command calculates and displays all four values. If the resulting display is too wide for your screen, the average days stayed will be broken between lines.

The CALCULATE command uses the following mathematical functions:

Option	Result
AVG()	arithmetic mean
CNT()	count records
MAX()	the largest value
MIN()	the smallest value

■ Programming Screen Displays

NPV()   net present value of a series

STD()   standard deviation of a series

SUM()   numeric total

VAR()   the variance in a series

The advantage of the CALCULATE command is that it eliminates an additional scan of the database. This is very important since the time it takes to scan a large database is significant.

Like the SUM and AVERAGE commands, CALCULATE can also use a FOR clause to select records. Suppose you want to calculate the total and average of the days stayed by male patients. Enter

```
CALCULATE SUM(Days_stay),AVG(Days_stay) FOR;
  Upper(Sex)="M"
```

The answers are 22 and 3.14.

Statistics in Programs

These statistics functions are capable of generating important information. But the screen displays they produce do not present the information clearly. How can the values generated by these commands be placed into screen display programs like the ones you have created in this chapter?

A key element is missing. You learned earlier in this chapter that if a value is stored in a field or a memory variable, you can use the ? command to control the display of that value. However, statistics such as sums and averages are not stored as part of the database. You need to find a way to store the value of the statistics functions into memory variables to control their display.

dBASE IV allows you to perform this operation by using the TO clause with any of the statistics functions. The TO clause must be followed by the name or names of the variables to which the values will be assigned. You can use the TO clause to store the number of days stayed by male patients in a variable named Male_stay. Enter

```
SUM Days_stay FOR Upper(Sex)="M" TO Male_days
```

The value is displayed as 22. But because the information was stored as a memory variable, you can display it again using the ? command. Clear the screen and display the value as part of a more complete statement. Enter

```
CLEAR
? "Total days, males:",Male_days PICTURE "999.9"
```

Statistical Programs ■ 119

The ability to store the value generated by statistics functions is not very significant when you are entering commands at the dot prompt. But it is crucial for use in a dBASE IV program. The assignment of values to variables is the link between the statistics functions and program displays. You can now use these two items to create a program that will display a statistical summary of information.

The program will be called Stats. Enter

```
MODIFY COMMAND Stats
```

The program begins with the standard screen control settings.

```
* create clear screen
SET TALK OFF
SET STATUS OFF
SET SCOREBOARD OFF
CLEAR
```

The next step is to open the database file. Enter

```
USE Admit
```

The next section of the program gathers the statistical information from the database records and stores it in memory variables. The goal of this program is to compute the total number of patients, the total number of days stayed, and the total amount of the charges. These statistics should be calculated by gender. Should you use SUM or CALCULATE? In this case, CALCULATE is the better choice because you need to count the number of patients as well as total their days and charges. Since CALCULATE can perform two operations in one pass through the database, it is the most efficient choice. Enter

```
* calculate statistical values
CALCULATE CNT(),SUM(Days_stay),SUM(Charges) TO;
  M_count,M_days,M_charges FOR UPPER(Sex)="M"
```

This command was divided into two lines by the semicolon (;) character. The semicolon lets you write a long command over several lines. When dBASE IV encounters the semicolon, it reads the next line as part of the same command. This makes the program instructions easier to enter and to read. When you enter this command, you can experiment by omitting the semicolon and typing the entire command on a single line. You find that since the command contains more than

■ **Programming Screen Displays**

80 characters, dBASE IV scrolls the screen display to the right as you enter. This will pose no problem when the command executes.

If you choose to break a command line with a semicolon, don't omit necessary spaces. For example, when split into two parts, a command like LIST CHARGES FOR MONTH(ADMIT) = 11 might look like this:

```
LIST CHARGES FOR;
 Month(Admit)=11
```

If you look carefully, you'll see that the second line begins with a blank space. This is necessary because you must place a blank between the FOR clause and the expression MONTH(ADMIT) = 11 even if they are on separate lines. The semicolon does not substitute for spaces.

The CNT() function of the CALCULATE command does not require a field argument since it merely counts records. The names M_count, M_days, and M_charges are the names of the variables that will hold the calculated values. The next command performs the same operation but selects the female patients' records.

```
CALCULATE CNT(),SUM(Days_stay),SUM(Charges) TO;
 F_count,F_days,F_charges FOR Upper(Sex)="F"
```

Up to this point in our program, no information has been displayed on the screen. The SET TALK OFF command suppresses the data normally displayed by the CALCULATE command.

One of the advantages of capturing values in memory variables is that you can perform calculations with those memory variables to create new values. In our current example, you can determine the total number of patients, days stayed, or charges by adding together the male and female variables for each statistic. The following commands combine the male and female variables into a total for all patients.

```
* combine male and female
All=M_count+F_count
Alldays=M_days+F_days
Allcharges=M_charges+F_charges
```

The next section of the program displays the statistics. Begin with a centered heading. You can use the method shown previously to store the heading as a memory variable and then display it centered on the screen. The ? by itself produces a blank line following the heading.

```
* display statistics
Title="Emergency Room Admit Statistics"
? SPACE((80-len(title))/2)+Title
?
```

The first display will show the number of male and female patients admitted. The statistics will be presented in table format.

The totals will display at column 40. You will also display the percentage at column 60. Use an AT clause to place the headings at the proper column locations.

```
* admission statistics
? "Admissions:","Total" at 40,"%" AT 60
```

You are now ready to place the data on the screen. The following command prints the word Male at the left edge of the screen. The second item printed is the value of M_count. A PICTURE clause controls the width of M_count. Remember that when you create a numeric variable, dBASE IV assigns it a width of 20 characters. A PICTURE clause of "999" limits the size of the displayed value to three characters. The AT clause places those three characters at column 40.

```
? "Male",M_count PICTURE "999" AT 40
```

The next entry uses the ?? command to place its data on the same line as the previous command. This command does not display a single variable but the results of a calculation using the M_count and All variables.

> *Note:* The *100 multiplies the results of dividing M_count and All by 100. This moves the decimal point two places to the right. For example, if M_count/All is .7, then multiplying by 100 changes the number to 70.

The use of columns 40 and 60 was simply an estimate of what locations might look right on the screen.

```
?? M_count/All*100 PICTURE "999.9" AT 60
```

To display the female data, use a pair of commands exactly like the previous two, with the female rather than the male variables.

```
? "Female",F_count PICTURE "999" AT 40
?? F_count/All*100 PICTURE "999.9" AT 60
```

The last set of data summarizes both the male and female values. To set off the totals, you can use the REPLICATE command to draw a line across the table.

? REPLICATE(Chr(196),65)

The Total line can allow some cheating. For example, since the percentages you have calculated are based on the value of the All variable, it is not necessary to calculate that All/All is 100%. You can simply tell the program to print 100%.

? "Total",All PICTURE "999" AT 40,"100.0" AT 60

Although the program is not complete, you have done enough to test the basic concept. Here is the current listing of the program.

```
* create clear screen
SET TALK OFF
SET STATUS OFF
SET SCOREBOARD OFF
CLEAR
USE Admit
* calculate statistical values
CALCULATE CNT(),SUM(Days_stay),SUM(Charges) TO;
 M_count,M_days,M_charges FOR UPPER(Sex)="M"
CALCULATE CNT(),SUM(Days_stay),SUM(Charges) TO;
 F_count,F_days,F_charges FOR UPPER(Sex)="F"
* combine male and female
All=M_count+F_count
Alldays=M_days+F_days
Allcharges=M_charges+F_charges
* display statistics
Title="Emergency Room Admit Statistics"
? SPACE((80-LEN(Title))/2)+Title
?
* admission statistics
? "Admissions:","Total" AT 40,"%" AT 60
? "Male",M_count PICTURE "999" AT 40
```

```
?? M_count/All*100 PICTURE "999.9" AT 60
? "Female",F_count PICTURE "999" AT 40
?? F_count/All*100 PICTURE "999.9" AT 60
? REPLICATE(CHR(196),65)
? "Total",All PICTURE "999" AT 40,"100.0" AT 60
RETURN
```

Save and execute the program by pressing (Alt)-e and typing r.

The program calculates and then displays a table of values summarizing the data in the Admit file (see Figure 3.7).

The display reveals that your program is on the right track. One detail that you might want to think about is the way the numbers align under the column headings Total and %. All the items are aligned at column 40. Because the word Total contains five characters and the numeric values are limited to three characters, the ones column of the numbers lines up with the third character in the heading. The % heading is only a single character. It displays exactly at column 60. However, the PICTURE clause used for that column creates five-character numbers, including the decimal point. The last digit of the number appears at column 45 and does not look properly aligned under the heading.

Figure 3.7

```
                        Emergency Room Admit Statistics
Addmissions:                         Total                    %
Male                                   7                     70.0
Female                                 3                     30.0
─────────────────────────────────────────────────────────────────
Total                                 10                    100.0
.
```

This problem is common with column layouts because the size of column headings often varies greatly from the information written into those columns. In this case, since you know the maximum size of each numeric value, you can compensate by changing the column locations of the headings.

Since the Total heading is two characters wider than the numbers in that column, you would subtract 2 from the column location. The % character is four characters shorter than the column's numeric data, so its location should be increased by four characters. This column heading adjustment may seem like a small point, but people using your programs often judge their quality by details such as this.

Place the Stats program into the editor by entering

```
MODIFY COMMAND Stats
```

Change line 20 so that the column locations properly align the headings with their associated numbers. Try this on your own. If you need help, the correct commands can be found at the end of the chapter in the Answers to Exercises section under exercise 5.

Save end execute the revised program by pressing (Alt)-e and typing r.

The display shows that you now have corrected the alignment problem.

Program Editing Techniques

To complete this program, you need to create two more tables with different variables. To display a table that summarizes the days stayed, you would change the M_count and F_count variables to the M_days and F_days variables. The commands to create the table display remain largely unchanged. This reuse of command sequences is quite common in programming.

Instead of entering all the commands a second time, you might want to take advantage of a word processing technique that allows you to copy blocks of text within a document. The dBASE IV editor can perform simple move or copy operations.

> *Note:* If you are familiar with a word processing program that creates standard MS-DOS text files (e.g., WordStar, WordPerfect, Microsoft Word), you might want to write your programs with the word processor to take advantage of advanced editing features to cut down on the amount of code you have to enter.

As an example, the next section of our tutorial will copy an existing block of comamnds and then revise them instead of entering the lines from scratch. Load the Stats program by entering

```
MODIFY COMMAND Stats
```

The block of commands you want to copy begins on line 21, which reads ? "Admissions:","Total" AT 38,"%" AT 64.

With a few exceptions, the commands on this and the next six lines can be copied and edited faster than entering the text from scratch.

Begin by positioning the cursor at the beginning of line 20.

To copy a block, you must first highlight the text that you want to copy. The [F6] function key turns on the highlighting mode. Press [F6].

The current character appears in reverse video. Moving the cursor extends the highlight over more text. Press

[↓] (6 times)

[End] [↵]

You have now highlighted the text that you want to copy (see Figure 3.8).

The dBASE IV editor uses [F7] to move text and [F8] to copy text. In this case the text should be copied. Press [F8] and [↵].

Figure 3.8

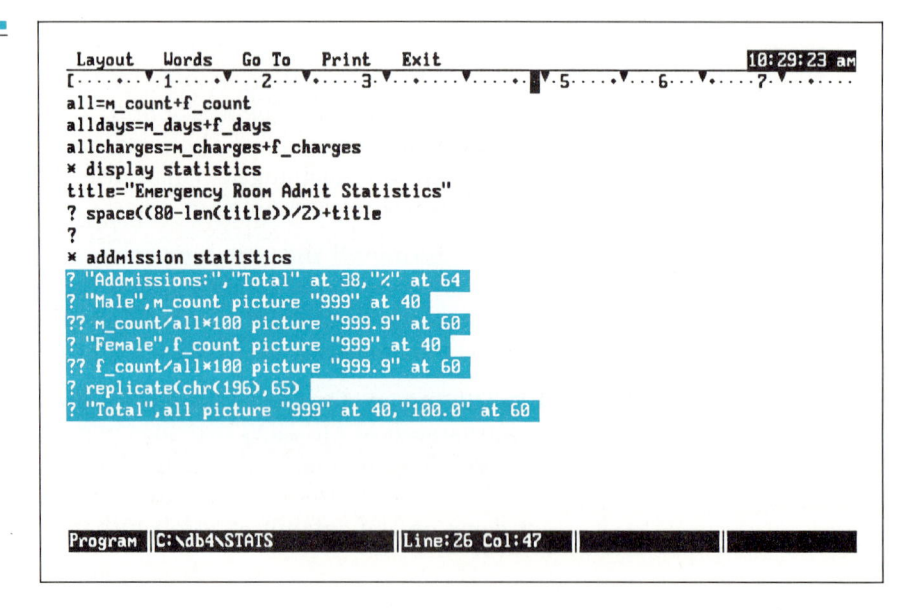

```
  Layout   Words   Go To   Print   Exit                    10:29:23 am
[.....V.1.....V....2....V....3.V.......V....V.5....V...6...V....7.V......
all=m_count+f_count
alldays=m_days+f_days
allcharges=m_charges+f_charges
* display statistics
title="Emergency Room Admit Statistics"
? space((80-len(title))/2)+title
?
* admission statistics
? "Addmissions:","Total" at 38,"%" at 64
? "Male",m_count picture "999" at 40
?? m_count/all*100 picture "999.9" at 60
? "Female",f_count picture "999" at 40
?? f_count/all*100 picture "999.9" at 60
? replicate(chr(196),65)
? "Total",all picture "999" at 40,"100.0" at 60




Program  C:\db4\STATS              Line:26 Col:47
```

126 ■ **Programming Screen Displays**

You have now selected to copy the block. The next step is to place the cursor at the position in the program where you want the copied lines to be inserted. In this case that is the next line below. Press ⏎.

To place a copy at that location, press F8.

The editor places a duplicate of the block into the text (see Figure 3.9).

Now modify the text to create the commands to display the second table. The first step is to add two blank lines between the first and second tables.

Move the cursor to the beginning of line 27.

Make sure that the editor is in the Insert mode. You can check the status line to see if the Ins indicator appears on the right section of the line. If not, press Ins to enter the insert mode. Then, enter

?

?

When the Insert mode is active, any text you enter is automatically inserted.

Change the command, which is now line 29, to display the heading "Hospital Days."

Figure 3.9

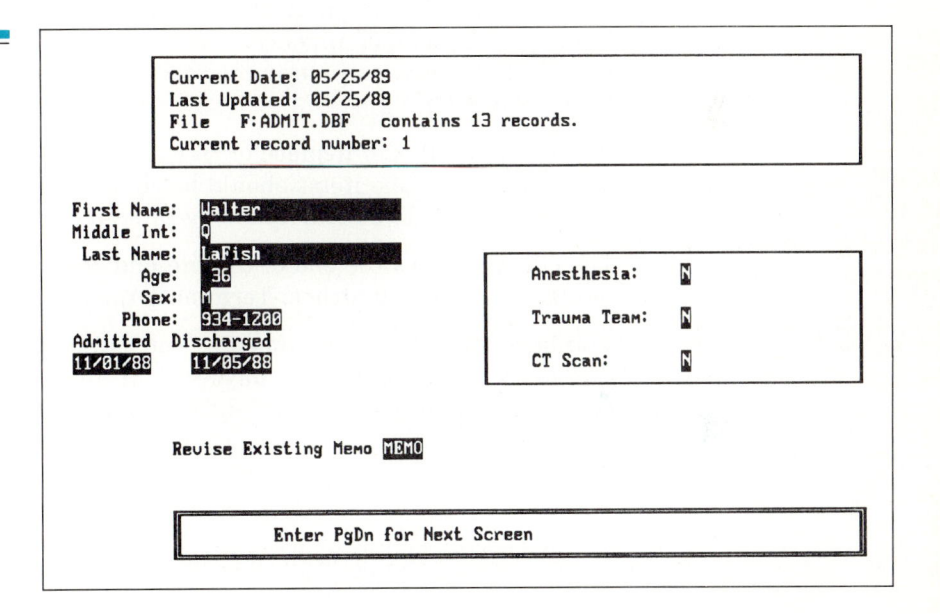

```
Current Date: 05/25/89
Last Updated: 05/25/89
File   F:ADMIT.DBF    contains 13 records.
Current record number: 1

First Name:  Walter
Middle Int:  Q
 Last Name:  LaFish
       Age:  36                         Anesthesia:   N
       Sex:  M
     Phone:  934-1200                   Trauma Team:  N
Admitted  Discharged
11/01/88   11/05/88                     CT Scan:      N


         Revise Existing Memo  MEMO


              Enter PgDn for Next Screen
```

Statistical Programs ■ 127

```
Old line:    ? "Admissions:","Total" AT 38,"%" AT 64
New Line:    ? "Hospital Days:","Total" AT 38,"%" AT 64
```

Replace

Another editing technique that can speed up the creation of program code is a word-processing technique called search and replace. This technique allows the editor to search for a text item and replace it with a different item. While this type of command is useful in word processing, it is even more useful in program editing because program commands tend to be more highly structured than normal text.

In this case, you have variable names that need to be swapped for other variable names, leaving the rest of the commands intact. This is an ideal use of search and replace. The dBASE IV editor provides a replace command that performs this operation. To activate the REPLACE command, press (Alt)-g.

This displays the Goto menu. Select Replace by pressing r.

Suppose you want to have the editor replace the M_count variable with M_days. Enter the item you want to locate.

```
M_count
```

Then enter the name of the variable you want to replace it with.

```
M_days
```

The editor begins searching the text from the current cursor position. When it locates an occurrence of the search text, M_count, the text is highlighted and you are prompted for a response: Replace/Skip/All/Quit? (R/S/A/Esc).

You can now elect to Replace or Skip the items one by one, or if you are sure that all the items should be changed, select All. In this case, change the next two occurrences by pressing r two times.

The editor reaches the end of the file and goes back to the beginning to search for more matches. Terminate the search by pressing (Esc).

You have made two replacements. You can perform this same operation to change F_count to F_days and All to Alldays. On the other hand, you might just want to edit the code manually. When you are done, the new section of the program should look like this:

```
?

?

? "Hospital Days:","Total" AT 38,"%" AT 64
```

```
? "Male",M_days PICTURE "999" AT 40
?? M_days/Alldays*100 PICTURE "999.9" AT 60
? "Female",F_days PICTURE "999" AT 40
?? F_days/Alldays*100 PICTURE "999.9" AT 60
? REPLICATE(CHR(196),65)
? "Total",Alldays PICTURE "999" AT 40,"100.0";
 AT 60
```

The next table we'll create is similar to the first two except that it uses the charge-related variables M_charges, F_charges, and Allcharges.

The use of the Charges variables also implies another change. Remember that the PICTURE clauses used so far have limited the values of variables to three characters. But the values for Charges are larger than that, at least five characters with two decimals. This means that you should change the PICTURE template for the Charges variables to "99,999.99." The percent calculations can use the same templates because percentages will never exceed 100%.

As soon as you consider changing the template for a number in a column, you should realize that this will affect the alignment between the column heading and the values in that column. The new template is nine characters wide. The heading Total has only five characters. That means the heading should be offset four columns farther to the right. Since the template is aligned at column 40, the heading should be moved to column 44.

The commands to create the third table, Hospital Charges, are listed below. You can enter the commands or use the COPY and/or REPLACE commands to enter these commands and reduce typing.

```
?
?
? "Hospital Charges:","Total" AT 44,"%" AT 64
? "Male",M_charges PICTURE "99,999.99" AT 40
?? M_charges/Allcharges*100 PICTURE "999.9" AT 60
? "Female",F_charges PICTURE "99,999.99" AT 40
?? F_charges/Allcharges*100 PICTURE "999.9" AT 60
? REPLICATE(CHR(196),65)
? "Total",Allcharges PICTURE "99,999.99" AT;
 40,"100.0" AT 60
```

The final section of the program contains the standard closing commands you used in the Scr1 program. Enter the following commands:

```
WAIT
* end of program routine
CLOSE DATABASE
SET SCOREBOARD ON
SET TALK ON
SET STATUS ON
RETURN
```

Here is the full listing of the STATS.prg program file:

```
* create clear screen
SET TALK OFF
SET STATUS OFF
SET SCOREBOARD OFF
CLEAR
USE Admit
* calculate statistical values
CALCULATE CNT(),SUM(Days_stay),SUM(Charges) TO;
 M_count,M_days,M_charges FOR Upper(Sex)="M"
CALCULATE CNT(),SUM(Days_stay),SUM(Charges) TO;
 F_count,F_days,F_charges FOR Upper(Sex)="F"
* combine male and female
All=M_count+F_count
Alldays=M_days+F_days
Allcharges=M_charges+F_charges
* display statistics
Title="Emergency Room Admit Statistics"
? SPACE((80-LEN(title))/2)+title
?
* admission statistics
? "Admissions:","Total" AT 38,"%" AT 64
? "Male",M_count PICTURE "999" AT 40
?? M_count/All*100 PICTURE "999.9" AT 60
```

130 ■ **Programming Screen Displays**

```
? "Female",F_count PICTURE "999" AT 40
?? F_count/All*100 PICTURE "999.9" AT 60
? REPLICATE(CHR(196),65)
? "Total",All PICTURE "999" AT 40,"100.0" AT 60
?
?
? "Hospital Days:","Total" AT 38,"%" AT 64
? "Male",M_days PICTURE "999" AT 40
?? M_days/Alldays*100 PICTURE "999.9" AT 60
? "Female",F_days PICTURE "999" AT 40
?? F_days/Alldays*100 PICTURE "999.9" AT 60
? REPLICATE(CHR(196),65)
? "Total",Alldays PICTURE "999" AT 40,"100.0";
 AT 60
?
?
? "Hospital Charges:","Total" AT 44,"%" AT 64
? "Male",M_charges PICTURE "99,999.99" AT 40
?? M_charges/Allcharges*100 PICTURE "999.9" AT 60
? "Female",F_charges PICTURE "99,999.99" AT 40
?? F_charges/Allcharges*100 PICTURE "999.9" AT 60
? REPLICATE(CHR(196),65)
? "Total",Allcharges PICTURE "99,999.99" AT;
 40,"100.0" AT 60
WAIT
* end of program routine
CLOSE DATABASE
SET SCOREBOARD ON
SET TALK ON
SET STATUS ON
RETURN
```

Save and execute the program by pressing (Alt)-e and typing r.

The program now displays three statistical tables that summarize the records in the Admit database file (see Figure 3.10).

Complete the program by pressing (↵).

Figure 3.10

```
                    Emergency Room Admit Statistics

Addmissions:                    Total                    %
Male                              7                     70.0
Female                            3                     30.0
                              ─────────────────────────────────
Total                            10                    100.0


Hospital Days:                  Total                    %
Male                             22                     51.2
Female                           21                     48.8
                              ─────────────────────────────────
Total                            43                    100.0


Hospital Charges:               Total                    %
Male                         65,200.00                  78.2
Female                       18,125.00                  21.8
                              ─────────────────────────────────
Total                        83,325.00                 100.0
Press any key to continue...
```

The statistical program will return an update report on the records in the Admit database. You can test this by adding a new record to the database and running the Stats program again.

Add the following record to the database file. Try this on your own. If you need help, the correct command can be found at the end of the chapter in the Answers to Exercises section under exercise 6.

Record #11

LAST	Sorenson
FIRST	Cynthia
MIDDLE	
ADMIT	11/28/88
DISCHARGE	12/02/88
AGE	35
PHONE	454-9999
SEX	f
DAYS_STAY	4
DAYS_ICU	
INSURED	T
PAYOR	Blue Shield

■ **Programming Screen Displays**

ANESTHESIA	T
TRUMA_TEAM	F
CT_SCAN	T
CHARGES	7556
REMARKS:	none

Remember to save the new record by entering (Ctrl)-(End). Execute the Stats program again to see the updated statistics. Enter

```
DO Stats
```

The program's summary now includes the new patient.

Complete the program by pressing (↵).

The statistical program illustrates how linear programs, when combined with custom screen displays, can generate important information about the database. The Stats program uses built-in dBASE IV commands but uses a customized screen display to present the information coherently.

The role of memory variables is crucial to the creation of this type of program. Memory variables enable you to defer the display of the value generated by CALCULATE commands until a specific point in a program.

Linear programs that use the ? command to display data represent the first level of programming sophistication in dBASE IV. These programs can perform a wide variety of useful and complicated tasks. Your programs rely on dBASE IV to automatically perform operations like scanning the database to determine the total of all charges for female patients. From a programming perspective, you do not have to think about how this operation is performed. You need only tell dBASE IV to carry out the operation.

A limitation of this type of program is its rigidity. Suppose you want to specify a range of dates for a report to gather data. You would have to modify the program code to select records by dates. But that change might prove too limiting. Every time you want to select a different range of dates, you would need to modify the program. A better solution would be to create a program that stops and asks what dates to use. If you wrote a program to ask some key questions, it could generate all types of statistical reports. Programs that allow you to enter selection criteria while they are running are called interactive programs. They are the subject of Chapter 4.

Summary

Here is a review of this chapter's key concepts.

Programs have four distinct sections:

1. Set the environment. This would also include opening the proper database file.

2. Calculate the values.

3. Display the information.

4. Close database—reset environment.

?. The ? command places data onto the screen display. The data is placed at the next available line on the screen. The command can output a single data item or a list of items separated by commas.

Clauses. The ? command accepts four different types of clauses that modify its output.

FUNCTION clause. The FUNCTION clause implements special operations on the output data such as capitalization, numeric formatting, and date formatting. Each function is represented by a letter entered as a text string, as in the command that prints the system date in European format: ? date() function "e"

PICTURE clause. A PICTURE clause formats the output with character-by-character control. This formatting controls the display of numeric values and character values. The PICTURE clause requires the entry of a template that indicates how the characters are to be formatted, as in the following command to display a number according to a numeric template: ? amount picture "$999,999.99"

AT clause. The AT clause allows you to specify the horizontal location for the display of data, as in the following command that prints the variable "Name" at column 25: ? NAME AT 25

STYLE clause. STYLE clauses add device-dependent attributes to the text sent to the screen or the printer. STYLE clauses use B for bold, U for underline, I for italic, R for superscript, and L for subscripted text. The actual appearance of the text depends upon the type of screen display used. Attributes not supported appear as normal text. The following command—? NAME STYLE "b"—will display names in bold text.

?. You can combine more than one clause with a ? command. The following command—? NAME STYLE "b" function "!"—will display the name variable in upper-case bold text.

??. The ?? command performs essentially the same function as ?, except that it places the output data at the next column on the current line; ? always places data on a new line.

REPLICATE(). Repeats a specific character or group of characters a specified number of times.

CHR(). Displays characters based on the numeric character value used as an argument to the function. Used to display characters not found on the keyboard but included as part of the IBM extended character set.

SPACE(). Creates a text string of blank spaces based on the number used as an argument.

LEN(). Returns a numeric value equal to the number of characters in a literal, variable, or field.

DATE(). Returns a date-type data item equal to the current system date. The actual value of the date is determined by MS-DOS and may require special hardware to keep an accurate date.

TIME(). Returns a character string representing the current system time.

SUM. The SUM command scans the database and produces a total for numeric fields. The total can be displayed on the screen and/or stored as a numeric variable.

AVERAGE. The AVERAGE function is similar to SUM except that it calculates the arithmetic mean.

CALCULATE. This command, which allows you to select among eight different types of calculations, is useful when you want to perform more than one type of calculation as you scan the database.

Editor Features. The dBASE IV editor contains word-processing functions to move blocks, copy blocks, and search and replace text blocks that can speed up the creation of programs with blocks of commands that repeat with only minor variations.

Review Problems for Chapter 3

1. Enter a sequence of two commands that will display the text **XYZ Disposable Supplies** horizontally centered on the screen. (Hint: use an @/say command with a calculation as the column value.)

2. List the Tax rate field so that the rates are displayed as percentages, for example, .06 as 6.0%.

3. Enter a command that will display the current system's date as part of a phrase such as Today is 11/01/88.

4. Enter commands that display the date in European date format.

5. Calculate the total amount of sales tax for all the records.

6. Create a program that displays the totals and averages for total amount and quantity. Also display the average price of the items sold.

7. Modify the previous program to use only records that have a sales date in August.

8. If you assume that the price for each item is marked up by 33%, create a program that calculates the total profit for all sales. (Hint: note that the amount of profit should be calculated on the total amount not including sales tax.)

Answers to Exercises

1. Display name variable.

    ? Name AT 35 STYLE "u" FUNCTION "!"

2. Draw a double line.

    ? Replicate(CHR(205),79)

3. Draw double line.

    ? Replicate(CHR(205),79)

4. Calculate average charges for female patients.

    AVERAGE Charges FOR UPPER(SEX)="F"

5. Revise line 20 in Stats program.

   Old line: ? "Admissions:","Total" AT 40,"%" AT 60
   New Line: ? "Admissions:","Total" AT 38,"%" AT 64

6. Add new record to database.

   ```
   USE Admit
   APPEND
   ```

4 Interactive Programming

The previous chapter described how to control the display of information on the screen. The Stats program, created at the end of Chapter 3, illustrated how the linear programming techniques shown in Chapter 2 and the screen display commands shown in Chapter 3 can be combined to create a program that generates statistical information about the database.

This chapter describes how you can create programs that actually allow you to enter information into the program while it is running. These programs are called interactive because the user must enter responses during the course of the program.

Fully Structured Screen Displays

In the previous chapter, you used the ? and ?? commands to display specific items of information on the screen. These commands control the display of information, including its horizontal location, through use of the AT clause. However, the vertical location of the text is automatically assumed to be the next available line on the screen. The effect of this type of display is that the data appears to scroll into the display area.

The @ command in dBASE IV is an option that lets you specify the vertical as well as the horizontal screen position of any data you wish to display. There are several important differences between @ and ?.

- The @ command requires a specific row and column location.
- The @ command can control the display of only a single item. The ? command can display a list of data items.
- The @ command can be used to display or input data. The ? command only displays data.
- Because you specify the row with the @ command, there is no need to print blank lines to separate items vertically.
- The ? command moves data down the screen one row at a time. The @ command allows you to place data at any vertical location on the screen. The display will no longer appear to scroll downward. You can display above the previous line if desired.
- The @ command is always followed by a pair of numeric values, the first for the row, 0 to 24, the second for the column, 0 to 79. Along with location, you will need to use one of two clauses.

The SAY clause places data at the specified screen location. The data item can be a field, memory variable, or any valid dBASE IV expression.

The GET clause establishes an input area on the screen at the specified location. The input area is displayed in reverse video and shows the current contents, if any, of the specified field or memory variable. The input area is not activated until a READ command is issued.

The SAY and GET clauses can be used individually or together in a single @ command. However, you can use only one of each in a single command. Also remember that unlike ?, you cannot display a list of items with @.

Open the Admit file by entering

```
USE Admit
```

By placing the Admit database in use, you now have access to the information stored in the first record of that file. You can display any part of the information stored in that record at any location on the screen by using an @ command with the SAY clause. Enter

```
@ 10,10 SAY Last
```

Fully Structured Screen Displays

The name LaFish appears at row 10, column 10 of the display. You can place the first name at row 8, column 10 by entering

```
@ 8,10 SAY First
```

The @/SAY command combination can be used to place literal text onto the screen as well. Enter

```
@ 8,0 SAY "First:"
@ 10,0 SAY "Last:"
```

You can combine the literal text with field information into a single command by using a dBASE IV expression. For example, to display a patient's admission date, you can combine the literal text "Admitted:" with the date-to-character conversion function for the Admit field. Enter

```
@ 12,0 SAY "Admitted: "+DTOC(Admit)
```

Display the day of the week the patient was admitted by entering

```
@ 12,20 SAY CDOW(Admit)
```

The @ command accepts the same PICTURE and FUNCTION clauses as the ? command. Numeric values can be displayed using a PICTURE clause. Enter

```
@ 14,0 SAY "Age:"
@ 14,10 SAY Age Picture "999"
```

If you want to combine a text literal with a numeric value, you can use the TRANSFORM() function to convert the numeric value to a formatted text string. Enter

```
@ 16,0 SAY "Charges:;
 "+TRANSFORM(Charges,"999,999.99")
```

One by one, the @/SAY commands begin to paint information on the screen (see Figure 4.1).

Clear the work area by entering

```
CLEAR
```

Input Areas

The @ command is very significant in dBASE IV because it provides a means to place input areas on the screen display. These input areas make interactive programming possible. An input area can represent either a memory variable or a field in a database record. When the

Figure 4.1

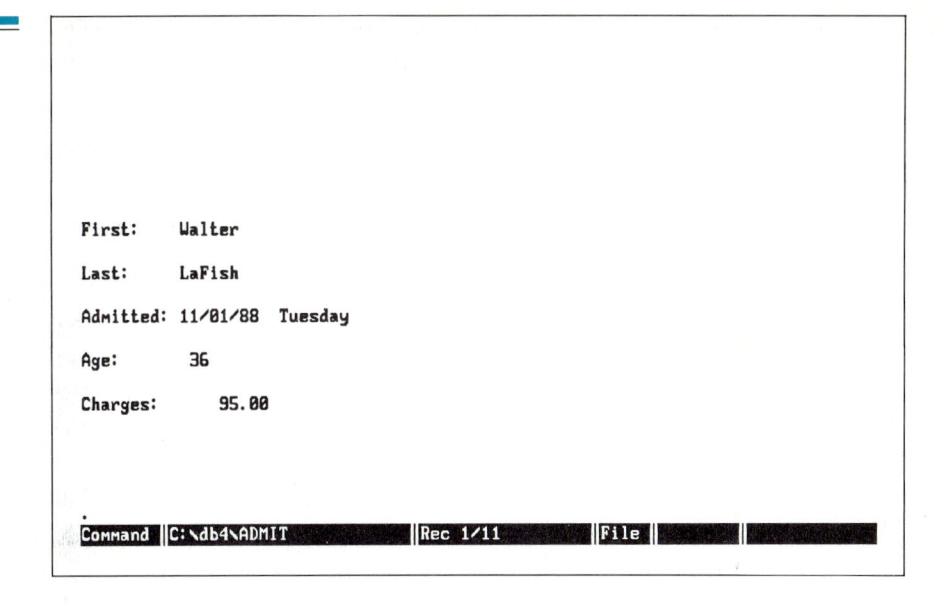

```
First:    Walter

Last:     LaFish

Admitted: 11/01/88  Tuesday

Age:      36

Charges:     95.00




Command  C:\db4\ADMIT         Rec 1/11    File
```

GET clause is used with the @ command, dBASE IV creates an input area on the screen for the field or variable.

Create a memory variable called test by entering

`TEST=1000`

Create an input area for this memory variable by entering

`@ 8,10 SAY "The value of the variable is" GET TEST`

dBASE IV displays the current value of the variable test in reverse video (see Figure 4.2.) The input area is 20 characters wide since dBASE IV assigns numeric variables a width of 20 characters when it creates them. However, the cursor is not positioned in the input area. In order to activate an input area you must enter a read command. Enter

`READ`

The READ command moves the cursor from the dot prompt to the input area. You can now enter a new value for the variable. Enter

`2500`

Fully Structured Screen Displays ■ **141**

Figure 4.2

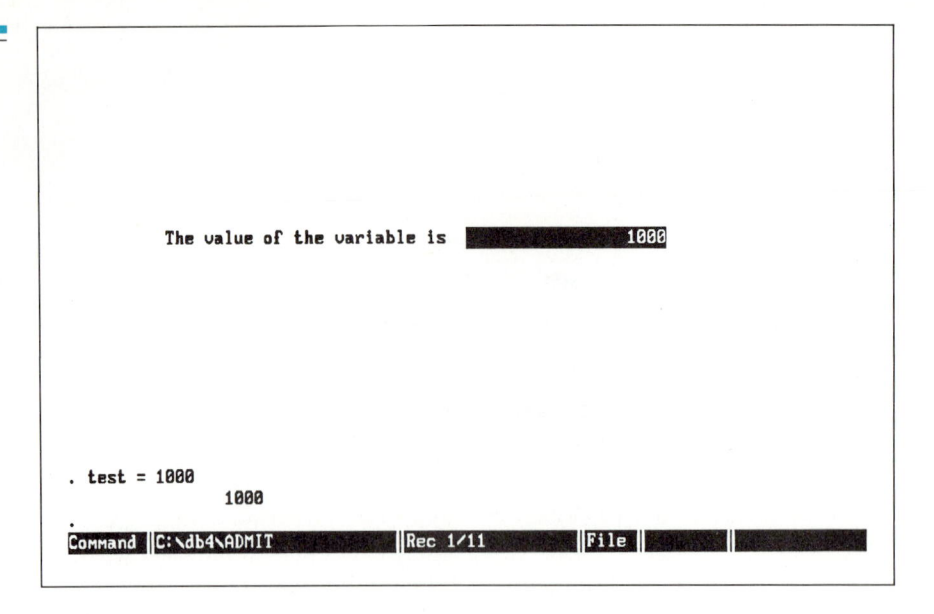

```
              The value of the variable is  ▓▓▓▓▓▓▓▓▓▓1000▓




. test = 1000
              1000
.
Command │C:\db4\ADMIT       │Rec 1/11   │File │
```

The change that you have entered into the input area changes the value of the memory variable just as if you had entered the command TEST=2500. To confirm this effect, clear the screen and display the value of the test memory variable.

CLEAR

? TEST

The value displays as 2500. The @/SAY/GET command provides you with an entirely new way to work with memory variables. You can now display and enter memory variables in a manner similar to the way you enter data into database fields with the EDIT or APPEND commands.

The @/SAY/GET combination allows you to use two display items in a single command. The SAY section is usually used to display a text prompt that labels the input area created by the GET clause. The @/SAY/GET combination also allows you to mix different data types, like display text with the SAY clause and numeric values with the GET clause, in a single command.

Mixing types in a single SAY clause is not quite so simple. Suppose you want to display the value of Test along with the phrase "The value of is." You have two options:

1. **@/SAY.** Use two @/SAY commands, as in

   ```
   @ 8,10 SAY "The value of Test is"
   @ 8, 26 SAY Test
   ```

2. **Convert.** Or, use an expression that converts the numeric value to characters.

   ```
   @ 8,10 SAY "The value of Test is "+STR(Test,20)
   ```

Both methods achieve the same result. In the case of the two @/SAY commands, you would have to count the number of characters in the phrase "The value of Test is" to know the correct column location for the second command. (This problem can be solved by using relative addressing, discussed later in this chapter.)

Calculation Programs

These new commands make it possible to construct programs that ask for user input and use that input to produce results. Once you have the ability to accept user input, you can create calculation-type programs. These programs first ask a user to furnish information and then proceed to perform some type of calculation based on the entry. For example, suppose you want to create a program that calculates the monthly payment for a loan. dBASE IV provides a function, PAYMENT(), and calculates a monthly payment when you supply the value for the loan amount, the interest rate, and the number of payment periods.

This function takes the following form:

PAYMENT(*Loan, Interest rate, Period*)

Create a program called Loan by entering

```
MODIFY COMMAND Loan
```

The first part of the program turns off the status bar, scoreboard, and talk, and clears the screen. Enter

```
SET TALK OFF
SET STATUS OFF
SET SCOREBOARD OFF
CLEAR
```

The next section of the program defines the memory variable you need to perform a calculation. In this case, you need three values: the amount of the loan, the interest rate, and the number of years. You will assume that the loan will be repaid on a monthly basis. Since the actual values will be entered by the user when the program is running, you will define all three variables as having a zero value. This process is called initialization of the variables.

The initialization of variables must be done before you attempt to create input areas. The @/SAY/GET command will only operate on variables or fields that already exist. Before your program asks for a response to be put into a variable, you must make sure that the variable exists.

It is customary to define numeric variables as zero, and character variables as blank spaces. However, there may be circumstances in which you would like to display a particular value as a default entry. The most common example is to display the current date in a date variable display instead of a blank date.

If you want to assign the same value, in this case zero, to more than one variable, you can use the STORE command. The STORE command allows you to assign the specified value to a list of variable names. Enter

```
* initialize variables
STORE 0 to Loan,Rate,Years
```

The next section of the program displays each of the variables and allows a user to enter values. Begin with the amount of the loan. You can use a PICTURE clause with a GET clause to limit the size of the input area. Keep in mind that dBASE IV will automatically assign the variables a width of 20 characters. Here, use a picture template to restrict the display area to "999,999.99." Enter

```
* display variables for input
@ 8,15 SAY "Loan Amount:" GET Loan PICTURE;
 "999,999.99"
```

Range Limits

The next item to display for input is the rate of interest to be charged. This type of entry is always a bit tricky because interest rates can be entered as decimal values or whole number percents. One way to address this situation is to use the PICTURE clause to indicate that a percent sign (%) is required here.

However, there is still no way to guarantee that the user will realize what method is required. Using a RANGE clause restricts numeric entries to a specific range of values. If you want the user to enter the value as a percent, you might restrict the entry to values from 1 to 25. Enter

```
@ 10,15 SAY "Interest:   " GET Rate PICTURE;
 "99.99%" RANGE 1,25
```

The text "Interest: " includes three spaces. This is done to make sure that the text literal has the same number of characters as "Loan Amount:" (the previous text item). This is a simple way of making sure that the input areas are displayed at the same column.

The third input area is for the number of years. Enter

```
@ 12,15 SAY "Years:   " GET Years PICTURE "99"
```

Once you have displayed the three input areas, you can activate them by issuing a READ command. The READ command activates all the input areas on the screen with a single command. In this case, there are three input areas on the screen. dBASE IV positions the cursor at the beginning of the first input area; first here refers to the order in which the @/SAY/GET commands were entered, not the row position on the screen. The cursor will then move forward and backward between the input areas, allowing you to enter and edit values. The READ operation is active until you move the cursor past the last input area. Enter

```
READ
```

When you have entered the value, the program calculates the monthly payment and displays the value on the screen.

You will notice that two @/SAY commands are used to display the payment value. In this case, it is simpler to use two commands rather than convert the calculation to a character expression.

```
@ 14,15 SAY "Payment:"
@ 14,26 SAY PAYMENT(Loan,Rate/100/12,Years*12);
 PICTURE "999,999.99"
```

The expression used for the interest rate includes a division by 100 to convert the percent to the proper decimal value.

Positioning the Cursor

The final section of the program uses a WAIT command to pause the program to enable the user to read the results of the calculation. The WAIT command automatically places the **Press any key to continue** message on the next available line on the screen. It would look better if that message was displayed at the bottom of the screen. This result

Fully Structured Screen Displays

can be achieved quite simply by using the @ command without a SAY or GET clause. For example, the command @ 23,0 will place the cursor at the beginning of line 23. If you then issue a WAIT command, the message will appear on line 24 because dBASE IV will see that as the next available line. This little trick enables you to skip to the bottom of the display without having to enter 10 ? commands.

```
@ 23,0
WAIT
```

The last section of the program resets the environment to the dBASE IV defaults.

```
SET TALK ON
SET STATUS ON
SET SCOREBOARD ON
RETURN
```

The entire Loan program looks like this:

```
SET TALK OFF
SET STATUS OFF
SET SCOREBOARD OFF
CLEAR
* initialize variables
STORE 0 to Loan,Rate,Years
* display variables for input
@ 8,15 SAY "Loan Amount:" GET Loan PICTURE;
 "999,999.99"
@ 10,15 SAY "Interest:  " GET Rate PICTURE;
 "99.99%" RANGE 1,25
@ 12,15 SAY "Years:     " GET Years PICTURE "99"
READ
@ 14,15 SAY "Payment:"
@ 14,26 SAY Payment(Loan,Rate/100/12,Years*12);
 PICTURE "999,999.99"
@ 23,0
WAIT
SET TALK ON
SET STATUS ON
```

```
SET SCOREBOARD ON
RETURN
```

This program has a distinct form that is typical of interactive programs.

Initialize. The program begins by initializing the variables into which the user will enter a response.

Display inputs. The next section of the program displays prompts and a typing area for the input of data.

Calculate. Once the user inputs are entered, you can perform any calculation that is necessary. Note that this calculation section may be expanded to include a variety of dBASE IV operations such as database calculations.

Display answer. When the values have been calculated, the results can be displayed for the user.

The last two steps can be compressed into a single calculate/display operation when the calculation tasks are simple.

Most of the interactive programs you create will use a similar sequence of operations.

Save and execute the program by pressing (Alt)-e and typing r. When the program executes, the three input areas appear in the center of the screen (see Figure 4.3).

Enter a value for the amount of the loan.

```
150000
```

The PICTURE clause automatically inserts the comma in the proper position within the number. Next, enter the interest rate, 9.75%.

```
975
```

What happened? Because you did not enter the decimal point, the entry of 975 was taken as 97.5%. The RANGE clause limits the values in this input area to values from 1 to 25. The RANGE clause caught the mistake. Enter

```
9.75
```

Figure 4.3

```
Loan Amount:        0.00
Interest:     0.00%
Years:      0
```

Fully Structured Screen Displays ■ 147

This time dBASE IV accepts the entry because it falls within the values specified in the RANGE clause.

You can move backward to a previous input area to make a revision as long as you have not moved past the last input area. Move back and change the interest rate to 10.5% by typing

[↑]

10.5

Complete the entry with the number of years.

30

The program displays the value of the monthly payment for the specified values (see Figure 4.4).

Complete the program by pressing [↵].

Special Screen Features

dBASE IV provides commands to enhance your screen displays with single- and double-line boxes and changes in screen color or video attributes.

@/TO. This command draws a single- or double-line box. The command requires two pairs of coordinates, one for the upper left and one for the lower right corners of the box.

Figure 4.4

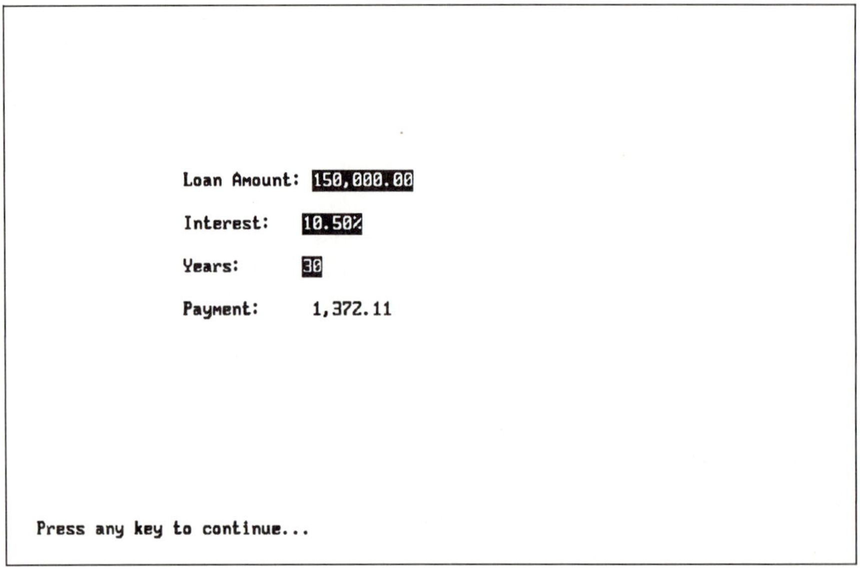

```
Loan Amount:  150,000.00
Interest:      10.50%
Years:         30
Payment:       1,372.11




Press any key to continue...
```

148 ■ Interactive Programming

@/FILL. The FILL command can change the color or video attribute of a block of screen text.

@/CLEAR. This command clears a specified area of the screen display.

Use the @/TO command to draw a box on the screen. Enter

`@ 5,10 TO 10,70`

dBASE IV draws a single-line box on the screen. To draw a double-line box, add the DOUBLE clause to the previous command. Press `↑``Spacebar` then type DOUBLE `↵`.

The PANEL clause draws a box in reverse video. Enter

`@ 5,10 TO 10,70 Panel`

These boxes can enhance the screen display quality of your programs. Load the Loan program into the editor.

`MODIFY COMMAND Loan`

Move the cursor to line 7 and insert the following command to draw a double-line box.

`@ 7,10 TO 13,70 Panel`

Add another command to draw a box where the answer will appear (see Figure 4.5).

Figure 4.5

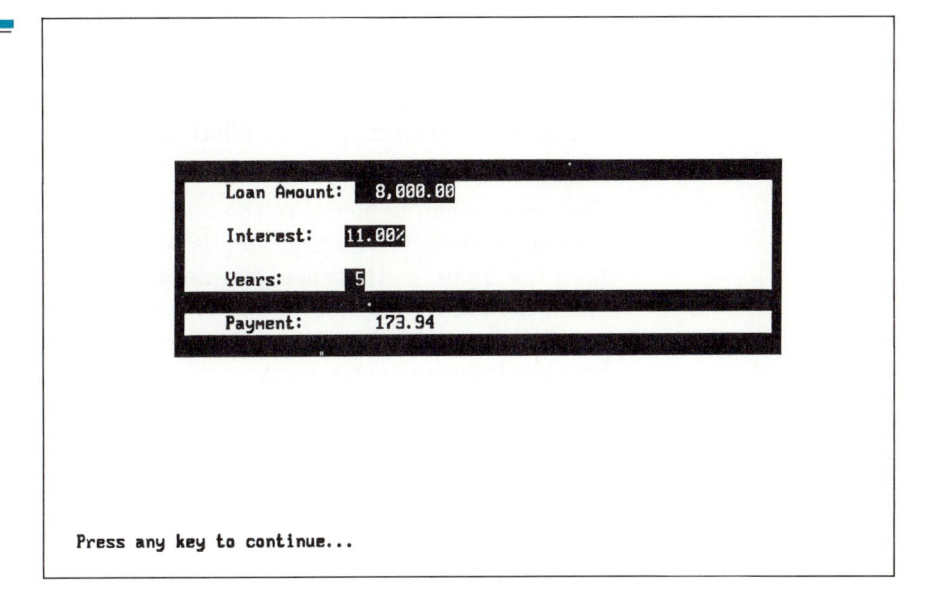

```
    Loan Amount:  8,000.00
    Interest:    11.00%
    Years:           5
    Payment:       173.94



    Press any key to continue...
```

Fully Structured Screen Displays ■ 149

```
@ 13,10 TO 15,70 Panel
```

Save and execute the program by pressing (Alt)-e and typing r. Enter the value to calculate.

```
8000
11
5
```

Complete the program by pressing (↵).

Passing Control Parameters

In the Loan program you saw how interactive screen displays can be used to input information into a program while it is running so that it can produce results based on the user's input. These calculator-type programs use the input as the raw data from which the calculation is made.

You can also use input to control the flow of a program. As an example, recall the Stats program created in Chapter 3 to display a statistical summary of the patient data. Suppose you want to be able to specify a range of dates for which the statistics would be selected. You can add a new section to the program that would interactively allow the user to enter the date range for the summary.

Load the Stats program into the editor by entering

```
MODIFY COMMAND Stats
```

Move the cursor to line 6, the line following the USE ADMIT command that places the database in use.

At this point in the program you should specify the dates for which the program should operate. What is the first step in the modification of this program?

The answer can be found in the outline of an interactive program shown previously. The first step is to initialize the variables that will hold the input. In this case, you need to create two date-type variables to hold the beginning and end dates. You can use the STORE command to define two variables, begin and end, as blank dates. Insert the following command.

```
STORE CTOD("00/00/00") TO Begin,End
```

Insert the next command to draw a box in the middle of the screen.

```
@ 8,10 TO 11,70 Double
```

Next, display the date variables as input areas so that the user can enter the desired range of dates.

```
@ 9,15 SAY "Beginning: " GET Begin
@ 10,15 SAY "End     : " GET End
READ
```

Once the dates have been entered, you can set a database filter based on comparing the beginning and end dates to the admission date field.

```
SET FILTER TO Admit>=Begin .AND. Admit<=End
```

The beginning of the Stats program now looks like this (the new program lines are highlighted in color):

```
* create CLEAR screen
SET TALK OFF
SET STATUS OFF
SET SCOREBOARD OFF
CLEAR
USE Admit
STORE CTOD("00/00/00") TO Begin,End
@ 8,10 TO 11,70 Double
@ 9,15 SAY "Beginning: " GET Begin
@ 10,15 SAY "End     : " GET End
READ
SET FILTER TO Admit>=Begin .AND. Admit<=End
* Calculate statistical values
CALCULATE CNT(),SUM(Days_stay),SUM(Charges) TO;
 M_count,M_days,M_charges FOR Upper(Sex)="M"
CALCULATE CNT(),SUM(Days_stay),SUM(Charges) TO;
 F_count,F_days,F_charges FOR Upper(Sex)="F"
* combine male and female
All=M_count+F_count
Alldays=M_days+F_days
```

Fully Structured Screen Displays

Save and execute the revised program by entering (Alt)-e and typing r. The program begins by displaying a box into which you can enter the beginning and end dates (see Figure 4.6).

Enter a range of dates to select records by.

```
110188
111588
```

The program will display a summary screen for only those records with an admission date included in the range you entered.

Complete the program by pressing (↵).

Selecting Defaults   In the case of character or numeric variables, the default values assigned during initialization are blank or zero values. In the just-revised Stats program, you use a function, DTOC(), to convert a text string into a blank date. While this method works, it is usually preferable to create more specific default values. In a program like Loan, the values entered are not related to database data but come entirely from the user. In Stats, it would be helpful if the default values for the variables reflected in a concrete way something about the records in the database. For example, it might be helpful to set the default for begin to the earliest date in the database and the default value end to the latest date in the database.

How can this be achieved? As usual, there are a variety of ways to attack the problem. One solution is to use the CALCULATE command with the MAX() and MIN() clauses. Open the Admit database by entering

```
USE Admit
```

If the MAX() clause of the CALCULATE command is applied to a date-type field such as admit or discharge, the result will be the most recent date. Enter

```
CALCULATE MAX(Admit)
```

The program returns the value of 11/28/88, the latest date in the file. You can achieve the desired default date values by initializing the begin and end variables with the result of a CALCULATE command,

Figure 4.6

```
Beginning: / /
End      : / /
```

152 ■ Interactive Programming

rather than a STORE command. Load the Stats program into the editor by entering

MODIFY COMMAND Stats

Line 6 contains the STORE command currently used to initialize the variables. Replace that command with a CALCULATE command that defines begin as the earliest date in the admit field and end as the latest date in the admit field. Try this on your own. If you need help, the correct command can be found at the end of the chapter in the Answers to Exercises section under exercise 1.

This change demonstrates that a variable can be initialized in more ways than one. In this case, a CALCULATE command assigns specific initial values to the variables. Here, the initialized variables actually provide useful information, as well as serving as input areas. A further benefit is that if the user wants to scan all the records, he merely presses ⏎ twice and accepts the default dates.

Validity Checks

The @/GET command also functions with a VALID clause. The VALID clause requires a logical expression. When data is entered into the input area, dBASE IV accepts the entry if the logical expression associated with the VALID clause is true. If the expression evaluates as false, the entry is rejected and the cursor will not leave the field until a new valid entry is made.

This type of validity check can avoid program problems or errors that result from the entry of values, characters, or dates that contradict the logic of the program. For example, the dates entered into the begin and end input areas should form a logical range of dates. The end date should always be equal to or greater than the begin date. You can use a VALID clause to compare the end date to the begin date to make sure that a date that is less than the begin date is not entered into the end variable.

Move the cursor to line 10 and add a VALID clause to the @ command.

```
Old Line:    @ 10,15 SAY "End    : " GET End
New Line:    10,15 SAY "End    : "GET End VALID;
             Begin<=End
```

Save and execute the revised program by pressing (Alt)-e and typing r. This time the dates are not blank but contain the first and last date values from the admit field (see Figure 4.7).

Figure 4.7

```
Beginning: 11/01/88
End      : 11/28/88
```

Test the operation of the VALID clause by entering

103188

dBASE IV rejects the date, i.e., beeps, and places the cursor back at the beginning of the field because the entry does not pass the validity check created by the logical expression attached to the VALID clause.

Replace the entry with a valid date.

111588

The program proceeds to calculate and display the summary information. Complete the program by pressing ⏎.

Customized Screen Displays

So far, you have applied the custom screen display abilities of the @-related commands to programs that use memory variables. Another major advantage of the @ command is that it can be used to create custom screen displays. These displays can be created by using the @ command to display the fields in any database file. The custom screen displays can be used for data entry, editing, or display.

dBASE IV provides two methods of using this type of custom screen display.

Format Files. A format file is a special type of program that contains only @/SAY/GET commands. Such a program file is designed to be used with the built-in dBASE IV commands EDIT and APPEND. The format file allows you to create a custom-programmed screen display while taking advantage of the built-in edit and append routines.

Programs Files. The custom screen formats can be written into a normal dBASE IV program or called as a subroutine. In this instance, you will be using screen displays as part of your own custom-designed edit and entry routines that you will substitute for the built-in dBASE IV functions.

In either case, the @ command allows you to create a custom-designed screen display including boxes and lines. You can also take advantage of the wide variety of PICTURE, FUNCTION, and other clauses that operate with @ to control the entry of data into variables or fields.

Format Files

dBASE IV format files enable you to blend a customized screen display with the built-in dBASE IV commands APPEND and EDIT. The APPEND and EDIT commands are used to add to or revise the records in the database. In order to operate, these commands must display the database fields as input areas on the screen. dBASE IV has a built-in method of displaying that information each time the APPEND or EDIT command is used. Display the default screen layout for the Admit file by entering

```
USE Admit
EDIT
```

The program creates an input display by listing all the field names down the left side of the screen. Next to each field name is an input area for that field (see Figure 4.8).

It is important to understand that this entry screen is only the default screen layout. dBASE IV allows you to create one or more custom-designed screen layouts that can substitute for the default style. The format file functions as a special-purpose subroutine directly re-

Figure 4.8

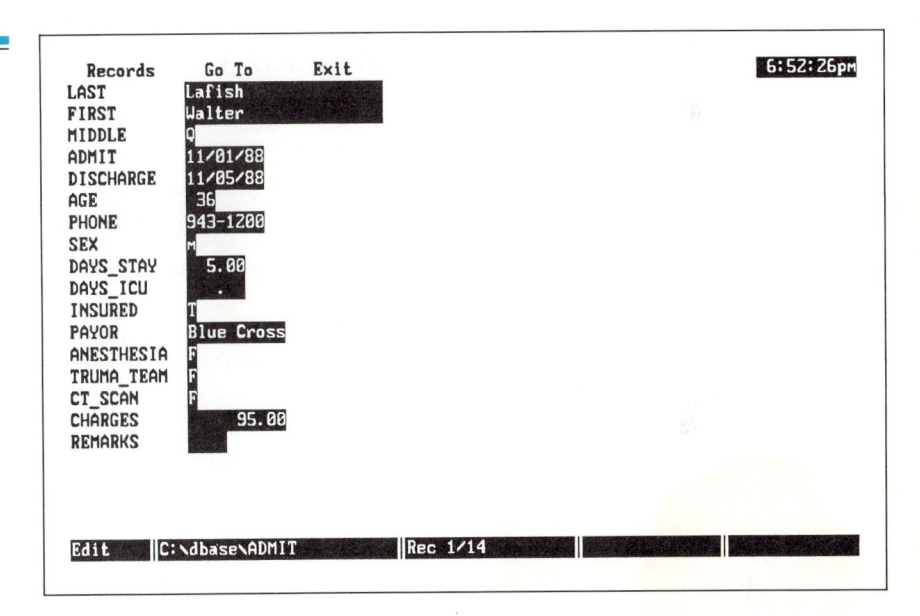

Customized Screen Displays ■ 155

lated to the use of the APPEND and EDIT commands within a program. Exit the current screen display by pressing (Esc).

A dBASE IV format file is a program file that contains a series of @/SAY/GET commands that create a custom screen layout. dBASE IV expects format files to have an .fmt extension. However, you can use any program file as a format file as long as it contains only @/SAY/GET and READ commands.

Begin the process of creating a format file by entering

```
MODIFY COMMAND Admit.fmt
```

The purpose of this format file is to create a customized screen layout for the Admit database.

Nonrecord Information

While the primary purpose of a format file is to display the information in the database's fields, you may want to include, as part of the customized screen display, certain system variables such as the current date, time, record number, and database file name. All of these items are available from the system functions that dBASE IV maintains.

Function	Meaning
DATE()	system date
TIME()	system time
DBF()	current database
RECNO()	current record number
RECCOUNT()	total records in database
VERSION()	program version number
MEMORY()	amount of free memory
LUPDATE()	date file was created or revised
DISKSPACE()	amount of disk space free

Each of these functions can be used as part of an expression. They can be included as part of the format file and will appear when the format file is used. Suppose you want to show the current date as well as the date that the file was last changed. You can use the DATE() and LUPDATE() functions as part of an expression with an @/SAY command, as seen in the two commands below. Since both functions return date-type values, it is necessary to convert the values to characters so that they can be combined with literal text.

Note: Insert the spaces inside the quotation marks to create the correct spacing. Leaving out the spaces will not cause errors in your programs, but items will not be properly aligned on the screen display.

```
@ 1,10 SAY "Current Date: "+DTOC(date())
@ 2,10 SAY "Last Updated: "+DTOC(LUPDATE())
```

The next line in the program displays a phrase that lists the name of the file and the total number of records in that file. The name of the database file can be included by using the DBF() function. Since this function returns character information, it is easy to integrate into an expression. The total number of records in the file can be accessed by the RECCOUNT() function. Since this function returns a numeric value, conversion is required to integrate this function with text.

The STR() function converts the RECCOUNT() function into a character string. Since record numbers in dBASE IV can be 12 characters in size, the text value created by the expression STR(RECCOUNT()) would also be 12 characters. Keeping in mind that the record numbers begin at 1, this creates a gap of blank spaces preceding the number of records. The problem can be eliminated by using the LTRIM() function. The LTRIM() function eliminates any blank spaces in a character item. These three functions can be used in a single expression LTRIM(STR(RECCOUNT())). This expression creates a text item that is only as wide as justified by the size of the record number, eliminating the unwanted spaces. Enter the next command.

```
@ 3,10 SAY "File "+DBF()+" Contains;
 "+LTRIM(STR(RECCOUNT()))+" Records."
```

The next command displays the current record number. The LTRIM(STR()) function converts the record number, given by the RECNO() function, into a trimmed character item.

```
@ 4,10 SAY "Current Record Number:;
 "+LTRIM(STR(RECNO()))
```

You can draw a box around the text displayed by these commands. Enter

```
@ 0,8 to 5,71
```

Displaying Fields

The major purpose of the format file is to display fields for entry or editing. A field entry area consists of two parts: An @/SAY displays the field name or equivalent text. This display is called the prompt because it identifies the meaning of the input area. Another @/GET displays an input area for the field that logically corresponds to the text.

There are two ways to display field input areas.

1. **Horizontal.** The horizontal approach is the one used by the dBASE IV default display. In this approach, the name of the field or some other text that identifies the input area is displayed, and an input area for that field is placed next to the prompt on the same line. This is the simplest type of command to use because it can be expressed as a single @/SAY/GET command.

2. **Vertical.** The vertical approach rotates the relationship between prompt and input areas 90 degrees. In this format an @/SAY is used to place the prompt on one line and an @/GET is used to place the input area on the next line below the prompt. This method requires separate @/SAY and @/GET commands.

Begin the fields section of the format file with the three fields that hold the patient's name: First, Last, and Middle. The simplest way to create an entry area is to use the horizontal approach. Enter

```
@ 7,0 SAY "First Name: " GET First
@ 8,0 SAY "Middle Int: " GET Middle
@ 9,0 SAY "Last Name: " GET Last
```

Add three more of these commands for the Age, Sex, and Phone field, on lines 10 though 12. Try this on your own. If you need help, the correct command can be found at the end of the chapter in the Answers to Exercises section under exercise 2. Remember to pad each prompt with blanks so that all of the prompts are 12 characters wide. This ensures that the input areas will all align at the same column.

The next two fields are the admit and discharge dates. In this case you will use the vertical method to place the prompts and the fields on different lines. First display the prompt for the admit field.

```
@ 13,0 SAY "Admitted"
```

The next command is also an @/SAY that places the discharge prompt on the same line. In order to know what column to use for the location, you need to count the characters in the previous prompt. The word Admitted has eight characters. This means that you should probably begin the next text item at column 10, at least. Enter

```
@ 13,10 SAY "Discharged"
```

The next command will place an input area for the Admit field directly below the prompt Admitted. Enter

```
@ 14,0 GET Admit
```

Where should the next input area, the area for discharge date, be placed? If you are thinking 14,10, you would be correct, with one possible exception. The placement of the admit field input area is simplified by the coincidence that the prompt word Admitted contains eight characters, the same width as a date field. But the prompt "Discharged" contains 10 characters. Should the eight-character date be aligned to the left or the right side of the prompt? The answer is a matter of personal preference. Suppose you want a right alignment. This means that instead of placing the input area at 14,10 you would move it in two characters to 14,12.

```
@ 14,12 GET Discharge
```

A vertical approach is more time consuming to plan and write than the horizontal approach to screen formats.

PICTURE Clauses

In creating a database, you will find that the entries made into some fields follow specific patterns. For example, a local phone number always uses a dash as the fourth character. Since this character is always the same, it is a waste of time to require a user to enter the dash character each time a phone number is added. It would be desirable to create a situation where the dash is automatically inserted into the field at that position, just as the slashes are inserted into the date fields. This effect can be achieved by using a PICTURE clause. In addition, you can restrict the entry in that character-type field to numbers only.

Move the cursor to the end of line 11, the line that displays the phone field. Add a PICTURE clause to the @/SAY/GET command.

Old line: `@ 12,0 SAY "Phone:    " GET Phone`
New Line: `@ 12,0 SAY "Phone:    " GET Phone PICTURE; "999-9999"`

PICTURE clauses can also be used in combination with other @ command clauses such as VALID. The sex field should be restricted to the entry of an F or M. You can use a PICTURE clause to convert the character to upper case and a VALID clause to restrict entry to the

Customized Screen Displays

letters F or M. Move the cursor to line 9 and modify the command as shown below. The order in which the clauses appear is not significant.

Old line: @ 11,0 SAY "Sex: " GET Sex
New Line: @ 11,0 SAY "Sex: " GET Sex PICTURE "!";
            Valid sex$"MF"

At this point the format file contains entry areas for only part of the 17 fields in the Admit database. You are not required to include all the fields in a format file. You may want to leave out certain fields in order to prevent accidental entry. For example, if you intend to calculate a value, like calculating Days_stay from the admit and discharge dates, you may want to eliminate that field from the entry screen.

End the format file at this point in order to use the format just created. Later in this chapter, you will return to this file and add more fields. The entire format file should read as follows:

```
@ 1,10 SAY "Current Date: "+DTOC(DATE())
@ 2,10 SAY "Last Updated: "+DTOC(LUPDATE())
@ 3,10 SAY "File "+DBF()+" contains;
 "+LTRIM(STR(RECCOUNT()))+" records."
@ 4,10 SAY "Current Record Number:;
 "+LTRIM(STR(RECNO()))
@ 0,8 TO 5,71
@ 7,0 SAY "First Name: " GET First
@ 8,0 SAY "Middle Int: " GET Middle PICTURE "!"
@ 9,0 SAY "Last Name:  " GET Last
@ 10,0 SAY "Age:        " GET Age
@ 11,0 SAY "Sex:        " GET Sex PICTURE "!";
VALID Sex$"MF"
@ 12,0 SAY "Phone:      " GET Phone PICTURE;
"999-9999"
@ 13,0 SAY "Admitted"
@ 13,10 SAY "Discharged"
@ 14,0 GET Admit
@ 14,12 GET Discharge
```

Save the file by entering Ctrl-End.

Using a Format File

Format files are a special form of subroutines. A format file subroutine is not activated with the DO command used for normal subroutines. Instead, dBASE IV uses the command SET FORMAT to activate a format file. Format files also differ from standard subroutines in that the commands contained in a format file do not become active immediately following the SET FORMAT TO. The use of a full screen editing command, such as EDIT or APPEND, is required to display the screen format. The SET FORMAT TO command loads the format file information into the computer so that when a full screen edit is required, dBASE IV uses the commands in the format file instead of the default screen display.

Create a program that displays records using the format file you have just made. Enter

```
MODIFY COMMAND Edit
```

Set the environment as you usually do while running a program.

```
SET TALK OFF
SET STATUS OFF
SET SCOREBOARD OFF
CLEAR
```

Open the database file.

```
USE Admit
```

Before you enter the EDIT command, you should activate the format file that you want to use, in this case Admit.fmt.

```
SET FORMAT TO Admit
```

The .fmt file extension is assumed by dBASE IV. Once the format file is active, you can perform the editing using the format file as the screen display.

```
EDIT
```

Complete the program by closing the files and setting the environment back to the default values.

```
CLOSE FORMAT
CLOSE DATABASE
SET SCOREBOARD ON
SET STATUS ON
SET TALK ON
RETURN
```

The program uses only two user-defined terms, the name of the database and the format files. Save and execute the program by pressing (Alt)-e and typing r. The program displays the first record in the Admit file using the format file to lay out the screen display. The box at the top of the screen displays the system information. The field information is displayed according to the commands in the format file. Note the difference in appearance between the horizontal and vertical layout styles (see Figure 4.9).

All of the normal edit mode commands will operate in this mode. Display record 2 by pressing (PgDn).

Move to the last record in the database by pressing (Ctrl)-(PgDn).

Add a new record by entering (PgDn) and typing

y

followed by (↵).

The program displays a blank entry screen for record 12. Enter

Scott

l

Fisher

Figure 4.9

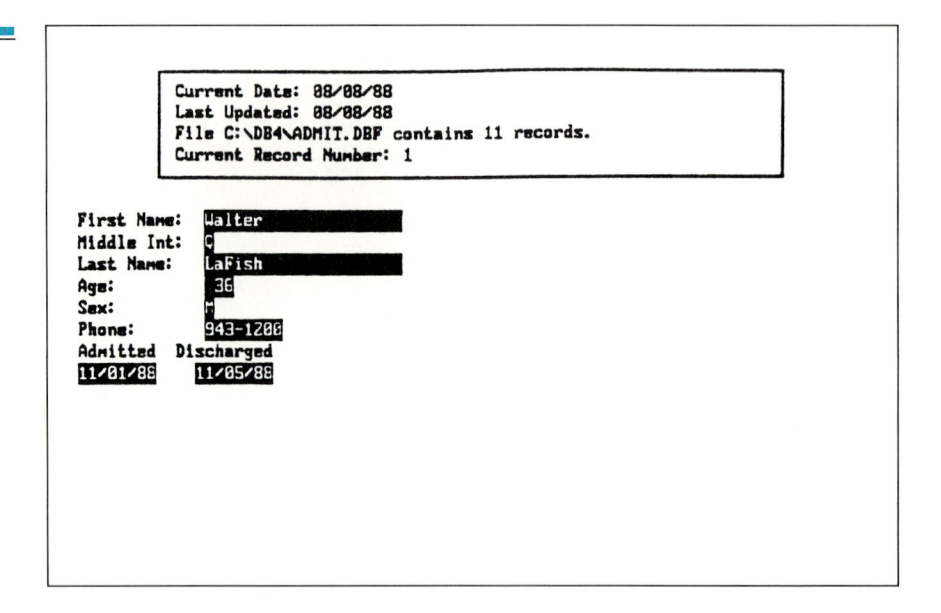

```
Current Date: 08/08/88
Last Updated: 08/08/88
File C:\DB4\ADMIT.DBF contains 11 records.
Current Record Number: 1
```

```
First Name: Walter
Middle Int:  C
Last Name:  LaFish
Age:         36
Sex:         M
Phone:       943-1200
Admitted  Discharged
11/01/88  11/05/88
```

162 ■ Interactive Programming

Notice that the middle initial is automatically capitalized because of the PICTURE function. Continue the entry.

`27`

`g`

The VALID function prevents the entry of the letter G in the sex field. Only M or F is valid. Change the entry.

`m`

The letter M fits the validity criterion and is accepted. Enter the phone number.

`2457788`

It is not necessary to enter the dash because it is already inserted by the PICTURE function. Continue the entry of the dates.

`120288`

`120688`

The program moves to another blank record. Terminate the program by pressing (Esc).

Run the program again and display the 12th record. Enter

`DO EDIT`

Press (Ctrl)-(PgDn). The new record, 12, is part of the database.

> *Note:* When a format file is used, dBASE IV creates an object file with an .fdo extension. This object file serves the same purpose as the .dbo files created for .prg files.

Exit the program by pressing (Esc).

Logical Fields

There are three logical fields, Anesthesia, Trauma_team, and Ct_scan, in the Admit file. Add these fields to the format file. Enter

`MODIFY COMMAND Admit.fmt`

Move the cursor to the end of the file by entering (Ctrl)-(PgDn).

All of the entry fields are currently located on the left side of the screen. Logical fields are designed to accept either T/F or Y/N entries. You can use a special PICTURE clause character, Y, to restrict the entry and display of the logical fields to only Y/N. This is useful when the logical field data is basically a yes/no response. Place the logical fields on the right side of the display pictured for yes/no entry. Enter

    @ 10,45 SAY "Anesthesia: " GET Anesthesia PICTURE;
    "Y"
    @ 12,45 SAY "Trauma Team: " GET Truma_team;
    PICTURE "Y"
    @ 14,45 SAY "CT scan: " GET Ct_scan PICTURE "Y"

Place a box around the three logical fields by entering

    @ 9,40 TO 15,70

Memo Fields

When a memo field is placed into a custom screen format, it appears just as it does in the default screen display. The memo field shows the word memo. In order to see the text stored in the memo, you need to position the cursor in the memo field and press (Ctrl)-(Home).

The display of the memo field has one major disadvantage. Because the word memo always appears in the field input area, it is not possible to tell whether any memo text has been entered or not. It would be helpful to know whether or not memo text has been entered by looking at the record. You could then tell at a glance whether or not you need to inspect the contents of the memo field.

In order to accomplish this, save the format file temporarily and return to the dot prompt so that you can experiment with some new functions. Press (Ctrl)-(End) and type

    USE Admit

Display the contents of the first record in the database file. Enter

    DISPLAY

You cannot tell from the normal display if this record contains memo text because only the word MEMO appears. But dBASE IV provides some special functions that allow you to test the contents of the memo field without having to display the text. The MEMLINES() function displays the number of lines of text stored in a memo field. The line count is based on 50-character text lines.

> *Note:* You can alter the size of the memo text line with the SET MEMOWIDTH TO command.

Enter

```
? Memlines(Remarks)
```

The program displays a value of 2, indicating that there is memo text in this record. Even a single character is counted as one line. Move to the end of the database by entering

```
GO BOTTOM
```

Display the number of lines of text in this memo field.

```
? Memlines(remarks)
```

This time the value is 0, informing you that no memo text has been entered for this record.

The MEMLINES() function makes it possible to test a memo field for text without having to actually display it. Use this function in an expression to list the names of the records that contain memo text.

```
LIST First,Last FOR Memlines(remarks)>0
```

Only three names are listed because those are the only records that contain memo field text.

The IIF() Function

Now that you have a method of determining what records contain memo text, you may want to create a display that indicates the status of the memo field. One way to accomplish this is to use the IIF() function, which operates in a similar manner to the VALID clause. The IIF() function requires a logical expression to evaluate. The VALID clause uses the results of its logical expression to determine if it should accept or reject the information that has been entered. The IIF() function allows you to specify two values. If the logical expression is true, the first value is used. If the logical expression is false, the second value is used.

The simplest way to use an IIF() function is with a logical field. For example, test the insured field. The following command will test each insured field and display **Insured** or **Not Insured** for each record.

```
LIST IIF(Insured,"Insured","Not Insured")
```

The IIF() function displays the first text item, **Insured,** for all records with a true value for insured, and **Not Insured** for all records with a false value for insured. The IIF() function is convenient for converting short data items such as logical fields into more elaborate displays. In this way, you have the advantage of making single-character entries while still displaying whole-word items in their place (see Figure 4.10).

You can use this function to convert the contents of the Sex field into the full words male and female. Enter

```
LIST IIF(Upper(Sex)="M","Male","Female")
```

The command lists the full text in place of the M and F characters.

You can use a MEMLINES() function as part of the logical test within the IIF() function. This means that if there is memo text in a record, the evaluation will be true. Enter

```
LIST IIF(Memlines(Remarks)>0,"Memo Text","No;
 Memo")
```

The command creates a list of the records that contain or do not contain memo (see Figure 4.11).

You can use the IIF() as part of the prompt in an @/SAY/GET command inside the format file. The effect is to display one prompt if the memo contains text and another if the memo is empty. You can then tell at a glance if the memo field in any record contains text or not. Open the format file for editing.

```
MODIFY COMMAND Admit.fmt
```

Figure 4.10

```
. list first,last for memlines(remarks)>0
Record#  first                last
      1  Walter               LaFish
      2  Harold               Tate
      3  Frank                Ivanovic

. list iif(insured,"Insured","Not Insured")
Record#  iif(insured,"Insured","Not Insured")
      1  Insured
      2  Not Insured
      3  Not Insured
      4  Insured
      5  Insured
      6  Insured
      7  Not Insured
      8  Insured
      9  Not Insured
     10  Insured
     11  Insured
     12  Not Insured
.
Command  C:\db4\ADMIT            Rec EOF/12       File                    Ins
```

Figure 4.11

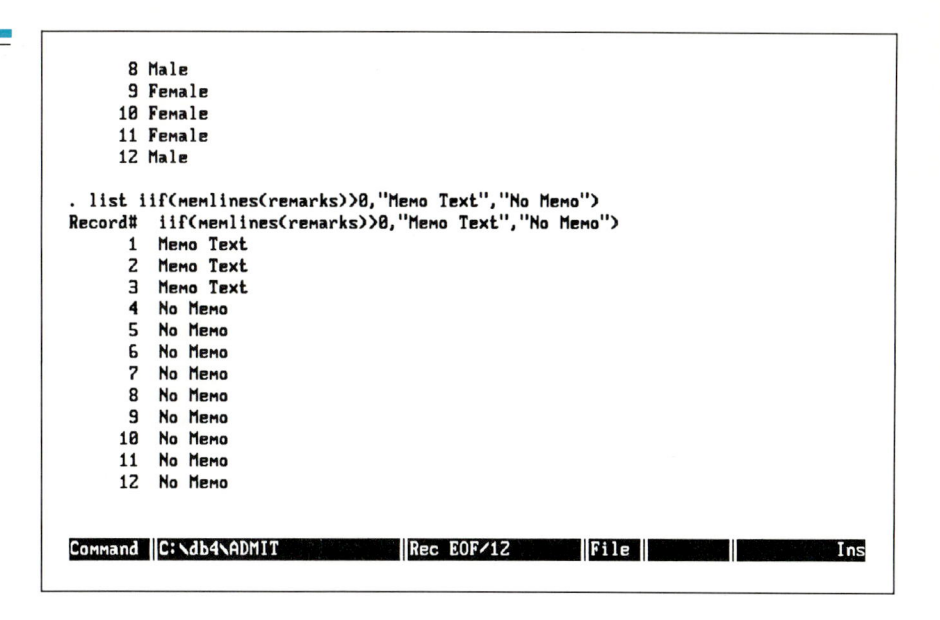

```
        8 Male
        9 Female
       10 Female
       11 Female
       12 Male
. list iif(memlines(remarks)>0,"Memo Text","No Memo")
Record#  iif(memlines(remarks)>0,"Memo Text","No Memo")
      1  Memo Text
      2  Memo Text
      3  Memo Text
      4  No Memo
      5  No Memo
      6  No Memo
      7  No Memo
      8  No Memo
      9  No Memo
     10  No Memo
     11  No Memo
     12  No Memo


Command  C:\db4\ADMIT            Rec EOF/12    File              Ins
```

Move the cursor to the end of the file by pressing Ctrl-PgDn.

The following command uses the IIF() function to alter the text of the prompt based on the contents of the memo field.

@ 18,10 SAY IIF(Memlines(Remarks)>0,"Revise;
 Existing Memo","Create New Memo") GET remarks

Multiple Pages

A format file does not have to fit all of the information onto a single screen display. dBASE IV allows you to create as many as 32 different screens within the same format file. To create another screen, a READ command is inserted into the format file at the position where you want that screen to begin. In our example, you can place the rest of the fields on a second screen.

Insert a message at the bottom of the current screen to alert the user that there is an additional screen of information for this record.

@ 20,10 TO 22,70 double

@ 21,20 SAY "Enter Pg Dn For Next Screen"

READ

The program fails to clear line 0 of the screen display when you move to the second page. To correct this, enter the following command.

Customized Screen Displays ■ 167

```
@ 0,0 SAY Space(78)
```

Complete the second page by entering

```
@ 4,10 SAY "Current Record Number:;
 "+LTRIM(STR(RECNO()))
@ 8,20 SAY "Payor Source:    " GET Payor
@ 10,20 SAY "Total Charges:  " GET Charges
@ 12,20 SAY "Days Stayed:    " GET Days_stay
@ 14,20 SAY "Days in ICU:    " GET Days_icu
@ 20,10 TO 22,70 Double
@ 21,20 SAY "Enter Pg Up For Previous Screen"
```

The entire format file now reads:

```
@ 1,10 SAY "Current Date: "+DTOC(date())
@ 2,10 SAY "Last Updated: "+DTOC(lupdate())
@ 3,10 SAY "File "+dbf()+" contains;
 "+LTRIM(STR(RECCOUNT()))+" records."
@ 4,10 SAY "Current Record Number:;
 "+LTRIM(STR(RECNO()))
@ 0,8 TO 5,71
@ 7,0 SAY "First Name: " GET First
@ 8,0 SAY "Middle Int: " GET Middle PICTURE "!"
@ 9,0 SAY "Last Name:  " GET Last
@ 10,0 SAY "Age:        " GET Age
@ 11,0 SAY "Sex:        " GET Sex PICTURE "!";
 Valid Sex$"MF"
@ 12,0 SAY "Phone:      " GET Phone PICTURE;
 "999-9999"
@ 13,0 SAY "Admitted"
@ 13,10 SAY "Discharged"
@ 14,0 GET admit
@ 14,12 GET discharge
@ 10,45 SAY "Anesthesia:  " GET Anesthesia;
 PICTURE "Y"
@ 12,45 SAY "Trauma Team: " GET Trauma_team;
 PICTURE "Y"
```

```
@ 12,45 SAY "Trauma Team: " GET Trauma_team;
  PICTURE "Y"
@ 14,45 SAY "CT Scan:      " GET Ct_scan PICTURE;
  "Y"
@ 9,40 TO 15,70
@ 18,10 SAY IIF(MEMLINES(Remarks)>0,"Revise;
  Existing Memo","Create New Memo") GET Remarks
@ 20,10 TO 22,70 Double
@ 21,20 SAY "Enter Pg Dn For Next Screen"
READ
@ 0,0 SAY Space(78)
@ 4,10 SAY "Current Record Number:;
  "+LTRIM(STR(RECNO()))
@ 8,20 SAY "Payor Source:   " GET Payor
@ 10,20 SAY "Total Charges: " GET Charges
@ 12,20 SAY "Days Stayed:   " GET Days_stay
@ 14,20 SAY "Days in ICU:   " GET Days_icu
@ 20,10 TO 22,70 Double
@ 21,20 SAY "Enter Pg Up For Previous Screen"
```

Save the revised format file by entering [Ctrl]-[End]. Run the Edit program again.

```
DO EDIT
```

The revised format screen is displayed. The prompt for the memo field indicates that this record contains text in the memo field.

Display the second screen in the format field by pressing [PgDn] (see Figure 4.12).

Move to the last record in the file by pressing [Ctrl]-[PgDn]. Notice that the prompt for the memo field in this record displays text indicating that the memo field is empty. Display the second screen for this record by pressing [PgDn]. Fill in the missing data.

```
Mutual of Omaha
4590
```

Exit the program by pressing [Ctrl]-[End].

Figure 4.12

```
         8 Male
         9 Female
        10 Female
        11 Female
        12 Male

. list iif(memlines(remarks)>0,"Memo Text","No Memo")
Record#  iif(memlines(remarks)>0,"Memo Text","No Memo")
     1   Memo Text
     2   Memo Text
     3   Memo Text
     4   No Memo
     5   No Memo
     6   No Memo
     7   No Memo
     8   No Memo
     9   No Memo
    10   No Memo
    11   No Memo
    12   No Memo

Command  C:\db4\ADMIT        Rec EOF/12    File                Ins
```

Seaching for Records

The Edit program that you are currently executing always begins the display with the first record in the database. But suppose you wanted to use this program to display a specific record, record #7. You can display a specific record by moving the pointer to that record before you activate the format screen with the EDIT command.

You can use the interactive program concepts described earlier in this chapter to allow a user to input the record number into a memory variable. You can then use that value to position the pointer and display the exact record requested.

Load the Edit program into the editor by entering

MODIFY COMMAND Edit

Move the cursor to line 6, which contains the command SET FORMAT TO ADMIT. It is here that you are to insert the commands necessary to allow a user to enter the record number to edit. The first step is to initialize the variable. Here, set the variable equal to 1 because there is no record 0.

Pick_rec=1

■ Interactive Programming

Use the @/SAY/GET commands to create an input area and prompt for this variable. How would you prevent the entry of an invalid record number? You can use a RANGE clause and set the upper limit to the function RECCOUNT(). In this way you cannot enter a record number greater than the total number of records in the file. Enter

```
@ 10,10 SAY "Enter the Record Number"
@ 12,10 GET Pick_rec RANGE 1,RECCOUNT()
READ
```

At this point, you have the value of the record number stored in the variable Pick_rec. You can position the pointer to that record by simply using the variable, which is a numeric value, with the GOTO command. This positions the pointer to that record.

```
GOTO Pick_rec
```

There is one last step. The EDIT command, on line 11, automatically places dBASE IV into the edit mode. Therefore, you can scroll back and forth between records by using the (PgUp) and (PgDn) keys. Here, however, you do not want that to take place. The objective is to allow editing of only the specified record. You can limit editing to a single record by adding a scope of NEXT 1 to the EDIT command.

> *Note:* In dBASE IV the NEXT scope begins with the current pointer position. Thus, the scope NEXT 1 actually refers to the current record.

Change the EDIT command by adding this scope.

Old line: EDIT
New Line: EDIT NEXT 1

The revised program looks like this (new program lines are highlighted in color):

```
SET TALK OFF
SET STATUS OFF
SET SCOREBOARD OFF
CLEAR
USE Admit
Pick_rec=1
@ 10,10 SAY "Enter the Record Number"
@ 12,10 GET Pick_rec RANGE 1,RECCOUNT()
READ
```

```
GOTO Pick_rec
SET FORMAT TO Admit
EDIT NEXT 1
CLOSE FORMAT
CLOSE DATABASE
SET SCOREBOARD ON
SET STATUS ON
SET TALK ON
RETURN
```

Save and execute the revised program by pressing (Alt)-e and typing r. The screen displays the prompt for entering the record number.

Enter the number of the record you want to edit. Enter

25

The program rejects the entry because there are only 12 records in the database. Enter a valid record number. Enter

7

The program displays the record that corresponds to the record number you entered (see Figure 4.13).

Figure 4.13

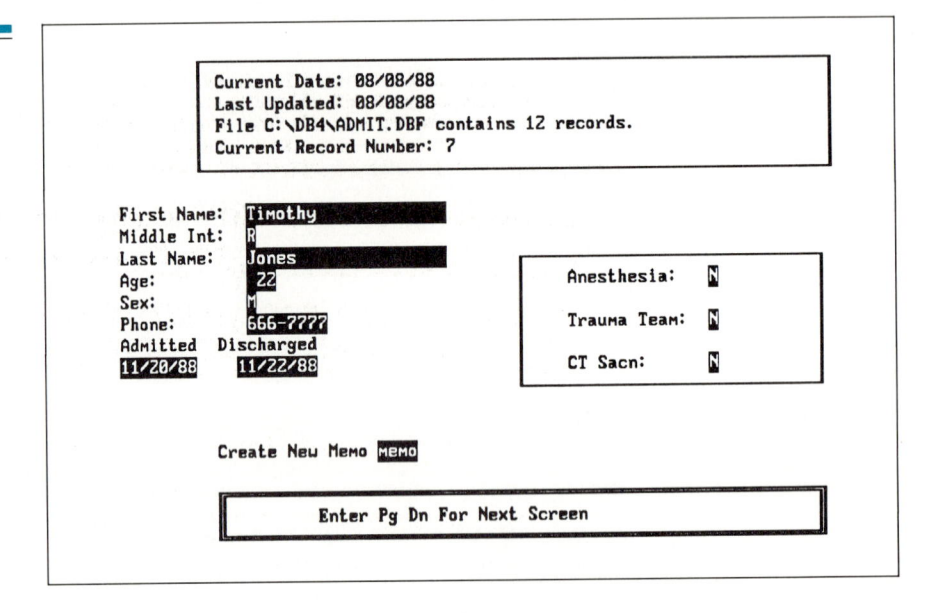

```
Current Date: 08/08/88
Last Updated: 08/08/88
File C:\DB4\ADMIT.DBF contains 12 records.
Current Record Number: 7

First Name: Timothy
Middle Int: R
Last Name: Jones
Age:         22                    Anesthesia:    N
Sex:         M
Phone:       666-7777              Trauma Team:   N
Admitted  Discharged
11/20/88  11/22/88                 CT Sacn:       N

           Create New Memo  MEMO

              Enter Pg Dn For Next Screen
```

172 ■ Interactive Programming

Display the next screen. Press (PgDn). Continue by pressing (PgDn).

Instead of displaying record 8, the program terminates after the specified record is displayed. This is due to the effect of the NEXT 1 scope, which limits the number of records to be edited to the current record.

Searching

The Edit program you have created functions perfectly well, but it is based on a dubious premise. In order to select a record for display or editing, you are required to know the record number. With a small database such as the one used in these examples, it is possible, though not desirable, to remember the record numbers associated with patients. The Edit program would be much more serviceable if you could enter the patient's name rather than the record number.

In order to make such a program function, you will need a command that searches the database to find the record that contains a specific name you are seeking. Such a command, the LOCATE command, uses a FOR clause to select a record based on a logical expression like Last="Smith". LOCATE then searches the database for a record that evaluates true for the expression. The pointer is positioned at that record. If no match is found, the pointer is positioned at the bottom of the file.

> *Note:* Recall that the bottom of the file is the last record in the database, not the end of file, which is beyond the last record in the database.

To see how LOCATE works, open the Admit file.

```
USE Admit
```

Locate the record that contains the last name Lutz by entering

```
LOCATE FOR Last="Lutz"
```

dBASE IV displays "Record =   4". This indicates that record 4 matches the expression. Display that record.

```
DISPLAY
```

The record contains the last name you are looking for.

In order to safeguard against differences in case, the LOCATE command should convert the field to upper case text. Enter

```
LOCATE FOR UPPER(Last)="TATE"
```

Searching for Records ■ 173

This time record 2 matches the criterion.

```
DISPLAY
```

The LOCATE command provides a tool to search the database for specific records based on the contents of the record, not the record numbers.

Modify the Edit program to perform this type of logical search.

```
MODIFY COMMAND Edit
```

The first line to be changed is the line that initializes the variable. In this case, create a character variable instead of a numeric variable. Move the cursor to line 5 and make the following change.

Old line: `Pick_rec=1`

New Line: `Pick_rec=SPACE(20)`

The next line should be changed to display a prompt that tells the user to enter the last name of the patient he wants to display.

Old line: `@ 10,10 SAY "Enter the Record Number"`

New Line: `@ 10,10 SAY "Enter the Last Name"`

Change the next command to display an input area for the character variable. You can use a FUNCTION clause to automatically capitalize the entry.

Old line: `@ 12,10 GET Pick_rec RANGE 1,RECCOUNT()`

New Line: `@ 12,10 GET Pick_rec FUNCTION "!"`

The last change in this program is on line #9, the line that currently contains the GOTO command. This line should be changed to perform a LOCATE, which compares the contents of the last field to the name entered into the Pick_rec variable. Try this on your own. If you need help, the correct command can be found at the end of the chapter in the Answers to Exercises section under exercise 3.

Save and execute the modified file by pressing (Alt)-e and typing r. The program displays an input area for the last name. Enter

```
Lutz
```

The program searches for and then displays the record with the matching last name.

Terminate the program by pressing (PgDn) twice.

Run the program again.

```
DO EDIT
```

■ **Interactive Programming**

Suppose you are not sure how to spell the last name. You may want to find the first entry that begins with a specific letter or two. For example, you may recall that one of the names begins with the letters "IV", but you can't remember the entire name. Enter

```
IV
```

What happened? The program displayed the record of a patient named Fisher because your program was not properly set up for partial matches. As a result it failed to locate the correct record and displayed the last record in the database. Exit the program by pressing (Ctrl)-(End).

The more significant question is why didn't the search locate a record with a last name that begins with "IV"? There are two possible answers.

1. There are no records in the database that have a last name that begins with "IV".

2. There is a logical error in your LOCATE command.

First, test to see if there really is a record in your database that has a last name that begins with the letters "IV." Enter

```
USE Admit
LIST Last
```

Record 3 should have been located. What is the logical error in the program? The answer lies in the way the input area for the search criterion operates. Remember that the variable was originally defined as 20 blank spaces. When you entered the last name you were seeking, you replaced some of the blanks with letters. However, the overall width of the variable remained 20 characters, two letters and 18 blanks.

When dBASE IV compared the contents of the variable to the last name field, it did so with a position-by-position comparison. In the case of the name IVANOVIC the program found that while the first two characters matched, the third, fourth and so on did not, i.e., the blank spaces in the variable did not match the letters in the field.

```
Field:      [IVANOVIC------------]
Variable:   [IV------------------]
```

How can this problem be resolved? dBASE IV allows the match if the variable does not contain all the trailing spaces but is simply a two-character entry.

```
Field:     [IVANOVIC-----------]
Variable:  [IV]
```

A partial match can be achieved through a function called TRIM(). TRIM() removes the trailing blanks from a variable or field. In this case, by adding the TRIM() function to the Pick_rec variable in the LOCATE command, you will make it possible to have a partial match.

Modify the Edit program by entering

`MODIFY COMMAND Edit`

Change line 9 to include a TRIM() function for the variable. Try this on your own. If you need help, the correct command can be found at the end of the chapter in the Answers to Exercises section under exercise 4.

Save and execute the program by pressing (Alt)-e and typing r. Enter the letters you want to search for.

IV

This time the correct record is located.

Exit the program by pressing (Ctrl)-(End).

Rapid Searches

The search performed by the current version of the Edit program is called a sequential search. A sequential search always begins with the first record in the database file. The search then moves, one record at a time, through the database until it finds a match, or it encounters the bottom of the file.

When the database file that you are working with is small, like the Admit file, the time it takes to perform a sequential search is quite short. But as the database grows larger, you will begin to notice that each search operation consumes a great deal of time.

Because a sequential search moves record by record, as the database grows the time it takes to move through all the records increases proportionally to the size of the database file. The solution to this problem requires some method to avoid a full sequential search of the database.

Imagine that you have a set of encyclopedias in which you need to search for the date of the Mexican-American war. How would you proceed? Searching sequentially requires that you begin reading on the first page of the first volume and continue until you find the Mexican War or reach the end of the last volume.

However, most people would never consider that approach. Instead, they would begin by selecting the M volume and jumping to the Mexican section to begin the actual search. What is there about the encyclopedia that makes this possible?

The answer is that you know in advance that all of the topics in all of the volumes have been organized in a specific order. Because the information is ordered, you can logically determine that volumes A through L and N though Z need not be searched. You have eliminated 25/26, or 96% of the data from your search, just by selecting the correct volume. This kind of search is called random access because it accesses database information at a number of different points, not just the beginning of the file.

How can this principle be applied to dBASE IV? Are there circumstances in which the records are arranged into a specific order? The answer is yes—when they are indexed.

Instead of performing a sequential search on the database file, you can locate records at a vastly higher rate of speed by searching the index file, which is already organized into a specific sequence.

The ability to perform rapid searches is one of the most important functions performed by index files.

To perform a random access search, you need to insure two factors:

- The database file must have an active index tag for the field you want to search.

- You must make sure that the index file contains all the records in the database.

The second point requires some explanation. The use of index files in dBASE IV is optional. The index files you created in Chapter 2 recorded the index order for the records that were entered into the database at that time. Since then, the database has been modified by adding two more records. Why aren't those records in the index files?

dBASE IV will update an index file only if it is open when changes—additions, deletions, or revisions—are made in the database file. At the moment, the Admit index file is not an accurate index of the Admit database.

Place the Admit database file in use.

```
USE Admit
```

Count the number of records.

`COUNT`

Twelve records are counted. Now activate the index file.

`SET INDEX TO Admit ORDER Last`
`COUNT`

This time the program reports only 10 records in the database because when this index file was updated, the Admit database file contained only 10 records.

You can update the index file by using the REINDEX command. Enter

`REINDEX`

dBASE IV rebuilds all four of the index tags contained in the Admit index file (see Figure 4.14).

Keeping index files up to date is a very important job, particularly when you intend to rely on those indexes for rapid searches. You will see that, as you create programs in future chapters, you will always open the appropriate index files each time the database is edited.

With the Admit index file updated, you can learn how to change the Edit program to a rapid-index based search.

Figure 4.14

```
. use admit
. count
     12 rec
. set indexords
. set index to admit tag last of admit
. set index to admit order last
Master index: LAST
. count
     10 records
.
. reindex
Rebuilding index - C:\DB4\ADMIT.MDX   Tag: LAST
   100% indexed        12 Records indexed
Rebuilding index - C:\DB4\ADMIT.MDX   Tag: DISCHARGE
   100% indexed        12 Records indexed
Rebuilding index - C:\DB4\ADMIT.MDX   Tag: CHARGES
   100% indexed        12 Records indexed
Rebuilding index - C:\DB4\ADMIT.MDX   Tag: SEX
   100% indexed        12 Records indexed
.
Command  C:\db4\ADMIT           Rec 5/12       File
```

The SEEK Command

The key to rapid searches is the SEEK command. The SEEK command searches the master index tag for a record that matches the specified expression. It is not necessary to use a logical expression such as Last = "Tate" because the SEEK command does not actually look at the fields in the database. SEEK searches the information stored in the master index tag for a match. If the index tag contains information from the last name field, then the search operates on last names.

Before you can issue a SEEK command, you need to determine that the key of the current master index contains the information you want to search. This can be done by using the DISPLAY STATUS command. Enter

DISPLAY STATUS

The display shows that the current master is sequenced by the contents of the last name field. It also shows that index tags are available for discharge date, charges, or sex (see Figure 4.15).

Return to the dot prompt by pressing (Esc).

With a properly updated master index tag in place, you can use the SEEK command to locate specific records. The following command locates a record with the last name of Lutz. Remember to enter "Lutz" as a literal, with the exact capitalization shown. Enter

Figure 4.15

```
Currently Selected Database:
Select area:   1, Database in Use: C:\DB4\ADMIT.DBF   Alias: ADMIT
          MDX file:    C:\DB4\ADMIT.MDX
     Master Index TAG:    LAST   Key: last
             Index TAG:    DISCHARGE  Key: discharge
             Index TAG:    CHARGES  Key: charges (Descending)
             Index TAG:    SEX   Key: upper(sex)
             Memo file:   C:\DB4\ADMIT.DBT

File search path:
Default disk drive: C:
Print destination:  PRN:
Margin =      0
Refresh count =    0
Reprocess count =   0
Number of files open =   6
Current work area =    1

ALTERNATE  - OFF   DESIGN    - ON    HEADING   - ON    SCOREBOARD - ON
AUTOSAVE   - OFF   DEVELOP   - ON    HELP      - ON    SPACE      - ON
Press any key to continue...
Command  C:\db4\ADMIT          Rec 2/12        File
```

Searching for Records ■ 179

```
SEEK "Lutz"
DISPLAY
```

Record 4, the one for Carol Lutz, is located. But what about this question of capitalization? Enter

```
SEEK "lutz"
```

dBASE IV displays the message **Find not successful.** Try all uppercase.

```
SEEK "LUTZ"
```

Once again the search fails. The reason is quite simple. The data in the index tag is exactly the same as the data entered into field because the key expression used to create the index is simply the field name. By using the field data exactly as entered, you create a situation whereby the value you are using as the search criterion, in this instance Lutz, must match the entry in terms of character and case exactly or the search will fail.

If you were searching with the LOCATE command, you could take advantage of the structure of the logical expression to compensate for vagaries in capitalization: for example,

```
LOCATE FOR UPPER(Last)="LUTZ"
```

The previous command is not sensitive to the case of the data in the database.

It is desirable to achieve the same sort of case insensitivity when you use a SEEK command. However, this cannot be achieved in exactly the same way. Because SEEK operates on the index key, the solution to case sensitivity must be handled by converting the information stored in the index file. You may recall that a similar problem occurred with the sex field. The solution was to index on the UPPER() value of the field, rather than simply the field itself.

In this case, you need to rewrite the Last index tag to use UPPER (Last) as the index key. Enter

```
INDEX ON UPPER(Last) TAG Last OF Admit
```

dBASE IV will warn you that you are about to overwrite an exiting index tag. Confirm your intention by pressing ⏎.

The index key has been changed to UPPER(Last). With the correct type of index key in place, you can change the Edit program to perform a rapid search rather than a sequential search. Load the Edit program into the dBASE IV editor.

■ **Interactive Programming**

MODIFY COMMAND Edit

What changes need to be made to this program in order to convert the search from the slower sequential method to the rapid search method?

The USE command now requires an INDEX and an ORDER clause so that the index file and proper index tag will be active when the search begins.

The LOCATE command is replaced with a SEEK command.

Move the cursor to line 4. Add the INDEX and ORDER clauses to the command. Try this on your own. If you need help, the correct command can be found at the end of the chapter in the Answers to Exercises section under exercise 5.

Another important aspect of opening a database and an index file at the same time is that any changes in the database that affect the index tags will automatically be included in the index tag sequences. If the index file is opened each time the database is revised, there will be no need to reindex the index tags.

Next, move the cursor to line 9. The LOCATE command needs to be replaced with a SEEK command. You will be seeking the same value, TRIM(Pick_rec). Since the use of the SEEK command implies searching the current master index, the command is much simpler in form than the LOCATE command. The fact that you are trying to match a value to UPPER(Last) is implied by the key used for the current master index, it does not have to be restated in the SEEK command.

Old line: LOCATE FOR UPPER(Last)=TRIM(Pick_rec)
New Line: SEEK TRIM(Pick_rec)

The revised program looks like this (new program lines are highlighted in color):

```
SET TALK OFF
SET STATUS OFF
SET SCOREBOARD OFF
CLEAR
USE Admit INDEX Admit ORDER Last
Pick_rec=space(20)
@ 10,10 SAY "Enter the Last Name"
@ 12,10 GET Pick_rec FUNCTION "!"
READ
```

Searching for Records

```
SEEK TRIM(Pick_rec)
SET FORMAT TO Admit
EDIT NEXT 1
CLOSE FORMAT
CLOSE DATABASE
SET SCOREBOARD ON
SET STATUS ON
SET TALK ON
RETURN
```

Save and execute the program by pressing (Alt)-e and typing r. Here, search for the first patient with a last name that begins with the letter S. Type

s

The record for Cynthia Sorenson appears. Exit the program by pressing (Ctrl)-(End).

The motivation for the last modification you made to the Edit program is different from previous changes. In the previous changes you made improvements and refinements in the interactive portion of the program. Each time you changed the program or format file, it changed the way information was displayed on the screen.

The last modification changes the program from sequential to rapid-indexed search but has no effect on what the user of the program sees. In fact, you cannot tell from the screen display that anything has been changed. The motivation for this change is performance, and the goal is to keep the speed of the search as fast as possible even when the database becomes quite large. Although this change has no effect on what a user sees, it is an important improvement in the way the program performs.

In creating programs you have two primary goals.

1. **Utility.** The program is designed to help the user carry out a task with greater ease and accuracy.

2. **Performance.** Your program should process the task as quickly as possible.

Both of these goals represent ideals. In this chapter you have seen that dBASE IV provides many ways to achieve the same result. Selecting the correct programming approach is often as much art as it is science. By looking at alternative solutions to the same problem, you can gain insights into the strengths and weaknesses of each approach.

The creation of a program is usually an evolutionary process in which procedures are seldom finished the first time through, but rather are revised and restructured several times as your concept of the program matures.

You may find that the goals even conflict at times. In such cases, you have to trade off benefits in one area for benefits in another. The quality of these decisions is what determines the quality of the programs you create.

Where does the Edit program stand in this process? Are there any obvious improvements that need to be made?

The most striking weakness in the Edit program is that it is still, for all its interactive quality, a linear program. It locates a single record and then stops. The program would be much more useful if you could repeat the search as many times as you want before you terminate it.

What does the program do about errors? Suppose you searched for someone who was not in the file. Enter

```
DO EDIT
Smith
```

What happened? The program displays the record for Milton Westrup. Why? The answer is that when the search failed to match Smith, the pointer was positioned on the last record in the index. Keep in mind that the last record in the index, which is currently ordered by last name, is the last name in alphabetical order rather than the last record number.

The fact that you asked for Smith and got Westrup is not a very clear indication of what happened. The program would be much better if it were able to react to this event in a way that is meaningful to the person using the computer.

Both of these problems require the use of nonlinear program structures called loops and conditionals, which are the subjects of the next chapter.

Exit the current program by entering (Ctrl)-(End).

Summary

In this chapter, you learned how to create programs that permit users to enter information or choices during the running of a program. These entry options created interactive programs, since the user's response controls the operation of the program, at least in part. Interactive structures make your programs more flexible and useful.

The @ command. This command is used to display information at exact row and column locations on the screen. The SAY clause is used to place the results of a dBASE IV expression at the specified location. The GET clause is used to place an input area for a variable or field at a specific screen location.

@ Clauses. The @ command accepts a variety of clauses. PICTURE uses a template to control the format of the data. FUNCTION allows you to enter special formatting functions. RANGE limits numeric input to a specific range of characters. VALID uses a logical expression to evaluate the validity of the entry.

Input areas. An input area is created with an @/SAY/GET or @/GET command. The input area is related to a specific field or variable. You can display up to 1,023 input areas on the screen (subject to memory limitations). The input areas become active when you issue a READ command. The cursor will move through the input areas in the same sequence as the @/GET commands were issued.

READ. The READ command activates all of the input areas currently on the screen. The cursor is positioned in the first input area. When the cursor is moved past the last input area, the command terminates.

Initialize variables. If a memory variable is used with an @SAY/GET or @/GET command, you must create the variable before you attempt to display an input area for it. This process is called initialization of the variable.

@/TO. This command draws a single, double, or highlighted box using the specified locations as the upper left and lower right corners.

Format files. A format file is a special form of a program subroutine that contains only @/SAY/GET and READ commands. Format files are used to add custom screen displays to existing dBASE IV commands, such as EDIT and APPEND. A format file is activated by the SET FORMAT TO command. Following the activation of a format file, any full screen editing commands—e.g., EDIT and APPEND—will display the information according to the format file commands. The format file is closed with the CLOSE FORMAT command.

LOCATE. This command requires a logical expression. It performs a sequential search of the database in order to find the first record for which the logical expression evaluates as true.

SEEK. This command performs a rapid search on the current master index tag or file. It positions the pointer to the first record that matches the key expression.

REINDEX. Updates the current index file Use/Index/Order. The INDEX and ORDER clauses can be used with the USE command to open an index file and select an index tag in a single operation. The ORDER clause selects an index tag as the master index. All open index tags update when modifications are made to the database.

Review Problems for Chapter 4

Chapter 4 teaches you how to create programs that incorporate user-entered information into their operations. The following problems will help you review these skills.

1. In the previous chapter's problem set, it was assumed that each item was marked up 33% from its wholesale price. Create a program that will calculate the wholesale price if you enter the selling price. (Hint: this program is a calculator-type program and does not use the SALES database file.)

2. Create a calculator-type program that calculates the total sales, including tax. The user needs to enter the quantity, the selling price, and the tax rate. The program calculates the cost, the tax, and the final total, cost plus tax.

3. Create a program that calculates the total and average sales for any specified period between two given dates.

4. Create a format file called SALES.fmt, which will display fields Company, Date_Sold, Inv_num (Character 10), Prod_code, Item_name, Price, Quantity, Total_amt, Taxable, Taxrate, Tax. The format should also include the file name and the record number. Use the format file to display records from the Sales database. (Hint:

you can create a format file by using the screen-painting program included with dBASE IV.

5. Using the format file you created in the review problems for Chapter 3, create a program that edits a specific record. Allow the user to search for the record by invoice number.

6. Modify the previous program to use an index tag to speed up the searching process.

Answers to Exercises

1. Find MAX and MIN dates for Admit.

    Old line: `STORE CTOD("00/00/00") to begin,end`
    New line: `CALCULATE min(admit),MAX(admit) to;`
                  `begin,end`

2. Create input areas for age, sex and phone.

    ```
    @ 10,0 SAY "Age:    " GET age
    @ 11,0 SAY "Sex:    " GET sex
    @ 12,0 SAY "Phone:  " GET phone
    ```

3. LOCATE command>

    Old line: `goto pick_rec`
    New line: `locate for upper(last)=pick_rec`

4. Trim blanks from variable.

    Old line: `locate for upper(last)=pick_rec`
    New line: `locate for upper(last)=trim(pick_rec)`

5. Open database and index file.

    Old line: `USE Admit`
    New line: `USE Admit index admit order last`

5 Loops and Branches

In the previous chapter, you created or modified the programs Edit and Stats to include a number of interactive elements. These programs showed how user input can be integrated into the operation of a running program. The programs in question were linear programs—the command logic ran from beginning to end and stopped.

These programs exhibit two major weaknesses:

1. Each program carries out an operation, like locating a patient, only once and then stops.

2. These programs cannot react to a record-search failure, displaying instead the last record in the file.

Both these problems have a common element: a program must evaluate conditions that occur during execution and carry out instructions based on those conditions. In the case of the first problem, you want the program to re-execute commands if the situation requires that they be repeated. The structure that allows this repetition is called a *loop*.

The second problem requires a structure called a *branch*. A branch is a program structure that contains alternate actions that take place under certain circumstances.

Loops and branches are two of the most powerful structures you can build with programming languages, and a combination of both is often required to solve a problem.

In this chapter, you will learn how dBASE IV creates loops and branches and how they can be applied to programming problems.

Branching Structures

Branching lets a program execute certain commands if an expression is true, while others execute if that expression is false. Programs with branches differ from the linear programs you have created where all of the commands in the program and subroutine files execute in a strict sequence. A program that contains a branch, or branches, may have commands that never execute because the proper conditions never exist. Branches create groups of alternate commands. These groups are mutually exclusive since no expression can be both true and false at the same time.

The program lines that implement branches create a block structure. Structures group together into blocks—the commands associated with specific conditions and the actions such conditions mandate.

The most common type of branching instruction uses the IF command followed by a logical expression. It employs the same concept as the IIF() function. If the expression after the IF is true, dBASE IV will execute one group of instructions. If it is false, dBASE IV will skip the instructions or execute an alternate set of instructions.

Unlike the commands used in a linear program, the IF command cannot be used by itself but must be used in conjunction with an ENDIF command. These commands define the beginning and end of the block structure. When the IF and ENDIF commands appear in a program, all of the commands in between the IF and ENDIF are treated as a group, or block, of commands.

dBASE IV treats such a command group in a special way. If the condition evaluates as true, the commands grouped between the IF and ENDIF commands execute. If the condition evaluates as false, the commands are skipped. dBASE IV then moves to the next instruction following the ENDIF and continues from that point (see Figure 5.1).

Figure 5.1

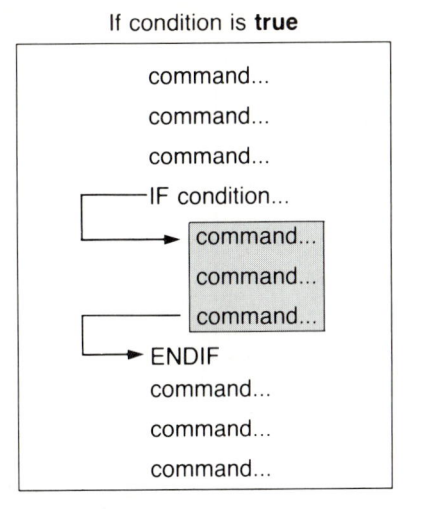

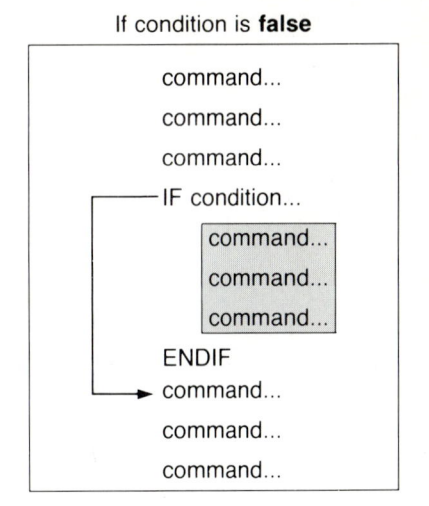

```
        If condition is true                    If condition is false
   ┌──────────────────────────┐           ┌──────────────────────────┐
   │   command...             │           │   command...             │
   │   command...             │           │   command...             │
   │   command...             │           │   command...             │
   │  ┌IF condition...        │           │  ┌IF condition...        │
   │  │   ┌──────────────┐    │           │  │   ┌──────────────┐    │
   │  │   │ command...   │    │           │  │   │ command...   │    │
   │  │   │ command...   │    │           │  │   │ command...   │    │
   │  │   │ command...   │    │           │  │   │ command...   │    │
   │  │   └──────────────┘    │           │  │   └──────────────┘    │
   │  └─►ENDIF                │           │   ENDIF                  │
   │     command...           │           │  └─►command...           │
   │     command...           │           │     command...           │
   │     command...           │           │     command...           │
   └──────────────────────────┘           └──────────────────────────┘
```

dBASE IV also permits the use of an alternate set of commands when the condition is false. The ELSE command divides into two parts the commands inside the IF/ENDIF structure. The portion before the ELSE executes when the condition is true, while the portion after executes when the condition is false. The ELSE keyword creates two mutually exclusive sets of instructions (see Figure 5.2).

The IF/ELSE/ENDIF structure provides the solution to a wide variety of programming problems—as when a search fails to locate a record in a database file. As the last chapter's Edit program currently stands, dBASE IV displays the last record in the file when no match is found. The key to improving the Edit program is the use of an IF command to test whether or not a match has been found. When a match is found, the program can proceed as usual. When no match is found, the program can display a message indicating that the search has failed.

Load the Edit program into the dBASE IV editor.

`MODIFY COMMAND Edit`

How can this program be modified to account for a possible search failure?

The key is to locate the point in the program where a decision can be made about the two possible options. That point is immediately following the SEEK command. When the SEEK command executes, the record pointer moves to the last record if the search has failed to locate a match. You will want to divide the operation of the program at

Branching Structures ■ 189

Figure 5.2

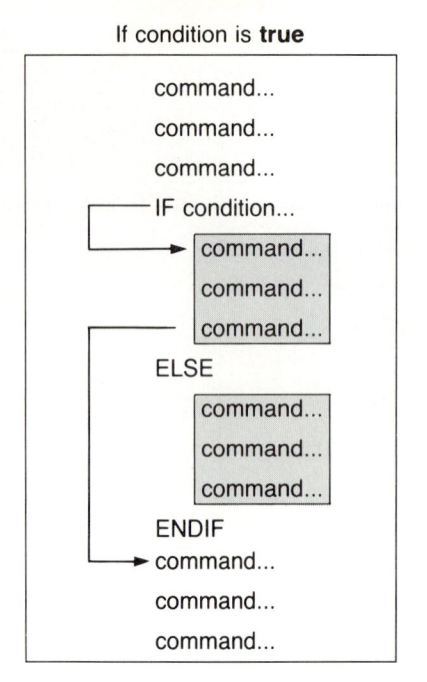

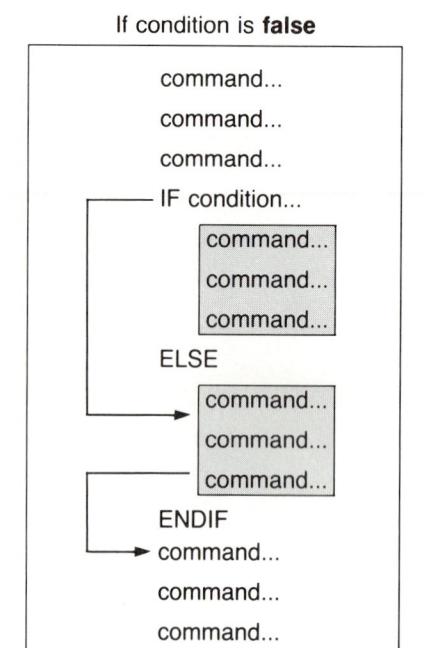

```
If condition is true

    command...
    command...
    command...
    IF condition...
        command...
        command...
        command...
    ELSE
        command...
        command...
        command...
    ENDIF
    command...
    command...
    command...
```

```
If condition is false

    command...
    command...
    command...
    IF condition...
        command...
        command...
        command...
    ELSE
        command...
        command...
        command...
    ENDIF
    command...
    command...
    command...
```

that point into two procedures, one for a successful match, the other for a failed search.

dBASE IV has a special function, FOUND(), that can evaluate searches. The FOUND() function's value is always false, unless a successful search has just been completed. The command IF FOUND() would test the success of the SEEK command and provide the condition to trigger program branching.

Move the cursor to line 10. Insert the following command.

```
IF FOUND( )
```

This command creates the first part of a conditional structure.

Indenting Commands

When you create programs that use logical structures such as IF/ELSE/ENDIF, it is helpful to format your program text to make the groups of related commands easier to read. The traditional formatting method is to indent all the commands that are part of an IF or ELSE group. These indents have no functional purpose as far as dBASE IV is concerned. In fact, dBASE IV eliminates all unnecessary spaces when it compiles your programs.

■ Loops and Branches

But this does not minimize the importance of writing well-formatted programs. The correct use of indents can make your program much easier to read and understand. In this book, all the programs with logical structures use indents. You can eliminate the indents without affecting the execution of the programs to save typing. However, it is strongly recommended that you indent all programs that you write.

The dBASE IV editor has a function called auto-indent. This feature automatically indents blocks of text in consecutive lines at the same indent as the previous line. When this option is active, the indents created by the (Tab) key are not stored as ASCII standard tabs.

> *Note:* ASCII stands for the American Standard Code for Information Interchange. This coding system is widely used for text file coding. In this system a (Tab) is stored as ASCII character 9. This means that any editor or word processor that reads standard ASCII files will recognize the characters as tabs.

To create standard tabs, you must turn off the auto-indent feature, which is on by default. Press (Alt)-w, type e, and press (Esc).

Remember that if you want to indent with standard tabs, you must turn off auto-indenting each time you enter the dBASE IV editor. If you do not, the indents you enter will not be stored with the file and all the text will be aligned on the left margin when you reload the file.

The purpose of an indent is to show that a command, or series of commands, exists within a logical structure. In this case, the next three commands are:

```
SET FORMAT TO Admit
EDIT NEXT 1
CLOSE FORMAT
```

These three commands should only execute when the expression following the IF command evaluates as true. If a matching record cannot be found, there is no reason to display the screen format or edit a record.

To show that these commands belong to the group of commands controlled by the IF, indent each line by placing a (Tab) character in front of each command (see Figure 5.3). Press (↓) (Tab) three times.

The next task is to add commands that execute when no match is found.

Branching Structures   ■   **191**

Figure 5.3

```
 Layout  Words  Go To  Print  Exit                    3:27:54 pm
[......▼.1.....▼.....2...▼......3.▼..•.....▼......▼.5....▼...6...▼.....?.▼......
set talk off
set status off
set scoreboard off
clear
use admit index admit order last
pick_rec=space(20)
@ 10,10 say "Enter the Last Name"
@ 12,10 get pick_rec function "!"
read
seek trim(pick_rec)
if found()
        set format to admit
        edit next 1
        close format
close database
set scoreboard on
set status on
set talk on
return


 Program  C:\db4\EDIT          Line:14 Col:0                        Ins
```

Move the cursor to the beginning of line 14 and mark the end of the IF/TRUE command section by inserting an ELSE command.

ELSE

The next group of commands executes when the search has failed. Here, display a message in the center of the screen. Notice that all of the following commands should be indented by one tab. Begin by clearing the display.

CLEAR

Next, create a boxed message in the center of the screen. Vertical centering is a simple matter. If you want to print a one-line message, line 12 is approximately the center of the screen. If you leave a blank line for space, that places the top and bottom lines of the box on rows 10 and 14, respectively.

Finding the horizontal location is more challenging because as part of the message you'll display, you should include the text entered as the search key, as in **No Match found for SMITH.** Since the entry text can vary from 1 to 20 characters, it is difficult to decide in advance where to place the side of the box or the beginning of the text.

The solution to this problem uses the technique discussed in Chapter 3. Instead of explicitly displaying the text as part of an @/SAY command, store the text as a variable. The command below stores the message, plus the search criterion, to a variable called Title.

```
Title="No Match found for "+TRIM(Pick_rec)
```

You can use the length of the text assigned to the variable title to determine where the text should be placed horizontally on the screen. That value will be stored in a variable called Placement.

```
Placement=(80-LEN(Title))/2
```

Placement can now let you calculate the location and width of the box, as well as the text. Suppose you want to draw the box five characters from the beginning and the end of the message. The left side of the box should be placed at Placement-5. The right side of the box should be placed five characters after the end of the message. That can be calculated by adding 5 to the sum of Placement plus the length of the text.

```
@ 10,Placement-5 to 14,Placement+5+LEN(Title)
@ 12,Placement SAY Title
```

Complete this section of the program by placing the cursor at the bottom of the screen and pausing the display.

```
    @ 23,0 WAIT
```

You have now concluded the section of the program that will execute if no match is found. The end of this section is marked by the ENDIF command, which is not indented.

```
ENDIF
```

The entire program will now look like this (new program lines are highlighted in color):

```
SET TALK OFF
SET STATUS OFF
SET SCOREBOARD OFF
CLEAR
USE Admit INDEX Admit ORDER Last
Pick_rec=SPACE(20)
@ 10,10 SAY "Enter the Last Name"
@ 12,10 GET Pick_rec FUNCTION "!"
READ
SEEK TRIM(Pick_rec)
```

Branching Structures ■ 193

```
    IF FOUND()
        SET FORMAT TO Admit
        EDIT NEXT 1
        CLOSE FORMAT
    ELSE
        CLEAR
        Title="No Match found for "+TRIM(Pick_rec)
        PLACEMENT=(80-LEN(Title))/2
        @ 10,Placement-5 to 14,Placement+LEN(Title)+5
        @ 12,Placement SAY Title
        @ 23,0
        WAIT
    ENDIF
    CLOSE DATABASE
    SET SCOREBOARD ON
    SET STATUS ON
    SET TALK ON
    RETURN
```

Save and execute the program by pressing [Alt]-e and typing rsmith[↵]. The program displays a message indicating that no match is found for the name Smith.

Complete the program by pressing [↵].

Execute the program again, using a valid name this time.

```
DO Edit
jones
```

Now, the patient's record is located. The program uses the section of the code that displays the record for editing (see Figure 5.4).

Complete the program by pressing [Ctrl]-[End].

The Edit program now uses an IF/ELSE/ENDIF structure to carry out different procedures depending upon the results of a record search.

Looping the Program

The Edit program now solves the first of the two problems identified at the beginning of this chapter.

Figure 5.4

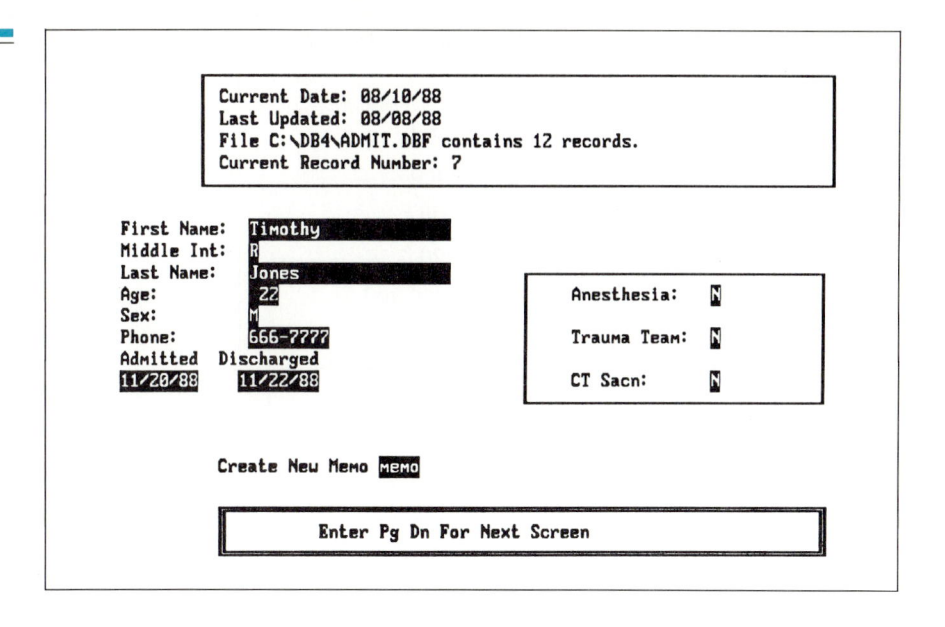

```
       Current Date: 08/10/88
       Last Updated: 08/08/88
       File C:\DB4\ADMIT.DBF contains 12 records.
       Current Record Number: 7

First Name:  Timothy
Middle Int:  R
Last Name:   Jones
Age:         22                      Anesthesia:  N
Sex:         M
Phone:       666-7777                Trauma Team: N
Admitted  Discharged
11/20/88  11/22/88                   CT Sacn:     N


       Create New Memo  MEMO


              Enter Pg Dn For Next Screen
```

The second problem—that of the program terminating after each search—can be solved by creating a loop to repeat a block of commands. The basic loop structure in dBASE IV is a DO WHILE loop. As with the IF structure, a loop does not function alone. Each DO WHILE requires a corresponding ENDDO command. The DO WHILE and ENDDO commands mark the group of commands that repeat while the loop is active.

The DO WHILE loop also requires a logical expression to control the number of repetitions. dBASE IV repeats the command contained within the loop structure as long as the logical expression associated with the loop is true. When the condition evaluates as false, the loop terminates and the program continues with the next command following the ENDDO (see Figure 5.5).

Their nature requires you to consider two important points when constructing loops.

1. **Starting condition.** Since a logical expression controls a loop, you must make sure that the expression is true the first time the DO WHILE command is encountered. If the condition is false, the loop will fail to execute and all of the commands inside the loop will be skipped.

Branching Structures ■ 195

Figure 5.5

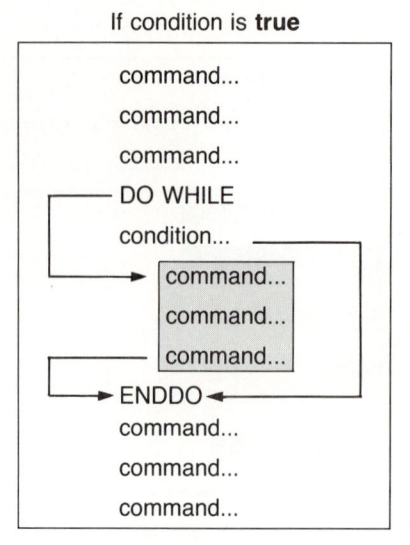

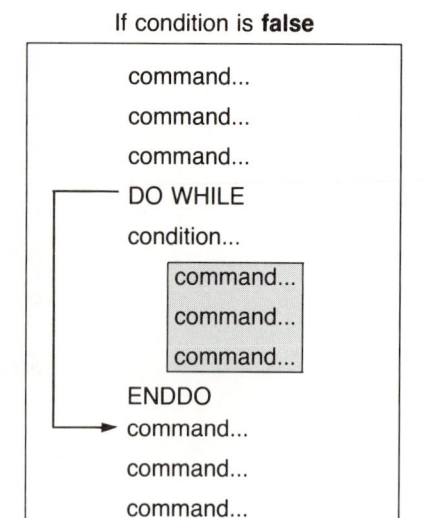

```
          If condition is true              If condition is false
          ┌──────────────────────┐          ┌──────────────────────┐
          │  command...          │          │  command...          │
          │  command...          │          │  command...          │
          │  command...          │          │  command...          │
     ┌────│  DO WHILE            │     ┌────│  DO WHILE            │
     │    │  condition...        │     │    │  condition...        │
     │    │    ┌──────────────┐  │     │    │    ┌──────────────┐  │
     └───▶│    │ command...   │  │     │    │    │ command...   │  │
          │    │ command...   │  │     │    │    │ command...   │  │
     ┌────│    │ command...   │  │     │    │    │ command...   │  │
     │    │    └──────────────┘  │     │    │    └──────────────┘  │
     └───▶│  ENDDO               │     └───▶│  ENDDO               │
          │  command...          │          │  command...          │
          │  command...          │          │  command...          │
          │  command...          │          │  command...          │
          └──────────────────────┘          └──────────────────────┘
```

2. **Exit condition.** A loop repeats until the logical expression associated with the DO WHILE command becomes false. This situation implies something very significant about the commands inside the loop: they must contain some operation that affects the logical expression that controls the loop. In practical terms this means that once you enter a loop, you have to provide some means of exiting the loop.

How can a DO WHILE/ENDDO loop be applied to the Edit program? One way is to create a loop that repeats the search until you specifically tell the program that you want to stop the search. In order to create this loop, you must do more than just enter the DO WHILE/ENDDO commands—you must also create a value, typically a memory variable, that indicates your desire to continue or terminate the search. You also have to create an interactive prompt to allow users to change the value of this variable while the program is running.

To begin these modifications, enter

```
MODIFY COMMAND Edit
```

Before you can add the new commands to the current program, you have to plan carefully how the loop will operate. The first step is to create a variable to control the loop. For example, suppose you create a variable called More and assign it the logical value of true, .T. You can then create a DO WHILE loop with a command that reads DO WHILE More.

Our strategy here is to allow the user an opportunity to change the value of the More variable by using an @/SAY/GET command. If the user enters a response that changes the value of MORE, the loop ter-

■ **Loops and Branches**

minates. If the user enters a response that leaves MORE true, the loop continues and the program repeats.

To determine where to insert these commands, you must examine the commands that begin the program. Many of these commands execute only once during the program. The SET commands at the beginning should not be included in the loop. Since all of the operations in the program will be carried out on the same database file, the USE command does not need to be included in the loop.

This brings you to line 5, where the command Pick_rec=SPACE(20) marks the start of the interactive portion of the program. You should begin the loop at this point because it is necessary to repeat the entry of the name for each record search.

Including the command Pick_rec=SPACE(20) brings to light an interesting subtlety.

If you include Pick_rec=SPACE(20) in the loop, a user will see a blank input area for the name each time the loop repeats because the command we've chosen to use sets the variable Pick_rec equal to 20 blanks each time. But if this command is left outside the loop, the effect is different. The first time through, the input area remains blank. But the second time through, it displays the previously searched for name because there is no command inside the loop to clear the old text out of the input area. You can envision situations when you want the last entry to appear as a default in the input area. But in this example, it is unlikely you would want to search for the same name twice in a row. It would make more sense to include Pick_rec=SPACE(20) within the loop so that the entry area is clean at the start of each search.

Since you have now decided that the loop should begin on line 5, move the cursor there.

The first command initializes a variable called More with a value of true. You will use this variable to control the operation of the loop.

```
More=.T.
```

Once the variable has been initialized, you can mark the beginning of the loop by entering the DO WHILE command. Because More is defined as a logical variable, you can use the short form of the logical expression.

```
DO WHILE More
```

The next step is to create the end of the loop. Before you proceed, however, let's discuss indenting again. In most cases it is proper to

Branching Structures ■ 197

indent all of the commands following a DO WHILE command until the corresponding ENDDO. But in this example, since the Edit program already exists, it requires some effort to indent all of the existing commands to another level. The listings in this book show the program correctly indented. You may choose to skip this additional indenting for convenience.

Move the cursor to line 23. The commands here and on line 24 pause the display so that you can read the "not found" message. In the looping version of this program, the user is asked if he wants to repeat the program at the end of each loop. This question pauses the program, making the two commands on lines 23 and 24 unnecessary. Delete the two lines by pressing Ctrl-y two times.

The End of the Loop

The final modifications to the program go at the end of the loop. Move the cursor to the beginning of line 23. The end of the loop occurs between the ENDIF and the CLOSE DATABASE commands. At this point in the program the first search, successful or unsuccessful, has been completed. You must ask the user if he wants to repeat the search or terminate the program. You can use an @/SAY/GET command to display the More variable with a prompt. Place this prompt at the bottom of the screen. Enter

```
@ 23,0 SAY "Continue searching? (Y/N) " GET More;
 PICTURE "Y" READ
```

The final command in the loop is the ENDDO command, which marks the end of the loop. When dBASE IV encounters ENDDO, it tests the value of the logical expression associated with DO WHILE. If the expression is true, the program recycles to the top of the loop and the commands contained within the loop execute again. If the expression is false, then the loop terminates and the program continues, beginning with the next command following the ENDDO. Enter

```
ENDDO
```

The program now contains the following commands. The unchanged lines are shown in a second color. The loop was created by adding only four new commands.

```
SET TALK OFF
SET STATUS OFF
SET SCOREBOARD OFF
CLEAR
```

```
USE Admit INDEX Admit ORDER Last
More=.T.
DO WHILE more
     Pick_rec=SPACE(20)
     @ 10,10 SAY "Enter the Last Name"
     @ 12,10 GET Pick_rec FUNCTION "!"
     READ
     SEEK TRIM(Pick_rec)
     IF FOUND()
SET FORMAT TO Admit
EDIT NEXT 1
CLOSE FORMAT
     ELSE
CLEAR
title="No Match found for "+TRIM(Pick_rec)
PLACEMENT=(80-LEN(Title))/2
@ 10,Placement-5 TO 14,Placement+LEN(Title)+5
@ 12,Placement SAY Title
     ENDIF
@ 23,0 SAY "Continue searching? (Y/N) " GET More;
 PICTURE "Y"
     READ
ENDDO
CLOSE DATABASE
SET SCOREBOARD ON
SET STATUS ON
SET TALK ON
RETURN
```

Save and execute the program by pressing (Alt)-e and typing r. Enter a name to search for.

```
tate
```

The program locates and displays the record for Harold Tate.

Exit the record by pressing (Ctrl)-(End). The prompt **Continue searching (Y/N)** appears at the bottom of the screen. The default value is Y because the more variable was initialized as .T. Press (⏎).

Branching Structures ■ 199

Because you have left the value of the More variable true, the program recycles to the top of the loop and displays the input area a second time.

Enter another search name.

`smith`

This time the program cannot find a match for Smith and displays the **No Match** message. The Continue prompt once again appears in the bottom-left corner of the display. Repeat the search one more time by pressing ⏎.

What has happened? The input area appears on the screen but it overlays part of the previous display (see Figure 5.6).

Why did this happen, and how can it be corrected? The fault lies in the placement of the CLEAR command in the program. The CLEAR command comes at the beginning of the program and is not included in the loop. Without a CLEAR command inside the loop, the program fails to clear the display when the loop repeats. This problem did not occur the first time you repeated the loop because a format file was used to display a database record. Because this format file contains two screens, when you exited the screen format with Ctrl-End, dBASE IV automatically cleared the screen display. The second time through

Figure 5.6

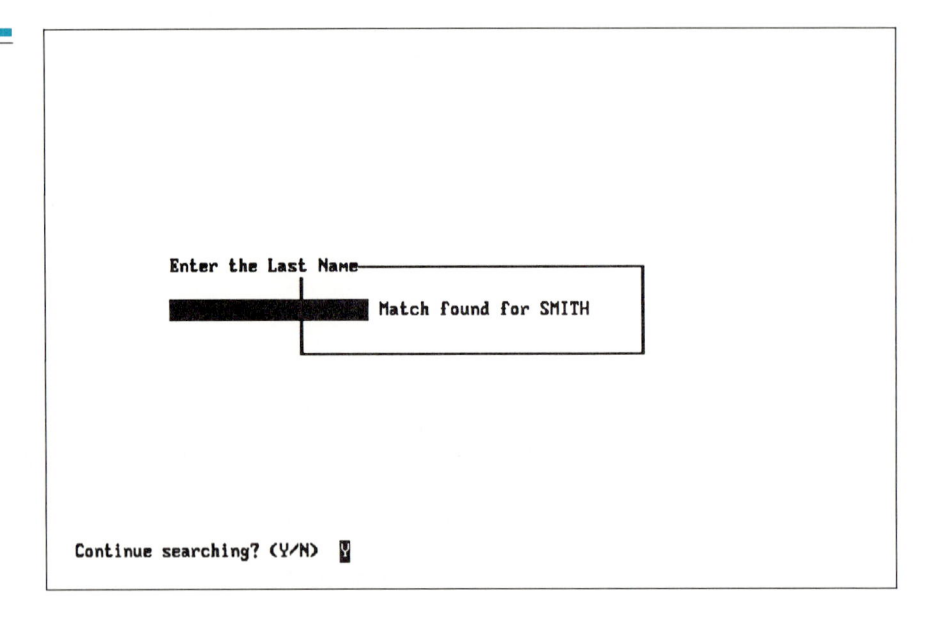

```
┌──────────────────────────────────────────────────────────┐
│                                                          │
│                                                          │
│              ┌─Enter the Last Name─────────────┐         │
│              │ ███████████████  Match found for SMITH │   │
│              └─────────────────────────────────┘         │
│                                                          │
│                                                          │
│                                                          │
│  Continue searching? (Y/N)  Y                            │
│                                                          │
└──────────────────────────────────────────────────────────┘
```

■ **Loops and Branches**

the loop no matching record was found so the format file was not invoked and the automatic screen clearing did not take place.

The solution to this problem is to include a CLEAR command inside the loop. Remove the current CLEAR command at the beginning of the program and place a CLEAR command inside the loop.

Complete the current search by entering

```
jones
```

and pressing Ctrl-End.

This time, terminate the program at the **Continue Y/N** prompt by pressing n. This value causes the loop condition to be false, terminating the loop and prompting the program to complete.

Modify the program by entering

```
MODIFY COMMAND Edit
```

Move the cursor to line 4. Delete this line by pressing Ctrl-y.

Move the cursor to line 7 and insert the CLEAR command. Line 6 is now inside the DO WHILE loop. This means that the screen will be cleared each time the loop repeats.

```
CLEAR
```

Save and execute the revised program by pressing Alt-e and typing r. Search for a name that is not in the file. Enter

```
Smith
```

When the **No match** message appears, continue the search by pressing y. This time the screen clears before the input area displays. Locate the Jones record by entering

```
jones
```

The record is displayed on the screen. Exit the program by pressing Ctrl-End and typing n.

Adding Records

The Edit program's current revision displays records that have already been entered into the database file. Suppose you want to create a program that adds new records to the database.

The program would be similar to Edit except that instead of the EDIT NEXT 1 command, it uses APPEND BLANK. The APPEND BLANK command is a special form of the APPEND command and adds a new, blank record to the end of the file then places the record pointer at that record.

With the record pointer positioned at the new blank record, you can use the SET FORMAT TO and READ commands, to allow entry of data into this new record. Create a new program by entering

```
MODIFY COMMAND Entry
```

The Edit program is quite close in structure to the Entry program you want to create. By making a few simple modifications to the Edit program, you can create an Entry program that adds new records. Instead of starting from scratch, you can save time and effort by loading a copy of the Edit program into the editor and then making the required changes.

To load a copy of an existing file into the editor you can press (Alt)-W and type w. You can select to read or write a file. Press r.

Remember that it is necessary to enter the file extension, .prg, for program files (see Figure 5.7). Enter

```
Edit.prg
```

Figure 5.7

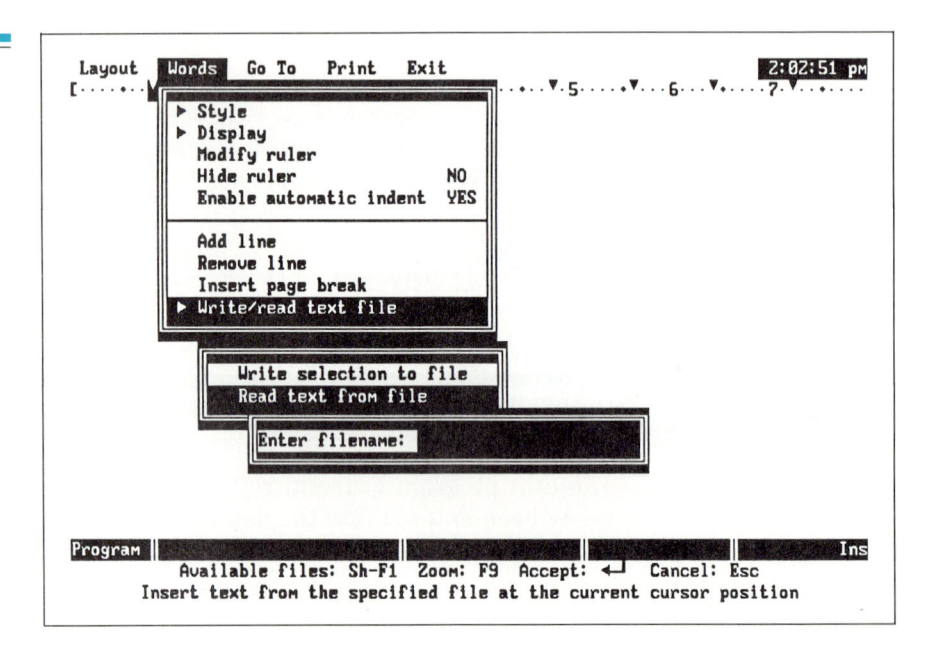

Loops and Branches

The editor loads a copy of the Edit program. What changes need to be made to this program in order to convert it to an entry program?

There is no need to search for records because you will be adding new records to the file. You can eliminate all of the commands that deal with locating records. Move the cursor to line 7. Delete the next six lines by pressing (Ctrl)-y six times.

The next command in the program is SET FORMAT TO Admit. This command should be retained because you want to use this format for the entry of the data into the new records.

The next command in the program, EDIT NEXT 1, should be replaced with APPEND BLANK to add a new blank record to the database.

Old line: EDIT NEXT 1
New line: APPEND BLANK

The APPEND BLANK command differs from EDIT and APPEND in that it does not automatically invoke the screen display format file. You must explicitly activate the format file with the READ command. Insert the following command on the line following APPEND BLANK.

READ

The CLOSE FORMAT command is in the proper position. Move the cursor to line 11. All of the commands in the ELSE/ENDIF group can be removed because they do not apply to adding new records. Press (Ctrl)-y seven times.

The next two lines display the More variable, which controls the loop. These commands belong in the Entry program because you need to allow the user to decide if more records should be added. The DO WHILE loop in this program will allow you to add as many new records as you desire.

You might want to change the text of the prompt to reflect the purpose of this program.

Old line: @ 23,0 SAY "Continue searching? (Y/N);
            " GET More PICTURE "Y"
New line: @ 23,0 SAY "Add more records? (Y/N);
            " GET More PICTURE "Y"

The Entry program is simpler than Edit. The entire program should read:

SET TALK OFF

Adding Records ■ 203

```
SET STATUS OFF
SET SCOREBOARD OFF
USE Admit INDEX Admit ORDER Last
More=.T.
DO WHILE More
     CLEAR
     GET FORMAT TO Admit
     APPEND BLANK
     READ
     CLOSE FORMAT
     @ 23,0 SAY "Add more records? (Y/N) " GET;
       More PICTURE "Y"
     READ
ENDDO
CLOSE DATABASE
SET SCOREBOARD ON
SET STATUS ON
SET TALK ON
RETURN
```

Save and execute the program by pressing Alt-e and typing r. When the program executes, it displays a new, blank record, 13 (see Figure 5.8).

Fill out the new record with the following information.

FIRST	Thomas
MIDDLE	A
LAST	Goren
AGE	36
SEX	m
PHONE	555-6666
ADMIT	12/05/88
DISCHARGE	12/07/88
ANESTHESIA	N
TRUMA_TEAM	Y
CT_SCAN	Y
MEMO	None

Figure 5.8

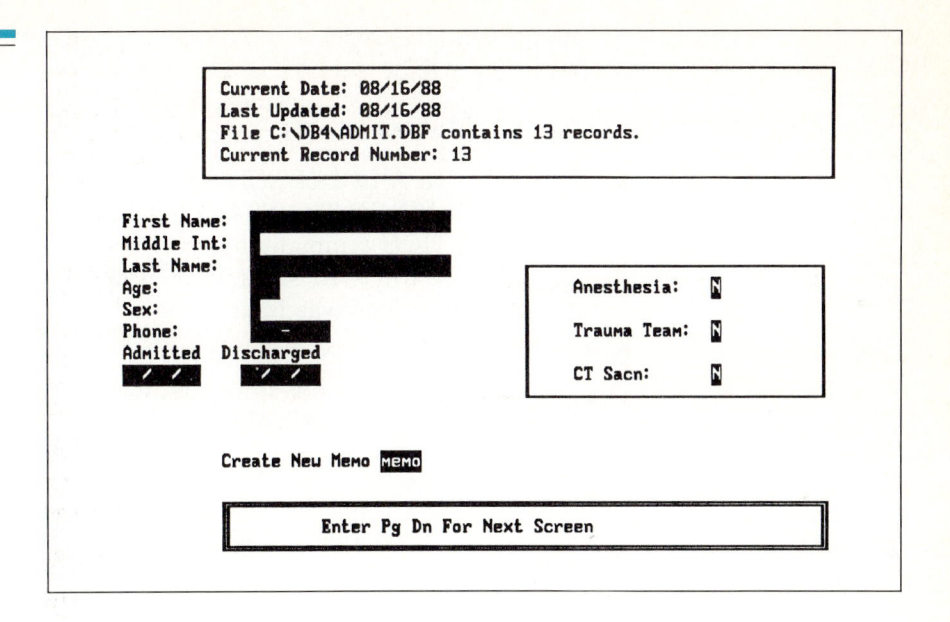

```
    Current Date: 08/16/88
    Last Updated: 08/16/88
    File C:\DB4\ADMIT.DBF contains 13 records.
    Current Record Number: 13


First Name:
Middle Int:
Last Name:
Age:                               Anesthesia:   N
Sex:
Phone:         -                   Trauma Team:  N
Admitted  Discharged
                                   CT Sacn:      N
  / /       / /


    Create New Memo  MEMO


        Enter Pg Dn For Next Screen
```

Display Page 2 of this entry screen by pressing (PgDn).

Enter the following information.

```
PAYOR     Travelers
CHARGES   3,400.00
```

Complete the entry by pressing (Ctrl)-(End). The prompt appears at the bottom of the screen asking you to decide if you want to enter additional records. If you press y or ⏎, the program adds another record. If you press n the program terminates. Press n.

Transactions and Rollbacks

When users make changes in a dBASE IV file, these changes overwrite the previous information as soon as the pointer moves to another record. If you make a mistake, there is no way to recover previously entered data.

dBASE IV provides a special set of commands to allow you to rollback changes in a database file. The term rollback refers to a process that restores the records and fields to their previous condition. There are three commands related to rollback operations.

1. **BEGIN TRANSACTION.** The BEGIN TRANSACTION command establishes a baseline for changes in the database. Once this command is entered, all changes made in the database with APPEND,

Adding Records ■ **205**

BROWSE, CHANGE, EDIT, RECALL, DELETE, REPLACE, and UPDATE will be recorded in a transaction log. This recording makes it possible to rollback, or undo, the changes made since entering the BEGIN TRANSACTION command.

2. **ROLLBACK.** A ROLLBACK command can be entered at any time following a BEGIN TRANSACTION command as long as no END TRANSACTION command has been issued. The command restores the database file to its state prior to the time the BEGIN TRANSACTION command was issued.

3. **END TRANSACTION.** The END TRANSACTION command saves the change, if any, made to the database since the entry of BEGIN TRANSACTION. Once an END TRANSACTION command executes, you cannot rollback the changes in the database.

These commands provide a method for accepting or rejecting changes made to the database file. The rollback is usually linked to some logical expression. The expression determines if the changes made to the database are correct. If they are not, the expression will trigger a rollback of the database to its previous condition.

These commands will operate at the dot prompt as well as within structured programs. Place the Admit database in use with the Admit index file. Enter

```
USE Admit INDEX Admit
```

Before you make any changes to the database, you can protect yourself against data loss by beginning a transaction session. Enter

```
BEGIN TRANSACTION
```

The command creates a transaction log file that will restore data should a rollback be necessary.

You can now proceed to make changes in the database by using the REPLACE command. Suppose you want to change all the first and last names to upper-case text. Enter a REPLACE command to change the text in the first and last fields to upper-case. Try this on your own. If you need help, the correct command can be found at the end of the chapter in the Answers to Exercises section under exercise 1.

List the current contents of the first and last fields. Enter

```
LIST First,Last
```

You can see that the names have been converted to upper-case characters (see Figure 5.9).

Figure 5.9

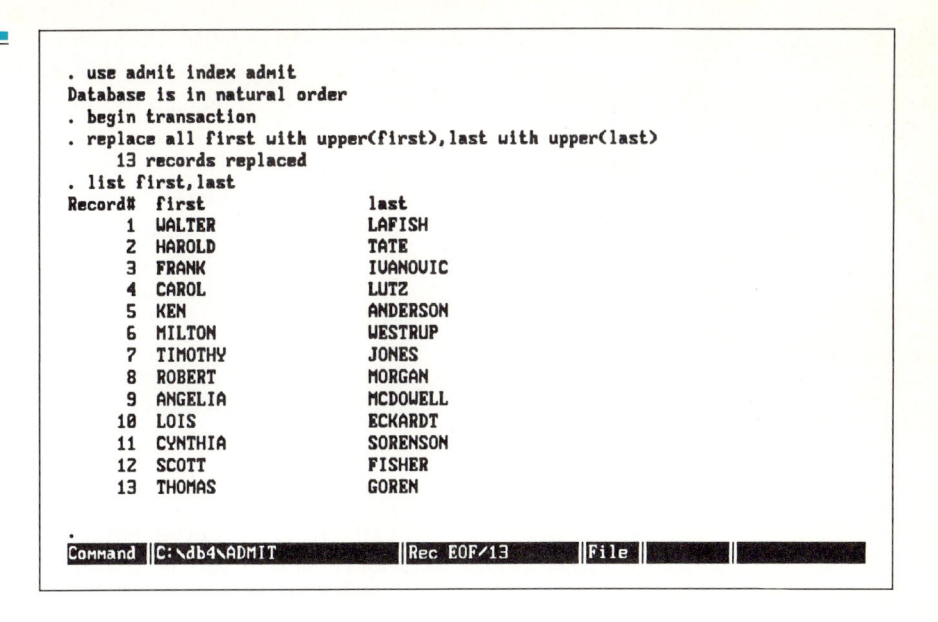

```
. use admit index admit
Database is in natural order
. begin transaction
. replace all first with upper(first),last with upper(last)
      13 records replaced
. list first,last
Record#  first              last
      1  WALTER             LAFISH
      2  HAROLD             TATE
      3  FRANK              IVANOVIC
      4  CAROL              LUTZ
      5  KEN                ANDERSON
      6  MILTON             WESTRUP
      7  TIMOTHY            JONES
      8  ROBERT             MORGAN
      9  ANGELIA            MCDOWELL
     10  LOIS               ECKARDT
     11  CYNTHIA            SORENSON
     12  SCOTT              FISHER
     13  THOMAS             GOREN
.
Command  C:\db4\ADMIT              Rec EOF/13     File
```

However, because of the transaction log, you can rollback these changes and restore that database to its former contents. Enter

ROLLBACK

dBASE IV compares the current contents of the database with the transaction log and returns it to the previous contents. Enter

LIST First,Last

The data is restored to its previous contents. Turn off the transaction operation by entering

END TRANSACTION

The BEGIN/END transaction operations provide a method to accept or reject one or more changes made to a database file.

How can you apply the transaction principle to the programs you are developing? One common problem with programs that add records to the database is that users often enter blank records. In our Entry program, the APPEND BLANK command adds a new record into the file each time the loop executes. Even if no data is entered into the record, it still becomes part of the database. If you select to enter a record by mistake, the blank record becomes part of the database.

Note: If a rollback operation fails, because of hardware problems or other reasons, the database file will be left in a corrupted state.

Adding Records ■ 207

dBASE IV will refuse to perform operations on the database because it will appear to have an uncompleted transaction. For this reason, you are advised to back up databases before you perform rollbacks.

One way to eliminate these blank records is to rollback the database if no data is entered into a record. In the current example, if no entry is made into the last name field, you can assume that the record is a blank. Even if there were some data in the record, without the last name of the patient it would be useless and should be discarded.

You can modify the Entry program so that it will reject empty records and rollback the database each time one is entered. Load the Entry program into the editor by entering

```
MODIFY COMMAND Entry
```

The first command to add to this program is the BEGIN TRANSACTION command. Where should this be placed? Since, in this program, you want to check each record as it is entered, the BEGIN TRANSACTION command should be placed before the APPEND BLANK command. In the event the new record is not filled in, the database will be rolled back to the point before the new record was appended.

Move the cursor to APPEND BLANK. Insert the BEGIN TRANSACTION command.

```
BEGIN TRANSACTION
```

The next set of commands encompasses the rollback structure. The term structure is employed here because a ROLLBACK command is seldom used unless it is part of a conditional structure like IF/ENDIF. A rollback is usually required only when it is determined that the changes in the file are in error. In this case, you will want to make the rollback conditional based upon the value of the key field, last name.

Move the cursor to line 13. Up to this point in the program, records are added to the database and the user makes whatever data entry is required. It is at this point that you can test the contents of the record to see if a last name has been entered. This can be done with an expression such as Last=SPACE(20). This expression is true if the entire last field is blank. In such a case you will want to issue a ROLLBACK command.

```
IF Last=SPACE(20)
    ROLLBACK
```

208 ■ **Loops and Branches**

```
ENDIF
END TRANSACTION
```

The modified program now looks like this. Changed commands appear in color.

```
SET TALK OFF
SET STATUS OFF
SET SCOREBOARD OFF
USE Admit INDEX Admit ORDER Last
MORE=.T.
DO WHILE MORE
     BEGIN TRANSACTION
     CLEAR
     SET FORMAT TO Admit
     APPEND BLANK
     READ
     CLOSE FORMAT
     IF Last=SPACE(20)
ROLLBACK
     ENDIF
     END TRANSACTION
     @ 23,0 SAY "Add more records? (Y/N) " GET;
       More PICTURE "Y"
     READ
ENDDO
CLOSE DATABASE
SET SCOREBOARD ON
SET STATUS ON
SET TALK ON
RETURN
```

Save and execute the program by pressing (Alt)-e and typing r. The blank record that appears is record 14. Do not enter any data. The record will be entered as a blank to test the effect of the rollback. Press (Ctrl)-(End). When you are asked if you want to add another record, press y.

When the blank screen appears, notice that it is record 14 once again. The rollback prevented the blank record from being added to the database. Enter another blank by pressing (Ctrl)-(End). This time, terminate the program by pressing n.

Batch Processing

When you executed the latest revision of the Entry program, you may have noticed that the program ran very slowly. This sluggishness is because the transaction/rollback procedure slows down the operation of dBASE IV significantly. You can create routines that have essentially the same purpose as a transaction/rollback operation but do not create unnecessary delays in processing. In the Entry program, dBASE IV rolls back all of the database in order to eliminate one record, the blank one at the end of the file. While this works, it is not the most efficient way to handle this particular type of rollback.

Another approach to this problem is called batch entry. In a batch entry approach, new records are entered into a separate file from the main database. This file is the batch file. When you have entered all of the new records into the batch file, your program can perform checking operations to make sure that all of the new records qualify for inclusion in the main database. The records in the batch file are added to the main database and filtered to include only legitimate records.

The batch processing approach is a more efficient way to deal with the problem of blank records because it operates exclusively on the new records being added. The transaction/rollback approach includes all of the records in the database, which is useful in many applications, but not the most appropriate method in this case since the transaction/rollback procedure needed to rollback each time a blank record was encountered. The batch method allows you to enter as many blanks as you like. The program filters out all of the blanks with a single command. This also increases the performance of the program.

The batch processing approach requires the use of three new commands.

1. **COPY STRUCTURE.** The COPY STRUCTURE command creates a new database file with the same structure as the active file but does not copy any of the records. In batch processing, this command creates a temporary database to hold all of the new records before they are integrated into the main database file.

2. **APPEND FROM.** The APPEND FROM command is another variation on APPEND. Here, APPEND FROM adds records stored in another database file to the current database. This command is essential to batch processing because it allows you to transfer records from the batch file to the main database. A FOR clause can filter the records as they are appended.

3. **Set safety.** dBASE IV will normally prompt you before overwriting a file. In batch processing, a new copy of the batch file is created each time the Entry program is run. By setting the safety off, you can avoid being prompted when you overwrite the previous batch file.

Load the Entry program into the editor by entering

```
MODIFY COMMAND Entry
```

Because you want to modify this program for batch processing, you should set safety off at the beginning of the program. Insert the following command at line 1 with Ctrl-n.

```
SET SAFETY OFF
```

The tactic in a batch processing program is to open the main database, make a copy of its structure, then have all of the new records entered into the duplicate database.

Move the cursor to line 6. Instead of allowing the program to proceed to modify the Admit database, you want to create a duplicate database and use that file for the new records. Insert the following commands.

```
COPY STRUCTURE TO Batch
USE Batch
```

Since Batch and Admit have the same structure, the Admit format file will operate with either file.

Move the cursor to line 10 and delete the BEGIN TRANSACTION command by pressing Ctrl-y

Move the cursor to line 15. Eliminate the next four commands by pressing Ctrl-y four times.

Move the cursor to line 17. At this point in the Entry program, the records will be entered into the Batch database file. The remaining task is to import these records into the Admit file while filtering out any records that are blank.

Adding Records ■ 211

The first step is to activate the Admit database. It is important to open the index file as well so that the index tags can be added as records are appended into the database. Insert the following command.

```
USE Admit INDEX Admit
```

In this case, you are not concerned with selecting a master index tag. Your only reason for opening the index file is to update the tags, so it does not matter which tag, if any, is the master tag. You can now use the APPEND FROM command to import the records from the Batch file and, at the same time, use a FOR clause to select records that are not blank. The # sign stands for "not equal to" in the command below. Insert this command.

```
APPEND FROM Batch FOR Last#SPACE(20)
```

Move the cursor to line 24 and insert the command that turns the safety back on.

```
SET SAFETY ON
```

The revised program looks like this. The new program lines are highlighted in color.

```
SET SAFETY OFF
SET TALK OFF
SET STATUS OFF
SET SCOREBOARD OFF
USE Admit INDEX Admit ORDER Last
COPY STRUCTURE TO Batch
USE Batch
More=.T.
DO WHILE More
    CLEAR
    SET FORMAT TO Admit
    APPEND BLANK
    READ
    CLOSE FORMAT
    @ 23,0 SAY "Add more records? (Y/N) " GET;
      More PICTURE "Y"
    READ
ENDDO
USE Admit INDEX Admit
```

212 ■ **Loops and Branches**

```
APPEND FROM Batch FOR Last#SPACE(20)
CLOSE DATABASE
SET SCOREBOARD ON
SET STATUS ON
SET TALK ON
SET SAFETY ON
RETURN
```

Save and execute this command by pressing (Alt)-e and typing r. The entry program displays a blank record screen. Observe that the file information at the top of the screen shows that this is the first record in the Batch file.

Enter several blank records. Press

(Ctrl)-(End) and type y

(Ctrl)-(End) and type y

(Ctrl)-(End) and type n.

If your batch processing program has worked correctly, there should still be only 13 records in the Admit file. Enter

```
USE Admit
COUNT
```

The records count shows that none of the blank records were appended to the file.

Implicit Conditions

Turn your attention back to the Edit program. The last modification you made to the Edit program concerned the use of the DO WHILE loop to repeat the search process. To terminate the loop, you entered n when asked if you wanted to continue.

This kind of loop requires an explicit entry. It might improve the feel of the program to exit when it is implicit in the entry made for the search. For example, if you leave the search input area blank, the program can take that as an implicit signal to terminate the search.

The advantage of this type of implicit condition is that you can terminate the loop without requiring the user to answer a specific question each time the loop executes. The elimination of the entry question makes the program more comfortable to use.

You can modify the Edit program so that it automatically terminates when the search key is a blank. Load the Edit program into the editor by entering

```
MODIFY COMMAND Edit
```

Exit and Automatic Loops

This modification changes the controlling mechanism in the Edit program from an explicit entry—"Continue? Y/N"—to an implicit entry, a blank search key to terminate the program. The modification introduces another way to look at loops and how to control their repetition.

The DO WHILE loop in the Edit program is controlled by the value of the More variable: DO WHILE More. Each time the ENDDO command is encountered, dBASE IV checks the value of the More variable to see if the loop should continue.

The next revision of the program will eliminate the need for the More variable. The control of the loop will be linked to the value of the Pick_rec variable, which is already used to search for a specific last name. Using the same variable for two purposes simplifies the structure of your program.

However, it poses a logical problem that requires a new approach to DO WHILE loops. To understand this logical problem, you need to look at how the Pick_rec variable is currently used.

At the beginning of each loop, the Pick_rec variable is set to 20 blanks. It is then displayed as an input area so that the user can enter the name that he wants to locate. The Pick_rec value is then used with the SEEK command to position the pointer to the correct record. The section of the program code shown below shows how to use Pick_rec.

```
Pick_rec=SPACE(20)
@ 10,10 SAY "Enter the Last Name"
@ 12,10 GET Pick_rec FUNCTION "!"
READ
SEEK TRIM(Pick_rec)
```

The new modified version of the program tests the contents of Pick_rec after the user has had a chance to enter a name. If Pick_rec is still blank, the program should terminate since the user has decided not to enter any name to search for.

It is here that a technical problem arises. This test ought to be performed following the READ but before the SEEK command. But what

■ Loops and Branches

good would that test do? It would occur in the middle of the loop. dBASE IV will not evaluate the loop conditional until it reaches the ENDDO command, which is preceded by the commands to display the record. We need some way to prompt the program to terminate the loop inside the loop without having to go all the way through the loop to reach the ENDDO. dBASE IV provides the EXIT command to automatically terminate the current loop, regardless of the condition of the logical expression used with the DO WHILE command.

The EXIT command is used in conjunction with a logical structure such as IF/ENDIF so that the EXIT command terminates the loop when a special condition exits. That condition here is that no entry is made into the Pick_rec variable. The commands below illustrate how to use EXIT. The EXIT command executes when Pick_rec is equal to 20 blank spaces.

```
IF Pick_rec=SPACE(20)
     EXIT
ENDIF
```

The EXIT command makes it possible to perform a test that terminates the loop immediately at any position within the loop. It is no longer necessary to perform a test only at the end of the loop.

When the EXIT command is added to the Edit program, it makes the value of MORE, used to control the loop, irrelevant. Once the loop begins, it should continue automatically until EXIT terminates the loop. It no longer matters what value or expression controls the loop.

In cases like this, dBASE IV allows you to take a short cut in creating the loop. Instead of using a logical expression with the DO WHILE command, you can simply turn on automatic looping by entering a logical true value, .T.; this command reads: DO WHILE .T.

By replacing the logical expression with the value .T., you are in effect creating a loop that will never evaluate as false, a loop called an endless loop. This type of loop is also called an automatic loop, since the DO WHILE/ENDDO commands are not related to any of the fields or variables in the program but simply cycle endlessly. The only way to terminate this type of loop is to use a command like EXIT.

Automatic loops with exits are useful when you want to turn on the loop and keep it running until some specific condition occurs.

Move the cursor to line 5. The MORE variable is no longer needed in this program. Delete that line by pressing Ctrl-y.

The next line in the program is the DO WHILE command. Change the DO WHILE to an automatic loop by substituting .T. for the More variable.

Old line: DO WHILE More
New line: DO WHILE .T.

Move the cursor to line 11. It is here that you want to test for entered search characters, or whether the key is blank. If it is blank, you want to exit the loop. Insert the following commands.

```
IF Pick_rec=SPACE(20)
     EXIT
ENDIF
```

The next step is to eliminate the commands that ask if you want to continue searching.

Move the cursor to line 25. A command needs to be inserted inside this section of the program to pause the screen display when no match is found. You need to enter two commands, one to position the cursor to line 23 on the screen, and the other to pause the program. Try this on your own. If you need help, the correct command can be found at the end of the chapter in the Answers to Exercises section under exercise 2.

Delete the @/SAY/GET and READ commands by pressing Ctrl-y two times.

The modified program now looks like this. The unchanged commands appear in a second color.

```
SET TALK OFF
SET STATUS OFF
SET SCOREBOARD OFF
USE Admit INDEX Admit ORDER Last
DO WHILE .T.
     CLEAR
     Pick_rec=SPACE(20)
     @ 10,10 SAY "Enter the Last Name"
     @ 12,10 GET Pick_rec FUNCTION "!"
     READ
     IF Pick_rec=SPACE(20)
EXIT
```

216   ■   **Loops and Branches**

```
        ENDIF
        SEEK TRIM(Pick_rec)
        IF FOUND()
SET FORMAT TO Admit
EDIT NEXT 1
CLOSE FORMAT
        ELSE
CLEAR
Title="No Match found for "+TRIM(Pick_rec)
Placement=(80-LEN(Title))/2
@ 10,Placement-5 TO 14,Placement+LEN(Title)+5
@ 12,Placement SAY Title
@ 23,0
WAIT
        ENDIF
ENDDO
CLOSE DATABASE
SET SCOREBOARD ON
SET STATUS ON
SET TALK ON
RETURN
```

Save and execute the program by pressing (Alt)-e and typing r. Enter a name to search for.

```
jones
```

The program finds the correct record. Exit that record by pressing (Ctrl)-(End). The program automatically cycles back to the beginning of the loop and displays the entry input area again. To terminate the program all you need do is press (↵).

The program terminates automatically. The change from an explicit to an implicit termination gives the program a smoother feel because the user responds only to one prompt to continue or terminate the program.

Frequency Distributions

In Chapter 4 you learned how to create programs that gather statistics about a database. The Stats program generated statistical summary information, such as totals and averages. You were able to gather that information without having to create loops or conditional structures because dBASE IV provides commands such as CALCULATE that automatically scan the database records.

Each record in the Admit database contains a value for the age of each patient. You could use the CALCULATE command to find the average age of the patients. Enter

```
USE Admit
CALCULATE AVG(Age)
```

The program displays the value 28.77, representing the average of the values in the Age field. But that Figure is not meaningful when you try to determine an age pattern for the patients admitted to the emergency room. A more meaningful way to analyze the ages is to count the number of patients in specific age groups, such as below 18, 18 to 44, 44 to 64, and 65 and over. Without a computer, you can perform this type of analysis by marking off columns on a piece of paper and putting marks in each column to represent the patients that fall into the groups represented by the columns (see Figure 5.10).

This kind of summary, called a frequency distribution, shows how many records fall into specific categories. The frequency distribution provides a more detailed and meaningful analysis of the pattern created by the ages of the admitted patients.

How can you create a program that calculates a frequency distribution? The question raises some interesting technical problems whose solutions will introduce some powerful programming concepts and methods. The methods are not entirely new because they use loops, conditional structures, and memory variables, constructs you already have some experience with. The difference is that you will apply these concepts differently to create the frequency distribution program.

Figure 5.10

```
Name:       Ken Anderson
Admit       11/13/88
Discharge   11/17/88
Days in       5.00
ICU days
```

218 ■ Loops and Branches

In order to create this program, there are some special techniques that you must master.

1. **Scanning the database.** In the previous chapters you relied on the built-in dBASE IV commands that automatically scan the records in the database—LIST, COPY, SUM, and CALCULATE. These commands automatically process all of the records in the database from beginning to end. However, as you begin to create programs that perform functions that vary from these standard operations, you must create structures to scan database records.

2. **Counters and accumulators.** Counters and accumulators are special uses of memory variables. These variables hold values created by counting or calculating during a database scan.

3. **DO CASE/ENDCASE structures.** The CASE structure is a variation on the IF/ENDIF structure. The DO CASE command selects from among a series, usually two or more, of mutually exclusive actions. The structure can contain any number of cases. A case uses a logical expression to select a group of commands in the same way as an IF command.

After you have experimented with these concepts, you will blend them together to create the frequency distribution program. Keep in mind that the frequency distribution is typical of an entire category of programs that search databases in order to classify information.

Scanning the Database

Scanning the database refers to the creation of a loop to process all the records in the database. Many of the commands in the dBASE IV database manager automatically scan the database. For example, the command LIST First,Last moves the record pointer to the top of the database and then lists the first and last name fields for all the records.

While these auto-scan commands are useful, as you create programs you will discover the need to create programs that perform special operations on the database records. This requires that you create loops to scan the database the way the LIST command moves automatically through the database.

The techniques involved in scanning the database involve some of the fundamental types of structures used in dBASE IV programs. You may recall that the field Days_icu, days in the Intensive Care Unit, has been left blank. Suppose that now you were ready to fill that field with data.

Frequency Distributions ■ 219

One way to do this is to simply use the EDIT command to edit the records. Since you are interested in filling in only one field, it might be useful to create a screen display that shows only the necessary information. For example, if you displayed a patient's name, days stayed, and the admit and discharge dates along with a single input area, it would simplify the entry of data into the Days_icu field. You could also make sure that the records are displayed in a special order, alphabetically by last name. The program could then step you through the database, record by record. To create this program, enter

```
MODIFY COMMAND Addicu
```

Begin the program by entering the usual SET commands.

```
SET TALK OFF
SET SCOREBOARD OFF
SET STATUS OFF
CLEAR
```

The next step is to open the database. In this case, open the Admit file and the Admit index, and select the index tag LAST. Try this on your own. If you need help, the correct command can be found at the end of the chapter in the Answers to Exercises section under exercise 3.

A Display Frame

The text section of this new program creates a display frame. A display frame is another way to approach the problem of creating a formatted screen display. The Edit and Entry programs use a format file to handle screen display layout. Each new record display causes dBASE IV to clear the screen and display the boxes, prompts, and input areas for the next record.

If you reflect upon the process, you will see that many of the items displayed as part of the format file could just as well remain on the screen for each record. The boxes and prompts remain the same for each record. The only information that changes are the fields because they related specifically to the record being displayed.

A display frame is a template placed on the screen before the first record. It generally consists of any prompts or boxes needed for the screen layout. The display frame remains on the screen as each record displays the field data. In effect, a display frame divides the information contained in a typical format file into two parts: the display frame, which is always the same for all of the records, and the field information, which changes with each record. The display-frame approach has several advantages over format files when the program displays a series of records. First, since only the field area of the screen needs to change each time a new record is displayed, the display-frame approach is faster. In addition, because only part of the screen display is rewritten for each new record, the screen no longer appears to jump each time a record is displayed. The effect is more pleasing to look at since your eye is not jolted by the clearing and rewriting of the entire screen, as happens with a format file.

Create the display frame for the records by entering

```
@ 8,10 to 14,60
@ 9,11 SAY "Name:"
@ 10,11 SAY "Admit"
@ 11,11 SAY "Discharge"
@ 12,11 SAY "Days in"
@ 13,11 SAY "ICU days"
```

End of File Loop

You have now reached the section of the Addicu program where you will display the fields for each record. This requires the creation of a scanning loop. There are two ways to accomplish this.

1. **DO WHILE .NOT. EOF().** This command uses a standard DO WHILE command to begin a loop. The logical expression used to control the loop is .NOT.EOF(). EOF() is a special dBASE IV function to indicate the end of a database file. When you scan through a database, the EOF() function is always true, .T., until you encounter the end of a database file; then, dBASE IV sets the value of EOF() to false, .F. The expression .NOT.EOF(), not end of file, will continue the loop until the program reaches the end of the file.

2. **SCAN.** The SCAN command is a variation on the DO WHILE command. It automatically assumes that you want to process the entire database. When you use SCAN in place of DO WHILE .NOT.EOF(), dBASE IV also automatically moves the record pointer back to the top of the database, which is not the case with DO WHILE.

Since both methods rely on a system function, EOF(), it is not necessary to create a variable to control the loop. Our example uses the DO WHILE method. Add this command to the program.

```
DO WHILE .NOT. EOF()
```

Once the loop has been started, you can begin the actual processing of records. Here, make sure that the total number of days stayed has been calculated by subtracting the admit date from the discharge date. You can use a REPLACE command to carry out this calculation. Following this replacement, display the values of the First, Last, Admit, Discharge, and Days_stay fields. Then create an input area for the ICU days.

Note: The commands below are all indented one tab stop. If you are working in the dBASE IV editor and want to add the indents, remember to turn off the automatic indent feature by pressing [Alt]-W and typing e.

```
REPLACE Days_stay with Discharge-Admit+1
@ 9,25 SAY TRIM(First)+SPACE(1)+Last
@ 10,25 SAY Admit
@ 11,25 SAY Discharge
@ 12,25 SAY Days_stay
@ 13,25 GET Days_icu VALID Days_icu<=Days_stay
READ
```

A VALID clause is used with the GET command here to make sure that the value entered for the ICU days is equal to, or less than, the stay days. It would not be logical for ICU days to exceed the stay days.

Moving the Pointer

At this point in the program you have entered the ICU days, if any, into the input area for the Days_icu field. You are now ready to move on to the next record. But before you allow the loop to cycle back to the top, move the record pointer to the next record in the database. This is done with the command SKIP, which changes the position of the pointer in a database file. The advantage of SKIP is that it moves the pointer 1 record down in the database relative to its current position. SKIP moves to the next record in the database.

Note: The SKIP command can also accept a numeric value as an argument. For example, SKIP 5 will move the record pointer 5 records ahead in the file. If the value is negative, the pointer moves toward the beginning of the file, e.g., SKIP -1.

Enter

```
SKIP
```

One of two things should happen now, depending upon whether you have reached the end of the file. If you have, the loop condition is false and the loop will terminate. If you have not reached the end of the file, you should go back to the top of the loop and repeat the commands contained within the loop. To test the EOF() condition, enter the ENDDO command.

```
ENDDO
```

The remainder of the program closes the database and index files and resets dBASE IV to the default settings.

```
CLOSE DATABASE
SET STATUS ON
SET SCOREBOARD ON
SET TALK ON
RETURN
```

The entire program reads:

```
SET TALK OFF
SET SCOREBOARD OFF
SET STATUS OFF
CLEAR
USE Admit INDEX Admit ORDER Last
@ 8,10 to 14,60
@ 9,11 SAY "Name:"
@ 10,11 SAY "Admit"
@ 11,11 SAY "Discharge"
@ 12,11 SAY "Days in"
@ 13,11 SAY "ICU days"
DO WHILE .NOT. EOF()
      REPLACE Days_stay with Discharge-Admit+1
      @ 9,25 SAY TRIM(First)+SPACE(1)+Last
      @ 10,25 SAY Admit
      @ 11,25 SAY Discharge
      @ 12,25 SAY Days_stay
      @ 13,25 GET Days_icu VALID Days_icu<=Days_stay
      READ
      SKIP
```

```
ENDDO
CLOSE DATABASE
SET STATUS ON
SET SCOREBOARD ON
SET TALK ON
RETURN
```

Save and execute the program by pressing Alt-e and typing r. The program displays the information for the first record with an input area for the ICU days.

Enter

2

The next record appears. Because only part of the screen was rewritten, the transition to the next display is smoother and faster than when the entire screen is rewritten. Also note that the index tag causes the records to be displayed in alphabetical order.

Skip this record by pressing ⏎. The next record is for Scott Fisher. Enter

15

dBASE IV rejects the entry because the ICU days would be greater than the total length of stay in the hospital. Revise the entry by entering

3

Skip the next four records by pressing ⏎ four times. This will bring you to Carol Lutz. Enter

2

Exit the program by skipping through the rest of the database. Press ⏎ five times.

You can check the results of the program by listing the ICU days. Try this on your own. If you need help, the correct command can be found at the end of the chapter in the Answers to Exercises section under exercise 4.

You can see that you have entered three items into the Days_icu field (see Figure 5.11).

Figure 5.11

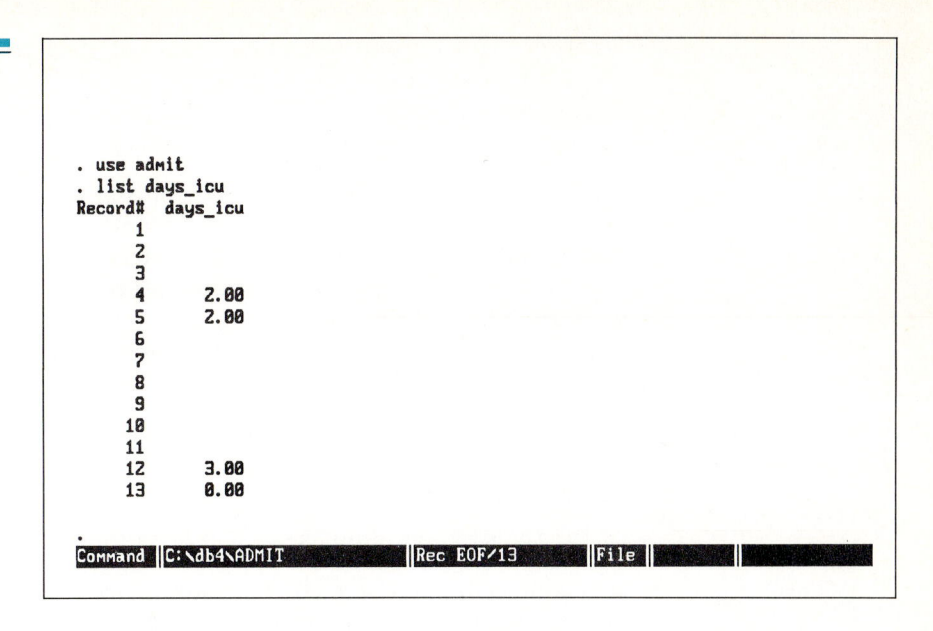

```
. use admit
. list days_icu
Record#   days_icu
     1
     2
     3
     4       2.00
     5       2.00
     6
     7
     8
     9
    10
    11
    12       3.00
    13       0.00
.
Command  C:\db4\ADMIT            Rec EOF/13     File
```

The SCAN Command

You can create a DO WHILE .NOT. EOF() loop with the SCAN command as well. SCAN is useful when you want to scan the database selectively. For example, suppose you want to run the ICU days program for records from a specific month. The SCAN command automatically processes records until reaching the end of the file. SCAN has the additional advantage of using a FOR clause to select specific records as the scan takes place.

Modify the Addicu program to scan specific months. Enter

`MODIFY COMMAND Addicu`

Move the cursor to line 4. If you want to select records for a specific month, you must allow the user to select the desired month. Create a character-type variable called Keymonth. Insert the following command.

> *Note:* The variable must be nine characters because the longest month name, September, has nine characters.

`Keymonth=SPACE(9)`

Choosing from a List

The next command in the Addicu program should be the @/SAY/GET command that displays the variable KEYMONTH as an input area. However, in this case, you know in advance the possible choices the user can make—one of the 12 months. In circumstances where you

Frequency Distributions ■ 225

know or want to limit the entries to a list of specific choices, dBASE IV allows you to create a variation on the standard @/SAY/GET command.

The variation involves the use of the @M function as part of a PICTURE clause. The @M function allows you to enter a list of options for entry. When the input area displays, the first item in the list appears. Instead of typing in another item, the user presses the space bar to display the next entry in the list. Upon reaching the end of the list, dBASE IV starts at the beginning again if the user continues pressing the space bar. List selection helps you eliminate typing and typing errors and insures that an entry is valid.

Before you enter the @/SAY/GET command for this field, you should display a prompt that tells the user to use the space bar to change values. Enter

```
@ 3,10 SAY "Press Space to Change Month"
```

The next command, and the input area for KEYMONTH, is going to be very long because it contains a list of the names of all 12 months. Begin by entering the following @/SAY/GET command. At the end of the line you should enter a space and then a semicolon. This procedure allows you to continue the remainder of the command on the next line.

```
@ 5,10 SAY "Records for " GET Keymonth PICTURE ;
```

The next line, which will be read by dBASE IV as a continuation of the previous line, consists of the function command @M, followed by a list of the items to display. The actual line that you will enter is wider than the screen display and wider than can be printed on a single line in this book. Even though the line below looks like it is broken into two parts, simply enter it as a single line. You should enter the names of the months in the same upper- and lower-case characters as shown here to match the format of the CMONTH() function.

```
"@ M January,February,March,April,May,June,July,
August,September,October,November,December"
```

Complete the interactive structure with a READ command that activates the input area.

```
READ
```

Now that the user has selected a month, the next step is to change DO WHILE to SCAN. The SCAN will use a FOR clause to select records with an admission date that has the same month as the keymonth variable.

Move the cursor to line 16. Replace DO WHILE with the correct form of SCAN. The FOR clause attached to the SCAN command will use the CMONTH() function to compare the name of the month of each Admit field to the selected month in the Keymonth variable. Try this on your own. If you need help, the correct command can be found at the end of the chapter in the Answers to Exercises section under exercise 5.

It is necessary to trim the Keymonth variable so that any of the blank spaces not taken up by characters do not affect the logical expression.

Another important difference between using DO WHILE and SCAN is that SCAN does not require a SKIP command inside the loop. SCAN automatically moves the pointer to the next record each time the loop executes. Because the SKIP command is no longer needed, SCAN further simplifies database processing loops.

Move the cursor to line 25. Delete the SKIP command by pressing Ctrl-y.

Change the ENDDO command to ENDSCAN.

Old line: ENDDO
New line: ENDSCAN

The modified Addicu program will look like this. The unchanged commands are shown in a second color.

```
SET TALK OFF
SET SCOREBOARD OFF
SET STATUS OFF
CLEAR
Keymonth=SPACE(9)
@ 3,10 SAY "Press Space to Change Month"
@ 5,10 SAY "Records for " GET Keymonth PICTURE ;"
   @ M January,February,March,April,May,June,July,
August,September,October,November,December"
READ
USE Admit INDEX Admit ORDER Last
@ 8,10 to 14,60
```

Frequency Distributions ■ 227

```
@ 9,11 SAY "Name:"
@ 10,11 SAY "Admit"
@ 11,11 SAY "Discharge"
@ 12,11 SAY "Days in"
@ 13,11 SAY "ICU days"
SCAN FOR CMONTH(Admit)=TRIM(Keymonth)
      REPLACE Days_stay WITH Discharge-Admit+1
      @ 9,25 SAY TRIM(First)+SPACE(1)+Last
      @ 10,25 SAY Admit
      @ 11,25 SAY Discharge
      @ 12,25 SAY Days_stay
      @ 13,25 GET Days_icu VALID Days_icu<=Days_stay
      READ
ENDSCAN
CLOSE DATABASE
SET STATUS ON
SET SCOREBOARD ON
SET TALK ON
RETURN
```

Save and execute the program by pressing Alt-e and typing r. The first item on the list, January, appears in the input area.

Press the space bar. The entry changes to February.

Press the space bar again. March appears in the input area. There is a short cut you can take that skips to a specific entry. If you enter the first letter of one of the list items, dBASE IV displays that item. Press j. June appears in the input area. If there is more than one choice with the same first letter, dBASE IV selects the next one based on the order in which the list was entered. In this case, you want to skip to December. Press d and ⏎

This time the program skips all of the records that do not match the criterion and displays the first admission in December (see Figure 5.12).

Press ⏎. The next matched record (Goren) appears. Enter

1

The program terminates because there are no more records that match the criterion.

Figure 5.12

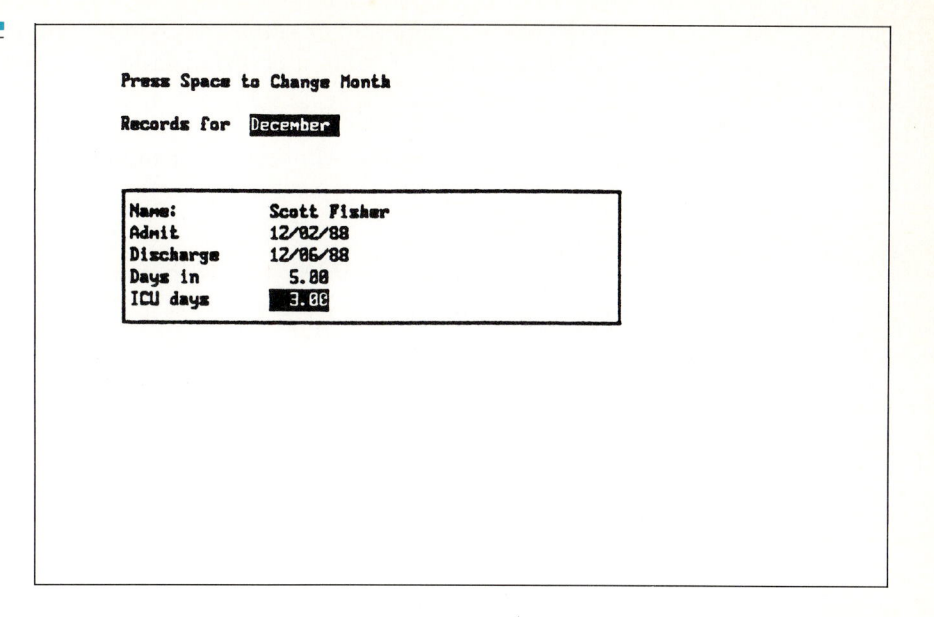

```
Press Space to Change Month

Records for  December

┌─────────────────────────────┐
│ Name:      Scott Fisher     │
│ Admit      12/02/88         │
│ Discharge  12/06/88         │
│ Days in     5.00            │
│ ICU days    3.00            │
└─────────────────────────────┘
```

Categories with Cases

It is easy to select groups of records when there are two mutually exclusive alternatives. For example, if you want to list all of the insured patients, you could use a LIST command with a FOR clause: LIST First,Last FOR Insured.

However, suppose a more complicated situation exists. When patients are admitted they fall into three classifications. One category includes people insured by Blue Cross or Blue Shield, companies that the hospital can bill directly. The second category includes patients using some other private insurance. The third category includes people who have no insurance.

One way to identify the individuals who belong to each classification is to scan the database three times, each time using a different criterion. It would be much more efficient if you could scan the database one time and divide the records into the three categories without having to cycle through the entire database two more times.

The solution to this problem is to use a DO CASE structure. The DO CASE structure allows you to list a number of logical expressions, each representing a category or special situation. Each CASE is associated with a command or set of commands that will execute if that CASE is selected. Create a program called Insured by entering

```
MODIFY COMMAND Insured
```

Begin the program by entering the usual environmental setting commands.

```
SET TALK OFF
SET SCOREBOARD OFF
SET STATUS OFF
CLEAR
```

The next command opens the database file and sets the index order to last name.

```
USE Admit INDEX Admit ORDER Last
```

This program creates a two-column list on the screen. The left column contains the names of the patients. The right column contains the insurance classification of the patient.

At the top of the screen, display the headings for each column with the following commands. In this program the left column will be aligned at 10 while the right column will be placed at 50. These locations are arbitrary. The REPLICATE function draws a line under the headings.

```
@ 0,10 SAY "Name"
@ 0,50 SAY "Insurance Classifications"
@ 1,0 SAY REPLICATE(CHR(196),79)
```

The remainder of the program consists of the data found in the records of the Admit file. You can use a SCAN command to process all of the records in the file. Enter

```
SCAN
```

This command begins the loop. The first action inside the loop is to display the name of the patient in the left column. Before you enter this command, you may want to consider how the loop affects @/SAY commands. Suppose you enter a command such as @ 2,10 SAY LAST to place the contents of the last name field in the first record at row 2 column 10. But remember that this command is part of a loop. When dBASE IV cycles through the loop the next time, it will encounter the same command again. The result is that the last name from the second record will be placed at row 2 column 10, writing over the previous name.

230 ■ Loops and Branches

If you want to place an @/SAY command inside a loop, you must take into consideration what will happen when the loop repeats. In this program, it would be better if each record displayed its data on the next line on the screen so that you could see a list of results, rather than having one record overwrite the previous record.

Therefore, you need to change the row/column values from absolute to relative values. An absolute value is a specific line or column number. A relative value changes its meaning relative to some previous value. dBASE IV provides two special functions that help you place items relative to other items on the display.

1. ROW(). The ROW() function returns the current line number of the cursor on the screen. The value varies from 0 to 24. When the screen is cleared, the value of ROW() is set to zero.

2. COL(). The COL() function returns the numeric value of the current cursor column. The value is a number from 0 to 79.

Used alone, the ROW() and COL() functions simply report the location of the cursor on the screen display. But the power of these functions is revealed when you realize you can use them in numeric expressions since they have numeric values. If the cursor is positioned on row 1, then the expression ROW()+1 will equal 2. What is important is that once the cursor is moved to a new line, line 2 for example, the expression ROW()+1 now evaluates as 3. The advantage of using a relative row value is that it increments as the program repeats the loop.

For example, the command @ ROW()+1,10 SAY LAST places the last name field in column 10 on the line below the current cursor position. This will cause the names to be listed down the screen instead of writing over each other. Enter

```
@ ROW()+1,10 SAY TRIM(Last)+", "+First
```

The DO CASE Structure

The next action to be performed by the Insured program displays text to indicate the insurance classification of patients. The IF/ENDIF structure provides a means of branching a program into one of two directions. The DO CASE structure provides a means to create multiple branch alternatives (see Figure 5.13). A DO CASE structure has four specific commands associated with it.

1. **DO CASE.** The DO CASE command marks the beginning of a series of case branches. The DO CASE command, unlike DO WHILE, SCAN, or IF, does not accept a logical expression; it is used by itself at all

Figure 5.13

0–17	//
18–44	⧸⧹⧸⧹ ///
45–64	⧸⧹⧸⧹ ⧸⧹⧸⧹
65+	⧸⧹⧸⧹ /

times. The logical expressions used to select the correct program branch are attached to the CASE commands that follow the DO CASE.

2. **CASE.** The DO CASE is followed by a number of specific CASE commands. Each CASE requires a logical expression to evaluate whether that branch is activated or skipped. Following the CASE, the commands that should be executed when that CASE is true are listed. dBASE IV activates the commands associated with the first CASE that evaluates as true. This means that if there are two or more cases that would be true, dBASE IV will always activate the first CASE and skip the others, even if they are also true. The logic used in a DO CASE structure dictates that all the cases represent mutually exclusive alternatives.

3. **OTHERWISE.** OTHERWISE is an optional command to create a branch that is activated if none of the cases is true. OTHERWISE is always placed following all the cases and requires no logical argument. If no OTHERWISE keyword is used and all the cases are false, no action is taken by the DO CASE. OTHERWISE serves as the action to take if none of the above cases is true.

4. **ENDCASE.** ENDCASE marks the end of the DO CASE structure. This command is required for each DO CASE in the program.

Begin the DO CASE structure by entering that command.

```
DO CASE
```

There are three potential branches for this Insured program block. The first question to ask about a patient is, "Does he have insurance?" If the answer is no, the insured field is false, and you can display a message about his status. If he has insurance, you then proceed to the next case, which attempts to separate those companies that you can bill directly. In this example, if the word Blue appears in the name, he is a direct billing patient.

Create the first CASE that selects all uninsured patients.

```
CASE .NOT. insured
    @ ROW(),50 SAY "No Insurance"
```

By using ROW() by itself, you tell dBASE IV to place the text on the same line as the previous item. The relative value in this case makes sure that patient name and classification fall on the same row.

The next CASE tests to see if insured patients belong to Blue Cross or Blue Shield. The sequence of the CASE clauses implies certain logical conditions. It is not necessary to test the insured field for true again because the first CASE acts as a filter, allowing only insured patients to move on to the second CASE.

```
CASE payor="Blue"
    @ ROW(),50 SAY "Direct Billing"
```

Any patients not selected by the first two cases fall into the classification of "Private Insurance." It would be logical to use an OTHERWISE command to print "Private Insurance" for any records that are not picked up by the first two classifications.

```
OTHERWISE
    @ ROW(),50 SAY "Private Insurance"
```

With all of the cases entered into the structure, complete it with the ENDCASE command.

```
ENDCASE
```

With the records evaluated and the classifications printed, you can end the loop.

```
ENDSCAN
```

Complete the program by pausing the display and resetting the environment.

```
@ 23,0
WAIT
CLOSE DATABASE
SET STATUS ON
SET SCOREBOARD ON
SET TALK ON
RETURN
```

Save and execute the program by pressing (Alt)-e and typing r. The program displays the patients and their insurance classifications in two columns (see Figure 5.14).

To complete the program, press (↵).

Accumulators

Suppose you also want the Insured program to show the total charges for insured and noninsured patients at the bottom of the list. There are two ways to produce this list. The first method might use the SUM or CALCULATE commands. These commands have their own built-in scanning functions and each would require a scan of the entire database. The program would have to scan the database three times to complete the task: once for the list, once for the total changes for insured, and once for the total charges for the uninsured.

The second approach requires only a single scan of the database. This approach performs the calculations at the same time it displays the records. This strategy creates memory variables and uses them as accumulators. An accumulator is a memory variable that adds together values from records as the database is scanned.

Figure 5.14

```
Name                          Insurance Classifications

Anderson, Ken                 Private Insurance
Eckardt, Lois                 Direct Billing
Fisher, Scott                 No Insurance
Goren, Thomas                 No Insurance
Ivanovic, Frank               No Insurance
Jones, Timothy                No Insurance
LaFish, Walter                Direct Billing
Lutz, Carol                   Private Insurance
Mcdowell, Angelia             No Insurance
Morgan, Robert                Direct Billing
Sorenson, Cynthia             Direct Billing
Tate, Harold                  No Insurance
Westrup, Milton               Private Insurance




Press any key to continue...
```

■ Loops and Branches

You create an accumulator by initializing a memory variable to zero, as in Total_chrg = 0. When the scan encounters a record that should be added into the total, you issue a command that looks like this:

```
TOTAL_chrg=Total_chrg+Charges
```

At first this command may seem odd. It doesn't make any sense if you read it as an algebraic equation. Instead, read it to mean, "let Total_chrg equal the current value of Total_chrg plus the value in the charge field." In this way, the value of the memory variable will grow larger—accumulate—as the loop processes each record and the statement executes over again. By the end of the scan, the value in the memory variable will equal the total of all the Charges fields.

This process of scanning and accumulating is similar to how SUM and CALCULATE operate. By programming your own accumulators, you can perform calculations while you carry out other operations during a single database scan.

To GET separate totals for different groups of records, you can use several accumulators embedded into IF/ENDIF structures.

Load the Insured program into the editor by entering

```
MODIFY COMMAND Insured
```

Move the cursor to line 9. Accumulators must be initialized before you begin the database scan. In this case, you will need two accumulators: one for the insured, and one for the noninsured patients. You can use the STORE command to initialize both variables in a single command. Insert the following command.

```
STORE 0 to Ins,Notins
```

The next step is to move inside the loop and place an IF/ENDIF structure into the program to accumulate the two totals.

Move the cursor line 11. Insert the following commands.

```
IF insured
Ins=Ins+charges
     ELSE
Notins=Notins+charges
     ENDIF
```

The final part of the modification displays the totals at the end of the program. Move the cursor to line 26. Insert the following commands to display the totals. The ROW() function once again determines the

Categories with Cases

row location of the totals. This is necessary because the location of the totals on the screen depends on the number of records in the database file. Insert the following commands.

```
@ ROW()+2,10 SAY "Total Charges Insured Patients"
@ ROW(),50 SAY Ins PICTURE "999,999"
@ ROW()+1,10 SAY "Total Charges Non-insured;
 Patients"
@ ROW(),50 SAY Notins PICTURE "999,999"
```

The modified program now looks like this. The new program lines are highlighted in color.

```
SET TALK OFF
SET SCOREBOARD OFF
SET STATUS OFF
CLEAR
USE Admit INDEX Admit ORDER Last
@ 0,10 SAY "Name"
@ 0,50 SAY "Insurance Classifications"
@ 1,0 SAY REPLICATE(CHR(196),79)
STORE 0 TO INS,Notins
SCAN
     IF Insured
Ins=Ins+charges
     ELSE
Notins=Notins+charges
     ENDIF
     @ ROW()+1,10 SAY TRIM(Last)+", "+First
     DO CASE
CASE .NOT. Insured
     @ ROW(),50 SAY "No Insurance"
CASE Payor="Blue"
     @ ROW(),50 SAY "Direct Billing"
OTHERWISE
     @ ROW(),50 SAY "Private Insurance"
     ENDCASE
ENDSCAN
```

```
@ ROW()+2,10 SAY "Total Charges Insured Patients"
@ ROW(),50 SAY Ins PICTURE "999,999"
@ ROW()+1,10 SAY "Total Charges Non-insured;
 Patients"
@ ROW(),50 SAY Notins PICTURE "999,999"
@ 23,0
WAIT
CLOSE DATABASE
SET STATUS ON
SET SCOREBOARD ON
SET TALK ON
RETURN
```

Save and execute the program by pressing (Alt)-e and typing r. The program now displays the total at the end of the list (see Figure 5.15).

Limiting the Display

In creating the previous modification to the Insured program, it may have crossed your mind that if the database was large enough, the value of the ROW() function would continue to increase until it exceeded 24, the last line on the screen. What would happen? When the

Figure 5.15

Name	Insurance Classifications
Anderson, Ken	Private Insurance
Eckardt, Lois	Direct Billing
Fisher, Scott	No Insurance
Goren, Thomas	No Insurance
Ivanovic, Frank	No Insurance
Jones, Timothy	No Insurance
LaFish, Walter	Direct Billing
Lutz, Carol	Private Insurance
Mcdowell, Angelia	No Insurance
Morgan, Robert	Direct Billing
Sorenson, Cynthia	Direct Billing
Tate, Harold	No Insurance
Westrup, Milton	Private Insurance
Total Charges Insured Patients	39,207
Total Charges Non-insured Patients	56,264

Press any key to continue...

Categories with Cases

value of ROW() reached 24, the command @ ROW()+1,10 would cause an error because it would indicate a location that was off the screen.

In order prevent this problem, you must limit the total number of records that can be displayed on the screen at one time. Each time this limit is reached, the display will pause. Pressing any key will clear the screen and the program will continue listing on the next screen.

The key to limiting the screen display is to place an IF command at the bottom of the loop. Each time the loop cycles, the IF command tests the current cursor row to see if it has reached the limit. You can set the limit to any value that seems appropriate. In this example, line 12 is used because you have only 13 records in the database. In most cases you would want to list more records on one screen so that the value of the limit might be set at 20 or 22.

Load the Insured program into the editor by entering

```
MODIFY COMMAND Insured
```

Move the cursor to line 24. This is the line that completes the display of each record. It is here that you want to insert the test to determine if the screen display has reached the limit. Insert the following command.

```
IF ROW()=12
```

This test becomes true when the program displays information on line 12 of the screen display. When that happens, the screen display pauses and waits until the user tells the program to continue. Insert the following commands.

```
@ 23,0 SAY "More ..."
WAIT
```

Next, the screen display will clear and the program will rewrite the headings. Insert the following commands.

```
CLEAR
@ 0,10 SAY "Name"
@ 0,50 SAY "Insurance Classifications"
@ 1,0 SAY REPLICATE(CHR(196),79)
     ENDIF
```

The modified program now looks like this. The new program lines are highlighted in color.

```
SET TALK OFF
```

```
SET SCOREBOARD OFF
SET STATUS OFF
CLEAR
USE Admit INDEX Admit ORDER Last
@ 0,10 SAY "Name"
@ 0,50 SAY "Insurance Classifications"
@ 1,0 SAY REPLICATE(CHR(196),79)
STORE 0 to Ins,Notins
SCAN
     IF Insured
Ins=Ins+Charges
     ELSE
Notins=Notins+Charges
     ENDIF
     @ ROW()+1,10 SAY TRIM(Last)+", "+First
     DO CASE
CASE .NOT. insured
     @ ROW(),50 SAY "No Insurance"
CASE Payor="Blue"
     @ ROW(),50 SAY "Direct Billing"
OTHERWISE
     @ ROW(),50 SAY "Private Insurance"
     ENDCASE
     IF ROW()=12
@ 23,0 SAY "More ..."
WAIT
CLEAR
@ 0,10 SAY "Name"
@ 0,50 SAY "Insurance Classifications"
@ 1,0 SAY REPLICATE(CHR(196),79)
     ENDIF
ENDSCAN
@ ROW()+2,10 SAY "Total Charges Insured Patients"
@ ROW(),50 SAY Ins PICTURE "999,999"
```

```
@ ROW()+1,10 SAY "Total Charges Non-insured;
 Patients"
@ ROW(),50 SAY Notins PICTURE "999,999"
@ 23,0
WAIT
CLOSE DATABASE
SET STATUS ON
SET SCOREBOARD ON
SET TALK ON
RETURN
```

Save and execute the program by pressing (Alt)-e and typing r. The program pauses when the display reaches row 12 (see Figure 5.16).

Continue the program by pressing ⏎. The program clears the screen and places the next set of records on the display (see Figure 5.17).

By adding the screen limit structure, the program operates properly no matter how many records are added to the database. Complete the program by pressing ⏎.

Figure 5.16

```
Name                          Insurance Classifications
--------------------------------------------------------
        Anderson, Ken         Private Insurance
        Eckardt, Lois         Direct Billing
        Fisher, Scott         No Insurance
        Goren, Thomas         No Insurance
        Ivanovic, Frank       No Insurance
        Jones, Timothy        No Insurance
        LaFish, Walter        Direct Billing
        Lutz, Carol           Private Insurance
        Mcdowell, Angelia     No Insurance
        Morgan, Robert        Direct Billing
        Sorenson, Cynthia     Direct Billing




More ...
Press any key to continue...
```

Figure 5.17

```
              Name                          Insurance Classifications
          ─────────────────────────────────────────────────────────────
              Tate, Harold                  No Insurance
              Westrup, Milton               Private Insurance

              Total Charges Insured Patients       39,207
              Total Charges Non-insured Patients   56,264




          Press any key to continue...
```

Counters

The Insured program now lists information about the insurance classification of each patient. However, in a large database, this type of list will be very long and you probably cannot absorb all of the information as it displays. It might be more useful to count the number of patients in each classification and display the totals. A program that performs this function is very similar in structure to the Insured program. The major difference is that instead of using the DO CASE structure to display different classes, you would use each CASE to count the number of patients.

This is made possible by a variation on the idea of an accumulator. In the Insured program, a typical accumulator command looks like this: Ins = Ins + Charges. Written in this way, the command increases the value of INS by the amount stored in Charges. But suppose that all of the charges fields contained the value of 1. As the program added up the charges, it would end up increasing the value of the variable by 1 for each record. In effect, it would give you a tally of the number of records.

However, the Charges field is unlikely to contain the value of 1 in all records. But you can change the accumulator to add the value of 1 instead of the value of the Charges field. The command now looks like this: Ins = Ins + 1.

Categories with Cases ■ **241**

This change from a field value to a numeric literal value changes the Ins variable to a counter. Each time the command Ins = Ins + 1 is processed during the loop, the value will increase by one.

Create a new program called Countins by entering

```
MODIFY COMMAND Countins
```

Begin the program with the usual opening commands.

```
SET TALK OFF
SET SCOREBOARD OFF
SET STATUS OFF
CLEAR
USE Admit INDEX Admit ORDER Last
```

The next command creates the variables to be used as counters. Because there are three classifications for records, you will need three variables.

```
STORE 0 to Class1,Class2,Class3
```

The next section of the program is the processing loop. This time when the database is scanned, the DO CASE structure selectively increments the counters for each classification.

```
SCAN
      DO CASE
CASE .NOT. Insured
      Class1=Class1+1
CASE Payor="Blue"
      Class2=Class2+1
OTHERWISE
      Class3=Class3+1
      ENDCASE
ENDSCAN
```

The last part of the program displays the value of the three counters.

```
@ 5,10 SAY "Non-insured patients"
@ ROW(),50 SAY Class1 PICTURE "999,999"
@ ROW()+1,10 SAY "Direct Billing Patients"
@ ROW(),50 SAY Class2 PICTURE "999,999"
@ ROW()+1,10 SAY "Private Insurance Patients"
```

■ **Loops and Branches**

```
@ ROW(),50 SAY Class3 PICTURE "999,999"
@ 23,0
WAIT
CLOSE DATABASE
SET STATUS ON
SET SCOREBOARD ON
SET TALK ON
RETURN
```

The entire program looks like this:

```
SET TALK OFF
SET SCOREBOARD OFF
SET STATUS OFF
CLEAR
USE Admit INDEX Admit ORDER Last
STORE 0 to Class1,Class2,Class3
SCAN
      DO CASE
CASE .NOT. Insured
      Class1=Class1+1
CASE Payor="Blue"
      Class2=Class2+1
OTHERWISE
      Class3=Class3+1
      ENDCASE
ENDSCAN
@ 5,10 SAY "Non-insured patients"
@ ROW(),50 SAY Class1 PICTURE "999,999"
@ ROW()+1,10 SAY "Direct Billing Patients"
@ ROW(),50 SAY Class2 PICTURE "999,999"
@ ROW()+1,10 SAY "Private Insurance Patients"
@ ROW(),50 SAY Class3 PICTURE "999,999"
@ 23,0
WAIT
CLOSE DATABASE
SET STATUS ON
```

```
SET SCOREBOARD ON
SET TALK ON
RETURN
```

Save and execute the program by pressing [Alt]-e and typing r. The program scans the database, counting the three classifications, and displays the results of the scan.

Complete the program by pressing [↵].

You have now learned how to use all of the structural elements you need to create the frequency distribution program discussed earlier.

Before you go on to the next section, you may want to try your hand at making some modifications to the Countins program. Your goal is to add percentages to the display as shown in Figure 5.18. Try this on your own. If you need help, the correct command can be found at the end of the chapter in the Answers to Exercises section under exercise 6.

Arrays

The previous program, Countins, performed a frequency distribution calculation based on the three insurance classifications. With this program, you have assembled all the tools necessary to calculate the frequency distribution for patient ages.

Figure 5.18

```
Non-insured patients              6    46.2%
Direct Billing Patients           4    30.8%
Private Insurance Patients        3    23.1%




Press any key to continue...
```

Loops and Branches

Why bother to create another program to calculate a frequency distribution for ages? Because in this case, you will create the program using a different type of memory variable called an array variable.

In the Countins program, you defined three variables to hold numbers of patients for each classification. The variables were named Class1, Class2, and Class3. In this type of calculation, you must define one variable for each classification. The simplest way to keep track of such variables is to use the same name and simply add a number for each variable.

dBASE IV gives you an easy way to create a series of variables with consecutive numbers. These variables are called a single-dimensional array. The command used to create this array is the DECLARE command. For example, you can create 10 variables with the name group by entering the following command; this command requires the use of square brackets ([ ]), not parentheses.

```
DECLARE Group[10]
DISPLAY MEMORY
```

dBASE IV shows the array of variables declared in memory. Each one of the numbered items within the array, e.g., Group[1], Group[2], etc., is called an element (see Figure 5.19).

Figure 5.19

```
              User Memory Variables

    GROUP        pub    A   [10]
       [1]      elem   L   .F.
       [2]      elem   L   .F.
       [3]      elem   L   .F.
       [4]      elem   L   .F.
       [5]      elem   L   .F.
       [6]      elem   L   .F.
       [7]      elem   L   .F.
       [8]      elem   L   .F.
       [9]      elem   L   .F.
      [10]      elem   L   .F.

    1 out of 500 memvars defined (and 10 array elements)

              User MEMVAR/RTSYM Memory Usage

    2800 bytes used for 1 memvar blocks (max=10)
     850 bytes used for 1 rtsym blocks (max=10)
    Press any key to continue...
    Command
```

Categories with Cases ■ 245

dBASE IV automatically defines the array elements as logical values. Return to the dot prompt by pressing (Esc).

When you want to refer to an element in the array, you do so by using the number of the element along with the array name. Enter

Group[2]=25

Group[3]=Group[2]*2

DISPLAY MEMORY

The memory now shows the values assigned to the elements in the array. Return to the dot prompt by pressing (Esc).

The main advantage of an array is that the number of the element can be any numeric value or expression. This means that you can indirectly refer to an element in the array by inserting a field or variable name into the array reference.

An array allows you to use loops to cycle through groups of variables, in a manner similar to the way that loops can scan database records. The next program you create will apply the structures used in the previous programs but also use arrays. You will see how the use of array variables improves the structure of a program. Create a new program called Ages by entering

MODIFY COMMAND Ages

The program begins with the standard opening sequence used in most of the previous programs.

SET TALK OFF

SET SCOREBOARD OFF

SET STATUS OFF

CLEAR

USE Admit INDEX Admit ORDER Last

You create and initialize memory variables with a single command such as STORE. The Ages program uses array variables. Such variables usually require two steps. The first step includes the DECLARE command to create the array variables. Because dBASE IV automatically defines all of the array variables as logical values, you must take the further step of initializing the variables as character, numeric, or date types, if you will not be using the variables as logical values.

In this program, you need two sets of variables, one for the name of each classification and the other for the value of the classification.

■ Loops and Branches

The following command creates two arrays, Class and Name, with four variables apiece.

```
DECLARE Class[4],Name[4]
```

The next step is to assign initial values to the array variables. The class variables should be initialized to zero. This can be done with a STORE command. Note that the class variables use the [] symbols to indicate the element to be defined.

```
STORE 0 to Class[1],Class[2],Class[3],Class[4]
```

The NAME variables display the names of the classifications.

```
Name[1]="Below 18"
Name[2]="18 to 44"
Name[3]="45 to 64"
Name[4]="Over 65"
```

With the variables defined, you can begin a scan loop.

```
SCAN
```

The loop contains a DO CASE structure that selects the element in the Class array that is to be incremented according to the value in the age field. The first case is Class 1, patients under 18.

```
DO CASE
CASE Age<18
     Class[1]=Class[1]+1
```

The next classification is patients from 18 to 44. In order to create this CASE, you must use a logical expression that combines two expressions with an .AND. conjunction.

```
CASE Age>=18 .AND. Age<45
     Class[2]=Class[2]+1
```

The next counter, for patients between 45 and 65, is created with the commands below.

```
CASE Age>=45 .AND. Age<65
     Class[3]=Class[3]+1
```

The program has now classified all the patients under the age of 65. This means that any records not already accounted for will fall into the last group, class 4. You can use an OTHERWISE command to implement this CASE.

```
OTHERWISE
    Class[4]=Class[4]+1
```

You can now close both the cases and the scanning loop.

```
ENDCASE
ENDSCAN
```

The values for the four classifications have now been captured in the elements of the CLASS array. All that is left is to display the data accumulated in the first part of the program. Begin by displaying the headings on the screen.

```
@ 0, 10 SAY "Classification"
```

```
@ 0, 50 SAY "Patients"
```

```
@ 1,0 SAY REPLICATE(CHR(196),79)
```

An Array Loop

The next section of the program demonstrates how the elements in array can be processed using a loop.

In the previous program, variable information was displayed by creating @/SAY commands for each variable. If you had 10 variables, you would need 10 individual @/SAY commands.

However, in this example the information is not stored in individual memory variables but is placed into elements in arrays. This makes possible the creation of a loop that processes the corresponding elements in the array. The key concept is that the elements in an array can be referred to by any numeric expression. For example, suppose you define a variable called Start as having the value of 1. You can then use that variable to refer to the first element in an array, as in Class[Start]. A reference such as Class[Start] is significant because it permits you to change the meaning of the reference by changing the value of the Start variable. If this command is placed into a loop and the value of Start incremented each time, a single command can operate on all the elements in an array.

The advantage of this approach is that the number of commands you need to display the information stored in the array is not tied to the size of the array. The loop can process many elements in the array without requiring any additional commands. The section of the program shown below demonstrates how to use this type of loop.

The first step is to create two variables that serve a dual purpose. A variable can be used to select the element within the array; it can also be used to determine when the end of the array has been reached. Unlike a file, an array does not have a special function such as EOF() to help determine the end of the array. Another variable is needed to determine the last element in the array. In the example below, the variables start and finish control the loop. The DO WHILE loop is controlled by the logical expression Start<=Finish.

```
Start=1
Finish=4
DO WHILE Start<=Finish
```

Inside the loop you can use the variable Start to create two @/SAY commands to display the element in the Class and Name arrays indicated by the value of Start.

```
@ ROW()+1,10 SAY Name[Start]
@ ROW(),50 SAY Class[Start] PICTURE "999,999"
```

Once these are displayed, the value of START should be incremented and the loop closed.

```
Start=Start+1
ENDDO
```

The program concludes with a pause and the usual resetting commands.

```
@ 23,0
WAIT
CLOSE DATABASE
SET STATUS ON
SET SCOREBOARD ON
SET TALK ON
RETURN
```

The entire program reads as follows:

```
SET TALK OFF
SET SCOREBOARD OFF
SET STATUS OFF
CLEAR
USE Admit INDEX Admit ORDER Last
DECLARE Class[4],Name[4]
STORE 0 to Class[1],Class[2],Class[3],Class[4]
Name[1]="Below 18"
Name[2]="18 to 44"
```

```
Name[3]="45 to 64"
Name[4]="Over 65"
SCAN
     DO CASE
CASE Age<18
     Class[1]=Class[1]+1
CASE Age>=18 .AND. Age<45
     Class[2]=Class[2]+1
CASE Age>=45 .AND. Age<65
     Class[3]=Class[3]+1
OTHERWISE
     Class[4]=Class[4]+1
     ENDCASE
ENDSCAN
@ 0, 10 SAY "Classification"
@ 0, 50 SAY "Patients"
@ 1,0 SAY REPLICATE(Chr(196),79)
Start=1
Finish=4
DO WHILE Start<=Finish
     @ ROW()+1,10 SAY Name[Start]
     @ ROW(),50 SAY Class[Start] PICTURE "999,999"
     Start=Start+1
ENDDO
@ 23,0
WAIT
CLOSE DATABASE
SET STATUS ON
SET SCOREBOARD ON
SET TALK ON
RETURN
```

Save and execute the program by pressing (Alt)-e and typing r. The program displays the frequency distribution of the patients classified by age (see Figure 5.20).

Complete the program by pressing (↵).

Figure 5.20

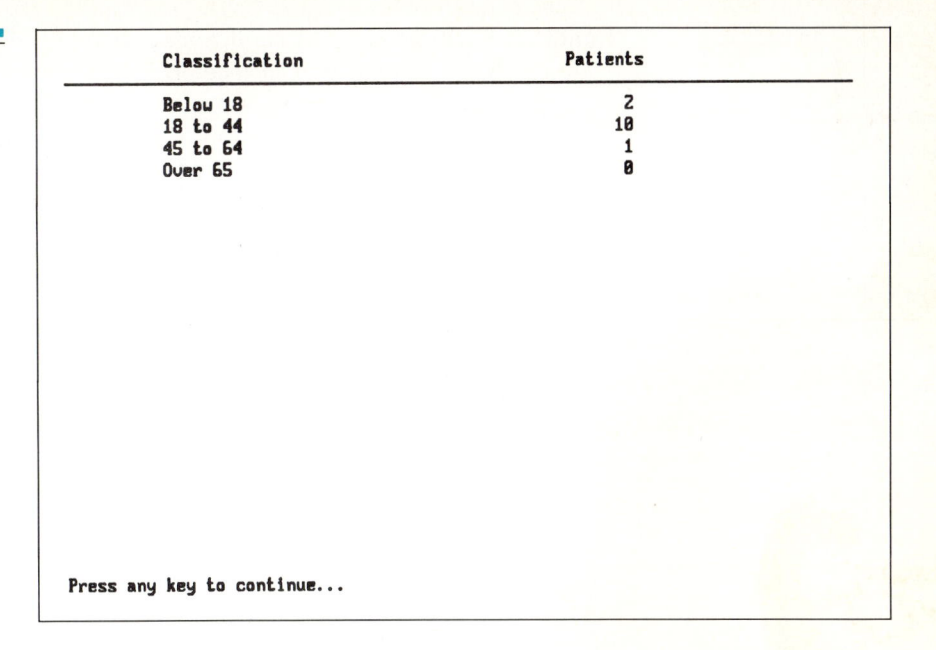

```
      Classification                     Patients
         Below 18                           2
         18 to 44                          10
         45 to 64                           1
         Over 65                            0




Press any key to continue...
```

The previous program demonstrates one of the advantages of using arrays to process variables that are part of related groups. The primary concept is to use loops to process data, rather than simply listing commands. The array-oriented loop that you used in the Ages program can process any number of records. In addition, the Ages program can be simply modified by increasing the number of elements in the arrays without having to change the loop that displays those values.

In the following chapters, we'll use these concepts to create programs that are not only successful in executing the specific task for which they were designed, but can easily be adapted to perform other functions.

Summary

Key concepts from this chapter include:

Branching. A branch is a path of execution that a program takes only under a specific condition. Branches allow a program to react to a condition or set of conditions. Programs with branches are more flexible than linear programs.

Conditional Structures. A conditional structure contains an expression that will evaluate to true or false to create the conditions for a program branch. If the test expression evaluates as true, the structure contains a command or group of commands to execute. The structure can also contain an alternate set of commands to execute when the condition is false.

IF/ELSE/ENDIF. These commands create a conditional structure. The structure always begins with an IF command and must end with an ENDIF command. The IF command requires a logical expression. The commands grouped between the IF and the ENDIF commands execute only when the logical expression associated with the IF is true. The ELSE command is an option that indicates a group of commands to execute when the logical expression associated with the IF command is false.

DO CASE/CASE/OTHERWISE/ENDCASE. These commands form another type of conditional structure. The DO CASE command precedes a series of individual CASE commands. The ENDCASE command terminates the list of cases. Each CASE requires a logical expression. Following the logical expression, a command or group of commands appears. These commands will execute only if the CASE is selected. dBASE IV selects the first CASE, if any, in the structure that evaluates as true. If more than one of the cases is true, dBASE IV selects the first and ignores all other cases, even ones that are true, that follow. If no cases are true, the program continues to execute commands following the ENDCASE. The OTHERWISE command, which is optional, creates a "none of the above" choice. When none of the cases evaluates as true, the structure automatically selects the commands grouped with OTHERWISE and executes them.

Loop. A loop is a structure that marks a group of commands to repeat until some condition changes. Loops allow small programs to perform a large number of tasks because the same commands are used over and over again while the loop is active. It is important to make sure that the commands inside the loop have a method of terminating the loop. Otherwise the loop could go on forever without stopping; this is called an endless loop. Loops can contain any dBASE IV command including branch structures and other loops.

DO WHILE/ENDDO. The DO WHILE and ENDDO keywords create a loop. The DO WHILE command requires a logical expression. The loop will continue to cycle through all of the commands between the DO WHILE and ENDDO as long as the expression evaluates as true. The logical expression is evaluated each time the loop reaches the ENDDO command. When the condition is false, execution continues following the ENDDO command.

Automatic loops. An automatic loop is one that uses the logical symbol .T. in place of a logical expression. The .T. causes the loop to always evaluate as true so that the loop will cycle automatically without reference to an actual condition. Automatic loops are terminated by an EXIT command embedded in a conditional structure within the loop.

SKIP. The SKIP command moves the record pointer one record down in the database. The command will accept a numeric expression. If the number is positive, the pointer moves that number of records toward the end of the file. If the expression is negative, the pointer aligns that number of records toward the beginning of the file.

SCAN/ENDSCAN. These commands create a special form of loop that will automatically process all the records in the current database. The SCAN loop automatically places the pointer at the top of the file and increments the pointer one record.

EXIT. The EXIT command jumps out of a loop. When an EXIT command is encountered, dBASE IV jumps to the first command following the next ENDDO command. EXIT is frequently used to terminate automatic loops. EXIT is usually embedded in a conditional structure, like an IF/ENDIF or DO CASE. EXIT allows you to terminate a loop without having to process all the commands in the loop.

TRANSACTION/ROLLBACK. The TRANSACTION commands provide a method of logging all changes made to a database before they are made a permanent part of the file. The commands BEGIN TRANSACTION and END TRANSACTION create a special form of conditional structure designed to prevent accidental modification of a database. All of the changes made following a BEGIN TRANSACTION command are temporary until an END TRANSACTION command executes. They then become part of the database. The ROLLBACK command can be executed before the END TRANSACTION command. ROLLBACK annuls the changes made in the database since the BEGIN TRANSACTION, and returns the database to is original state. You can rollback transactions as many times as you like. Once an END TRANSACTION command has been executed, ROLLBACK will have no effect.

Batch Processing. Batch processing refers to entering new records into a separate file before they are added to the main database.

APPEND FROM. The APPEND FROM command adds records to the current database by copying records from another database. Only fields with the same names in both databases are appended. You can use a FOR clause to filter records as they are appended.

Counters and Accumulators. A counter or an accumulator is a special use of a memory variable within a loop. A counter is a memory variable that is incremented by a fixed value each time the loop cycles, as in Kounter=Kounter+1. An accumulator is a memory variable that adds the contents of a field each cycle of the loop. Accumulators are used to accumulate totals during loops.

Arrays. An array is an organized set of related memory variables. The simplest type is a single dimension array. Each variable within an array is called an element. One advantage of arrays is that you can refer to elements in the array using numbers or numeric variables, fields, or expressions.

DECLARE. The DECLARE command creates an array of variables.

Review Problems for Chapter 5

Chapter 5 introduces the use of programming structures called loops and branches. The following problems will help you review how these structures are used in writing programs.

1. Create a program that will search the Sales database for a specific invoice number. The program will display the company and the date if the invoice number is found, and a message if the invoice number is not in the database.

2. Modify the previous program so that it will loop continuously until you enter a value of zero for the invoice number.

3. Create a program that will allow you to append new records onto the Sales database. Use the format file you have already created as the input screen for the program. The program should loop until you specify that you want to exit.

4. Create a program that lists the company, sales date, item name, and total amount in date order. The program should automatically pause at the end of each full screen of data.

5. Create a program that sums the total amounts for three classifications of products: those with the word "wipe" in the product name, those with the word "mask" in the product name, and all others. Also display the percentages for each category of the total of all sales.

6. Create a frequency distribution program that categorizes the total amount of sales. The sales should be grouped into the following categories:
0–500
501–1,000
1,001–2,000
2,001–3,000
over 3,000

Answers to Exercises

1. Convert first and last to upper-case.

   ```
   REPLACE all first with UPPER(First)
   REPLACE all last with UPPER(Last)
   ```

2. Pause the program.

   ```
   @ 23,0
   WAIT
   ```

3. Open database and index.

   ```
   USE Admit INDEX Admit ORDER Last
   ```

4. List the ICU days.

   ```
   USE Admit
   LIST Days_icu
   ```

5. Scan for a specific month.

   Old line: `DO WHILE .NOT. EOF()`

   New line: `SCAN FOR CMONTH(Admit)=TRIM(Keymonth)`

6. Add percentages to program with the new program lines highlighted in color.

   ```
   SET TALK OFF
   SET SCOREBOARD OFF
   SET STATUS OFF
   ```

```
CLEAR
USE Admit INDEX Admit ORDER Last
STORE 0 to Class1,Class2,Class3
SCAN
     DO CASE
CASE .NOT. Insured
Class1=Class1+1
CASE Payor="Blue"
     Class2=Class2+1
OTHERWISE
     Class3=Class3+1
     ENDCASE
ENDSCAN
All_class=Class1+Class2+Class3
@ 5,10 SAY "Non-insured patients"
@ ROW(),50 SAY Class1 PICTURE "999,999"
@ ROW(),60 SAY Class1/All_class*100 PICTURE;
  "99.9%"
@ ROW()+1,10 SAY "Direct Billing Patients"
@ ROW(),50 SAY Class2 PICTURE "999,999"
@ ROW(),60 SAY Class2/All_class*100 PICTURE;
  "99.9%"
@ ROW()+1,10 SAY "Private Insurance Patients"
@ ROW(),50 SAY Class3 PICTURE "999,999"
@ ROW(),60 SAY Class3/All_class*100 PICTURE;
  "99.9%"
@ 23,0
WAIT
CLOSE DATABASE
SET STATUS ON
SET SCOREBOARD ON
SET TALK ON
RETURN
```

6 Menus and Debugging

In this book's earlier chapters, you learned to write single-purpose programs: Each of these programs operated separately from the other programs you created and performed a discrete task, like editing or appending records. To build a coherent system of database-management routines, you need to bring these disparate individual programs together. The best way to tie all these routines together is to create menu programs that run the separate programs when they are chosen from the menu. These menu programs can use built-in dBASE IV menu tools, or you can create menus of your own custom design.

While menu programs can vary in their appearance and design, they have a common purpose: to present users with a list of options from which they can select the action they want to perform. The actions can be a simple series of commands or an entire program.

Menus are an important element in program design because they offer the user a road map of the application. A well-structured menu or series of menus can guide a user through the various steps of an application and reduce the time and effort needed to learn how it operates.

Because menus are so important, dBASE IV includes a variety of special tools that allow you to use some of the same design elements employed in the dBASE IV database manager in your own programs. These elements include menu bars, pull-down menus, pop-up menus, and windows.

In this chapter, you will learn about creating menus and about the facilities dBASE IV provides for designing menus and menu systems.

The Standard Menu

The term standard menu refers to a menu that does not use one of the special screen elements provided by dBASE IV, such as menu bars, pull-own menus, or pop-up menus. A standard menu program employs many of the same tools you have already used—interactive commands, loops, and conditional structures.

A menu program has three basic parts.

1. **Display options.** The first part of any menu program displays a list of available options.
2. **Pause for selection.** After the menu choices have been displayed, the program pauses to allow a user to select an item from that menu.
3. **Branch on selection.** When the user makes a selection, the program then reacts by branching to the commands or subroutines that correspond to that selection.

From work done in previous chapters, you have a series of routines related to the Admit database file. Some of them relate to data entry: Edit, Entry, and Addicu; others are statistical programs like Insured, Ages, and Countins.

Suppose you want to create a menu program that ties together the Edit, Entry, and Addicu programs. Enter the following to begin creating a program called Admitmnu (Admit menu):

```
MODIFY COMMAND admitmnu
```

The program begins with the usual SET commands.

```
SET TALK OFF
SET SCOREBOARD OFF
SET STATUS OFF
```

One goal in writing this menu program is to create a standard menu that not only runs the three programs specified but can also be quickly modified for more or different options. To make the program easier to modify, the options listed on the menu will be stored as elements in an array called OPTION. Each element in the array will be the text for one of the options that appear on the menu. To create this array, you need to use a DECLARE command followed by code to define the text for each element. Using an array has the additional advantage of keeping all the text for the options used in the menu at the beginning of the program where they are easy to locate and modify.

The first command in the sequence specifies the number of prompts that will appear on the menu. In this case there will be four, three for the programs, and one for exiting the menu. Relating the DECLARE command to the value of PROMPTS means that if you should expand the menu, you must change only the value of PROMPTS to increase the number of elements in the array. Enter the following commands.

```
PROMPTS=4
DECLARE Option[Prompts]
Option[1]="Enter New Admission Records"
Option[2]="Edit Existing Records"
Option[3]="Enter ICU Care Days"
Option[4]="Exit Menu"
```

The next section of the program starts an automatic loop. The loop will continue until you specifically select to exit the menu.

```
DO WHILE .T.
```

When the loop begins, clear the screen, place a heading at the top of the display, and initialize a variable called START to 1. This variable selects the element in the OPTION array for displays.

```
CLEAR
action=0
@ 2,25 SAY "Admission File Menu"
@ 3,0 SAY REPLICATE(CHAR(196),79)
Start=1
```

Because the prompts for our menu have been stored in an array, you can use a loop to display the items in the menu. Using a loop to per-

The Standard Menu ■ 259

form this action makes it easy to expand the number of options in the menu by simply increasing the number of elements in the array.

The Start variable serves three functions in this loop.

1. **Control loop.** The Start variable controls the number of cycles the loop goes through. It appears in the expression Start<=Prompts to terminate the loop after all the elements in the array have been processed.

2. **Number options.** The Start variable also numbers the options that appear on the menu. A user enters this number to select one of the options.

3. **Array element.** The Start variable will also select elements in the option array.

The following five commands create a loop that displays the menu options. If the number of elements in the array increases, the loop simply repeats more times. It is not necessary to add additional commands. This is the advantage of using an array.

```
DO WHILE Start<=Prompts
@ ROW()+1,25 SAY STR(Start,1)
@ ROW(),COL()+1 SAY "."+SPACE(1)+Option[Start]
Start=Start+1
     ENDDO
```

Following the display of the option, you have to allow the user to enter a choice. The choice is recorded by allowing the user to enter a single digit corresponding to the options listed on the menu. In this example, the variable Action captures the user's input.

The code that creates the input area for Action contains some special items. First, the CHR() function displays a character in the IBM extended character set that looks like an arrow pointing to the right. In addition, a FUNCTION clause, Z, formats the input area. The Z function displays a zero value as a blank. Because Action is initialized as zero, the Z function suppresses the display of the zero and shows a blank instead.

```
@ ROW()+1,0 SAY REPLICATE(CHR(196),79)
@ ROW()+1,25 SAY "Enter Selection"+CHR(16)
GET Action FUNCTION "Z"
PICTURE "9"
READ
```

Once the entry has been made into the Action input area, the program must evaluate the entry and branch to the corresponding subroutine. This is accomplished with a DO CASE structure. Each case in the structure tests the value of action for a specific value from 1 to 4. The first three cases branch to subroutines. The final case terminates the loop with an EXIT command.

```
DO CASE
CASE Action=1
     DO Entry
CASE Action=2
     DO Edit
CASE Action=3
     DO Addicu
CASE Action=4
     EXIT
     ENDCASE
```

When the subroutine ends, dBASE IV returns to the calling program and continues reading commands following ENDCASE. Here, you want to redisplay the menu and allow the user to make additional selections from the menu, so enter an ENDDO command.

```
ENDDO
```

The loop continues until 4 is pressed, activating the EXIT command and terminating the automatic loop. Conclude the program with the environment reset commands.

```
SET STATUS ON
SET SCOREBOARD ON
SET TALK ON
RETURN
```

Save and execute the program by pressing (Alt)-e and typing r. The menu displays the four options created as part of the menu (see Figure 6.1).

Select the first option on the menu, **Enter new records,** by pressing 1. Because you "pictured" the variable as only a single character, it was not necessary to press (↵).

The program branches to the subroutine Entry and displays the entry screen for a new record.

The Standard Menu ■ 261

Figure 6.1

```
                    Admmssion File Menu
               ─────────────────────────────
                    1 . Enter New Addmission Records
                    2 . Edit Existing Records
                    3 . Enter ICU Care Days
                    4 . Exit Menu
               ─────────────────────────────
                    Enter Selection▶ ▮
```

Exit the Entry program by pressing Ctrl-End and typing n.

The Entry program ends and control passes back to the Admitmnu program. Since the DO WHILE loop is still active in the Admitmnu program, the menu is redisplayed on the screen (see Figure 6.2).

But something is wrong with the menu. It appears more spread out than before. In addition, a set of numbers appears along the left side of the menu and the status bar is displayed. Why?

The answer has to do with the subroutines that you are using. The Entry, Edit, and Addicu programs have commands that reactivate the status bar, scoreboard, and talk functions at the end of each program. Because these programs were originally conceived as stand-alone modules, the environment setting commands that made sense in those programs cause a problem when the modules are accessed as subroutines.

Figure 6.2

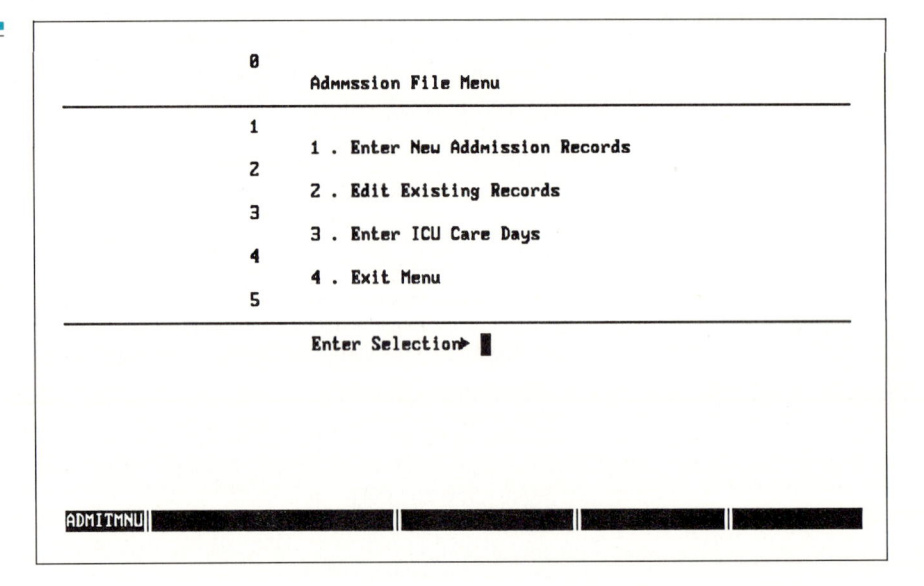

```
                  0
                            Admmssion File Menu
                  ─────────────────────────────
                  1
                            1 . Enter New Addmission Records
                  2
                            2 . Edit Existing Records
                  3
                            3 . Enter ICU Care Days
                  4
                            4 . Exit Menu
                  5
                  ─────────────────────────────
                            Enter Selection▶ ▮




  ▌ADMITMNU▐        ▐         ▐         ▐         ▐
```

262 ■ Menus and Debugging

One solution is to edit the subroutines and remove the set commands. When you are using a number of subroutine programs, it is not necessary for each routine to set the environment. This is usually done in the main program only, and establishes an environment that stays in effect for all of the subroutines.

However, in this case it is simpler to include the SET commands as part of the loop. In this way the environment can be set each time a subroutine terminates.

Exit the current menu by pressing 4.

Load the Admitmnu program into the editor by entering

`MODIFY COMMAND Admitmnu`

Move the cursor to line 34. Insert the SET commands at the bottom of this loop. When the subroutine is complete, dBASE IV will execute the next command following ENDCASE. This is where you want to place the commands to reset the environment. Try this on your own. If you need help, the correct command can be found at the end of the chapter in the Answers to Exercises section under exercise 1.

Save and execute the program by pressing (Alt)-e and typing r. The menu appears correctly. Now run the Addicu program from the menu by pressing 3.

The program asks you to select the month. Enter

d

Skip the records by pressing (PgDn) two times.

This time when you return to the menu, it displays properly.

Implicit Exit

In chapter 5 you became familiar with the idea of an implicit command to exit a loop. An implicit command is one that is inferred from an entry. In the case of the Admitmnu program, you require the user to enter the value of 4 in order to terminate the program. But suppose the user pressed (↵) instead of a number. You could conclude that the user meant to exit the menu. This means that pressing (↵) is an implicit exit command. You can adjust the Admitmnu program to respond to either the explicit exit command, 4, or an implicit entry command, (↵).

Load the Admitmnu program by entering

`MODIFY COMMAND Admitmnu`

The Standard Menu ■ 263

Move the cursor to line 9. Change the prompt to indicate that pressing ⏎ will exit the menu. Instead of using the word "return" you might want to display a symbol that looks like the ⏎ symbol used on many PC keyboards. You can do this by using three characters found in the IBM extended character set, characters 17, 196, and 217.

Old line: `Option[4]="Exit Menu"`

New line: `Option[4]="Exit Menu - Press;`
           `"+CHR(17); +CHR(196)+CHR(217)`

The next command you need to edit is the CASE command that controls exiting. Move the cursor to line 32.

The logical expression used with the CASE command should be changed to include an action value of 0 as well as a value of 4.

Old line: `CASE action=4`

New line: `CASE action=4.or.action=0`

Save and execute the program by pressing Alt-e and typing r. The menu appears with the symbol for the ⏎ key included (see Figure 6.3).

To exit the program press ⏎. The program now accepts ⏎ as an implicit command to exit the menu.

Menu Modification

The second goal of the Admitmnu program was to create a menu program that could be easily adapted to operate with any group of subroutines. Suppose you want to create a second menu program to run the statistical programs Insured, Ages, and Countins. It would not be necessary to create a new menu program from scratch. You could simply modify a copy of the Admitmnu program so that it executed the statistical programs rather than the data entry programs currently used by Admitmnu.

Begin by creating a new program called Statsmnu (statistic menu).

`MODIFY COMMAND Statsmnu`

Figure 6.3

```
Admmssion File Menu

    1 . Enter New Addmission Records
    2 . Edit Existing Records
    3 . Enter ICU Care Days
    4 . Exit Menu - Press ⏎

Enter Selection▶
```

264 ■ Menus and Debugging

You can avoid entering the entire program by loading a copy of the Admitmnu program into the editor. Press (Alt)-w and type w r.

```
Admitmnu.prg
```

What changes must be made for this program to function as the statistical menu? You need to change two parts: the text used for the title, and options 1 through 3. These menu lines should read as follows:

Admission Statistics Menu

List Insurance Status

Distribution of Patient Ages

Distribution of Insurance Classifications

Option 1 should run the Insured program, option 2 the Ages program, and option 3 the Countins program. Try this on your own. If you need help, the correct command can be found at the end of the chapter in the Answers to Exercises section under exercise 2.

When you have completed the modifications, save and execute the new program by pressing (Alt)-e and typing r. The program displays the new menu options in the same format (see Figure 6.4).

Execute the Ages program by pressing 2.

The summary of the distribution of patient ages is displayed on the screen. Return to the menu by pressing (↵).

Exit the Statsmnu program by pressing (↵).

A Menu That Runs Menus

So far in this chapter, you have created two menu programs that coordinate the execution of programs. A menu program can also tie together other menu programs. For example, suppose you want to create a master menu program that would provide the user with access to either the Admitmnu or the Statsmnu menu. This master menu would use the two other menu programs as subroutines.

Figure 6.4

```
               Admission Statistics Menu
               ─────────────────────────
               1 . List Insurance Status
               2 . Distribution of Patient Ages
               3 . Distribution of Insurance Classifications
               4 . Exit Menu - Press ↵

               Enter Selection▶ ▌
```

The Standard Menu ■ 265

You can begin by creating a new program called Mainmnu (main menu) by entering

`MODIFY COMMAND Mainmnu`

Load a copy of one of the previous menu programs into the editor by pressing (Alt)-W and typing W r. Then enter

`Admitmnu.prg`

Move the cursor to line 6. Change the next two lines to display options for running the two menu programs you have already created.

Old line:	`OPTION[1]="Enter New Admission Records"`
New line:	`OPTION[1]="Patient Data Entry"`
Old line:	`OPTION[2]="Edit Existing Records"`
New line:	`OPTION[2]="Patient Statistics"`

Since this menu has only two options, you can delete option 3. Move the cursor line 8. Press (Ctrl)-y.

The next two lines need to be modified to work with a three-option menu.

Old line:	`OPTION[4]="Exit Menu - Press;`
	`"+CHR(17)+CHR(196)+CHR(217)`
New line:	`OPTION[3]="Exit Menu - Press;`
	`"+CHR(17)+CHR(196)+CHR(217)`

Move the cursor to line 4 and change that line to:

Old line:	`Prompts=4`
New line:	`Prompts=3`

Move the cursor to line 12. Change the title of the menu.

Old line:	`@ 2,25 SAY "Admission File Menu"`
New line:	`@ 2,25 SAY "Main Menu"`

Move the cursor to line 26. Change the name of the subroutine from Entry to Admitmnu.

Old line:	`DO Entry`
New line:	`DO Admitmnu`

Move the cursor to line 28 and change the name of the program from Edit to Statsmnu.

Old line: `DO Edit`

New line: `DO Statsmnu`

Move the cursor to line 29 and delete the next two lines by pressing Ctrl-y two times.

The last change alters the option number in the final CASE from 4 to 3.

Old line: `CASE Action=4.OR.action=0`

New line: `CASE Action=3.OR.action=0`

Save and execute the program by pressing Alt-e and typing r. The main menu appears with options that will access the other two menu programs (see Figure 6.5).

Press 2. The Statsmnu program executes and displays its menu. To return to the main menu, press ⏎.

What does the screen show? The display is labeled Main Menu, but the options are not those of the Main Menu but those of the Statsmnu program.

Exit the menu by pressing ⏎.

Why didn't the menus work correctly? Is there something wrong with the programs?

It seems unlikely that the programs are incorrect because all three of the programs involved have run individually without error. In fact all three programs use exactly the same structure because they were created by making copies of the first menu program, Admitmnu.

However, it is clear that when the three programs are combined something is not correct. The menu options from the Get menu were mixed up with the menu options from the subroutine. What caused this problem and how can it be corrected?

Figure 6.5

```
                    Main Menu
_____
                 1 . Patient Data Entry
                 2 . Patient Statistics
                 3 . Exit Menu - Press ⏎
_____
                 Enter Selection▶ ▌
```

Debugging a Program

Rather than simply divulge the answer, we'll use this opportunity to learn how to use the tools provided by dBASE IV for situations just like this. The DEBUG command lets you operate your programs in a debugging mode. This mode allows you to examine a program as each command executes. The DEBUG command is a powerful tool for finding problems in programs. Learning to use DEBUG can save you a tremendous amount of time when you are trying to isolate a problem in a program or series of programs with subroutines.

To enter the debug mode, use the DEBUG command along with the name of the program you want to debug.

```
DEBUG Mainmnu
```

dBASE IV displays the debug screen display. The screen is divided into five different windows (see Figure 6.6).

1. **Program list.** The window that appears in the top left portion of the screen is the program listing window. It shows the commands in the program that you are debugging. The name of the program appears on the left side of the window's top border. Each command is num-

Figure 6.6

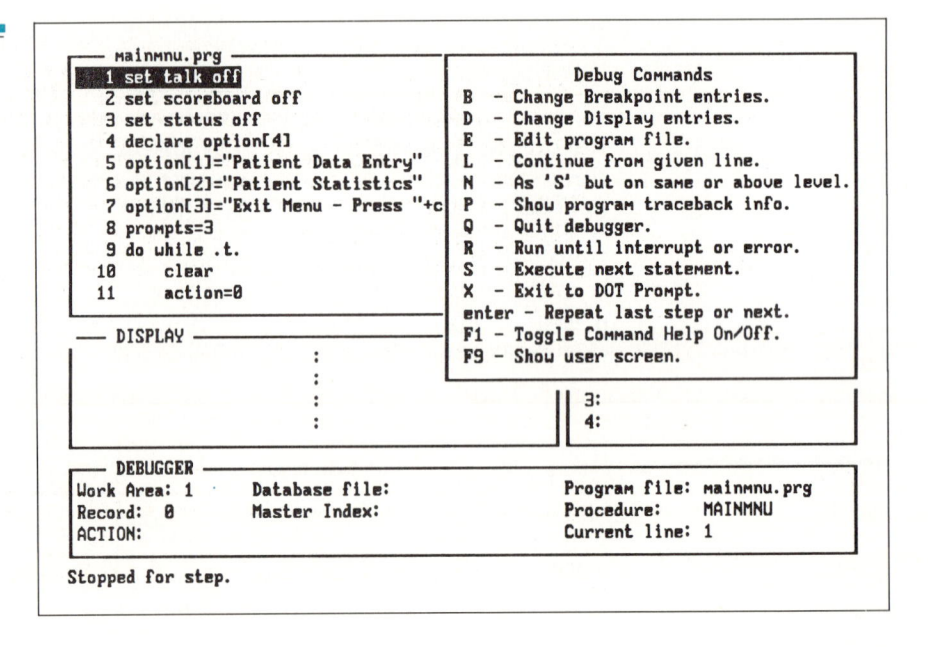

```
┌─ mainmnu.prg ──────────────────────┐┌──────────────────────────────────┐
│ 1 set talk off                     ││         Debug Commands           │
│ 2 set scoreboard off               ││ B - Change Breakpoint entries.   │
│ 3 set status off                   ││ D - Change Display entries.      │
│ 4 declare option[4]                ││ E - Edit program file.           │
│ 5 option[1]="Patient Data Entry"   ││ L - Continue from given line.    │
│ 6 option[2]="Patient Statistics"   ││ N - As 'S' but on same or above level. │
│ 7 option[3]="Exit Menu - Press "+c ││ P - Show program traceback info. │
│ 8 prompts=3                        ││ Q - Quit debugger.               │
│ 9 do while .t.                     ││ R - Run until interrupt or error.│
│ 10    clear                        ││ S - Execute next statement.      │
│ 11    action=0                     ││ X - Exit to DOT Prompt.          │
│                                    ││ enter - Repeat last step or next.│
┌─ DISPLAY ──────────────────────────┐│ F1 - Toggle Command Help On/Off. │
│                              :     ││ F9 - Show user screen.           │
│                              :     │└──────────────────────────────────┘
│                              :     │   3:
│                              :     │   4:
┌─ DEBUGGER ─────────────────────────────────────────────────────────────┐
│ Work Area: 1    Database file:        Program file: mainmnu.prg         │
│ Record:    0    Master Index:         Procedure:    MAINMNU             │
│ ACTION:                               Current line: 1                   │
└────────────────────────────────────────────────────────────────────────┘
  Stopped for step.
```

268 ■ **Menus and Debugging**

bered to make reference simpler. The command that is about to execute is highlighted.

2. **Help.** The window that appears in the upper right corner of the screen is the help window. It is automatically displayed when you enter the debugging mode but will be removed as soon as you enter your first command. Pressing (F1) redisplays this window.

3. **Display.** The display window shows the current value of specified fields, variables, or system functions. This window is updated each time a command executes. It allows you to see how various commands affect the values that control your program.

4. **Breakpoints.** The breakpoint window is positioned next to the display window (and is completely hidden by the help window at this moment). The breakpoint window is used to enter one or more logical expressions that will serve as breakpoints for the program during debugging.

5. **Debugger.** The debugger window is positioned at the bottom of the screen. This window shows the current work area (work areas are discussed in chapter 8 on multiple databases), database file, record number, master index, program file, procedure name (discussed later in this chapter), and program line number.

The cursor is positioned in the debugger window next to a prompt called **Action.** All the actions you can take in the debugger are single-letter commands, plus (F1) for help and (F9) to display the program screen, and the up and down arrow keys to select the next or previous line.

Pressing (↵) tells dBASE IV to execute the highlighted command. Press (↵).

Pressing (↵) executes command line 1 in the program. It also causes dBASE IV to remove the help window and reveal the full program and breakpoint windows.

The highlight bar now moves to the next command and awaits your instruction. Execute the next 13 commands by pressing (↵) 13 times.

The debugger is now positioned on line 15, the DO WHILE command (see Figure 6.7).

When the debugger is active, you cannot see the screen as it looks when the program is actually running. You can toggle between the screen display and the debugger display by using the (F9) key. Press (F9).

Figure 6.7

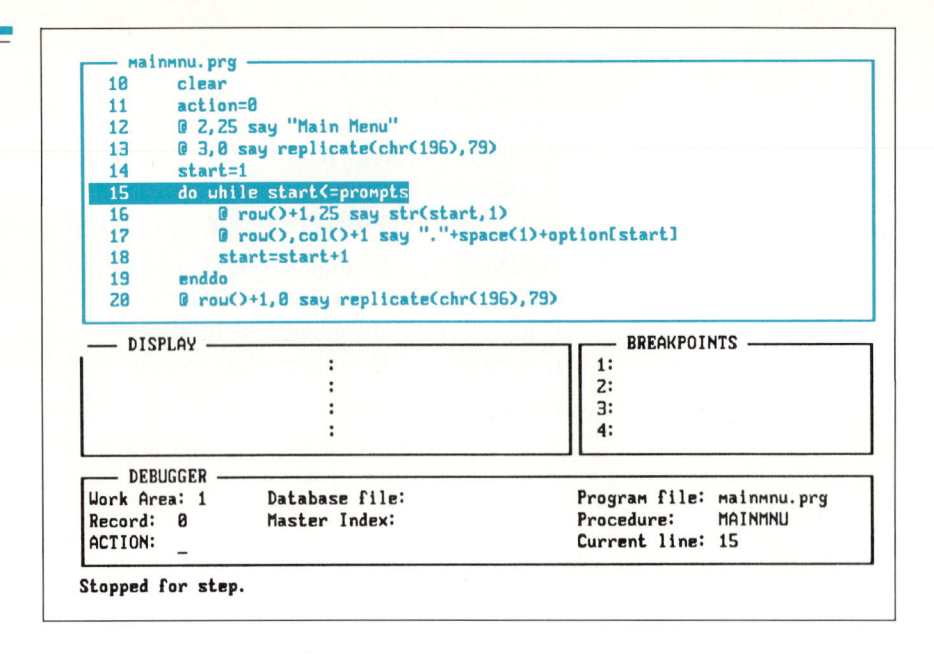

```
┌─ Mainmnu.prg ──────────────────────────────────────┐
│  10    clear                                        │
│  11    action=0                                     │
│  12    @ 2,25 say "Main Menu"                       │
│  13    @ 3,0 say replicate(chr(196),79)             │
│  14    start=1                                      │
│  15    do while start<=prompts                      │
│  16        @ row()+1,25 say str(start,1)            │
│  17        @ row(),col()+1 say "."+space(1)+option[start]│
│  18        start=start+1                            │
│  19    enddo                                        │
│  20    @ row()+1,0 say replicate(chr(196),79)       │
└─────────────────────────────────────────────────────┘
┌─ DISPLAY ──────────────────┐  ┌─ BREAKPOINTS ──────┐
│                    :       │  │ 1:                 │
│                    :       │  │ 2:                 │
│                    :       │  │ 3:                 │
│                    :       │  │ 4:                 │
└────────────────────────────┘  └────────────────────┘
┌─ DEBUGGER ──────────────────────────────────────────┐
│ Work Area: 1    Database file:     Program file: mainmnu.prg│
│ Record:    0    Master Index:      Procedure:    MAINMNU│
│ ACTION:    _                       Current line: 15 │
└─────────────────────────────────────────────────────┘
Stopped for step.
```

dBASE IV displays the screen display as it would appear after 14 commands in the Mainmnu program.

Return to the debugger display by pressing [F9].

Displaying Values in Debug

One of the most important functions of the debugger is its ability to display the value of certain key fields, system functions, or variables as each command executes. The reason you are debugging this program is that something goes wrong with the main menu when you return from one of the submenus. In order to find out exactly what goes wrong, you might want to monitor the status of some key elements in the program.

In the case of the menu programs, the values of the variables Start, Prompts, Action, and Option control the way the program behaves. You might gain some insight into the problem by observing how these values are affected by the commands in the program.

The display window allows you to keep track of 10 variables while the program is running. This window will show only four of the values at any one moment; you will have to scroll the display window to see the other values. You can enter valid dBASE IV expressions as display items.

To display values press

d

The highlight bar and the cursor move to the display window. Enter the values or expressions that you want to track.

PROMPTS

ACTION

START

OPTION[Start]

Move the highlight bar to the top of the display window by pressing (PgUp).

The right side of the window displays the current values of these expressions (see Figure 6.8).

Return to the debugger window by pressing (Esc).

Advance the program four more commands. Press (↵) four times.

If you look at the display window, the value of Start and OPTION[Start] have changed because line 18, Start=Start+1, has just executed.

Figure 6.8

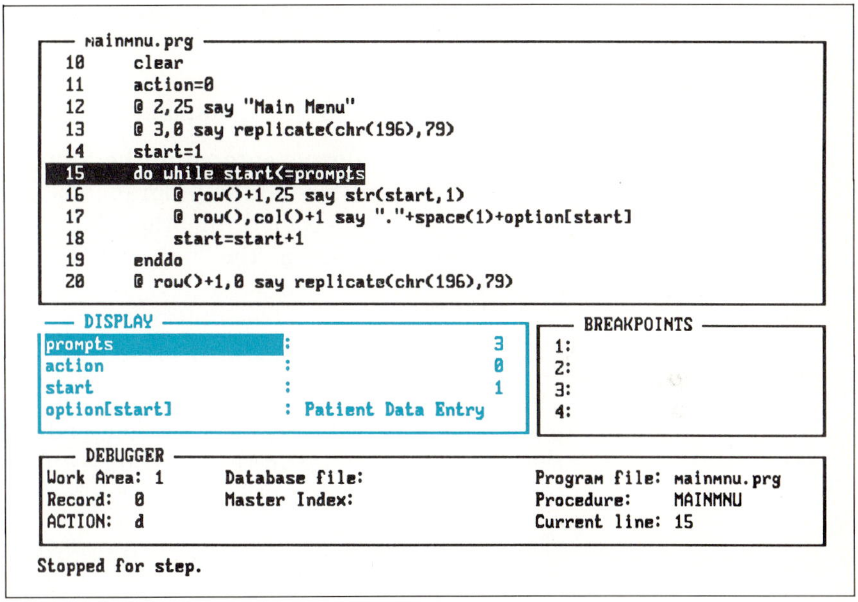

```
── mainmnu.prg ──
10    clear
11    action=0
12    @ 2,25 say "Main Menu"
13    @ 3,0 say replicate(chr(196),79)
14    start=1
15    do while start<=prompts
16       @ row()+1,25 say str(start,1)
17       @ row(),col()+1 say "."+space(1)+option[start]
18       start=start+1
19    enddo
20    @ row()+1,0 say replicate(chr(196),79)
```

```
── DISPLAY ──                              ── BREAKPOINTS ──
prompts          :              3          1:
action           :              0          2:
start            :              1          3:
option[start]    : Patient Data Entry      4:

── DEBUGGER ──
Work Area: 1    Database file:       Program file: mainmnu.prg
Record:    0    Master Index:        Procedure:    MAINMNU
ACTION:    d                         Current line: 15

Stopped for step.
```

Debugging a Program ■ 271

The program window highlight bar is located at line 19, the ENDDO command. Press ⏎.

The ENDDO command, a loop instruction, causes the program highlight bar to move backwards to command 15. The debugger demonstrates visibly the effect of a loop. You can learn a lot about the way a program actually works by watching it in the debugger.

Breakpoints

While it is sometimes necessary to step though each command in a program while debugging, this is often a tedious chore. In order to make it easier to concentrate on those points in the program that really affect the outcome, you can set breakpoints. A breakpoint is a device to break, or stop, a program's run at the point, or place, in the program where it appears. In the dBASE IV debugger, a breakpoint uses a logical expression. The debugger halts the program as soon as that expression is true.

For example, the loop that is currently executing will repeat three more times. It would be more convenient to allow the program to process automatically until it reaches a point where you might expect some important development. In this case, you might want the program to run until one of the key variables changes.

You can accomplish this by setting a breakpoint or breakpoints. To access the breakpoint window, press

b

The cursor moves to the breakpoint window (see Figure 6.9).

A breakpoint is always entered in the form of a logical expression. In this case we want to stop the program when the value of the Action variable changes to something other than zero. The expression below uses the # sign to act as the "not equal to" symbol. Enter

`ACTION#0`

Exit the breakpoint window by pressing Esc.

The breakpoint is now set for a specific condition. Once the breakpoint is set, you will enter the R command. The R command, run, tells the debugger to run the program as if you were in normal program execution mode until the breakpoint condition is true. Press r.

The program displays the main menu exactly as it would during normal execution. Enter option 2 to run the Statsmnu program.

■ **Menus and Debugging**

Figure 6.9

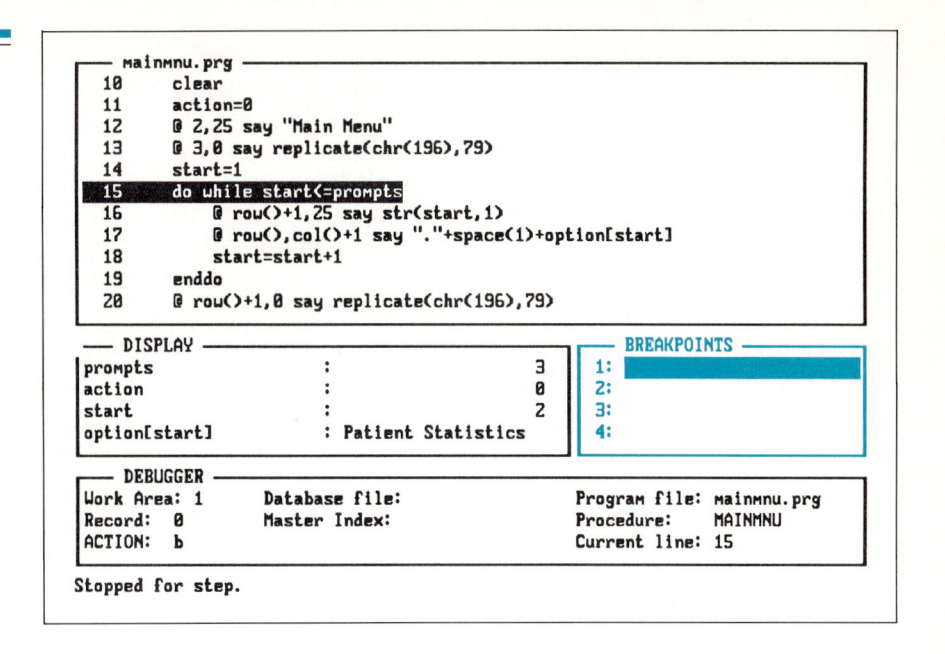

```
┌─ mainmnu.prg ─────────────────────────────────────────────┐
│  10      clear                                             │
│  11      action=0                                          │
│  12      @ 2,25 say "Main Menu"                            │
│  13      @ 3,0 say replicate(chr(196),79)                  │
│  14      start=1                                           │
│  15      do while start<=prompts                           │
│  16         @ row()+1,25 say str(start,1)                  │
│  17         @ row(),col()+1 say "."+space(1)+option[start] │
│  18         start=start+1                                  │
│  19      enddo                                             │
│  20      @ row()+1,0 say replicate(chr(196),79)            │
├─ DISPLAY ──────────────────────────┬─ BREAKPOINTS ─────────┤
│ prompts            :           3   │ 1:                    │
│ action             :           0   │ 2:                    │
│ start              :           2   │ 3:                    │
│ option[start]      : Patient Statistics │ 4:               │
├─ DEBUGGER ─────────────────────────┴───────────────────────┤
│ Work Area: 1    Database file:        Program file: mainmnu.prg │
│ Record:    0    Master Index:         Procedure:    MAINMNU │
│ ACTION:    b                          Current line: 15     │
├────────────────────────────────────────────────────────────┤
│ Stopped for step.                                          │
└────────────────────────────────────────────────────────────┘
```

Following your entry, dBASE IV will return to the debugger screen. Why? The answer is that your entry changed the value of the action variable from zero to 2. Since your breakpoint was set for "action is not equal to zero," the debugger halts the program and returns to the debugging mode (see Figure 6.10).

The highlight bar in the command window is now located on the DO CASE command. Execute the DO CASE by pressing ⏎ three times.

The highlight bar jumps to line 27. The DO CASE command selects the CASE Action = 2 choice based on your entry. The highlight bar is on the command DO Statsmnu. When this command executes, control shifts to the subroutine program. Press ⏎ four times.

The debugger screen now displays the commands in the subroutine file, Statsmnu.

The breakpoint is still set for Action#0. You need to think about the problem you encounter with this program and where it occurs. When you ran the program before, the problem occurred when you tried to return to the main menu from the Statsmnu subroutine. One way to find the problem is to examine the state of the system at the point when dBASE IV switches control back to the Mainmnu program.

Debugging a Program ■ 273

Figure 6.10

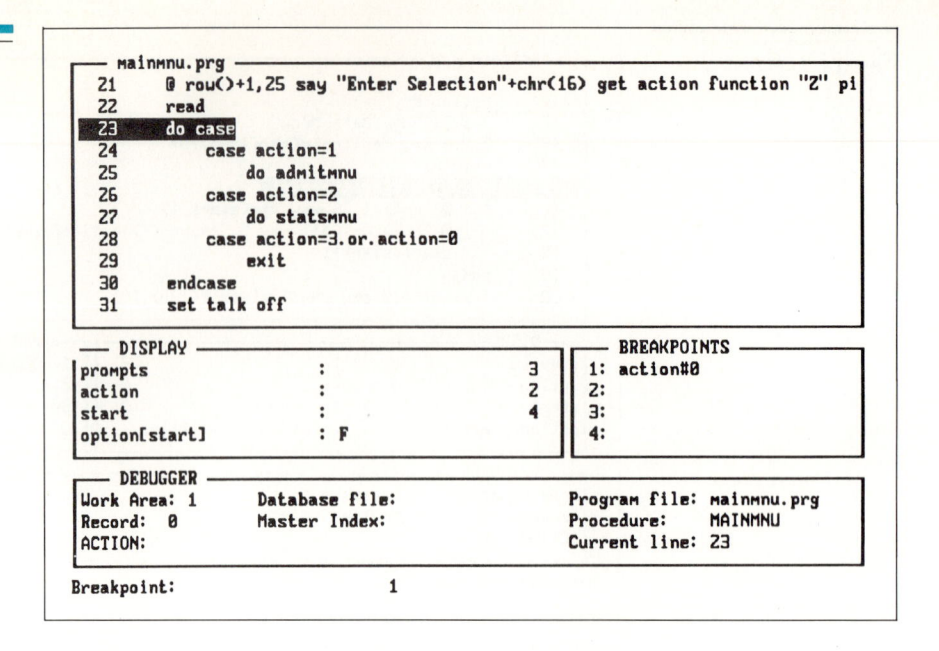

```
┌─ mainmnu.prg ─────────────────────────────────────────────────────┐
│  21      @ row()+1,25 say "Enter Selection"+chr(16) get action function "Z" pi │
│  22      read                                                      │
│  23      do case                                                   │
│  24          case action=1                                         │
│  25              do admitmnu                                       │
│  26          case action=2                                         │
│  27              do statsmnu                                       │
│  28          case action=3.or.action=0                             │
│  29              exit                                              │
│  30      endcase                                                   │
│  31      set talk off                                              │
└────────────────────────────────────────────────────────────────────┘
┌─ DISPLAY ──────────────────────────┐ ┌─ BREAKPOINTS ──────────────┐
│ prompts           :          3     │ │ 1: action#0                │
│ action            :          2     │ │ 2:                         │
│ start             :          4     │ │ 3:                         │
│ option[start]     : F              │ │ 4:                         │
└────────────────────────────────────┘ └────────────────────────────┘
┌─ DEBUGGER ─────────────────────────────────────────────────────────┐
│ Work Area: 1      Database file:         Program file: mainmnu.prg │
│ Record:    0      Master Index:          Procedure:    MAINMNU     │
│ ACTION:                                  Current line: 23          │
│                                                                    │
│ Breakpoint:                   1                                    │
└────────────────────────────────────────────────────────────────────┘
```

How can you set a breakpoint to halt the program at that point? dBASE IV has a system function called PROGRAM(). This function returns the name of the currently executing program. You could create a breakpoint expression that reads PROGRAM()="Mainmnu".

Note: The program name should always be in upper-case characters.

This expression would stop execution as soon as control switched back to the Mainmnu module. Create this breakpoint by entering

b

PROGRAM()="Mainmnu"

and pressing (Esc). Run the program by pressing r. The Statsmnu menu displays as it would be during normal execution. To duplicate the problem you encountered when you were running the program, press ⏎ just as you did when you ran the program before.

The debugger halts the program at the point where control returns to the Mainmnu program (see Figure 6.11).

You have now returned to the main program. Look at the debugger's display area. You will see that the value of Action is zero because the subroutine Statsmnu changed the value of the variable. When the

Figure 6.11

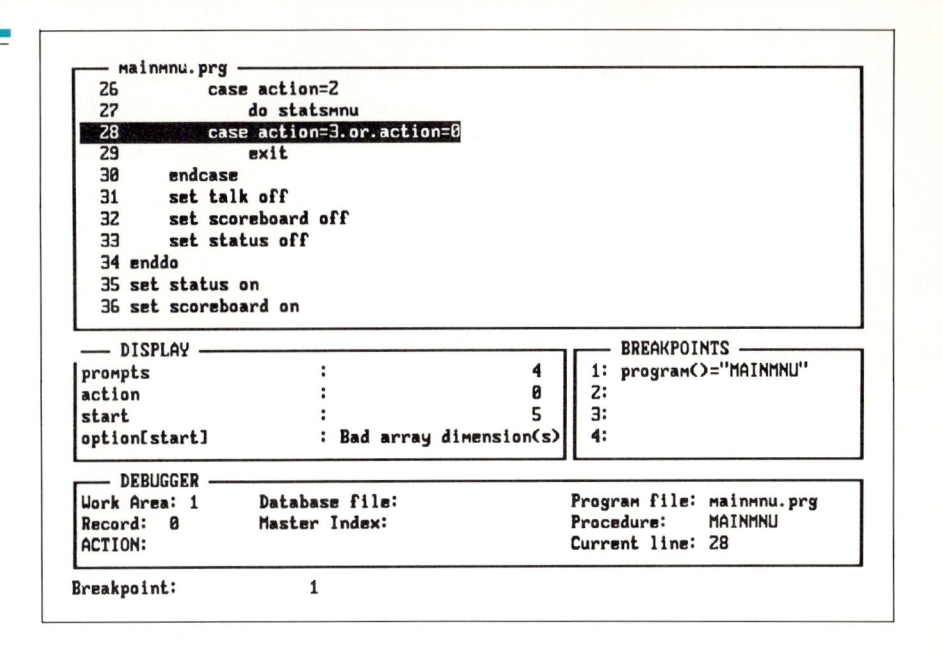

```
┌─ mainmnu.prg ─────────────────────────────────────────┐
│ 26          case action=2                             │
│ 27             do statsmnu                            │
│ 28          case action=3.or.action=0                 │
│ 29             exit                                   │
│ 30          endcase                                   │
│ 31          set talk off                              │
│ 32          set scoreboard off                        │
│ 33          set status off                            │
│ 34 enddo                                              │
│ 35 set status on                                      │
│ 36 set scoreboard on                                  │
└───────────────────────────────────────────────────────┘
┌─ DISPLAY ──────────────────────────┐┌─ BREAKPOINTS ───┐
│ prompts          :            4    ││ 1: program()="MAINMNU" │
│ action           :            0    ││ 2:              │
│ start            :            5    ││ 3:              │
│ option[start]    : Bad array dimension(s) ││ 4:       │
└────────────────────────────────────┘└─────────────────┘
┌─ DEBUGGER ────────────────────────────────────────────┐
│ Work Area: 1   Database file:      Program file: mainmnu.prg │
│ Record:    0   Master Index:       Procedure:    MAINMNU     │
│ ACTION:                            Current line: 28          │
│                                                       │
│ Breakpoint:          1                                │
└───────────────────────────────────────────────────────┘
```

Mainmnu program called the subroutine Statsmnu, the value of Action was 2. During the Statsmnu program, dBASE IV encountered commands that changed the value of Action. When the Statsmnu program terminated and control returned to the Mainmnu program, the action variable maintained this last value. Execute the next five commands by pressing ⏎ five times.

The Mainmnu program has recycled to the top of the DO WHILE loop. This may seem odd because the value of Action was zero and the program was designed to exit if the value of Action was zero. But the DO CASE structure in Mainmnu had already chosen an option when it ran the Statsmnu subroutine. Since a DO CASE only selects one of the cases each time it is activated, the current value of Action has no effect. The DO CASE will not select an option until the loop cycles again. The net effect is exactly what you desire—the program will redisplay the menu and allow you to choose another option.

Dot Command Access

In the previous section you saw how a subroutine changed the value of the Action variable so that when program control returned to the main menu routine, Action had a different value. If Action changed, what has happened to the other variables? Have they changed? Will the changes affect the Mainmnu program?

These questions are at the heart of the problem with our menus. The debugger display window also shows that the Prompts value is now 4 rather than the original value of 3. Would this change affect the way Mainmnu operates? The answer is yes. Remember that the number of menu options displayed is controlled by the value of Prompts. The Mainmnu program has only three options. The value of prompts must be 3 in order for this program to function correctly. The fact that the value is currently 4 means that Mainmnu will operate incorrectly, if at all.

What other variables have been affected by subroutines? The debugger provides a way to suspend debugging and exit to the dot prompt where you can enter as many dBASE IV commands as you need to analyze the current status of a program. The X (exit) command provides access to the dot prompt. This exit command does not terminate either the program or the debugger. Rather, it suspends the debugging process until you enter the RESUME command at the dot prompt. RESUME then reactivates the debugger at exactly the point you exited. Press x.

The dot prompt appears. You can now enter commands. The command you are most interested in is DISPLAY MEMORY, since it is the status of memory variables that you are concerned about. Enter

DISPLAY MEMORY

The display shows the current status of all memory variables (see Figure 6.12). This display is a bit different from the memory display shown when no program was running. There are two very important differences.

1. **Private.** If you look at the variable names, you will notice that to the right of the name the word **priv** appears. **Priv** is an abbreviation for private. You may not have noticed but when you create a memory variable at the dot prompt, dBASE IV inserts the word **pub** next to the variable name. **Pub** means public. What is the difference between public and private variables?

    Private variables are created when dBASE IV executes a program. They are associated with the program commands STORE or DECLARE that define variables. dBASE IV automatically erases these variables when the program that created the variables terminates. This means that when a program ends, all of the memory variables used by that program are erased from memory.

Figure 6.12

```
            User Memory Variables

    START       priv   N        5  (5.000000000000000000)   MAINMNU @ mainmnu.prg
    ACTION      priv   N        0  (0.000000000000000000)   MAINMNU @ mainmnu.prg
    OPTION      elem   A    [4]
      [1]       elem   C   "List Insurance Status"     MAINMNU @ mainmnu.prg
      [2]       elem   C   "Distribution of Patient Ages"    MAINMNU @ mainmnu.prg
      [3]       elem   C   "Distribution of Insurance Classifications"   MAINMNU @ mai
    nmnu.prg
      [4]       elem   C   "Exit Menu"    MAINMNU @ mainmnu.prg
    PROMPTS     priv   N        5  (4.000000000000000000)   MAINMNU @ mainmnu.prg

         4 out of 500 memvars defined (and 4 array elements)

              User MEMVAR/RTSYM Memory Usage

     2800 bytes used for 1 memvar blocks (max=10)
      850 bytes used for 1 rtsym blocks (max=10)
      224 bytes used for 4 array element memvars
       99 bytes used for 4 memvar character strings

     3973 bytes total

    Press any key to continue...
```

A public variable, created at the dot prompt, operates like the dBASE IV system variables DATE(), EOF(), and so on, in that they are maintained at all times until you CLEAR them from the memory.

2. **Program name.** On the right end of each variable line, following its value, dBASE IV displays the name of the program that created the variable. For example, the Start variable shows Mainmnu @ Mainmnu.prg. This identifies the variable start as being associated with the Mainmnu program.

   Note: The notation dBASE IV uses to identify the source program for a variable is written as *"procedure @ program."* dBASE IV allows you to define up to 32 procedures within a program file. When a program has no procedures, dBASE IV assigns the program name as the procedure name. This is why Mainmnu appears twice. Procedures are discussed later in this chapter.

All of the variables on the display are associated with the Mainmnu program. However, if you look at the text in the OPTION array, you will see that they are the options used in the Statsmnu program, not the ones needed for the Mainmnu program. This is the source of the problem with the execution of these programs. Because all the programs use the same memory variable names, OPTION[Start], the

Debugging a Program ■ 277

subroutines change the original values. When the program returns to the main routine, the values of the OPTION[] variables no longer match up with the main program's needs, creating the wrong menu display.

The debugging process has revealed how the connections between the programs cause the problem you encountered. The Admitmnu or Statsmnu programs individually do not cause problems because none of their subroutines have variable names in common. But when you use three menu programs all with the same variable names, conflicts can arise.

To make the program run correctly, you must revise the programs to avoid memory variable conflicts.

Now that you have located the problem, you can return to the debugger. Return to the dot prompt by pressing (Esc).

Resume the debugger by entering

RESUME

Exit the debugger with the Q (quit) command. Press q.

> *Note:* Remember that Q quits the debugger while X only suspends the debugger.

Private Variables

You have now used the debugger to identify a flaw in the logic of your programs. Next, you need to find a way to prevent the values used in the subroutines from affecting the values used in higher-level routines. In the case of the Mainmnu program, you need to differentiate between the OPTION array values for Mainmnu, Statsmnu, and Admitmnu. Because all three programs are largely duplicates of each other, the memory variable names are exactly the same in each program. Only the value assigned to these variables is different.

One solution would be to edit each of the programs and enter names that will not conflict. For example, you might change the variable name Prompts in Statsmnu to Pmtsstats (prompts for statistics). This solution has a number of significant drawbacks.

Changing the variable names is tedious and time-consuming. When you change the name of a variable, you not only have to change its initial use, but every command in the program that refers to that variable as well. If you forget to change any of the references, an error will occur.

Changing all the variables names in a program would negate much of the advantage of trying to write programs that can be copied and quickly modified. If each program requires a unique set of variable names to avoid conflict, it would be just as simple to write the programs from scratch.

Even if you accepted the task of editing the programs to make the variable names unique, these is no guarantee that you will actually do so. You might forget that you had used a variable name in a subroutine, which would lead to a conflict. If you are using unique names in many programs, the list of variable names you have to remember will quickly become enormous.

What is the best solution? The answer lies in something that you saw during the debugging process—the concept of a private variable. Privacy of variables causes dBASE IV to associate a variable with a specific program. For example, a private variable called Prompts created in the Statsmnu program would carry the label Prompts Statsmnu @ Statsmnu.prg. The same variable name created in the Mainmnu program would be Prompts Mainmnu @ Mainmnu.prg. dBASE IV would be able to avoid conflicts by using the program name to differentiate between variables of the same name.

Why didn't this happen automatically when you ran the programs before? The reason is sequence. When a variable is defined as private, it will be erased when the program ends. But when you run a subroutine from a program, the program's variables are still around and can be affected by the subroutine. These variables are called shared variables because they are common to both the main program and its subroutines.

In the case of the programs you are working with, this meant that when you created Prompts in the Mainmnu program, all of the subroutines that used the variable name Prompts were seen by dBASE IV to be sharing the variable from the Mainmnu program, not a variable unique to each subroutine.

These conflicts can be resolved by using the PRIVATE command. The PRIVATE command tells dBASE IV what variables used in a subroutine should be considered as private variables.

For example, placing the command PRIVATE Prompts into the Statsmnu program would cause dBASE IV to create a new variable,

Prompts Statsmnu @ Statsmnu.prg that would be used in the subroutine but would leave Prompts Mainmnu @ Mainmnu.prg unchanged.

The problem created by private and shared variables is complicated. It involves the interaction among a number of programs that function as a system of subroutines. The solution is to add to each subroutine a PRIVATE command that allows dBASE IV to distinguish between similar variable names created in different routines. This solution preserves the advantages of writing generalized programs and avoids the necessity of making all variable names unique.

Modify the Statsmnu program by entering

```
MODIFY COMMAND Statsmnu
```

Insert a PRIVATE modifier at the beginning of the program. The command is followed by the list of variables you want to protect from conflict with variables in the calling routine. Insert the following command.

```
PRIVATE Action,Prompts,Start,Option
```

Save the program by pressing (Ctrl)-(End).

Add the same command to Admitmnu.

```
MODIFY COMMAND Admitmnu
```

Insert the PRIVATE modifier.

```
PRIVATE Action,Prompts,Start,Option
```

Save the program by pressing (Ctrl)-(End).

Recall that Statsmnu and Admitmnu have been altered since they last executed. This means that they need to be recompiled. dBASE IV will automatically recompile the programs when they are called as subroutines, but it will be faster to manually compile the programs before you execute the Mainmnu program. Enter

```
COMPILE Admitmnu
COMPILE Statsmnu
```

Execute the Mainmnu program.

```
DO Mainmnu
```

Access the Statsmnu by pressing 2.

Return to the main menu by pressing (↵)

Figure 6.13

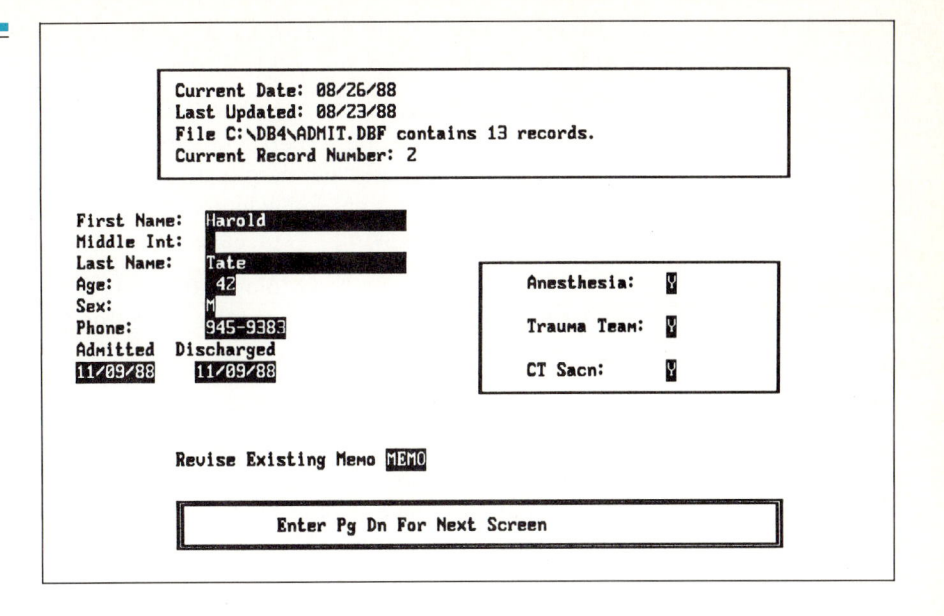

```
    Current Date: 08/26/88
    Last Updated: 08/23/88
    File C:\DB4\ADMIT.DBF contains 13 records.
    Current Record Number: 2

First Name:  Harold
Middle Int:
Last Name:   Tate
Age:         42                    Anesthesia:  Y
Sex:         M
Phone:       945-9383              Trauma Team: Y
Admitted   Discharged
11/09/88   11/09/88                CT Sacn:     Y


         Revise Existing Memo MEMO

            Enter Pg Dn For Next Screen
```

The main menu redisplays correctly because each subroutine menu protects the variable names from conflict with the other menus. Access the Admit menu program by pressing 1.

Run option 2 from this menu by pressing 2. Locate the record for Tate by entering

Tate

The Edit program, running as a sub-subroutine of the Mainmnu program, locates the desired record (see Figure 6.13).

Return to the main menu by pressing (Ctrl)-(End) once and (↵) twice. The main menu displays correctly. Exit the menu by pressing (↵).

Popup Menus

The beginning of this chapter explained how to create standard program menus and to tie them together as a system of subroutines. Menus are a crucial part of any application because they represent the most common form of communication between the program and the person using the application. Because this area of operation is so important, dBASE IV provides special tools to help you create other types of menus. These tools make it fairly simple to create the types of menus used in the dBASE IV database manager. dBASE IV provides tools to create two types of menus.

1. **Popup menus.** A popup menu is a window that can be displayed at any position on the screen. The menu consists of options listed inside a box. A highlight bar is placed on the first option. The options in the popup menu can be selected by moving the highlight bar to an option and pressing ⏎ or entering the first letter of the option.

   Note: For this method to operate correctly, you must make sure that no two options begin with the same first character.

2. **Menu bars.** A menu bar lists options on a bar across the top of the screen.

Popup menus and menu bars can be combined in different ways to achieve a wide variety of screen layouts, each with a unique look and feel. We'll begin the exploration of these tools by creating programs that use dBASE IV popup menus.

Popup menus require the use of six specific commands.

1. **DEFINE POPUP.** The DEFINE POPUP command defines a popup menu. The command sets the location and optionally the size of the popup window. It also assigns a logical name for the popup menu.

2. **DEFINE BAR.** The DEFINE BAR command creates the bars that appear inside the popup menu. Each bar is assigned a numeric value and a text string that will be displayed inside the popup menu. DEFINE BAR commands must be preceded by a DEFINE POPUP command.

3. **ACTIVATE POPUP.** The ACTIVATE POPUP command instructs dBASE IV to display the specified popup menu on the screen and activate the menu. Activate means transfer control of the program to the popup menu routine built into dBASE IV. The user can move the highlight bar up and down in the popup menu display and select an item by pressing ⏎. Selecting an item from a popup menu has no meaning unless an ON POPUP SELECTION command has been used to tell dBASE IV what to do when ⏎ is pressed. As a general rule, never activate a popup until you have executed an ON POPUP SELECTION command. Without an ON POPUP SELECTION command, a popup menu forms an endless loop.

4. **SHOW POPUP.** The SHOW POPUP command displays the popup menu but does not activate the menu. Use this command to show the options listed in a popup menu without actually transferring control to the popup menu routine.

5. **DEACTIVATE POPUP.** The DEACTIVATE POPUP command removes the popup menu from the screen and transfers control to the next command in the program.

6. **RELEASE POPUP.** The RELEASE POPUP command clears a popup menu definition from memory. Unlike memory variables, popup menu definitions cannot be defined as private. This means that once a popup menu is created with a program or subroutine, it will stay in memory until it is specifically released. As with SET commands, your programs should release popup definitions when the program terminates.

In addition there are three system functions that relate to popup menus.

1. **POPUP().** The POPUP() function returns the name of the active popup menu, if any. If no popup is active, the value of POPUP() is a null; POPUP()="" is true when no popup is active.

2. **BAR().** The BAR() function is the key to using popup menus. dBASE IV assigns a numeric value to BAR() that corresponds to the option on the popup menu that is selected when the user presses ⏎. The BAR() function makes it possible for a program to react to a selection made in a popup menu by testing the value of BAR() and using an IF/ENDIF or DO CASE structure to branch based on the value of BAR().

3. **PROMPT().** The PROMPT() function operates in a manner similar to BAR() except that it returns the text of the prompt rather than the number of the bar selected in the popup menu.

To illustrate how popup menus operate, you will create a program, Admitpop, that performs the same function as Admitmnu except that it uses a popup menu rather than a standard menu. Before you get directly into the Admitpop program, there is a side issue to deal with. In the programs that you have been developing, you have been using the SET commands at the beginning and the end of each program to turn on and off the environmental settings. When the programs are combined, the SET ON/OFF commands in each of the subroutines create some awkward problems.

To avoid this problem, while you are working on the rest of the routines in this chapter, remove the SET TALK, STATUS, SAFETY, and SCOREBOARD commands from the six subroutines you have been using. Load the Entry program into the editor.

```
MODIFY COMMAND Entry
```

Delete the first four commands by pressing Ctrl-y four times.

Move the cursor to line 16. Delete the four SET commands by pressing Ctrl-y four times.

Save the program by pressing Ctrl-End.

Repeat the process for the Edit, Addicu, Insured, Ages, and Countins programs.

When you have completed these deletions, create a program called Setoff that contains all the SET OFF commands you would normally use in a standard program.

```
MODIFY COMMAND Setoff
```

Enter the following commands

```
SET TALK OFF
SET SCOREBOARD OFF
SET STATUS OFF
SET SAFETY OFF
RETURN
```

Save the program by pressing Ctrl-End.

Create a program called Seton that contains all the SET ON commands that you would normally use in a program. Enter

```
MODIFY COMMAND Seton
```

Enter the following commands:

```
SET TALK ON
SET SCOREBOARD ON
SET STATUS ON
SET SAFETY ON
RETURN
```

Save the program by pressing Ctrl-End.

You can now run these programs or call them as subroutines instead of burdening each program with its own SET commands. Execute the Setoff program so that all of the programs will run in the SET OFF mode.

```
DO SETOFF
```

You are now ready to create a popup menu program called Admitpop.

■ Menus and Debugging

```
MODIFY COMMAND Admitpop
```

Begin the program by clearing the screen. This makes sure that the popup menu will have a clear background upon which to be displayed.

```
CLEAR
```

Any program that uses a popup menu will need to follow this basic outline.

1. **Define the menu.** This action sets the name for the popup menu and selects the location on the screen where it will be displayed.

2. **Define the bars.** This part of the procedure defines the text of the bars, the lines that appear within the menu.

3. **On selection.** The ON SELECTION command is very important because it determines what action will be taken when a selection is made. Without this command, the popup menu stays active even when you press ⏎. It is important that this command be used before you activate the popup menu.

4. **Activate menu.** This step is taken at the point in the program when you want the user to make a selection from the menu. By including this command in a loop, the user can make repeated selections from the menu.

5. **Release menu.** When the program is over, you should remember to release the popup menu from memory.

According to this outline, the next step in the program is to define the menu. In this case you will give the menu the name Admitmnu. You also need to specify a location on the screen for the popup. All that is required is that you enter a location for the upper left corner of the menu box. dBASE IV will automatically create a box based on the size and number of bars you define. You could enter a second coordinate for the lower right corner of the menu box to define the exact size of the menu box.

Note: If the menu box you define is too small for the number or width of the bars defined, dBASE IV will scroll the bars vertically in the menu box and truncate any lines that are too long.

In this example, you will let dBASE IV calculate the size of the menu box.

```
DEFINE POPUP Admitmnu from 5,20
```

Once a popup menu has been defined, you need to create one or more menu bars. The bars are the items that will be listed in the menu. In this example there will be four menu bars, one for each option that appeared on the standard menu created with the Admitmnu program.

The DEFINE BAR command requires that you specify three things:

1. **Number.** The number is a numeric value or expression that indicates the line in the menu you are defining. You do not have to define the bars in numeric order. If you skip a number, dBASE IV simply displays a blank line in the popup menu for that bar number.

2. **Popup menu.** You need to specify the name of the popup menu, already defined with DEFINE POPUP, in which this bar should be displayed.

3. **Prompt text.** You can enter text or a character expression that will be displayed in the popup menu when activated.

The command below specifies that the first bar in the Admitmnu popup menu will display the text **Add Admission Records.**

```
DEFINE BAR 1 OF Admitmnu PROMPT "Add Admission;
 Records"
```

Define the other three bars for this menu.

```
DEFINE BAR 2 OF Admitmnu PROMPT "Revise Existing;
 Records"
DEFINE BAR 3 OF Admitmnu PROMPT "ICU Care Days"
DEFINE BAR 4 OF Admitmnu PROMPT "Exit Menu"
```

Event Management Commands

You have now defined the menu and the bars it will display. The next step is to decide what should happen when a menu selection is made. This is done by using the ON SELECTION POPUP command. This command uses a structure that is a bit different from other dBASE IV structural commands—IF/ENDIF, DO CASE, DO WHILE—that you have used so far. In the case of IF/ENDIF, DO CASE, and DO WHILE, you were able to specify one or more commands to be executed when certain conditions were met.

dBASE IV has another class of commands that operate on events. An event is a specific action such as selecting a bar from a popup menu or pressing of the (Esc) key. An event-oriented command is one that sets up an action to take if the specified event takes place. In dBASE IV, commands that begin with the word ON are event-oriented commands. Popup and bar menus require event management commands that tell dBASE IV what to do when an event takes place. Unlike conditional structures, event management commands specify only a single operation.

Note: One way around the limit of one command for each event is to use a subroutine, for example, DO INSURED, with the event management command. This technique will be demonstrated later in this chapter.

The ON SELECTION POPUP command is an event management command that precedes another command, and it executes its argument command as soon as a selection is made from the popup menu. Each ON SELECTION POPUP is related to a specific popup menu. If the program encounters several ON SELECTION POPUP commands for the same menu, the last command before the popup is activated is the one used. You cannot have more than one selection option for a given menu.

The most common command to use with a popup selection is DEACTIVATE POPUP. This command causes the popup menu routine to terminate and control passes to the next command in the program. In this case, the function of the menu is simply to set the value of the BAR() function so that you can branch based on its number. In effect, the BAR() function plays the same role as the Action variable did in the Admitmnu program. The difference is that in the popup menu, the user selects the option by moving a highlight bar rather than by entering a number.

The ON SELECTION POPUP and other event commands are different in that they do not cause an action to take place when the commands are encountered in the program. Instead, they set up an action that will take place later in the program if the specified event does take place.

Enter the following command to deactivate the popup when a selection is made.

```
ON SELECTION POPUP Admitmnu DEACTIVATE POPUP
```

You have now defined all the elements necessary to use a popup menu as part of the program. The remainder of the program is a simple loop. At the beginning of the loop the screen is cleared and the popup menu activated. In this way the popup menu serves as a sort of subroutine for selecting options.

```
DO WHILE .T.
CLEAR
ACTIVATE POPUP Admitmnu
```

When an item is selected from the menu, the ON SELECTION POPUP command entered previously will deactivate the menu. There are no commands contained within the loop that indicate what will happen when the selection is made from the popup menu. To figure out what that action will be, you would need to read backwards through the program to locate the previous ON SELECTION POPUP command.

The remainder of the loop consists of a DO CASE structure that evaluates the BAR() function to define the option selected from the menu. Bars 1 through 3 call subroutine programs while bar 4 exits the loop.

```
DO CASE
CASE BAR()=1
    DO Entry
CASE BAR()=2
    DO Edit
CASE BAR()=3
    DO Addicu
CASE BAR()=4
    EXIT
    ENDCASE
ENDDO
```

The final two commands release the popup menu definition and terminate the program.

```
RELEASE POPUP Admitmnu
RETURN
```

The entire program looks like this:

```
CLEAR
DEFINE POPUP Admitmnu from 5,20
DEFINE BAR 1 OF Admitmnu PROMPT "Add Admission;
 Records"
DEFINE BAR 2 OF Admitmnu PROMPT "Revise Existing;
 Records"
```

```
          DEFINE BAR 3 OF Admitmnu PROMPT "ICU Care Days"
          DEFINE BAR 4 OF Admitmnu PROMPT "Exit Menu"
          ON SELECTION POPUP Admitmnu DEACTIVATE POPUP
          DO WHILE .T.
               CLEAR
               ACTIVATE POPUP Admitmnu
               DO CASE
          CASE BAR()=1
               DO Entry
          CASE BAR()=2
               DO Edit
          CASE BAR()=3
               DO Addicu
          CASE BAR()=4
               EXIT
               ENDCASE
          ENDDO
          RELEASE POPUP Admitmnu
          RETURN
```

The program is 23 lines long as compared with the Admitmnu program, which is 43 lines long. Using the dBASE IV built-in popup menu routines makes it simpler to program menus because many operations are embedded in the popup menu commands. Save and execute the program by pressing Alt-e and typing r. The program displays a popup menu box with the four options appearing as bars in the menu (see Figure 6.14).

You can move the highlight bar by using the ↑ and ↓ arrow keys. Press ↓.

To select this option, press ↵.

The menu deactivates and the Edit program runs.

Figure 6.14

```
Add Addmission Records
Revise Existing Records
ICU Care Days
Exit Menu
```

Popup Menus ■ 289

Exit the program by pressing ⏎.

The popup menu appears again. You can also select a popup menu option by typing the first letter of the option. In this case, all four options use text that begins with different first characters. To run the Addicu program press

i

Exit the program by pressing ⏎.

The menu appears again because the ACTIVATE POPUP command is contained within a loop. To exit the loop and the program press

e

The program terminates and returns you to the dot prompt.

Non-Option Text in Popup Menus

dBASE IV allows you to add bars to the popup menu that do not serve as selection items but can add informational text to the menu. This means that you can add headings and separators to the menu.

Load the menu Admitpop program into the editor.

`MODIFY COMMAND Admitpop`

Suppose you want the first line in the popup menu to serve as the heading "Admission Records Menu." You would create a command that defines bar 1 as Admission Records Menu. The trick is to add the SKIP clause. The SKIP clause causes dBASE IV to display the text as part of the menu but to skip that bar when the highlight bar is moved. In effect this makes the bars created with the SKIP clause informational text that enhances the appearance of the popup menu without interfering with the selection process.

Move the cursor to line 4 and insert the following command.

```
DEFINE BAR 1 OF Admitmnu PROMPT "Admission Records;
 Menu" SKIP
```

Another addition to the menu that improves its appearance is a separator line. This line usually consists of a line of dashes to mark off one section of the menu from another. You can use character 196 to draw a single line or character 205 to draw a double line across the menu. Insert the following command to draw a double line below the heading.

```
DEFINE BAR 2 OF Admitmnu PROMPT
REPLICATE(CHR(205),30) SKIP
```

■ Menus and Debugging

You can insert skip lines at any part of the menu. For example, you might want to draw a line between the three subroutine options and the exit option. To figure out what bar that would be, you need to count through the items that will be displayed. Lines 1 and 2 are headings, and lines 3 through 5 are the subroutine options. That means the line should be drawn at bar 6. Insert the following.

```
DEFINE BAR 6 OF Admitmnu PROMPT
REPLICATE(CHR(196),30) SKIP
```

The addition of the skip lines creates a small problem. You now have duplicate bar definitions for bars 1 and 2. You now need to change the bar numbers of the other options so that they will all fit onto the same menu. The commands below show the new bar numbers, in bold. Change the numbers in the program to match the commands below.

```
DEFINE BAR 3 OF Admitmnu PROMPT "Add Admission;
 Records"
DEFINE BAR 4 OF Admitmnu PROMPT "Revise Existing;
 Records"
DEFINE BAR 5 OF Admitmnu PROMPT "ICU Care Days"
DEFINE BAR 7 OF Admitmnu PROMPT "Exit Menu"
```

Now that you have altered the position of the bars in the popup menu, you need to change the values in the DO CASE structure to match the new bar locations. Move the cursor to line 14. Change the numbers in the program to match the commands below. The commands below show the new bar numbers, in bold.

```
      DO CASE
CASE BAR()=3
      DO Entry
CASE BAR()=4
      DO Edit
CASE BAR()=5
      DO Addicu
CASE BAR()=7
      EXIT
      ENDCASE
```

Popup Menus ■ **291**

Save and execute the modified program by pressing (Alt)-e and typing r. The modified menu now contains headings and separator lines.

Press ⬇ three times. The highlight bar skips all the lines created with the SKIP clause. Exit the program by pressing ⏎.

Messages

Another optional feature of a built-in popup menu routine is message text. A popup menu message is a line of text that appears centered on the bottom line of the screen and corresponds to the currently highlighted menu bar. The purpose of the message is to provide additional information about the option so that the user can get an idea what operation each menu option carries out.

The message feature assumes that no other information is currently being displayed on the bottom line of the screen. If there is, the message may overwrite that information.

Load the Admitpop menu program into the editor.

```
MODIFY COMMAND Admitpop
```

You can create a message by adding a MESSAGE clause to a menu bar definition command. Move the cursor to line 5. The command on this line defines bar 3. You can use the MESSAGE clause to add an explanation of this option's function.

Old line: `DEFINE BAR 3 OF Admitmnu`
           `PROMPT "Add Admission Records"`
New line: `DEFINE BAR 3 OF Admitmnu`
           `PROMPT "Add Admission Records"`
           `MESSAGE "Use for new patients only."`

The new command will display the phrase **Use for new patients only** at the bottom of the screen when bar 3 is highlighted. Add messages to the next two bars also.

Old line: `DEFINE BAR 4 OF Admitmnu`
           `PROMPT "Revise Existing Records"`
New line: `DEFINE BAR 4 OF Admitmnu`
           `PROMPT "Revise Existing Records"`
           `MESSAGE "Uses last name to locate patient."`
Old line: `DEFINE BAR 5 OF Admitmnu`
           `PROMPT "ICU Care Days"`

■ **Menus and Debugging**

New line: `DEFINE BAR 5 OF Admitmnu`
            `PROMPT "ICU Care Days"`
            `MESSAGE "Selects patients by month."`

Save and execute the revised program by pressing Alt-e and typing r. The message associated with bar 3 appears at the bottom of the screen (see Figure 6.15).

Press ↓. The message changes to correspond to the highlighted menu bar. Exit the menu by pressing e.

Popups in Programs

The popup menu created in the Admitpop program demonstrates how a popup menu can replace the standard menu like the one created in the Admitmnu program. But popup menus can be used to help users make selections in all types of programs.

Two of the programs that serve as subroutines to the Admitpop menu program begin by asking the user to make a selection. The Addicu program asks the user to select a month, and the Edit program asks the user to select the last name of the patient.

Figure 6.15

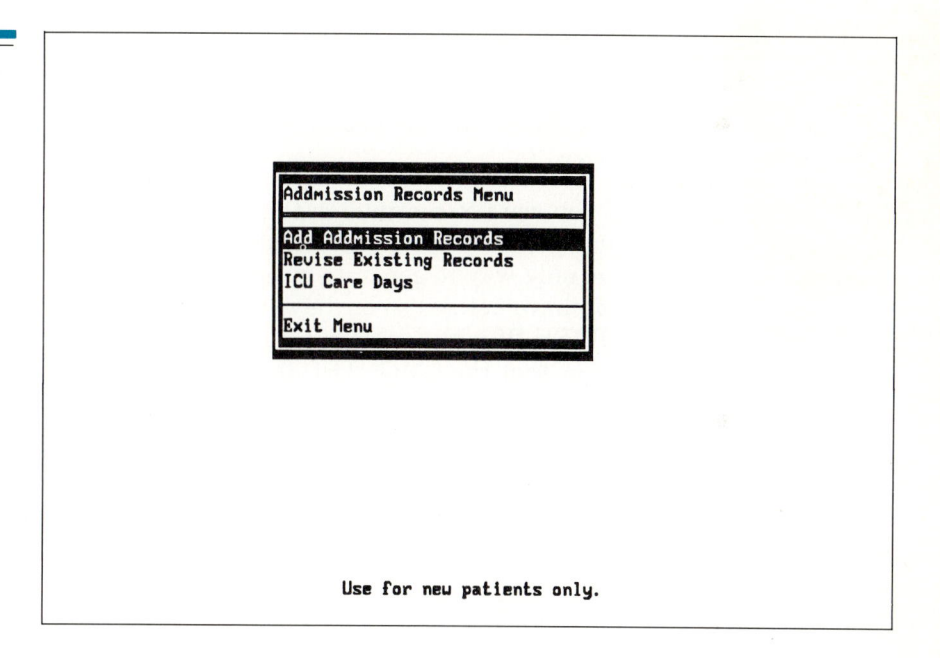

```
┌─────────────────────────────────────────┐
│                                         │
│                                         │
│                                         │
│      ┌──────────────────────────┐       │
│      │Addmission Records Menu   │       │
│      ├──────────────────────────┤       │
│      │Add Addmission Records    │       │
│      │Revise Existing Records   │       │
│      │ICU Care Days             │       │
│      │                          │       │
│      │Exit Menu                 │       │
│      └──────────────────────────┘       │
│                                         │
│                                         │
│                                         │
│                                         │
│           Use for new patients only.    │
└─────────────────────────────────────────┘
```

Popup Menus ■ 293

You could replace these user input prompts with popup menus that allow the user to select from the menu rather than make a manual entry.

Begin with the Addicu program. This program asks the user to select a month. This is currently done using an entry area and an @M function to allow the user to move among the 12 months. Create a new version of this program that uses a popup menu in place of the entry area.

```
MODIFY COMMAND Addicu2
```

Begin the program by clearing the screen and defining a popup menu. In this case you will specify the actual size of the menu box by adding the TO clause to the DEFINE POPUP command.

```
CLEAR
DEFINE POPUP Pick_month FROM 2,20 TO 18,45
```

The next task is to create the bars for the menu. Begin by creating three skip lines to serve as the heading for the popup menu.

```
DEFINE BAR 1 OF Pick_month PROMPT "Add ICU Days"
SKIP
DEFINE BAR 2 OF Pick_month PROMPT "Select Month;
 To Edit" SKIP
DEFINE BAR 3 OF Pick_month PROMPT;
 REPLICATE(CHR(205),25)
SKIP
```

If you were to continue in this manner you would have to enter 12 more DEFINE BAR commands, one for each month. But that is not the only way to generate a series of menu bars. While the menu bars you have defined so far have used numbers and character strings, dBASE IV will also accept numeric and character expressions. You know that the CMONTH() function generates the text equal to the name of a month. The MONTH() function generates a numeric value equal to the number of the month. It seems as if it ought to be possible to get dBASE IV to generate the month menu bars automatically.

You can accomplish this task by creating a loop. The loop will be structured around a variable called Month. Month is a date value that can be used to determine the month number and name. In this case use the date 1/1/88 as the starting value. Enter

```
month={01/01/88}
```

You may wonder about the way we entered this date value. dBASE IV allows you to use a short cut form of the CTOD() conversion function. When a date is surrounded by {}, curly brackets, dBASE IV automatically assumes that you want to perform a character-to-date conversion. The command Month={01/01/88} is equivalent to Month=CTOD("01/01/88"). The result is the same in either case, but the {} symbols save you a few keystrokes.

With the initial date value stored as the variable month, you can create a loop that will cycle through all 12 months. The loop can be stopped by using a logical expression to test the year of the date. The loop should cycle through all 12 months of 1988 but terminate when you reach January of 1989. The expression YEAR(Month)=1988 will limit the loop to a 12-month cycle.

```
DO WHILE YEAR(Month)=1988
```

The next command defines the menu bar for each month. Instead of using numbers and text, this command uses numeric and character expressions. The number of the menu bar is calculated by using the MONTH() function's value of Month plus 3 to allow for the three heading lines. In this way the date 01/01/88 will be bar 4, month 1 +3. The text of the bar is generated by the expression CMONTH(Month).

```
DEFINE BAR MONTH(Month)+3 of Pick_month PROMPT;
   CMONTH(Month)
```

To create the next month, the value of the date stored in the Month variable should be incremented to the next month. dBASE IV does not provide any direct means of changing the month. However, you can approximate the operation by adding 31 days to the month value each time. Since you are only interested in the month portion of the date, the exact day—02/01/88 or 02/02/88—makes no difference. Assuming that each month has 31 days fits our purpose.

```
Month=Month+31
```

You can now end the loop and have it cycle until a menu bar is created for all 12 months.

```
ENDDO
```

The loop requires only four commands in place of the 12 define bar commands you otherwise would have to enter.

Popup Menus ■ 295

The next task is to set the ON SELECTION POPUP action. In this CASE, you can use the DEACTIVATE POPUP commands as the action.

```
ON SELECTION POPUP Pick_month DEACTIVATE POPUP
```

With all the elements defined, activate the menu and allow the user to select a month.

```
ACTIVATE POPUP Pick_month
```

The next set of commands draws the editing frame on the screen and opens the Admit database file.

```
USE Admit
@ 8,10 TO 14,60
@ 9,11 SAY "Name:"
@ 10,11 SAY "Admit"
@ 11,11 SAY "Discharge"
@ 12,11 SAY "Days in"
@ 13,11 SAY "ICU days"
```

This is the point in the Addicu program that a scan loop scans the database and selects records for the selected month. What type of expression can we use to relate the selection in the popup menu to the record in the database? You could use either a numeric or character test. The BAR() function could be compared to MONTH(Admit) or the PROMPT() function could be compared to the value of CMONTH(Admit). Recall that PROMPT() returns the text of the menu bar prompt that was selected. In this case, use the text comparison.

```
SCAN FOR CMONTH(Admit)=TRIM(Prompt())
```

The remainder of the program is exactly the same as it is in the Addicu program with the exception of the RELEASE POPUP command.

```
    REPLACE Days_stay WITH Discharge-admit+1
    @ 9,25 SAY TRIM(First)+SPACE(1)+Last
    @ 10,25 SAY Admit
    @ 11,25 SAY Discharge
    @ 12,25 SAY Days_stay
    @ 13,25 GET Days_icu Valid Days_icu<=;
Days_stay
    READ
```

■ Menus and Debugging

```
ENDSCAN
CLOSE DATABASE
RELEASE POPUP Pick_month
CLEAR
RETURN
```

Save the program by pressing (Ctrl)-(End).

Manually compile and run this program by entering

```
COMPILE Addicu2
DO Addicu2
```

The program displays a popup menu listing all 12 months (see Figure 6.16).

Press (↑)-(↵). This selects the records for December. Exit the program by pressing (↵) two times.

You may have noticed that this program delays about 7 to 10 seconds before displaying the menu. This delay is the result of the loop you created at the beginning of the program. The loop made it simpler for you to write the program by eliminating the need to enter long, repetitive commands. However, you will find that dBASE IV takes longer to execute loops than sequential statements. If you want to go back and manually enter the commands for defining all 12 months, eliminating the loop, you will find that the program will run faster.

As an optional exercise, modify the program to perform more quickly. Try this on your own. If you need help, the listing of the modified program can be found at the end of the chapter in the Answers to Exercises section under exercise 3.

Figure 6.16

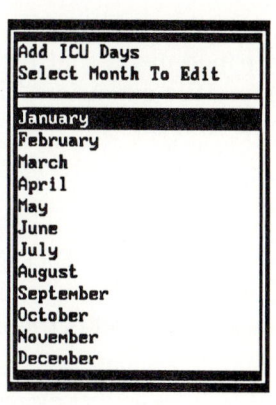

```
Add ICU Days
Select Month To Edit

January
February
March
April
May
June
July
August
September
October
November
December
```

Popup Menus ■ 297

Special Item Lists

The previous program, Addicu2, demonstrates how popup menu bar items can be generated by a loop rather than be defined individually. dBASE IV provides built-in options for popup menus that automatically generate menu bars. These options can let your popup menu list the files stored on disk, the structure of an open database, file or the contents of the fields in a database.

A basic example of how to use this feature is a program to aid in the selection of programs for editing program files. The program will automatically generate a popup menu that contains all of the program files on disk listed as bars in a popup menu. Create a program called Editprgs by entering

```
MODIFY COMMAND Editprgs
```

The first command simply clears the screen display.

```
CLEAR
```

The key to displaying a list of items in a popup menu is in the special clauses that the DEFINE POPUP command accepts:

1. **FILES, FILES LIKE.** The FILES and FILES LIKE options allow you to list a file or group of files in a popup menu. The FILES LIKE clause allows you to enter a wildcard such as *.dbf, which selects all files that end with a .dbf extension.

    Note: Wildcards are used with MS-DOS to select groups of files for MS-DOS commands. You can use any valid MS-DOS wildcard with the FILES LIKE clause.

2. **STRUCTURE.** The STRUCTURE option lists the field names of the currently active database as bars in a popup menu.

3. **FIELD.** The FIELD option lists the contents of the specified field in the popup menu.

Here, you want to create a popup menu that lists the names of all of the files that end with the .prg file extension. The following DEFINE POPUP command will create that menu.

```
DEFINE POPUP Programs FROM 0,20 PROMPT FILES LIKE;
   *.prg
```

When you use a special list option with a DEFINE POPUP command, there is no need to create menu bars. The bars are automatically generated by dBASE IV. The next command is the ON SELECTION POPUP command.

```
ON SELECTION POPUP Programs DEACTIVATE POPUP
```

Next, activate the menu.

```
ACTIVATE POPUP Programs
```

Save the program by pressing Ctrl-End.

Run the program by entering

```
COMPILE Editprgs
DO Editprgs
```

dBASE IV automatically generates a popup menu that lists all of the files with a .prg extension. Your disk may list different files than the screen image below shows (see Figure 6.17).

dBASE IV will scroll the names in the box if the disk has more files than can be shown in one screen. Press PgDn two times and PgUp two times.

Move the highlight bar to the file name Addicu.prg. Press ↵.

The program terminates and returns to the dot prompt.

The program you have just executed helps you select program files for editing by displaying a list of the program files in a popup menu box. So far, the program generates the list of files correctly. But how can you get the program to edit the selected file?

You want the program to issue the command MODIFY COMMAND Edit.prg when you select the filename Edit.prg. The Editprgs program

Figure 6.17

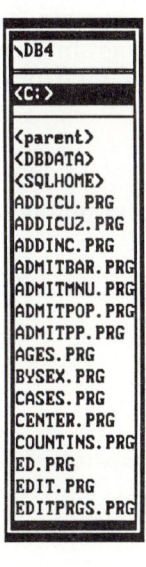

```
\DB4
<C:>

<parent>
<DBDATA>
<SQLHOME>
ADDICU.PRG
ADDICU2.PRG
ADDINC.PRG
ADMITBAR.PRG
ADMITMNU.PRG
ADMITPOP.PRG
ADMITPP.PRG
AGES.PRG
BYSEX.PRG
CASES.PRG
CENTER.PRG
COUNTINS.PRG
ED.PRG
EDIT.PRG
EDITPRGS.PRG
```

Popup Menus ■ 299

is able to display a list of files from which you can select a name. However, what the program does not do, as of yet, is to connect that name with a command. Enter

```
? PROMPT()
```

dBASE IV displays the name of the file that you selected from the popup menu. Since you did not release the popup at the end of the program, the popup menu and its functions, BAR() and PROMPT(), are still active.

> *Note:* The filename selected is stored with its full MS-DOS pathname. An MS-DOS pathname includes the drive and directory names as well as the filename. For example, C:\DB4=YAddicu.prg reads "Addicu.prg located on drive C in the DB4 directory." The drive and directory names that appear on your screen will reflect the installation of dBASE IV on your computer system.

Ideally, you should tell dBASE IV to edit the file indicated by the text of the PROMPT() function. This can be done by using the PROMPT() function in place of the filename following MODIFY COMMAND. Enter

```
MODIFY COMMAND PROMPT()
```

The program loads the Addicu.prg file into the program editor. Using the PROMPT() function in place of the filename allows dBASE IV to perform a symbolic substitution, called a macro substitution, of the function with the file name that it relates to. The next step is to apply the same logic to the Editprgs program. Load the Editprgs file into the editor by using the LAYOUT MODIFY COMMAND. Press (Alt)-l and type m.

```
Editprgs.prg
```

Move the cursor to the end of the program and add the following commands.

```
MODIFY COMMAND PROMPT()
COMPILE PROMPT()
RELEASE POPUP programs
RETURN
```

Save and execute the program by pressing (Alt)-e and typing r. Move the highlight bar to Addicu.prg. Press (↵). The program loads the file that you selected, Addicu.prg, into the editor.

Exit the editor by pressing (Ctrl)-(End).

Another way to get the Editprgs program to work using a macro substitution is to transfer the PROMPT() value to a memory variable. Modify the Editprgs program to use this technique.

```
MODIFY COMMAND Editprgs
```

Move the cursor to line 6. Insert a command that creates a memory variable for the filename.

```
Filename=PROMPT()
```

Change line 7 to use macro substitution.

Old line: COMPILE PROMPT()
New line: COMPILE &Filename

Save and compile the program by entering

```
COMPILE Editprgs
```

Execute the program by entering

```
DO Editprgs
```

Move the highlight bar to Addicu.prg and press (↵). Save the file by pressing (Ctrl)-(End).

The program is saved and compiled by the Editprgs program. This program demonstrates two important concepts: The first is the use of a specialized type of popup menu with automatically generated menu bars. The second is the use of macro substitution, where a value that would otherwise be interpreted by dBASE IV as a literal is actually treated as a symbol. One of the most common uses of this technique is using a variable name in place of an actual filename when a program selects a file from disk.

A Field Popup

Another powerful clause that works with the DEFINE POPUP command is the FIELD clause. FIELD, like FILES, causes dBASE IV to generate menu bars in a popup menu. In this instance, the contents are the contents of a specified database field. This means that you can use the popup menu to select a record by highlighting the item in the key field and pressing (↵).

The Edit program asks the user to enter the last name of a patient so that the program can select records to edit. Instead of using an interactive input area you can operate the same program by using a popup menu to list the last names of the patients.

Create a program called Editpop by entering

```
MODIFY COMMAND Editpop
```

Begin the program with the command to open the database file with the correct index order.

```
USE Admit INDEX Admit ORDER Last
```

The next command creates a popup menu that uses the data stored in the last name field for each record in the database. Using the PROMPT FIELD clause, the fields will appear as menu bars. The FIELD clause specifies the name of the field that appears in the menu box.

> *Note:* The PROMPT FIELD clause is limited to displaying the contents of a single field in the popup menu. There may be instances where you want to display data from more than one field. In this example you might want to display the first and last names in the menu box. You can accomplish this by adding a new field to the structure of the file with the MODIFY STRUCTURE command, a field called Fullname. Then, use the REPLACE command to fill in the field with the desired data: REPLACE ALL FULLNAME WITH TRIM(First)+" "+Last. You can then use the Fullname field with the popup menu command.

The size of the menu box is restructured by using coordinates. dBASE IV scrolls the bars in the box to accommodate all the records in the database.

```
DEFINE POPUP Patients FROM 4,20 TO 14,60;
 PROMPT FIELD Last
```

Next, specify the action to take when the selection is made in the popup menu.

```
ON SELECTION POPUP Patients DEACTIVATE POPUP
```

The next section of the program begins an automatic loop that lets users choose a popup menu name and edit the record related to that name. Begin the loop and clear the screen display.

```
DO WHILE .T.
     CLEAR
```

Activate the popup menu so that the user can select the record to edit.

```
ACTIVATE POPUP Patients
```

302 ■ **Menus and Debugging**

Once the selection is made, the popup menu deactivates. Positioning the pointer to the correct record is a simple matter. When a FIELD clause is used in a popup menu, the value of BAR() and PROMPT() directly correspond to the record number and field contents of the record you selected. You can edit the selected record by using the value of the BAR() function as the numeric argument of a record scope. RECORD BAR() positions the pointer to the record selected in the popup menu. The Admit format file controls the screen display of the record.

```
      SET FORMAT TO Admit
      EDIT record BAR()
      CLOSE FORMAT
```

Finally, close the loop, and database, and release the popup menu.

```
ENDDO
CLOSE DATABASE
RELEASE POPUP Patients
RETURN
```

The entire program reads like this:

```
USE Admit INDEX Admit ORDER Last
DEFINE POPUP Patients FROM 4,20 TO 14,60 PROMPT;
 FIELD Last
ON SELECTION POPUP Patients DEACTIVATE POPUP
DO WHILE .T.
      CLEAR
      ACTIVATE POPUP Patients
      SET FORMAT TO Admit
      EDIT record BAR()
      CLOSE FORMAT
ENDDO
CLOSE DATABASE
RELEASE POPUP Patients
RETURN
```

Save the program by pressing [Ctrl]-[End].

Popup Menus ■ 303

Compile and execute the program by entering

COMPILE Editpop

DO Editpop

The popup menu appears on the screen with the last names of the patients appearing as bars in the menu (see Figure 6.18).

Move the highlight bar to the name LaFish. Press ⏎.

The program deactivates the menu and displays the contents of the record that corresponds to the selection made in the popup menu.

Exit the editing display by pressing Ctrl-End.

The program recycles back to the popup menu and allows you to make another selection.

But there is a problem. Suppose that you don't want to edit another record but want to exit the program—what do you enter?

Since each bar in the menu corresponds to a record, pressing ⏎ on any bar will cause another record to be edited. dBASE IV recognizes the Esc key as an instruction to deactivate the popup menu without making a selection. Press Esc.

The menu deactivates but triggers an error on encountering the command, EDIT record BAR() (see Figure 6.19).

Since you pressed Esc instead of making a selection, BAR() has a value of zero. The error occurs because there is no record zero in the database. You must resolve this problem to complete the program. Cancel the program by pressing ⏎.

Figure 6.18

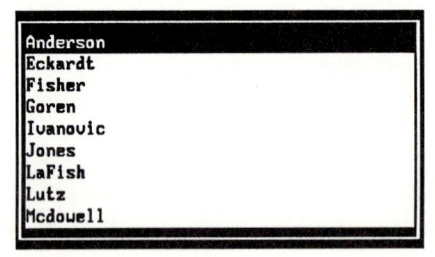

```
Anderson
Eckardt
Fisher
Goren
Ivanovic
Jones
LaFish
Lutz
Mcdowell
```

■ **Menus and Debugging**

Figure 6.19

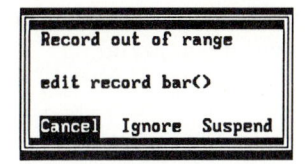

```
Record out of range
edit record bar()
Cancel  Ignore  Suspend
```

Error Trapping

The solution to this problem lies in the use of dBASE IV event-management functions. The encountered event, in this case, is the error that occurred during the execution of a program. Normally, dBASE IV has a built-in routine that occurs with every error. The error message box that displays is part of that routine. However, dBASE IV provides an event command called ON ERROR that allows you to specify a command to execute when an error occurs. That command can be a single command or a call to execute a subroutine. When an ON ERROR command is active, dBASE IV does not display the default error message box. The specified ON ERROR command executes in its place.

How can ON ERROR solve the problem with the Editpop program? The error occurs when no record is selected from the menu box and the EDIT command attempts to find record zero. You could use the command ON ERROR EXIT to respond to the kind of event that caused the error. With that command in place, the program would exit the loop when no record was selected.

Load the Editpop program into the editor by entering

```
MODIFY COMMAND Editpop
```

Move the cursor to line 3. Add a MESSAGE clause to the popup menu definition that tells the user to press (Esc) to exit the program. When a MESSAGE clause is attached to the DEFINE POPUP command, instead of to individual DEFINE BAR commands, the message appears for all the bars in that menu.

Old Line: `DEFINE POPUP Patients FROM 4,20 TO 14,60;`
            `PROMPT FIELD Last`

New line: `DEFINE POPUP Patients FROM 4,20 TO 14,60;`
            `PROMPT FIELD Last MESSAGE "Press Esc;`
            `To Exit"`

Move the cursor to line 6 to turn on event management for an error condition. Insert the following command:

ON ERROR EXIT

Move the cursor to line 13 to add two commands to the closing routine. First, release the ON ERROR setting so that dBASE IV will return to the normal error handling procedure following the termination of the program.

The revised program looks like this. The new program lines are highlighted in color.

```
USE Admit INDEX Admit ORDER Last
DEFINE POPUP Patients FROM 4,20 TO 14,60 PROMPT;
 FIELD Last
MESSAGE "Press Esc To Exit"
ON SELECTION POPUP Patients DEACTIVATE POPUP
ON ERROR EXIT
DO WHILE .T.
    CLEAR
    ACTIVATE POPUP Patients
    SET FORMAT TO Admit
    EDIT record BAR( )
    CLOSE FORMAT
ENDDO
ON ERROR
CLOSE FORMAT
CLOSE DATABASE
RELEASE POPUP Patients
RETURN
```

Save and execute the program by pressing Alt-e and typing r.

Summary

This chapter's key concepts include

Menus. A menu is a screen display that lists the program options that a user can select. Menus appear in almost every application and are part of the basic repertoire of any programmer. dBASE IV provides a variety of methods to create and use menus as part of a dBASE IV application.

Standard menus. A standard menu is one created by using @/SAY commands to construct the menu. A variable used with an @/GET statement captures the user's selection. A DO CASE structure evaluates the menu options and branches to the appropriate subroutine.

Debug. dBASE IV provides a complete interactive debugging system. The system can be accessed from the editor by pressing [Alt]-e and typing d or from the dot prompt with the DEBUG command. The debugger displays five windows on the screen. The command window displays the commands of the program as they execute. You can toggle between the debugger display and the actual screen display using [F9]. The display window allows you to check on the status of dBASE IV fields, variables, and expressions.

Breakpoints. The debugger allows you to establish breakpoints in a program. A breakpoint in the dBASE IV debugger uses a logical expression. The debugger halts the execution of the program when the breakpoint expression is true. You can set up to 10 different breakpoints. Breakpoints speed up the process of debugging by halting the program only at crucial points.

Private variables. Variables created by a program are automatically released when the program terminates. If a program is called as a subroutine, all the variables in the calling program are available for use and modification in the subroutine. When the program returns to the calling routine, the modifications performed on the variables in the subroutine flow through. If you wish to protect the calling program's variables from the subroutine, you should use a PRIVATE command in the subroutine for those variables subject to name conflict with variables in the calling routine.

Public variables. A public variable is available to all programs. When you create a variable at the dot prompt, it is automatically a public variable. When a variable is created in a program, it functions as a public variable for any subroutines that are called from that program.

Popup menus. Popup menus are a special built-in subroutine provided by dBASE IV to facilitate creating menus. A popup menu is a box with a list of options. The user selects an option from this type of menu by moving the cursor to an item and pressing [↵].

DEFINE POPUP. The DEFINE POPUP command defines a popup menu. The command sets the location and (optionally) the size of the popup window. It also assigns a logical name for the popup menu.

DEFINE BAR. The DEFINE BAR command creates the bars that will appear inside the popup menu. Each bar is assigned a numeric value and a text string that displays inside the popup menu. DEFINE BAR commands must be preceded by a DEFINE POPUP command.

ACTIVATE POPUP. The ACTIVATE POPUP command causes dBASE IV to display the specified popup menu on the screen and activate that menu. Activate means that control of the program transfers to the popup menu routine built into dBASE IV. The user can move the highlight bar up and down the popup menu display and select an item by pressing ⏎.

SHOW POPUP. The SHOW POPUP command displays the popup menu but does not activate the menu. You would use this menu to show the options listed in a popup menu without actually transferring control to the popup menu routine.

DEACTIVATE POPUP. The DEACTIVATE POPUP command removes the popup menu from the screen and transfers control to the next command in the program.

RELEASE POPUP. The RELEASE POPUP command clears a popup menu definition from memory. Once a popup is created by a program or subroutine, it stays in the memory until specifically released. Your programs should RELEASE POPUP definitions when the program terminates.

POPUP(). The POPUP() function returns the name of the ACTIVATE POPUP menu, if any.

BAR(). The BAR() function is the key to using popup menus. dBASE IV assigns a numeric value to BAR() that corresponds to the bar in the popup menu that is selected when the user presses ⏎. The BAR() function makes it possible for a program to react to a selection made in a popup menu by testing the value of BAR() and using an IF/ENDIF or DO CASE structure to branch based on the value of BAR().

PROMPT(). The PROMPT() function operates in a manner similar to BAR() except that it returns the text of the prompt rather than the number of the bar selected in the popup menu.

Event Management. Event management is the control of actions that occur during program operations. An event is an action that may occur in the program, like the selection of an item from a popup menu, or an error condition. When the event happens, dBASE IV executes the specified command or subroutine. The ON SELECTION POPUP command is an example of an event-management command.

Popup Prompt Files. The PROMPT FILES clause used with a popup menu causes dBASE IV to generate automatically the bars of the popup menu by listing the files available in the current directory. This type of popup menu does not require DEFINE BAR commands because the bars are generated from the disk directory. The LIKE clause allows you to specify an MS-DOS wildcard that filters the filenames to restrict the names that appear in the popup. The name of the selected file, including drive, directory, and filename, are stored in the PROMPT() function. The BAR() function is of limited use with this command since it is unlikely the numeric sequence of the files will be useful in evaluating a selection.

Popup Prompt Field. Like the PROMPT FILES clause, this option also automatically generates the bars of a menu. The bars in this popup will be the information stored in selected fields of the database. Make sure that the database contains the field you want to use for the popup. When a selection is made, the PROMPT() function will contain the contents of the selected field. Selection from a field's popup menu does not move the record pointer. That can be done by searching for the record that matches the PROMPT() contents. If the file is not indexed, you can use the BAR() value as the record number. Remember that if the file is indexed, the BAR() function's value will not correspond to the record number.

ON ERROR. The ON ERROR command is an event-management command that allows you to specify a command or subroutine to execute when an error takes place. The command that is selected replaces the dBASE IV error message routine. ON ERROR stays in effect until another ON ERROR, without an argument, is executed. This is true even after the program terminates.

Review Problems for Chapter 6

Chapter 6 teaches the various methods to create menus of options. The following problems will help you review the techniques and skills explained in this chapter.

1. One use of menus is to organize individual programs. In the previous review sections, you created two calculation programs (Chapter 4, problems 1 and 2.) Create a standard menu program that allows you to run either of these programs.

   In the listing below, the calculator programs are assumed to have the name P04-01.prg and P04-02.prg

2. Create a program that carries out the same function as the program you created for the first review problem but uses a dBASE IV popup menu to list the menu options.

3. Create a standard menu program that allows the user to select to list the company, date, product name, and sales amount by date order, company name, product name, or total sale amount order.(Hint: The menu is used to select the desired index tag for each type of listing.)

4. Create a program that duplicates the function of the previous program using popup menus.

5. Create a program that uses a field popup menu to allow the user to select an invoice for editing. The popup menu will list the invoice numbers.

Answers to Exercises

1. Set commands

   ```
   SET TALK OFF
   SET SCOREBOARD OFF
   SET STATUS OFF
   ```

2. Modify Admitmnu program.Changed lines are printed in color.

   ```
   SET TALK OFF
   SET SCOREBOARD OFF
   SET STATUS OFF
   DECLARE OPTION[4]
   ```

```
OPTION[1]="List Insurance Status"
OPTION[2]="Distribution of Patient Ages"
OPTION[3]="Distribution of Insurance
Classifications"
OPTION[4]="Exit Menu - Press
"+CHR(17)+CHR(196)+CHR(217)
Prompts=4
DO WHILE .T.
    CLEAR
    Action=0
    @ 2,25 SAY "Admission Statistics Menu"
    @ 3,0 SAY REPLICATE(CHR(196),79)
    Start=1
    DO WHILE Start<=Prompts
@ ROW()+1,25 SAY STR(Start,1)
@ ROW(),COL()+1 SAY "."+SPACE(1)+OPTION[Start]
Start=Start+1
    ENDDO
    @ ROW()+1,0 SAY REPLICATE(CHR(196),79)
    @ ROW()+1,25 SAY "Enter Selection"+CHR(16)
GET Action FUNCTION "Z"PICTURE "9"
    READ
    DO CASE
CASE Action=1
    DO Insured
CASE Action=2
    DO Ages
CASE Action=3
    DO Countins
CASE Action=4.OR.Action=0
    EXIT
    ENDCASE
    SET TALK OFF
    SET SCOREBOARD OFF
    SET STATUS OFF
```

```
ENDDO
SET STATUS ON
SET SCOREBOARD ON
SET TALK ON
RETURN
```

3. Modify Addicu2 program. Changed lines are highlighted in colored type.

```
CLEAR
DEFINE POPUP Pick_month FROM 2,20 TO 18,45
DEFINE BAR 1 OF Pick_month PROMPT "Add ICU Days" SKIP
DEFINE BAR 2 OF Pick_month PROMPT "Select Month; To Edit" SKIP
DEFINE BAR 3 OF Pick_month PROMPT REPLICATE(CHR(205),25) SKIP
DEFINE BAR 4 OF Pick_month PROMPT "January"
DEFINE BAR 5 OF Pick_month PROMPT "February"
DEFINE BAR 6 OF Pick_month PROMPT "March"
DEFINE BAR 7 OF Pick_month PROMPT "April"
DEFINE BAR 8 OF Pick_month PROMPT "May"
DEFINE BAR 9 OF Pick_month PROMPT "June"
DEFINE BAR 10 OF Pick_month PROMPT "July"
DEFINE BAR 11 OF Pick_month PROMPT "August"
DEFINE BAR 12 OF Pick_month PROMPT "September"
DEFINE BAR 13 OF Pick_month PROMPT "October"
DEFINE BAR 14 OF Pick_month PROMPT "November"
DEFINE BAR 15 OF Pick_month PROMPT "December"
ON SELECTION POPUP pick_month DEACTIVATE POPUP
ACTIVATE POPUP pick_month
USE Admit
@ 8,10 to 14,60
@ 9,11 SAY "Name:"
@ 10,11 SAY "Admit"
@ 11,11 SAY "Discharge"
```

```
      @ 12,11 SAY "Days in"
      @ 13,11 SAY "ICU days"
SCAN FOR CMONTH(Admit)=TRIM(PROMPT())
      REPLACE Days_stay WITH Discharge-Admit+1
      @ 9,25 SAY TRIM(First)+SPACE(1)+Last
      @ 10,25 SAY Admit
      @ 11,25 SAY Discharge
      @ 12,25 SAY Days_stay
      @ 13,25 GET Days_icu VALID Days_icu<=;
Days_stay
      READ
ENDSCAN
CLOSE DATABASE
RELEASE POPUP Pick_month
CLEAR
RETURN
```

7 Using Multiple Databases

In the previous six chapters, you carried out a variety of operations on and wrote several programs for using the data stored in the Admit database. This chapter will teach you dBASE IV techniques for constructing programs that use more than one database.

One-to-Many Relationships

The database you have been working with stores the records of individual patients. For each patient admitted to the emergency ward, the database utilities we've written let us add new records. The Admit database stores the patient's name, gender, insurance carrier, and other information. All these entries have one thing in common: for each field, only one entry is necessary. For example, a patient is either a male or a female. A patient's discharge date is a particular day—you cannot be discharged on more than one date. There is a one-to-one relationship between each patient record and the field information recorded for that patient.

Not all pieces of information have a one-to-one relationship. For example, suppose you want to keep track of the doctors who treat the patients in the emergency room. While a given patient can have only one name or phone number, it is likely that a single patient will be treated by more than one doctor. Since one patient can be attended by multiple doctors, the relationship between patient and doctor is a one-to-many relationship. You can view that relationship from two points of view. From the doctor's point of view, one doctor will treat more than one patient.

How can you use dBASE IV to record information that exhibits such complex relationships? One way is to create several fields in the patient database to record physician's names. But this method has a major disadvantage: you have no way of knowing in advance exactly how many physicians will treat a given patient. When you create extra fields, you will find that some of the records do not have enough space for all the doctors, while others will have too many fields, leaving the space empty and wasted.

The answer lies in using more than one database to record the information. For example, you might create a database where you can record the names of the doctors and the patients they treat. In this database, the name of the patient can appear in as many records as necessary to list all the doctors involved in a patient's treatment. The name of a doctor can also appear multiple times for all the different patients treated by that physician. In such a database, each record would not stand for a person, doctor or patient, but for an interaction between a specific doctor and a specific patient. You can then use dBASE IV multiple-database techniques to relate the two databases.

Relating these databases is efficient because you do not need to repeat or duplicate all the patient information in the doctor file. All you need to do is enter information, patient name for example, that will link the records in the doctor file to the patients in the Admit file.

dBASE IV allows you to extend this logic to more than just two databases. You can operate on up to 10 databases at one time. Why would you need so many databases open at one time? If you extend the logic of the current example, you can quickly see how many files can be related. If you wanted to record information about the doctors' medical specialities and their home and work telephone numbers, you would not want to repeat this information for every patient that the doctor treats. Therefore, you would make a third database to store the information about each doctor. This file is a one-to-one type file.

You've now envisioned three databases, one for patients, one for physicians, and one that relates the two. You can produce reports that draw some information from all three files.

Later, you might want to record information about the patient's treatment and what procedures were carried out during the treatment. Once again, you could generate two more databases: one that lists standard types of treatment, and another, a one-to-many file, to link patients to various types of treatment. So far, you have envisioned a system that uses five database files to record information about a single patient.

While such a system may seem complex, it is more efficient than duplicating information in many files or trying to accommodate complex relationships in a single database. Storing information in multiple databases and linking those files logically constitutes a relational database system.

In this chapter, you will learn the basic techniques to relate multiple dBASE IV files.

New Databases

To learn about related databases, you must first create the databases. To begin, create two new database files. The first file, Doctors, contains a list of the physicians who work in the emergency room of the hospital.

Use the CREATE command to create a database, with the following structure, called Doctors.

Structure for database: Doctors.dbf

Field	Field Name	Type	Width
1	FIRST	Character	20
2	LAST	Character	20
3	MED_REC_NO	Character	10
4	FIELD	Character	20
5	HPHONE	Character	8
6	WPHONE	Character	8
7	RESIDENT	Logical	1

■ Using Multiple Databases

Enter the following six records.

Record #1
FIRST	Victor
LAST	Erlich
MED_REC_NO	999-777-11
FIELD	Anesthesiology
HPHONE	777-5555
WPHONE	999-4500
RESIDENT	F

Record #2
FIRST	Mark
LAST	Craig
MED_REC_NO	333-000-90
FIELD	Cardiology
HPHONE	999-9999
WPHONE	888-8888
RESIDENT	T

Record #3
FIRST	Amanda
LAST	Christenson
MED_REC_NO	333-000-55
FIELD	Internist
HPHONE	333-3333
WPHONE	444-4444
RESIDENT	F

Record #4
FIRST	Donald
LAST	Westfall
MED_REC_NO	666-999-00
FIELD	Dermatology
HPHONE	222-3333
WPHONE	299-9999
RESIDENT	T

One-to-Many Relationships ■ 317

Record #5
FIRST   Norman
LAST   Bates
MED_REC_NO   000-999-00
FIELD   Surgery
HPHONE   666-7777
WPHONE   888-7777
RESIDENT   T

Record #6
FIRST   Rebecca
LAST   LaFish
MED_REC_NO   444-999-12
FIELD   Pediatrics
HPHONE   444-4444
WPHONE   999-5000
RESIDENT   Y

Opening Multiple Databases

Before begining to write multiple-database programs, let's outline the basic dBASE IV concepts for operating with multiple database files. Begin by closing all open databases by entering

```
CLEAR ALL
DO SETON
```

Open the Admit database by entering

```
USE Admit
```

The Admit database is now active. If you look at the status line, you will see the name of the active database, Admit.dbf, and the number of records, 13. What will happen if you open the Doctors database? Enter

```
USE Doctors
```

When dBASE IV opens the Doctors database, it automatically closes the Admit database. The name in the status bar changes to Doctors.dbf, and the number of records changes to six. With the USE command, you can only open one database file at a time. Each time you open a new file, the previous database is closed.

If this were the only way to use database files in dBASE IV, it would be very difficult to relate data in different databases. But dBASE IV has a method to let you have access to more than one database at a time, using a concept called a work area. dBASE IV has 10 work areas. Each work area can contain one database file. This means that dBASE IV can have up to 10 different databases open at once, as long as each database is assigned to a different work area.

The reason that the USE command closes the open database when you open a new file is because dBASE IV assumes that you want to work in work area 1, unless you specify otherwise. Thus, the fact that only one database at a time can be open applies only to a single work area. By activating other work areas, you will find that you can keep more than one database open at a time.

Use the SELECT command to activate another work area. By default, dBASE IV automatically selects work area 1 when the program loads. However, you can open database files in other work areas by first selecting one of those other work areas, 2 through 10, before you open a new database.

> *Note:* dBASE IV permits you to refer to work areas by letter as well as number. Work area 1 is A, 2 is B, and so on. The commands SELECT 1 and SELECT A are equivalent. You should avoid creating files with single-letter names such as A, B, and C, because dBASE IV will confuse them with work area names.

Close all files by entering

```
CLEAR ALL
```

Open the Admit file in work area 2 by entering

```
SELECT 2
```

The SELECT command does not change any aspect of the screen display. Even the status line does not tell you what area is currently active. Open the Admit database by entering

```
USE Admit
```

Before you open the Doctors database, change the work area to 3 and then open that database file.

```
SELECT 3
USE Doctors
```

To see what you've accomplished, use the DISPLAY STATUS command to list the current database status (see Figure 7.1).

```
DISPLAY STATUS
```

The listing shows that there are two database files open, one in work area 2 and one in work area 3. It also indicates that work area 3 is currently selected. It is important to understand that while you can have more than one database open, only one can be selected, or active, at any moment.

The display reveals an important feature of the dBASE IV work area. On the right side of the status display, the word **alias** appears. An alias is a name assigned to a work area that contains an open database. This is one distinction that can be made between work areas with open database files and empty work areas.

The alias name can be used to refer to the work area and the data contained within it. The alias name is automatically set to the filename when you open a database. Thus, work area 2 has the alias Admit while work area 3 is assigned Doctors.

Once a database has been opened and an alias assigned, you can refer to the work area by its alias rather than the work area number or letter. Exit the status display by pressing (Esc).

Figure 7.1

```
Select area:  2, Database in Use: D:DBASE\ADMIT.DBF    Alias: ADMIT
Production    MDX file:  D:\DBASE\ADMIT.MDX
            Index TAG:      ADMIT  Key: UPPER(SEX)+DTOS(ADMIT)
            Index TAG:      DISCHARGE  Key: DISCHARGE
            Index TAG:      CHARGES  Key: CHARGES Descending)
            Index TAG:      SEX  Key: UPPER(SEX)
            Index TAG:      DAYS  Key: UPPER(SEX)+STR(DAYS_STAY)
            Index TAG:      NAMES  Key: UPPER(SEX)+LAST+FIRST
            Index TAG:      LAST  Key: upper(last)
            Memo file:   D:\DBASE\ADMIT.DBT

Currently Selected Database:
Select Area:  3, Database in Use: D:\DBASE\DOCTORS.DBF    Alias: DOCTORS

File search path:
Default disk drive: D:
Print destination:  PRN:
Margin =     0
Refresh count =    0
Reprocess count =   0
Press any key to continue...
Command  |D:\dbase\DOCTORS        |Rec 1/6        |File
```

320 ■ Using Multiple Databases

Change the work area by entering

`SELECT Admit`

The work area changes to work area 2, the one that contains the Admit database.

You can assign an alias name that is different from the filename by using an ALIAS clause with the USE command. Suppose you want to assign the name Patients to the work area that contains the Admit database file. Enter

`USE Admit ALIAS Patients`

Display the status by entering

`DISPLAY STATUS`

This time the alias name appears as Patients (see Figure 7.2).

Exit the display by pressing (Esc).

Besides naming the work areas that contain databases, the alias name can be used to create an extended field name. The extended field name includes both the alias and the field name so that dBASE IV can determine the work area to draw the data from.

Figure 7.2

```
Currently Selected Database:
Select area:  2, Database in Use: D:\DB4\ADMIT.DBF    Alias: PATIENTS
         Memo file:    D:\DB4\ADMIT.DBT

Select area:  3, Database in Use: D:\DB4\DOCTORS.DBF   Alias: DOCTORS

File search path:
Default disk drive: D:
Print destination:  PRN:
Margin =      0
Refresh count =    0
Reprocess count =    0
Number of files open =    6
Current work area =    2

ALTERNATE  - OFF   DESIGN      - ON    HEADING    - ON   SCOREBOARD - ON
AUTOSAVE   - OFF   DEVELOP     - ON    HELP       - ON   SPACE      - ON
BELL       - ON    DEVICE      - SCRN  HISTORY    - ON   SQL        - OFF
CARRY      - OFF   ECHO        - OFF   INSTRUCT   - ON   STATUS     - ON
CATALOG    - OFF   ENCRYPTION  - ON    INTENSITY  - ON   STEP       - OFF
Press any key to continue...
Command ||D:\db4\ADMIT          ||Rec 1/13      ||File||
```

One-to-Many Relationships ■ 321

For example, both files contain fields called FIRST and LAST. The fields in the Admit file refer to patients, while the same fields in the Doctors file refer to physicians.

> *Note:* If no alias name is used, dBASE IV assumes that you are referring to a field in the current work area or a memory variable.

Enter

? Last

dBASE IV displays the name LaFish because the pointer is positioned to record 1 in the Admit database. If you want to refer to the last name field in the Doctors database, you would need to include the alias along with the field name. The alias always precedes the field name and is followed by two characters, ->. This means that the last field in the Doctors database would be referred to as Doctors->Last. Enter

? Doctors->Last

dBASE IV returns the name Erlich because that is the name stored in the last name field of the the first record in the Doctors database. While it is not necessary, you can refer to the fields in the selected work area with an alias as well. Enter

? Patients->Last

The program displays LaFish. Remember, the alias of the Admit file was reset to Patients. You must use the alias name, not the filename, when you make an extended field reference.

> *Note:* Memory variables are automatically assigned the alias M. If you define a memory variable called Last, the extended reference M->Last would refer to that variable. This is useful when a memory variable and a field in the current database have the same name. Using the M alias enables the program to distinguish the variable from the field.

Pointer Independence

When you are working with multiple database files, each database has its own record pointer. This means that you can position the pointer in each work area to different records. The currently selected

322 ■ Using Multiple Databases

work area is the Admit file. Locate the record for patient Ken Anderson by entering

```
LOCATE FOR Last="Ander"
```

The pointer in this database is now positioned at record 5. Change to the Doctors database by entering

```
SELECT Doctors
```

Position the pointer to the record for Dr. Westfall. Enter

```
LOCATE FOR Last="West"
```

The pointer is now positioned on record 4. The ability to position the file pointers independently within each work area is an important feature of dBASE IV multiple file operations. You will see in the next section how this pointer positioning can be applied to linking files.

Using Data from Open Files

There are many ways to use data stored in different database files. In the next example program, you will create a file that relates the doctors to patients so that you can keep records that show patient care as well as doctor activity. This task requires that you create a separate database file that records three items:

1. The name of the patient
2. The name of the doctor
3. The date

This information provides the link between the doctors and the patients. It is not necessary to insert all the information about the doctor or the patient. The new file forms a logical link between the other two files. Later you will learn how programs can retrieve information from both files based on this link.

To create this new file, select work area 1. Enter

```
SELECT 1
```

Create a new database called Patcare (patient care) with the following structure.

Field	Field Name	Type	Width
1	DOCTOR	Character	30
2	PATIENT	Character	30
3	DATE_CARE	Date	8

One-to-Many Relationships ■ 323

There are now three open database files, Patcare, Admit alias Patients, and Doctors.

Inserting Data from Other Databases

Suppose you want to record the fact that on 11/13/88, Ken Anderson was treated by Dr. Westfall. One way to do this is to simply enter those items into the Patcare file. However, this information is stored in the two databases open in the other work areas.

The pointers in work areas 2 and 3 are positioned at the records for Ken Anderson and Dr. Westfall respectively. Enter

```
? Patients->Last,Doctors->Last
```

The command prints the values from the different work areas.

To display the full name of the patient, you could use an extended field reference in a dBASE IV expression. Enter

```
? TRIM(Patients->Last)+", "+Patients->First
```

Enter a command to print the last and first name of the doctor in the same format we just used for the patient. Try this on your own. If you need help, the correct command can be found at the end of the chapter in the Answers to Exercises section under exercise 1.

To create a record that records the relationship between Ken Anderson and Dr. Westfall, you could use the REPLACE command to insert the data from the other databases into a record in the Patcare database.

First, create a blank record in Patcare by entering

```
APPEND BLANK
```

Insert the patient's last and first names into the patient field of the Patcare database. Enter

```
REPLACE Patient WITH TRIM(Patients->Last)+",;
  "+Patients->First
```

The command draws the information from the database, Admit, in the Patients work area. Use the REPLACE command again to insert the last and first name of the doctor into the record. Try this on your own. If you need help, the correct command can be found at the end of the chapter in the Answers to Exercises section under exercise 2.

Complete the record by inserting the date into the record. Since the date of the treatment happens to be the admission date of the patient, you can draw that information from the Admit database as well. Enter

    REPLACE Date_care WITH Patients->Admit

The resulting record contains the information that notes the interaction between doctor and patient. Save the information by entering

    USE Patcare

> *Note:* Why is it necessary to enter a USE command at this point? The reason has to do with the dBASE IV memory buffering system. If you were to exit without closing the database, and then reopen the file with USE, dBASE IV will show the last field as a blank. This is because the data in the last field is not actually transferred to the database but is being held in the memory buffer until the next entry is made. The USE command forces dBASE IV to write all the information entered into the buffer to the file.

Display the record by entering (see Figure 7.3)

    EDIT

Figure 7.3

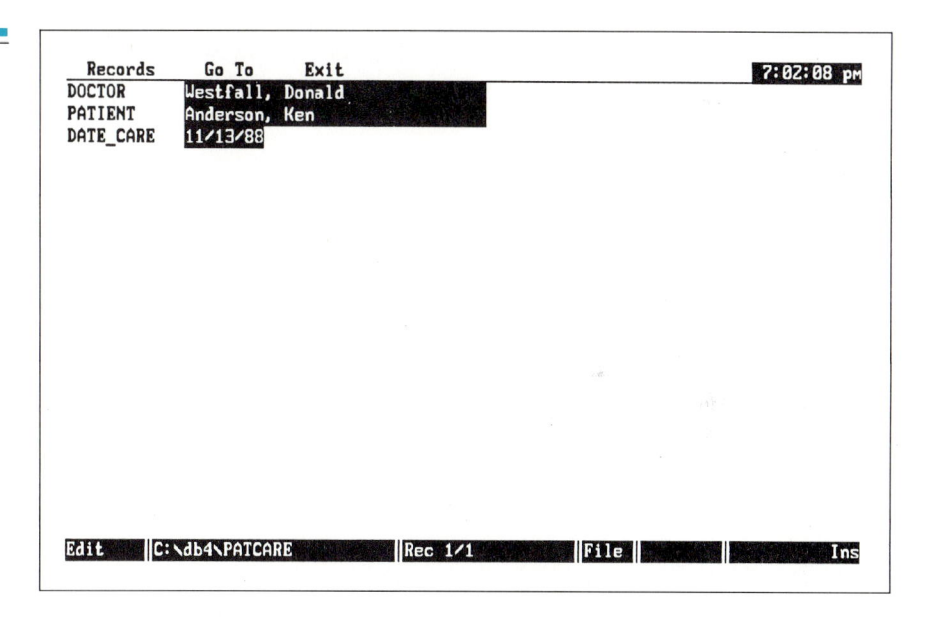

```
    Records    Go To    Exit                                   7:02:08 pm
    DOCTOR     Westfall, Donald
    PATIENT    Anderson, Ken
    DATE_CARE  11/13/88




    Edit    C:\db4\PATCARE         Rec 1/1       File              Ins
```

One-to-Many Relationships   ■   325

You've now established the basic procedure for entering records about patient treatment with the following sequence of manually entered commands.

1. **Open files.** Three different database files are required for entering records about patient care. Each of the files, Patcare, Admit, and Doctors, is placed into separate work areas by using the SELECT command.

2. **Position pointers.** In this step you position the pointers in the contributing databases, Admit and Doctors, to the records with the correct patient and doctor information.

3. **Activate entry database.** If you want to insert data from other work areas into a database, the database that will receive the data must be the selected database.

4. **Append blank.** Add a blank record to the database into which the record is to be inserted.

5. **Replace fields.** Use the REPLACE command to copy data stored in the other databases into the appropriate fields in the currently selected database.

These steps will create a new record that links a doctor and a patient. The link between the files is a logical link, not a physical link. dBASE IV does not actually keep track of the relationship. You will see later in this chapter that in order to retrieve the linked data, you must perform operations based on the information stored in Patcare. The only use of Patcare records is to let you locate the records in the larger databases Admit and Doctors.

Exit the record by pressing (Esc).

The next task is to use the logic just outlined to create a program that makes entries into the patient care database. Close all the databases by entering

CLOSE DATABASE

Programming Multiple Databases

The next program you'll create makes it easy to enter records into the Patcare database. A key concept to remember when writing multiple-file applications is that a user is not concerned with the number of databases he is working with. The user only wants to record the information as quickly and as accurately as possible. The process of information being passed between different databases in different work areas is invisible to the user. Your job as the programmer is to use the tools provided by dBASE IV to deal with all the details without users being aware that they are taking place.

What dBASE IV tools should you use? Because the files are small, you might want to create popup menus to let users select the patients and the doctors that should be recorded. Begin by creating a program called Addcare. Enter

```
MODIFY COMMAND Addcare
```

To begin the program, use the Setoff program created in the previous chapter to turn off the environment attributes.

```
DO SETOFF
```

The next sequence of commands opens the databases needed by the program and places them into work areas so that data from each file is available for use. The ALIAS clause assigns the alias Patients to the Admit file.

```
* place databases in use
USE Patcare
SELECT B
USE Admit ALIAS Patients
SELECT C
USE Doctors
```

The next step is to display a status box at the bottom of the screen. The purpose of this box is to display the names of patients and doctors as they are selected by a user. When a popup menu is deactivated, the screen is cleared of the menu. It is helpful to display the name selected to ensure the correct name was picked from the popup menu.

```
* selection status box
@ 19,0 TO 23,55
@ 20,5 SAY "Patient:"
@ 21,5 SAY "Doctor:"
@ 22,5 SAY "Date:"
```

With the box displayed, the next step is to allow the user to select the name of a patient. This means that you need to activate the Patients work area.

```
* patients popup menu
SELECT Patients
```

It might be advantageous to display the names of the patients in alphabetical order. This requires you to index the database by last name.

```
INDEX ON Last TO Lastpat
```

Define a popup menu using PROMPT FIELD so that the menu automatically lists all of the patients' last names. The MESSAGE clause displays the message **Select Patient** at the bottom of the screen while the popup menu is active.

```
DEFINE POPUP Patients FROM 1,0 TO 10,30
PROMPT FIELD Last MESSAGE "Select Patient"
```

Set the ON SELECTION command to deactivate the popup menu when a selection is made.

```
ON SELECTION POPUP Patients DEACTIVATE POPUP
```

Once the popup menu has been defined, it can be displayed. In order to give the user some idea of the total number of names that can be scrolled through the menu, display a message just above the menu, on line 0, that lists the total number of records in the Admit database. The RECCOUNT() function returns a value equal to the total number of records in the database.

```
@ 0,0 SAY LTRIM(STR(RECCOUNT()))+" Patients"
```

With this prompt displayed, activate the menu.

```
ACTIVATE POPUP Patients
```

This menu deactivates when a selection is made. Following that selection, you need to position the pointer to the record that corresponds to the selection from the popup menu. This is done by using the PROMPT() function to locate the record that corresponds to the selection made from the menu. Since the database is indexed on the last name field, use the SEEK command to position the pointer.

> *Note:* It is important to understand that using a popup field menu on an indexed database changes the relationship between menu bar number and database record number. In an indexed database, the first patient name will be the first alphabetical name, in this case Anderson. The popup menu will assign the bar number 1 to that item. However, Anderson may not be record 1. You could not locate the selected item by entering GOTO BAR(). Instead, you need to perform a logical search to find the record that matches the displayed item as captured by the PROMPT() function.

```
SEEK PROMPT()
```

The pointer is now positioned to the correct patient record. To confirm this selection, you can display the name of the selected patient in the box at the bottom of the screen. This operation has no logical function in the program. Its sole purpose is to allow the user to remember or confirm the selected item. Such confirmation displays help users since people sometimes find it difficult to remember what they have chosen. Your program functions the same way whether you display a confirmation prompt or not. However, programs always have a better feel when you display this type of information following a selection.

```
@ 20,15 SAY TRIM(Last)+", "+First
```

With the patient selected and the name displayed, you can go on and repeat the same procedure using the doctors work area and the doctors popup menu.

```
* doctor's popup menu
SELECT Doctors
INDEX ON Last TO Lastdoc
DEFINE POPUP Doctors FROM 1,0 TO 10,30 PROMPT;
  FIELD Last MESSAGE "Select Doctor"
ON SELECTION POPUP Doctors DEACTIVATE POPUP
@ 0,0
@ 0,0 SAY LTRIM(STR(RECCOUNT()))+" Doctors";
  ACTIVATE POPUP Doctors
SEEK PROMPT()
@ 21,15 SAY TRIM(Last)+", "+First
```

There is an additional command in the doctor's procedure that was not in the patient's procedure. That command, @ 0,0, has the effect of clearing line 0 without affecting the rest of the screen. The reason this is done is that the display of the number of doctors on line 1 will not completely overwrite the previous number of patients display. By clearing the line before you write the number of doctors, you avoid the display of the extra characters.

With the doctor and patient databases positioned to the correct records, you can record that information in the Patcare database. This is done by selecting the Patcare work area and adding a blank record. The REPLACE command then inserts data from the records in the other work areas into the new record. The assumption is made that the treatment date is the admission date of the patient.

```
* enter date
SELECT Patcare
@ 0,0
@ 1,0 to 4, 50
APPEND BLANK
REPLACE Date_care WITH Patients->Admit,;
 Patient WITH TRIM(Patients->Last)+",;
 "+Patients->First,;
 Doctor WITH TRIM(Doctors->Last)+",;
 "+Doctors->First
```

While it is likely that the patient received treatment on the admission date, it may not always be the case. The program should allow the user to edit the date so that it can be changed when necessary. You can also use a VALID clause to make sure that a treatment date does not exceed the discharge date stored in the patient record.

```
@ 2,10 SAY "Enter Date of Treatment"
@ 3,10 GET Date_care VALID Date_care<=;
Patients->Discharge
READ
```

Display the revised date in the box at the bottom of the screen and pause to allow the user to inspect the entry.

```
@ 22,15 SAY Date_care
@ 23,79
WAIT
```

Finally, close the databases, release the menus, and run the Seton program to reset the environment.

```
*close databases and popups
CLOSE ALL
RELEASE POPUP Patients,Doctors
DO Seton
RETURN
```

Save the program by pressing (Ctrl)-(End). Execute the program by entering the following command; dBASE IV automatically compiles the program for you.

```
DO Addcare
```

The program begins by displaying the box at the bottom of the screen and the patients popup menu (see Figure 7.4).

Move the highlight bar to the name Goren. Select that patient by pressing (↵). The patient's name is placed into the box at the bottom of the screen, and the doctors menu is displayed.

Move the highlight bar to the name Craig. Select that doctor by pressing (↵). The doctor's name is inserted into the box at the bottom of the screen and an entry area for the treatment date is displayed at the top of the screen. The admission date of the patient is entered as a default value.

Enter a new date for the treatment.

```
122588
```

dBASE IV beeps to warn you that the date you entered was invalid because it was beyond the discharge date for the patient. The cursor remains in the entry field. Enter a valid date.

```
120688
```

Figure 7.4

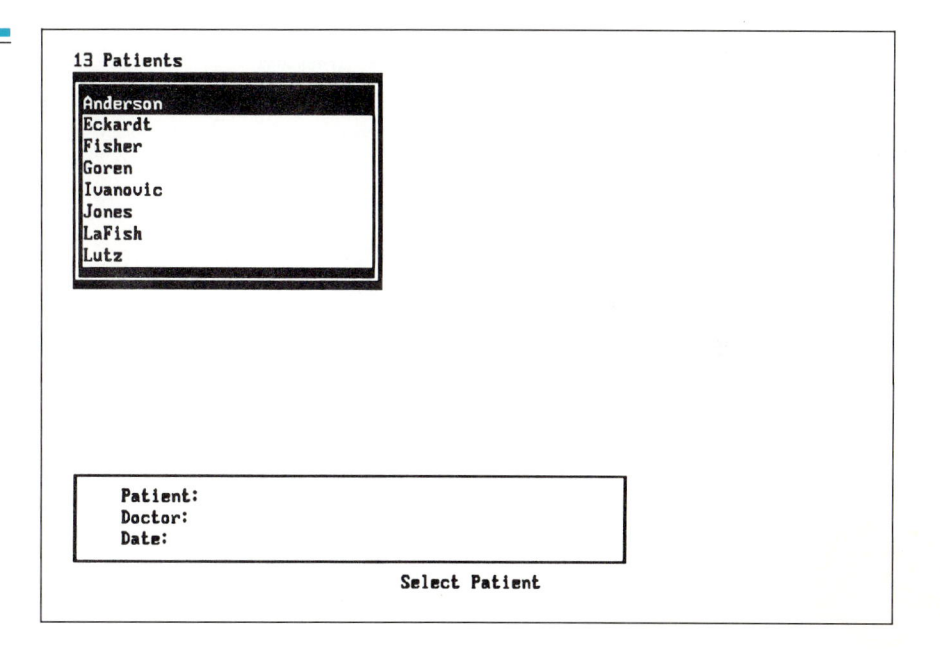

```
13 Patients
┌─────────────┐
│ Anderson    │
│ Eckardt     │
│ Fisher      │
│ Goren       │
│ Ivanovic    │
│ Jones       │
│ LaFish      │
│ Lutz        │
└─────────────┘




    ┌──────────────────────────┐
    │ Patient:                 │
    │ Doctor:                  │
    │ Date:                    │
    └──────────────────────────┘
                Select Patient
```

One-to-Many Relationships ■ 331

The box at the bottom of the screen now contains the complete record entered into the Patcare file (see Figure 7.5).

Complete the program by pressing ⏎.

To confirm the results of the program, open and list the contents of the Patcare database.

```
USE Patcare
LIST
```

Record 2 registers the information entered through the menus of the Addcare program (see Figure 7.6).

Procedures and Bar Menus

The previous program pulled together the concepts of multiple databases and popup menus. However, the program was written in a strictly linear fashion. It ran through the entry items in a strict order—patient, doctor, and date—and exited at the end. The program, though a good demonstration of basic techniques, is not a practical application yet. To make this a useful program you need to build in the following features:

Figure 7.5

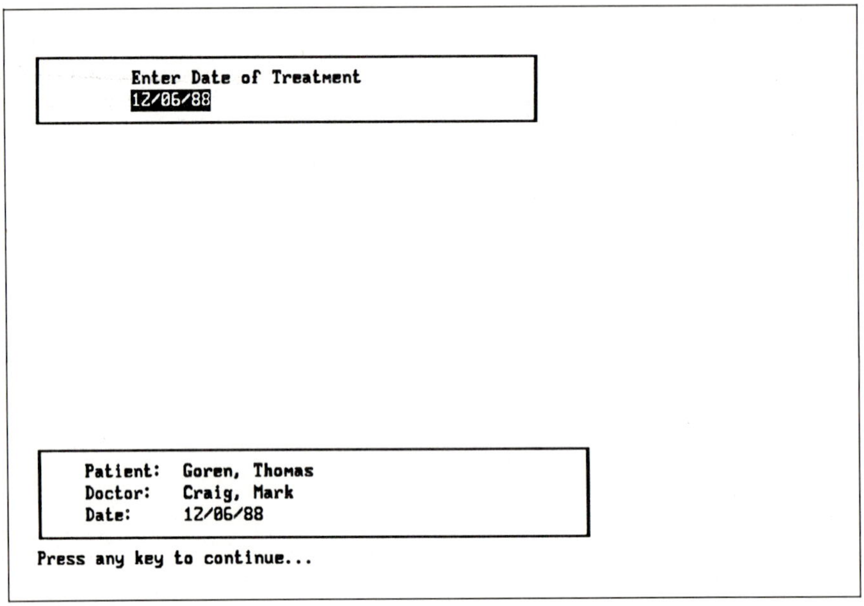

```
       Enter Date of Treatment
       12/06/88




       Patient:  Goren, Thomas
       Doctor:   Craig, Mark
       Date:     12/06/88
Press any key to continue...
```

332 ■ Using Multiple Databases

1. **Select operations.** Since the entry of each record requires the selection of three items, you should be able to select the entry of the items in any order.
2. **Revise items.** You should be able to go back and change a selection—doctor, patient, or date—as often as needed.
3. **Accept.** You should offer the user the opportunity to add the information after it has been selected. This gives the user a chance to reject or correct a mistaken choice.
4. **Looping.** The program ought to be able to allow the user to enter as many records as necessary.

To accomplish these goals, you must learn two new techniques. The first is a built-in dBASE IV feature called a menu bar. A menu bar, similar in its use to popup menus, displays options horizontally across the top of the screen. The cursor can be moved to the left or right in order to highlight and then select menu items.

The typical use of menu bars is to consolidate and organize programs that use several popup menus. The menu bar contains a list of options, each of which activates a popup menu. The menu bar makes it easy to create a program to access popup menus in random order. Because the multi-database program Addcare is built around the use of

Figure 7.6

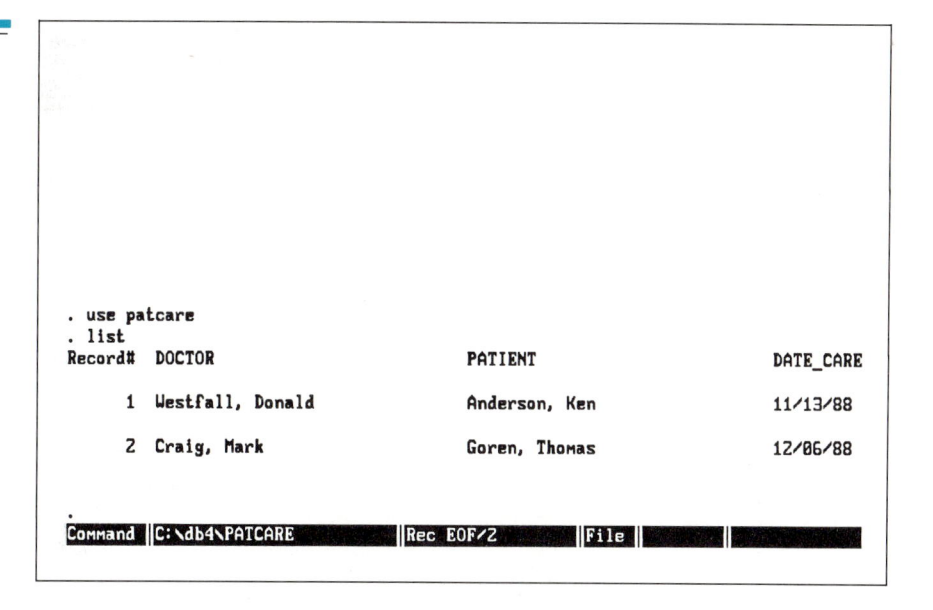

```
. use patcare
. list
Record#  DOCTOR                    PATIENT              DATE_CARE
      1  Westfall, Donald          Anderson, Ken        11/13/88
      2  Craig, Mark               Goren, Thomas        12/06/88
.
Command  C:\db4\PATCARE            Rec EOF/2     File
```

several popup menus, the menu bar system is a good way to consolidate and manage those menus.

The second technique involves the use of program procedures, a special form of subroutines. A normal subroutine as we have defined it in this book is a program file accessed, or called, by another program. If you have a program requiring a large number of subroutines, you must call many individual .prg files, each one containing a subroutine.

This technique has several disadvantages. When you create these programs, it is difficult to coordinate the routines because you have to load a disk file for each program to read or edit its commands. When the program executes, dBASE IV is slowed down by loading each of the separate files called as a subroutine.

Using procedures is an alternate way to string together subroutines. Procedures are individual subroutines grouped into a single .prg file, each functioning separately. A procedure is a group of commands beginning with the PROCEDURE command and ending with the RETURN statement. dBASE IV allows you to create up to 1,170 procedures in one .prg file.

> *Note:* The total number of commands in a procedure file is limited by the amount of RAM available to dBASE IV.

Procedures overcome the editing problems of program subroutines by storing all the commands in a single .prg file. The speed of execution is increased because dBASE IV has only to load one .prg file containing all of the routines.

The nature of the next program you will create requires the use of several subroutines. This is almost always the case when you use menu bars and popup menus together in the same program.

Using a Menu Bar

Menu bars have much in common with popup menus. They differ only in that menu bars assume each menu option will activate some special operation. Each popup menu triggers only one event that occurs no matter how many bars appear in the window. When you create a menu bar, you can set a separate event for each of the items in the bar. This means that if you have four menu-bar options, you can define four ON SELECTION event-management commands. The menu bar operates in a manner similar to the DO CASE structure—menu bar 1 = case 1 = do something.

The menu bar is ideal for coordinating subroutines.

To learn the basic use of menu bars and the commands that create them, let's return to the Statsmnu program. This program coordinates the selection of the three statistical programs, Insured, Ages, and Countins. Another program, Statspop, implemented a popup menu to run the same subroutines as the Statsmnu program. Create a new program, called Statsbar, to use a bar menu to coordinate the statistical programs.

```
MODIFY COMMAND Statsbar
```

Begin the program by running the Setoff program and clearing the screen.

```
DO SETOFF
CLEAR
```

The next command defines the bar menu. The command does not require location coordinates, as does DEFINE POPUP, because dBASE IV assumes the menu bar will appear on line zero of the display.

```
DEFINE MENU Patients
```

Once a bar menu is defined, you can proceed to define pads for the menu. Each one of the options listed on the menu bar requires a pad. When you define a pad, you assign it a name. This is different from popup menus where each bar is assigned a numerical value. The text that appears in the menu bar pad is a prompt.

The command below creates a pad called "insured." The pad shows the text Insurance Status. In this program, the name of the menu pad matches the name of the subroutine activated by that pad. This is not required but it makes it simpler to remember the name of the pad.

```
DEFINE PAD insured of Patients PROMPT "Insurance
Status"
```

The next two pad definitions create pads corresponding to the other two subroutines you want to run from this menu.

```
DEFINE PAD Ages of Patients PROMPT "Patient Ages"
DEFINE PAD Countins of Patients PROMPT "Insurance
Summary"
```

The last pad, the exit pad, terminates the program.

```
DEFINE PAD Exit OF Patients PROMPT "Exit"
```

The pads appear on the menu bar in the order of their defintion; thus, the bar will read **Insurance Status, Patient Ages, Insurance Summary,** and **Exit**.

The next section of the program uses an event-management command, ON SELECTION PAD, to execute a command when a pad is selected. ON SELECTION PAD requires you to enter the name of the pad and the bar menu to which it relates. In each case, the event for each pad is set as a DO command that executes a subroutine.

```
ON SELECTION PAD Insured OF Patients DO Insured
ON SELECTION PAD Ages OF Patients DO Ages
ON SELECTION PAD Countins OF Patients DO Countins
```

The final ON SELECTION PAD deactivates the menu when Exit is selected.

```
ON SELECTION PAD Exit OF Patients DEACTIVATE MENU
```

The remainder of the program is quite simple because the activation of a bar menu creates a loop making the bar menu options available until the bar menu is specifically deactivated. This built-in loop cuts down on the amount of code and the work you have to perform as a programmer. Complete the rest of the program.

```
ACTIVATE MENU Patients
RELEASE Patients
DO Seton
RETURN
```

The entire program reads as follows:

```
DO Setoff
CLEAR
DEFINE MENU Patients
DEFINE PAD Insured OF Patients PROMPT "Insurance;
 Status"
DEFINE PAD Ages OF Patients PROMPT "Patient Ages"
DEFINE PAD Countins OF Patients PROMPT "Insurance;
 Summary"
DEFINE PAD Exit OF Patients PROMPT "Exit"
ON SELECTION PAD Insured OF Patients DO Insured
ON SELECTION PAD Ages OF Patients DO Ages
ON SELECTION PAD Countins OF Patients DO Countins
```

Figure 7.7

```
 Insurance Status   Patient Ages   Insurance Summary   Exit
```

```
ON SELECTION PAD Exit OF Patients DEACTIVATE MENU
ACTIVATE MENU Patients
RELEASE Patients
DO Seton
RETURN
```

This program has just 15 lines of code, as compared to Statsmnu's 43 lines. Save and execute the program by entering (Ctrl)-(End),

```
DO Statsbar
```

The program displays a menu bar at the top of the screen. dBASE IV automatically highlights the first pad on the bar (see Figure 7.7).

To execute a program, you highlight the pad and press (↵). Suppose you want to run the Ages program. Press (→)-(↵). The menu bar program calls the subroutine Ages and executes the program.

Conclude the subroutine by pressing (↵). The menu bar reappears at the top of the screen (see Figure 7.8).

You'll notice that because the Ages program does not clear the screen after it concludes, the last display from that program remains on the

Figure 7.8

```
 Insurance Status   Patient Ages   Insurance Summary   Exit

            Below 18                              2
            18 to 44                             10
            45 to 64                              1
            Over 65                               0
```

Procedures and Bar Menus ■ 337

screen. Also notice that the highlight bar remains on the last selected pad when the menu is redisplayed. Run the Insured program by pressing ⬅-↵.

Exit the program by pressing ↵ two times.

dBASE IV provides a second way to highlight a menu pad. Entering a combination of the (Alt) key and the first letter of the text in a pad causes the highlight bar to move to that option. If two or more options have the same first letter, dBASE IV moves to the next matching pad. Press (Alt)-e. The highlight bar moves to the Exit pad. Exit the menu bar program by pressing ↵.

Procedures

The previous program, Statsbar, calls three subroutines, Insured, Ages, and Countins. At the moment, these subroutines reside in separate files. But you can combine all four subroutines into one program file containing four procedures.

Create a new program file called Statspro by entering

```
MODIFY COMMAND Statspro
```

This program will use four procedures, the Statsbar program being the first. All procedures begin with the PROCEDURE command, followed by the name of the program.

```
PROCEDURE Statsbar
```

Since the Statsbar program already exists, simply copy the commands in that program into the procedure. Press (Alt)-w and type w r.

```
Statsbar.prg
```

The entire contents of the Statsbar program loads into the editor following the PROCEDURE command.

> *Note:* The editor always inserts an extra blank line. Blank lines have no effect on dBASE IV programs and are automatically eliminated when the program is compiled.

All procedures must end with a RETURN command. Because the Statsbar program already ends with RETURN, the procedure is complete. You can now move the cursor to the end of the program and create a second procedure. Press (Ctrl)-(PgDn). Insert some blank lines by pressing ↵ two times.

■ Using Multiple Databases

The entry order of the procedures is not significant. Define the next procedure, the Insured program, by entering another PROCEDURE command.

```
PROCEDURE Insured
```

Load the contents of the Insured file by pressing (Alt)-w and typing w r. Then, enter

```
Insured.prg
```

Move to the bottom of the program by pressing (Ctrl)-(PgDn).

The second program has been added to the procedure file. Repeat the process for two more programs, Ages and Countins. Try this on your own. If you need help, the correct command can be found at the end of the chapter in the Answers to Exercises section under exercise 3.

Save the program by pressing (Ctrl)-(End). Compile the program.

```
COMPILE Statspro
```

Executing a Procedure File

Procedure files do not execute exactly the same way as programs. Since the Statspro program contains a number of procedures, entering DO STATSPRO confuses dBASE IV as to which of the procedures in the file to execute.

Instead, use a procedure file like a database file. Once a procedure file is opened, you can execute any one of its procedures by using a DO command. But the procedure file is never directly accessed with a DO command.

To open a procedure file, use the SET PROCEDURE TO command. Enter

```
SET PROCEDURE TO Statspro
```

Execute the Statsbar procedure by entering

```
DO Statsbar
```

The program executes exactly as if your were using separate files. In running the programs from the menu, you should notice a slight increase in performance because dBASE IV does not have to fetch each subroutine from the disk.

Execute the Countins program by entering (Alt)-i. Return to the menu by pressing (↵). Exit the program by entering (Alt)-e.

Procedures and Bar Menus ■ 339

A procedure file remains open until you explicitly close it, or open another procedure file. dBASE IV permits only one active procedure file at a time. To close the current procedure file, enter

```
SET PROCEDURE TO
```

Menu Bars and Multi-Database Applications

You are now ready to use the principles of multiple databases, menu bars, popup menus, and procedures to create a program that allows you to create patient care records.

Begin by creating a new procedure file. Enter

```
MODIFY COMMAND Addpro
```

To create a program for entering the patient care information outlined earlier, it is necessary to create several procedures. A final procedure ties all the parts into a single program.

The first procedure, Setup, executes the commands to set up the screen, files, and menus. The procedure begins by running the Setoff program.

```
PROCEDURE Setup
DO SETOFF
```

The next section of the Setup procedure opens the databases needed for the program. The SELECT command assigns the work areas for the database. The Doctors and Admit databases use an index you created to order the records alphabetically by last name.

Note: You can speed up the application by creating indexes for the files and, to maintain their accuracy, always use those index files when entering data into those files. Then you could simply open the index files instead of creating them from scratch.

```
* open databases
SELECT a
USE Patcare
SELECT b
USE Admit ALIAS Patients
INDEX ON Last TO Lastpat
SELECT c
USE Doctors
INDEX ON Last TO Lastdoc
```

With the files assigned to work areas, opened, and indexed, the next task is to define the program's menus. The first menu, the popup menu for the Admit file, is called PATIENTS. The DEFINE POPUP command uses PROMPT FIELD to automatically generate the bars based on the contents of the Last Name field. The ON SELECTION POPUP command deactivates the menu.

```
* define popups
DEFINE POPUP Patients FROM 1,0 TO 10,30 PROMPT
FIELD Last MESSAGE
     "Select Patient"
ON SELECTION POPUP Patients DEACTIVATE POPUP
```

The next set of commands performs the same function, defining a popup menu, for the Doctors file. The position of the upper left corner of this popup menu is moved to 1,16 to display the popup menu below the second pad, Select Doctor, in the menu bar.

```
DEFINE POPUP Doctors FROM 1,16 TO 10,46 PROMPT;
 FIELD Last MESSAGE "Select Doctor"
ON SELECTION POPUP Doctors DEACTIVATE POPUP
```

The last popup menu, Exit, does not use the PROMPT FIELD clause. Instead, it displays two options: one that saves the current selection as a record in the Patcare database and the other that exits the program. If data is entered but not saved with the "Insert Data As Shown" option, no record is created.

```
DEFINE POPUP EXIT FROM 1,35 TO 4,60
DEFINE BAR 1 OF EXIT PROMPT "Insert Data As Shown"
DEFINE BAR 2 OF EXIT PROMPT "Exit Program"
ON SELECTION POPUP Exit DEACTIVATE POPUP
```

The final definitions in the Setup procedure define the menu bar itself. The bar will have four pads, Select Patient, Select Doctor, Date, and Exit.

```
* define menu bar
DEFINE MENU Addcare
DEFINE PAD Pick_pat OF Addcare PROMPT "Select;
 Patient"
DEFINE PAD Pick_doc OF Addcare PROMPT "Select;
 Doctor"
```

```
DEFINE PAD Pick_date OF Addcare PROMPT "Date"
DEFINE PAD EXIT OF Addcare PROMPT "Exit"
```

Each of the four pads calls a different procedure. To make writing the program easier, the names of the pads match the names of the procedures.

Note: This is not required.

```
ON SELECTION PAD Pick_pat OF Addcare DO Pick_pat
ON SELECTION PAD Pick_doc OF Addcare DO Pick_doc
ON SELECTION PAD Pick_date OF Addcare DO Care_date
ON SELECTION PAD EXIT OF Addcare DO End_prog
```

With these definitions in place, you can end the Setup procedure.

```
RETURN
```

The next procedure draws the data box that appears at the bottom of the screen. The box starts out empty but will eventually display the selected patient, doctor, and treatment date.

```
Procedure Draw_box
* selection status box
@ 19,0 to 23,55
@ 20,5 SAY "Patient:"
@ 21,5 SAY "Doctor:"
@ 22,5 SAY "Date:"
RETURN
```

The next procedure is called Pick_pat (pick patient). The routine begins by selecting the correct database and takes advantage of the popup menu. To select the patient, the popup menu is activated. When a selection is made, the PROMPT() function positions the pointer to the correct record. The last line of the procedure displays the selected name in the box at the bottom of the screen.

```
PROCEDURE Pick_pat
SELECT Patients
ACTIVATE POPUP Patients
SEEK PROMPT()
@ 20,15 SAY TRIM(Last)+", "+First
RETURN
```

The next procedure, Pick_doc (pick doctor), is structured like the Pick_pat procedure.

```
PROCEDURE Pick_doc
SELECT Doctors
ACTIVATE POPUP Doctors
SEEK PROMPT()
@ 21,15 SAY TRIM(Last)+", "+First
RETURN
```

The Care_date procedure enters the date. The procedure defines a public variable, Care_date. The variable is made public because it is created in a procedure. If it were not made public, it would be released when the procedure ended. By declaring the variable public it is accessible to the other procedures. The variable is set equal to the admission date for the selected patient. This will serve as a default value. In this program, the entry of the date is made to a variable rather than directly into the Date_care field of the Patcare database so that no data will be inserted into Patcare database until the user approves of the choices made.

```
PROCEDURE Care_date
PUBLIC Care_date
Care_date=Patients->Admit
```

The variable appears in a box to allow the user to edit the date if necessary. A VALID clause prevents the entry of a date that exceeds the discharge date.

```
@ 10,0 to 14, 50
@ 12,10 SAY "Enter Date of Treatment"
@ 13,10 GET Care_date Valid Care_date<=;
Patients->Discharge
READ
```

Once the entry has been made, clear that area of the screen by using a CLEAR clause with the @ command. This command functions to clear the area of the screen indicated by the coordinates. The date is also displayed in the box at the bottom of the screen.

```
@ 10,0 CLEAR TO 14,50
@ 22,15 SAY Care_date
RETURN
```

Procedures and Bar Menus

The End_prog procedure saves the selected data and/or exits the program. The procedure begins with the activation of the exit popup menu.

```
PROCEDURE End_prog
ACTIVATE POPUP Exit
```

Following the menu, a DO CASE structure evaluates the results. Menu highlight bar 1 indicates that the user selected to save the data shown in the box at the bottom of the screen. This save operation appends a blank record and replaces the fields with the information stored in the other databases and the Care_date memory variable. An @/CLEAR TO command erases the information in the box at the bottom of the screen to allow the user to select another record.

```
DO CASE
     CASE BAR()=1
          SELECT Patcare
          APPEND BLANK
          REPLACE Date_care WITH Care_date,;
          Patient WITH TRIM(Patients->Last)+",;
           "+Patients->First,;
          Doctor WITH TRIM(Doctors->Last)+",;
           "+Doctors->First
          @ 20,15 CLEAR TO 22,49
```

Highlight bar 2 indicates the user wants to exit the program. The commands below close the databases, release the menu bar, popup menus, and memory variables.

Note: Since Care_date was declared as a public variable, it must be explicitly released or it will remain active after the program terminates.

```
     CASE BAR()=2
          CLOSE DATABASE
          DEACTIVATE MENU
          RELEASE MENU Addcare
          RELEASE POPUP Patients, Doctors,Exit
          RELEASE Care_date
```

```
        DO Seton
        CLEAR
        RETURN
ENDCASE
RETURN
```

The final procedure, called the main line of the program, ties all the parts together. In this case, the main line is quite simple. Activating the menu bar links most of the procedures together because of the way the menus are defined. The procedure Add_menu is the one you will execute in order to run the program.

```
PROCEDURE Add_menu
DO Setup
DO Draw_box
ACTIVATE MENU Addcare
DO Seton
RETURN
```

Save the program by presssing Ctrl-End. Compile the procedure file by entering

`COMPILE Addpro`

To use the procedure file, enter

`SET PROCEDURE TO Addpro`

Run the program by executing the main line procedure, Add_menu.

`DO Add_menu`

The program displays the menu bar at the top of the screen and the empty data box at the bottom of the screen (see Figure 7.9).

To select a patient, press ↵. The popup menu for patients appears (see Figure 7.10).

Move the highlight bar to Jones. Press ↵. The name of the patient appears in the box at the bottom of the screen. Select a doctor by pressing Alt-s.

Move the highlight bar to LaFish. Press ↵. Enter the date. Press Alt-d.

Procedures and Bar Menus ■ **345**

Figure 7.9

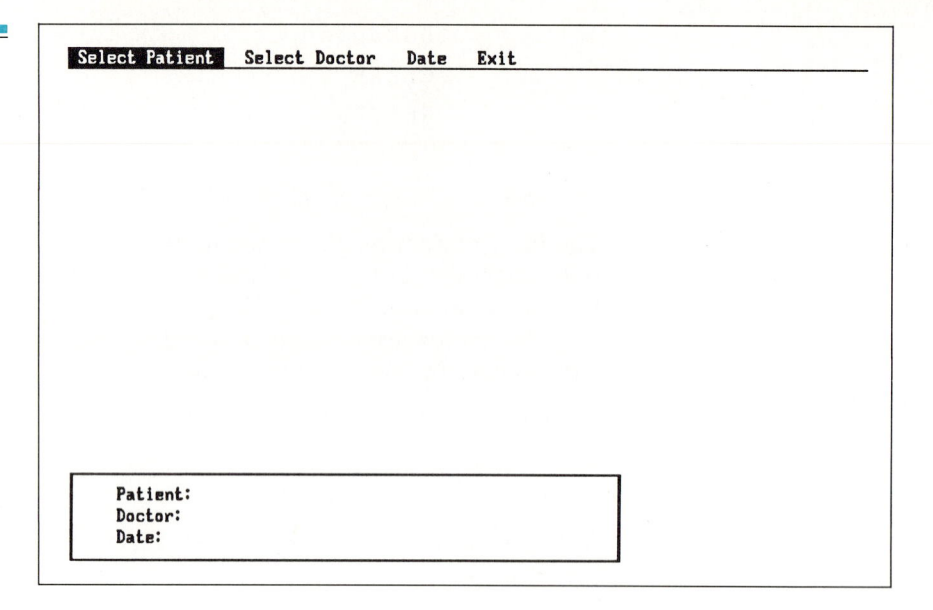

```
Select Patient   Select Doctor   Date   Exit




                    Patient:
                    Doctor:
                    Date:
```

Figure 7.10

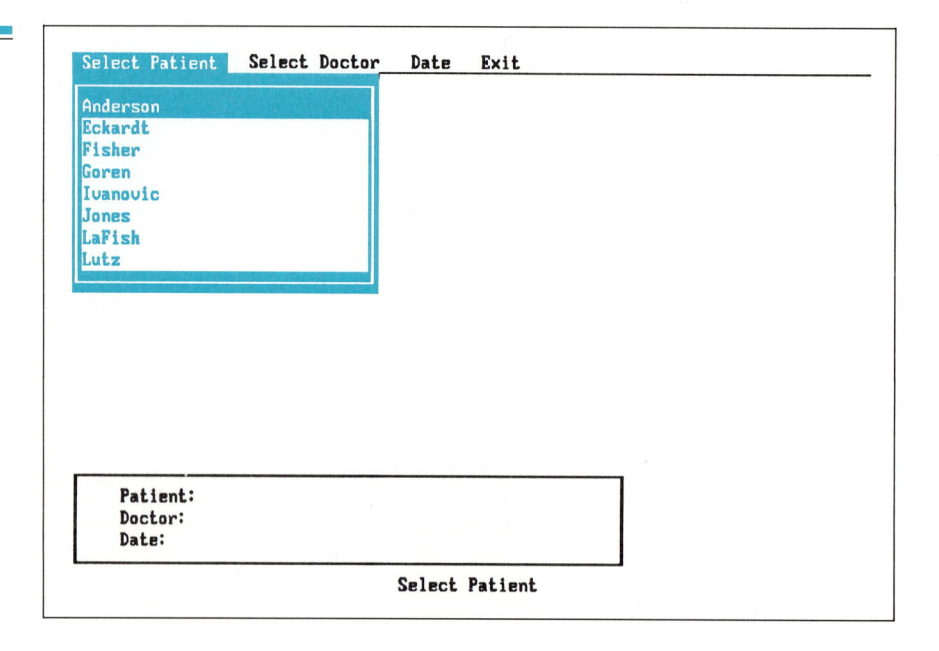

```
Select Patient   Select Doctor   Date   Exit
  Anderson
  Eckardt
  Fisher
  Goren
  Ivanovic
  Jones
  LaFish
  Lutz



                    Patient:
                    Doctor:
                    Date:
                                       Select Patient
```

346 ■ Using Multiple Databases

The program displays a box in the center of the screen for entering the date. The admission date of the patient is displayed as the default (see Figure 7.11).

Accept the date by pressing ⏎.

You can change any of the items as many times as you wish. For example, you can change the name of the doctor to Westfall by pressing ← and typing W.

The box at the bottom of the screen shows the new doctor.

Display the Exit menu by pressing Alt-e. Figure 7.12 shows the Exit menu.

Save the currently displayed data by pressing ⏎. The box clears, indicating the program is ready for another record.

Exit the program by pressing E. The program terminates and dBASE IV returns to the dot prompt. One last step is required to close the procedure file. Enter

CLOSE PROCEDURE

Figure 7.11

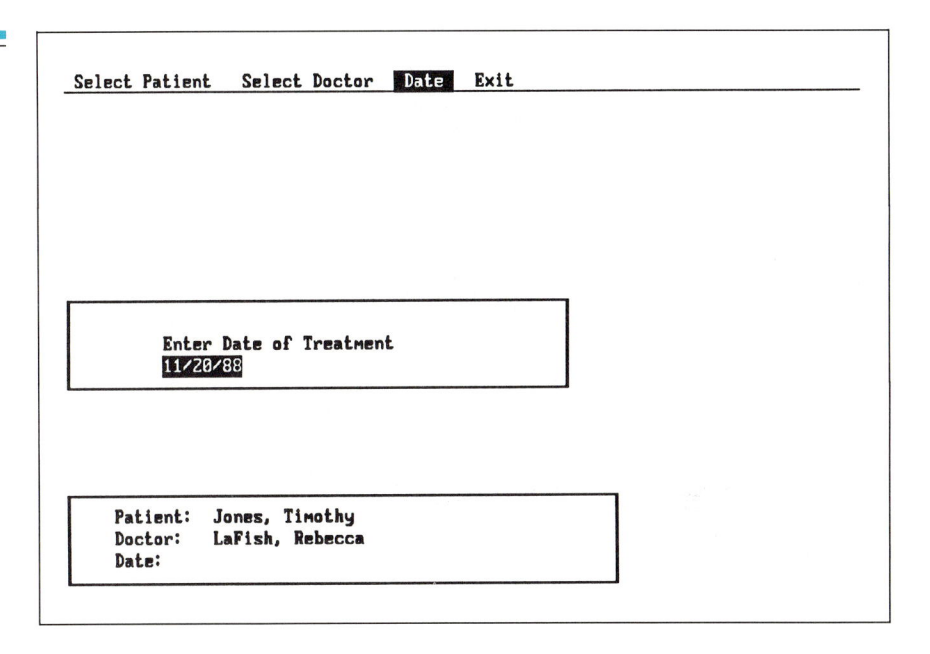

```
Select Patient    Select Doctor    Date    Exit
────────────────────────────────────────────────




              ┌─────────────────────────────────┐
              │    Enter Date of Treatment      │
              │    11/20/88                     │
              └─────────────────────────────────┘



        ┌─────────────────────────────┐
        │  Patient:  Jones, Timothy   │
        │  Doctor:   LaFish, Rebecca  │
        │  Date:                      │
        └─────────────────────────────┘
```

Procedures and Bar Menus ■ 347

Figure 7.12

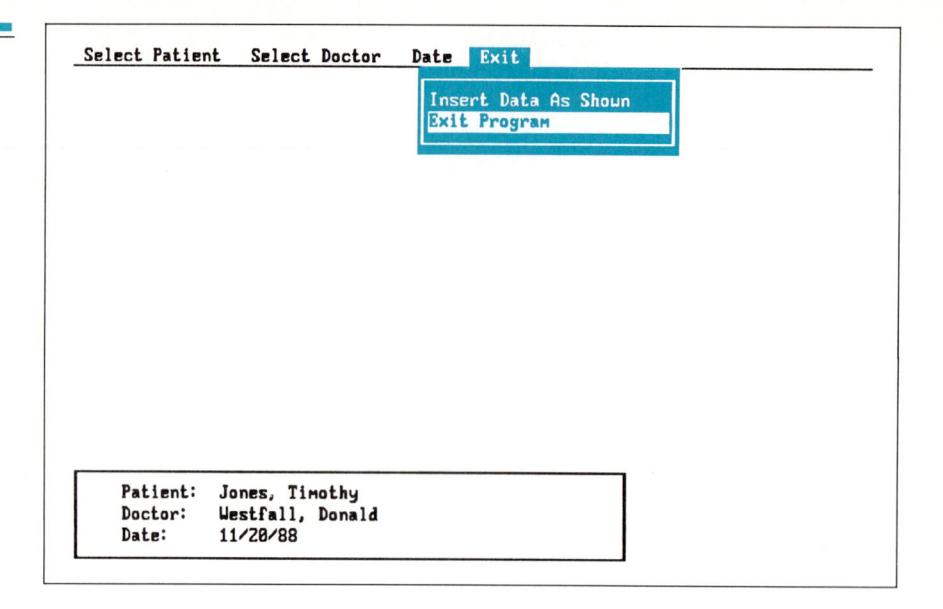

```
Select Patient    Select Doctor    Date   Exit
                                          ┌─────────────────────┐
                                          │ Insert Data As Shown│
                                          │ Exit Program        │
                                          └─────────────────────┘




                  ┌──────────────────────────────────┐
                  │ Patient:  Jones, Timothy         │
                  │ Doctor:   Westfall, Donald       │
                  │ Date:     11/20/88               │
                  └──────────────────────────────────┘
```

SET PROCEDURE TO and CLOSE PROCEDURE perform the same function.

Running a Procedure

You can compress the commands needed to load, run, and close a procedure file by creating a simple program containing these three commands. Enter

MODIFY COMMAND Runpro

The commands needed for this file comprise one that opens the procedure, one that executes the main routine, and one that closes the procedure.

SET PROCEDURE TO Addpro

DO Add_menu

CLOSE PROCEDURE

Save and execute the program by pressing (Ctrl)-(End). Enter

DO Runpro

The small program loads the procedure file and then executes the main routine.

Use the menus to add the following records to the Patcare database.

Doctor	Patient	Date
Craig, Mark	Goren, Thomas	2/06/88
Westfall, Donald	Jones, Timothy	1/20/88
Westfall, Donald	Eckardt, Lois	1/24/88
Bates, Norman	Eckardt, Lois	1/24/88
Christenson, Amanda	Fisher, Scott	2/02/88
LaFish, Rebecca	Fisher, Scott	2/02/88
Craig, Mark	Fisher, Scott	2/02/88
Christenson, Amanda	Sorenson, Cynthia	1/28/88
Christenson, Amanda	Morgan, Robert	1/21/88

Exit the program using the Exit menu option.

When the program terminates, the procedure file automatically closes and dBASE IV returns to its normal status.

Retrieving Data from Multiple Databases

The previous program demonstrates one way to enter data into a database from other databases. Once you have stored the data, you will eventually need to retrieve it. It is this kind of program that you will create next.

Before you begin writing the program, let's explore some of the retrieval tools dBASE IV provides by executing commands at the dot prompt. Begin by opening the databases involved with patient records. Keep in mind that you are starting in work area 1. Enter

```
USE Patcare
```

Open the next database, the Admit file, in the second work area. In the previous section you used the SELECT command to activate work area 2 in order to place a database in that work area. dBASE IV allows you to skip that extra step by using the IN clause with the USE command. The IN clause allows you to indicate a work area. The following command opens the Admit file in work area 2.

Note: You could use the work area letters, A through J, instead of the numbers 1 through 10.

```
USE Admit in 2
```

Open the Doctors database in work area 3. Try this on your own. If you need help, the correct command can be found at the end of the chapter in the Answers to Exercises section under exercise 4.

Procedures and Bar Menus ■ 349

Linking Pointers

The previous section explained how dBASE IV moves the record pointer in each of its work areas independently of other work areas. You used this facility in the Add_menu program to position the pointer to different records in the Admit and Doctors databases. Then, you copied the patient and doctor names into a new record in the Patcare file.

When you retrieve data, you reverse this process. The records in the Patcare file provide the key values for positioning pointers to the records that relate to each other. Suppose you want to know the Medical Record Number (field Med_rec_no) and the specialty (field Field) of the doctor who treated the patients stored in Patcare file. You would need to perform the following actions:

1. Open three databases in separate work areas. (You have already accomplished this step.)

2. Use the doctor's name stored in a Patcare database record to search the Doctors database to locate the record for that doctor.

3. Use extended field references, alias names, along with field names, to draw the information Med_rec_no and Field from the Doctors database.

4. Return to the Patcare file, move the pointer to the next record, and repeat the process.

dBASE IV has a built-in command and a function to perform this type of operation automatically: SET RELATION and LOOKUP(). Both of these constructs relate files by a key value that links records logically. The next section demonstrates how to use these operations.

The SET RELATION command creates a link between two related database files. Linking refers to the process of relating pointer movement in the current database to pointer movement in another database in a different work area. In our current example, your goal is to reposition the pointer in the Doctors database each time the pointer in Patcare moves to a new record.

The link is a logical operation. Both databases must share common key information. Each time the pointer moves within Patcare, dBASE IV uses the key information in the current record to locate a matching record in Doctors. In this example, that information is the last name of the doctor. By using the last name of the doctor, as stored in Patcare, to search for a matching name in Doctors, you can find the additional information you need, Med_rec_no and Field.

The key technical requirement of this scheme is that the database to be searched, in this case Doctors, must be indexed on the key information. Select the Doctors database by entering

SELECT Doctors

Create an index for the Doctors last name by entering

INDEX ON Last TAG Last OF Doctors

Return to the Patcare database work area by entering

SELECT a

The LOOKUP() function will search a specified database for a match and return a specific field from the matching record. The LOOKUP() function requires three arguments.

1. **Get item.** Get item is the item that you want to get from the unselected database. For example, the speciality of the doctor stored in the Field field.

2. **Key value.** The key value is the name of a field or an expression that indicates the value to search for.

3. **Search where.** Search where is the name of the field in the unselected database to search for the key value. This field should be the field upon which the unselected database is indexed.

There is one small problem. The field structure of the Patcare and Doctors databases are not identical. The Patcare file has a single field called Doctor in which the doctor's name appears last name first. The Doctors file uses two fields, First and Last, to hold the name of the doctor. This means that the field Patcare->Doctor is not an exact match for Doctors->Last.

This problem can be solved by using dBASE IV functions to manipulate the contents of the Doctor field so that you can isolate the last name from the first. You will need to use two functions to perform this manipulation.

1. **SUBSTR().** The SUBSTR() (substring) function allows you to select a fragment of a character field or variable. The function takes three arguments: SUBSTR*(Character string,Begin at,Stop at)*. *Character String* is any dBASE IV character field or expression. *Begin at* and *Stop at* are numeric values that indicate the first and last characters to include. This function allows you to isolate part of a field or variable.

2. **AT()**. The AT() function locates a character within a character string: AT*(Search for,Within field or variable)*. It returns a numeric value equal to the the search character's location in the string.

In this case you can use the AT() function to find the location of the comma, since the comma separates the last name from the first name. Enter

```
? AT(",",Doctor)
```

dBASE IV returns the value of 9. This means that the comma is the ninth character in the doctor field. You can infer from this that characters 1 though 8 make up the doctor's last name. Enter

```
? SUBSTR(Doctor,1,8)
```

This time, the last name of the doctor, Westfall, is displayed. By using the two functions together you can create a command that separates the last name from the rest of the doctor field. Enter

```
? SUBSTR(Doctor,1,AT(",",Doctor)-1)
```

With the problem of the field's structure resolved, you can return to the task of using the LOOKUP() function. Your goal is to display information currently stored in the Doctors database that relates to the doctor named in this record, Westfall. This means that you want to retrieve Field from the Doctors database based on the doctor's name stored in the current record. Enter

```
? LOOKUP(Doctors->Field,"Westfall",Doctors->Last)
```

The LOOKUP() function performs a search for the name Westfall in the LAST NAME field of the Doctors database and returns the Field for that doctor (see Figure 7.13).

Of course, the actual name of the doctor will not always be Westfall. You can create a generalized command by inserting the SUBSTR/AT expression used earlier to isolate the last name of the doctor. The following command combines all the elements discussed so far. Enter

```
? LOOKUP(Doctors->Field,SUBSTR(Doctor,1,;
   AT(",",Doctor)-1),Doctors->Last)
```

Once again the function locates the information in the Doctors database. You can repeat the operation by using a command to automatically scan all the records in the selected database, such as LIST.

Figure 7.13

```
. use patcare
. use admit in 2
. use doctors in 3
. select doctors
. index on last tag last of doctors
  100% indexed          6 Records indexed
. sele a
. ? at(",",doctor)
         9
. ? substr(doctor,1,8)
Westfall
. ? substr(doctor,1,at(",",doctor))
Westfall,
. ? substr(doctor,1,at(",",doctor)-1)
Westfall
. ? lookup(doctors->field,"Westfall",doctors->last)
Dermatology
```
```
Command  C:\db4\PATCARE         Rec 1/10       File            Ins
         Type a dBASE IV command and press the ENTER key (⏎)
```

Enter

```
LIST Patient,LOOKUP(Doctors->Field,SUBSTR;
(Doctor,1,AT(",",Doctor)-1),Doctors->Last)
```

The command generates a list of patients and the field of medicine practiced by their doctors (see Figure 7.14).

Suppose you want to list two items from the Doctors database. You must use a complete LOOKUP() function for each field you want to retrieve; this results in a very complicated command. Below is an example:

```
LIST Patient,LOOKUP(Doctors->Field,SUBSTR;
(Doctor,1,AT(",",Doctor)-1),Doctors->Last),;
LOOKUP(Doctors->Med_rec_no,SUBSTR(Doctor,1,;
AT(",",Doctor)-1),Doctors->Last);
```

dBASE IV offers a solution to this problem. Instead of simply using the LOOKUP() function each time you want to establish a link between two files, you can just establish a relation. A relation sets up a lookup relationship between two databases that automatically acti-

Procedures and Bar Menus ■ **353**

Figure 7.14

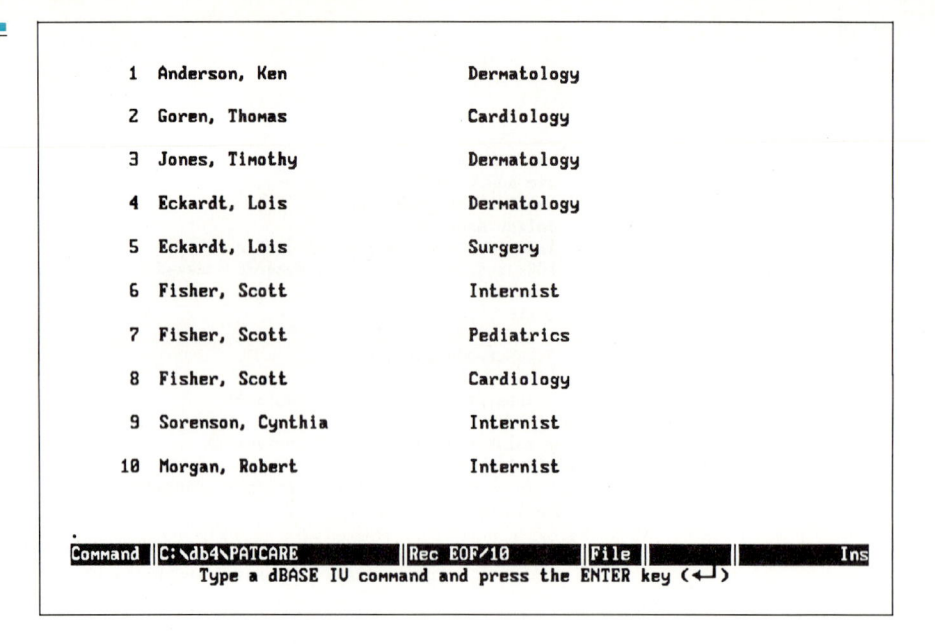

```
  1  Anderson, Ken          Dermatology

  2  Goren, Thomas          Cardiology

  3  Jones, Timothy         Dermatology

  4  Eckardt, Lois          Dermatology

  5  Eckardt, Lois          Surgery

  6  Fisher, Scott          Internist

  7  Fisher, Scott          Pediatrics

  8  Fisher, Scott          Cardiology

  9  Sorenson, Cynthia      Internist

 10  Morgan, Robert         Internist


Command ||C:\db4\PATCARE      ||Rec EOF/10    ||File ||              Ins
       Type a dBASE IV command and press the ENTER key (↵)
```

vates each time an extended reference is made to a field in the related database. The command that establishes a relation is SET RELATION TO. This command requires you to specify the key value to lookup and the alias name of the database to search: SET RELATION TO LOOKUP INTO *Name of Database*. Keep in mind, in this case, the two databases do not share an identical field. Here, the lookup value is an expression, not a field name.

```
SET RELATION TO SUBSTR(Doctor,1,AT(",",Doctor)-1);
 into Doctors
```

The Patcare and Doctors databases are now linked so that any reference to a field in the Doctors database will be treated as a lookup operation. Enter

```
LIST Patient,Doctor,Doctors->Field,;
 Doctors->Med_rec_no
```

This relation prompts dBASE IV to perform lookups for the Doctors->Field and Doctors->Med_rec_no (see Figure 7.15).

When a relation is set you can automatically generate a lookup by referring to a field in the linked database. This holds true for @/SAY

Figure 7.15

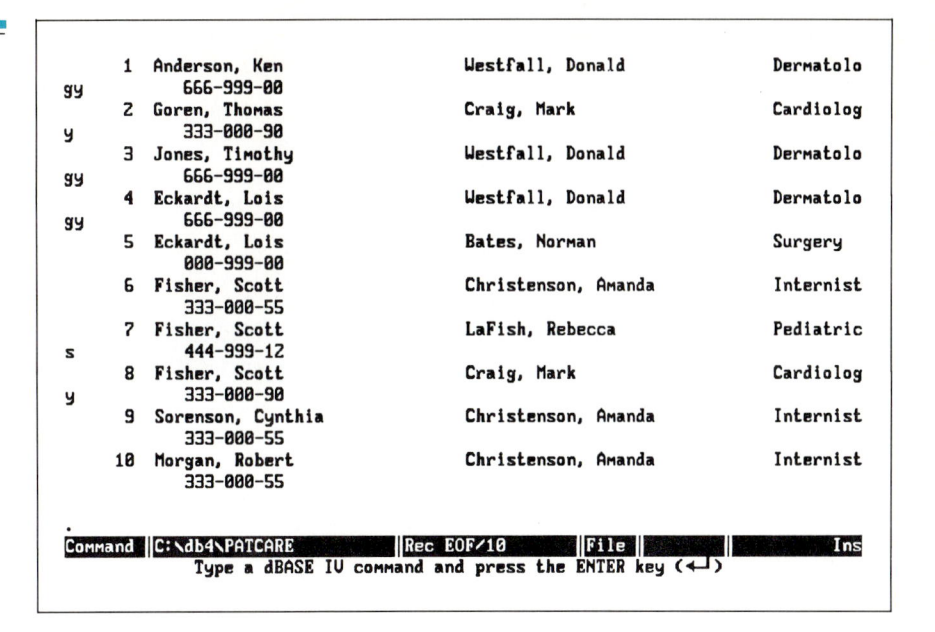

```
    1  Anderson, Ken        Westfall, Donald      Dermatolo
gy     666-999-00
    2  Goren, Thomas        Craig, Mark           Cardiolog
y      333-000-90
    3  Jones, Timothy       Westfall, Donald      Dermatolo
gy     666-999-00
    4  Eckardt, Lois        Westfall, Donald      Dermatolo
gy     666-999-00
    5  Eckardt, Lois        Bates, Norman         Surgery
       000-999-00
    6  Fisher, Scott        Christenson, Amanda   Internist
       333-000-55
    7  Fisher, Scott        LaFish, Rebecca       Pediatric
s      444-999-12
    8  Fisher, Scott        Craig, Mark           Cardiolog
y      333-000-90
    9  Sorenson, Cynthia    Christenson, Amanda   Internist
       333-000-55
   10  Morgan, Robert       Christenson, Amanda   Internist
       333-000-55

Command  C:\db4\PATCARE      Rec EOF/10    File           Ins
        Type a dBASE IV command and press the ENTER key (⏎)
```

commands as well as ?, LIST, etc. Clear the screen display by entering

CLEAR

Position the pointer to record 5 in the database. Type 5 and press ⏎.

Display the information about the patient's doctor using @/SAY commands. Enter

@ 10,10 SAY Doctors->Field

The program places the word Surgery at the specified location. Skip to the next record and repeat the command.

SKIP

Press ↑ two times.

This time, the specialty related to record 6, Internist, appears.

This demonstrates that once a relation is set, you can automatically perform lookups using @/SAY commands like those found in a format file. This allows you to combine multi-database lookups with operations such as format files that were previously performed only on a single database.

Procedures and Bar Menus ■ 355

The next step is to use the concepts you have just explored to create programs that take advantage of these features.

It is important to remember to close the open databases before you go on, since dBASE IV maintains them until you specifically close them. The CLOSE DATABASE command also removes any relations currently set between databases. Enter

```
CLOSE DATABASE
```

Programming with Multiple Databases

The principles of multi-database operation can be used in programs as well as from the dot prompt. Used in a program, multiple database operations are hidden from the user. You can combine the information stored in different files on one screen display.

To illustrate how to apply multiple database operations to programs, you will create a program called Browpat (browse patients). The program uses a popup menu to list the patients stored in the Patcare file. When you select a patient, your program will search both the Admit and Doctors databases in order to display a summary screen about the patient and his or her treatment.

Begin by entering

```
MODIFY COMMAND browpat
```

Begin this program by running the Setoff program.

```
DO SETOFF
```

The next section of the program opens the required database and index files. The first file is the Patcare database. Since it is the names in this file that you will display, create an index for that file to sort the patients' names alphabetically.

```
* open databases and indexes
USE Patcare
INDEX ON Patient TAG Last OF Patcare
```

The next two database files go in separate work areas. Because the Admit and the Doctors files already have index files, you can open the index files at the same time you open the databases. Use the IN clause to specify the work areas for each database.

```
USE Admit ALIAS Patients INDEX Admit ORDER Last;
 IN 2
USE Doctors INDEX Doctors ORDER Last IN 3
```

With the files opened and indexed, the next step is to define a popup menu that lists the names of the patients stored in the Patcare database. Use popup menu commands to create this list.

```
* create menu
DEFINE POPUP Names FROM 1,0 TO 20,30 PROMPT FIELD;
 Patient
ON SELECTION POPUP Names DEACTIVATE POPUP
```

Since the popup menu is located on the left side of the screen, 1,0 to 20,30, you can place the patient information on the right side of the screen, beginning at column 35. First, display the labels for the data. Because these will be the same for all the records you display, these items form a frame in which to place the each record.

```
* display information frame
@ 1,35 SAY "Patient Information"
@ 3,35 SAY "Name:"
@ 4,35 SAY "Dates:"
@ 5,35 SAY "Age:"
@ 6,35 SAY "Days:"
@ 7,35 SAY "Charges:"
@ 8,35 SAY "Insured:"
@ 9,35 SAY "Payor:"
@ 12,35 SAY "Physician:"
@ 13,35 SAY "Med. #"
@ 14,35 SAY "Speciality"
@ 15,35 SAY "Resident:"
```

The program has now set up the conditions for processing records. The processing begins with an automatic loop, DO WHILE .T., followed by activation of a popup menu. This menu allows the user to select the patient whose records are to be reviewed.

```
* start processing loop
DO WHILE .T.
     ACTIVATE POPUP names
```

When a selection is made from this menu, you must position pointers to the corresponding records in all three databases. In the dot prompt mode, you position pointers by using a LOOKUP() function or by setting a relation. These methods also work in a program. However, in a program, it is often just as easy to perform SEEK operations in each database.

The first pointer is the one in the currently selected database. Remember that selecting a name from a popup menu does not affect the pointer position in that file. In this example, the SEEK command finds the record that matches the text returned by the PROMPT() function.

```
* position pointers
SET ORDER to TAG Last OF Patcare
SEEK PROMPT()
```

To position the pointer to the correct record in the Admit file, select that database and perform another SEEK. What should you see in this database? You are trying to locate the record for the patient listed in the current record in the Patcare database. The command below uses an extended reference that employs part of the Patcare patient field. Note also the use of the UPPER() function because the last index tag in the Admit file is indexed on UPPER(LAST).

```
    SELECT Patients
    SEEK UPPER(SUBSTR(Patcare->Patient,1,AT;
    (",",Patcare->Patient)-1))
```

You can perform a similar operation in the Doctors database work area. The only change is that you are drawing the key value from the Doctor field of the Patcare database.

```
SELECT doctors
SEEK SUBSTR(Patcare->Doctor,1,
AT(",",Patcare->Doctor)-1)
```

The pointers in all three databases are now aligned at corresponding records. You can return to the Patcare work area to display the information about this patient.

```
SELECT Patcare
```

The information about the patient can be displayed by a series of @/SAY commands. Data can be drawn from any of the databases, even those that are currently unselected, by using the alias name to create an extended field reference. The name of the patient can be drawn from Patcare. The admission and discharge dates, age, days, and charges can be accessed from the work area containing the patients alias file.

```
@ 3,50 SAY Patient
@ 4,50 SAY DTOC(Patients->Admit)+" to;
 "+DTOC(Patients->Discharge)
@ 5,50 SAY Patients->Age
@ 6,50 SAY Patients->Days_stay
@ 7,50 SAY Patients->Charges
```

You can use IIF() functions to substitute phrases from logical or potentially blank fields.

```
@ 8,50 SAY IIF(Patients->Insured,"Yes","No;
 Insurance")
@ 9,50 SAY IIF(Patients->Insured,Patients->Payor,;
 "Does not apply")
```

The next part of the display comes from the Doctors database.

```
@ 12,50 SAY Doctor
@ 13,50 SAY Doctors->Med_rec_no
@ 14,50 SAY Doctors->Field
@ 15,50 SAY IIF(Doctors->Resident,"Yes","No ")
```

At this point, the program displays the data for the selected patient. The next step is to allow the user to decide to continue or exit the program. Display two lines that prompt the user about how to continue or exit.

```
@ 23,35 SAY "Press any key to continue"
@ 24,35 SAY "F10 to Exit"
```

We offered to let the user press a function key, F10, to exit. In order to integrate function keys, or other special keys such as Home, End, arrow keys, and others into a program, you need to use a special method to pause the program for input. The standard screen input methods @/GET and READ do not recognize all keys as valid entries. For example, the Home key is used for cursor position inside an input area. In order to use keys like Home or F10, you must create a special loop. The loop uses the INKEY() function to sense when a key has been pressed. The INKEY() function returns a numeric value corresponding to the last key pressed. The value returned by the INKEY() function is the ASCII code value of that key. If no key is pressed, INKEY() equals zero.

If a key does not use one of the standard ASCII codes, dBASE IV assigns a special value to that key. The function keys are assigned the following values.

Key	Value
F1	28
F2	-1
F3	-2
F4	-3
F5	-4
F6	-5
F7	-6
F8	-7
F9	-8
F10	-9

There are many ways to use the INKEY() function. The most common is a key-capture loop. A key-capture loop begins by setting a variable equal to zero, the value that INKEY() would have when no key is pressed. You then start a loop that will repeat as long as the value of the variable is zero. The only command inside the loop is one that assigns the value of INKEY() to the variable. This means that as long as no key is pressed, the loop runs endlessly and the program hovers in the same position. As soon as a key is pressed the value of the variable is no longer zero, and the loop terminates allowing the program to continue. The commands below illustrate a typical key-capture loop. Key is simply a variable name.

```
Key=0
DO WHILE Key=0
    Key=INKEY()
ENDDO
```

Once a key is pressed and its value passed to the variable, you can test the variable to see if the user has selected to exit the program. The test requires that you know the value of the special key you want to test for, in this case F10, which equals -9.

```
IF Key=-9
    CLEAR
    EXIT
ENDIF
```

If the user selects to repeat the loop, clear the prompt from the bottom right section of the screen.

```
@ 20,35 CLEAR to 21,50
```

This ends the processing portion of the program. End the loop and enter the commands to complete the program.

```
ENDDO
* close program
CLOSE DATABASE
RELEASE POPUP Patients
DO Seton
RETURN
```

Save and execute the program by pressing (Ctrl)-(End). Enter

```
DO Browpat
```

The popup menu appears with the names of the patients entered into the bars of the menu (see Figure 7.16).

Figure 7.16

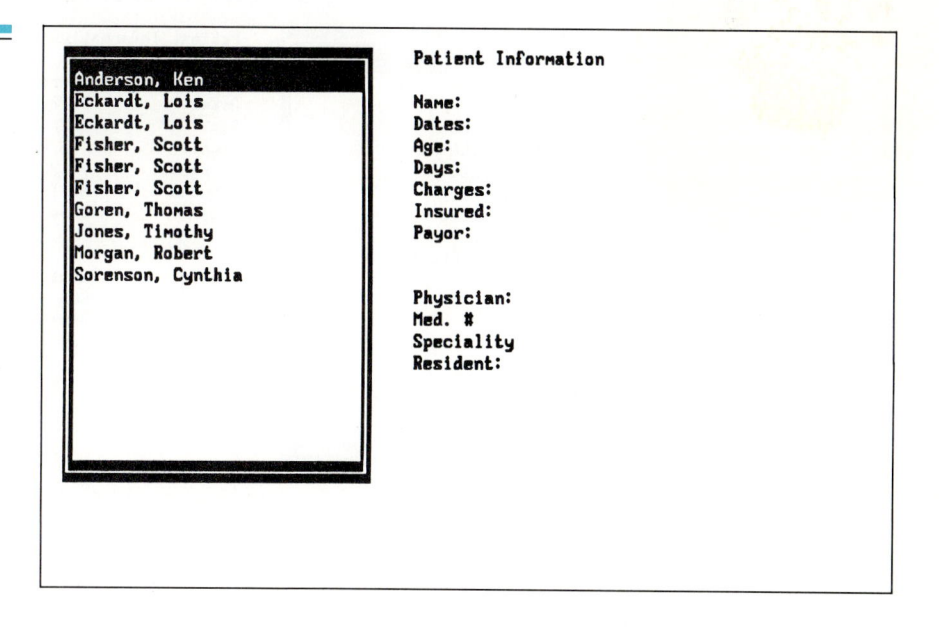

```
Anderson, Ken              Patient Information
Eckardt, Lois
Eckardt, Lois              Name:
Fisher, Scott              Dates:
Fisher, Scott              Age:
Fisher, Scott              Days:
Goren, Thomas              Charges:
Jones, Timothy             Insured:
Morgan, Robert             Payor:
Sorenson, Cynthia
                           Physician:
                           Med. #
                           Speciality
                           Resident:
```

Programming with Multiple Databases ■ 361

You will notice that some patients appear more than once because they have more than one record in the Patcare database. This is a problem you must resolve, but for the moment put that concern aside and see what the program accomplishes as it stands.

To display the information about Timothy Jones, move the highlight bar to Jones, Timothy and press ⏎. The program locates and displays on the right side of the screen the information related to that record. The display itself gives no clue that the information is drawn from three separate databases. The multiple database operation is transparent to users; they cannot distinguish single or multiple database applications by simply viewing the data. As a programmer, you are performing a type of optical illusion that makes the data appear more unified than it actually is.

Continue to another record by pressing ⏎. The menu reappears on the left side of the screen. The information from the previous record is left on the display (see Figure 7.17).

Select the first record for Eckardt, Lois, by moving the highlight bar to her name and pressing ⏎.

The program fetches the information for that patient.

If you look at the insurance information, you'll see that the display for this patient overlays the previous item. This is because the pro-

Figure 7.17

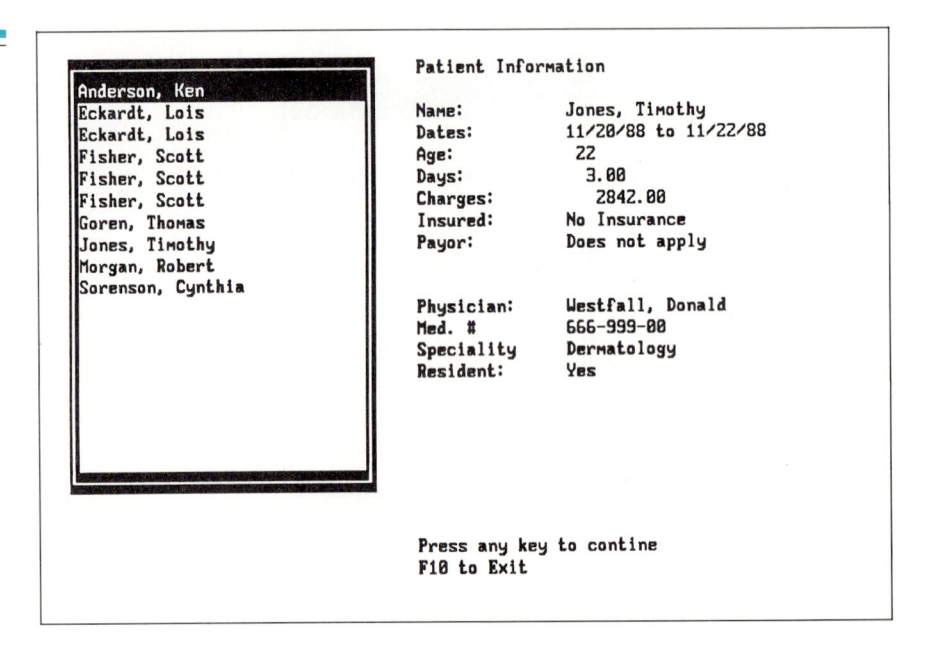

```
Anderson, Ken           Patient Information
Eckardt, Lois
Eckardt, Lois           Name:       Jones, Timothy
Fisher, Scott           Dates:      11/20/88 to 11/22/88
Fisher, Scott           Age:        22
Fisher, Scott           Days:       3.00
Goren, Thomas           Charges:    2842.00
Jones, Timothy          Insured:    No Insurance
Morgan, Robert          Payor:      Does not apply
Sorenson, Cynthia
                        Physician:  Westfall, Donald
                        Med. #      666-999-00
                        Speciality  Dermatology
                        Resident:   Yes




                        Press any key to contine
                        F10 to Exit
```

■ **Using Multiple Databases**

gram did not erase the old data before it wrote the new data. Also, take note of the doctor's information. The current physician is Westfall. This patient has a second record that ought to show another physician's name. Continue by pressing ⏎.

Move the highlight bar to the second occurrence of Eckardt, Lois, and press ⏎. The screen displays the same physician's information. This cannot be correct. Why didn't the second physician for that patient appear?

The answer is related to the method you used to position the pointer in the Patcare file. When you use a SEEK command, dBASE IV locates the first record that matches the key. In this case, the key for both records is the same, Eckardt. Each time the program seeks that record, it stops at the first record and never reaches the second.

The program you have created is perfectly adequate when a one-to-one relationship exists between records in the various databases. But when there is more than one record for the same patient, the program fails to display the additional data. This is a major flaw in the program and it needs to be corrected. Exit the program by pressing F10. The program terminates and returns you to the dot prompt.

Programming One-to-Many Relationships

The primary problem with the Browpat program is that it fails to account for the possibility that patients might have more than one record in the Patcare file. To correct this weakness, you can create another program that is similar in many ways to Browpat but takes into account that more than one physician may be treating the same patient.

Create a new program called Browpat1 by entering

```
MODIFY COMMAND Browpat1
```

The program begins by running the Setoff subroutine to set the environment for running a program. It is followed by the opening of the databases.

```
DO SETOFF
* open databases and indexes
USE Patcare
```

Unique Indexes

The first problem to address is duplicate names in the popup menu. The duplicate names appear because the Patcare database contains more than one record for each of several patients. When the popup

Programming with Multiple Databases ■ 363

menu displays, each record occupies one bar, causing the duplicates. The problem of eliminating the duplicates is tricky because you don't actually want to eliminate those records. Your goal is to display a list of the patients with each name appearing only once.

The solution to this problem is supplied by a special clause called UNIQUE that can be used with the INDEX command. The UNIQUE clause prompts dBASE IV to create only one index entry when two or more records have the same index key value.

A unique index has some very important and, in this example, useful characteristics. The indexing process can also locate records with duplicate keys because it already arranges the records in order. Since indexing does not actually alter the database, an index file, or index tag, creates the processing order for records. With a unique index, dBASE IV simply skips records that have the same key value; thus, a normal index would contain all 10 records in the Patcare file while a unique index would contain only the seven unique records.

Because indexing does not actually delete the record, you can change back to the full database by closing the index or activating a normal index. For example, suppose you created two index tags using the patient's LAST NAME field as the key. If one were unique and the other normal, you could switch back and forth between a full or a unique database by activating the appropriate index.

This is exactly the strategy you will use in this program. The first step is to create the two index tags. First, create an index tag called last to sort all the records by patient name. This is the same index you used with the original Browpat program.

```
INDEX ON Patient TAG Last OF Patcare
```

The next index is called names. It also employs a patient's name as the key value but uses the UNIQUE clause to eliminate duplicate patient names.

```
INDEX ON Patient TAG Names OF Patcare UNIQUE
```

Because the unique index is the last one to be created, it is currently the master index; thus, until you activate the other index tag, last, the database lists only unique names.

With the dual index tags established for the Patcare file, you can proceed to open the other database files exactly as in the previous program.

```
USE Admit ALIAS Patients INDEX Admit ORDER Last;
 IN 2
USE Doctors INDEX Doctors ORDER Last IN 3
```

The popup menu and the display of labels for the data is also the same as in the previous program, except for the physician section. You will deal with physicians later in the program.

```
* create menu
DEFINE POPUP names from 1,0 to 20,30 PROMPT FIELD
Patient
ON SELECTION POPUP Names DEACTIVATE POPUP
* display information frame
@ 1,35 SAY "Patient Information"
@ 3,35 SAY "Name:"
@ 4,35 SAY "Dates:"
@ 5,35 SAY "Age:"
@ 6,35 SAY "Days:"
@ 7,35 SAY "Charges:"
@ 8,35 SAY "Insured:"
@ 9,35 SAY "Payor:"
```

You are now at the point in the program where the main processing loop begins. Start the loop and activate the popup menu.

```
* start proceeding loop
DO WHILE .T.
    ACTIVATE POPUP Names
```

The next section of the program positions the record pointers. Here, you will process all the records for the selected patient; therefore, you will want to switch the index tag in the Patcare database from the unique index tag, names, to the full index tag, last. This is done with the SET ORDER TO TAG command.

```
* position pointers
SET ORDER TO TAG Last OF Patcare
```

Positioning the pointer proceeds exactly as it did in the previous version of this program.

Programming with Multiple Databases ■ **365**

```
SEEK PROMPT()
SELECT Patients
SEEK UPPER(SUBSTR(Patcare->Patient,1,AT;
 (",",Patcare->Patient)-1))
SELECT Doctors
SEEK SUBSTR(Patcare->Doctor,1,;
 AT(",",Patcare->Doctor)-1)
SELECT Patcare
```

Before you display patient information, you can eliminate any data from the previous records by using the @/CLEAR TO command to clear columns 50 to 79.

```
@ 3,50 CLEAR TO 24,79
@ 3,50 SAY Patient
@ 4,50 SAY DTOC(Patients->Admit)+" TO;
 "+DTOC(Patients->Discharge)
@ 5,50 SAY Patients->Age
@ 6,50 SAY Patients->Days_stay
@ 7,50 SAY Patients->Charges
@ 8,50 SAY IIF(Patients->Insured,"Yes","No;
 Insurance")
@ 9,50 SAY IIF(Patients->Insured,Patients->Payor,;
 "Does not apply")
```

Up to this point in the program, only a few commands have been added or altered from the structure used in the Browpat program. But it is at this point, following the display of patient information, that the real change appears.

The records with duplicate patient names stored in the Patcare database represent the treatment of one patient by one doctor. To get an accurate summary of a patient's care you must list all the doctors who treated that patient. You cannot know in advance if that is one, two, three, or more doctors. The goal of the program is to process as many records as necessary until all the records for the selected patient have been exhausted.

To do this you need to create a loop. The PROMPT() function holds the name of the selected patient. Therefore a loop that uses the command DO WHILE PATIENT=PROMPT() will process all the doctor records for the selected patient. It is important to recognize the role the index file plays in making this loop work correctly. By indexing the database according to patient name, you can be sure that all the records for a given patient are contiguous. The SEEK command locates the first matching record. The loop then processes that record and any records following that contain the same patient's name.

The first step in implementing this loop begins by defining a variable called Line as 12.

```
Line=12
```

This variable changes the line value for the @/SAY command because it cannot be a literal value that would be the same each time the loop executes. It must be a variable that will change relative to the number of times the loop cycles. The value of 12 merely serves as the starting position for the display. Begin the loop.

```
DO WHILE Patient=PROMPT()
```

The next set of commands displays the labels for the physician data. The first command uses the variable name Line as the row value. The other commands use the ROW() function so that their display is relative to the location of the first line.

```
@ LINE,35 SAY "Physician:"
@ ROW()+1,35 SAY "Med. #"
@ ROW()+1,35 SAY "Speciality"
@ ROW()+1,35 SAY "Resident:"
```

The process is repeated with the data display commands.

```
@ LINE,50 SAY TRIM(Doctor)
@ ROW()+1,50 SAY Doctors->Med_rec_no
@ ROW()+1,50 SAY TRIM(Doctors->Field)
@ ROW()+1,50 SAY IIF(Doctors->Resident,"Yes",
"No ")
```

Following this display of information, the program must prepare for the possibility that there are more physician records for this patient. First, the value of the Line variable is incremented so that a second cycle through the loop will write data below the current position, rather than writing over data at the same position.

```
Line=Line+5
```

Next, a SKIP command moves the record pointer to the next record in the database. This is a crucial step. When the loop reaches the

ENDDO command it performs the logical test associated with the DO WHILE command. If the record now being pointed to contains a patient name different from the one selected from the menu, the loop terminates. If they still match, the loop cycles again displaying more physician data for that patient.

```
    SKIP
ENDDO
```

Following the end of that loop, the program pauses to allow the user to read the displayed material.

```
@ 23,35 SAY "Press any key to continue"
@ 24,35 SAY "F10 to Exit"
Key=0
DO WHILE Key=0
    Key=INKEY()
ENDDO
IF Key=-9
    CLEAR
    EXIT
ENDIF
@ 12,35 CLEAR to 24,79
```

The final addition to the program reactivates the unique index tag, names, before the popup menu is displayed again.

```
    SET ORDER TO TAG Names OF Patcare
ENDDO
* close program
CLOSE DATABASE
RELEASE POPUP Patients
DO Seton
RETURN
```

Save and execute the program by pressing (Ctrl)-(End). Enter

```
DO BROWPAT1
```

This time, the program displays a list of unique patient names.

Test the program by selecting Eckardt, Lois. Move the highlight bar to Eckardt, Lois and press ⏎. This patient record lists two physi-

368 ■ **Using Multiple Databases**

cians. The loop display cycles twice to show both physicians (see Figure 7.18).

Continue by pressing ⏎. This time choose Fisher, Scott. Move the highlight bar to Fisher, Scott and press ⏎. This patient has three physicians. As the program attempts to display the data, an error occurs (see Figure 7.19).

The cause of this error is quite simple. As the program attempted to display the last physician, it ran out of room. The value of the ROW() function exceeded 24, the maximum value allowed. This makes sense because the screen display has only 25 lines, 0 through 24, on which to display data. Cancel the program by pressing ⏎.

Paging the Screen

The solution to this problem is to modify the program to display the physicians in groups that fit on the screen display. In this case, the physicians should be displayed two at a time. The exact number is not important. What is significant is that the program can accommodate any number of physician records by dividing the display into a series of pages. The term page refers to the limit that can fit on the screen at any one moment.

Figure 7.18

```
Patient Information

Name:         Eckardt, Lois
Dates:        11/24/88 to 12/03/88
Age:          49
Days:         10.00
Charges:          3929.00
Insured:      YesInsurance
Payor:        Blue Cross


Physician:    Westfall, Donald
Med. #        666-999-00
Speciality    Dermatology
Resident:     Yes




Press any key to contine
F10 to Exit
```

Figure 7.19

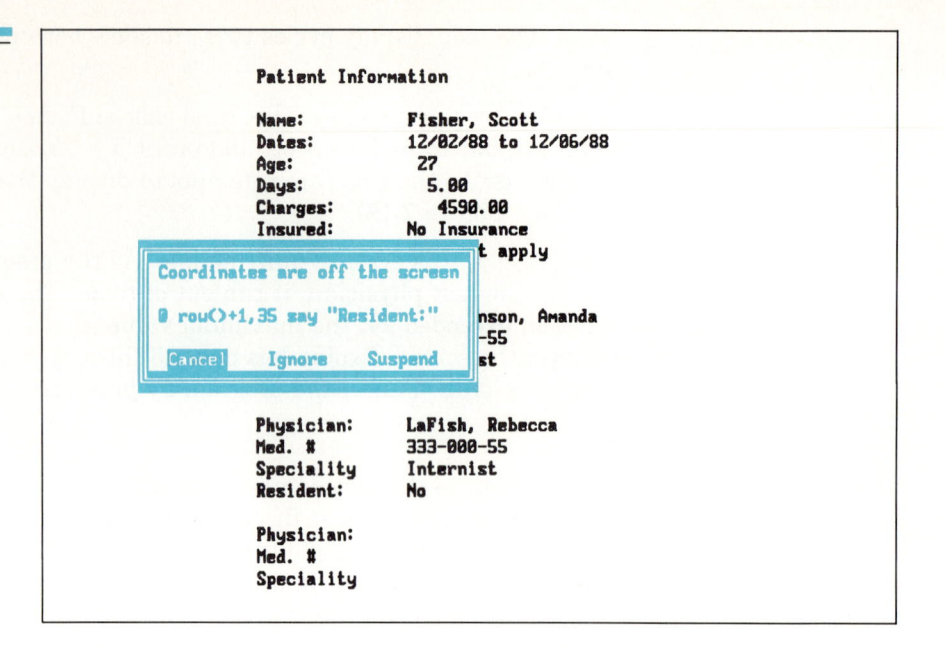

```
                Patient Information

         Name:       Fisher, Scott
         Dates:      12/02/88 to 12/06/88
         Age:        27
         Days:       5.00
         Charges:    4590.00
         Insured:    No Insurance
                                         t apply
    ┌─────────────────────────────────┐
    │ Coordinates are off the screen  │nson, Amanda
    │                                 │ -55
    │ @ row()+1,35 say "Resident:"    │
    │                                 │ st
    │ [Cancel]   Ignore    Suspend    │
    └─────────────────────────────────┘

         Physician:  LaFish, Rebecca
         Med. #      333-000-55
         Speciality  Internist
         Resident:   No

         Physician:
         Med. #
         Speciality
```

Load the Browpat1 program into the editor by entering

`MODIFY COMMAND Browpat1`

Move the cursor to line 41, the line that immediately follows the physician display loop, DO WHILE PATIENT = PROMPT().

It is here that you need to perform a test before you allow the loop to display any physician records. The test that you want to perform is based on the position of the last record, if any, displayed as part of this loop. In this example, line 12 is the first line of the physician display. Each display is 5 lines long. This means that by the time two physicians records have been displayed the value of Line would be 22. When the value of 5 is added to the value of Line at the bottom of the loop, a full page of data has been displayed. Thus a test, Line>22, would determine when a page was filled. Insert the following command.

`IF Line=22`

If the test is true, pause the program until the user is ready to see more information.

`@ 23,0`
`WAIT "More, Press any key"`

When the user wants to continue, the program should clear the physician display area, reset the value of Line to 12, the top of the page, and allow the loop to start over again at that point.

```
    @ 12,35 CLEAR to 24,79
    Line=12
ENDIF
```

The modified section of the program reads as follows. The new program lines are highlighted in color.

```
DO WHILE Patient=PROMPT()
    IF Line=22
        @ 23,0
        WAIT "More, Press any key"
        @ 12,35 CLEAR to 24,79
        Line=12
    ENDIF
    @ Line,35 SAY "Physician:"
    @ ROW()+1,35 SAY "Med. #"
    @ ROW()+1,35 SAY "Speciality"
    @ ROW()+1,35 SAY "Resident:"
    @ line,50 SAY TRIM(doctor)
    @ ROW()+1,50 SAY doctors->med_rec_no
    @ ROW()+1,50 SAY TRIM(doctors->field)
    @ ROW()+1,50 SAY IIF(doctors->resident,;
      "Yes","No ")
    Line=Line+5
    SKIP
ENDDO
```

Save and execute the program by pressing (Ctrl)-(End). Enter

```
DO BROWPAT1
```

Move the highlight bar to Fisher, Scott and press (↵). This time the program inserts a pause after the first two doctors have been listed.

Press (↵). The third physician is listed.

Exit the program by pressing (F10).

The use of limited pages of information allows you to create screen displays offering more information than can be displayed at any one moment.

Summary

The key concepts covered in this chapter include:

Popup prompt field. Like the PROMPT FILES clause, the PROMPT FIELD option also automatically generates the bars of a popup menu. The bars in this menu contain the information stored in selected fields of the database. Make sure that the currently open database contains the field you want to use for the menu. When a selection is made, the PROMPT() function will contain the contents of the selected field. Selection from a field popup menu does not move the record pointer. This is done by searching for the record that matches the PROMPT() function's contents. If the file is not indexed, use the BAR() value as the record number. Remember, if the file is indexed, the BAR() function's value will not correspond to the record number.

Multiple databases. dBASE IV allows you to work with more than one database at a time. Multiple database applications allow you to create groups of related files that share common links. The links between the files are not created or maintained by dBASE IV but are logical links that must be implemented through your programs.

Work areas. When a database file is opened, it is placed into a work area. dBASE IV normally places all database files into work area 1. Since each work area can have only one open database, each new file closes the previous database. By selecting a new work area before opening another database, you can open up to 10 database files at the same time. The 10 work areas can be referred to by number, 1 through 10, or letter, A through J.

Select. The SELECT command activates a work area. Only one work area can be selected at a time. The SELECT command can operate on work area numbers or letters—SELECT 2 or SELECT B both select the second work area.

Alias. When a database is opened in a work area, dBASE IV assigns an alias name to the work area/database combination. The alias is the same as the database filename unless you specifically alter the name by using an ALIAS clause with the USE command, as in USE ADMIT ALIAS Patients. The alias name serves two purposes. First, you can use the alias name with the SELECT command to activate a work area, as in SELECT Patients. The second function of the alias name is to create an extended field name reference. This extended reference begins with the work area alias name, a two-character symbol (->), and the field name. This allows dBASE IV to draw information from a field in an unselected database. For example, the extended reference Patients->Last tells dBASE IV to use the contents of the Last field from the database in the work area with the alias Patients.

You have the option of using the alias name with fields in the current database if you desire. Field names with no alias are assumed to be references to the database in the currently selected work area. Memory variables are given the alias M;M—>Last refers to a memory variable called Last, distinct from any field with the same name.

Menu bars. A menu bar lists options across the top of the screen. Menu bars are similar to popup menus with one major difference. In a popup menu, you define a single event-management command, ON SELECTION POPUP, to execute no matter what item in the popup menu you select. In a menu bar you can define a separate event-management command, ON SELECTION MENU, for each option listed on the menu bar. The options on the menu bar are called pads. Unlike popup bars, which are assigned numbers, each pad has a descriptive name.

Procedures. dBASE IV employs the concept of procedures to enable you to cluster multiple programs or subroutines in a single program file. Procedures have two major advantages. First, they allow you to write a program and all of its subroutines in the same file. This makes it easier to create and edit a series of related routines because you do not have to load each routine as a separate file. Second, dBASE IV will load all the commands from all the procedures, if RAM memory is sufficient, at one time. This will improve program execution speed.

Review Problems for Chapter 7

Chapter 7 discusses the use of multiple databases. The review problems in this section require the use of additional databases that can be found on the Examples disk.

You will need to use two additional .dbf files supplied on the Examples disk. The first file is called Prods and has the following structure. This file contains product information.

Structure for database: C:\DBASE\PRODS.DBF

Number of data records: 40

Date of last update : 10/11/88

Field	Field Name	Type	Width	Dec	Index
1	PROD_CODE	Character	10		N
2	ITEM_NAME	Character	30		N
3	PRICE	Numeric	6	2	N
4	MAKER	Character	15		N
5	DISCOUNT	Numeric	4	2	N
6	EPA	Logical	1		N
** Total **			67		

The second file is called Cust and contains information about the customers.

Structure for database: C:\DBASE\CUST.DBF

Number of data records: 22

Date of last update: 10/11/88

Field	Field Name	Type	Width	Dec	Index
1	COMPANY	Character	30		N
2	STREET	Character	30		N
3	CITY	Character	30		N
4	STATE	Character	2		N
5	ZIP	Character	5		N
6	AREA	Character	3		N
7	PHONE	Character	8		N
8	CONTACT	Character	30		N
** Total **			139		

You will use these databases in conjunction with SALES in the following problems.

1. Enter a series of commands that open the three databases, Sales, Prods, and Cust in workareas 1, 2, and 3 respectively.

2. To relate databases, you must create indexes on the key fields. Create an index for Prods on the Prod_code field. Make that index a tag called NAME in an index file called Prods.

3. Create an index for Cust on the Company field to a tag called Name in an index file called Cust.

4. Use a lookup function command to list the name and discount on each item in the Sales database by looking up product code in the Prods database.

5. List the company, area code, phone number, and contact name for each company listed in the Sales database. Use the set relation to command link the databases.

6. Create a program that searches for a record in Sales by invoice number. When the record is displayed use the Prods and Cust databases to display the customer's address drawn from the Cust database and maker, discount, and Epa value from Prods.

Answers to Exercises

1. Display doctor's name

   `? TRIM(Doctors->Last)+", "+Doctors->First`

2. Insert doctor's name in record

   `REPLACE Doctor WITH TRIM(Doctors->Last)+", "+Doctors->First`

3. Create two procedures
   ⏎ (2 times)

   `PROCEDURE ages`

   Press Alt-W and type W r.

   `Ages.prg`

   Ctrl – PgDn

⏎ (two times)

`PROCEDURE Ages`

Press Alt-w and type w r.

`Countins.prg`

4. Place Doctors database in area 3

    `USE Doctors IN 3`

8 Reports and Printing

This chapter explores the creation of printed reports from dBASE IV. You used many of the techniques required for printing reports when you created programs to generate screen summaries. The primary difference between a screen summary and a printed report is the format of the data. Data written on a screen limits you to an 80-column, 25-line grid that makes up the standard PC screen display. Programs that display more information than fits on the screen must pause the display until a user is ready to see more information. The same screen area gets overwritten with new information. Screen displays also allow you to place information at any position on the screen, in any order.

Printed reports are just the opposite. A printed report assumes that you have limitless paper supplies. This paper stream eliminates the need to pause the program during processing. However, processing records on paper is strictly sequential; thus, printing takes place starting at the top, left corner of the page and moves to the right and down the page. Printing does not allow you to move backwards on the page.

The printed report also requires you to be aware of the size and shape of the page. A printed page often requires headings, page numbers, and margins—elements not usually needed for a screen summary.

Finally, printers are capable of printing characters with different fonts, point sizes, and special characteristics, like bold and underlined text. The exact characteristics depend on the design of your printer. These features are called printer-dependent features because they differ depending on the actual printer being used.

Printed reports always pose two problems for the programmer. The first concerns data processing: How can the data be organized and summarized to fit the purpose of the report? The second concerns the typography associated with placing information onto a printed page. Therefore, you must be concerned about the report's content (data processing) and the report's form (layout on the page).

dBASE IV provides built-in facilities for generating many useful report and label forms. However, as a programmer, you will learn to build customized reports and label printing programs of your own.

Turning the Printer On

The basic process of printing information in dBASE IV is quite simple. dBASE IV, like most programs, considers the screen display and the printer as output devices. By default, most dBASE IV commands automatically use the screen as the output device, like the LIST command. Open the Patcare database by entering

```
USE Patcare
```

The first command normally displays the data on the screen. Enter

```
LIST
```

This command lists the 10 records stored in the Patcare file. If you want that list sent to the printer, you have to tell dBASE IV to use a different device as the output destination. This can be done in two ways:

1. **By command.** Changing the output device by command means each command intended for output to the printer will use the clause TO PRINT to redirect data to the printer. This redirection affects only that specific command.

2. **By environment.** You can change the default device by using a SET command to redirect all output to the printer. The SET command

affects all the output commands that follow until you issue another SET command.

The change device by command method uses the TO PRINT clause. Enter

```
LIST TO PRINT
```

This time the output appears both on the screen and on the printer. dBASE IV does not automatically feed the entire page through the printer. When the printing stops, the paper is left at the middle of the page. dBASE IV continues printing at this spot when you issue the next print command.

> *Note:* If you are working with a laser printer, you don't see any printing taking place at all. This is because a laser printer does not feed a printed page until the entire page is full, or a specific command to feed the form is issued. Most laser printers have an indicator light, labeled Form Feed, that tells you there is data, that is, a partial page, waiting for the rest of the page so it can be printed.

If you want to begin printing at the top of the next page, you must issue a form feed command. A form feed command tells the printer to advance to the top of the next page. In dBASE IV that command is called EJECT. Enter

```
EJECT
```

If you intend to issue several print commands, you might find the environmental solution more efficient. The environmental approach begins with a command that sets up the printer as an output device, SET PRINT ON. Enter

```
SET PRINT ON
```

Now enter two LIST commands.

```
LIST Doctor
```

```
LIST Patient
```

With the command SET PRINT ON, both LIST commands send their output to the printer. This output redirection continues until you specifically change it. Enter

```
SET PRINT OFF
```

Turning the Printer On ■ **379**

All the commands you enter while printing is set to on are sent to both the screen and the printer. With the print setting now off, the LIST command outputs on the screen only. Enter

LIST

The data appears on the screen only. But wait, you have forgotten to feed the form. Enter

EJECT

Even with printing set to off, the EJECT command sends the form feed instruction to the printer. This tells you that EJECT is a command specifically related to the printer and affects the printer regardless of whether or not print is set on or off.

Consider how the EJECT command actually works. Both dBASE IV and your printer make an assumption about the length of a printed page. The assumption is that each page you send to your printer consists of exactly 66 lines of text with each line exactly 1/6 of an inch in height. If you multiply 66 by 1/6, you arrive at 11 inches of vertical space. This is the most common size paper used with computers but it is not the only size. You will learn later how to adjust printing to fit forms of different sizes.

When you send information to the printer, many printers keep track of the number of lines being sent. Upon encountering a form feed command, the printer skips an amount of space equal to the unused portion of the current page. The printer then starts counting lines for the next page. This skip is called a form feed because, if all goes correctly, the printer will reposition to the top of the next form.

What if the printer does not keep count of lines? While most printers today offer a line count, it was not always so. A few years ago it was common to encounter printers that did not recognize a form feed. If the printer did not keep count, then the printing program did. The program had to issue a series of blank lines equal to the amount of unused space on the page.

You will see that dBASE IV still keeps track of the number of lines printed on a page. This is useful in writing programs because it helps you know how close printed text appears to the bottom or top of a page.

dBASE IV has two functions, PROW() and PCOL(), that contain the row and column position of the printer's print head. They function in a manner similar to the ROW() and COL() functions for the screen cursor. Enter

```
? PROW(),PCOL()
```

The two functions return the value of zero because you have just ejected a page. This means that the printer is at the top of the new page, at row 0, column 0. Like the screen display, dBASE IV counts the printer position starting with 0 as the first row and column, not 1. List the patients' names to the printer. Try this on your own. If you need help, the correct command can be found at the end of the chapter in the Answers to Exercises section under exercise 1.

To see what this print operation did to the value of the PROW() and PCOL() functions, enter

```
? PROW(),PCOL()
```

The row function is now 12, 10 records, plus one line for the heading making the next line to print, line 12. List the structure of the file to the printer. Try this on your own. If you need help, the correct command can be found at the end of the chapter in the Answers to Exercises section under exercise 2. Check the status of the PROW() and PCOL() functions by entering

```
? PROW(),PCOL()
```

The line number has increased to 21. Eject the page by entering

```
EJECT
? PROW(),PCOL()
```

The functions take on the value of zero because you are starting a new page.

Printing with @/SAY

dBASE IV also allows you to send information to the printer using the full formatting ability of the @/SAY command.

Note: Since the printer is an output-only device, there is no use for @/GET. @/GET commands are ignored if they are sent to the printer.

Output generated by the full screen command @/SAY is handled differently than output created with ?, DISPLAY, or LIST. dBASE IV uses the command SET DEVICE TO handle the output from @/SAY commands. To send @/SAY commands to the printer, enter

```
SET DEVICE TO PRINT
```

Position the record pointer to the beginning of the file and print the name of the patient at line 5, column 20 of the page.

```
GO TOP
```

```
@ 5,20 SAY "Patient: "+Patient
```

The printer advances to the row and column designated and prints the text. Display the values of the PROW() and PCOL() variables. Enter

```
? PROW(),PCOL()
```

The values are row = 5 and column = 59. The PROW() and PCOL() functions are affected by any type of printing. When the device is the printer, information displayed with the ? command also prints on the screen display. Enter another @/SAY command.

```
@ 10,20 SAY "Doctor: "+Doctor
```

The printer advances to line 10 and prints the data. Enter

```
@ 9,20 SAY "Date of Care: "+DTOC(Date_care)
```

Did the command operate as you expected? The command placed the data on line 9, but on the next page. This is an important lesson when it comes to formatting output for the printer. dBASE IV does not permit you to move backwards on a page. Since you already printed on line 10, attempting to print on line 9 causes dBASE IV to reference line 9 on the next page. When you are working with @/SAY commands for the printer, you must make sure that your commands print in the correct sequence.

When you complete printing, direct the @/SAY output back to the screen by entering

```
SET DEVICE TO SCREEN
EJECT
```

Close the current database by entering

```
CLOSE DATABASE
```

Printing Forms

As with screen displays, there are two basic approaches to printing data. The full screen command @/SAY allows you to specify the column and row location. The unstructured commands such as ?, LIST, and DISPLAY print consecutively on the page. Both of these methods have strengths and weaknesses when it comes to programming. Suppose you want to print a form for each patient in the Admit file. To get a feel for the two printing methods, you will create two programs, one using unstructured commands, the other using structured commands. Create a program called Pform1 (print form 1) by entering

```
MODIFY COMMAND Pform1
```

The program begins by running the Setoff program and opening the Admit database. The file is ordered alphabetically by last name. The records will print in this order.

```
DO SETOFF
USE Admit INDEX Admit ORDER Last
```

The next command tells dBASE IV to direct the standard output to the printer.

```
SET PRINT ON
```

To process all the records in the database, you can begin a scan loop. Because printing all 10 records in the database is time-consuming, you can demonstrate the principle by printing only those records that have an admission date in the month of December. The SCAN command accepts a FOR clause, to make the selection of records simple.

```
SCAN FOR MONTH(Admit)=12
```

Because SET PRINT ON does not affect output generated with the @/SAY command, you can use an @/SAY command to display information about the print job on the screen. This display has no functional purpose in printing the forms; but it does inform a user about what is going on with the printing. Display messages keep users informed about printing activity, useful when users cannot see or hear the printing taking place, either because the printer is in a remote location or it is a laser printer. In this case, the command displays the name of the patient in the record being printed.

```
@ 10,10 SAY "Printing Patient: "+Last
```

When using the SET PRINT ON command, the selected information appears both on the screen display and on the printer. This is usually confusing to users and has a slight effect on operating speed. You can eliminate the display of information on the screen by using the command SET CONSOLE OFF.

Printing with @/SAY ■ 383

Note: This command suppresses all screen display. If you turn the console off but forget to turn it back on, dBASE IV will accept your commands but nothing will appear on the screen. Quitting dBASE IV by entering quit will terminate the program and return the screen display to normal.

```
SET CONSOLE OFF
```

With the console off and the printer on, you are ready to place information on the page. The primary print command is the ? command. When using this command you must account for each line to be printed, even the blank lines. The next section of the program prints five blanks, a title, and skips two more lines.

```
?
?
?
?
?
? "Patient Admission Data"
?
?
```

The next section prints the name of the patient. You may recall the ?? and ? commands from Chapter 3. The ?? does not issue a linefeed before it prints. This means that if you use ? and follow it with ??, the two items appear on the same line. The AT clause places the second item on the line at a specific column location so all the items align horizontally. The STYLE clause allows you to take advantage of print attributes such as bold or underline, if supported by your printer.

```
?  "Last Name:" style "B"
?? Last AT 30
?  "First Name:" style "B"
?? First AT 30
?
```

The remainder of this section lists other information you might want to display. To save some effort, we'll not include all of the fields. Many of the commands require some additional functions to get correct printouts. For example, to combine the two dates into a single phrase it is necessary to use the DTOC(), date to character conversion, function. The single character in the Sex field is converted by means of an IIF() function into either Male or Female. The $ operator in the expression SEX$"Mm" searches for the letters "m" or "M." The TRANSFORM() function formats and converts a numeric value.

```
? "Dates:"
?? DTOC(Admit)+" to "+DTOC(Discharge) AT 30
? "Sex:"
?? IIF(Sex$"Mm","Male","Female") AT 30
? "Age:"
?? Age AT 30
? "Insurance:"
?? IIF(Insured,Payor,"Not Insured") AT 30
? "Charges:"
?? TRANSFORM(Charges,"999,999.99") AT 30
```

At the end of the record-printing operation, issue a form feed instruction with the EJECT command.

```
EJECT
```

This ends the processing within the loop. Since the program now recycles to the top of the loop where the @/SAY command displays the name of the next patient, it is necessary to turn the screen display on once again.

```
    SET CONSOLE OFF
ENDSCAN
```

The final section completes the program by turning off the printer, closing the database, and running the Seton program.

```
SET PRINT OFF
CLOSE DATABASE
DO Seton
RETURN
```

Save and execute the program by pressing Ctrl-End.

Selecting a Printer

Before you execute this program, consider the type of printer you are working with. Each printer has its own special set of features that can enhance the output of your programs. Almost all printers will print the raw data, letters, and numbers that dBASE IV produces. This type of output is considered generic computer output.

However, other features such as bold or italic print, continuous underlines, and changes in pitch are printer dependent. This means that even though you have used a command or clause designed to produce a special effect, it operates only if the printer supports it.

The STYLE clause used in the Pform1 program is an example of a printer-dependent feature. In order for dBASE IV to perform the printer-dependent operations you must tell dBASE IV what printer you are using. This is done by using a special system memory variable called _pdriver, printer driver. A printer driver is a special file that contains information aboput how special printing effects are implemented on specific printers. dBASE IV is supplied with a number of these special files which contain data dBASE IV needs to access features on various printers.

Note: Note that the name of this variable begins with an underscore character.

By selecting the correct driver, dBASE IV can match up the desired effect, for example, bold print, with the way that effect is implemented on your printer.

Note: Keep in mind that not all printers can produce all effects. For example, most laser printers will not produce italic text with their resident fonts. Italic print requires the addition of font cartridges or fonts loaded from the disk into the memory of the printer. These are called soft fonts.

You can display the name of the current print driver by entering

```
? _pdriver
```

The name of the current print driver appears. If no special print driver has been installed, the driver will be Generic.pr2. If the driver contains the name of your printer, then you do not have to change it.

Note: The name of the printer is an abbreviation. For example, the IBM Graphics Printer is abbreviated as Ibmgp.pr2.

Since a printer driver is a file, then the name of the print driver corresponds to a filename on the disk. In order to select the correct print driver, you must have the print driver file on the disk. List all of the available print drivers by entering

```
DIR *.pr2
```

The program lists the printer drivers, if any, currently stored on disk (see Figure 8.1).

Figure 8.1

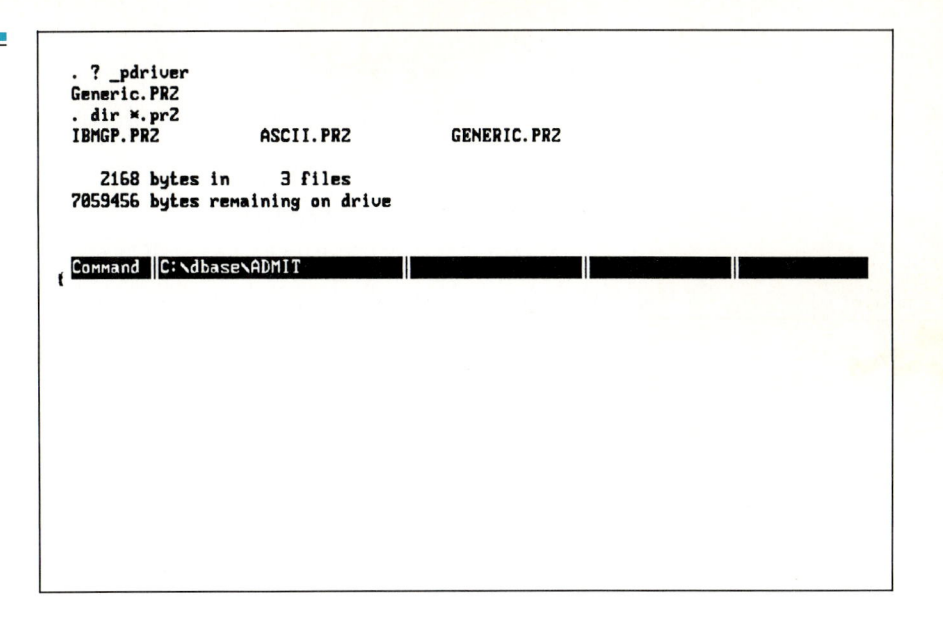

```
. ? _pdriver
Generic.PR2
. dir *.pr2
IBMGP.PR2          ASCII.PR2          GENERIC.PR2

    2168 bytes in    3 files
7059456 bytes remaining on drive


Command  C:\dbase\ADMIT
```

Suppose you are working with an IBM graphics printer or one compatible with that printer. You would want to set the printer driver to Ibmgp.pr2 by defining the system variable to equal the filename of the print driver you want to use.

`_pdriver="Ibmgp.ps2"`

You can now run the program and produce any of the effects supported by the printer. The STYLE clause used in the Pform1 program is an example of a printer-dependent feature. Enter

`DO Pform1`

The program prints the selected records, one on each page.

Printing Using @/SAY Commands

The next task is to create another similar program that accomplishes the same result but uses @/SAY commands rather than ? commands. Create the new program by entering

`MODIFY COMMAND Pform2`

This program begins the same way as the Pform1 program. One small addition is a command that prints the name of the database on the screen.

Printing with @/SAY ■ 387

```
DO SETOFF
USE Admit INDEX Admit ORDER Last
@ 10,10 SAY "Printing Records from "+dbf()
```

Begin a scanning loop and display the name of the first patient.

```
SCAN for MONTH(Admit)=12
     @12,10 SAY "Patient: "+Last
```

The next command is the one that sends the output of the @/SAY commands to the printer.

```
SET DEVICE TO PRINT
```

With the @/SAY commands, data is not echoed to the screen display after the SET DEVICE TO PRINT command. You do not need to turn off the console display off in order to suppress the echo of this data.

You can use the @/SAY command to print the heading centered on the page assuming the page is 85 columns wide.

> *Note:* The number of columns or characters depends on the size of the print. The default print size for most printers is 10-pitch. The term pitch measures the number of characters per horizontal inch. 10-pitch printing places 10 characters in each horizontal inch, making an 8.5-inch wide sheet of paper 85 columns wide. Many narrow-carriage printers will print only 80 columns even though the paper placed in such printers can be up to 8.5-inch wide. In this book, the printing programs assume your printer is not capable of printing beyond the 80th character and limits the width of the printing accordingly.

```
     Title="Patient Admission Data"
     @ 5,(80-LEN(Title))/2 SAY Title
```

The next line prints the first data label at the beginning of line 7. When you use @/SAY commands, it is not necessary to insert blank lines manually. By skipping from line 5 to line 7, dBASE IV knows to leave a blank line; skipping lines is implicit in the command.

```
@ 7,0 SAY "Last Name:"
```

Once you have established the starting row, you can use the PROW() function to place the rest of the data on the page relative to that starting line. This makes it easy to adjust lines to print lower or higher on the page, since they are all relative to the first line. The PROW() function can save you a tremendous amount of editing should it be necessary later to change the starting location of the text on the page. When you are developing an application, you will probably need to adjust the location of text more than once until you find the best position.

In the commands below, each PROW()+1 expression moves the text to a new line. Each PROW() statement tells dBASE IV to print the text on the same line as the last item. Spacing makes sure that all the PROW() numbers, column numbers, and @/SAY commands line up at the same horizontal position. Adding spaces to each line ensures this alignment. The spaces have no effect on the execution of the program. In fact, they are removed from the program object file when it is compiled. The spaces are placed there to illustrate a useful editing technique. By making the items line up in columns, you can more easily pick out the row or column values should it be necessary to edit them. Entering these extra characters is optional.

```
@ PROW()    ,30 SAY Last
@ PROW()+1  ,0  SAY "First Name:"
@ PROW()    ,30 SAY First
@ PROW()+2  ,0  SAY "Dates:"
@ PROW()    ,30 SAY DTOC(Admit)+" TO;
  "+DTOC(Discharge)
@ PROW()+1  ,0  SAY "Sex:"
@ PROW()    ,30 SAY IIF(Sex$"Mm","Male",;
"Female")
@ PROW()+1  ,0  SAY "Age:"
@ PROW()    ,30 SAY Age
@ PROW()+1  ,0  SAY "Insurance:"
@ PROW()    ,30 SAY IIF(Insured,Payor,"Not;
  Insured")
@ PROW()+1  ,0  SAY "Charges:"
@ PROW()    ,30 SAY Charges PICTURE;
  "999,999.99"
```

Next, eject the current page and end the scan loop.

```
    EJECT
    SET DEVICE TO SCREEN
ENDSCAN
```

Complete the program by closing the database and running the Seton program.

```
CLOSE DATABASE
DO Seton
RETURN
```

Save and execute the program by pressing (Alt)-e and typing r. The program produces an output that is almost exactly like the results of the Pform1 program.

Relative Addressing

You may have noticed that the printed text is placed at the top of the page leaving the bottom mostly empty. You can move the text farther down the page quite easily because you created the program with relative addressing. Load the program into the editor by entering

```
MODIFY COMMAND Pform2
```

Move the cursor to line 9. Change the row address of this command to 25.

Old line: @ 7,0 SAY "Last Name:"

New line: @ 25,0 SAY "Last Name:"

Because all of the other print statements are addressed relative to this command, all of them move as a unit when you change the first command. This is one of the advantages of using relative addressing with @/SAY commands.

Save and execute the program by pressing (Alt)-e and typing r.

The program prints the text farther down the page. The method used to create the program enabled you to readjust the printed output. This is another example of how easily modular or flexible programs can be modified. If you had used explicit row locations, like @ 10,0, you would have to edit all of the commands in order to shift the location of the printing on the page.

Preprinted Forms

One of the major advantages of using @/SAY commands in printing operations is that you can easily adapt programs to work with preprinted forms. Today you can purchase a variety of preprinted business forms with lines, boxes, or item labels already printed on the form.

You can use dBASE IV to fill in these forms by using @/SAY commands to place information at exact locations on the form. Most preprinted forms are supplied with a sample grid that helps you count line and character locations so you can use the forms with your program.

The use of preprinted forms speeds up form processing because the printer need only print data from the database instead of printing data labels, lines, and other information that is the same on each form.

Column Reports

The previous two programs, Pform1 and Pform2, placed one record on each page. A column report places as many records as possible on the same page. The basic structure of a column report program can be modified to create programs with various types of totals, subtotals, and summaries. Let's write a simple column report program. Enter

```
MODIFY COMMAND Colrpt
```

A column report program begins like a form printing program by opening the database and the desired index.

```
DO Setoff
USE Admit INDEX Admit ORDER Last
```

Unlike the form printing program, a column report program must print the column headings before it goes on to print the data stored in database records. The method we use below creates a variable called HD. This variable defines where to print the first line of the page heading. The rest of the print lines are addressed relative to that first line. The replicate function draws a line of dashes across the page.

```
* print headings
SET DEVICE TO PRINT
Hd=5
Title="Admission File Data"
@ Hd,(80-LEN(Title))/2 SAY Title
@ Hd+1, 0 SAY REPLICATE("=",75)
@ Hd+2, 5 SAY "Patient"
@ Hd+2,30 SAY "Admitted"
```

```
@ Hd+2,40 SAY "Dischar."
@ Hd+2,50 SAY "Age"
@ Hd+2,55 SAY "Sex"
@ Hd+2,60 SAY "Insured"
@ Hd+3, 0 SAY REPLICATE("=",75)
```

Following the headings, the output device is set back to the screen to allow the program to display processing information about the progress of the report. In this case, the report displays a status prompt showing what percentage of the database has been processed to let the user gauge how much longer the report will take to complete. The process of making this status display begins by defining a variable called printed that keeps count of the number of records printed.

Note: You cannot use the record number, RECNO(), as a guide if the database is indexed because the record numbers will appear out of order.

```
SET DEVICE TO SCREEN
Printed=1
```

The loop begins with a SCAN command. Following that command the program displays the percentage of completed processing using the value of PRINTED divided by the total number of records in the database as determined by the RECCOUNT() function. To display this value as a percentage, it must be multiplied by 100. The STR() function converts the result into a character string so that the percent (%) character can be printed after the value.

```
SCAN
    @ 10,10 SAY STR(Printed/RECCOUNT()*100,4,1);
    +"% Printed."
```

The next section of the program begins the record processing. The device is set to the printer so that the @/SAY commands will send output to that device.

```
SET DEVICE TO PRINT
```

Th next command adds a number next to each record. This is not the record number but simply a number to label each line in the report. Since you are already using a variable to count records, you can simply print that number at the beginning of the line.

```
@ PROW()+1,0 SAY STR(Printed,2)+"."
```

The next series of @/SAY commands actually prints the data from the database. The first command prints the name of the patient. Since the first and last names have been allocated 20 spaces each in the database structure, it is possible but not likely, that a name might be as large as 40 characters. You can fix a limit on the size of a printed name using a PICTURE clause. In this case, a PICTURE clause with 24 X characters limits the largest name to 24 characters. If the name is longer than 24 characters, the extra letters are simply not printed. It is important in column reports to set the maximum width for each column. Otherwise, you may find that an unexpectedly long entry prints over into the next column.

```
@ PROW() ,5 SAY Trim(Last)+", "+First;
  PICTURE "XXXXXXXXXXXXXXXXXXXXXXXX"
```

The next three lines print information at columns 30, 40, 50, and 55 respectively.

```
@ PROW() ,30 SAY Admit
@ PROW() ,40 SAY Discharge
@ PROW() ,50 SAY Age PICTURE "999"
@ PROW() ,55 SAY UPPER(Sex)
```

The next command uses the IIF() function to evaluate the contents of the insured field to decide whether to print the payor, or the phrase, "Not Insured." A PICTURE clause with 20 X's limits the amount of text printed in this column.

```
@ PROW() ,60 SAY IIF(Insured,Payor,"Not Insured");
  PICTURE "XXXXXXXXXXXXXXXXXXXX"
```

The print line for each record is now complete. Before the loop recycles to the top you need to increment the value of Printed by 1 and set the output device back to the screen.

```
    Printed=Printed+1
    SET DEVICE TO SCREEN
ENDSCAN
```

In this program, use the EJECT command at the end of the program because all the records are printed on the same page. After the page has been ejected, close the database and conclude the program in the usual manner.

```
EJECT
CLOSE DATABASE
DO Seton
RETURN
```

The entire program looks like this:

```
DO Setoff
USE Admit INDEX Admit ORDER Last
* print headings
SET DEVICE TO PRINT
hd=5
Title="Admission File Data"
@ hd,(80-LEN(Title))/2 SAY Title
@ hd+1, 0 SAY REPLICATE("=",75)
@ hd+2, 5 SAY "Patient"
@ hd+2,30 SAY "Admitted"
@ hd+2,40 SAY "Dischar."
@ hd+2,50 SAY "Age"
@ hd+2,55 SAY "Sex"
@ hd+2,60 SAY "Insured"
@ hd+3, 0 SAY REPLICATE("=",75)
SET DEVICE TO SCREEN
Printed=1
SCAN
     @ 10,10 SAY STR(Printed/RECCOUNT()*100,4,1);
     +"% printed."
     SET DEVICE TO PRINT
     @ PROW()+1,0 SAY STR(Printed,2)+"."
     @ PROW() ,5  SAY TRIM(last)+", "+First;
     PICTURE "XXXXXXXXXXXXXXXXXXXXXX"
     @ PROW() ,30 SAY Admit
     @ PROW() ,40 SAY Discharge
     @ PROW() ,50 SAY age PICTURE "999"
     @ PROW() ,55 SAY UPPER(Sex)
     @ PROW() ,60 SAY IIF(Insured,Payor,"Not;
```

```
        Insured") PICTURE "XXXXXXXXXXXXXXXXXXX"
        Printed=Printed+1
        SET DEVICE TO SCREEN
ENDSCAN
EJECT
CLOSE DATABASE
DO Seton
RETURN
```

Save and execute the program by pressing [Alt]-e and typing r.

The program displays the percentage of records left to print on the screen while the print operations runs.

Pagination

The previous program printed out all 13 records from the Admit database on one page. But suppose records in that database could not fit onto a single page? The number of pages required for a column report will vary depending on the size of the database being printed. For a program to operate properly regardless of the number of records to print, it should be able to stop printing, eject the page, and begin again at the top of a new page. This process is called pagination.

Before you create a program to handle this situation, it might occur to you that none of the databases you have created so far is large enough to test your pagination program once you create it. You can create another database made up of several copies of each record in the Admit database for testing purposes. This would provide a database large enough to test the pagination program without requiring you to make a lot of entries. Begin by creating a copy of the Admit file called Admitbig. Enter

```
USE Admit
COPY TO Admitbig
```

At this point, you now have two databases with 13 records each. The trick is to find a way to expand the Admitbig file without manually entering more records. Place the Admitbig file in use. Enter

```
USE Admitbig
```

Instead of manually entering records, use the APPEND FROM command to import records from the Admit file. Enter

```
APPEND FROM Admit
```

Column Reports ■ **395**

The file is now double in size. Repeat the process two more times. Try this on your own. If you need help, the correct command can be found at the end of the chapter in the Answers to Exercises section under exercise 3.

You can vary the import of records by selecting certain files, such as those with a December admission date, by attaching an appropriate FOR clause. Try this on your own. If you need help, the correct command can be found at the end of the chapter in the Answers to Exercises section under exercise 4. Repeat that command twice more by pressing

[↑] [↵]

[↑] [↵]

There are now 58 records in the Admitbig database.

To create some variety in these records, you can use the REPLACE command to alter the dates in some random fashion. If you add the value of the record number to the admission and discharge dates, they would extend into other months. Enter

```
REPLACE ALL Admit WITH Admit+RECNO(),
Discharge WITH Discharge+RECNO()
```

The admission dates now stretch to February of 1989. Index the file on last name to an index file called Admitbig. Try this on your own. If you need help, the correct command can be found at the end of the chapter in the Answers to Exercises section under exercise 5.

You now have a database large enough to test a column report program that paginates. Close the database by entering

```
CLEAR ALL
```

Programs That Paginate

A program that paginates has three basic parts.

1. **Page header.** This section of a report program prints information that ought to appear at the top of every page, such as the report title and the column headings.

2. **Page ending.** This section of the program creates the page ending information, such as printing the page number, and issues the form feed to prepare the printer for the next page. In many cases the page

ending routine will be followed by the page header routine for the next page.

3. **Main line printing loop.** This section of the program is the part that prints the lines of data on the page. The loop is interupted only when it is necessary to handle a page end, a page beginning, or you have reached the end of the data that needs to be printed.

The primary part of the program, the main processing loop, is similar to the processing loop in the Colrpt program. For the most part, the loop prints the records exactly as it did in that program. There are, however, two exceptions: when the printing begins at the top of a page, and when it reaches the end of a page. At these two times, the program deviates from the printing of individual records and performs special operations.

At the top of the page the program must print the report title, the column headings, and other information normally appearing there. At the bottom of the page, it should print a page number and then skip to the top of the next page. The two routines that deal with the top and the bottom of the page are closely related. When the end of page routine executes, it leaves the program at the top of a new page and creates the need to perform the top of the page routine.

The only exceptions to this link include the first page, which by definition begins at the top of the page, and the last page, which does not require another page to begin.

The best way to create a paginated column report is to create a file with three procedures: one to print the page headings, one to print the page's ending, and the other for the main processing loop.

> *Note:* It is possible to write a single program that will print a column report. Using procedures avoids entering the same set of heading commands at two points in the program.

Create a new program called Colrpt1 by entering

```
MODIFY COMMAND Colrpt1
```

The first procedure is the page heading routine. This routine prints the column headings at the top of the page. The variable HD is set at 5 to place the heading at line 5.

```
PROCEDURE HEADING
SET DEVICE TO PRINT
Hd=5
```

```
TITLE="Admission File Data"
@ Hd,(80-LEN(Title))/2 SAY Title
@ Hd+1, 0 SAY REPLICATE("=",75)
@ Hd+2, 5 SAY "Patient"
@ Hd+2,30 SAY "Admitted"
@ Hd+2,40 SAY "Dischar."
@ Hd+2,50 SAY "Age"
@ Hd+2,55 SAY "Sex"
@ Hd+2,60 SAY "Insured"
@ Hd+3, 0 SAY REPLICATE("=",75)
SET DEVICE TO SCREEN
RETURN
```

The second procedure is the page-end routine. This routine performs a number of tasks. The first task is to print the page number at the bottom of the page. The variable Pageno will be defined as part of the main procedure in the program. To make your programs more readable, enter a blank line in between each procedure.

```
PROCEDURE Endpage
SET DEVICE TO PRINT
@ 60,37 SAY "-"+LTRIM(STR(Pageno,2))+"-"
```

Once the page number has been printed, the remainder of the page can be ejected.

```
EJECT
```

Before you execute the top of the page routine, display the next page number on the screen to allow the user to see the number of pages remaining to print in this report.

```
SET DEVICE TO SCREEN
PAGENO=Pageno+1
@ 12,10 SAY STR(Pageno,2)+"pages."
```

The last step in the page ending routine calls the page heading routine. This makes sense because the top of a new page always follows the end of the last page, unless you have reached the end of the file.

```
DO Heading
RETURN
```

The next routine, the main processing routine, must print the records from the database. In addition, it must contain the commands that trigger the execution of the heading and page-end routines. The main procedure begins by running Setoff and opening the database, Admitbig, in this case.

```
PROCEDURE Report
DO SETOFF
USE Admitbig INDEX Admitbig ORDER Last
```

Since the report always begins at the top of a page, the main routine should execute the heading routine and create three variables to control various aspects of processing.

The variable Printed counts records and prints numbers next to each record. The variable is initialized as 1. The Pageno variable keeps track of the pages that are printed and holds the value for the page numbers. The Marg_bot variable sets a limit on the number of lines printed on each page. In this case, the bottom is set at line 50.

```
* print headings
Printed=1
Pageno=1
Marg_bot=50
DO Heading
```

With the headings printed on the first page, the program can begin printing records as part of the main processing loop. This loop is identical, for the most part, to the loop in the Colrpt program.

```
SCAN
        @ 10,10 SAY STR(Printed/RECCOUNT()*100,4,1);
        +"% printed."
        SET DEVICE TO PRINT
        @ PROW()+1,0 SAY STR(Printed,2)+"."
        @ PROW() ,5   SAY TRIM(Last)+", "+First;
          PICTURE "XXXXXXXXXXXXXXXXXXXXXX"
        @ PROW() ,30 SAY Admit
        @ PROW() ,40 SAY Discharge
        @ PROW() ,50 SAY Age PICTURE "999"
        @ PROW() ,55 SAY IIF(UPPER(Sex)="M","M","F")
        @ PROW() ,60 SAY IIF(Insured,Payor,"Not;
```

Programs That Paginate

```
       Insured") PICTURE "XXXXXXXXXXXXXXXXXXX"
   PRINTED=Printed+1
   SET DEVICE TO SCREEN
```

Following the printing of each record, the program must check to see if it has reached the bottom of the page by comparing the value of the PROW() function to the value established for the page end by the Marg_bot variable. If the print row exceeds that value, the end-of-page routine should be executed.

```
IF PROW()>Marg_bot
      DO ENDPAGE
ENDIF
```

The loop conditional can now be evaluated to see if there are more records to print.

```
ENDSCAN
```

The last part of the program executes when the scan loop terminates and all the records in the database have been processed. The program might be somewhere in the middle of a page. To end the routine properly the program should skip to the bottom of the page, print the page number, and eject.

```
SET DEVICE TO PRINT
@ 59,37 SAY "-"+LTRIM(STR(Pageno,2))+"-"
SET DEVICE TO SCREEN
EJECT
```

Following the ejection of the last page, the program can conclude with the usual closing commands.

```
CLOSE DATABASE
DO Seton
RETURN
```

Save the program by pressing (Ctrl)-(End). Because this program is a procedure file, it needs to be compiled before it can be used. Enter

```
COMPILE Colrpt1
```

Run the program by loading the procedure file and executing the main routine called Report. Try this on your own. If you need help, the correct command can be found at the end of the chapter in the Answers to Exercises section under exercise 6.

The program generates a two-page report listing the 58 records stored in the Admitbig file. Close the procedure file by entering

CLOSE PROCEDURE

Reports with Totals

Another element often included in column reports are totals, averages, or other summary data. For example, suppose you change the Colrpt1 program to create a report listing the days stayed and the charges incurred. You might want to print the sum and average of these values at the end of the report.

Load the Colrpt1 program into the editor by entering

MODIFY COMMAND Colrpt1

Move the cursor to line 10. Remove the headings for age, sex, and insurance. Press Ctrl-y three times.

Insert two new headings for days and charges.

@ Hd+2,50 SAY "Days"

@ Hd+2,60 SAY "Charges"

Move the cursor to line 33, the line in the Report procedure beginning with DO HEADING.

Note: If you did not insert blank lines between your procedures, your cursor might show this command on line 31. Make sure that you insert these commands in front of the DO HEADING command.

In order to accumulate totals for days and charges you need to create two variables. Insert the following command:

STORE 0 TO Sumdays,Sumcharges

Move the cursor to line 42 (@ PROW() ,50 SAY AGE PICTURE "999"). This program does not require you to print Age, Sex, or Insured. Delete the lines by entering Ctrl-y three times.

To replace these commands, insert commands that print the number of days stayed and the charges. While you have created a field for the days stayed, you can ensure accuracy by simply calculating that value from the difference between the admit and discharge dates. The charges can be printed from the Charges field. Insert the following commands:

Programs That Paginate ■ 401

```
@ PROW() ,50 SAY Discharge-Admit+1 PICTURE;
  "99,999"
@ PROW() ,60 SAY Charges PICTURE "99,999,999.99"
```

You may wonder why the PICTURE clauses are larger than the values allowed in the fields themselves. While no individual records will have a value as large as the PICTURE clause permits, the total of all the records may be that large. In a PICTURE clause, the left-most character aligns at the specified column with the rest of the number being placed to the right. To have the decimal places for the total and the items in the column line up, you should use the same PICTURE clause for both the column items and the total.

In addition to printing these values, you need to add them to the value of the accumulator variables for the totals.

```
Sumdays=Sumdays+Discharge-Admit+1
Sumcharges=Sumcharges+Charges
```

The final step is to print out the total and calculate averages at the end of the report. Move the cursor to line 53 (@ 59,37 SAY "-"......).

Insert the following commands to print totals and averages for the days and charges. The variable PRINTED is used for a third purpose here, too. Since it already has the correct value for the number of records printed, it makes the ideal divisor for the averages calculation.

```
@ PROW()+1,0 SAY REPLICATE("=",75)
@ PROW()+1,0 SAY "Totals"
@ PROW(),50  SAY Sumdays PICTURE "99,999"
@ PROW(),60  SAY Sumcharges PICTURE;
  "99,999,999.99"
```

Before calculating the average, adjust the value of the Printed variable. In this program the value of Printed increments following each record. Thus, the value of Printed at the bottom of each cycle of the loop is actually 1 greater than the actual number of records printed. When the last record has been printed, the variable Printed is 1 larger than it ought to be. Before you use the variable to calculate the average, reduce its value by 1.

```
Printed=Printed-1
```

Calculate and print the averages.

```
@ PROW()+1,0 SAY "Averages"
@ PROW(),50  SAY Sumdays/Printed PICTURE "99,999"
```

```
@ PROW(),60  SAY Sumcharges/Printed PICTURE;
  "99,999,999.99"
```

The revised program looks like this. New commands are highlighted in color.

```
PROCEDURE Heading
SET DEVICE TO PRINT
Hd=5
title="Admission File Data"
@ Hd,(80-LEN(Title))/2 SAY Title
@ Hd+1, 0 SAY REPLICATE("=",75)
@ Hd+2, 5 SAY "Patient"
@ Hd+2,30 SAY "Admitted"
@ Hd+2,40 SAY "Dischar."
@ Hd+2,50 SAY "Days"
@ Hd+2,60 SAY "Charges"
@ Hd+3, 0 SAY REPLICATE("=",75)
SET DEVICE TO SCREEN
RETURN
PROCEDURE Endpage
SET DEVICE TO PRINT
@ 59,37 SAY "-"+lTRIM(STR(Pageno,2))+"-"
EJECT
SET DEVICE TO SCREEN
@ 12,10 SAY STR(Pageno,2)+"pages."
Pageno=Pageno+1
DO Heading
RETURN
PROCEDURE Report
DO Setoff
USE Admitbig INDEX Admitbig ORDER Last
* print headings
Printed=1
Pageno=1
Marg_bot=50
STORE 0 TO Sumdays,Sumcharges
```

Programs That Paginate

```
DO Heading
SCAN
    @ 10,10 SAY STR(Printed/RECCOUNT()*100,4,1);
    +"% printed."
    SET DEVICE TO PRINT
    @ PROW()+1, 0 SAY STR(Printed,2)+"."
    @ PROW()   , 5 SAY TRIM(Last)+", "+First;
     PICTURE "XXXXXXXXXXXXXXXXXXXXXX"
    @ PROW()   ,30 SAY Admit
    @ PROW()   ,40 SAY Discharge
    @ PROW()   ,50 SAY Discharge-Admit PICTURE;
     "99,999"
    @ PROW()   ,60 SAY Charges PICTURE;
     "99,999,999.99"
    Sumdays=Sumdays+Discharge-Admit
    Sumcharges=Sumcharges+Charges
    Printed=Printed+1
    SET DEVICE TO SCREEN
    IF PROW()>Marg_bot
        DO Endpage
    ENDIF
ENDSCAN
SET DEVICE TO PRINT
@ PROW()+1,0 SAY REPLICATE("=",75)
@ PROW()+1,0 SAY "Totals"
@ PROW(),50 SAY Sumdays PICTURE "99,999"
@ PROW(),60 SAY Sumcharges PICTURE "99,999,999.99";
 Printed=Printed-1
@ PROW()+1,0 SAY "Averages"
@ PROW(),50 SAY Sumdays/Printed PICTURE "99,999"
@ PROW(),60 SAY Sumcharges/Printed PICTURE;
 "99,999,999.99"
@ 59,37 SAY "-"+lTRIM(STR(Pageno,2))+"-"
SET DEVICE TO SCREEN
EJECT
```

```
CLOSE DATABASE
DO Seton
RETURN
```

Save the program by entering Ctrl-End. Compile and execute the program. Try this on your own. If you need help, the correct command can be found at the end of the chapter in the Answers to Exercises section under exercise 7.

The report prints with the summary information at the end. After the report has printed, close the procedure file by entering

```
CLOSE PROCEDURE
```

Programs with Subtotals

The previous report printed a grand total for all of the records processed. Another useful variation on the column report prints totals for a subgroup within the report. You might want to produce a report grouping together patients discharged in the same month. The program could print a total and average for each month, then a final grand total and average.

Subtotal programs introduce the concept of a controlled break within the main processing loop. The previous reports we developed used a scan loop to process the entire database without interruption, except for the page end routine.

In the case of a subtotal report, a second loop inside the full database scan loop prints records that belong to the same group, like the same discharge month. This loop stops when all the records for the group have been processed. The program then prints the summary information for this group and starts another inner loop for the next group, the next month, if any.

The key to creating a subtotal report is to get the records in the database grouped correctly before the report begins by creating a file or index tag that sequences the records according to the type of grouping you desire. If you do not create the correct type of index sequence, the subtotal report will not work properly.

Suppose you want to print a report similar to Colrpt1 but with the patients grouped and subtotaled by month. What is the nature of the index sequence for such a report? The first task would be to index the records according to the discharge date arranged in chronological order. But what about the sequence within each monthly group? You may want the patients listed alphabetically by name within that group. You could index by date and then by last name.

Place the Admitbig file in use along with its index file by entering

`USE Admitbig INDEX Admitbig`

Create an index that orders the records first by discharge date and then by last name. To combine a date with a character field like last name, you must convert the date to character string. Enter

`INDEX ON DTOC(Discharge)+Last TAG Monthly OF;`
`  Admitbig`

To see the results of this indexing, enter

`DISPLAY ALL Discharge,Last`

The screen lists the records in the current index order (see Figure 8.2).

But this is not the order you expected. If you look carefully at the sequence of records, you will notice several problems.

The order of the dates places January 1989 ahead of November 1988. Because you indexed on the text conversion of the date, the program ranked the dates first by month, then by day, without taking the year into consideration.

Because you indexed on the full value of the date, the names are not alphabetized in monthly groups but in daily groups. Only if two peo-

Figure 8.2

```
Record#  discharge  last
    26   01/02/89   Goren
    46   01/07/89   Jones
    48   01/07/89   Mcdowell
    36   01/08/89   Eckardt
    37   01/08/89   Sorenson
    47   01/10/89   Morgan
    38   01/13/89   Fisher
    39   01/15/89   Goren
    49   01/21/89   Eckardt
    50   01/21/89   Sorenson
    51   01/26/89   Fisher
    53   01/28/89   Fisher
    52   01/28/89   Goren
    55   01/30/89   Fisher
    54   01/30/89   Goren
    57   02/01/89   Fisher
    56   02/01/89   Goren
    58   02/03/89   Goren
     1   11/06/88   LaFish
     2   11/11/88   Tate
Press any key to continue...
Command  C:\db4\ADMITBIG   Rec 26/58   File
```

Reports and Printing

ple were discharged on the same day would the names be listed alphabetically.

Stop the display by pressing (Esc).

To get the correct sequence for subtotal grouping, you must index the records differently. The first improvement we'll make uses the DTOS(), date to index sequence, function. This function changes the date into a string of characters that begins with the year followed by the month and day. Enter

```
LIST DTOS(Discharge)
```

This format (see Figure 8.3) ranks the dates correctly by year before they are sequenced by month or day. Create a revised index using this function. In order to overwrite the previous version of this tag without generating an error message, turn safety off before you index.

```
SET SAFETY OFF
INDEX ON DTOS(Discharge)+Last TAG Monthly of;
 Admitbig
DISPLAY ALL Discharge,Last
```

Figure 8.3

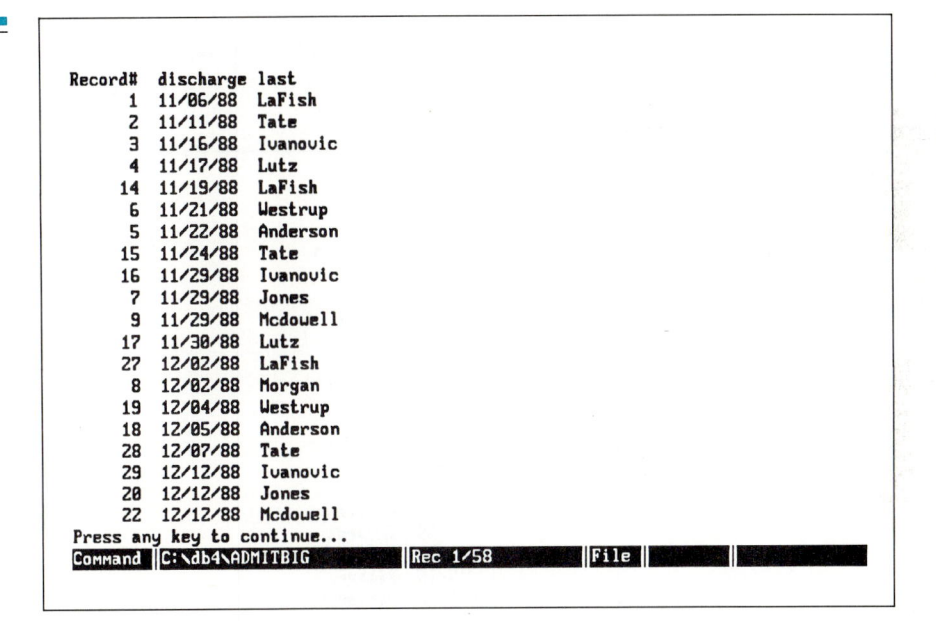

```
Record# discharge last
      1 11/06/88  LaFish
      2 11/11/88  Tate
      3 11/16/88  Ivanovic
      4 11/17/88  Lutz
     14 11/19/88  LaFish
      6 11/21/88  Westrup
      5 11/22/88  Anderson
     15 11/24/88  Tate
     16 11/29/88  Ivanovic
      7 11/29/88  Jones
      9 11/29/88  Mcdowell
     17 11/30/88  Lutz
     27 12/02/88  LaFish
      8 12/02/88  Morgan
     19 12/04/88  Westrup
     18 12/05/88  Anderson
     28 12/07/88  Tate
     29 12/12/88  Ivanovic
     20 12/12/88  Jones
     22 12/12/88  Mcdowell
Press any key to continue...
Command  C:\db4\ADMITBIG    Rec 1/58    File
```

Programs That Paginate ■ 407

The DTOS() function solves part of the problem. The dates are in the correct sequence but they still break up the records into daily, not monthly groups. The current index key is too detailed. You need to reduce the precision to use only the yearly and monthly parts of the date. Exit the display by pressing (Esc).

You can create the correct index sequence by using the SUBSTR() function to limit the number of characters included in the index key. Try this on your own. If you need help, the correct command can be found at the end of the chapter in the Answers to Exercises section under exercise 8.

List the records again.

```
DISPLAY ALL Discharge,Last
```

This time the records are correctly grouped by last name within the month (see Figure 8.4).

Exit the display by pressing (Esc).

You have solved half of the problem. With the records correctly sequenced, you are ready to create a program that prints subtotals for each group.

To save some effort, you can start by making modifications to a copy of the Colrpt1 program. You can use the basic printing and pagination routines in this program in the new program. A quick way to

Figure 8.4

```
Record# discharge last
     5  11/22/88  Anderson
     3  11/16/88  Ivanovic
    16  11/29/88  Ivanovic
     7  11/29/88  Jones
     1  11/06/88  LaFish
    14  11/19/88  LaFish
     4  11/17/88  Lutz
    17  11/30/88  Lutz
     9  11/29/88  Mcdowell
     2  11/11/88  Tate
    15  11/24/88  Tate
     6  11/21/88  Westrup
    18  12/05/88  Anderson
    31  12/18/88  Anderson
    44  12/31/88  Anderson
    10  12/13/88  Eckardt
    23  12/26/88  Eckardt
    12  12/18/88  Fisher
    25  12/31/88  Fisher
    13  12/20/88  Goren
Press any key to continue...
Command  C:\db4\ADMITBIG        Rec 5/58      File               Ins
```

copy a file is to use the MS-DOS COPY command. You can access MS-DOS commands without quitting dBASE IV by using the RUN command. Simply enter RUN, followed by the MS-DOS command you want to execute.

Note: The amount of memory in your computer will determine your ability to use the RUN command. If you do not have sufficient memory, dBASE IV displays an error message when you attempt to use RUN.

Enter

```
RUN COPY Colrpt1.prg Grprpt.prg
```

Load the new file into the editor.

```
MODIFY COMMAND Grprpt
```

The first two procedures in this program can remain as they are. Move the cursor to the beginning of the third procedure, Report.

You will create several new procedures in this program, each to accomplish one part of the program. The current Report procedure changes to a procedure that prints a line of data. Change the name of the procedure to Prtline.

Old line: `PROCEDURE Report`
New line: `PROCEDURE Prtline`

Move the cursor to the next line and eliminate the next nine commands. Press Ctrl-y nine times.

Move the cursor to the line that reads IF RROW()>Marg_bot. Delete the next 18 commands. Press Ctrl-y 18 times.

One final alteration changes the variable in the command @ 10,10 SAY STR(Printed/Reccount()*100,4,1)+"% printed.". Move the cursor backwards to line 27. Change Printed to All. This is done because the printed variable counts records in each group, not in the database as a whole.

Old line: `@ 10,10 SAY STR(Printed/RECCOUNT()`
            `*100,4,1)+"% printed."`
New line: `@ 10,10 SAY STR(All/RECCOUNT()`
            `*100,4,1)+"% printed."`

The revised procedure looks like this:

```
PROCEDURE Prtline
@ 10,10 SAY STR(All/RECCOUNT()*100,4,1)+"%;
 printed."
SET DEVICE TO PRINT
@ PROW()+1, 0 SAY STR(Printed,2)+"."
@ PROW() , 5 SAY TRIM(Last)+", "+First PICTURE;
 "XXXXXXXXXXXXXXXXXXXXXXX"
@ PROW() ,30 SAY Admit
@ PROW() ,40 SAY Discharge
@ PROW() ,50 SAY Discharge-Admit+1 PICTURE;
 "99,999"
@ PROW() ,60 SAY Charges PICTURE "99,999,999.99"
Sumdays=Sumdays+Discharge-Admit+1
Sumcharges=Sumcharges+Charges
Printed=Printed+1
SET DEVICE TO SCREEN
RETURN
```

Move the cursor to the end of the file. Add a blank line and begin a new procedure. This procedure will be called Prtsubs. This routine prints the total for each group.

```
PROCEDURE Prtsubs
SET DEVICE TO PRINT
```

The first part of the procedure is similar to the part of the Colrpt1 program that printed the total at the end of the report.

```
@ PROW()+1, 0   SAY REPLICATE("=",75)
@ PROW()+1, 0   SAY "Total"
@ PROW()  , 50 SAY Sumdays PICTURE "99,999"
@ PROW()  , 60 SAY Sumcharges PICTURE;
 "99,999,999.99" SET DEVICE TO SCREEN
```

In the next section of this procedure, the values printed represent the totals for one group of patients. Before the program proceeds, two things must happen. First, the totals for this group must be added to accumulators holding the grand total for all groups. Second, the group total variables should be reset to zero so that they can start fresh for the next group. These operations must proceed in order. If you were to clear the values before you transferred them to the grand total accumulators, the program would not work.

In this program the variables Gnddays (grand total days) and Gndcharges (grand total charges) hold the overall database totals. The variable All keeps count of all of the records processed. It is necessary to subtract 1 from the value of Printed for each group, just as it was at the end of the Colrpt1 program.

```
Gnddays=Gnddays+Sumdays
Gndcharges=Gndcharges+Sumcharges
All=All+Printed-1
STORE 0 TO Sumdays,Sumcharges,
STORE 1 TO Printed
RETURN
```

The next procedure prints the grand totals and averages at the end of the program.

```
PROCEDURE Prtgrand
SET DEVICE TO PRINT
@ PROW()+1, 0 SAY REPLICATE("=",75)
@ PROW()+1, 0 SAY "Grand Totals"
@ PROW(), 50 SAY Gnddays PICTURE "99,999"
@ PROW(), 60 SAY Gndcharges PICTURE;
 "99,999,999.99"
@ PROW()+1, 0 SAY "Averages"
@ PROW(), 50 SAY Gnddays/All PICTURE "99,999"
@ PROW(), 60 SAY Gndcharges/All PICTURE;
 "99,999,999.99" @ 60,37 SAY "-"+lTRIM;
(STR(Pageno,2))+"-"
SET DEVICE TO SCREEN
EJECT
RETURN
```

It is useful in a subtotal report program to print a special heading for each subtotal group. The Grphead procedure prints this heading. The heading takes advantage of the DMY() function that returns a text string with the day-month, name-year format; DMY(11/01/88) returns 1 November 88. In order to eliminate the day number, the SUBSTR() function displays the text beginning at the third character in the string.

Programs That Paginate ■ **411**

```
PROCEDURE Grphead
SET DEVICE TO PRINT
@ PROW()+3,0 SAY "Patients for "+subSTR;
 (Dmy(Discharge),3)
@ PROW()+1,0 SAY REPLICATE("=",75)
SET DEVICE TO SCREEN
RETURN
```

You have now assembled six procedures to create the subtotal report.

1. **Heading.** Print page headings.

2. **Endpage.** End page routine, prints page number, ejects page, and executes page headings.

3. **Prtline.** Print one line for each record.

4. **Prtsubs.** Prints group subtotals.

5. **Prtgrand.** Print grand totals for report.

6. **Grphead.** Prints heading for each subtotal group.

All these procedures contain separate SET DEVICE TO PRINT and SET DEVICE TO SCREEN commands so that the main procedure does not have to turn print output on or off. From the main program the assumption is made that @/SAY is directed to the screen and that each procedure is responsible for turning printing on or off when necessary.

The next routine, the main program, places each of the individual subroutines into a logical structure. By placing most of the detailed commands in procedures, the main line of the program's logic is easier to layout and understand. It makes little difference to dBASE IV how you create the program. But modularizing your programs helps isolate errors and makes program revision and modification faster.

The main procedure begins by running the Setoff program and opening the Admitbig file with the new index tag you created for this report.

```
PROCEDURE Report
DO Setoff
USE Admitbig INDEX Admitbig ORDER Monthly
```

The next task is to create the variables used in the program.

```
STORE 0 TO Sumdays,Sumcharges,Gnddays,;
Gndcharges,All
STORE 1 TO Printed,Pageno
Marg_bot=55
```

The actual report printing begins with the printing of the headings at the top of the first page by the Heading subroutine.

```
DO Heading
```

With the heading printed, begin the main processing loop. In this case, you cannot use a scan loop because the main processing loop is tested after each group, not after each record has printed. Here, the main processing loop is a DO WHILE .NOT. EOF() command.

```
DO WHILE .NOT. EOF()
```

The first task in the main processing loop is to establish the control value. The control value determines when the last record from a particular group has been processed. A subtotal program begins by assuming that the values stored in the first record in the database comprise the criterion for the first subtotal group. In this program, each subtotal group represents all the patients discharged in the same month. If the first record in the database has a November 1988 discharge date, that date becomes the first subtotal group control value.

In this example, the control value for a group is the first six characters of the discharge date and the program will group together all of the records that match the control value.

```
Control=SUBSTR(DTOS(Discharge),1,6)
```

With the control value set, you can call the subroutine that prints the subtotal group heading.

```
DO Grphead
```

With the heading printed, you are ready to begin the inner or group processing loop. This loop prints records as long as the discharge date, year, and month match the control value. There is one other reason to stop the loop: if the last record in the file has been reached. To account for both possible conditions, the loop is controlled by a compound expression. The expression SUBSTR(DTOS(Discharge),1,6) = Control tests to see if the records belong to the same monthly grouping, and WHILE .NOT.EOF() tests to see if the program has reached the end of the file. Without this additional test, the program would

Programs That Paginate ■ 413

work perfectly until it reached the last record in the file. Then it would print endlessly.

```
DO WHILE SUBSTR(DTOS(Discharge),1,6)=;
Control.AND..NOT.EOF()
```

The inner loop is the one that actually prints the lines for each record using the procedure Prtline.

```
    DO Prtline
```

Following the line printing, the pointer skips to the next record in the file.

```
    SKIP
```

At this point, we must perform a series of tests. First, the program tests the value of PROW() to determine if more records should be printed on this page. If not, the Endpage routine is executed to start a new page.

```
    IF PROW()>=Marg_bot
       DO Endpage
    ENDIF
```

The next test is performed by the ENDDO command associated with the inner loop. The program tests for the end of the file, or if the date in the new record matches the value in the control variable. If they match, the program cycles back to the beginning of the inner loop and prints another record as part of the same group. If the test fails, the loop terminates.

```
ENDDO
```

If the ENDDO command fails to recycle the loop, you can assume that the last record in the current control group has been printed. This means that you will want to print the subtotals for that group. This is done by executing the Prtsubs routine.

```
DO Prtsubs
```

When the Prtsubs routine completes, the ENDDO associated with the main processing loop is evaluated. If the pointer is not at the end of the file, there are more records, and implicitly, another subgroup to process. This ENDDO will recycle processing back to the top of the loop where the old control value used to create the previous group gets replaced with the new control value, and the group processing begins again. If the end of file marker has been reached, the program proceeds to the next command.

ENDDO

When the program reaches this point, all the records have been processed in their subtotal groups. The last task of the program is to print the grand totals and the averages for all of the records using the procedure Prtgrand.

```
DO prtgrand
```

The final program commands are the standard program closing routines.

```
CLOSE DATABASE
DO Setoff
RETURN
```

The entire program reads as follows:

```
PROCEDURE Heading
SET DEVICE TO PRINT
Hd=5
Title="Admission File Data"
@ Hd,(80-LEN(title))/2 SAY Title
@ Hd+1, 0 SAY REPLICATE("=",75)
@ Hd+2, 5 SAY "Patient"
@ Hd+2,30 SAY "Admitted"
@ Hd+2,40 SAY "Dischar."
@ Hd+2,50 SAY "Days"
@ Hd+2,60 SAY "Charges"
@ Hd+3, 0 SAY REPLICATE("=",75)
SET DEVICE TO SCREEN
RETURN
PROCEDURE Endpage
SET DEVICE TO PRINT
@ 59,37 SAY "-"+lTRIM(STR(Pageno,2))+"-"
EJECT
SET DEVICE TO SCREEN
@ 12,10 SAY STR(Pageno,2)+"pages."
Pageno=Pageno+1
DO Heading
RETURN
```

```
PROCEDURE Prtline
@ 10,10 SAY STR(All/RECCOUNT()*100,4,1)+"%;
 printed."
SET DEVICE TO PRINT
@ PROW()+1, 0 SAY STR(Printed,2)+"."
@ PROW() , 5 SAY TRIM(Last)+", "+First PICTURE;
 "XXXXXXXXXXXXXXXXXXXXXXX"
@ PROW() ,30 SAY Admit
@ PROW() ,40 SAY Discharge
@ PROW() ,50 SAY Discharge-Admit+1 PICTURE;
 "99,999"
@ PROW() ,60 SAY charges PICTURE "99,999,999.99"
Sumdays=Sumdays+Discharge-Admit+1
Sumcharges=Sumcharges+Charges
Printed=Printed+1
SET DEVICE TO SCREEN
RETURN
PROCEDURE Prtsubs
SET DEVICE TO PRINT
@ PROW()+1, 0 SAY REPLICATE("=",75)
@ PROW()+1, 0 SAY "Total"
@ PROW(), 50 SAY Sumdays PICTURE "99,999"
@ PROW(), 60 SAY Sumcharges PICTURE
"99,999,999.99" SET DEVICE TO SCREEN
Gnddays=Gnddays+Sumdays
Gndcharges=Gndcharges+Sumcharges
All=All+Printed-1
STORE 0 TO Sumdays,Sumcharges,
STORE 1 TO Printed
RETURN
PROCEDURE Prtgrand
SET DEVICE TO PRINT
@ PROW()+1, 0 SAY REPLICATE("=",75)
@ PROW()+1, 0 SAY "Grand Totals"
@ PROW(), 50 SAY Gnddays PICTURE "99,999"
@ PROW(), 60 SAY Gndcharges PICTURE;
```

```
      "99,999,999.99"
   @ PROW()+1, 0 SAY "Averages"
   @ PROW(), 50 SAY Gnddays/All PICTURE "99,999"
   @ PROW(), 60 SAY Gndcharges/All PICTURE;
    "99,999,999.99"
   @ 60,37 SAY "-"+LTRIM(STR(Pageno,2))+"-"
   SET DEVICE TO SCREEN
   EJECT
   RETURN
   PROCEDURE Grphead
   SET DEVICE TO PRINT
   @ PROW()+3,0 SAY "Patients for "+SUBSTR(DMY;
   (Discharge),3)
   @ PROW()+1,0 SAY REPLICATE("=",75)
   SET DEVICE TO SCREEN
   RETURN
   PROCEDURE Report
   DO Setoff
   USE Admitbig Index Admitbig ORDER Monthly
   STORE 0 TO Sumdays,Sumcharges,Gnddays,;
   Gndcharges,All
   STORE 1 TO Printed,Pageno
   Marg_bot=55
   DO Heading
   DO WHILE .NOT. EOF()
        Control=SUBSTR(DTOS(Discharge),1,6)
        DO Grphead
        DO WHILE SUBSTR(DTOS(Discharge),1,6)=;
        Control.AND..NOT.EOF()
             DO Prtline
             SKIP
             IF PROW()>=Marg_bot
                  DO Endpage
             ENDIF
        ENDDO
        DO Prtsubs
```

```
ENDDO
DO Prtgrand
CLOSE DATABASE
DO Setoff
RETURN
```

Save and run the program by entering

Ctrl-End

```
SET PROCEDURE TO Grprpt
DO Report
```

The last procedure outlining the basic flow of the program is very easy to follow because all the details are handled in procedures. This is the advantage of writing a program in a series of procedures. You can see that many programs can be built by combining the subroutines in different ways under different conditions.

Block Format Reports

In a form report, each page contains only one record. In a column report, each record prints on one line of the page. In a block-type report, each record prints two or more lines on the same page. This makes the block-type report a cross between the two standard formats you have already programmed.

Block-type reports cover such tasks as printing mailing labels, either one or several across, or printing lists with too much data to fit on one line. All the formats have in common the fact that each record is no longer equal to one line on the report.

The most common type of block report is a label printing program.

> *Note:* dBASE IV does not know or care what type of paper you have in your printer. Label reports can be printed on normal paper or on mailing labels. To learn how to write these programs, you do not have to have mailing labels in your printer. Normal computer printing paper will do.

You will create two label-print programs: one to print one label across, and one to print three labels across.

Begin by creating a program that prints a single label.

```
MODIFY COMMAND Label1
```

Begin this program by running the Setoff program and opening the Admit database indexed by last name.

```
DO Setoff
USE Admit INDEX Admit ORDER Last
```

Setting Page Length

The major difference between printing on labels and printing on paper is that while standard computer paper is 11 inches wide and 66 lines long, labels come in many sizes, all smaller than a standard page. The most common mailing label is one inch long and 3.5 inches wide.

> *Note:* Mailing labels for computer printers will sometimes be sold in boxes in what appear to be very odd sizes. For example, the labels referred to in this text as 1 inch in length are often sold as 15/16 of an inch. The difference in size, 1/16 inch, is the difference between measuring the label and measuring the distance from one label to the next. Labels are placed on the backing paper with a small space, 1/16 inch, between each label. The label itself is therefore slightly smaller than one inch, 15/16 inch. When you are writing a program to print, you are not very concerned with the actual physical dimensions of the label but the distances, horizontal and vertical, you need to position the printed text. In this case, you want to measure the distance between the top of one label and the top of the next label. It is this distance that tells you how far the program must move in order to reach the top of the next label.

A 1-inch label means that your form length is six lines. A 1.5-inch label would be nine lines, a 2-inch label 12, and so on.

To work with this type of label, you need to change the value dBASE IV uses for the length of the form so that the eject command positions the printhead at the top of the next label. Without this change, dBASE IV would skip the full 11 inches each time you used eject.

There are two ways to accomplish this change in form length.

1. **Printer codes.** The EJECT command operates by sending a form feed command to the printer. The printer is usually set to react to the single command sent by dBASE IV, form feed, to skip to the top

of the next form. Most printers allow you to alter the setting for form length by sending a special sequence of codes to the printer. For example, the following commands would set an Epson FX-80 printer to a one-inch form length. These commands are not part of a program, do not enter them.

```
SET PRINT ON
?? CHR(27)+"C"+CHR(0)+CHR(1)
SET PRINT OFF
```

In this command it is the value in the last CHR() function that sets the number of inches. A seven-inch form length would look like this:

```
SET PRINT ON
?? CHR(27)+"C"+CHR(0)+CHR(7)
SET PRINT OFF
```

2. **Line feeds.** Another way to approach this problem is to eliminate the use of the form feed command, and instead, send enough line feeds—blank lines—to complete the page when EJECT is issued.

    The line feed method is the better one to employ because it is not printer specific. The line feed method works with almost any printer. However, the form feed method requires you to know the exact coding sequence that will work with your specific printer.

    Note: The form feed method has an advantage. If you are working with a fairly large form, like 7 inches, a form feed works faster than a series of line feeds. In the case of a 1-inch label you will find that form feeds offer little advantage over line feeds.

A shorthand form of the line feed method requires you to reset two of the built-in dBASE IV printer system variables.

1. **_plength.** The _plength value sets the number of lines on the form. The default value is 66.

2. **_padvance.** This variable selects the method used by dBASE IV when the EJECT command is issued. By default, _padvance is set to FORMFEED, meaning it will use the form feed method.

    Note: A form feed is accomplished, on most printers, when escape character 12 is sent. For example, ?? CHR(12) with the print set on would be the equivalent of EJECT.

By setting this value to Linefeeds, the EJECT command issues a series of line feed commands in order to reach the top of the next form.

Enter the commands that set up dBASE IV to print on one-inch labels.

```
* set page length
_plength=6
_padvance="Linefeeds"
```

The next step is to start a scan loop that prints all the records.

```
* start loop
SCAN
     @ 10, 10 SAY "Printing "+Last
```

Set the device to print and use @/SAY commands to place the data on the label.

```
SET DEVICE TO PRINT
@ 1,        0 SAY TRIM(Last)+", "+First
@ PROW()+1, 0 SAY "Admitted "+DTOC(Admit)
@ PROW()+1, 0 SAY "Discharged "+DTOC(Discharge)
```

For the most part, relative addressing has been in terms of the PROW() function controlling the vertical position of the data. In the next two commands, relative addressing places two items on the same line. The @/SAY command uses the expression PCOL()+2 to place the data on the same line, two columns from the last character printed.

```
     @ PROW()+1, 0         SAY "Age: "+STR(Age)
     @ PROW(), PCOL()+2 SAY "Sex: "+UPPER(Sex)
```

Complete the printing, eject the rest of the form, and end the loop.

```
     @ PROW()+1, 0         SAY
IIF(Payor=Space(20),"Not Insured",Payor)
     EJECT
     SET DEVICE TO SCREEN
ENDSCAN
```

The program concludes with the usual commands and the addition of two commands that set the page length and page advance variables back to their default settings.

```
_Plength=66
_Padvance="FORMFEED"
CLOSE DATABASE
DO Seton
RETURN
```

The entire program reads as follows:

```
DO Setoff
USE Admit INDEX Admit ORDER Last
* set page length
_plength=6
_padvance="Linefeeds"
* start loop
SCAN
    @ 10, 10 SAY "Printing "+Last
    SET DEVICE TO PRINT
    @ 1,          0        SAY TRIM(Last)+",;
     "+First
    @ PROW()+1, 0          SAY "Admitted;
     "+DTOC(Admit)
    @ PROW()+1, 0          SAY "Discharged
"+DTOC(Discharge)
    @ PROW()+1, 0          SAY "Age: "+STR(Age)
    @ PROW(), PCOL()+2 SAY "Sex: "+UPPER(Sex)
    @ PROW()+1, 0          SAY IIF(Payor=Space(20),;
    "Not Insured",Payor)
    EJECT
    SET DEVICE TO SCREEN
ENDSCAN
_plength=66
_padvance="FORMFEED"
CLOSE DATABASE
DO SETON
RETURN
```

Save and execute the program by pressing Alt-e and typing r. The program prints the information as labels, a block of data exactly one inch in length.

Multiple Column Blocks

The basic label program is quite simple; however, many users like to use label forms that have three columns of labels across a full 8.5-inch page.

> *Note:* The advantage of these labels is that most printers move faster horizontally than they do vertically. If you are printing a large number of labels, you can reduce the number of line feeds by printing several labels on the same line. In theory this will shorten the time it takes to print labels. The actual savings depends on the design and capacity of the printer you use.

The main problem in printing more than one label horizontally is that the flow of the data in the database goes in a different direction. For example, if you want to print three names on the same line, you have to access three consecutive records. When you come to the second line of the label, you have to print the admission date from the first label. However, since you just printed the name from the third record, you have to move the pointer backwards to the first record. This problem occurs for each line you want to print. This is a very confusing procedure to write and it wastes a lot of time and effort moving back and forth between the same records.

The solution to this problem is to move sequentially through the database, from top to bottom. However, instead of printing the data as it is encountered, store the data in memory variables. When the data from three records is stored, you can then print the information in the memory variables without moving the pointer backwards.

This process takes advantage of the ability of dBASE IV to store data in arrays. An array, discussed in Chapter 6, is a special memory variable. An array is not a single value but a sequence of related values, called elements. How does using arrays apply to the problem with multi-labels?

You want to print three labels, consisting of five lines of data, across the page. Think of the labels as a grid of items arranged in rows (one for each line) and columns (one for each label.) The grid they form is a two-dimensional array. You can refer to any one of the items by its line and column position. For example, the admission date on the second label can be referred to as the item in row 2, column 2 of the label array.

In Chapter 6 you used one-dimensional arrays. But you can create a two-dimensional array to hold all of the elements needed for printing three-across labels.

The advantage of using array variables is they can be referred to indirectly by number. This makes it possible to use a loop, with counters, to cycle through the elements of an array, simplifying programming.

The best way to attack the multi-label program is to use a two-dimensional array to store the data, and then print out the elements in the array. Begin by creating a new program called Label2. Enter

```
MODIFY COMMAND Label2
```

The program begins with the same commands used in the Label1 program to open the database and set the form length to one inch.

```
DO Setoff
USE Admit INDEX Admit ORDER Last
* set page length
_plength=6
_padvance="Linefeeds"
```

The next command, the DECLARE command, creates an array of the proper size to store the items from the records. This process is called dimensioning an array. Here, you want five lines, one for each row of the labels, by three columns across.

```
DECLARE Line[5,3]
```

Once the array is declared, you must fill the elements with data. The array solves the basic problem of the program by allowing you to move vertically in the database. This means that you will fill column 1 with the first record, column 2 with the second record, and column 3 with the third record. When you print, the operation turns 90 degrees. Then you will move across the array, printing all of the columns from each row before moving to the next row.

The main line of processing begins with a DO WHILE .NOT.EOF() loop.

```
*start loop
DO WHILE .NOT.EOF()
```

In order to fill the array, you must define a set of five items from each of the three records that will print together. This can be done by using a loop that cycles three times. Each time the loop cycles, it fills in a different column of the array. A variable named Position selects the column, 1, 2, or 3, to fill. The loop begins with column 1.

```
POSITION=1
```

The loop processes until the value of position reaches 3. You must take into account that during one of the passes the program may encounter the end of the file before it can fill all three columns. The following command creates a loop controlled by those conditions.

```
DO WHILE Position<=3.AND..NOT.EOF()
```

As the loop begins, its first command stores the name field into an element in the array. Line[1,Position] indicates that the contents of the First and Last fields will be placed in row 1 of the array. The column position will be determined by the value of Position, which changes as the loop cycles.

```
LINE[1,Position]=TRIM(Last)+", "+First
```

The next four lines store information into the next four elements of the array.

```
Line[2,Position]="Admitted "+DTOC(Admit)
Line[3,Position]="Discharged "+DTOC(Discharge)
Line[4,Position]="Age: "+STR(age)+" Sex:;
 "+UPPER(Sex)
Line[5,Position]=IIF(Payor=Space(20),"Not;
 Insured",Payor)
```

When the first record has been placed into the array, you are ready to skip to the next record in the database.

```
     SKIP
```

You now want to begin placing data into the second column of the array. This is done by adding 1 to the value of POSITION, which then directs the data into the elements in the second column of the array.

```
     Position=Position+1
ENDDO
```

The loop cycles three times, and fills all the elements of the array. The next step is to print the elements of the array using a single @/SAY command inside a dual loop. The loops use two variables: Label ln to select the row of the array and Position to select the column of the array. The loops begin with the first line of the array, print all the columns, then move on to the second, print all columns, and so on. The only @/SAY command needed is one that prints the selected element in the array.

The first task is to start a loop that cycles five times, once for each row in the label.

```
Label_ln=1
DO WHILE Label_ln<=5
```

Within each line, you need to cycle three times, one for each column.

```
Position=1
DO WHILE Position<=3
```

You are now ready to print the items in the array. You can take advantage of the array structure to calculate the location for the @/SAY command. First, the row position for printing would be the same as the line number in the array; line 1 of the array would be line 1 of the label. You can therefore use the Label_ln variable as the line value with the @/SAY command.

The column position is a bit trickier but it can also be calculated. You are working with three labels across a page. Labels of this kind are usually about 2.5 inches wide, making the start of the next label to the right about 26 columns. This means that label 1 should be positioned at 0, label 2 at 26, and label 3 at 52. Since the distance between labels is constant you can simply multiply the column number by 26. Because you want the first column at zero you should subtract 1 from the value of the array column; thus, the expression (Position−1)*26 will create the correct column position.

```
SET DEVICE TO PRINT
@ Label_ln,(position-1)*26
SAY Line[Label_ln,Position]
SET DEVICE TO SCREEN
```

Following that printing of the element, move to the next column.

```
           Position=Position+1
```

You can then end this loop so it will cycle through the columns 1 to 3 before terminating. The && symbols let you add a program note on the same line as ENDDO command. This is another method to add notations to a program. In this case, it helps you match ENDDO and DO WHILE commands.

```
    ENDDO && column position 1 through 3
```

When this column loop is complete, the row value is incremented and the cycle begins over for the next line of the label.

```
      Label_ln=Label_ln+1
ENDDO && label lines 1 through 5
```

When all five lines, three columns apiece, are completed, eject the rest of the form and process the next group of records.

```
      EJECT
ENDDO && processing all records
```

When all the records have processed, conclude the program with the usual commands.

```
_plength=66
_padvance="Formfeed"
CLOSE DATABASE
DO Seton
RETURN
```

Using an array makes it possible to print all the data with a single command encased in a series of loops that cycle through all the elements of the array. This structure not only saves some programming time but is very easy to modify. By changing only a few of the controlling values the same program could print 2.5-inch labels 2 across.

Save and execute the program by entering (Alt)-e and typing r. (You may have to issue an EJECT command if you're using a laser printer.) The labels print in three columns. If you look at the last line of labels, you will notice the second and third labels on the line are a repetition of the labels on the previous line. Why?

Because the current database contains exactly 13 records; thus, the last line of labels begins with the 13th record and then encounters the end of the file. The end of file stops the loop that defines the array. However, the second and third columns in the array still maintain their value from the previous row, and they repeat.

The repetition is not harmful but it may confuse someone using the program. In order to eliminate printing these extra records, you must clear all the old values from the array before it adds a new row of values.

Load the Label2 program into the editor.

```
MODIFY COMMAND Label2
```

The modification to eliminate the repetition of labels in the last row requires you to create a dual loop. This dual loop is like the one used to print the elements in the array and sets each of the items in the array to a blank.

Move the cursor to line 19. You can create this loop with a minimum of effort by simply copying the current loop. Turn on the text highlighting by pressing F6.

Move the cursor to line 29. Press End. Move to the beginning of line 31. Press F8. You now have a duplicate of the dual loop structure. You need to modify this loop so that it does not print, but sets each element equal to a blank.

Move the cursor to line 35. Remove the SET DEVICE commands and substitute a command that sets each element equal to SPACE(1).

Old lines:
```
SET DEVICE TO PRINT
@ Label_ln,(position-1)*26 SAY;
  Line[Label_ln,position]
SET DEVICE TO SCREEN
```

New line:
```
Line[Label_ln,Position]=SPACE(1)
```

Save and execute the modified program by entering Alt-e and typing r. The program executes. This time the last label appears alone at the end of the sequence without the repetition of the other records.

When you have completed this printing make sure you position the paper in your printer to the top of the form so you will be ready to print the next report with the proper pagination.

Reports from Multiple Databases

The reports you have generated up to this point all have drawn data from only a single database. In the previous chapters you learned how to use multiple databases to store related groups of data and assemble this data using relationships between the databases. The same concepts can be applied to produce a report that draws data from a number of related database files.

Suppose you want to create a report listing information about patient care. This report uses the Patcare file to locate patients and the doctors who treat them. The problem posed by such a report is that for every patient there may be one or more doctors to list.

You can combine the techniques you learned about block-format and column-format reports to produce a report that prints out as many physician names as necessary for each patient.

Create a new program called Treatrpt (treatment report) by entering

MODIFY COMMAND Treatrpt

Because a report like this has so many parts, it is best to attack this program with a series of procedures.

The first procedure is a page heading routine. This procedure prints the title of the report at the top of the page.

```
PROCEDURE Pagehead
Title="Patient Care Report"
SET DEVICE TO PRINT
@ 5,(80-LEN(Title))/2 SAY Title
@ 6,0 SAY REPLICATE("=",75)
@ 10,0
SET DEVICE TO SCREEN
RETURN
```

The second procedure is the page-ending routine. This routine executes when the printed lines fill a page. It will print the page number, eject the page, and then execute the page heading routine to place the heading at the top of the next page.

```
PROCEDURE Pageend
SET DEVICE TO PRINT
@ 60,39 SAY "-"+LTRIM(STR(Pageno))+"-"
SET DEVICE TO SCREEN
Pageno=Pageno+1
EJECT
DO Pagehead
RETURN
```

The next two routines print column headings for the information in the report. The report will print eight items about each patient (name, admit and discharge date, age, gender, anesthesia, trauma team, and CT scan). The routine below prints the headings for these columns.

```
PROCEDURE Pathead
SET DEVICE TO PRINT
@ PROW()+3,  5 SAY "Patient"
@ PROW()   , 30 SAY "Admit"
@ PROW()   , 40 SAY "Dischrg."
@ PROW()   , 50 SAY "Age"
@ PROW()   , 55 SAY "Sex"
@ PROW()   , 60 SAY "Anest"
@ PROW()   , 65 SAY "Team"
@ PROW()   , 70 SAY "Scan"
@ PROW()+1,  0 SAY REPLICATE("-",75)
SET DEVICE TO SCREEN
RETURN
```

The next procedure prints column headings for physician information. In this case, there are five items to print about each physician.

```
PROCEDURE Dochead
SET DEVICE TO PRINT
@ PROW()+2,  3 SAY "Number"
@ PROW()   , 15 SAY "Physician"
@ PROW()   , 40 SAY "Date"
@ PROW()   , 50 SAY "Specialty"
@ PROW()   , 70 SAY "Resident"
@ PROW()+1,  3 SAY REPLICATE("-",72)
SET DEVICE TO SCREEN
RETURN
```

The next procedure prints a line of information about a patient. The assumption is made that the selected database is the Admit database, but the patient's name is drawn from the open, not selected, Patcare database. With the exception of the patient's name, all other data is drawn from the Admit database. Use the IIF() function to convert logical fields into the words Yes and No.

```
PROCEDURE Infopat
* print patient data
SET DEVICE TO PRINT
@ PROW()+1,  0 SAY STR(Printed,3)+"."
```

```
@ PROW()   ,  5 SAY Patcare->Patient;
 PICTURE "XXXXXXXXXXXXXXXXXXXXX"
@ PROW()   , 30 SAY Admit
@ PROW()   , 40 SAY Discharge
@ PROW()   , 50 SAY Age
@ PROW()   , 55 SAY UPPER(Sex)
@ PROW()   , 60 SAY IIF(Anesthesia,"Yes","No")
@ PROW()   , 65 SAY IIF(Truma_team,"Yes","No")
@ PROW()   , 70 SAY IIF(Ct_scan,"Yes","No")
SET DEVICE TO SCREEN
RETURN
```

The following procedure prints a line of information about a physician. The assumption is that the printing will take place while the Doctors database is selected. All of the fields are drawn from the Doctors database with the exception of the physician's name, which is drawn from the open, but not selected, Patcare database.

```
PROCEDURE Infodoc
SET DEVICE TO PRINT
@ PROW()+1,  3 SAY Med_rec_no
@ PROW()   , 15 SAY Patcare->Doctor PICTURE;
 "XXXXXXXXXXXXXXXXXXXXX"
@ PROW()   , 40 SAY Patcare->Date_care
@ PROW()   , 50 SAY Field PICTURE "XXXXXXXXXXXXX"
@ PROW()   , 70 SAY IIF(Resident,"Yes","No")
SET DEVICE TO SCREEN
RETURN
```

You now have six procedures defined. These will be your tools for creating the main procedure that organizes the printing of the report.

1. **Pagehead.** Prints the headings at the top of each page.

2. **Pageend.** Prints page number and starts new page.

3. **Pathead.** Prints the headings for patient information.

4. **Dochead.** Prints the headings for doctor information.

5. **Infopat.** Prints information about a patient.

6. **Infodoc.** Prints information about a doctor.

The next procedure is the main program called Report. This procedure begins with the Setoff program followed by the USE commands that open the three databases needed for this report: Patcare, Admit, and Doctors. All three files are indexed on the last name of the patient, Patcare and Admit, or the doctor, Doctors. Admit is assigned the alias name of Patients.

```
PROCEDURE Report
DO Setoff
USE Patcare INDEX Patcare ORDER Last
USE Admit INDEX Admit ORDER Last ALIAS Patients;
  IN 2
USE doctors INDEX Doctors ORDER Last in 3
```

You need three variables during this program. Pageno produces the page numbers, Printed counts the records printed, and Marg_bot sets the bottom line for each page. In this program, the value of Printed does not correspond to the number of records in any of the databases; instead, it counts only the unique names in the Patcare file.

```
Pageno=1
Printed=1
Marg_bot=55
```

The first printing command in the program runs the Pagehead subroutine to print the page heading at the top of the first page.

```
DO Pagehead
```

The program is now ready to begin the main processing loop, a DO WHILE .NOT.EOF() loop. When you are working with multiple databases, you must match the end of file with the proper database. In this case, the end of file controlling the program is the end of the Patcare database. The goal is to process all the records in the Patcare database and use Admit and Doctors as lookup databases to supply detail about the patients and doctors respectively. This means that when the ENDDO corresponding to this command is encountered, Patcare must be the active database.

```
DO WHILE .NOT.EOF() && File Patcare
```

The next command displays the name of the patient being processed.

```
@ 10,10 SAY "Patient "+Patient
```

You have now arrived at the key logical structure in the program; the part of the program that actually processes the information about

432 ■ **Reports and Printing**

each patient. You must address the possibility that a patient may have multiple records in the Patcare database. You want to print the patient information only once. But you want to print the doctor information for as many records as that patient has in the Patcare database.

The solution is to print the patient information first. Then start a loop, structured like a subtotal group loop, that will print the doctor information for the group of records for the same patient. The report will print patient information only once for each unique patient name in Patcare, but is capable of printing multiple doctors for any of those patients.

The first step is to create a control value to control the doctor processing loop. In this case, that value will be the name of the patient since all of the records are related to that patient.

```
Control=Patient
```

With the control value set as the patient name, you can locate the patient's record in the Admit, alias Patients, database.

```
SELECT Patients
```

The SEEK command positions the pointer to the correct patient record. The UPPER() function is used in the SEEK expression because the index key created for the Admit file is UPPER(LAST). The SUBSTR() function isolates the last name portion of the patient field.

```
SEEK UPPER(SUBSTR(Patcare->Patient,1,;
  AT(",",Patcare->Patient)-1))
```

With the pointer positioned to the correct record in Admit, you can execute the routines to print the patient information. Because this report combines patient and doctor information, it is necessary to print headings for each type of data. Run the Pathead and Infopat procedures to print the patient data.

```
DO Pathead
```

```
DO Infopat
```

The patient's information has been printed. The next step is to print one or more doctors who are related to that patient's treatment. Begin by printing the headings for doctor information.

```
DO Dochead
```

The next step is to start a subtotal loop. This loop processes all the records grouped together for one patient. The loop is controlled by the

Reports from Multiple Databases ■ **433**

expression PATCARE->PATIENT=CONTROL. This means that the loop will print doctor information as long as the name of the patient in the Patcare file remains the same as the value in the control variable.

```
DO WHILE Patcare->Patient=Control
```

Once the loop has been initiated, you can select the Doctors database.

```
    SELECT Doctors
```

Position the record pointer to the proper doctor record by using a SEEK command. The SEEK expression uses a substring of the doctor's name stored in the Patcare database.

```
SEEK SUBSTR(Patcare->Doctor,1,;
AT(",",Patcare->Doctor)-1)
```

With the pointer positioned to the correct record in the Doctors database, you can run the Infodoc routine to print physician information.

```
    DO Infodoc
```

Following the printing of the doctor information, you must determine if there are more doctors for the current patient. This is done by returning to the Patcare database and moving the pointer to the next record. If that record has the same patient name, Patcare->Patient=Control, the loop will recycle and print another doctor under the current patient. If the values do not match, the inner loop terminates and the program recycles to the top of the patient loop so a new patient record can be printed.

```
SELECT Patcare
SKIP
```

Before the program encounters the ENDDO commands, you need to test for the end of the page.

```
IF PROW()>=Marg_bot
        DO Pageend
    ENDIF
ENDDO && doctor records
```

Following the doctor loop, the value of PRINTED—the number of patient records processed—is incremented. This means the numbering of items on the report will count only unique blocks of patient/doctor information, not actual records.

```
      Printed=Printed+1
ENDDO && patient record
```

Following the end of the loops, which means all of the records have been processed, you can conclude the program by printing the final page number and running the usual closing commands.

```
SET DEVICE TO PRINT
@ 59,39 SAY "-"+lTRIM(STR(Pageno))+"-"
SET DEVICE TO SCREEN
EJECT
CLOSE DATABASE
DO Seton
RETURN
```

The entire program reads as follows:

```
PROCEDURE Pagehead
Title="Patient Care Report"
SET DEVICE TO PRINT
@ 5,(80-LEN(Title))/2 SAY Title
@ 6,0 SAY REPLICATE("=",75)
@ 10,0
SET DEVICE TO SCREEN
RETURN
PROCEDURE Pageend
SET DEVICE TO PRINT
@ 59,39 SAY "-"+lTRIM(STR(Pageno))+"-"
SET DEVICE TO SCREEN
Pageno=Pageno+1
EJECT
DO Pagehead
RETURN
PROCEDURE Pathead
SET DEVICE TO PRINT
@ PROW()+3, 5 SAY "Patient"
@ PROW()   ,30 SAY "Admit"
@ PROW()   ,40 SAY "Dischrg."
```

```
@ PROW()    , 50 SAY "Age"
@ PROW()    , 55 SAY "Sex"
@ PROW()    , 60 SAY "Anest"
@ PROW()    , 65 SAY "Team"
@ PROW()    , 70 SAY "Scan"
@ PROW()+1, 0 SAY REPLICATE("-",75)
SET DEVICE TO SCREEN
RETURN
PROCEDURE Dochead
SET DEVICE TO PRINT
@ PROW()+2, 3 SAY "Number"
@ PROW()    , 15 SAY "Physician"
@ PROW()    , 40 SAY "Date"
@ PROW()    , 50 SAY "Specialty"
@ PROW()    , 70 SAY "Resident"
@ PROW()+1, 3 SAY REPLICATE("-",72)
SET DEVICE TO SCREEN
RETURN
PROCEDURE Infopat
* print patient data
SET DEVICE TO PRINT
@ PROW()+1, 0 SAY STR(Printed,3)+"."
@ PROW()    , 5 SAY Patcare->Patient PICTURE;
  "XXXXXXXXXXXXXXXXXXXXXX"
@ PROW()    , 30 SAY Admit
@ PROW()    , 40 SAY Discharge
@ PROW()    , 50 SAY Age
@ PROW()    , 55 SAY UPPER(Sex)
@ PROW()    , 60 SAY IIF(Anesthesia,"Yes","No")
@ PROW()    , 65 SAY IIF(Truma_team,"Yes","No")
@ PROW()    , 70 SAY IIF(Ct_scan,"Yes","No")
SET DEVICE TO SCREEN
RETURN
PROCEDURE Infodoc
SET DEVICE TO PRINT
```

```
@ PROW()+1,  3 SAY Med_rec_no
@ PROW()   , 15 SAY Patcare->Doctor PICTURE;
 "XXXXXXXXXXXXXXXXXXXXX"
@ PROW()   , 40 SAY Patcare->Date_care
@ PROW()   , 50 SAY Field PICTURE "XXXXXXXXXXXXX"
@ PROW()   , 70 SAY IIF(Resident,"Yes","No")
SET DEVICE TO SCREEN
RETURN
PROCEDURE Report
DO Setoff
USE Patcare INDEX Patcare ORDER Last
USE Admit INDEX Admit ORDER Last ALIAS Patients
IN 2
USE Doctors Index Doctors ORDER Last 3
Pageno=1
Printed=1
Marg_bot=55
DO Pagehead
DO WHILE .NOT.EOF() && File Patcare
     @ 10,10 SAY "Patient "+Patient
     Control=Patient
     SELECT Patients
     SEEK UPPER(SUBSTR(Patcare->Patient,1,;
     AT(",",Patcare->Patient)-1))
     DO Pathead
     DO Infopat
     DO Dochead
     DO WHILE Patcare->Patient=Control
          SELECT Doctors
          SEEK SUBSTR(Patcare->Doctor,1,;
          AT(",",Patcare->Doctor)-1)
          DO Infodoc
          SELECT Patcare
          SKIP
          IF PROW()>=Marg_bot
```

```
                DO Pageend
              ENDIF
          ENDDO && doctor records
          Printed=Printed+1
    ENDDO && patient records
    SET DEVICE TO PRINT
    @ 59,39 SAY "-"+lTRIM(STR(Pageno))+"-"
    SET DEVICE TO SCREEN
    EJECT
    CLOSE DATABASE
    DO Seton
    RETURN
```

Save the program by pressing Ctrl-End. Compile the program by entering

```
COMPILE Treatrpt
```

To execute the program, you must open the procedure file and run Report. Try this on your own. If you need help, the correct command can be found at the end of the chapter in the Answers to Exercises section under exercise 9.

As the report executes, notice that some patients, Scott Fisher for instance, have all of the physicians related to their treatment listed, while other patients have only a single physician. This program illustrates how the concept of a subtotal loop can be applied to printing databases with one-to-many relationships.

Close the procedure file after the printing is complete, by entering

```
CLOSE ALL
```

Summary

This chapter focused on the most common type of printed reports generated by database programs, and introduced the following concepts:

Accessing printer. dBASE IV uses two methods to send information to the printer. The SET PRINT ON command sends standard screen output, such as output from ?, LIST, and DISPLAY, to the printer. When SET PRINT is on, the output appears both on the screen and the printer. If you want to suppress the screen display, you can use SET CONSOLE OFF to blank the screen while printing. Remember to SET CONSOLE OFF following printing or your screen will remain blank. The SET DEVICE TO PRINT command redirects the output of @/SAY commands to the printer. These commands will not echo on the screen when the device is set to print. @/GET commands are not redirected to the printer. To change @/SAY output back to the screen, use the SET DEVICE TO SCREEN command.

Eject. The EJECT command feeds the remainder of the page. dBASE IV requires a specific instruction to feed the remainder of the page.

System variables. dBASE IV maintains a series of special memory variables that help monitor activity directed toward the printer. The most important variables, PROW() and PCOL(), report the current position of the print element on the page. These functions make it possible to perform relative addressing in reports just as ROW() and COL() do for screen displays.

Form feeds. Most printers keep track of the number of lines printed on a page. This means you can send a single printer command, usually CHR(12), to feed the rest of the form. dBASE IV uses this method of page advance by default.

Line feeds. A line feed causes the printer to move one line at a time. You can control forms by using dBASE IV to send a series of line feeds equal to the number of lines left on the page. This method is generally a bit slower than using form feeds. However, it can be used to control printing on forms that are not 11 inches in length.

The _plength system variable sets the number of lines on a printed page. The default value is 66 and assumes that vertical printing is set for a line height of 1/6 inch per line.

The _padvance variable controls the method to advance a page. By default it is set to Formfeed, meaning the EJECT command will operate by issuing CHR(12). If set to Linefeeds, the EJECT command will use the value in _plength to determine how many blank lines to send to the printer in order to feed the form.

Printer driver. Some dBASE IV printer tasks, such as the STYLE clause of the ? command, require printer-specific information to implement effects such as bold, underline, or italic printing. dBASE IV supplies this information in the form of printer driver files. These files have a .pr2 file extension. The system variable _pdriver selects a printer driver file. By default the printer driver is set for Generic.pr2.

Form reports. A form report is one that prints one record on each page of the report. Form reports can also be used to fill out preprinted forms.

Column reports. Column reports print as many records as possible on a page. Each record prints one line of data. Column reports can print summary information at the end of the report such as column totals.

Subtotal reports. A subtotal report prints summary information at the end of each subtotal group, as well as a summary for the entire report. Subtotal reports require that the database be indexed so that all of the records that belong to the same group are physically grouped together.

Label reports. A label report prints more than one line of information for each record. Label reports are often used with small forms that require a change in the page length and page advance variables.

Multiple database reports. These reports combine information stored in several databases to create a single report. By using the subtotal and label techniques, they can print several lines of data for each item on the report. This allows you to report one-to-many relationships.

Review Problems for Chapter 8

1. Create a program that prints the information from the Sales database on a individual form.

2. Create a column report program for the data from the Sales database that lists the company, date, item name, quantity, and total amount.

3. Modify the previous report to include subtotals for each company.

4. Use the Cust database to create a mailing label program for printing 3.5-inch by 1-inch labels.

5. Create a report that scans the Sales database and prints the company's name and address on one line. That line should be followed by one line for each sale for that company by printing the date,

product name, maker, and EPA status for each. Note that each company may have one or more products.

Answers to Exercises

1. Print patients' names.

   `LIST Patient TO PRINT`

2. List file structure.

   `LIST STRUCTURE TO PRINT`

3. Expand file with append from.

   ⬆ ⏎

   ⬆ ⏎

4. Import December records only.

   `APPEND FROM Admit FOR MONTH(Admit)=12`

5. Index Admitbig file.

   `INDEX ON Last TAG Last OF Admbig`

6. Execute procedure file.

   `SET PROCEDURE TO Colrpt1`

   `DO Report`

7. Compile and execute procedure program.

   `COMPILE Colrpt1`

   `SET PROCEDURE TO Colrpt1`

   `DO Report`

8. Index with SUBSTR() of DTOS().

   `INDEX ON SUBSTR(DTOS(Discharge),1,6)+Last;`
   ` TAG Monthly OF Admitbig`

9. Execute procedure file.

   `SET PROCEDURE TO Treatrpt`

   `DO Report`

9 SQL

The topic of this chapter, SQL (Structured Query Language), is different from other elements in dBASE IV. SQL is not unique to dBASE IV. In fact, SQL is a database system in itself, used on many computer systems.

The existence of SQL as part of dBASE IV raises some basic questions. What is SQL? What purpose does it serve? Why is it included in dBASE IV? Before you go on to learn to use SQL, let's answer these questions.

Personal vs. Shared Computing

To use dBASE IV, you work on a micro or personal computer. The many technical definitions of a micro or personal computer usually involve the amount of memory or storage capacity, speed of operation, and the cost of the machine. These definitions become obsolete almost before they are written because of the tremendous growth of the microcomputer industry.

Microcomputers were originally designed as personal productivity tools. The earlier computers, mainframe and mini, were designed to be used by groups of people. By way of analogy, when you purchase a telephone, you need a phone jack to connect the phone to the phone system. A telephone is designed to be part of an integrated system. On the other hand, if you buy a calculator, you can use that calculator without reference to any outside network or system. All of the operational power needed for the device is built into the device. The calculator is similar in operation to a personal computer, while the telephone is similar to computers in a network. The calculator is not designed to share information with other calculators, but the telephone is designed to share information with other people on the system.

This basic design difference between personal and shared computers is also reflected in the software used on each kind of system. Microcomputer software tends to store information in formats unique to the currently running application. When dBASE IV stores data, it places the data into a format that cannot be understood by other programs, like Lotus 1-2-3, without some special conversion. The data stored in dBASE IV is organized in fields and records and does not match the data storage methods used by Lotus 1-2-3, which produces financial spreadsheets in rows and columns. The ideas are similar but the implementation is very different. Sharing data between microcomputer applications has traditionally been difficult, and data conversion usually loses information in the translation.

The problem, even with conversion from one format to another, is that users have to know enough about the command structure of both programs to perform the translation. This situation is analogous to that of an interpreter, who must have a working knowledge of both Spanish and English in order to translate from one to the other.

On mini and mainframe computer systems, the problem of sharing data created with different applications is more critical because the computers were designed to share information. In the late 1970s, IBM introduced a new concept meant to eliminate, at least from the user's point of view, the differences in the data formats in database files. The idea was to develop a standard set of database commands that worked with any application to manipulate data stored in a database. This concept took the name SQL: Structured Query Language.

SQL is a standard language for expressing database storage, retrieval, selection, and sequencing tasks and eliminates the need to know the exact storage format of data. The user or programmer does not need to know the exact structure of the file: fields and records, rows and columns, or comma-separated text. People can use the same set of commands for any file. It no longer matters what application creates the file or wants to use its data. To share data, all a user needs is the proper SQL command.

SQL Databases

SQL databases are organized differently than dBASE IV databases. In fact, SQL terminology conflicts with the meaning of many dBASE IV terms.

SQL databases. The term database has a very different meaning in SQL than it does in dBASE IV. In dBASE IV, a database is a collection of fields and records. In the examples in this book, you need several database files, Admit, Doctors, Patcare, to store information related to emergency room activity. In SQL, all the information stored in all these dBASE IV database files constitutes a single SQL database. SQL places all the information under a single umbrella. In dBASE IV, each database represents one set of fields and records. In SQL, a database holds any number of different groups similar to dBASE IV database files.

SQL tables. SQL databases store groups of information, which dBASE IV calls databases, in tables. A table groups data into columns (the equivalent of fields) and rows (the equivalent of records). Each SQL table performs the same task as a dBASE IV database file.

Object Orientation

In addition to changes in structure and terminology, SQL approaches database operations from a different point of view. In Chapters 1 and 2, you learned how dBASE IV's verb-oriented language carries out operations. Each command verb performs some operation either on a database file, a field, a record, a memory variable, or other dBASE IV object. Verb-oriented languages, like dBASE IV are process-oriented. For example, when you enter the dBASE IV command LIST Last,First, do the records list in alphabetical order? The answer is, it depends upon what command you entered prior to LIST. In dBASE IV, the indexing process and the listing process are independent operations. To get an alphabetical list, you must make sure you execute the correct operations, command verbs, in the proper sequence.

SQL attempts to insulate the user or programmer from these details. Each SQL command is a complete set of specifications describing a table of answers to a question called a query—thus the name query language. SQL is more object-oriented than dBASE IV because each query describes the table of answers you want to display. Here is an example of an SQL command that lists doctors by last name.

```
SELECT Last,First ORDERED BY Last;
```

In dBASE IV, your commands tell the program what actions to take. These actions produce the object—a table of information. In SQL, each command is a complete description of the object you want to produce. The exact process that creates this object is hidden from your view and from your control.

Why Use SQL?

SQL insulates users or programmers from the details of database operation. In the dBASE IV programs you have created, you use commands that move record pointers, perform seek operations, and many other details to produce the displays and listings you want. You cannot write a dBASE IV application unless you understand how the data is organized, how pointers move, what alias names are, how to test for the end of a file, and a long list of other skills covered in the previous chapters. When you work in SQL, pointers, end of file markers and the like, are hidden from you. The SQL program works out the details of these operations for you.

There are several reasons why SQL is useful.

1. **Importing Data.** SQL makes it possible to import data stored in foreign databases into a common structure. This is important for users working on networks with SQL file servers. SQL makes data sharing simpler because users are insulated from variations in file structure and format.

2. **Transfer Skills.** If a user is already familiar with SQL commands, she can use dBASE IV SQL without having to learn an entire new language.

3. **Simpler Approach.** The SQL table-object orientation handles database relational operations more clearly than using the dBASE IV approach that requires work areas, record pointers, and alias names.

4. **Networking.** dBASE IV programs are structured toward single-user databases. If you run dBASE IV on a computer network, you may encounter situations where more than one person is attempting to modify a dBASE IV database at the same time. dBASE IV provides special tools to avoid this type of conflict. However, if you do not conspicuously apply these tools, dBASE IV will not protect network users from potentially destructive conflicts. Using SQL for database management tasks automatically implements file protection. This

is a reflection of SQL's origins on mini and mainframe computer networks. As with other database tasks, SQL insulates the user or programmer from network-specific concerns and simplifies the task of working with databases open to a network of users.

SQL is designed as a query language, not a full programming language, and therefore is not meant to stand alone. Rather, it serves as a database query tool box from which a programmer can draw. SQL cannot create screen formats, menus, or printed reports. Its only purpose is to handle database query operations efficiently.

Why Use SQL with dBASE IV?

Why would you want to use SQL with dBASE IV? The answer differs depending on whether you are using dBASE IV simply as a database application, or whether you are writing programs.

When dBASE IV is used as a database application, SQL offers the advantage of using familiar commands. Also, relational operations are generally simpler to script in SQL than in dBASE IV.

dBASE IV SQL can also be used within programs, just as it is used in the manual command mode. Programmers can take advantage of SQL to simplify relational database operations.

SQL also provides a potential link between mini and mainframe applications written in traditional high-level programming languages like Cobol to form broadly based database applications. dBASE IV allows you to write similar applications that combine the sophisticated dBASE IV interfaces, like pop-up menus, and menu bars, with SQL database features.

SQL alone cannot create a complete application. SQL consists of a set of roughly 30 commands and is an alternate means of handling database management tasks. These commands provide an optional way of storing and retrieving data. You still need to use dBASE IV commands and structures to create menus, screens, and reports. SQL, even on minis and mainframes, does not replace, but enhances, existing languages like Cobol or Fortran.

SQL approaches the concepts of data management in a different way from dBASE IV. Depending upon the task, you can use standard dBASE IV databases or SQL databases to handle particular tasks. As you will see, information can be moved back and forth between standard dBASE IV files and dBASE IV SQL files quite easily.

dBASE IV SQL provides a tool box of commands that works interactively from the dot prompt, or inside programs. This dual character allows you to follow the same learning process with SQL as you did with dBASE IV. You can explore individual commands, then once you understand the concepts, place those commands into applications.

You will begin by interactively learning the basics of SQL.

Starting an SQL Session

Because SQL and dBASE IV were developed independently, many of the command names conflict. Both dBASE IV and SQL use commands such as SELECT, CREATE, and INSERT, but these commands have vastly different meanings and uses.

The commands in dBASE IV break down into two categories: those that operate in both dBASE IV and SQL modes and those that are dBASE IV- or SQL-only commands. You may be surprised to learn that most dBASE IV commands and functions, about 180 commands and 100 functions, can be used in either dBASE IV or dBASE IV SQL. Most of the commands that are mode-specific relate to data entry and retrieval, like USE, EDIT, APPEND, SELECT, and others.

In order to avoid conflict, dBASE IV has two operating modes. The first is the normal dBASE IV operation mode in which you have performed all manual and program operations up to this point. The second is the SQL mode. To enter the SQL processing mode, use the command SET SQL ON.

> *Note:* Programs that contain SQL commands use a .prs rather than a .prg file extension so that dBASE IV can identify the mode in which the programs should run. Enter

```
SET SQL ON
```

The dot prompt changes from the normal dot to the "SQL dot." In addition, the status bar shows the word SQL instead of Command.

If you have used dBASE III or dBASE III Plus you might be have used a short-cut method of entering commands. This method is called the four-character rule. It states that all dBASE command verbs or clause names can be shortened to the first four characters when entering a command. For example the command DISPLAY STRUCTURE could be entered as DISP STRU. This method will work with dBASE IV as well. If you are used to using this shortcut, it is very important to remember that the four-character rule, which applies to dBASE IV commands entered at the dot prompt, does not apply to

SQL commands. dBASE IV commands such as REPLACE, SELECT, or CLOSE can be shortened to four-character abbreviations, as in REPL, SELE, and CLOS. However, SQL commands such as SELECT, CREATE, or INSERT cannot be shortened. All SQL commands must be entered without abbreviation. The dBASE IV commands that are allowed in SQL, and there are many, can still be shortened.

Creating a Database

The first step in an SQL session is to open an existing database or create a new one. Remember that the term database refers to an SQL database, not a dBASE IV database file. An SQL database consists of all the tables (an SQL table is roughly the same as a dBASE IV database file) related to that database. In SQL, the database is defined by the organizational structure of the individual tables.

For example, suppose you want to create an SQL system that contains information about emergency room activity, the same project you have been using as an example for dBASE IV databases. In dBASE IV, you create individual databases to store the various types of information, such as Admit, and Doctors. In SQL, the first step is to create the umbrella database that contains all the individual elements. To create a new database, use the command CREATE DATABASE. The following SQL command creates a new database called Emerg. The command ends with a semicolon character, another difference between SQL and normal dBASE IV commands.

Note: In normal dBASE IV syntax, the semicolon indicates that the current command is continued on the next line.

Failure to place the semicolon at the end of the name creates an error. Enter

```
CREATE DATABASE Emerg;
```

The program creates an SQL database called Emerg. This process may take a few moments. When it is complete, dBASE IV SQL displays a message confirming the creation of the new database (see Figure 9.1).

A dBASE IV SQL database requires a new directory on the disk. dBASE IV automatically creates this directory as a subdirectory of the active MS-DOS directory. If the current directory is called DBASE, then the new SQL database is stored in D\BASE\EMERG. The status line shows the directory that stores all the information related to the current SQL database.

Figure 9.1

```
. set sql on
SQL. create database emerg;
Database EMERG created
SQL.
SQL
          Type a dBASE IV command and press the ENTER key (⏎)
```

It is not necessary to know how dBASE IV SQL uses these files. However, should you wish to back up an SQL database, remember to include the files stored in the SQL directories or you will not have backed up the SQL databases.

Tables

Once you have created a new database, you can begin to define tables. SQL table definition is equivalent to the action of the CREATE command in dBASE IV. The command requires you to specify the data rows and columns, equivalent to records and fields, to include in the table.

Here you will notice one of the major differences between dBASE IV and dBASE IV SQL: The field creation process in dBASE IV takes place in an interactive, full-screen display mode. SQL does not provide this type of user-friendly entry environment. Instead, you enter all SQL commands as command sentences beginning with an SQL command and ending with a semicolon.

Suppose you want to create an SQL table that has a structure similar to the Patcare database file. The dBASE IV structure of Patcare is:

Field	Field Name	Type	Width
1	DOCTOR	Character	30
2	PATIENT	Character	30
3	DATE_CARE	Date	8

SQL tables are created with the CREATE TABLE command:

`CREATE TABLE Tablename (Name Type, Name Type,..)`

SQL tables can contain the following fields.

1. **smallint.** Stores integer values (whole numbers with no decimals) of six or fewer digits, like 999999. Negative numbers are limited to five digits, −99999.

2. **Integer.** Holds 11-digit whole numbers from 99999999999 to −9999999999.

Starting an SQL Session ■ **449**

3. **Decimal.** Holds numbers with decimal values. You must specify the total number of digits and the number of decimal places. Example, decimal(7,2) allows values from 9,999.99 to −999.99; the maximum is 19 digits.

4. **Numeric.** Holds a maximum size decimal number of 20 digits.

5. **Float.** Holds a floating-point decimal number of up to 19 digits.

6. **Char.** Holds text data from 1 to 254 characters in length.

7. **Date.** Holds date fields with a mm/dd/yy format.

8. **Logical.** Functions in the same manner as a dBASE IV logical field. It is always a true or false value, represented by the symbols .T. or .F.

Create a table called Patcare by entering the following command. SQL will not accept a table name longer than eight characters. Enter

```
CREATE TABLE patcare(Doctor Char(30),Patient Char(30),
Date_care Date);
```

dBASE IV SQL responds with the message **Table Patcare created.**

SQL commands work with list-type syntax. The specifications for a command, such as CREATE TABLE, appear after the command separated by commas. This procedure can create very long commands. Suppose you want to create a second table called Arrival that contains information about how the patient got to the emergency room. The table would have the following columns.

	Column	Type
1	Last	Character(20)
2	First	Character(20)
3	County	Character(15)
4	City	Character(15)
5	Injury	Character(15)
6	How	Character(15)
7	Date_inj	Date
8	Transpt	Character(15)
9	Time_arv	Character(5)

The SQL command to create this table is:

```
CREATE TABLE Arrival (Last char(20),
First char(20),County char(15),City char(15),
Injury char(15),How char(15),Date_inj Date,
Time char(5),Transpt char(15));
```

In order to make the entry of SQL commands easier and more accurate, dBASE IV allows you to open a special editing window when you want to enter long SQL commands by using the (Ctrl)-(Home) keys. Enter (Ctrl)-(Home). dBASE IV displays an editing window with the editor menu and places the cursor at the top of the display.

The editing window allows you to enter and revise SQL commands using all of the editing functions available in the program editor, including block move and copy. You can take advantage of SQL syntax to break up a long and complicated SQL command into a series of short lines, or you can simply type the entire SQL command with wraparound typing. Remember, SQL commands end with a semicolon. The Enter key or extra spaces are simply ignored. The earlier example's text can be written in short lines to make them easier to read.

Enter the CREATE TABLE command into the editing window (see Figure 9.2).

Figure 9.2

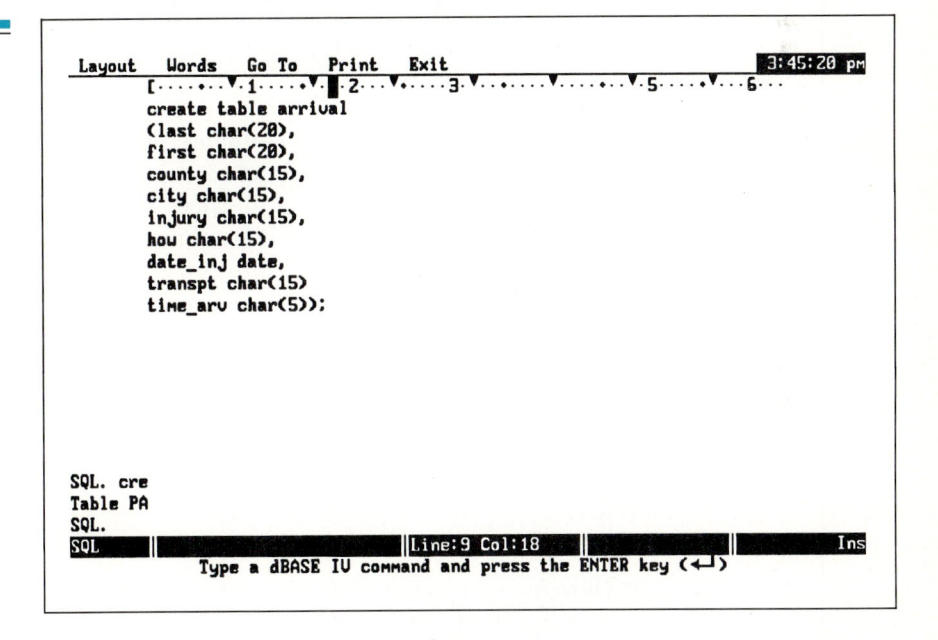

```
Layout   Words   Go To   Print   Exit                         3:45:20 pm
      [......V.1.....V..2...V.....3.V........V.....V.5....V...6...
      create table arrival
      (last char(20),
      first char(20),
      county char(15),
      city char(15),
      injury char(15),
      how char(15),
      date_inj date,
      transpt char(15)
      time_arv char(5));




















SQL. cre
Table PA
SQL.
SQL                              Line:9 Col:18                        Ins
              Type a dBASE IV command and press the ENTER key (⏎)
```

Starting an SQL Session ■ 451

```
CREATE TABLE Arrival
(Last char(20),
First Char(20),
County char(15),
City char(15),
Injury char(15),
How char(15),
Date_inj date,
Transpt char(15),
Time_arv char(5));
```

When the command is complete, tell dBASE IV SQL to execute the command by entering Ctrl-End. The editor transfers the entered text to the command line. dBASE IV executes the SQL command and confirms the operation by displaying the message **Table Arrival created.**

Adding Columns to Databases

dBASE IV SQL permits you to add columns to an existing table with the ALTER TABLE command. Suppose you want to add a column called Occup for the patient's occupation. Enter

```
ALTER TABLE arrival ADD (occup char(15));
```

dBASE IV SQL confirms the addition of the column by displaying the message **Column OCCUP added to table Arrival.**

Data Entry

Since SQL does not directly support full-screen interactive modes, like the dBASE IV edit and append modes, data entry in dBASE IV SQL is also done through command lines. The data entry command is the INSERT INTO command. This command adds rows of data into a table. Suppose you want to add to the Arrival table a data row of the following information:

Column	Data
Last	Johnson
First	Harold
County	-
City	-
Injury	-
How	-
Date_inj	12/05/88

Transpt   Ambulance
Time_arv   08:45
Occup   -

The command below inserts this data into the respective columns. But before you enter this command, look at its structure. The command consists of three parts. The first part of the command contains the name of the operation, INSERT INTO, and the name of the table, Arrival. That command is followed by two lists. The first list specifies the columns that will have data placed into them. The second list begins with a keyword, VALUES, followed by the actual data list. The VALUES list requires that the data items be the same data type as the columns into which they will be inserted. The character items are enclosed in quotation marks. The date requires a CTOD() function (character to date conversion) so it can be stored in a date-type column. Enter

```
INSERT INTO Arrival
(Last,First,Date_inj,Transpt,Time_arv)
VALUES
("Johnson","Harold",CTOD("12/05/88"),
"Ambulance","08:45");
```

dBASE IV SQL responds with the message **1 row(s) inserted.** You do not have to enter the names of the columns if your VALUES list sequences the items in the same order as the destination columns. Suppose you want to enter the following data:

Column	**Data**
Last	Parker
First	Walter
County	Contra Costa
City	Walnut Creek
Injury	-
How	-
Date_inj	12/09/88
Transpt	Drove Himself
Time_arv	15:45
Occup	Accountant

This data list has two fields that have no data. You must enter blanks for those fields if you want to enter the data without writing the column names. Enter

```
INSERT INTO Arrival
VALUES
("Parker","Walter","Contra Costa","Walnut Creek","
", " ",CTOD("12/09/88"),"Drove Himself","15:45",
"Accountant");
```

to insert a second row into the Arrival table. To confirm that you have actually added data to the SQL table, use the SELECT command to display its information. SELECT is the most powerful and most commonly used SQL command.

```
SELECT column names FROM table
```

In this case, you will use SELECT in its simplest form. This form lists all the rows and columns in the specified table. The * symbol acts as a wildcard for all rows and columns. Before you execute the SELECT command, clear the screen using the dBASE IV CLEAR command. Enter

```
CLEAR
```

dBASE IV allows you to enter many standard dBASE IV commands, just as you would in the normal dBASE IV operational mode. Enter the SQL SELECT command.

```
SELECT * FROM arrival;
```

All the information from the table displays on the screen.

Loading Information into a Table

Inserting individual rows of data into an SQL table is a tedious process. The dBASE IV process of full-screen entry is much easier and faster. SQL was never designed for easy data entry. Entering data in an SQL table would be highly impractical if SQL was meant to stand alone.

dBASE IV provides two ways to get data into an SQL database table, other than using the INSERT command:

1. **Loading data from non-SQL files.** dBASE IV SQL allows you to insert data into SQL tables by importing information stored in non-SQL files. This information can be stored in ASCII text files, dBASE IV, dBASE III, Framework II database or spreadsheet files, Lotus

1-2-3 .WKS files, spreadsheet .DIF (data interchange format), or Microsoft SYLK format.

Note: More details about files from other applications can be found in Chapter 10.

2. **Convert dBASE IV databases.** You can add a complete table, columns and rows, by importing an entire dBASE IV file into dBASE IV SQL.

Let's investigate the importance of data stored in other types of files. You can create the simplest type of file, an ASCII text file, with a text editor, most word processing programs, and the dBASE IV editor. You can create a text file with the dBASE IV editor and load that data into a dBASE IV SQL table. Create a text file by entering

```
MODIFY COMMAND Addrows.txt
```

Enter the following information into the file. This file is structured as a list of data items separated by commas, and character information is enclosed in quotations. Dates are handled in a special way. The date 12/10/88 is entered as a number value, 19881210. This type of file uses a structure dBASE IV calls a delimited file.

Each of the two rows of data should have only a single ⏎ character at the end of each record.

```
"Green","Janet","San Francisco","","","",19881210,
"Ambulance","09:00","",


"Lee","Mark","Alemeda","Oakland","","",19881208,
"Ambulance","15:45","Accountant"
```

Save the file by pressing (Ctrl)-(End). There is now a file called Addrows.txt in the \DBASE directory on the hard disk. You can load the data from that file into the Arrival SQL table by using the LOAD DATA FROM command. To use this command with non-dBASE IV files, you need to add a TYPE clause to identify the structure of the source file. In this case, you have created a text file with the dBASE IV comma-delimited structure. Enter

```
LOAD DATA FROM Addrows.txt INTO TABLE Arrival TYPE
DELIMITED;
```

List the information in the Arrival table to confirm the data was loaded.

```
SELECT * FROM Arrival;
```

Starting an SQL Session ■ **455**

The Arrival table now contains two new records imported from the delimited text file (see Figure 9.3).

Importing from text files lets you acquire data from users who do not have dBASE IV. Information obtained from mini and mainframe computers is often furnished in the form of ASCII comma-delimited files similar to the one you just created.

Note: Dates are typically one area where mainframe files will not usually conform to the dBASE IV numeric yyyy/mm/dd format. It is more common to get dates as character strings in the mm/dd/yy format. In this case, you would probably create a character column for the date. You would use the ALTER command to add a date column to your table and then use UPDATE to copy the CTOD() of the character date column into the new column. The SQL command UPDATE operates like the dBASE IV command REPLACE.

You can also use a dBASE IV .dbf file as the source of import data. This is very handy because you can take advantage of all of the dBASE IV data entry tools and then transport the information directly into an SQL table.

Using a dBASE IV .dbf file has one drawback over using text files. The dBASE IV file must have a structure before you can begin to en-

Figure 9.3

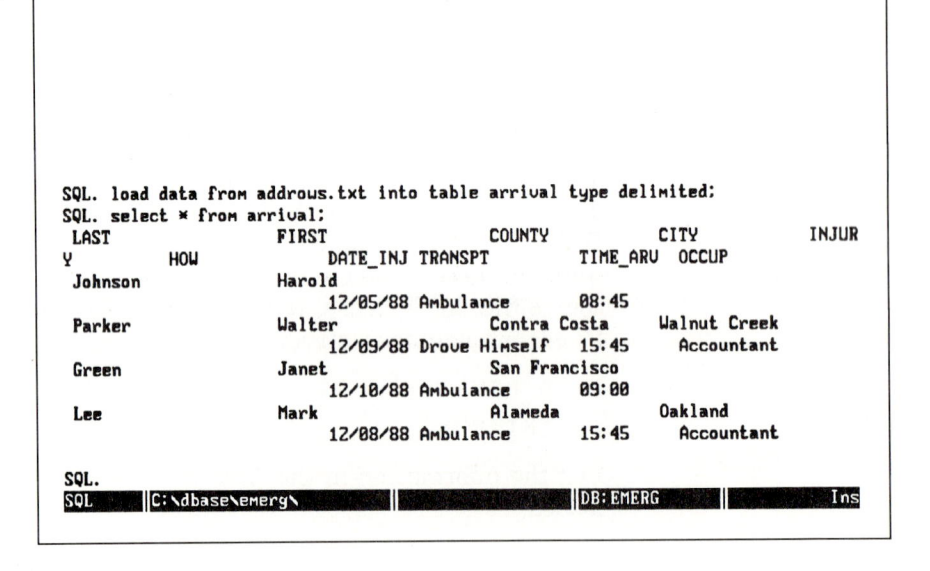

```
SQL. load data from addrows.txt into table arrival type delimited;
SQL. select * from arrival;
  LAST              FIRST                COUNTY            CITY              INJUR
Y         HOW           DATE_INJ TRANSPT        TIME_ARV  OCCUP
  Johnson           Harold
                              12/05/88 Ambulance        08:45
  Parker            Walter               Contra Costa      Walnut Creek
                              12/09/88 Drove Himself   15:45      Accountant
  Green             Janet                San Francisco
                              12/10/88 Ambulance        09:00
  Lee               Mark                 Alameda           Oakland
                              12/08/88 Ambulance        15:45      Accountant

SQL.
SQL      C:\dbase\emerg\                         DB: EMERG                  Ins
```

456 ■ SQL

ter data. In this case, it would mean that you would have to duplicate the structure used to create the SQL table before you could enter data.

dBASE IV SQL has a feature that can serve to create a dBASE IV file automatically with the same structure as the SQL table. The command is UNLOAD DATA TO. This command moves information in the opposite direction, from an SQL table to a dBASE IV .dbf file. When you want to work with dBASE IV .dbf files, no TYPE clause is needed. Enter

UNLOAD DATA TO Addrows.dbf FROM Arrival;

You have now created a dBASE IV .dbf file with the same structure and data as the SQL table Arrival. You cannot access .dbf files while SQL is active. Turn off the SQL mode by entering

SET SQL OFF

The SQL database is not closed, it is merely suspended. When you return to the SQL mode, the Emerg database will be still be open in exactly the state it was in when you left the SQL mode.

> *Note:* Quitting dBASE IV will automatically close all files, including SQL databases.

Access the Addrows database file by entering

USE Addrows
LIST

The .dbf file contains the same structure and information as the SQL table (see Figure 9.4).

Here, you are not interested in the date, but in the file structure. Remove the records from the database by using the ZAP command. ZAP deletes all records from a database but leaves the structure unchanged.

> *Note:* You can achieve the same results with DELETE ALL and PACK, but ZAP is much faster. DELETE ALL and PACK cannot automatically assume you intend to remove all records and must therefore perform a sequential search of the database.

ZAP

The ZAP command requires a confirmation when safety is on.
Press y.

Figure 9.4

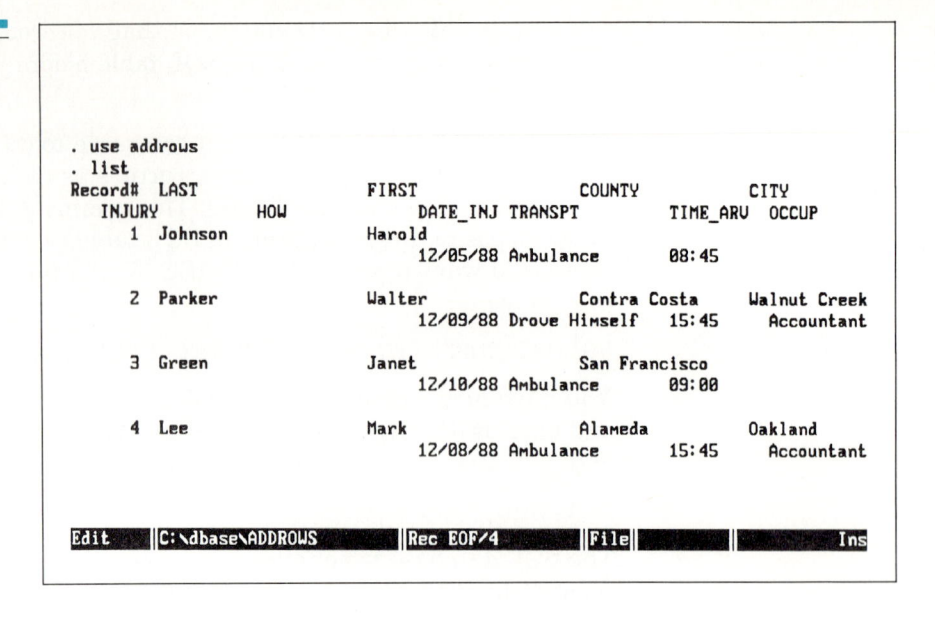

```
. use addrows
. list
Record# LAST                FIRST              COUNTY            CITY
    INJURY          HOW         DATE_INJ TRANSPT       TIME_ARV  OCCUP
     1  Johnson             Harold
                                12/05/88 Ambulance       08:45

     2  Parker              Walter             Contra Costa      Walnut Creek
                                12/09/88 Drove Himself   15:45        Accountant

     3  Green               Janet              San Francisco
                                12/10/88 Ambulance       09:00

     4  Lee                 Mark               Alameda           Oakland
                                12/08/88 Ambulance       15:45        Accountant


 Edit    C:\dbase\ADDROWS       Rec EOF/4       File                    Ins
```

Now that you have a structure, you can use the dBASE IV editing features to add records to the database. Enter

APPEND

The default dBASE IV record editing screen is displayed for this database (see Figure 9.5).

Enter a new record with the following information.

Column	Data
Last	Ross
First	Rachel
County	Alameda
City	Berkeley
Injury	broken arm
How	auto accident
Date_inj	12/15/88
Transpt	Police
Time_arv	18:30
Occup	

Figure 9.5

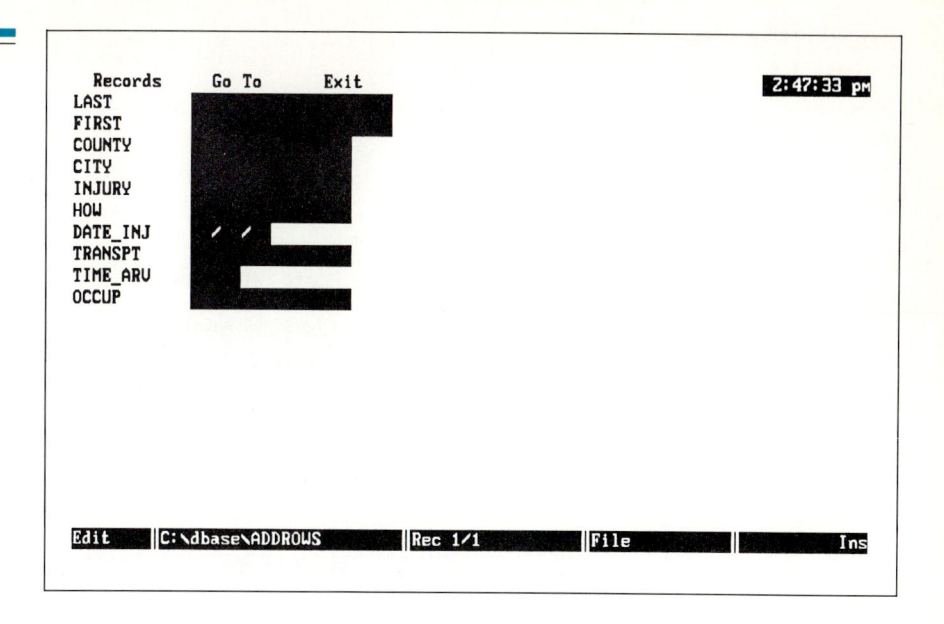

```
    Records      Go To      Exit                           2:47:33 pm
 LAST
 FIRST
 COUNTY
 CITY
 INJURY
 HOW
 DATE_INJ          / /
 TRANSPT
 TIME_ARV
 OCCUP




 Edit    C:\dbase\ADDROWS       Rec 1/1      File                Ins
```

Save the record by pressing Ctrl-End. Then, enter

CLOSE DATABASE

Return to SQL by entering

SET SQL ON

You return to the Emerg database at the exact point you left. You can now use the LOAD DATA FROM command to add information stored in the Addrows.dbf file. Try this on your own. If you need help, the correct command can be found at the end of the chapter in the Answers to Exercises section under exercise 1.

Display the contents of the Arrival table by entering

SELECT * FROM Arrival;

The data from the .dbf file appears as the last row in the table (see Figure 9.6).

In addition to the Arrival table, the Emerg database should also contain a table called Patcare corresponding to the Patcare database file. You can add this table to the SQL database with the LOAD DATA FROM command. Try this on your own. If you need help, the correct command can be found at the end of the chapter in the Answers to Exercises section under exercise 2.

Starting an SQL Session ■ **459**

Figure 9.6

```
                        Press the F1 key for HELP
. set sql on
SQL. start database emerg;
SQL. select * from arrival;
 LAST              FIRST               COUNTY              CITY            INJUR
Y         HOW         DATE_INJ TRANSPT          TIME_ARV OCCUP
 Johnson           Harold
                            12/05/88 Ambulance           08:45
 Parker            Walter              Contra Costa      Walnut Creek
                            12/09/88 Drove Himself 15:45          Accountant
 Green             Janet               San Francisco
                            12/10/88 Ambulance           09:00
 Lee               Mark                Alameda           Oakland
                            12/08/88 Ambulance    15:45          Accountant
                                                Alameda           Berkeley           broke
n arm     auto accident  12/15/88 Police           18:38
SQL.
┌────┐┌─────────────────┐                        ┌─────────┐                    ┌───┐
│SQL │││C:\dbase\emerg\  │                        │DB: EMERG│                    │Ins│
└────┘└─────────────────┘                        └─────────┘                    └───┘
         Type a dBASE IV command and press the ENTER key (↵)
```

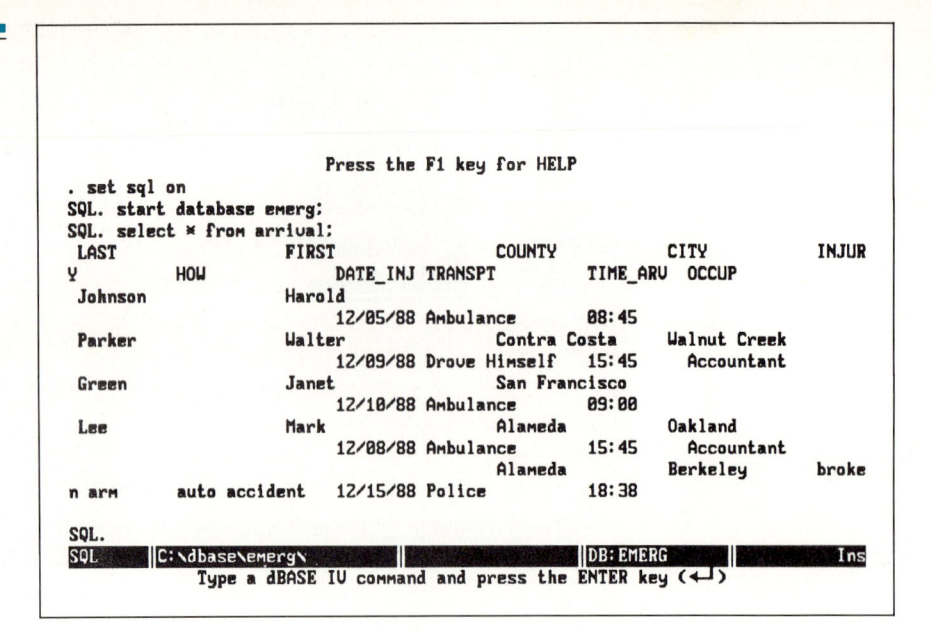

Adding Complete .dbf Files

Another way to add data to an SQL database is to import not only data from a dBASE IV .dbf file, but the entire file—structure and data. This procedure adds new tables to the open SQL database. The process uses a special command found in dBASE IV SQL but not in the normal SQL family of commands. The command is DBDEFINE and can be used in two ways:

1. **With a filename.** If you specify a dBASE IV .dbf filename, dBASE IV SQL searches the SQL database directory for the file and creates an SQL table for that file.

2. **With no filename.** If no filename follows the command, dBASE IV SQL searches the SQL database directory for any dBASE IV .dbf files. Each file encountered is added to the SQL database as a table.

The key to using this command is that the .dbf files must be stored in the SQL database directory. You can determine whether this is the SQL database directory by looking at the left side of the status bar. In this example, the assumption is made that dBASE IV is stored in the DBASE directory and therefore the Emerg SQL database directory is \DBSAMPLE\EMERG.

In order to perform the DBDEFINE operation, the databases you want to incorporate into the SQL database must be copied into the

SQL directory using the COPY FILE command or with the MS-DOS Copy command.

Note: If you have sufficient memory in your computer, you can use the dBASE IV RUN command to execute an MS-DOS command.

Be sure to copy all the files related to a given file, including the .dbt (for memo fields) and .mdx (index fields in structure) files.

In this example, you want to incorporate the Admit and Doctors files into the SQL database. Copy the files from their current directory, assumed to be \DBSAMPLE, to the SQL directory, assumed to be \DBSAMPLE\EMERG. The dBASE IV copy cannot be used in the SQL mode because you cannot use the USE command to open a .dbf file in the SQL mode. Instead, you can use the COPY FILE command. Enter

```
COPY FILE \DBSAMPLE\Admit.dbf TO \Dbase\Emerg\Admit.dbf
```

Repeat the command to copy the .dbt file.

```
COPY FILE \DBSAMPLE\Admit.dbt TO \Dbase\Emerg\Admit.dbt
```

If you exit the SQL mode, the USE and COPY commands will be available. Enter the following sequence of commands that use the standard dBASE IV method of copying .dbf and related files.

```
SET SQL OFF
USE Doctors
COPY TO \DBSAMPLE\Emerg\Doctors
CLOSE DATABASE
SET SQL ON
```

With the .dbf and .dbt files copied to the SQL database directory, you can employ the DBDEFINE command to integrate those files into the SQL database. You can add a specific file by using the name with the DBDEFINE command. Enter

```
DBDEFINE doctors;
```

SQL responds with the messages **Table(s) DBDEFINED: Doctors** and **DBDEFINE successful.** If you use DBDEFINE without a specific filename, the command searches the directory for any .dbf files to be integrated into the SQL database.

```
DBDEFINE;
```

Starting an SQL Session ■ **461**

The program searches the directory and finds the Admit database and incorporates it into the current SQL database. The Emerg database now has four tables: Arrival, Patcare, Doctors, and Admit.

The program displays a message box that looks like an error message, but which simply confirms that the DBDEFINE; command executed without errors. The message reads **DBDEFINE completed; error/warnings found.** Since no errors are listed, this means that no problems were encountered in the definition process. Exit the message by pressing ⏎.

Selecting Information

The heart of all SQL operations is the SELECT command. It is the power of SQL that a single command, by using special clauses, can perform a wide variety of database retrieval operations on individual tables or form relations between different tables.

The idea that a single command should perform a wide variety of tasks is the basic concept behind SQL. It is clear from the programs you created earlier that the procedures required to perform simple retrievals or multiple file retrievals based on linking information are quite different. But SQL is object- rather than process-oriented. In that sense, SQL performs a wide variety of operations under the umbrella command, SELECT.

Before you can write SQL programs, you need to learn some of the ways SELECT can perform data retrieval operations. The SQL command SELECT performs a wide variety of queries with the addition of clauses similar to those used in dBASE IV. In standard dBASE IV, each command performs a specific operation. In dBASE IV SQL, each clause attached to a SELECT command represents an additional operation performed by SELECT.

The simplest form of SELECT is SELECT FROM. This command creates lists of information from a specified table in the open database. The FROM clause is required in all SQL select operations. All other clauses are optional.

The simple SELECT FROM command displays information from all the rows in the specified table. You have the option of entering a list of columns or using the asterisk symbol, (*), to include all the columns in the table. The command below lists the last names, first names, admission, and discharge dates from the Admit table. Enter

```
SELECT Last,First,Admit,Discharge FROM Admit;
```

dBASE IV SQL displays the information you requested (see Figure 9.7).

Enter a command that selects the doctors' first names, last names, and specialty fields from the Doctors table. Try this on your own. If you need help, the correct command can be found at the end of the chapter in the Answers to Exercises section under exercise 3. The command will yield the list shown in Figure 9.8 below.

You have just seen one of the key differences between standard dBASE IV operations and dBASE IV SQL operations. There was no need to close the Admit file in order to access data in the Doctors file. The SELECT command uses the FROM clause to indicate the data table to use for each selection.

In addition to selecting columns in tables, dBASE IV SQL will accept dBASE IV expressions as objects for selection. You may want to use a character expression to select a combination of first and last name. You may also want to convert date information to a different format. Enter the following command.

```
SELECT TRIM(First)+" "+Last,MDY(Admit),
MDY(Discharge)
FROM Admit;
```

Figure 9.7

```
SQL. select last,first,admit,discharge from admit;
   LAST            FIRST           ADMIT    DISCHARGE
   LaFish          Walter          11/01/88 11/05/88
   Tate            Harold          11/09/88 11/09/88
   Ivanovic        Frank           11/12/88 11/13/88
   Lutz            Carol           11/10/88 11/13/88
   Anderson        Ken             11/13/88 11/17/88
   Westrup         Milton          11/14/88 11/15/88
   Jones           Timothy         11/20/88 11/22/88
   Morgan          Robert          11/21/88 11/24/88
   Mcdowell        Angelia         11/14/88 11/20/88
   Eckardt         Lois            11/24/88 12/03/88
   Sorenson        Cynthia         11/28/88 12/02/88
   Fisher          Scott           12/02/88 12/06/88
   Goren           Thomas          12/05/88 12/07/88

SQL.
SQL      |C:\dbase\emerg\                       |DB:EMERG
            Type a dBASE IV command and press the ENTER key (⏎)
```

Selecting Information ■ 463

Figure 9.8

```
Ivanovic      Frank        11/12/88 11/13/88
Lutz          Carol        11/10/88 11/13/88
Anderson      Ken          11/13/88 11/17/88
Westrup       Milton       11/14/88 11/15/88
Jones         Timothy      11/20/88 11/22/88
Morgan        Robert       11/21/88 11/24/88
Mcdowell      Angelia      11/14/88 11/20/88
Eckardt       Lois         11/24/88 12/03/88
Sorenson      Cynthia      11/28/88 12/02/88
Fisher        Scott        12/02/88 12/06/88
Goren         Thomas       12/05/88 12/07/88

SQL. select first,last,field from doctors:
  FIRST         LAST           FIELD
  Victor        Erlich         Anesthesiology
  Mark          Craig          Cardiology
  Amanda        Christenson    Internist
  Donald        Westfall       Dermatology
  Norman        Bates          Surgery
  Rebecca       LaFish         Pediatrics

SQL.
SQL    C:\dbase\emerg\                    DB: EMERG
      Type a dBASE IV command and press the ENTER key (<┘)
```

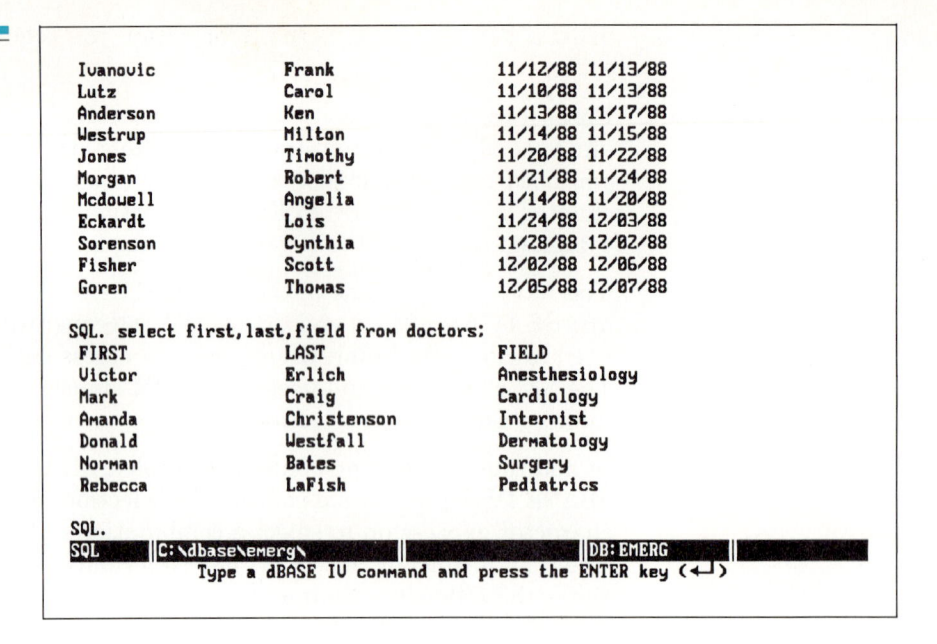

dBASE IV SQL displays the information according to the expression used in the command. The expression TRIM(First)+" "+Last causes the leftmost column to vary in width, a factor that distorts the alignment of the dates in the column to the right. This is a problem caused by the expression, not SQL. The same results would occur with a dBASE IV LIST command (see Figure 9.9).

dBASE IV SQL also has a set of functions that perform mathematical operations.

AVG()   Calculates the average of the column values
COUNT()   Counts the number of rows in a table
MAX()   Finds the largest values in a column
MIN()   Finds the smallest value in a column
SUM()   Calculates the sum of the values in a column

For example, suppose you want to count the number of rows in the Patcare table. Enter

```
SELECT COUNT(*) FROM Patcare;
```

SQL displays the value 10.00, indicating a count of 10 rows in that table.

Figure 9.9

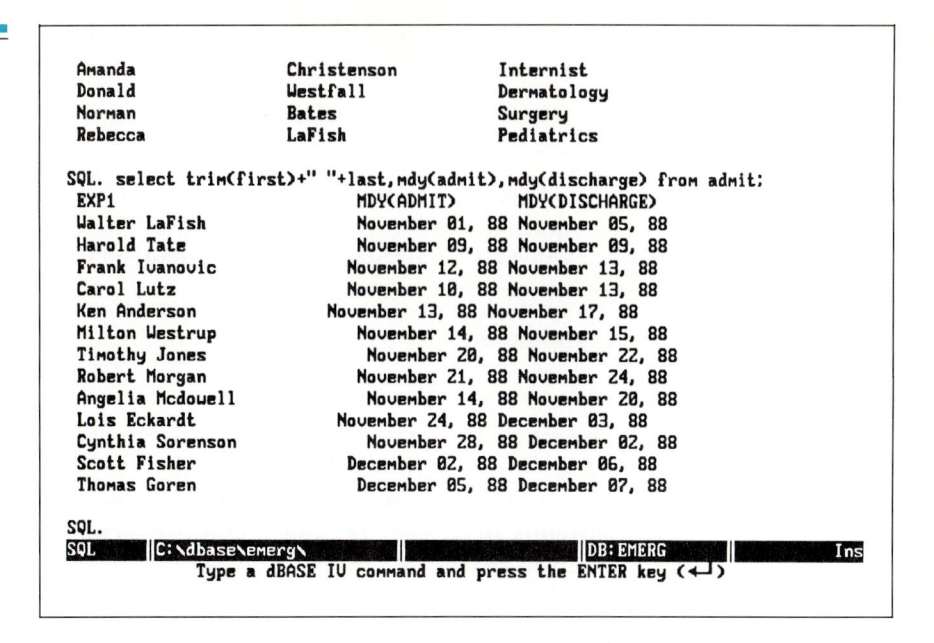

```
Amanda          Christenson        Internist
Donald          Westfall           Dermatology
Norman          Bates              Surgery
Rebecca         LaFish             Pediatrics

SQL. select trim(first)+" "+last,mdy(admit),mdy(discharge) from admit;
EXP1                    MDY(ADMIT)        MDY(DISCHARGE)
Walter LaFish           November 01, 88   November 05, 88
Harold Tate             November 09, 88   November 09, 88
Frank Ivanovic          November 12, 88   November 13, 88
Carol Lutz              November 10, 88   November 13, 88
Ken Anderson            November 13, 88   November 17, 88
Milton Westrup          November 14, 88   November 15, 88
Timothy Jones           November 20, 88   November 22, 88
Robert Morgan           November 21, 88   November 24, 88
Angelia Mcdowell        November 14, 88   November 20, 88
Lois Eckardt            November 24, 88   December 03, 88
Cynthia Sorenson        November 28, 88   December 02, 88
Scott Fisher            December 02, 88   December 06, 88
Thomas Goren            December 05, 88   December 07, 88

SQL.
SQL      C:\dbase\emerg\                          DB: EMERG         Ins
         Type a dBASE IV command and press the ENTER key (↵)
```

You can use the SUM() and AVG() functions to calculate values. Enter the following example.

`SELECT SUM(Charges),AVG(Charges) FROM Admit;`

Select Clauses

The SELECT command can perform more complicated data management tasks when used with clauses. The SELECT command can be modified by the following optional clauses:

1. **INTO.** The INTO clause transfers values created by SQL mathematical functions, such as SUM() and AVG(), into dBASE IV memory variables. The INTO clause enables you to integrate SQL values into a program.

2. **WHERE.** The WHERE clause creates data subsets from SQL tables by selecting rows according to a logical expression. The SQL WHERE clause performs a function similar to the FOR clause in standard dBASE IV.

3. **GROUP BY.** The GROUP BY clause creates subtotal groups within a selection.

4. **HAVING.** The HAVING clause creates a qualification for subtotal groups produced by group clauses.

5. **UNION.** The UNION clause links several selection commands together into a single operation.
6. **ORDER BY.** The ORDER BY clause sets an order to display the selected information.
7. **SAVE TO TEMP.** The SAVE TO TEMP clause transfers the selected data into a dBASE IV database file. This enables you to use the data selected by an SQL query in a dBASE IV program.

Using these clauses is the key to operating within the dBASE IV SQL environment.

The WHERE Clause

The single most important SQL clause is the WHERE clause. This clause works with logical expressions identical to the types of expressions used in standard dBASE IV. Suppose you want to select male patients. In dBASE IV, you would use a command like LIST FOR UPPER(Sex)="M". In SQL the command would be written as SELECT * FROM ADMIT WHERE UPPER(Sex)="M";.

Use the WHERE clause to list the male names of the patients (see Figure 9.10).

Figure 9.10

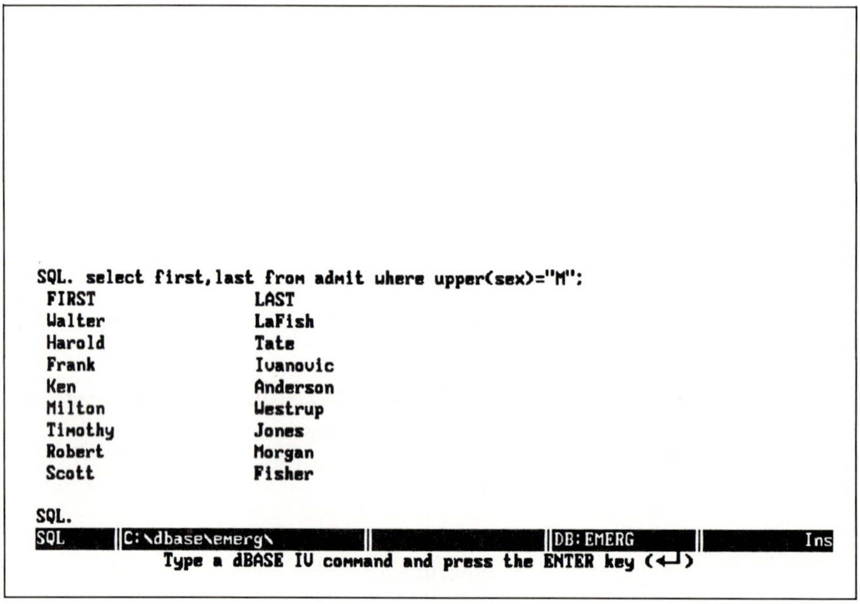

```
SQL. select first,last from admit where upper(sex)="M":
 FIRST          LAST
 Walter         LaFish
 Harold         Tate
 Frank          Ivanovic
 Ken            Anderson
 Milton         Westrup
 Timothy        Jones
 Robert         Morgan
 Scott          Fisher
SQL.
SQL    ||C:\dbase\emerg\                    ||DB:EMERG         ||  Ins
        Type a dBASE IV command and press the ENTER key (↵)
```

```
SELECT First,Last
FROM Admit
WHERE UPPER(Sex)="M";
```

The expression used with the WHERE clause can include most dBASE IV functions. For example, to select patient records for the month of December, enter the following command:

```
SELECT First,Last
FROM Admit
WHERE MONTH(Admit)=12;
```

You can combine expressions with the and/or operators just as you would use the .AND./.OR. operators in standard dBASE IV. For example, suppose you want to list the male patients admitted in November. Enter

```
SELECT First,Last
FROM Admit
WHERE MONTH(Admit)=12 and UPPER(Sex)="M";
```

SQL also uses operators not available in dBASE IV. SQL refers to these operators as predicates. These predicates are:

1. **BETWEEN.** BETWEEN selects data that falls within a numeric range.

2. **IN.** The IN predicate performs a function similar to the dBASE IV $ operator and allows you to enter a list of values for which matching records should be included.

3. **LIKE.** The LIKE predicate permits you to create a wildcard criterion for selection.

Suppose you want to select all the patients admitted from the 15th to the 30th of November. In dBASE IV, you would use an expression like Admit>=CTOD("11/15/88").AND.Admit<=CTOD("11/30/88")

The BETWEEN clause simplifies this syntax. Enter the following command.

Note: You can use curly brackets to indicate a character to date conversion—Admit>={11/15/88}. This format can be substituted for Admit>=CTOD("11/15/88").

```
SELECT First,Last,Admit
FROM Admit
```

Selecting Information ■ **467**

```
WHERE Admit BETWEEN CTOD("11/15/88") AND
Admit<=CTOD("11/30/88");
```

SQL displays the table of patients meeting the qualification (see Figure 9.11).

The IN predicate also creates a specialized selection criterion. With IN, you can specify a list of values. If any one of the values matches the column data, the row is included. Suppose you want to list patients insured by either Blue Shield or Mutual of Omaha (see Figure 9.12). Enter

```
SELECT First,Last,Admit,Payor
FROM Admit
WHERE Payor IN("Blue Shield","Mutual of Omaha");
```

The LIKE predicate creates a wildcard operation in which you create a template of the data you want to select. The template can contain the wildcard characters, _ or %. The _ (underscore character) matches any single character, while % matches any group of characters.

> *Note:* If you are familiar with MS-DOS wildcards, the _ plays the same role as ?, and % plays the same role as * in MS-DOS wildcards.

Figure 9.11

```
SQL. select first,last from admit where month(admit)=11 and upper(sex)="M":
     FIRST              LAST
     Walter             LaFish
     Harold             Tate
     Frank              Ivanovic
     Ken                Anderson
     Milton             Westrup
     Timothy            Jones
     Robert             Morgan

SQL. select first,last,admit from admit where admit between ctod("11/15/88") and
ctod("11/30/88"):
     FIRST              LAST               ADMIT
     Timothy            Jones              11/20/88
     Robert             Morgan             11/21/88
     Lois               Eckardt            11/24/88
     Cynthia            Sorenson           11/28/88

SQL.
SQL     ||C:\dbase\emerg\              ||          ||DB: EMERG       ||       Ins
             Type a dBASE IV command and press the ENTER key (↵)
```

Suppose you want to find a patient, but are not sure of the exact spelling of the name. It could be Sorenson, Sorinson, Soransen, Soranson, etc. The LIKE predicate could select rows by putting underscore characters in place of the vowels in the name. Enter the following command as an example.

SELECT *

FROM Admit

WHERE Last LIKE "S_r_ns_n";

SQL displays the record for Cynthia Sorenson.

You can combine WHERE clauses with statistical functions. You might want to total the charges paid by Blue Shield. Enter

SELECT SUM(Charges)

FROM Admit

WHERE Payor="Blue Shield";

The SQL command calculates the value, $13,341, for the selected rows from the Admit table.

Enter an SQL command to calculate the total number of days stayed (Days_stay column) for patients discharged in November. Try this on

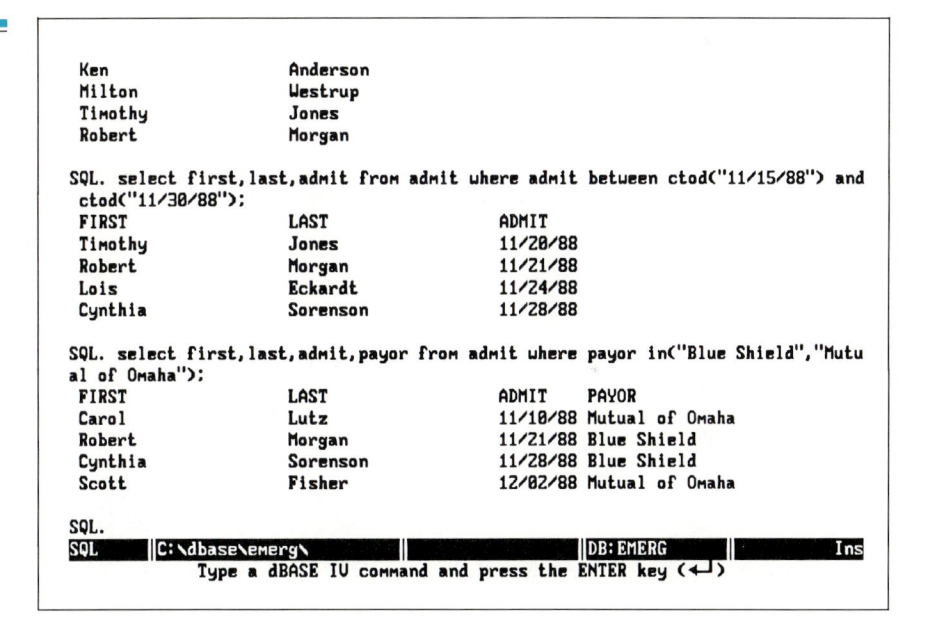

Figure 9.12

```
Ken                 Anderson
Milton              Westrup
Timothy             Jones
Robert              Morgan
SQL. select first,last,admit from admit where admit between ctod("11/15/88") and
ctod("11/30/88");
FIRST               LAST                ADMIT
Timothy             Jones               11/20/88
Robert              Morgan              11/21/88
Lois                Eckardt             11/24/88
Cynthia             Sorenson            11/28/88

SQL. select first,last,admit,payor from admit where payor in("Blue Shield","Mutu
al of Omaha");
FIRST               LAST                ADMIT       PAYOR
Carol               Lutz                11/10/88    Mutual of Omaha
Robert              Morgan              11/21/88    Blue Shield
Cynthia             Sorenson            11/28/88    Blue Shield
Scott               Fisher              12/02/88    Mutual of Omaha

SQL.
SQL     ||C:\dbase\emerg\              ||DB:EMERG                    Ins
        Type a dBASE IV command and press the ENTER key (↵)
```

Selecting Information ■ **469**

your own. If you need help, the correct command can be found at the end of the chapter in the Answers to Exercises section under exercise 4.

The DISTINCT Clause

Suppose you want to list the names of the patients in the Patcare table (see Figure 9.13). Enter

SELECT patient FROM patcare;

Some names appear more than once in this listing. Suppose you want to list only the unique names. In standard dBASE IV operations, you would have to create an index with the UNIQUE clause. SQL can perform the same function by using the DISTINCT clause with the SELECT command. Enter

SELECT DISTINCT Patient FROM Patcare;

This time each name appears only once (see Figure 9.14).

Grouping Data

The SELECT command can also create subtotal groups from a table. The GROUPED BY clause generates group sums or totals. For exam-

Figure 9.13

```
Sorenson            Cynthia                        11/28/88 12/02/88   35 454-999
9  f       5.00              .T.     Blue Shield                .T.         .F.
 .T.       7556.00

SQL. select sum(charges) from admit where payor = "Blue Shield":
           SUM1
           13431.00

SQL. select patient from patcare:
 PATIENT
 Anderson, Ken
 Goren, Thomas
 Jones, Timothy
 Eckardt, Lois
 Eckardt, Lois
 Fisher, Scott
 Fisher, Scott
 Fisher, Scott
 Sorenson, Cynthia
 Morgan, Robert

SQL.
SQL    ||C:\dbase\emerg\                              ||DB: EMERG              Ins
         Type a dBASE IV command and press the ENTER key (↵)
```

ple, if you want to sum the charges for different insurance carriers, you would enter the following command (see Figure 9.15).

SELECT Payor,SUM(Charges)

FROM Admit

GROUP BY Payor;

If you want to count the number of patients treated by each physician, you would use the Patcare table for this display (see Figure 9.16).

SELECT Doctor,COUNT(*)

FROM Admit

GROUP BY Doctor;

You could reverse the logic and count the physicians for each patient. Try this on your own. If you need help, the correct command can be found at the end of the chapter in the Answers to Exercises section under exercise 5.

The GROUP BY clause imposes some additional restrictions on the use of the SELECT command. The columns specified following SE-

Figure 9.14

```
Anderson, Ken
Goren, Thomas
Jones, Timothy
Eckardt, Lois
Eckardt, Lois
Fisher, Scott
Fisher, Scott
Fisher, Scott
Sorenson, Cynthia
Morgan, Robert

SQL. select distinct patient from patcare;
PATIENT
Anderson, Ken
Eckardt, Lois
Fisher, Scott
Goren, Thomas
Jones, Timothy
Morgan, Robert
Sorenson, Cynthia

SQL.
```
SQL   C:\dbase\emerg\   DB:EMERG   Ins
        Type a dBASE IV command and press the ENTER key (↵)

Selecting Information ■ 471

Figure 9.15

```
SQL. select payor,sum(charges) from admit group by payor;
G_PAYOR                          SUM1
                                 48832.00

Blue Cross                        4024.00

Blue Shield                      13431.00

Glaziers & Glass                  7324.00

Mutual of Omaha                  15693.00

National                          3325.00

Progressive Casualty              2842.00

SQL.
SQL    |C:\dbase\emerg\           |DB: EMERG         Ins
       Type a dBASE IV command and press the ENTER key (←)
```

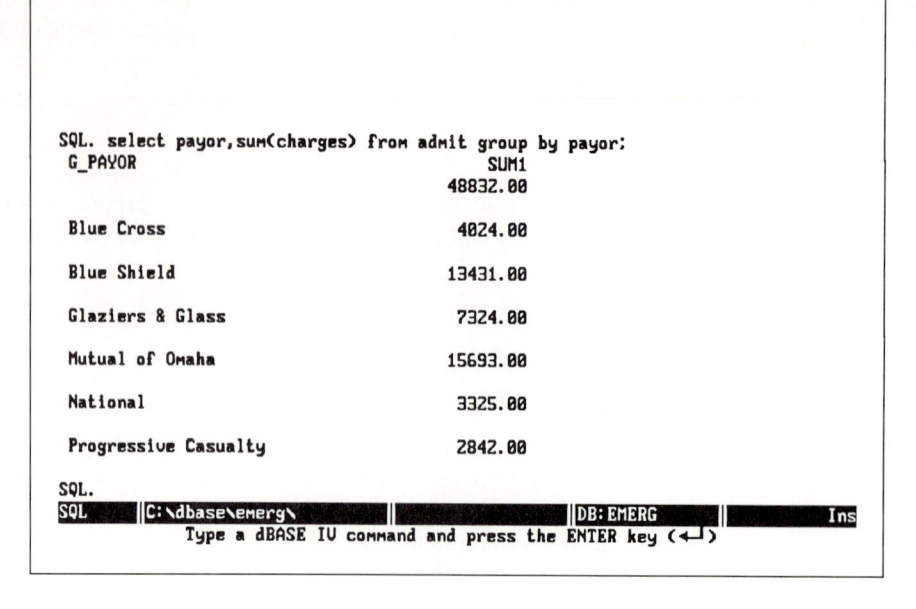

LECT must also appear in the GROUP BY clause. The only exceptions are SQL mathematical functions, such as SUM() and COUNT(). This restriction makes sense when you think about what the command means. Including a column name that is not a group key would pose a logical problem for SQL. Should it simply display the first row value in the group for that column or the last row value in the group? In SQL, this problem is avoided by making such commands illegal. Suppose you entered a command like the one below.

SELECT Last,Payor,SUM(Charges)

FROM Admit

GROUP BY Payor;

This command would not be a legal SQL query because the last column is not included in the GROUP BY clause. You must use a column name with the GROUP BY clause. You cannot use an expression such as UPPER(Sex) or MONTH(Admit).

You can use more than one column name if you want to create a subgroup within a group. Suppose you want to find the amount of charges for each insurance carrier, but also divide those groups by sex. In this case, you would select and group by payor,sex. Enter the following command.

Figure 9.16

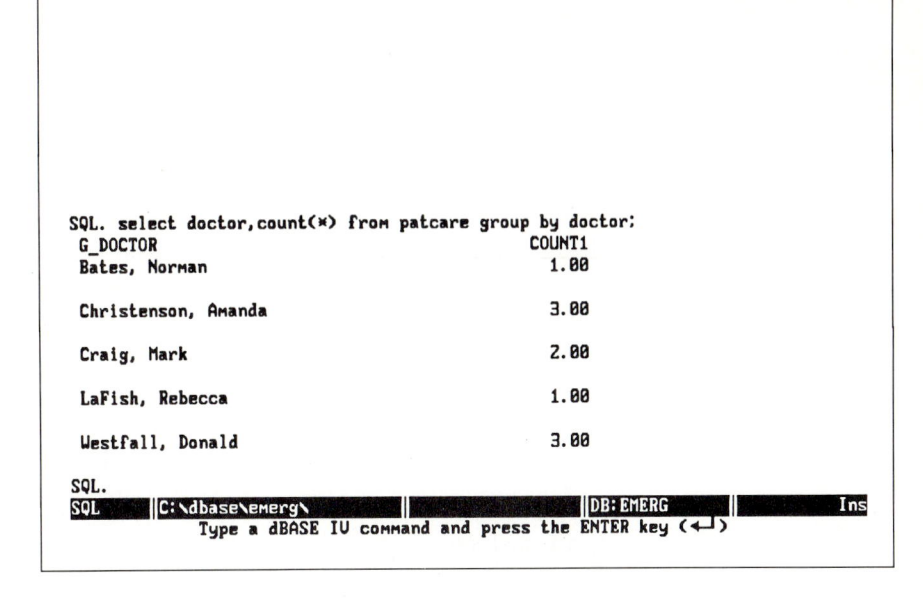

```
SQL. select doctor,count(*) from patcare group by doctor;
G_DOCTOR                                   COUNT1
Bates, Norman                              1.00

Christenson, Amanda                        3.00

Craig, Mark                                2.00

LaFish, Rebecca                            1.00

Westfall, Donald                           3.00

SQL.
SQL      ||C:\dbase\emerg\          ||        ||DB:EMERG||       Ins
              Type a dBASE IV command and press the ENTER key (↵)
```

```
SELECT Payor,Sex,SUM(Charges)
FROM Admit
GROUP BY Payor,Sex;
```

The program ran into one problem during the execution of the command. You will recall that data entered into the Admit database field Sex was entered inconsistently in terms of upper- or lower-case letters. This caused SQL to generate groups for both the upper- and lower-case M and F characters. dBASE IV handles this problem by using the expression UPPER(Sex). However, dBASE IV SQL will not accept that expression, UPPER(Sex), as a column name in the GROUP BY clause.

Updating Information

SQL provides a command that performs the same function as the dBASE IV command REPLACE. REPLACE changes data in one or more records. In dBASE IV SQL, the UPDATE command performs a similar function.

You can use UPDATE to replace the data in a column with other data created from dBASE IV expressions and functions. In the previous command, you encountered a problem caused by having both upper- and lower-case characters stored in the Sex column.

UPDATE uses syntax similar to the SELECT command. UPDATE is followed by the table name. A SET clause precedes the name of the column to change and the expression that determines the value to place into that column. To change the Sex column to all upper-case characters, enter the following UPDATE command:

```
UPDATE Admit
SET Sex=UPPER(Sex);
```

dBASE IV SQL issues a warning that no WHERE clause was used with the command. This warning reminds you that this command will automatically affect all the rows in the table. Since this is exactly what you want to do, press ⏎.

SQL confirms that 13 rows have been updated. With the Sex column now uniform in terms of case, you can reenter the grouping command to see if you can get a more coherent display.

```
SELECT Payor,Sex,SUM(Charges)
FROM Admit
GROUP BY Payor,Sex;
```

This time, there are only M and F groups, where required, for each carrier.

Suppose you want to group by month. This poses a bit of a problem since SQL cannot use an expression, such as MONTH(Admit), to group the rows by month. The only way to get around this problem is to add a new column to the database that contains a value representing only the month portion of the admission date. To add a new column, you must use the ALTER command. Here, add a column called Month and make it a character column wide enough to contain the name of the month. Enter

```
ALTER TABLE Admit ADD (MONTH(CHAR(15));
```

SQL rejects the command with an error message. Exit the error by pressing ⏎.

What caused the error? The message displayed read **name expected.** What does that mean? By simply reading your command, you would find nothing to which SQL should object. However SQL is much fussier about name conflicts than standard dBASE IV. The name of the column you wanted to insert was Month, which is also a dBASE IV function name. Standard dBASE IV would allow Month as a field or variable name. But SQL will not allow this name as a data column or table. You will need to change the name of the column to something unambiguous to add the column to the table. Enter

```
ALTER TABLE admit ADD (mname char(15));
```

This time, the command executes perfectly. Now use the ALTER command to place the CMONTH() value of Admit into the Mname column. In order to avoid the warning message, you can add a WHERE clause that will have no effect. For example, the expression CMONTH(ADMIT)#SPACE(10) allows updating when the name of the month is not equal to 10 spaces. This expression will not exclude any rows because all the rows contain valid dates. It will, however, satisfy SQL that a WHERE clause has been used to select records.

```
UPDATE Admit
SET Mname=CMONTH(Admit)
WHERE CMONTH(Admit)#SPACE(10);
```

This time, SQL updates 13 rows but does not pause the operation for a warning.

With a month column established, you can create a command that groups information by month. For example, you can display the monthly totals and averages for charges and days stayed.

```
SELECT Mname,SUM(Charges),AVG(Charges),SUM(Days_;
stay),
AVG(Days_stay)
FROM Admit
GROUP BY Mname;
```

The query results in two sets of values, one for each month (see Figure 9.17).

The HAVING Clause

The HAVING clause relates to queries that use the GROUP BY clause. HAVING allows you to qualify the group information to select groups of data that fit certain criteria. The HAVING clause is generally used when you have generated a large number of groups and want to select only those that are significant. You may want to display the dates, if any, on which more than one patient was admitted. To do this, you would use a SELECT command with a GROUP BY clause. Adding a HAVING clause would enable you to select groups with more than a single record. The expression used with the HAVING clause is different from ordinary expressions because it operates

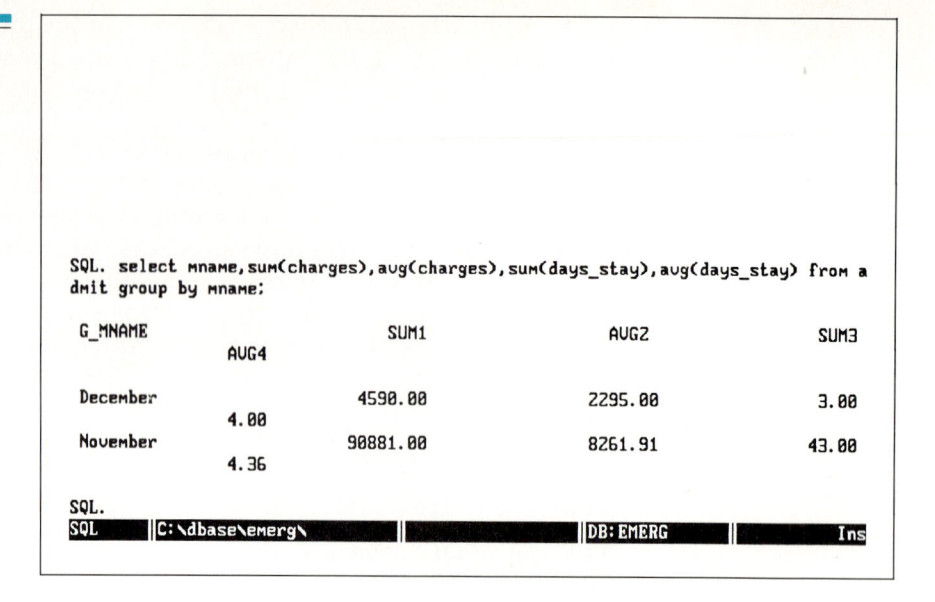

Figure 9.17

```
SQL. select mname,sum(charges),avg(charges),sum(days_stay),avg(days_stay) from a
dmit group by mname;

G_MNAME                    SUM1              AVG2              SUM3
              AVG4
December                  4590.00           2295.00            3.00
              4.00
November                  90881.00          8261.91            43.00
              4.36
SQL.
SQL      C:\dbase\emerg\                          DB: EMERG              Ins
```

on a group rather than a row value. For example, if one of the select functions is COUNT(*), the HAVING expression uses this function as part of the expression, COUNT(*)>1. Enter the following command.

```
SELECT Admit,COUNT(*)
FROM Admit
GROUP BY Admit
HAVING COUNT(*)>1;
```

Sequencing Output

The output of a SELECT command can be sequenced by adding an ORDER BY CLAUSE. The ORDER BY clause is subject to the same restrictions as the GROUP BY clause. First, the ORDER BY clause can operate only on column names. You cannot use an expression like UPPER(Sex), as an order key. Second, the order column must be included in the selection list. This means if you list the first and last names only, you cannot sequence them by the admission date unless you add the Admit column to the selection list.

Let's display the first and last names and admission dates sequenced by last name. In this example, we use the number 1 as the ordered by key. (SQL permits you to use the column number in place of the column name.) Here, since the first column in Admit is Last, then the value 1 indicates the use of column 1, Last.

Figure 9.18

```
SQL. select last,first,admit from admit order by 1:
LAST              FIRST           ADMIT
Anderson          Ken             11/13/88
Eckardt           Lois            11/24/88
Fisher            Scott           12/02/88
Goren             Thomas          12/05/88
Ivanovic          Frank           11/12/88
Jones             Timothy         11/28/88
Lafish            Walter          11/01/88
Mcdowell          Angelia         11/14/88
Morgan            Robert          11/21/88
Sorenson          Cynthia         11/28/88
Tate              Harold          11/09/88
Westrup           Milton          11/14/88

SQL.
SQL       C:\dbase\emerg\                    DB: EMERG         Ins
```

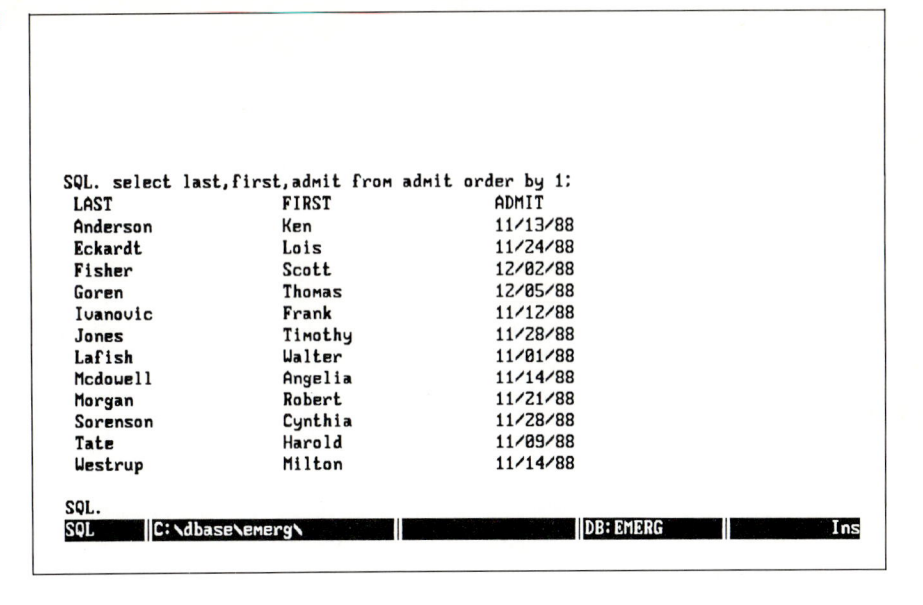

```
SELECT Last,First,Admit
FROM Admit
ORDER BY 1;
```

The columns are sequenced by last name (see Figure 9.18).

You can also select ascending or descending order. Display the same selection ordered by admit date in descending order. Adding ACS or DESC following the column name or number indicates the sequence order. The default is ascending order.

```
SELECT Last,First,Admit
FROM Admit
ORDER BY Admit DESC;
```

You can also use multiple keys to sequence columns that contain repetitions. The command below sequences the information in the Patcare table according to doctors, with the patients alphabetized within each doctor group (see Figure 9.19).

```
SELECT *
FROM Patcare
ORDER BY Doctor,Patient;
```

Selecting Information ■ 477

Figure 9.19

```
SQL. select * from patcare order by doctor,patient:
DOCTOR                      PATIENT                 DATE_CARE
Bates, Norman               Eckardt, Lois           11/24/88
Christensen, Amanda         Fisher, Scott           12/02/88
Christensen, Amanda         Morgan, Robert          11/21/88
Christensen, Amanda         Sorenson, Cynthia       11/22/88
Craig, Mark                 Fisher, Scott           12/02/88
Craig, Mark                 Goren, Thomas           12/06/88
Lafish, Rebecca             Fisher, Scott           12/02/88
Westfall, Donald            Anderson, Ken           11/13/88
Westfall, Donald            Eckardt, Lois           11/24/88
Westfall, Donald            Jones, Timothy          11/28/88

SQL.
SQL     C:\dbase\emerg\                    DB: EMERG          Ins
```

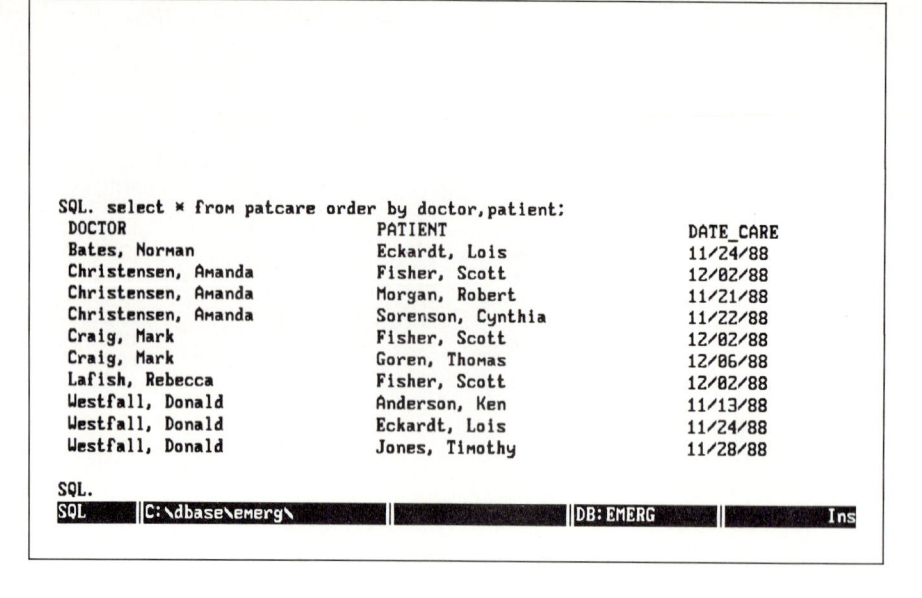

Multiple Table Selections

You have now come to the heart of SQL, the ability to perform selections involving more than one table of information. In Chapter 7 you learned how to create relational programs that involved linking data from more than one database file. In the SQL environment, all the data tables are available to any of the selections. This enables you to perform multiple database operations by using a single SQL command.

It is this area where the contrast between standard dBASE IV methods and the dBASE IV SQL method of obtaining data is the greatest. In standard dBASE IV operations, relations between two or more files require a series of commands, the use of work areas, and control of independent record pointers in each database.

In SQL, these operations are handled with a single command. The command is a variation on the SELECT/FROM/WHERE commands you have been working with. The difference is that you can use the name of more than one table with the FROM clause. For example, a FROM clause that reads FROM ADMIT,PATCARE would allow you to draw data from columns in both tables. For the data in different tables to make sense when displayed, however, you need to supply a logical expression to relate the information in each table.

When using multiple tables, it may be necessary to distinguish between columns with the same name in different tables. You can add a table name to the column name by using a period to indicate the table name prefix. For example, the last name column in the Doctors table would be written DOCTORS.LAST.

To understand how an SQL multiple table query operates, you can create commands that duplicate some of the listings you created using standard dBASE IV commands in Chapter 7. For example, one of the lists used the patients in the Patcare file to list the names of the doctors and their specialty fields. This requires data from both Patcare and Doctors tables. In standard dBASE IV operations, the following commands would produce this list:

```
USE Patcare in 1
USE Doctors in 2
SELECT Doctors
INDEX ON Last TAG Last OF Doctors
SELECT Patcare
SET Relation TO SUBSTR(Doctor,1,at(",",doctor)-1)
INTO Doctors
LIST Patient,Doctor,Doctors->Field
```

How would SQL operations differ from the standard dBASE IV procedure? Because SQL is object- rather than process-oriented, a single command with the proper clauses replaces the sequence of commands used in standard dBASE IV. This means the proper sequencing of commands, so crucial in standard dBASE IV, would be eliminated by SQL. In SQL, the important task would be to write the one command, a SELECT command, with the proper clauses. An SQL command is an all-or-nothing task. In standard dBASE IV, you must enter the correct commands in correct sequence. A mistake in any part of the sequence causes an error. In SQL, the entire operation is concentrated in a single command that either works or not.

An SQL command to create the same information list as the dBASE IV commands just used requires two clauses. The FROM clause lists the tables to be used in the query. In addition, a WHERE clause functions as the expression linking the data in the two tables.

To work out the SQL command, you can take each part of the command and determine what specifications to use with each part of the command. This allows you to work out, in parts, what can become a complex single command.

Begin with the column list that follows the SELECT command. In this case, there are two columns, Patient and Field. The next clause is the FROM clause. Here, you will enter the name of two tables, Patcare and Doctors. The final clause is the WHERE clause. In a multiple table display, the WHERE clause links the records in the tables. In this case, you want to match the name of the doctor in the Patcare table with the last name of the doctor in the Doctors table. This ensures the medical field displayed is the correct one. The WHERE clause can use the same type of expression used in the standard dBASE IV SET RELATION TO command—SUBSTR(Doctor,1,AT (",",Doctor)-1). With the WHERE clause, the expression would be converted to a logical expression by testing its equality to the last name in the Doctors table—LAST=SUBSTR(Doctor,1,AT(",",Doctor)-1).

With these three clauses worked out, you can create the SQL command that will display the desired information.

```
SELECT Patient,Field
FROM Patcare,Doctors
WHERE Last=SUBSTR(Patcare.Doctor,1,at
(", ",Patcare.Doctor)-1);
```

SQL correlates the speciality fields with the name of the doctor associated with the patient and displays the list of patients and the field of treatment (see Figure 9.20).

You can link the Patcare table to the Admit table by using the last name of the patients. The following command lists all of the patients and doctors where treatments required the use of anesthesia. In this query the link between the tables selects rows from the Patcare table based on the value of the anesthesia column in the Admit table. None of the columns in Admit are displayed; they are only used to qualify rows in the Patcare table. Enter

```
SELECT Patient,Doctor
FROM Patcare,Admit
WHERE Patient=TRIM(Last) and Anesthesia;
```

SQL lists the patients and doctors who used anesthesia.

The link between patient names in Patcare and Admit was written in a simple fashion. It may be useful to understand why this works the same way as the more complicated dBASE IV expression. The patient column contains data stored in a last name, first name format. The last column in Admit contains only the last name of the patient. To

Figure 9.20

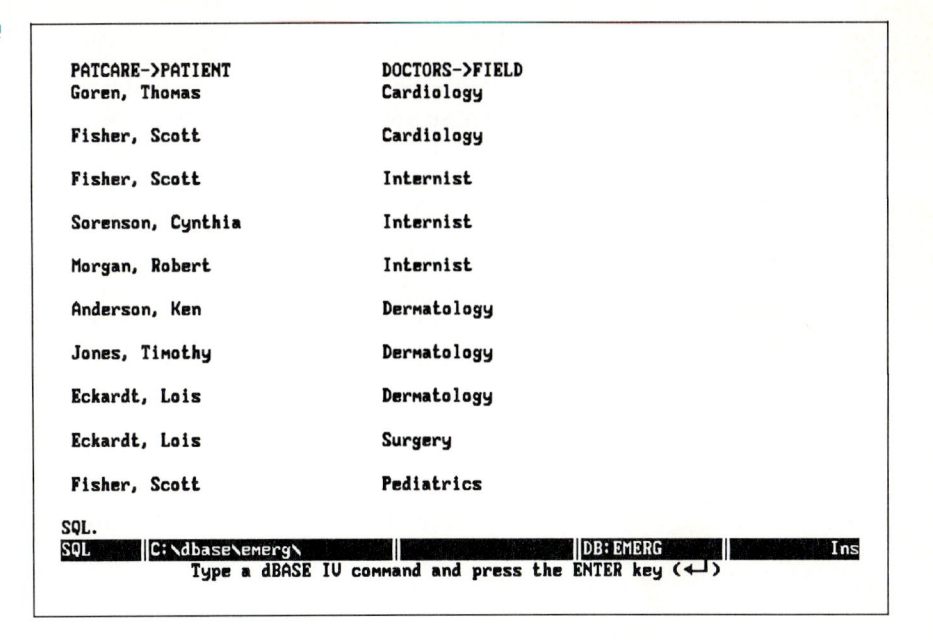

```
PATCARE->PATIENT           DOCTORS->FIELD
Goren, Thomas              Cardiology

Fisher, Scott              Cardiology

Fisher, Scott              Internist

Sorenson, Cynthia          Internist

Morgan, Robert             Internist

Anderson, Ken              Dermatology

Jones, Timothy             Dermatology

Eckardt, Lois              Dermatology

Eckardt, Lois              Surgery

Fisher, Scott              Pediatrics
SQL.
SQL      C:\dbase\emerg\                    DB:EMERG              Ins
         Type a dBASE IV command and press the ENTER key (↵)
```

compare the last names only, you previously used a complicated expression to create a substring that separated the last name from the first name. But suppose you compared the column data directly, Patient=Last. Would this work? The answer is no. At first, it seems it should. If you imagined text, rather than column names, the expression would yield Anderson, Ken=Anderson. This would match correctly. But remember in SQL and dBASE IV, a column or field value is always padded with spaces to fill the entire column or field width. The actual comparison would include any spaces in the columns, as well as the characters. The comparison would be as follows, where x is used to indicate a space.

"Anderson, Kenxxxxxxxxxxxxxxx";

="Andersonxxxxxxxxxxx"

To make the expression work, the TRIM() function eliminates the spaces from the last name column value to allow the correct match.

You can sequence the list by using the ORDER BY clause. Enter

SELECT Doctor,Patient
FROM Patcare,Admit
WHERE Patient=TRIM(Last) and Anesthesia
ORDER BY Doctor;

Multiple Table Selections ■ **481**

The results are displayed in the form of a table (see Figure 9.21).

You can create SELECT commands to draw data from more than two tables. Suppose you want to list the names of the patients in the Patcare table, along with their admission date and the field of medicine related to their treatment. To assemble all the items, you have to link three tables, Patcare, Admit, and Doctors. This can still be done with a single SQL command.

The command below lists the column names Patient, Admit, and Field, from the tables Patcare, Admit, Doctors. The tricky part is to form links between all of the tables. This is done by making a compound expression for use with the WHERE clause. One part of the clause relates the patient's name to the Admit table, while the other links the patient's name to the Doctors table. The ORDER BY clause then sequences the results according to patient name. Since both the Admit and Doctors tables contain last columns, the table name is used with the column name to remove any ambiguity.

```
SELECT Patient,Admit,Field
FROM Patcare,Admit,Doctors
WHERE Patient=TRIM(Admit.Last)
      and Patcare.Doctor=TRIM(Doctors.Last)
ORDER BY Patient;
```

Figure 9.21

```
SQL. select doctor,patient from patcare,admit where patient=trim(last) and anesthesia order by doctor:
  DOCTOR                    PATIENT
  Bates, Norman             Eckardt, Lois
  Christenson, Amanda       Sorenson, Cynthia
  Christenson, Amanda       Morgan, Robert
  Westfall, Donald          Anderson, Ken
  Westfall, Donald          Eckardt, Lois

SQL.
SQL     C:\dbase\emerg\                        DB:EMERG              Ins
        Type a dBASE IV command and press the ENTER key (↵)
```

dBASE IV SQL displays the table of results (see Figure 9.22).

You can see that SQL syntax, though not simple, is a bit less complex than standard dBASE IV when it comes to complex data relations. SQL is simpler in the sense that all of the operations needed to perform the task are united into a single command rather than distributed among a series of procedurally oriented commands, as they would be in standard dBASE IV. On the other hand, the relationship formed between the tables exists only for that query. In standard dBASE IV, a relation link remains in place until it is removed. Both approaches to database management have strengths and weaknesses and fit some tasks better than others.

Subqueries

SQL operations are single commands. This means that each command generates a single result. There are some database management tasks that require consecutive operations. Suppose you want to list all of the patients who stayed in the hospital longer than average. The problem with this query is: How can you determine whether the days stayed are longer than average when you have to calculate the average at the same time? In standard dBASE IV operations, you would solve this problem by using consecutive commands to pass information forward by means of a memory variable. For example:

Figure 9.22

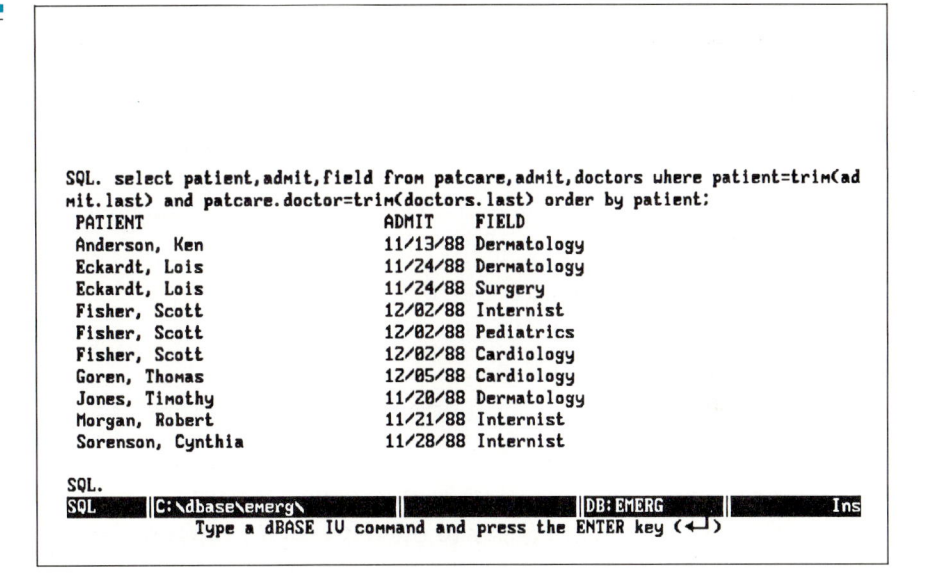

```
SQL. select patient,admit,field from patcare,admit,doctors where patient=trim(ad
mit.last) and patcare.doctor=trim(doctors.last) order by patient:
  PATIENT              ADMIT     FIELD
  Anderson, Ken        11/13/88  Dermatology
  Eckardt, Lois        11/24/88  Dermatology
  Eckardt, Lois        11/24/88  Surgery
  Fisher, Scott        12/02/88  Internist
  Fisher, Scott        12/02/88  Pediatrics
  Fisher, Scott        12/02/88  Cardiology
  Goren, Thomas        12/05/88  Cardiology
  Jones, Timothy       11/20/88  Dermatology
  Morgan, Robert       11/21/88  Internist
  Sorenson, Cynthia    11/28/88  Internist

SQL.
SQL      C:\dbase\emerg\                          DB:EMERG              Ins
           Type a dBASE IV command and press the ENTER key (↵)
```

```
Average Days_stay TO Avgdays
LIST Last,First FOR Days_stay>Avgdays
```

The logic involved in this operation requires the program to first determine, by looking at the data in the Admit table, the average number of days stayed. That value can then be fed into another query that looks at days in excess of this average. You can see that in trying to answer the query, one operation must precede the other. Since all SQL queries are single commands, you cannot relate two queries in sequence.

The solution is to nest one query within another, similar to the way functions nest inside each other in a complex expression. By nesting one SELECT command within the WHERE clause of another SELECT command, you create a subquery.

Subquery commands consist of at least two SELECT commands—outer and inner. The inner query is nested as an argument for the WHERE clause of the outer query. SQL executes the inner query first. The outer query then uses the results of the inner query as its starting point.

To return to the example, the inner query would be one that calculates the average of the days stayed. Enter the query below:

```
SELECT AVG(Days_stay) FROM Admit;
```

This query evaluates as a value 4.31. The trick is to nest the entire query within another query. The idea is to write a WHERE clause that depends upon the results of the inner query; **WHERE Days_stay =** *(SELECT AVG(Days_stay) FROM Admit)*. The bold text represents the WHERE clause of the outer query, which uses the results of the inner query, in italics, as a starting point. The command below lists the patients names for those who have more than the average number of days in the hospital.

```
SELECT Last,First
FROM Admit
WHERE Days_stay.
     (SELECT AVG(Days_stay) FROM Admit)
ORDER BY Last;
```

The query lists the names selected by comparing the results of the inner query to the days stayed column.

Ending an SQL Session

When you complete an SQL session, you must close the open database by using the STOP DATABASE command. Enter

STOP DATABASE;

The Emerg database is closed. You can now exit the SQL mode.

SET SQL OFF

You are returned to the dot prompt mode.

Starting an SQL Database

Once you have closed an SQL database, you can reopen it by using the START DATABASE command. First, place dBASE IV into the SQL mode.

SET SQL ON

Enter the start database SQL command.

START DATABASE Emerg;

The Emerg database is now ready for more SQL operations. As an example, list the doctors.

SELECT Last,First FROM Doctors;

Close the database and exit the SQL mode by entering

CLOSE DATABASE;

SET SQL OFF

Summary

This chapter introduced concepts associated with the use of dBASE IV SQL.

SQL. SQL, Structured Query Language, was developed for use on mainframe and mini computers as a standard method of addressing the retrieval of data from database files created by a variety of applications. SQL represents an approach toward the main activity of database management, data retrieval. SQL insulates users from data-handling mechanisms. SQL queries let users describe the data they want to retrieve. SQL then implements the operations necessary to retrieve that data.

SQL databases. An SQL database holds one or more groups of related data. Unlike standard dBASE IV, where a database corresponds to a single file, SQL databases coordinate data storage in a variety of files. Databases are created with the CREATE command. A dBASE IV SQL database creates its own directory to store all files related to the SQL database. The database requires access to the SQLHOME directory in order to copy the basic file needed for an SQL database.

SQL tables. Data in SQL databases is organized into tables. A table consists of columns that divide information into classifications. The table is expanded by adding rows of information to the table. An SQL database contains one or more tables. A table is created by using the DEFINE TABLE command to specify the columns for the table. Columns can be numeric, character, logical, or date types. There is no SQL equivalent of the dBASE IV memo field.

SQL objects. SQL views database management from an object-orientation rather than a verb- or process-orientation. By hiding the process from users, SQL queries can be implemented by a variety of systems that use different procedures and structures to store data. The most common SQL object is a result table. A result table consists of all the columns and rows in a database that fit the description entered into a SELECT query. The results must be treated as a block, not as a group of individual items, as is the case in standard dBASE IV database management.

SQL selection. A selection consists of all the rows and columns that meet the specified query description. The SELECT command finds the related information.

SQL data entry. SQL does not provide interactive editing tools for data entry and revision. SQL assumes data entry will be handled by some other application and the results imported into a SQL database. The INSERT command adds rows of data to a table. dBASE IV provides the LOAD command to add data stored in common microcomputer formats, such as delimited text files, Lotus 1-2-3 worksheet files, and dBASE IV database files, into SQL tables. You can integrate a complete dBASE IV database file into an SQL database using the DBDEFINE command.

WHERE clause. The WHERE clause selects rows from tables during an SQL query. The WHERE clause requires a logical expression that can be evaluated in terms of the tables involved in the query. Most dBASE IV functions are allowed in SQL expressions. The exceptions are functions that refer directly to dBASE IV standard database file operations, such as LOOKUP() and RECNO(). SQL WHERE clauses can also make use of special SQL predicates. BETWEEN tests for a range of values, IN compares an item to a list of values, and LIKE allows you to create a wild-card template.

DISTINCT clause. The DISTINCT clause causes SQL to include only the table rows with a unique value in specified column or columns.

SQL functions. SQL provides statistical functions SUM(), AVG(), MAX(), MIN(), and COUNT(). These functions return summary values for specified columns.

GROUP BY clause. The GROUP BY clause produces subtotal group results based on a specified column. The column used as the grouping criterion must appear in both the selection and the group by list.

HAVING clause. The HAVING clause selects subtotal groups that meet a specified criterion.

Nesting. Complex queries can be handled by nesting one selection within another query.

ORDER BY. The ORDER BY clause selects a column to sequence the contents of a row. You must specify a column name as the order by key. dBASE IV expressions are not allowed.

Multiple table queries. A SELECT command can include data from more than one table. When one-to-one relationships do not exist, use the WHERE clause to specify a relationship between the two or more tables designated in the query.

Review Problems for Chapter 9

1. Create an SQL database called SELLING.
2. Add the three .dbf files Prods, Sales, and Cust to the Selling SQL database.
3. Enter an SQL command that lists the date, amount, and tax for all sales in July.
4. Repeat the previous query by ordering the rows by item name.
5. Find the total amount of sales and sales tax.
6. List the company, date, product name, and total amount, with subtotals for company.

7. List the date, total amount, product code, EPA status, and maker of each product in the Sales table.

8. List the company, contact, phone number, and city for each company listed in the Sales table.

Answers to Exercises

1. Load data from .dbf file.

   ```
   LOAD DATA FROM Addrows.dbf INTO TABLE Arrival;
   ```

2. Load data from Patcare file.

   ```
   LOAD DATA FROM Patcare.dbf INTO TABLE Arrival;
   ```

3. SELECT doctor information.

   ```
   SELECT First,Last,Field FROM Doctors;
   ```

4. Calculate total days stayed.

   ```
   SELECT SUM(Days_stay)
   FROM Admit
   WHERE MONTH(Discharge)=11;
   ```

5. Patients grouped.

   ```
   SELECT Patient,COUNT(*)
   FROM Admit
   GROUP BY Patient;
   ```

10 Programming in SQL

In the previous chapter, you learned the basic operations and concepts related to SQL and its dBASE IV implementation. In this chapter, you will learn how SQL databases and queries can be integrated into dBASE IV programs.

How dBASE SQL Works

Before you begin to create programs using dBASE IV SQL commands, it might be useful to examine how dBASE IV and SQL operate and what it means to use dBASE IV SQL. Some questions are: What actually happens when you create an SQL database? Where is the data stored? How does that data relate to standard dBASE IV?

The answers to these questions reveal an important point about SQL. As you saw in Chapter 9, SQL concepts are different from those used by standard dBASE IV. When you use dBASE IV SQL, dBASE IV uses standard dBASE IV operations to carry out SQL tasks. Put another way, SQL is a type of dBASE IV program that responds to SQL commands. When you enter an SQL command, dBASE IV breaks the command up into a sequence of SQL operations. Suppose you entered an SQL query like the one below:

```
SELECT Last,First FROM Admit;
```

dBASE IV looks at this SQL command and carries out standard dBASE IV operations that achieve this result. The command below demonstrates approximately what dBASE IV does in response to this SQL command.

```
USE Admit
LIST Last,First
CLOSE DATABASE
```

The more complex the SQL command, the greater the complexity of the dBASE IV command sequence needed to carry out that command. dBASE IV SQL acts as a translator program that generates the dBASE IV operations needed to carry out SQL instructions.

SQL is simply a different way of attacking database management and is useful for two reasons. First, SQL operations are easier to write when using multiple file applications; second, SQL allows people familiar with programming in SQL to work with dBASE IV with a minimum of training.

SQL is also a common language that allows different types of databases and database management applications to respond to a common set of commands.

dBASE SQL Files

For SQL to work, dBASE IV uses a special set of files called system files. These files are stored in a directory whose default name, as suggested in the dBASE IV installation process, is \DBSAMPLE \SQLHOME.

> *Note:* If you did not install dBASE IV on your computer, you may have to use MS-DOS to examine the directory structure to determine the location of the SQL files on your computer.

You can list the files in this directory by entering

```
DIR \dbsample\sqlhome\*.*
```

The list will show 13 files. Eleven of these files are .dbf, dBASE IV database files and form the basis of all dBASE IV SQL operations. These database files are used by dBASE IV to hold information about your SQL databases, tables, indexes, columns names, and others. When you create a new SQL database, dBASE IV creates a new directory with the name of that database. Creating the SQL database

Emerg created a new directory called \DBSAMPLE\EMERG. By creating this directory, dBASE IV SQL has a place to store all the files required for an SQL database.

dBASE IV then copies the SQL system files to the new directory. These files then record information about the SQL database.

List the name of the files in the \DBSAMPLE\EMERG directory by entering

```
DIR \dbsample\emerg\*.*
```

This time, there are 17 files (see Figure 10.1). There is a .dbf file for each of the tables in the Emerg SQL database, Arrival.dbf, Patcare.dbf, Admit.dbf, and Doctors.dbf. This tells you that the data in the SQL database is actually stored in .dbf files.

SQL is not an actual product, but a set of conventions any database program may choose to follow. For example, most MS-DOS applications allow you to use MS-DOS wildcards, like *.*, in commands that require disk operations. These programs allow you to follow MS-DOS conventions from within the application, an advantage to anyone familiar with MS-DOS wildcards. People who are familiar with SQL enjoy a similar advantage when they want to work in dBASE IV.

You can access the information in the SQL database files from the dot prompt, just as you would any other .dbf file. The Systabls.dbf file

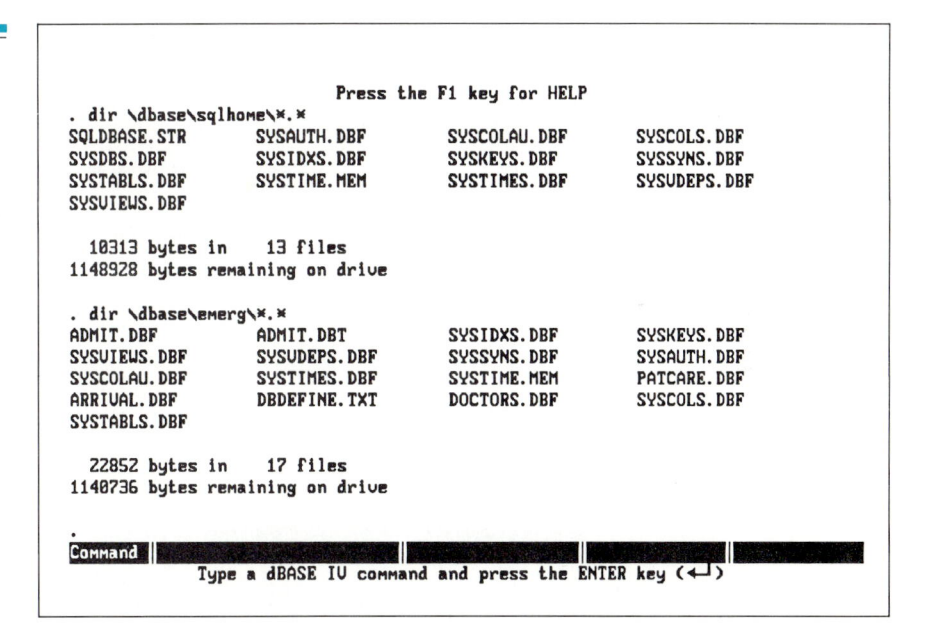

Figure 10.1

```
                        Press the F1 key for HELP
. dir \dbase\sqlhome\*.*
SQLDBASE.STR      SYSAUTH.DBF       SYSCOLAU.DBF      SYSCOLS.DBF
SYSDBS.DBF        SYSIDXS.DBF       SYSKEYS.DBF       SYSSYNS.DBF
SYSTABLS.DBF      SYSTIME.MEM       SYSTIMES.DBF      SYSUDEPS.DBF
SYSVIEWS.DBF

   10313 bytes in    13 files
 1148928 bytes remaining on drive

. dir \dbase\emerg\*.*
ADMIT.DBF         ADMIT.DBT         SYSIDXS.DBF       SYSKEYS.DBF
SYSVIEWS.DBF      SYSUDEPS.DBF      SYSSYNS.DBF       SYSAUTH.DBF
SYSCOLAU.DBF      SYSTIMES.DBF      SYSTIME.MEM       PATCARE.DBF
ARRIVAL.DBF       DBDEFINE.TXT      DOCTORS.DBF       SYSCOLS.DBF
SYSTABLS.DBF

   22852 bytes in    17 files
 1140736 bytes remaining on drive

.
Command
        Type a dBASE IV command and press the ENTER key (↵)
```

How dBASE SQL Works ■ 491

contains the names of all the tables in that directory's SQL database. Set the dBASE IV search path to the \DBSAMPLE\EMERG directory. Enter

```
SET PATH TO \dbsample\emerg
```

Open the SYSTABLS database.

```
USE Systabls
```

Look at the right side of the status line. dBASE IV displays the words **read only,** meaning the file can be read but not written to prevent you from accidentally changing the information in an SQL system file. These files can be displayed, but not changed, from the dot prompt mode. List the structure of the file.

```
LIST Structure
```

You can see the file consists of fields such as Tbname (table name) and Colcount (column count) (see Figure 10.2).

This database records and maintains information about the tables assigned to the Emerg SQL database. Enter

```
LIST Tbname,Colcount
```

This list (see Figure 10.3) shows the names of all of the .dbf files in the Emerg directory, including the four database files you created.

Figure 10.2

```
     25584 bytes in    14 files
 1132544 bytes remaining on drive

 . use systabls
 . list stru
 Structure for database: C:\DBASE\EMERG\SYSTABLS.DBF
 Number of data records:     14
 Date of last update   : 09/15/88
 Field  Field Name  Type         Width    Dec    Index
     1  TBNAME      Character      10               N
     2  CREATOR     Character      10               N
     3  TBTYPE      Character       1               N
     4  COLCOUNT    Numeric         3               N
     5  CLUSTERRID  Numeric        10               N
     6  INDXCOUNT   Numeric         3               N
     7  CREATED     Date            8               N
     8  UPDATED     Date            8               N
     9  CARD        Numeric        10               N
    10  NPAGES      Numeric        10               N
 ** Total **                       74

 Command  C:\dbase\emerg\SYSTABLS  Rec 1/14         File  ReadOnly
          Type a dBASE IV command and press the ENTER key (⏎)
```

The Colcount field holds values that correspond to the number of fields in each file. You will recall Patcare has 3 fields, Admit 17 fields, and so on.

You can access these files to obtain information about the SQL databases. Knowing about these files enables you to perform SQL operations on these files as well as on the user-defined files. All of the SQL system files are listed as tables in the Systabls file. This means Systabls is the name of a table in the SQL database that SQL should recognize.

Place dBASE IV in the SQL mode by entering

```
CLOSE DATABASE
SET SQL ON
```

Start the Emerg database. Enter

```
START DATABASE Emerg;
```

You can produce a list of the tables in your SQL database by entering

```
SELECT Tbname,Colcount FROM Systabls;
```

SQL accesses the same data you accessed earlier from the dot prompt (see Figure 10.4).

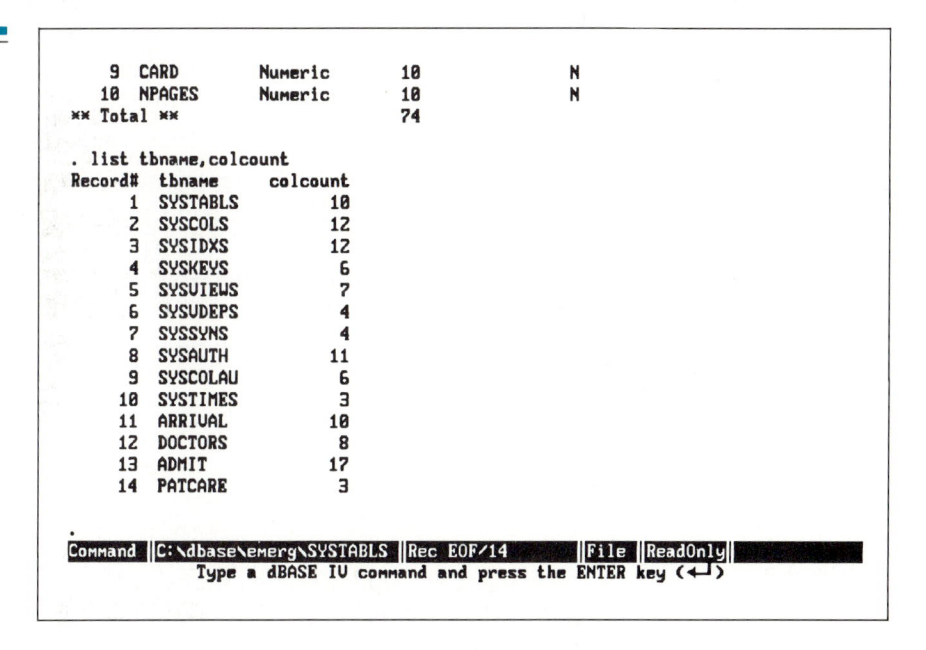

Figure 10.3

```
    9   CARD        Numeric       10           N
   10   NPAGES      Numeric       10           N
** Total **                       74

. list tbname,colcount
Record#  tbname      colcount
      1  SYSTABLS        10
      2  SYSCOLS         12
      3  SYSIDXS         12
      4  SYSKEYS          6
      5  SYSVIEWS         7
      6  SYSUDEPS         4
      7  SYSSYNS          4
      8  SYSAUTH         11
      9  SYSCOLAU         6
     10  SYSTIMES         3
     11  ARRIVAL         10
     12  DOCTORS          8
     13  ADMIT           17
     14  PATCARE          3
.
Command  C:\dbase\emerg\SYSTABLS   Rec EOF/14        File  ReadOnly
         Type a dBASE IV command and press the ENTER key (←)
```

How dBASE SQL Works ■ 493

Figure 10.4

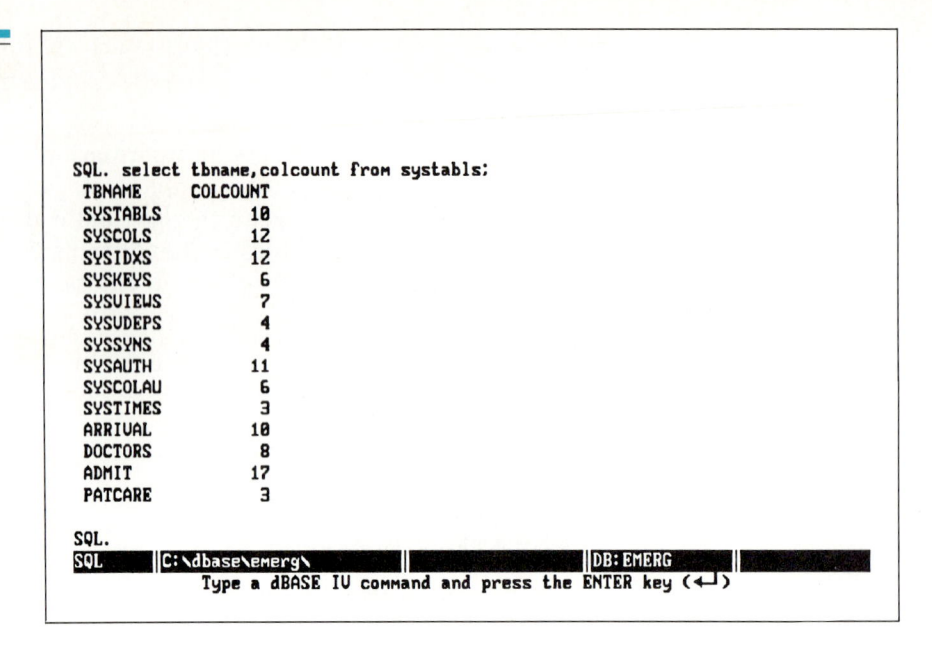

```
SQL. select tbname,colcount from systabls:
  TBNAME      COLCOUNT
  SYSTABLS       10
  SYSCOLS        12
  SYSIDXS        12
  SYSKEYS         6
  SYSVIEWS        7
  SYSUDEPS        4
  SYSSYNS         4
  SYSAUTH        11
  SYSCOLAU        6
  SYSTIMES        3
  ARRIVAL        10
  DOCTORS         8
  ADMIT          17
  PATCARE         3

SQL.
SQL    C:\dbase\emerg\                          DB: EMERG
       Type a dBASE IV command and press the ENTER key (⏎)
```

This demonstrates that SQL manipulates databases in a way similar to dBASE IV. You can see even though SQL uses different terms, the data is still stored in dBASE IV database (.dbf) files. Keep in mind that standard dBASE IV uses the term database to refer to a single .dbf file. dBASE IV SQL uses the term database to refer to a collection of .dbf and other disk files that function as a logical unit even though they are composed of numerous individual files.

To get a list of the columns in an SQL table, access the Syscols table. This table contains information about all the columns in all the tables in the SQL database. Two of the column names in this table are COLNAME (column name) and TBNAME (table name). To list the column names for the Doctors table, you would select the COLNAME for each row containing the table name Doctors. You enter the name of the table using the WHERE clause, in upper-case characters. Enter

```
SELECT Colname
FROM Syscols
WHERE Tbname="Doctors";
```

By accessing the Systabls and Syscols tables, you can display information about the tables and columns in the SQL database. These tables provide the same type of information provided by the dBASE IV command DISPLAY STRUCTURE.

494 ■ Programming in SQL

Close the SQL database by entering

```
STOP DATABASE;
SET SQL OFF
```

Programs That Use SQL Commands

SQL database operations can be used within dBASE IV programs provided that they conform to the following specifications:

1. All programs that contain SQL commands have a .prs file extension. This enables dBASE IV to compile the program as a dBASE IV SQL program rather than a standard dBASE IV program.

2. Programs that use SQL commands cannot use dBASE IV commands that access .dbf files. These commands include APPEND, ASSIST, AVERAGE, BROWSE, CALCULATE, CHANGE, CONTINUE, COPY, CREATE, DISPLAY, EDIT, GOTO, INDEX, INSERT, JOIN, LIST, LOCATE, PACK, REPLACE, SCAN, SEEK, SELECT, SKIP, SORT, TOTAL, USE, and ZAP.

The disadvantage of many SQL commands—their lack of an interactive, full-screen entry mode—can be viewed as an advantage in some programming situations. For example, the dBASE IV process for making changes to a file's structure requires you to manually enter the new fields. The SQL command ALTER allows you to perform this operation with a one-line command.

For example, throughout the last few chapters, you had to adjust the links between the Patcare file and other databases because the names of the patients and doctors were stored in a single field, not two different fields. It would be simpler if you could create fields in the Admit and Doctors files (tables) that matched the contents of the Patcare fields (columns). You can use an SQL program to make this change. Standard dBASE IV does not contain an explicit command that lets you alter the structure of a file (table).

SQL programs are created exactly like standard dBASE IV programs, with the exception that the file extension is .prs rather than .prg. Enter

```
MODIFY COMMAND Addcols.prs
```

The key to creating SQL programs is that all the commands that deal with data storage and retrieval must use SQL command syntax. The rest of the commands can be written as normal dBASE IV commands.

You do not explicitly turn the SQL mode on or off in an SQL program. dBASE IV will automatically enter the SQL mode when the program executes, and exits the SQL mode when it terminates. As long as the file is compiled with a .prs extension, the commands will execute in the proper mode.

In this case, the first step is to open the Emerg SQL database.

```
START DATABASE Emerg;
```

Add new columns to the Admit and Doctors tables.

```
ALTER TABLE Admit ADD (Patient char(30));
ALTER TABLE Doctors ADD (Doctor char(30));
```

Next, use the UPDATE command to fill in the new columns with data. Here, we'll use the last and first name columns to create the full names for the new columns.

```
UPDATE Admit
SET Patient=TRIM(Last)+", "+First;
UPDATE Doctors
SET Doctor=TRIM(Last)+", "+First;
```

You may want to confirm the operation by displaying the information, using SQL SELECT commands.

```
CLEAR
SELECT Patient
FROM Admit
ORDER BY Patient;
WAIT
SELECT Doctor
FROM Doctors
ORDER BY Doctor;
WAIT
```

The non-SQL commands WAIT and CLEAR should not have semicolons as command terminators. Only specific SQL command sequences—in this example spread over 3 lines—require that syntax.

The last step is to close the revised database.

```
STOP DATABASE;
CLEAR
RETURN
```

■ **Programming in SQL**

The entire program should look like this:

```
START DATABASE Emerg;
ALTER TABLE Admit ADD (Patient CHAR(30));
ALTER TABLE Doctors ADD (Doctor CHAR(30));
UPDATE Admit
SET Patient=TRIM(Last)+", "+First;
UPDATE Doctors
SET Doctor=TRIM(Last)+", "+First;
CLEAR
SELECT Patient
FROM Admit
ORDER BY Patient;
WAIT
SELECT Doctor
FROM Doctors
ORDER BY Doctor;
WAIT
STOP DATABASE;
CLEAR
RETURN
```

Save the program by pressing Ctrl-End. When you compile and/or execute an SQL program, you must remember to specify the file extension .prs. If you do not add this extension, dBASE IV will look for a .prg file with the same name and execute that program if one is found. Compile the program by entering

COMPILE Addcols.prs

dBASE IV recognizes this program as an SQL program because of its file extension. Execute the program by entering

DO Addcols.prs

As the program executes, the status line changes, indicating access of the Emerg SQL database. As the columns are added to the database, SQL displays messages confirming each action. When the SQL program arrives at the UPDATE commands, SQL pauses the program because you did not include a WHERE clause with the UPDATE command. An UPDATE command without a WHERE clause causes SQL to wait for you to confirm your intention to update all the rows in a table. This is not an error message but merely a warning about the scope of the command (see Figure 10.5).

Confirm the command by pressing ⏎. The next UPDATE command prompts the same warning. Press ⏎. Next, the program displays the contents of the newly created column in the Admit file.

Continue the program by pressing ⏎. The next SQL query displays the contents of the doctor column. Complete the program by pressing ⏎. The program concludes and returns you to the dot prompt demonstrating that SQL programs function in much the same manner as any other dBASE IV program.

Interactive Programs With SQL Databases

The previous SQL program is an example of a linear program. Linear programs carry out a list of commands without using block structures, like loops or branches. However, SQL programs do not limit programs to carrying out a sequence of SQL commands. You can use SQL databases in much the same way you can use standard dBASE IV databases. As an example, suppose you want to create a program that displays information about a specific patient.

Begin by creating a new program file, Findpat.prs (find patient SQL).

```
MODIFY COMMAND Findpat.prs
```

This program combines standard dBASE IV commands with dBASE IV SQL commands. First, run the Setoff program to set the environment.

```
DO Setoff
```

The next command sequence uses standard dBASE IV commands to create a memory variable, display an input area for the variable, and allow the user to enter a last name into that variable. The @/GET command uses a PICTURE clause with the function "@!". This function automatically converts text to upper-case.

Figure 10.5

```
. compile addcols.prs
Compiling line     20
. do addcols.prs
Column PATIENT added to table ADMIT
Column DOCTOR added to table DOCTORS
Warning - No WHERE clause specified in UPDATE statement
Press ESC to abandon operation, any other key to continue...
ADDCOLS  C:\dbase\emerg\                           DB:EMERG
```

498 ■ Programming in SQL

```
Findlast=SPACE(20)
@ 10, 10 SAY "Enter Last Name of Patient: "
GET Findlast PICTURE "@!"
READ
CLEAR
```

Once the variable is filled in, you can use its value as part of the SQL operation that retrieves information for that patient. The next SQL command opens the SQL database Emerg and must be terminated with a semicolon.

```
START DATABASE Emerg;
```

With the database open, you can use an SQL select command to retrieve the data.

```
SELECT *
FROM Admit
WHERE Upper(Last)=TRIM(Findlast);
```

To achieve an accurate match, it is necessary to convert the last column to upper-case and trim any trailing blanks from the FINDLAST variable.

The final step requires the program-end command and the addition of the SQL command, STOP DATABASE. It is important to remember to close the SQL database at the end of your program. Otherwise, the SQL database remains open. This is significant because SQL operations use dBASE IV work areas for files. For example, when the SQL database accesses the Admit table, dBASE IV places the file \DBSAMPLE\EMERG\ADMIT.DBF in use, in work area 9. Work area 10 stores SQL system tables. If you do not close the SQL database, these work areas remain in use and can potentially conflict with other operations. For example, if you attempted to open the standard Admit dBASE IV database file, it would be assigned the same alias name, Admit, as an already open file and would cause an error.

```
WAIT
STOP DATABASE;
DO Seton
RETURN
```

The entire program reads as follows:

```
DO Setoff
Findlast=SPACE(20)
```

```
@ 10, 10 SAY "Enter Last Name of Patient: "
GET Findlast PICTURE "@!"
READ
CLEAR
START DATABASE Emerg;
SELECT *
FROM admit
WHERE Upper(Last)=TRIM(Findlast);
WAIT
STOP DATABASE;
DO Seton
RETURN
```

Save this program by pressing (Ctrl)-(End). Compile the program by entering

```
COMPILE Findpat.prs
```

It is necessary to use the .prs extension so that the compile process will know this is an SQL program. The compiling process seems to take a long time, considering the small size of the program. When an SQL program is compiled, dBASE IV actually checks the logic of the commands against the SQL database's contents. This is a more detailed compiling process than that performed with standard dBASE IV programs. If you make a typographical error in a filename in a standard dBASE IV command, the compiler will not find that mistake, like typing AdmitX instead of Admit. It will become an error only when dBASE IV attempts to carry out that command and finds that no such file exists.

The SQL compilation process actually attempts to locate the files specified. For example, if you entered "START DATABASE Emergx;" the compiler would attempt to find that database; if it could not, it would issue an error aborting the compilation. This helps you eliminate bugs from your programs before you attempt to execute them. It also makes the compilation process much slower than it is for standard dBASE IV programs.

However, you could not compile the program on a computer that did not have the Emerg database installed.

When the compilation is complete, you can execute the SQL program. Enter

```
DO Findpat.prs
```

Enter the name of a patient.

```
Jones
```

The program will search for, and then display, the data for the specified patient stored in the SQL database table (see Figure 10.6).

The information is displayed exactly as it is when you perform a SELECT command in the SQL mode. Complete the program by pressing ⏎. The SQL database closes and the program returns you to the dot prompt.

The INTO Clause

The next program demonstrates how user input passes to an SQL command, accesses the SQL database, but insulates a user from SQL commands. The EDIT program, created earlier using standard dBASE IV commands, locates records for the user and serves as a model for our next effort.

The most obvious problem with this new program involves the data display format. The standard SQL display structure is basically unformatted, similar to the output of the dBASE IV LIST command.

You can get a row of SQL data to appear in a formatted display by using the INTO clause. The INTO clause used with the SELECT command sends the information stored in SQL table columns to dBASE IV memory variables. Here is an SQL command to display the last and first name of the selected patient.

```
SELECT Last,First
FROM Admit
WHERE UPPER(Last)=TRIM(Findlast);
```

This command places data on the screen. The INTO clause can direct the output away from the screen and into dBASE IV memory variables. In the following command, the values stored in the first and last columns are stored in memory variables mv1 and mv2.

Figure 10.6

```
LAST                FIRST              MIDDLE ADMIT    DISCHARGE AGE PHONE
    SEX DAYS_STAY DAYS_ICU INSURED PAYOR              ANESTHESIA TRUMA_TEA
M CT_SCAN    CHARGES MNAME         PATIENT
    Jones              Timothy         R        11/20/88 11/22/88  22 666-777
7  M        3.00     0.00 .F.    Progressive Casualty     .F.       .F.
    .F.         2842.00 November    Jones, Timothy

Press any key to continue...
```

Interactive Programs With SQL Databases ■ 501

```
SELECT Last,First
INTO mv1,mv2
FROM Admit
WHERE UPPER(Last)=TRIM(Findlast);
```

Columns match to variables sequentially. The number of columns must correspond to the number of variables, so each column referenced has a corresponding variable to fill.

The INTO clause accomplishes two things:

1. It suppresses the unformatted display of the information from the SQL database.
2. It places the information into memory variables that operate with standard dBASE IV output formatting commands, such as @/SAY/GET.

With the INTO clause, you can control the format of the information retrieved from an SQL database. Create a new program Findpat1.prs by entering

```
MODIFY COMMAND Findpat1.prs
```

The program begins with the Setoff subroutine.

```
DO Setoff
```

This program displays the information stored in the Admit table in a formatted manner. You will use the INTO clause to store the column information as memory variables. The Admit table has 18 columns; therefore, you will need 18 variables. You may recall when you are working with a group of related memory variables, it is sometimes simpler to create an array of variables. Here, you will create an array of 18 variables to hold data from each of the 18 columns in the table.

```
DECLARE mv[18]
```

Next open the SQL database.

```
START DATABASE Emerg;
```

In this program, you will embed the retrieval routine in a loop so you can search for as many patients as you desire. The loop will be controlled by a memory variable called More. The loop begins with the display of the Findlast variable so the user can enter the last name of the patient.

```
More=.T.
DO WHILE More
    CLEAR
    Findlast=SPACE(20)
    @ 10, 10 SAY "Enter Last Name of Patient: "
    GET Findlast PICTURE "@!"
    READ
    CLEAR
```

With the name entered into the variable, you can perform the selection. The SQL SELECT command contains an INTO clause that lists the 18 memory variables. The selection uses * to select all columns. The brackets are used to indicate the element number of the mv array.

```
SELECT *
INTO mv[1],mv[2],mv[3],mv[4],mv[5],mv[6],
  mv[7],mv[8],mv[9],mv[10],mv[11],mv[12],
  mv[13],mv[14],mv[15],mv[16],mv[17],mv[18]
FROM Admit
WHERE UPPER(Last)=TRIM(Findlast);
```

The data from the selection is now stored in the array of variables. The array allows you to create a formatted display using a loop, rather than creating individual @/SAY commands for each element. The following loop uses a value called Field to cycle through the first 16 elements in the array. Each element is displayed next to a label that says Column #1, Column #2, and so on. Only the first 16 elements in the array are displayed. This is done to suppress the display of the Mname and Patient columns because they display duplicate information.

```
Field=1
DO WHILE Field<=16
    @ ROW()+1,0 SAY "Column;
     #"+LTRIM(STR(Field))
    @ ROW(),15 SAY mv[Field];
     Field=Field+1
ENDDO
```

With the data displayed, you can ask the user if he wants to continue the search, or exit the program.

```
    @ 24,0 SAY "Search again? (Y/N) " GET More;
      PICTURE "Y"
    READ
ENDDO
```

Conclude the program in the usual manner.

```
STOP DATABASE;
DO Seton
RETURN
```

Save and execute the program by pressing (Alt)-e and typing r. The compiling process will take a few moments because SQL programs open and check the actual SQL databases. When the program executes, you can enter the name of a patient. Enter

Jones

This time the patient information is displayed in a formatted manner, as a series of lines containing one column each (see Figure 10.7).

Search for another patient by pressing ⏎ and entering

Anderson

Figure 10.7

```
Column #1     Jones
Column #2     Timothy
Column #3     R
Column #4     11/20/88
Column #5     11/22/88
Column #6                          22
Column #7     666-7777
Column #8     M
Column #9                           3
Column #10                          0
Column #11    F
Column #12    Progressive Casualty
Column #13    F
Column #14    F
Column #15    F
Column #16                       2842



Search again? (Y/N)  Y
```

■ Programming in SQL

The loop performs another selection, transferring the information into the memory variable array, and displays the information in the same format.

Exit the program by pressing n. The database is closed and you return to the dot prompt mode.

Temporary Tables

The Findpat1.prs program demonstrates how SQL data can be captured in a form that allows you to perform standard dBASE IV display manipulations. But what about the names of the columns? The value of the patient charges appeared next to a label that read Column #16. While this tells you something about the structure of the SQL database, it does nothing to identify the meaning of the value.

You can use @/SAY commands to place meaningful labels next to the data items, but it is easier to place the column names next to the values. This saves you the effort of explicitly writing commands to display column labels. Also, by using actual column names, you create a generalized routine that can be adapted to any SQL table.

You can get access to the column names from the SQL system files. dBASE IV SQL maintains a table called Syscols with information about all the columns in all the tables in the SQL database. The table contains columns called Tbname (table names) and Syscols (system column names) that hold the table names and column names. You can use this table to find the names of the columns in the Admit table.

How can this information produce the column names as part of the formatted display? Place the column name information into memory variables using the INTO clause. But gathering the information from the Syscols table poses a different problem than you faced with the patient information.

When you use the SELECT/INTO command, the assumption is made that only one row of the table will qualify for selection. The INTO command then places the column values for that row into memory variables.

But when you select records from the Syscols table, you will be retrieving more than one row. For example, the column names for the Admit table will produce 18 rows. This means you need to develop a method to handle selections that consist of more than one row.

dBASE IV SQL includes a special clause called SAVE TO TEMP. This clause creates a temporary SQL table in the current database to contain the output of a SELECT command. The temporary table can then be used as the basis for other operations on this selected data. The temporary table is deleted when you stop the database. The SAVE TO TEMP clause can select rows and columns from the Syscols table, creating a new table, Cnames. This table will have one column, Colname (column name), and as many rows as the Admit table has columns, in this case 18. Each row will contain the name of one of the columns.

You can experiment with the SAVE TO TEMP clause in the SQL mode. Enter

```
SET SQL ON
```

Start the Emerg database.

```
START DATABASE Emerg;
```

Create the temporary table discussed above by entering

```
SELECT Colname
FROM Syscols
WHERE Tbname="ADMIT"
SAVE TO TEMP Cnames;
```

Because the results of the selection were sent to another table, they did not appear on the screen. You can list the information stored in the temporary table by entering another SQL command.

```
SELECT * FROM Cnames;
```

The column names are listed from the temporary table (see Figure 10.8). How many are there? You can determine the number by counting, but this method is impractical in a program. dBASE IV maintains a system variable called SQLCNT. This variable equals the number of rows selected in the most recent SQL operation. Enter

```
? SQLCNT
```

dBASE IV displays the value 18, indicating there are 18 column names. You now have a way of isolating the column names in a table and determining the number of rows in that table.

It is necessary to create a temporary table for another reason— dBASE IV will not allow you to perform certain operations on the SQL system tables, Syscols or Systabls. These tables are designated as read-only. If you want to work with system table values, you must place them in a temporary table. Exit the SQL mode by entering

Figure 10.8

```
SQL. select * from cnames:
 COLNAME
 LAST
 FIRST
 MIDDLE
 ADMIT
 DISCHARGE
 AGE
 PHONE
 SEX
 DAYS_STAY
 DAYS_ICU
 INSURED
 PAYOR
 ANESTHESIA
 TRUMA_TEAM
 CT_SCAN
 CHARGES
 MNAME
 PATIENT

SQL.
SQL      C:\dbase\emerg\                              DB:EMERG
         Type a dBASE IV command and press the ENTER key (↵)
```

```
STOP DATABASE;
SET SQL OFF
```

You are ready to begin a new program that will be able to locate the column names as well as the data from an SQL table. Begin by entering

```
MODIFY COMMAND Findpat2.prs
```

The program begins by running Setoff and opening the SQL database.

```
DO Setoff
START DATABASE Emerg;
```

The first task in this program is to obtain the column names. This makes sense because each of the patient displays will use the same set of column names. The column name routine needs to run only once during the program, while the patient routine can execute any number of times.

The first command creates the temporary table for the column names.

```
* define column names
SELECT Colname
FROM Syscols
```

Interactive Programs With SQL Databases ■ **507**

```
WHERE Tbname="ADMIT"
SAVE TO TEMP Cnames;
```

The names are now isolated in the table Cnames. You now need two sets of memory variables: one for the column names, and one for column contents. Both these sets will have the same number of elements as the current value of the system variable SQLCNT (SQL count). You can use that value to create two arrays of the same size.

```
DECLARE mv[SQLCNT],Colnm[SQLCNT]
```

The value of SQLCNT will change after each SQL command. If you want to refer to the current SQLCNT value at some later point in the program, you should copy the value into a user-defined memory variable.

```
Total_rows=SQLCNT
```

You have now created the arrays to hold the column names and the column contents.

SQL Cursors

So far, you have accomplished two things: You have created a new table, Cnames, which contains the names of columns, and you have created an array of memory variables for the names of the columns.

How can you get the information from the SQL table Cnames into the array Colnm? The SELECT/INTO clause transfers one row at a time into memory variables. What you would like to do is move one row at a time through the SQL table and transfer each row value into a different memory variable.

In SQL programming, you can implement this operation with the SQL cursor commands. In SQL, the cursor refers to a database concept, not the flashing screen symbol. The term cursor in SQL is roughly equivalent to the concept of a pointer in standard dBASE IV. An SQL cursor allows you to move through an SQL table, one row at a time. Each row can be used individually in operations like transfers from SQL columns to dBASE IV memory variables.

SQL uses four commands to operate SQL cursors.

1. **DECLARE.** DECLARE sets up the relationship between an SQL table and an SQL cursor. The DECLARE command contains an SQL SELECT command that specifies the data available to the cursor.

   Note: This command does not actually access the data. It merely sets up the operation that will be performed by other commands accessing the cursor. This means the SQL count function's value following a DECLARE command is always zero.

2. **OPEN.** OPEN begins the cursor operation by extracting from the table the rows that meet the cursor qualification. This command will change the value of the SQLCNT variable based on the number of rows selected by the SELECT command.

3. **FETCH.** FETCH increments the cursor location to the next row in the table. FETCH also transfers the data in the current cursor row into a memory variable. The FETCH command moves the cursor before it extracts data. The first FETCH command following an OPEN command positions the cursor to the first selected row in the table.

4. **CLOSE.** CLOSE completes a cursor operation. The cursor values are released. If you reopen a closed cursor, the cursor is positioned to the first row in cursor table.

SQL cursor commands function only in SQL programs. They cannot be used from the SQL entry mode.

These commands combine to let you move through a series of selected rows and perform operations on each row separately. The concept of the SQL cursor brings you full circle in terms of object vs. process orientation. The SQL cursor requires you to construct a program that moves through the data, one step at a time. These programs usually consist of a loop that repeats until all the rows have been processed. The FETCH command plays the role of both the SKIP and STORE dBASE IV commands. It places the current information into memory variables and positions the SQL cursor to the next row. SKIP can move more than one row at a time, always in a forward direction.

You can now apply these commands to the task at hand. The first step is to declare the cursor. A DECLARE command creates a cursor name that is used by all subsequent cursor-related commands. SQL allows you to have multiple cursors operating during the same program. The cursor names are necessary so each cursor command operates on the correct cursor.

The following command creates a cursor called COLNAMES. The cursor consists of all the columns and all the rows of the temporary table, CNAMES. Since CNAMES has only 1 column, all the rows contain valid column names.

```
DECLARE Colnames CURSOR FOR
SELECT *
FROM Cnames;
```

With the cursor declared, you can use the cursor to create memory variables. The first step is to open the cursor.

```
OPEN Colnames;
```

This positions the cursor to the first row of data. The next task is to place the first row of data into the first element in the column array; the second row into the second element, and so on. This is an ideal situation to use a loop. A variable called Position controls the loop. Position begins at 1 and recycles the loop until all the rows have been accessed. For the program to know when this has happened, use the variable Total_rows. Total_rows was set equal to SQLCNT when you created the Cnames table. Thus, the expression Position<=Total_rows will function as a "do until end of table" command.

```
Position=1
DO WHILE Position<=Total_rows
```

Once the loop begins, use the FETCH command to extract the value from the row and place it into a memory variable. Then the memory variable defines the element in the array that corresponds to the row, as indicated by the value of position.

```
    FETCH Colnames INTO Ar_value;
    Colnm[Position]=Ar_value
```

You may wonder why two commands were used to make the transfer. For example, you might enter the command FETCH Colnames INTO Colnm[Position] and accomplish the transfer in one command. While the command looks perfectly valid, dBASE IV SQL will not accept this command. Because the dBASE IV compiler checks SQL commands for accuracy, an array variable, like Colnm[Position] cannot be evaluated properly. The name has no specific meaning until the array subscript variable Position is assigned a definite numeric argument. dBASE IV will not compile a command that uses this type of variable name.

> *Note:* An array variable used with a literal value, like Colnm[1], would be acceptable because 1 is a literal value indicating a definite element in an array.

To circumvent this problem, the data from FETCH is placed into a variable called Ar_value. This value is in turn transferred to the array element. The compiler does not object to the second command because the dBASE IV compiler does not check non-SQL commands in the same way it checks SQL commands.

Complete the loop by incrementing the value of position so each subsequent cycle places its values into the next element in the array.

```
    Position=Position+1
ENDDO
```

When the cycles are complete, you have an array of values equaling a list of the column names. These names will remain constant throughout the rest of the program and will provide the text for the data labels. You can close the cursor.

```
CLOSE Colnames;
```

The next stage of the program begins the main processing loop where patient information is retrieved from the database table. These commands are identical to the previous program, Findpat1.prs.

```
More=.T.
DO WHILE More
    CLEAR
    Findlast=SPACE(20)
    @ 10, 10 SAY "Enter Last Name of Patient: ";
     GET Findlast PICTURE "@!"
    READ
    CLEAR
    SELECT *
    INTO mv[1],mv[2],mv[3],mv[4],mv[5],mv[6],
    mv[7],mv[8],mv[9],mv[10],mv[11],mv[12],
    mv[13],mv[14],mv[15],mv[16],mv[17],mv[18]
    FROM Admit
    WHERE UPPER(Last)=TRIM(Findlast);
```

You have two arrays of the same size: one with the column names, the other with the column data. You can now create a loop to display the corresponding element in each array.

```
    Field=1
    DO WHILE Field<=Total_rows
        @ ROW()+1,0 SAY Colnm[Field]
```

```
            @ ROW(),15 SAY mv[Field]
            Field=Field+1
    ENDDO
```

The remainder of the commands are identical to the Findpat1.prs program.

```
        @ 24,0 SAY "Search again? (Y/N) " GET More;
          PICTURE "Y"
        READ
ENDDO
STOP DATABASE;
DO Seton
RETURN
```

Save and execute the program by pressing Alt-e and typing r. The program takes a few moments to compile and then executes. The first display is the input prompt for the name of the patient. Enter

Jones

This time, the program shows the data with the column names displayed next to each item (see Figure 10.9).

Figure 10.9

```
LAST           Jones
FIRST          Timothy
MIDDLE         R
ADMIT          11/20/88
DISCHARGE      11/22/88
AGE                               22
PHONE          666-7777
SEX            M
DAYS_STAY                          3
DAYS_ICU                           0
INSURED        F
PAYOR          Progressive Casualty
ANESTHESIA     F
TRUMA_TEAM     F
CT_SCAN        F
CHARGES                         2842
MNAME          November
PATIENT        Jones, Timothy




Search again? (Y/N) Y
```

512   ■ Programming in SQL

Display information for another patient by pressing ⏎ and entering

```
Tate
```

The information for the next patient appears. Exit the program by entering n.

Editing an SQL Row

The previous program created a display with data drawn from an SQL database table that looks very much like the display used by dBASE IV for editing a standard dBASE IV database file. It would be useful to alter the program so you can edit the data displayed to make corrections, additions, or updates.

dBASE IV SQL does not have a command that allows you to see and change information at the same time. SQL editing requires a series of commands. For example, suppose the charges for TATE read $4,500. First, you have to display the charges, then use an UPDATE command to place a new value back into the table. Here are sample commands to accomplish this (do not enter them).

```
SELECT Last,First,Charges
FROM Admit
WHERE Last="Tate";
UPDATE Charges
SET Charges=4500
WHERE Last="Tate";
```

This process of editing records is very cumbersome. The solution is to create a program, similar to Findpat2.prs, that allows you to edit the records in a manner similar to the full-screen display modes in standard dBASE IV. The main difference in the new version is that you need to find a way to put any changes made during full-screen editing back into the SQL table. Begin by creating a new program called Editsql.prs.

```
MODIFY COMMAND Editsql.prs
```

The program's beginning is almost identical to the beginning of Findpat2.prs.

Note: You may wish to save time by copying the Findpat2.prs and editing it, rather than starting from scratch.

One change is to display a message at the beginning of the program informing users of the delay caused by the opening of the SQL database.

```
DO Setoff
CLEAR
@ 8,10 to 12,70
@ 10,30 SAY "Opening SQL Database"
DECLARE mv[18],Colnm[18]
START DATABASE Emerg;
```

Create the temporary table for the column names. Remember it is necessary to transfer the names to a temporary table because dBASE IV SQL will not define a cursor for a table marked as read-only.

```
* define column names
SELECT Colname
FROM syscols
WHERE Tbname="ADMIT"
SAVE TO TEMP Cnames;
```

Use the cursor method to extract the data from the table and place it into an array of memory variables.

```
Total_rows=SQLCNT
DECLARE Colnames CURSOR FOR
SELECT *
FROM Cnames;
OPEN Colnames;
Position=1
DO WHILE Position<=Total_rows
    FETCH Colnames INTO Ar_value;
    Colnm[Position]=Ar_value
    Position=Position+1
ENDDO
CLOSE Colnames;
```

The next section of the program lets a user enter a patient's name.

```
* find data for selected patient
More=.T.
DO WHILE more
    CLEAR
    Findlast=SPACE(20)
```

```
@ 10, 10 SAY "Enter Last Name of Patient: "
GET Findlast PICTURE "@!"
READ
CLEAR
```

It is here that you arrive at the the point where the program diverges from the Findpat2.prs program. The old program merely displays the data from the table. In such a case, it is a simple matter to use a SELECT/INTO command to fill an array of variables for the display. Here, the matter is more complex because you are not through with the row after you have extracted the data. Because you intend to allow changes and modifications to the data, you must find a way to place the revised data back into the table.

This can be done by creating a cursor for the Admit table. The cursor you need to create is different from the Colnames cursor. Here, it must be an update cursor, which uses two special clauses:

1. **FOR UPDATE OF.** This clause, used with the DECLARE command, opens certain columns for updating. The clause allows SQL to automatically direct an UPDATE command to the specific row and columns indicated by the cursor. This clause creates a link between the cursor operations and the UPDATE command that would not otherwise exist.

2. **WHERE CURRENT OF.** This clause indicates UPDATE should place data into the current cursor row of the table. This clause corresponds to the FOR UPDATE OF clause used with the DECLARE command.

Begin by creating a cursor for the Admit table. The cursor selects all the columns for the row that matches the specified last name. The FOR UPDATE OF is followed by the names of the columns allowed to accept new data. Since this is an editing program, all the columns are declared as open for updating.

```
DECLARE ED CURSOR
FOR SELECT *
FROM Admit
WHERE UPPER(Last)=TRIM(Findlast)
FOR UPDATE OF
    Last,First,Middle,Admit,Discharge,Sex,Age,
Phone,Days_stay,Days_icu,Insured,Payor,Anesthesia,
Truma_team,CT_scan,Charges,Mname,Patient;
```

With the cursor declared, the program will open this cursor.

```
OPEN ED;
```

The FETCH command transfers the data in the columns to the array of memory variables.

```
FETCH ED INTO mv[1],mv[2],mv[3],mv[4],mv[5],mv[6],
mv[7],mv[8],mv[9],mv[10],mv[11],mv[12],mv[13],mv[14],mv[15],
mv[16],mv[17],mv[18];
```

You are now ready to display the information for editing. The loop contains an @/GET command so the values in the mv[] array can be edited as well as displayed. Notice only the first 16 items are displayed. This is because the last two columns, Cname and Patient, are values that can be calculated from other entries. These can be updated based on changes to the Last, First, and Admit columns.

```
Line=1
DO WHILE Line<=18
    @ ROW()+1,0 SAY Colnm[Line]
    @ ROW(),15 GET mv[Line]
    Line=Line+1
ENDDO
READ
```

Following the editing of the variables, you must return to the active SQL cursor row and replace the current values in the columns with the revised values. This is done with UPDATE commands. The UPDATE command is linked to the cursor row by the inclusion of the WHERE CURRENT clause. This clause carries the name of the cursor to indicate the row to be updated. There is no requirement that you update all the columns designated as update columns. In this case, update all the columns to record any changes made during editing. The update instructions can be listed in any order.

```
* update database with
UPDATE Admit SET
Last=mv[1],First=mv[2],Middle=mv[3],Admit=mv[4],
Discharge=mv[5],Age=mv[6],Phone=mv[7],Sex=mv[8],
Days_icu=mv[10],Insured=mv[11],Payor=mv[12],
Anesthesia=mv[13],Truma_team=mv[14]
    WHERE CURRENT OF ED;
```

It is not necessary to update all the columns in one command. Here, a second command completes the updates based on logical values. For example, the Days_stay field is calculated by subtracting the admission date from the discharge date and adding 1.

```
UPDATE Admit
   SET Ct_scan=mv[15],Charges=mv[16],Days_stay=
Discharge-Admit+1,
   Patient=TRIM(Last)+", "+First,Mname=
CMONTH(Admit)
   WHERE CURRENT OF ED;
```

Following the updating, you can close the cursor for that row.

```
         CLOSE ED;
```

The remainder of the program is the same as the previous version, with the exception that a message box has been added to tell the user the SQL database is being closed. One more addition is the DBCHECK command. This command checks the tables against the information stored in the system tables. For example, the command compares the column names listed in the Syscols table with the actual column names of each table. The command is designed to detect problems in the SQL database. It is a good idea to run this command before you close that SQL database.

```
     @ 24,0 SAY "Edit more patients? (Y/N) " GET More PICTURE "Y"
     READ
ENDDO
CLEAR
@ 8,10 TO 12,70
@ 10,30 SAY "Closing SQL Database"
DBCHECK;
STOP DATABASE;
DO Seton
RETURN
```

The entire program reads as follows. The new command lines are highlighted in color.

```
DO Setoff
CLEAR
```

Interactive Programs With SQL Databases ■ 517

```
@ 8,10 TO 12,70
@ 10,30 SAY "Opening SQL Database"
DECLARE mv[18],Colnm[18]
START DATABASE Emerg;
* define column names
SELECT Colname
FROM Syscols
WHERE Tbname="ADMIT"
SAVE TO TEMP Cnames;
Total_rows=SQLCNT
DECLARE Colnames CURSOR FOR
SELECT *
FROM Cnames;
OPEN Colnames;
Position=1
DO WHILE Position<=Total_rows
    FETCH Colnames INTO Ar_value;
    Colnm[Position]=Ar_value
    Position=Position+1
ENDDO
CLOSE Colnames;
* find data for selected patient
More=.T.
DO WHILE More
    CLEAR
    Findlast=SPACE(20)
    @ 10, 10 SAY "Enter Last Name of Patient: ";
     GET Findlast PICTURE "@!"
    READ
    CLEAR
    DECLARE ED CURSOR
    FOR SELECT *
    FROM Admit
    WHERE UPPER(Last)=TRIM(Findlast)
    FOR UPDATE OF
```

```
     Last,First,Middle,Admit,Discharge,Sex,Age, Phone,
     Days_stay,Days_icu,Insured, Payor,Anesthesia,
     Truma_team,Ct_scan, Charges,Mname,Patient;
          OPEN ED;
          FETCH ED INTO mv[1],mv[2],mv[3],mv[4],mv[5],mv[6],
     mv[7],mv[8],mv[9],mv[10],mv[11],mv[12],mv[13],mv[14],mv[15],
     mv[16],mv[17],mv[18];
          Line=1
          DO WHILE Line<=18
               @ ROW()+1,0 SAY Colnm[Line]
               @ ROW(),15 GET mv[Line]
               Line=Line+1
          ENDDO
          READ
          * update database with
          UPDATE Admit SET
     Last=mv[1],First=mv[2],Middle=mv[3],Admit=mv[4],
     Discharge=mv[5],Age=mv[6],Phone=mv[7],
     Sex=mv[8],Days_icu=mv[10],Insured=mv[11],Payor=mv[12],
     Anesthesia=mv[13],Truma_team=mv[14]
          WHERE CURRENT OF ED;
          UPDATE Admit
          SET Ct_scan=mv[15],Charges=mv[16],Days_stay=
     Discharge-Admit+1,
          Patient=TRIM(Last)+", "+First,Mname=
     CMONTH(Admit)
          WHERE CURRENT OF ED;
          CLOSE ED;
          @ 24,0 SAY "Edit more patients? (Y/N) " GET;
           More PICTURE "Y"
          READ
ENDDO
CLEAR
@ 8,10 to 12,70
@ 10,30 SAY "Closing SQL Database"
```

```
DBCHECK;
STOP DATABASE;
DO Seton
RETURN
```

Save and execute the program by pressing Alt-e and typing r. The program displays a message indicating it is opening the SQL database. When the program is ready, you are asked to enter a name.

Tate

The program displays the record for Tate in a format that looks very similar to the dBASE IV edit mode (see Figure 10.10).

Move the cursor down to the middle initial area and press r. Save the record by pressing PgDn. To test the effectiveness of your editing, enter

y
Tate

This time, the record is displayed with an R as the middle initial. This demonstrates you can insert data back into the SQL row from which the information was drawn.

Press PgDn, ↵, and then type

Smith

and press ↵. The program displays the record for Tate again because there is no Smith in the file. When the SELECT command failed to return a row, the program simply continued and displayed the last group of values stored in the memory variables. Press PgDn. This time the program encounters an error (see Figure 10.11).

Figure 10.10

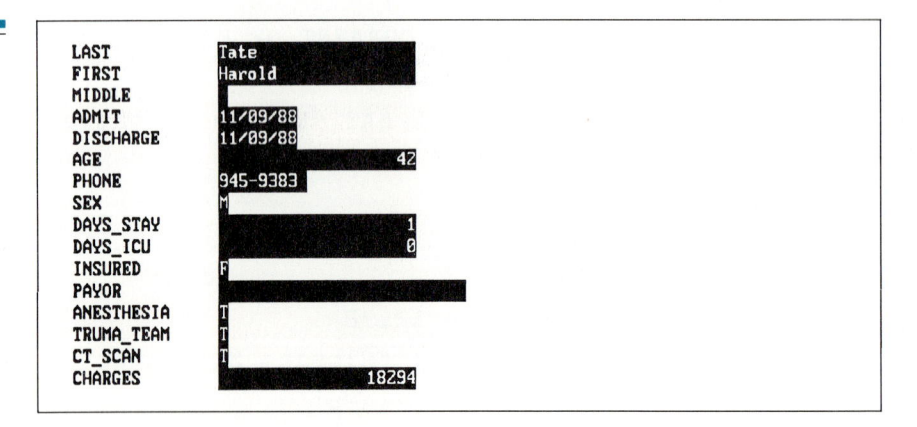

```
LAST        Tate
FIRST       Harold
MIDDLE
ADMIT       11/09/88
DISCHARGE   11/09/88
AGE                                42
PHONE       945-9383
SEX         M
DAYS_STAY                           1
DAYS_ICU                            0
INSURED     F
PAYOR
ANESTHESIA  T
TRUMA_TEAM  T
CT_SCAN     T
CHARGES                         18294
```

Why? The answer relates to a problem with the SELECT command. Because no row was selected, the UPDATE commands related to the cursor position caused dBASE IV to encounter an error. Cancel the program by pressing ⏎. When the dot prompt appears, enter a CLOSE ALL command to free any dBASE IV work areas that were in use at the time the error occurred. Before you do so, use the DISPLAY STATUS command to observe that dBASE IV has been using work areas while executing SQL procedures. Enter

DISPLAY STATUS

The display reveals that work area 9 holds the open database file in the \DBSAMPLE\EMERG directory. This is part of the SQL procedure dBASE IV carries out (see Figure 10.12).

Close the open databases and free up the work areas by pressing Esc and entering

CLOSE DATABASE
DO Seton

SQL Codes

dBASE IV maintains a system variable called SQLCODE. This variable helps programs test the results of an SQL operation. In the Editsql.prs program, entering a name that does not match the contents of the Admit table creates an error. To deal with the error, you need to test the results of the selection before allowing the program to display the information and attempting to perform a replacement.

The SQLCODE variable is set to zero if the SQL command is successful. However, if the SQL command, a SELECT or INSERT, for example, cannot locate any matching rows, the value of SQLCODE

Figure 10.11

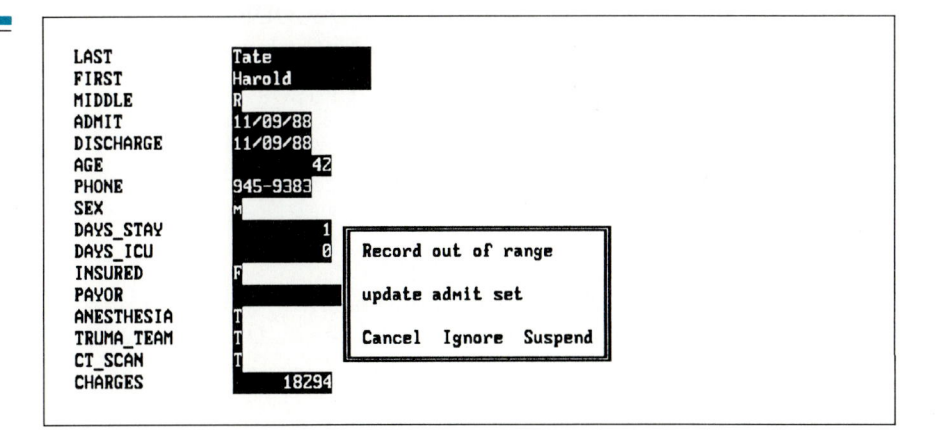

```
LAST         Tate
FIRST        Harold
MIDDLE       R
ADMIT        11/09/88
DISCHARGE    11/09/88
AGE                42
PHONE        945-9383
SEX          M
DAYS_STAY           1
DAYS_ICU            0     ┌─────────────────────────┐
INSURED      F            │ Record out of range     │
PAYOR                     │                         │
ANESTHESIA   T            │ update admit set        │
TRUMA_TEAM   T            │                         │
CT_SCAN      T            │ Cancel  Ignore  Suspend │
CHARGES         18294     └─────────────────────────┘
```

Interactive Programs With SQL Databases ■ 521

Figure 10.12

```
File search path:     \dbsample\emerg
Default disk drive:   D:
Print destination:    PRN:
Margin =       0
Refresh count =       0
Number of files open =    5
Current work area =   1

ALTERNATE  - OFF   DELIMITERS - OFF   FULLPATH  - OFF   SAFETY     - OFF
AUTOSAVE   - OFF   DESIGN     - ON    HEADING   - ON    SCOREBOARD - ON
BELL       - ON    DEVELOP    - ON    HELP      - ON    SPACE      - ON
CARRY      - OFF   DEVICE     - SCRN  HISTORY   - ON    SQL        - OFF
CATALOG    - OFF   ECHO       - OFF   INSTRUCT  - ON    STATUS     - ON
CENTURY    - OFF   ENCRYPTION - ON    INTENSITY - ON    STEP       - OFF
CONFIRM    - OFF   ESCAPE     - ON    LOCK      - ON    TALK       - ON
CONSOLE    - OFF   EXACT      - OFF   NEAR      - OFF   TITLE      - ON
DEBUG      - OFF   ESCAPE     - OFF   PAUSE     - OFF   TRAP       - OFF
DELETED    - OFF   FIELDS     - OFF   PRINT     - OFF   UNIQUE     - OFF

Press any key to continue...
Command                                                                Ins
```

variable is set to 100. You can use SQLCODE to determine if a match has been found for the name.

Load the Editsql.prs program into the editor.

MODIFY COMMAND Editsql.prs

The challenging part to making modifications to programs is the correct placement of the testing commands. In this case, the command IF SQLCODE=0 can permit editing. An ELSE command can display a message if no matching row is found.

Where should the IF SQLCODE=0 command be placed? Your first guess might logically be to place it on line 39, following the command

```
DECLARE ED CURSOR
FOR SELECT *
FROM Admit
WHERE UPPER(Last)=TRIM(Findlast)
FOR UPDATE OF
    Last,First,Middle,Admit,Discharge,Sex,Age,
Phone,Days_stay,Days_icu,Insured,Payor,Anesthesia,
Truma_team,Ct_scan,Charges,Mname,Patient;
```

However, this is not correct because dBASE IV does not actually perform the SELECT indicated in the DECLARE until after an open cursor command. Placing the test after this command fails to detect the difference between a match and a miss.

In order to work properly, the command should be inserted on line 40 following the OPEN ED command. It is the OPEN command that actually seeks the row and subsequently sets the SQLCODE variable according to the results of that search. Make the following change in the program:

Old line: OPEN ED;

                FETCH ED INTO

                mv[1],mv[2],mv[3],mv[4],mv[5],mv[6],

                mv[7],mv[8],mv[9],mv[10],mv[11],mv[12],

                mv[13],mv[14],mv[15],mv[16],mv[17],mv[18];

New line: OPEN ED;

                IF SQLCODE=0

                FETCH ED INTO

                mv[1],mv[2],mv[3],mv[4],mv[5],mv[6],

                mv[7],mv[8],mv[9],mv[10],mv[11],mv[12],

                mv[13],mv[14],mv[15],mv[16],mv[17],mv[18];

The placement of the ELSE/ENDIF structure is also awkward. Keep in mind the IF command occurs after the OPEN cursor command. This means no matter what the value of the SQLCODE variable, there is still an active cursor. It is important to close this cursor before the loop can recycle. If it is not closed, any attempt to search for another name will cause an error. This means the ELSE/ENDIF option should be inserted on line 59, between the UPDATE and CLOSE commands. This makes sense because the UPDATE commands create the error when the cursor command fails to locate a valid row in the table. By branching over the UPDATE commands, you arrive at a point in the program where an alternative action can be taken when no row qualifies. The important point is to make sure the CLOSE cursor command is executed regardless of the number of rows selected. Thus, neither the open or close commands are included in the conditional structure.

Insert the following commands between the UPDATE and CLOSE commands.

Old line: UPDATE Admit
```
          SET Ct_scan=mv[15],Charges=mv[16],Days_
          stay=Discharge-Admit+1,Patient=
          TRIM(Last)+",
          "+First,Mname=CMONTH(Admit)
          WHERE CURRENT OF ED;
          CLOSE ED;
```
New line: UPDATE Admit
```
          SET Ct_scan=mv[15],Charges=mv[16],Days_
          stay=Discharge-Admit+1,Patient=
          TRIM(Last)+",
          "+First,Mname=CMONTH(Admit)
          WHERE CURRENT OF ED;
          ELSE
          CLEAR
          @ 8,10 to 12,70
          @ 10,30 SAY "No Match Found"
          ENDIF
          CLOSE ED;
```

The entire program reads as follows. The new commands appear in color.

```
DO Setoff
CLEAR
@ 8,10 to 12,70
@ 10,30 SAY "Opening SQL Database"
DECLARE mv[18],Colnm[18]
START DATABASE Emerg;
* define column names
SELECT Colname
FROM Syscols
WHERE Tbname="ADMIT"
SAVE TO TEMP Cnames;
Total_rows=SQLCNT
DECLARE Colnames CURSOR FOR
```

```
SELECT *
FROM Cnames;
OPEN Colnames;
Position=1
DO WHILE Position<=Total_rows
    FETCH Colnames INTO Ar_value;
    Colnm[Position]=Ar_value
    Position=Position+1
ENDDO
CLOSE Colnames;
* find data for selected patient
More=.T.
DO WHILE More
    CLEAR
    Findlast=SPACE(20)
    @ 10, 10 SAY "Enter Last Name of Patient: ";
     GET Findlast PICTURE "@!"
    READ
    CLEAR
    DECLARE ED CURSOR
    FOR SELECT *
    FROM Admit
    WHERE UPPER(Last)=TRIM(Findlast)
    For UPDATE OF
Last,First,Middle,Admit,Discharge,Sex,Age,Phone,
Days_stay,Days_icu,Insured,Payor,Anesthesia,
Truma_team,Ct_scan,Charges,Mname,Patient;
    OPEN ED;
    IF SQLCODE=0
        FETCH ED INTO mv[1],mv[2],mv[3],mv[4],mv[5],
mv[6],mv[7],mv[8],mv[9],mv[10],mv[11],mv[12],
mv[13],mv[14],mv[15],mv[16],mv[17],mv[18];
        Line=1
        DO WHILE Line<=18
```

```
                    @ ROW()+1,0 SAY Colnm[Line]
                    @ ROW(),15 GET mv[Line]
                    Line=Line+1
              ENDDO
              READ
              * UPDATE DATABASE WITH
              UPDATE Admit SET Last=mv[1],First=mv[2],
Middle=mv[3],Admit=mv[4],Discharge=mv[5],
Age=mv[6],Phone=mv[7],Sex=mv[8],
Days_icu=mv[10],Insured=mv[11],Payor=mv[12],
Anesthesia=mv[13],Truma_team=mv[14]
              WHERE CURRENT OF ED;
              UPDATE Admit
              SET Ct_scan=mv[15],Charges=mv[16],Days_
stay=Discharge-Admit+1,Patient=TRIM(Last)+",
"+First,Mname=Cmonth(Admit)
              WHERE CURRENT OF ED;
        ELSE
              CLEAR
              @ 8,10 TO 12,70
              @ 10,30 SAY "No Match Found"
        ENDIF
        CLOSE ED;
        @ 24,0 SAY "Edit more patients? (Y/N) "
        GET more PICTURE "Y"
        READ
ENDDO
CLEAR
@ 8,10 TO 12,70
@ 10,30 SAY "Closing SQL Database"
DBCHECK;
STOP DATABASE;
DO Seton
RETURN
```

Save and execute the program by pressing (Alt)-e and typing r. When the program runs, the message **Opening SQL Database** appears on the screen. When the database is opened, you can enter a name to locate. Enter

```
Smith
```

This time, the program tests the results of the OPEN cursor command to determine if a match has been made. In this case, it finds no match and the message **No Match Found** appears.

Continue the search by pressing (⏎). Then enter

```
Goren
```

Since this name is found in the table, a record can be displayed for editing (see Figure 10.13).

Exit the program by pressing (PgDn)-n.

Reports

The previous program demonstrated how SQL databases can be used in programs that create interactive screen displays. Such programs can also allow users easy access for data entry and updates to SQL databases. Programs that provide a user interface for SQL databases are called frontpiece applications. Most SQL systems require programmers to create frontpiece applications. In mainframe computers, these applications are created in standard programming languages like Cobol and Fortran.

Figure 10.13

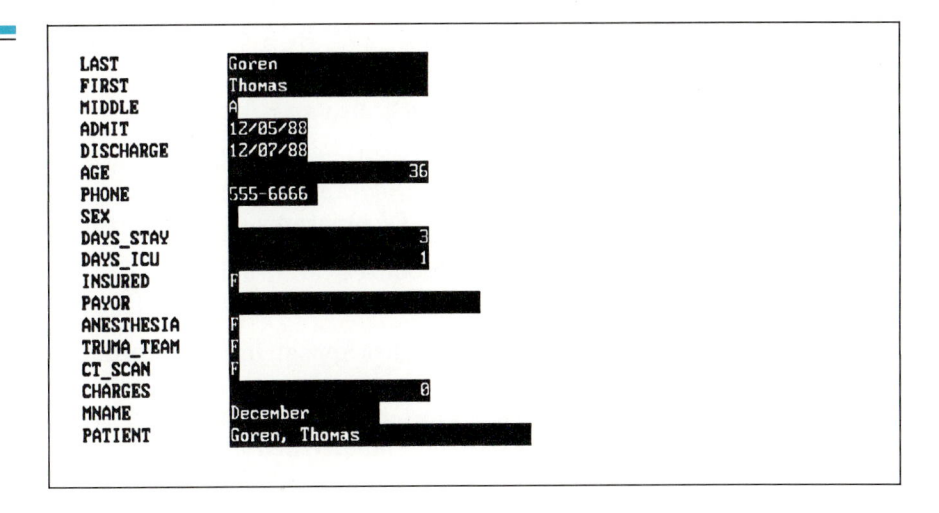

```
LAST         Goren
FIRST        Thomas
MIDDLE       A
ADMIT        12/05/88
DISCHARGE    12/07/88
AGE                                36
PHONE        555-6666
SEX
DAYS_STAY                           3
DAYS_ICU                            1
INSURED      F
PAYOR
ANESTHESIA   F
TRUMA_TEAM   F
CT_SCAN      F
CHARGES                             0
MNAME        December
PATIENT      Goren, Thomas
```

In addition to frontpiece applications, it is usually necessary to create programs that generate reports. There are two ways to handle SQL database information when it comes to reports:

1. **Keep tables.** The KEEP option is used with the SAVE TO TEMP clause of the SELECT command. This command clause creates a standard dBASE IV database file that contains the information transferred to the temporary table. If you perform a selection and place the results into a temporary table with SAVE TO TEMP TABLE NAME KEEP, dBASE IV creates a .dbf file with the same name as the table name in the DBASE directory. The purpose of this is to create a standard dBASE IV database that can be used with normal dBASE IV programs to print reports. This operation avoids the need to create a full dBASE IV SQL print program. Instead, you can simply adapt routines used with standard dBASE IV database files.

2. **SQL direct access.** You can directly access data stored in SQL databases by writing .prs-type programs. These programs use the techniques of declaring SQL cursors and temporary tables, as in the previous application.

If you are familiar with writing dBASE IV report programs, the first solution is the simplest. However, in the following examples, you will learn how to use SQL commands to access SQL database data directly for reports. You will create two types of reports: a simple report that draws data from one table only, and a more complex report that draws data from three tables.

The first report lists the patients in the Admit table with a total and average of the charges and days stayed.

Begin by creating a new program called Rptsql.prs (report SQL) by entering

```
MODIFY COMMAND Rptsql.prs
```

Like normal dBASE IV reports, SQL reports can be written using procedures. SQL programs can use procedures in the same way that standard dBASE IV programs can, with two exceptions.

None of the procedures can use dBASE IV file-related commands or functions like USE, APPEND, LOOKUP(), or RECNO().

SQL commands must appear in logical order. You should avoid using SQL commands in procedures except for the main procedure. Suppose you create a subroutine at the beginning of the file that contains an SQL FETCH command. When dBASE IV compiles the program, it will reject the FETCH command in the subroutine because it has not yet encountered the related DECLARE and OPEN commands in a different procedure farther down in the file. The subroutines in a .prs procedure program should be restricted to standard dBASE IV commands when possible.

With these two provisions in mind, begin to create the application. The first procedure prints the headings at the top of the page.

```
PROCEDURE Heading
SET DEVICE TO PRINT
Title="Patient Report"
@ 5,(80-LEN(Title))/2 SAY Title
@ PROW()+2,  5 SAY "Patient"
@ PROW(),   27 SAY "Admit"
@ PROW(),   37 SAY "Disch."
@ PROW(),   52 SAY "Charges"
@ PROW(),   63 SAY "Day"
SET DEVICE TO SCREEN
RETURN
```

The next procedure, the page-end routine, creates a page break and resumes printing at the top of the next page.

```
PROCEDURE Endpage
SET DEVICE TO PRINT
@ 59,38 SAY "-"+LTRIM(STR(Pageno))+"-"
SET DEVICE TO SCREEN
Pageno=Pageno+1
EJECT
DO Heading
RETURN
```

The third procedure, a summary procedure, prints the totals and averages at the end of the program.

```
PROCEDURE Summary
SET DEVICE TO PRINT
@ PROW()+1,  0 SAY REPLICATE("=",75)
@ PROW()+1,  0 SAY "Totals"
@ PROW(),   47 SAY t1 PICTURE "9,999,999.99"
```

Reports ■ 529

```
@ PROW(),    62 SAY t2 PICTURE "9,999"
@ PROW()+1,   0 SAY "Averages"
@ PROW(),    47 SAY t1/Total_rows PICTURE;
 "9,999,999.99"
@ PROW(),    62 SAY t2/Total_rows PICTURE "9,999.9"
@ 59,38 SAY "-"+LTRIM(STR(Pageno))+"-"
SET DEVICE TO SCREEN
EJECT
RETURN
```

With these three subroutines in place, you are ready to create the main procedure of the report. Begin the procedure by running the Set-off program and printing the headings at the top of the first page.

```
PROCEDURE Report
DO Setoff
DO Heading
```

The program requires three memory variables: two to accumulate totals for charges and days, and a third to count pages.

```
STORE 0 TO t1,t2
Pageno=1
```

The next step is to gain access to the SQL database.

```
START DATABASE Emerg;
```

In order to print a formatted report, it is necessary to create an SQL cursor for the information you want to print. In this case, use a cursor called RPT for the Patient, Admit, Discharge, and Charges columns. Days stayed can be calculated from the discharge and admit dates and does not need to be transferred from the SQL database. The ORDER BY clause sequences the records by patient name.

```
DECLARE RPT CURSOR FOR
SELECT Patient,Admit,Discharge,Charges
FROM Admit
ORDER BY Patient;
```

Next, open the cursor so you can gain access to the data in the first row of the selection.

```
OPEN RPT;
```

For a report, you want to create a loop that cycles once for each row in the selection. In dBASE IV, the test .NOT. EOF() controls a loop such as this. There is no EOF() function in SQL. However, in SQL the selection actually takes place before you begin the loop. The system variable SQLCNT (SQL count) can determine the number of cycles necessary to print all the rows. This value is transferred to a user variable, Total_rows, because SQL changes SQLCNT after each SQL command. The variable line counts the rows as they print.

```
Total_rows=Sqlcnt
Line=1
DO WHILE Line<=Total_rows
```

The first command inside the loop is the SQL FETCH command. This command transfers the values from the first row of the selection into a series of memory variables. The number of variables used in the selection must exactly match the number of columns specified in the cursor selection.

```
    FETCH RPT INTO mv1,mv2,mv3,mv4;
```

The first use of the memory variables is to display a message indicating how much of the selected data has been processed.

```
    @ 10,10 SAY "Printing ";
     +STR(Line/Total_rows*100)+"% complete."
```

You are now ready to set the DEVICE TO the printer and output the contents of the first row as stored in the memory variables. LINE prints a number for each row. The mv3 and mv2 variables, which hold discharge and admit dates respectively, are used to calculate the value of the days stayed.

```
        SET DEVICE TO PRINT
        @ PROW()+1,  0 SAY LTRIM(STR(Line))+"."
        @ PROW(),    5 SAY mv1;
         PICTURE "XXXXXXXXXXXXXXXXXXXX"
        @ PROW(),   27 SAY mv2
        @ PROW(),   37 SAY mv3
        @ PROW(),   47 SAY mv4 PICTURE "9,999,999.99"
        @ PROW(),   62 SAY mv3-mv2 PICTURE "9,999"
        SET DEVICE TO SCREEN
```

Following the printing, the counters and accumulators are incremented.

```
Line=Line+1
t1=t1+mv4
t2=t2+mv3-mv2
```

Before the loop concludes, test for the end of page. The ENDDO then cycles the program back to the top of the loop to print the next row in selection.

```
    IF PROW()>55
        DO Endpage
    ENDIF
ENDDO
```

When all the rows in the selection have been printed, you can close the SQL cursor, run the subroutine that prints the totals and averages, and then close the files.

```
CLOSE RPT;
DO Summary
STOP DATABASE;
DO Seton
RETURN
```

The entire program's four procedures looks like this:

```
PROCEDURE Heading
SET DEVICE TO PRINT
Title="Patient Report"
@ 5,(80-LEN(Title))/2 SAY Title
@ PROW()+2, 5 SAY "Patient"
@ PROW(),   27 SAY "Admit"
@ PROW(),   37 SAY "Disch."
@ PROW(),   52 SAY "Charges"
@ PROW(),   63 SAY "Days"
SET DEVICE TO SCREEN
RETURN
PROCEDURE Endpage
SET DEVICE TO PRINT
```

```
@ 59,38 SAY "-"+LTRIM(STR(Pageno))+"-"
SET DEVICE TO SCREEN
Pageno=Pageno+1
EJECT
DO Heading
RETURN
PROCEDURE Summary
SET DEVICE TO PRINT
@ PROW()+1, 0 SAY REPLICATE("=",75)
@ PROW()+1, 0 SAY "Totals"
@ PROW(),   47 SAY t1 PICTURE "9,999,999.99"
@ PROW(),   62 SAY t2 PICTURE "9,999"
@ PROW()+1, 0 SAY "Averages"
@ PROW(),   47 SAY t1/Total_rows PICTURE;
 "9,999,999.99"
@ PROW(),   62 SAY t2/Total_rows PICTURE "9,999.9"
@ 59,38 SAY "-"+LTRIM(STR(Pageno))+"-"
SET DEVICE TO SCREEN
EJECT
RETURN
PROCEDURE Report
DO Setoff
DO Heading
STORE 0 to t1,t2
Pageno=1
START DATABASE emerg;
DECLARE RPT CURSOR FOR
SELECT Patient,Admit,Discharge,Charges
FROM Admit
ORDER BY Patient;
OPEN RPT;
Total_rows=Sqlcnt
Line=1
DO WHILE Line<=Total_rows
```

```
            FETCH RPT INTO mv1,mv2,mv3,mv4;
            @ 10,10 SAY "Printing "+STR(Line/Total_;
             rows*100)+"% complete."
            SET DEVICE TO PRINT
            @ PROW()+1,  0 SAY LTRIM(STR(Lline))+"."
            @ PROW(),    5 SAY mv1 PICTURE;
             "XXXXXXXXXXXXXXXXXXXX"
            @ PROW(),   27 SAY mv2
            @ PROW(),   37 SAY mv3
            @ PROW(),   47 SAY mv4 PICTURE "9,999,999.99"
            @ PROW(),   62 SAY mv3-mv2 PICTURE "9,999"
            SET DEVICE TO SCREEN
            Line=Line+1
            t1=t1+mv4
            t2=t2+mv3-mv2
            IF PROW()>55
                DO Endpage
            ENDIF
     ENDDO
     CLOSE RPT;
     DO Summary
     STOP DATABASE;
     DO Seton
     RETURN
```

Save the program by pressing (Ctrl)-(End). Compile the procedure file by entering

```
COMPILE Rptsql.prs
```

To execute a procedure file, you need to open the procedure file by entering

```
SET PROCEDURE to Rptsql.prs
```

Execute the report program by entering

```
DO Report
```

The program opens the SQL database and prints the data selected by the process used in the program of transferring data, one row at a time, to dBASE IV memory variables and prints those variables with @/SAY commands.

Remember to close the procedure file by entering

CLOSE PROCEDURE

Multi-Table Reports

The Rptsql.prs program demonstrates how information stored in SQL databases can be transferred to dBASE IV reports. The program is a simple one because only a single table of data is involved. But the techniques used in the program can be expanded to create reports capable of gathering related data from more than one table in the SQL database. Since the primary advantage of SQL databases is access to multiple tables, this type of direct access report is an important tool.

The report you are about to create requires data from three SQL tables in the Emerg database: Admit, Patcare, and Doctors. The report prints information about each patient in the Admit table. However, unlike the previous program, it also lists physician information, if any, for that patient.

To do this, the program checks the Patcare table as each record is printed to see if there is any physician information for that patient. If there is, you must draw data from Patcare and Doctors in order to list the physician data on the report.

As with the previous program, we'll use procedures to write this program. The procedures contain standard dBASE IV only. All the SQL operations take place in the main procedure of program, the last procedure in the file.

Create the program by entering

MODIFY COMMAND Rptsql1.prs

The program begins with seven procedures. Each of these is a subroutine used to print one part of the report.

1. **Head_page.** Print the headings at the top of the page.
2. **End_page.** Print the page number at the bottom of a page and the headings at the top of the next page.
3. **End_rpt.** Print the final page number on the last page of the report.
4. **Head_pat.** Print the headings for the patient information. This routine will be printed before each line of patient data.

5. **Head_doc.** Print the headings for the physician information. This routine will print before each group of physicians.
6. **Prt_pat.** This routine prints one row of patient information.
7. **Prt_doc.** This routine prints one row of doctor information.

Begin with the page heading, ending, and final page routines.

```
PROCEDURE Head_page
SET DEVICE TO PRINT
Title="Patient Report"
@ 5,(80-LEN(Title))/2 SAY Title
@ 6,0 SAY REPLICATE("=",75)
SET DEVICE TO SCREEN
RETURN
PROCEDURE End_page
SET DEVICE TO PRINT
@ 59,38 SAY "-"+LTRIM(STR(Pageno))+"-"
SET DEVICE TO SCREEN
Pageno=Pageno+1
EJECT
DO Head_page
RETURN
PROCEDURE End_rpt
SET DEVICE TO PRINT
@ 59,38 SAY "-"+LTRIM(STR(Pageno))+"-"
SET DEVICE TO SCREEN
EJECT
RETURN
```

The next two procedures print the headings before the patient and doctor information lines.

```
PROCEDURE Head_pat
SET DEVICE TO PRINT
@ PROW()+2,  5 SAY "Patient"
@ PROW(),   27 SAY "Admit"
@ PROW(),   37 SAY "Disch."
@ PROW(),   52 SAY "Charges"
```

```
@ PROW(),   63 SAY "Days"
SET DEVICE TO SCREEN
RETURN
PROCEDURE Head_doc
SET DEVICE TO PRINT
@ PROW()+1, 5 SAY "Physician"
@ PROW(),   35 SAY "Date"
@ PROW(),   45 SAY "Field"
@ PROW(),   65 SAY "Med Rec #"
SET DEVICE TO SCREEN
RETURN
```

You are now ready to prepare procedures that actually print the data drawn from the SQL database. In the following procedure, four memory variables, pv1, pv2, pv3, and pv4, are used to print the data transferred by the FETCH command. Days stayed is calculated by subtracting the discharge and admit dates.

```
PROCEDURE Prt_pat
SET DEVICE TO PRINT
@ PROW()+1, 0 SAY LTRIM(STR(Line))+"."
@ PROW(),   5 SAY pv1;
  PICTURE "XXXXXXXXXXXXXXXXXXX"
@ PROW(),   27 SAY pv2
@ PROW(),   37 SAY pv3
@ PROW(),   47 SAY pv4 PICTURE "9,999,999.99"
@ PROW(),   62 SAY pv3-pv2 PICTURE "9,999"
SET DEVICE TO SCREEN
RETURN
```

The final subroutine prints a row of physician information. It uses four memory variables, dv1, dv2, dv3, and dv4. The dv3 variable holds the name of the medical field and uses a PICTURE clause of 19 characters to make sure it does not overflow into the next column.

```
PROCEDURE Prt_doc
SET DEVICE TO PRINT
@ PROW()+1, 5 SAY dv1
@ PROW(),   35 SAY dv2
```

```
  @ PROW(), 45 SAY dv3;
  PICTURE "XXXXXXXXXXXXXXXXXX"
  @ PROW(), 65 SAY dv4
SET DEVICE TO SCREEN
RETURN
```

You are ready to attempt the main program procedure, which begins with running Setoff and printing the heading at the top of the first page.

```
PROCEDURE Report
DO Setoff
DO Head_page
```

Next, set the page number to 1.

```
Pageno=1
```

Now access the SQL database.

```
START DATABASE Emerg;
```

The first operation in the database is to select the information from the Admit table. This information is the patient data stored in the Patient, Admit, Discharge, and Charges columns. The first command creates an SQL cursor for the data ordered by the patient's name.

```
DECLARE RPT CURSOR FOR
SELECT Patient,Admit,Discharge,Charges
FROM Admit
ORDER BY Patient;
```

With the cursor declared, you can open the cursor so you can gain access to the information.

```
OPEN RPT;
```

To control the main processing loop, the value of SQLCNT determines the number of cycles the main processing loop should make. This value is copied into the Total_rows variable. The Line variable counts the number of patients. The value of SQLCNT is set to the number of rows in the selection following the OPEN, not the DECLARE command.

```
Total_rows=Sqlcnt
Line=1
DO WHILE Line<=Total_rows
```

538 ∎ **Programming in SQL**

The first operation inside the loop uses the FETCH command to draw information from the current row in the selection. This is the same procedure used in the previous program to access each row of information.

```
FETCH RPT INTO pv1,pv2,pv3,pv4;
```

With the information stored in the variables, you can print the patient data using the two subroutines Head_pat, to print the headings, and Prt_pat to print the data under the headings.

```
DO Head_pat
```

```
DO Prt_pat
```

The screen display is updated to tell the user how much of the data in the selection has been printed.

```
@ 10,10 SAY "Printing "+STR(Line/Total_;
rows*100)+"% complete."
Line=Line+1
```

With the patient information sent to the printer, you must consider how to obtain the physician information related to this patient, if any.

The key is the Patcare table, which contains the names of patients and the doctors who treated them. Determine if the current patient has records in the Patcare table by selecting records from Patcare, based on the current value of the memory variable pv1, which holds the name of the patient as drawn from the current cursor row.

If there are rows in the Patcare table that match the patient's name, you must print those rows. The simplest procedure is to perform a selection on the Patcare table and save the results in a temporary table. Using the temporary table to hold the results then allows you to create a cursor for the physician information so it can be sent to the printer. In this example, the temporary table is called Doclist.

```
* search for treatment data
SELECT *
FROM Patcare
WHERE Patient=pv1
SAVE TO TEMP Doclist;
```

Immediately following the selection, you must determine if any rows in the Patcare table match the current patient name. You can test the system variable, SQLCODE. Remember that this variable is 0 if one or more rows are selected, and 100 if no rows are selected. In this case, test for a zero value.

```
IF SQLCODE=0
```

If the value of SQLCODE is zero, you know you have at least one physician for that patient. Thus, you must declare a cursor for the temporary table. In this report there are two cursors active at one time: the RPT cursor, which is related to the Admit table, and the DOCS cursor, which is used for physician information.

The DOCS cursor is the result of a multiple table selection. The report requires two columns from Patcare, physician name and care date, and two columns from the Doctors table, Field and Medical record number. To obtain this information, the selection must create a logical link between the data in the Patcare and Doctors tables using the WHERE clause. The expression Doclist.Doctor=Doctors.Doctor causes dBASE IV SQL to link the rows of the two tables by matching doctor's names. The name of the table is used along with the column name to avoid ambiguity when both tables have columns with that name.

```
* PRINT Doctor List
DECLARE DOCS CURSOR FOR
    SELECT Doclist.Doctor,Date_care,Field,
Med_rec_no
    FROM Doclist,Doctors
    WHERE Doclist.Doctor=Doctors.Doctor;
```

The DOCS cursor can now access the row or rows of physician information. The second cursor is opened.

```
OPEN DOCS;
```

When the OPEN command executes, you can determine the number of physicians related to this patient. The variable Total_docs is assigned this value. The variable Docline counts the number of physicians printed.

```
Total_docs=SQLCNT
Docline=1
```

Before the doctor data prints, the headings are printed using a subroutine.

```
DO Head_doc
```

The next step is to enter an inner loop that FETCHes the data for each of the doctors and prints the data.

```
DO WHILE Docline<=Total_docs
    FETCH Docs INTO dv1,dv2,dv3,dv4;
    DO Prt_doc
    Docline=Docline+1
ENDDO
```

When the loop completes, the patient information and all the physician information, if any, related to that patient, is printed. You have finished printing a complete unit of data. In this type of report the number of lines printed for each unit will vary.

The next step is an important one: You must close the DOCS cursor and remove the temporary table, Doclist, from the database. SQL maintains a temporary database until you close the SQL cursor. In this situation, the Emerg database is still open. However, as the loop moves through the next cycle, the program attempts to create another temporary table called Doclist for the next patient. If there was already a table called Doclist in the database, an error would occur. Thus, it is necessary to remove the table using the DROP TABLE command. Also keep in mind the cursor must be closed before you attempt to drop the table.

```
    CLOSE DOCS;
ENDIF
```

It is important to understand the correct placement of the DROP TABLE command following the ENDIF. This means DROP TABLE executes whether or not the temporary table Doclist contains any rows. Put another way, when the SELECT command creates a temporary table, the table exists even if no rows of data are added to it. In dBASE IV terms, SQL creates a data file as part of the command before it determines if any rows qualify. This means once the SELECT/SAVE TO TEMP clause is executed, a DROP TABLE command is needed regardless of the number of rows, if any, transferred to this table.

```
    DROP TABLE Doclist;
```

The outer loop concludes with a test for the end of the page.

```
        IF PROW()>55
            DO End_page
        ENDIF
ENDDO
```

When the outer loop is complete, the program completes the last page of printing and closes the SQL database.

```
CLOSE RPT;
DO End_rpt
STOP DATABASE;
DO Seton
RETURN
```

Save the program by pressing (Ctrl)-(End). Compile and run the procedure. Try this on your own. If you need help, the correct command can be found at the end of the chapter in the Answers to Exercises section under exercise 1.

The program executes and prints a report listing all the patients and any physicians who treated those patients. The program executes more slowly than typical dBASE IV reports because dBASE IV SQL operates more slowly than standard dBASE IV.

Note: In programming terms, dBASE IV acts as an interpreter for dBASE IV SQL. Since dBASE IV is already an interpreter of the dBASE IV language, you find a situation where dBASE IV translates dBASE IV SQL, which in turn is translated back to machine level commands. This process degrades the performance of SQL databases compared to standard dBASE IV databases.

When the program completes printing, close the procedure file by entering

```
CLOSE PROCEDURE
```

The Rptsql1.prs program illustrates the use of multiple cursors to draw blocks of related information from SQL database tables and transfer them to standard dBASE IV output routines. The result is a report that directly accesses multiple SQL data tables.

Summary

This chapter covered the creation of dBASE IV programs that directly access information stored in SQL databases, and emphasized the following concepts:

dBSE IV SQL system. The dBASE IV SQL system uses a series of related dBASE IV files to create an SQL-type environment. All of the files related to an SQL database are stored in a single MS-DOS directory with the same name as the database. In this directory there are two types of files: SQL system files and data files. The SQL system files are used by dBASE IV SQL to maintain a catalog of tables, columns, and other SQL data. The system files can be accessed by using SQL table selection commands aimed at the system tables, Systabls or Syscols. The system files are marked as read-only, in order to prevent accidental changes to these files.

SQL programs. dBASE IV allows you to create programs to perform SQL operations. Program files that work with SQL databases, rather than standard dBASE IV databases, must use a .prs file extension. These files are compiled by dBASE IV differently than normal dBASE IV program files. SQL programs are checked against the information stored in the current SQL database. Normal dBASE IV compiling does not check references to files or fields. SQL compiling checks references to databases, tables, and columns to make sure they match the existing information. You can execute programs that use dBASE IV databases as subroutines.

SQL procedures. SQL programs can be written with modular procedure techniques available for normal dBASE IV programs. You cannot use standard dBASE IV file commands, USE, APPEND, etc., in SQL procedures. Also note the dBASE IV SQL compiler will not allow SQL commands in procedures if they are not in logical sequence. It is best to group all SQL commands in a single procedure.

SQL cursors. The basic tool in SQL programming is the cursor. The SQL cursor is roughly equivalent to the record pointer in standard dBASE IV file operations. In SQL, a cursor is created by performing a selection from a database table. The cursor can then be used to move row by row though the database. SQL cursors can move only one row at a time and always in a forward direction.

DECLARE. Creates a cursor. An SQL cursor is a logical object. This means when you declare a cursor, SQL records the logical requirements but does not physically draw the data from tables. This is important to remember when you want to test the results of a cursor operation because a DECLARE command does not reset the system variables SQLCODE or SQLCNT. That occurs following the OPEN command. The DECLARE command requires an SQL SELECT command nested as the argument for the cursor. When the declared cursor is opened, SQL executes the selection.

OPEN. This command opens a cursor. **Opening** means the selection specified in the DECLARE command is actually implemented.

FETCH. FETCH transfers the information from the current cursor row into a series of memory variables. Following an OPEN command, FETCH will operate on the first row of the cursor selection. Each subsequent FETCH command draws data from the next row. The number of variables in a FETCH command must equal the number of columns in the DECLARE/SELECT command.

CLOSE. This command closes a specified cursor. Closing a cursor does not release the specification. You can reopen the same cursor at a later point in the same program. If so, the FETCH command will begin again at the first row in the selection.

SAVE TO TEMP. This clause can be used with a SELECT command to create a new, temporary table that contains only the information extracted by the selection. The temporary table will remain in the SQL database until it is stopped. If you add the KEEP option to the clause, dBASE IV SQL will create a standard dBASE IV database file with the same contents and structure as the temporary table.

DROP. This command deletes tables or entire databases. This command can be used to remove a temporary table from a database without stopping the database.

DBCHECK. This command performs a check in which the information in the SQL system files is checked against the actual SQL tables in the database. Any inconsistencies are reported with messages.

System variables. dBASE IV SQL maintains two memory variables. SQLCNT contains a value corresponding to the number of rows affected by the last SQL command. SQLCODE contains a value indicating the status of the last SQL command. A value of zero indicates a normal execution. A value of 100 indicates normal execution but no rows selected. This is usually the result of a selection criterion that does not match the database information. If an error occurs during execution, the value is set to −1.

Review Problems for Chapter 10

1. Create an SQL program that allows the user to display the customer information for a selected customer from the Cust table.

2. Create an SQL program that allows you to edit a row of information from the Prods table.

3. Create an SQL program that prints a list of data from the Sales table including date, company, item name, and total amount.

4. Create an SQL program that prints the products listed in the Sales table, their price, discount, and total amount.

Answers to Exercises

1. Compile and run Rptsql1.PRS program.

   ```
   COMPILE Rptsql1.prs
   SET PROCEDURE TO Rptsql1.prs
   DO Report
   ```

Index

accumulators,
  setting up; 234
  summary description; 254
ACTIVATE POPUP command,
  creating popup menus with; 282
  summary description; 308
activating,
  See Also returning to;
  Assist mode; 5
  input areas; 145
ALIAS clause (USE command),
  creating aliases with; 321
aliases,
  creating; 321
  summary description; 372
aligning,
  numbers under column headings; 124
Alt-e,
  saving text with; 53
altering,
  See changing;
.AND.,
  logical connective, using for selecting records; 66
append,
  mode, how different from edit mode; 23
APPEND BLANK command,
  how different from EDIT and APPEND; 203

APPEND command,
  adding records with; 155
  how different from APPEND BLANK; 203
APPEND FROM command,
  batch processing with; 210
  summary description; 254
Append/Edit/Browse display,
  entering data with; 23
appending records,
  in append mode, 23
  with APPEND BLANK command, 202
application,
  definition; 2
arrays,
  data management using; 244
  handling SQL cursors with; 510
  menu options storage as; 259
  printing reports with; 425
  processing with a loop; 248
  single-dimensional, setting up; 245
  summary description; 254
assigning,
  values to more than one variable; 144
Assist mode,
  characteristics of; 4
  exiting; 5
  returning to; 5
* (asterisk) character,

  wildcard in SQL; 462
AT clause (? question command),
  controlling horizontal screen location with; 105
  purpose; 103
  summary description; 134
@ (at) command,
  clauses summary description; 184
  controlling vertical screen location with; 139, 193
  drawing boxes with TO clause; 148
  summary description; 184
AT function,
  locating characters with; 352
@ (at) M function,
  selection control with; 226
auto-indent,
  indenting commands with; 191
AVERAGE command,
  using in statistical programs; 117
AVERAGE function,
  summary description; 135
AVG function,
  CALCULATE command use of; 118
  SQL; 464

backing up,
  database files; 40
  before rollbacks, 208
BAR function,
  creating popup menus with; 283

Index   ■   I-1

Bar function (*continued*)
    summary description; 308
batch processing,
    data entry handling by; 210
    summary description; 254
BEGIN TRANSACTION command,
    rollback operations handling with; 205
BETWEEN SQL operator,
    description; 467
boxes,
    drawing; 148
branching,
    control structures; 188
    summary description; 251
breakpoints,
    debugging with; 272
    summary description; 307
CALCULATE command,
    using in statistical programs; 118
CALCULATE function,
    summary description; 135
calculation,
    programs; 143
Caps Lock key,
    status monitoring by scoreboard; 98
case,
    converting to text strings to upper case; 104
    sensitivity,
        methods for handling, 65
        SQL problems with, 473
CASE command,
    summary description; 252
categories,
    handling with a DO CASE command; 229
CDOW function,
    purpose; 63
changing,
    See Also editing;
    data; 35
        with SQL UPDATE, 473
    field types from character to date; 11
    files; 205
    memo text line length; 164
    record display,
        from forms view to table view, 22
    screen color; 149
characters,
    data, entering; 18
    field type, changing to data field type; 11
    fields,
        concatenating with +, 82
        extracting substrings from, 351
        syntax and use, 10
    graphics, designing screen displays with; 109
    repeating, using in screen displays; 108
    special, how to insert in text string; 108

variables, length of; 97
CHR function,
    inserting special characters with; 108
    summary description; 135
clauses,
    command components; 58
    question mark (?) command
        summary description; 134
CLEAR clause (@ at command),
    clearing screen areas with; 149
CLEAR command,
    clearing screens with; 30
    summary description; 43
    suppressing text output with; 99
clearing,
    screen areas with; 149
    screen display
        areas; 343
        lines; 329
    screens; 30
CLOSE DATABASE command,
    closing database files with; 36
    summary description; 43
CLOSE SQL command,
    handling cursors with; 508
    summary description; 544
closing,
    See Also ending, terminating;
    files; 36
CMONTH function,
    purpose; 63
CNT function,
    CALCULATE command use of; 118
    using in statistical programs; 121
COL function,
    obtaining current cursor column with; 231
color,
    changing screen; 149
columns,
    headings, aligning numbers under; 124
Command mode,
    characteristics of; 5
    entering; 5
    terminating commands in; 5
commands,
    components of; 57
    history, using commands from; 34
    indenting; 190
    sequence types description,
        branched, 49
        linear, 49
        looped, 49
comments,
    program, creating; 99
comparing,
    data items using logical comparison operators ; 60
compile,
    differences between dBASE IV use and traditional use; 4

compiling,
    how different in dBASE IV; 53
    summary description; 88
concatenating,
    character fields with + operator; 82
conditional,
    processing implicit contrasted with explicit; 213
    structures summary description; 252
control structures,
    DO CASE; 229
    IIF function; 167
    interactive; 138
    linear; 50
    loops and branches (chapter); 187
    techniques for managing; 150
controlling,
    program flow; 150
converting,
    numbers into strings; 157
COPY command,
    summary description; 43
COPY STRUCTURE command,
    batch processing with; 210
    copying database structures with; 41
COPY TO command,
    copying database files with; 41
copying,
    files; 40
        cautions , 10
    text blocks; 126
COUNT command,
    counting records with; 29
COUNT function,
    SQL; 464
counters,
    setting up; 241
    summary description; 254
counting,
    records; 28
CREATE command,
    creating database files with; 8
creating,
    aliases; 321
    array variables; 246
    calculation programs; 143
    display frames; 220
    filters; 68
    frequency distribution programs; 218
    global field lists; 75
    index files in descending order; 80
    links; 350
    menu bars; 334
    menus; 257
        popup, 282
    multiple screen displays; 167
    popup menu item lists; 298
    procedures; 338
    programs,
        linear, 51
        modular, 72
        using MODIFY COMMAND command, 51
    relations; 354

screen displays,
  customized, 154
  fully structured, 138
SQL databases; 448
statistical programs; 117
subroutines; 77
variables,
  date, 95
  private, 278
Ctl-End,
  saving text with; 53
Ctl-Home keys,
  viewing memo field contents with; 164
CTOD function,
  creating date variables with; 96
  description; 63
{} (curly brackets),
  character to date conversion with; 467
cursors,
  positioning; 145
  SQL; 508

data entry,
  See Also entering data;
  batch processing of; 210
  mode characteristics; 23
  REPLACE command use for; 35
data items,
  as structure component; 6
data types,
  mixing in indexes; 83
  mixing with @/SAY/GET; 142
databases,
  creating SQL; 448
  files,
    characteristics, 6
    copying, 10
    creating, 8
    how different from word processing files, 6
    summary description, 42
  listing contents of; 31
  manager, summary description; 42
  multiple,
    differences between SQL handling and dBASE handling, 478
    handling (chapter), 314
    opening, 318
    selecting information in SQL, 478
    summary description, 372
  object, command component description; 57
  relational, handling (chapter); 314
  scanning the; 219
  SQL, how different from dBASE IV databases; 444
  structure,
    building, 11
    definition, 6
    listing the, 32
    saving, 17
    size limit, 17

date,
  displaying the current; 112
  entering a; 18
  field type,
    changing field types from character to date, 11
  fields,
    summary description, 42
    syntax and use, 10
    using to select records, 62
  functions, description and table of; 63
  variables,
    creating, 95
    length of, 97
DATE function,
  obtaining the current date with; 112
  summary description; 135
DAY function,
  purpose; 63
dBASE III,
  differences from dBASE IV, memo fields, 16
dBASE IV,
  advantages as database application programming language; 3
  characteristics as programming language and as application; 2
  SQL system summary description; 543
,DBASE,SQLHOME,
  directory for dBASE SQL files; 490
DBCHECK SQL command,
  checking SQL tables with; 517
  summary description; 544
.dbf,
  field information file extension (except memo fields); 10
DBF function,
  meaning; 156
.dbo,
  compiled file extension; 53
.dbt,
  memo file extension; 10
DEACTIVATE POPUP command,
  creating popup menus with; 283
  summary description; 308
DEBUG command,
  debugging programs with; 268
debugging,
  (chapter); 257
  programs, techniques for; 268
  summary description; 307
decimal,
  numbers, entering; 19
  variables, length of; 97
Decimals option (CREATE command),
  syntax and use; 10
DECLARE command,
  setting up arrays with; 245
  summary description; 254
DECLARE SQL command,
  handling cursors with; 508
  summary description; 544

default mode,
  Assist mode as; 4
DEFINE BAR command,
  creating popup menus with; 282
  summary description; 308
DEFINE POPUP command,
  creating popup menus with; 282
  summary description; 308
delete attribute of current record,
  status monitoring by scoreboard; 98
DELETE command,
  marking records for deletion with; 29
deleting,
  all records with ZAP; 457
  records,
    advantages of two-step method, 30
    method for, 29
    summary description, 43
DIR command,
  listing files in a directory with; 41
directory,
  dBASE SQL files; 490
  listing the files in; 41
disk,
  free space; 156
DISKSPACE function,
  meaning; 156
DISPLAY command,
  summary description; 43
display frames,
  advantages over format files; 221
  creating; 220
DISPLAY MEMORY command,
  listing memory variables with; 95
DISPLAY STATUS command,
  listing available index tags with; 85
displaying,
  field input areas; 157
displaying ,
  multiple pages; 167
displaying,
  records using forms view; 22
  SQL database information; 494
  values in the debugger; 270
DISTINCT clause (SELECT SQL command),
  selecting unique values with; 470
  summary description; 487
DO CASE command,
  handling CASE structures with; 231
  summary description; 252
DO command,
  executing programs with; 74
  summary description; 88
DO WHILE command,
  controlling program loops with; 195
  differences with the SCAN command; 227
  summary description; 252
DO WHILE .NOT. EOF command,
  controlling a scanning loop with; 221
documenting,
  programs, indenting conventions for; 190

Index   I-3

$ (dollar) operator,
  case sensitivity handling with; 65
  IN SQL operator simularity to; 467
  logical connective use with; 67
  restrictions on use; 60
  string handling with; 64
dot prompt,
  accessing from the debugger; 276
  meaning and use; 5
DOW function,
  purpose; 63
drawing,
  boxes with @ command TO clause; 148
DROP command,
  summary description; 544
DTOC function,
  description; 63
dumps,
  listing information; 31

edit,
  mode, how different from append mode; 23
EDIT command,
  adding records with; 155
  how different from APPEND BLANK; 203
editing,
  See Also changing;
  programs, techniques for; 125
  SQL rows; 513
EJECT command,
  See Also reports;
  ejecting pages with; 36
  summary description; 43, 439
ELSE command,
  branching control structure use of; 189
  summary description; 252
End key,
  moving to record end in table display; 22
end of file,
  detecting; 39
  loop to handle; 221
END TRANSACTION command,
  rollback operations handling with; 206
ENDCASE command,
  handling CASE structures with; 232
  summary description; 252
ENDDO command,
  summary description; 252
ENDIF command,
  branching control structure use of; 188
  summary description; 252
ending,
  See Also terminating;
ENDSCAN command,
  summary description; 253
entering,
  character data; 18

Command mode; 5
data,
  batch processing of, 210
  from other databases, 324
  in Command mode, 23
  in SQL, 452
date,
  data, 18
logical,
  data, 19
memo,
  data, 15, 20
numeric,
  data, 19
environment,
  setting up for screen displays; 98
environmental commands,
  summary description; 87
EOF,
  See end of file;
errors,
  calculation, how to avoid those due to representation; 13
  detecting in SQL with DBCHECK; 517
  handling, rollbacks as a method for; 205
  trapping; 305
Esc key,
  entering Command mode with; 5
event management,
  concepts and commands for; 286
  detecting key press events with INKEY function; 359
  error trapping using; 305
  summary description; 309
executing,
  procedures; 339
  programs using DO command; 74
execution,
  deferred,
    advantages of, 48
    contrasted with immediate execution, 47
    how to, 49
  immediate,
    contrasted with deferred execution, 47
EXIT command,
  summary description; 253
  terminating loops with; 215
exiting,
  Assist mode; 5
expressions,
  calculations permitted in (table); 58
  definition; 33
  index key use of; 82
  LIST command use of; 33
  restriction on use; 35
  summary description; 43, 88

.F. logical field symbol,
  LIST command use of; 31

F2 function key,
  changing record display between forms view and table view; 22
  returning to Assist mode with; 5
F6 function key,
  highlighting text with; 126
F7 function key,
  moving text with; 126
F8 function key,
  copying text with; 126
F9 function key,
  toggling between screen display and debugger display with; 269
.fdo,
  format file extension; 153
FETCH SQL command,
  handling cursors with; 508
  summary description; 544
FIELD option (DEFINE POPUP command),
  creating item lists with; 298
field types,
  changing from character to date; 11
  floating-point characteristics; 13
  numeric, description of the two kinds; 12
fields,
  as structure component; 6
  creating; 9
  definition; 7
  global,
    lists, creating new, 75
    selection of, 70
  input areas, displaying; 157
  logical, advantages and use; 15
  names,
    LIST command use of, 33
    syntax and use, 9
  numeric,
    handling decimal point in, 14
    summary description; 42
  types, syntax and use; 10
files,
  closing; 36
  copying; 40
  creation and revision date, obtaining; 156
  dBASE SQL, using; 490
  format See format files;
  index,
    purpose, 11
    types of, 79
  listing directory; 41
  opening; 36
  recovering data from; 205
  structure,
    See database structure,
FILES LIKE option (DEFINE POPUP command),
  creating item lists with; 298
FILES option (DEFINE POPUP command),
  creating item lists with; 298

FILL clause (@ at command),
  filling screen areas with; 149
filling,
  screen areas; 149
filters,
  controlling program flow with; 151
  definition and use; 68
  summary description; 89
fixed decimal,
  numbers,
    how different from floating point, 13
  stored as numeric field type, 13
fixed-length,
  fields, implications of; 8
fixed-point numbers,
  See fixed decimal;
floating-point,
  field type, characteristics; 13
  numbers,
    how different from fixed decimal, 13
  stored as floating-point field type, 13
flow of control,
  program, techniques for managing; 150
.fmt,
  format file extension; 156
fonts,
  soft, description; 396
FOR clause,
  selecting records with; 60
  selective command execution with; 67
  summary description; 88
FOR UPDATE OF clause (DECLARE SQL command),
  updating records with; 515
form feeds,
  See Also reports;
  ejecting pages with; 36
  setting page length with; 419
  summary description; 439
format files,
  advantages of display frames over; 221
  building customized screen displays; 155
  creating customized displays with; 154
  creating customized screen displays with; 154
  summary description; 184
  techniques for using; 161
formatting,
  fields,
    logical, 163
    memo, 164
  input areas; 159
  screen displays; 107
    using format files, 154
forms,
  preprinted, printing with; 390

  printing; 382
  view, changing to table view from; 22
FOUND function,
  evaluating searches with; 190
frequency distribution,
  programs, creating; 218
function,
  definition; 63
FUNCTION clause,
  question mark (?) command,
    summary description; 134
FUNCTION clause (? question command),
  purpose; 102
  special symbols (table) and use of; 103
function keys,
  ASCII values; 360
functions,
  summary description; 89

GET clause (@ at command),
  purpose; 139
GROUP BY clause (SELECT SQL command),
  grouping data with; 470
  summary description; 487
grouping,
  data in SQL; 470

HAVING clause (SELECT SQL command),
  summary description; 487
highlighting,
  text; 126
history,
  command, using commands from; 34
housekeeping tasks,
  methods for handling; 30

IF command,
  branching control structure use of; 188
  limiting screen displays with; 238
  summary description; 252
IIF function,
  controlling program flow with; 165
implicit,
  conditions, controlling loop exit conditions with; 213
  exit, setting up; 263
importing,
  See Also entering data;
  data into SQL; 454
IN clause (USE command),
  retrieving data from multiple databases with; 349
IN SQL operator,
  description; 467
  using; 468
indenting,
  commands; 190
index,
  active, selecting; 85

files,
  purpose, 11
  relationship to database files, 78
  types of, 79
order,
  creating descending, 80
  tag as synonym for, 79
tags,
  listing available, 85
  selecting, 84
INDEX clause (USE command),
  opening index files with; 85
INDEX ON command,
  creating indexes with; 80
Index option (CREATE command),
  syntax and use; 11
indexed,
  database, popup menu implications for; 328
indexes,
  adding to programs; 86
  data type mixing in; 83
  multiple, creating; 79
  selecting; 365
  unique,
    creating, 364
    in multiple database applications, 363
indexing,
  records; 78
  summary description; 89
information,
  dumps, listing; 31
initializaing,
  array variables; 246
INKEY function,
  detecting key press events; 359
input areas,
  activating; 145
  creating; 140
  summary description; 184
Ins key,
  status monitoring by scoreboard; 98
inserting,
  special characters in text strings; 108
INTO clause (SELECT SQL command),
  obtaining user input with; 501

labels,
  displaying; 113
  literals used as labels for variables; 113
  printing; 418
language concept,
  summary description; 88
LEN function,
  determining text string length with; 110
  summary description; 135
LIKE SQL operator,
  description; 467
  using; 468

Index I-5

line feeds,
    See Also reports;
    setting page length with; 420
    summary description; 439
linear programming,
    (chapter); 47
    summary description; 87
linking,
    memo files with database files; 16
    multiple databases; 350
links,
    description; 350
LIST command,
    listing database contents with; 31
    summary description; 43
listing,
    database
        contents; 31
        structure; 32
    memo fields; 39
    SQL files; 493
literals,
    definition; 61
    screen display use of; 113
LOCATE command,
    searching for records; 173
    summary description; 184
logical,
    connectives, using for selecting
        records; 66
    data, entering; 19
    expressions,
        comparison operators (table); 60
        selecting groups of records with; 60
        summary description, 89
    fields,
        advantages and use, 15
        formatting, 163
        selecting records with; 61
        summary description, 42
        syntax and use, 10
LOOKUP function,
    searching databases with; 351
loops,
    automatic, summary description; 253
    exit conditions; 213
    processing arrays with; 248
    program control, concepts and
        methods; 194
    summary description; 252
LTRIM function,
    trimming blank spaces with; 157
LUPDATE function,
    meaning; 156
mathematical,
    operations in SQL (table); 464
MAX function,
    CALCULATE command use of; 118
    SQL; 464
.mdx,
    multiple index file extension; 11, 79
MEMLINES function,
    testing for memo text existance with;
        164

memo,
    data, entering; 20
    fields,
        dBASE IV differences from dBASE
            III, 16
        entering data into, 15
        formatting, 164
        listing, 39
        storage characteristics, 15
        summary description, 42
        syntax and use, 10
        viewing, 164
    files,
        how linked with database file, 15
    width,
        controlling memo field width
            with, 40
memory,
    free; 156
    variables,
        characteristics and use, 94
        listing, 95
        using as accumulators, 234
        using as array variables, 245
MEMORY function,
    meaning; 156
menu bars,
    creating; 334
    description; 333
    multiple database applications for;
        340
    summary description; 372
menus,
    advantages; 257
    creating (chapter); 257
    popup,
        adding informational text to, 290
        adding messages to, 292
        creating, 281
        indexed database implications of,
            328
        item list creation for, 298
        summary description, 307
    standard,
        creating, 258
        summary description, 307
    summary description; 306
    that run menus, creating; 265
MIN function,
    CALCULATE command use of; 118
    SQL; 464
modes of operation,
    dBASE IV; 4
MODIFY COMMAND command,
    summary description; 88
    writing programs with; 51
modular,
    programs, principles of creating; 72
MONTH function,
    purpose; 63
moving,
    See Also copying;
    record end; 22
    text; 126

MS-DOS commands,
    accessing from dBASE IV; 409
.ndx,
    index file extension; 11
    single index file extension; 79
nesting,
    queries summary description; 487
.NOT.,
    negation connective, testing for false
        values with; 61
NPV function,
    CALCULATE command use of; 119
Num Lock key,
    status monitoring by scoreboard; 98
numbers,
    converting into strings; 157
    difference between fixed decimal and
        floating point; 13
    representation of, impact on
        calculation accuracy; 13
numeric,
    data, entering; 19
    field types, description of the two
        kinds; 12
    fields,
        handing decimal point in, 14
        syntax and use, 10
    variables, length of; 97

object orientation,
    vs procedure orientation, as a
        difference between SQL and
        dBASE IV; 444
ON ERROR command,
    error trapping with; 305
    summary description; 309
ON SELECTION PAD,
    creating menu bars with; 336
ON SELECTION POPUP command,
    event management with; 287
one-to-many relationships,
    handling; 314
    programming; 363
OPEN SQL command,
    handling cursors with; 508
    summary description; 544
opening,
    files; 36
.OR.,
    logical connective, using for selecting
        records; 67
ORDER BY clause (SELECT SQL
    command),
    sequencing output in SQL with; 476
    summary description; 487
OTHERWISE command,
    handling CASE structures with; 232
    summary description; 252

PACK command,
    deleting records with; 29
pads,
    description of menu bar; 336

I-6   ■   Index

highlighting; 337
_padvance system variable,
  summary description; 439
pages,
  See Also reports;
  definition; 369
  displaying multiple; 167
  setting length of; 419
paging,
  reports; 395
  screen displays; 369
pausing,
  programs; 145
PCOL function,
  obtaining current printer column with; 381
PgDn key,
  appending records with; 23
PICTURE clause (@ at command),
  formatting input areas with; 159
PICTURE clause (? question command),
  purpose; 102
  special symbols (table) and use of; 104
  summary description; 134
_plength system variable,
  summary description; 439
+ (plus) symbol,
  concatenation operator, linking character fields with; 82
popup,
  menus See menus, popup;
  prompt
    field summary description; 309, 372
    files summary description; 309
POPUP function,
  creating popup menus with; 283
  summary description; 308
positioning,
  cursor; 145
(pound) character,
  "not equal to" sign; 212
.prg,
  procedure file extension; 334
  program file extension; 51
printers,
  accessing, summary description; 438
  codes, controlling with STYLE clause (? question command); 106
  default print size; 388
  drivers for,
    characteristics of, 386
    summary description, 439
  selecting; 385
  turning on; 378
printing,
  column reports; 391
  data and database structures; 35
  forms; 382
  reports,
    with page headers and footers, 395
    with subtotals, 405

with totals, 401
reports (chapter); 377
using @/SAY for; 381
with ? command; 384
with @/SAY command; 387
PRIVATE command,
  setting up private variables with; 279
PROCEDURE command,
  creating procedures with; 338
procedure orientation,
  vs object orientation, as a difference between SQL and dBASE IV; 444
procedures,
  creating; 338
  description; 334
  executing; 339
  running; 348
  summary description; 372
program,
  defaults, selecting; 152
PROGRAM function,
  breakpoint handling with; 274
Program mode,
  characteristics of; 5
programming,
  interactive (chapter); 138
  language definition; 2
  modular; 72
  multiple databases; 326
  SQL; 489
  with multiple databases; 356
programs,
  adding indexes to; 86
  calculation; 143
  compiling, how different in dBASE IV; 53
  control structures; 150
    DO CASE, 229
    IFF function, 165
    IIF function, 167
    interactive, 138
    linear, 50
    loops and branches (chapter), 187
    techniques for managing, 150
  creating SQL; 498
  debugging; 268
  documenting, indenting conventions for; 190
  editing; 125
  executing using DO command; 74
  frequency distribution; 218
  interactive,
    contrasted with linear programs, 92
    structure of, 147
    with an SQL database, 498
  pausing; 145
  sections of, summary description; 134
  SQL, restrictions and conventions; 495
  statistical; 117
  structure (diagram); 50

terminating with RETURN command; 52
validity checking of; 153
version number; 156
PROMPT FIELD option (DEFINE POPUP command),
  creating menu bars with; 302
PROMPT function,
  creating popup menus with; 283
  summary description; 308
PROW function,
  obtaining current printer line number with; 381
.prs,
  SQL file extension; 447

queries,
  See selecting;
  multiple database summary description; 487
? (question) command,
  @ (at) command differences with; 139
  clauses; 102
  examples of program use; 100
  outputing to the screen with; 94
  printing with; 384
  summary description; 134
?? (question double) command,
  how printing differs from ? command; 384
  summary description; 135

RANGE clause (@ at command),
  establishing numeric entry limits with; 144
ranges,
  establishing limits for numeric entries; 144
  numeric, SQL use of; 467
READ command,
  activating input areas with; 145
  summary description; 184
RECALL command,
  removing deletion mark from records with; 29
RECCOUNT function,
  counting records with; 29
  meaning; 156
RECNO function,
  cautions on use with indexed databases; 392
  meaning; 156
record pointers,
  definition and use; 37
  linking; 350
  moving with the SKIP command; 222
  multiple databases, independence of; 322
  summary description; 43
records,
  adding to a database; 201
  appending,
    in append mode, 23

Index ■ I-7

records, appending *(continued)*
   with APPEND BLANK command, 202
  as structure component; 6
  blank, how to check for; 23
  counting; 28
  current record number; 156
  definition; 7
  deleting; 29
  indexing; 78
  moving to end in table display; 22
  searching,
    random access, 177
    sequential, 170
  selecting,
    using date fields for, 62
    using logical expressions for, 60
    using logical fields for, 61
    using multiple criteria for, 66
    with FOR clause, 60
  sequencing,
    methods for, 78
  summary description; 42
  total records in database; 156
recovery,
  file, rollbacks as a method for; 205
REINDEX command,
  random access searching with; 177
  summary description; 184
relational databases,
  handling (chapter); 314
relations,
  creating; 354
  description of; 353
relative addressing,
  printing with; 390
RELEASE POPUP command,
  creating popup menus with; 283
  summary description; 308
removing,
  See Also deleting;
  trailing blanks; 176
reopening,
  SQL databases; 485
REPLACE command,
  replacing data with; 35
  rollback operations handling with; 206
  searching and replacing text with; 128
replacing,
  data; 35
  text, searching and; 128
REPLICATE function,
  summary description; 135
reports,
  See Also pages;
  block format, printing; 418
  column,
    printing, 391
    summary description, 440
  form feeds, setting page length with; 423
  forms summary description; 440

label summary description; 440
line feeds, setting page length with; 423
multiple database, printing; 429
multiple database, summary description; 440
printing (chapter); 377
SQL; 527
  creating, 528
  creating multi-table, 535
subtotals,
  printing, 405
  summary description, 440
totals, printing; 401
with page headers and footers, printing; 395
retrieving,
  See Also selecting,
    searching;
  data from multiple databases; 349
RETURN command,
  terminating programs with; 52
returning to,
  Assist mode; 5
ROLLBACK command,
  rollback operations handling with; 206
  summary description; 253
rollback operations,
  handling; 205
rounding problems,
  avoiding; 13
ROW function,
  obtaining current cursor line number with; 231
RUN command,
  accessing MS-DOS commands with; 409
running,
  procedures; 348

SAVE TO TEMP clause (SELECT SQL command),
  summary description; 544
saving,
  database structure; 17
  text,
    commands for; 53
@/SAY,
  printing with; 387
SAY clause (@ at command),
  purpose of @/SAY; 139
SCAN command,
  controlling a scanning loop with; 225
  differences with the DO WHILE command; 227
  summary description; 253
scanning,
  databases; 219
scope,
  summary description; 89
  command,
    definition and use; 58

types of (table); 59
scoreboard,
  screen display environment; 98
screen displays,
  centering text on; 109
  clearing; 30
    areas of, 149, 343
    lines on, 329
  customized,
    creating, 154
  date and time stamps on; 112
  enhancing appearance of; 148
  filling areas of; 149
  horizontal location control; 105, 192
  how different from printed reports; 377
  input area creation; 140
  limiting, using IF for; 238
  multiple, creating; 167
  paging; 369
  programming (chapter); 92
  structured,
    creating fully, 138
    setting up, 107
  structured compared with unstructured; 93
  suppressing information display on; 383
  unstructured, program characteristics; 97
  vertical location control; 139, 192
searches,
  evaluating with FOUND function; 190
searching,
  databases, using LOOKUP for; 351
  for records; 170
  records, random access; 177
  replacing text and; 128
SEEK command,
  random access searching with; 177
  summary description; 184
SELECT command,
  multiple database handling with; 319
  summary description; 372
SELECT SQL command,
  clauses for; 465
  selecting information with; 462
selecting,
  active index; 85
  fields globally; 70
  index tags; 84
  information with SQL; 462
  information with SQL SELECT command; 467
  program defaults; 152
  records,
    using date fields for, 62
    using logical expressions for, 60
    using logical fields for, 61
    using multiple criteria for, 66
    with FOR clause, 60

; (semicolon) character,
  long command line breaking with; 120
  SQL use different from dBASE IV; 448
sequencing,
  output in SQL; 476
  records; 78
SET CONSOLE OFF,
  suppressing information display with; 383
SET FIELDS TO command,
  globally selecting fields with; 71
SET FILTER TO command,
  creating filters with; 68
SET INDEX TO command,
  creating index files with; 78
  opening index files with; 85
SET MEMOWIDTH TO command,
  changing memo text line size with; 164
  setting memo field width with; 40
SET ORDER TO command,
  selecting active index with; 85
SET ORDER TO TAG command,
  selecting indexes with; 365
SET PRINT ON command,
  turning the printer on with; 379
SET RELATION command,
  creating a link with; 350
SET RELATION TO command,
  creating relations with; 354
SET SAFETY command,
  batch processing with; 210
SET SQL ON command,
  starting an SQL session with; 447
SET verb,
  environmental commands use of, summary description; 87
shared computing,
  SQL appropriate for; 442
SHOW POPUP command,
  creating popup menus with; 282
  summary description; 308
SKIP command,
  moving the record pointer with; 222
  summary description; 253
sorting,
  See Also indexing;
  records compared with indexing; 78
SPACE function,
  creating strings of blanks with; 110
  summary description; 135
SQL,
  as a set of conventions; 491
  codes, testing operation results with; 521
  command syntax; 450
  concepts and commands (chapter); 442
  creating a database; 448
  cursors summary description; 543
  data entry summary description; 486

databases,
  how different from dBASE IV databases, 444
  summary description, 485
editing rows; 513
ending a session; 485
functions, summary description; 487
how dBASE SQL works; 489
loading dBASE IV files into; 456, 460
loading information into a table; 454
objects, summary description; 486
operations, dBASE IV differences; 463
procedures; 543
programs, summary description; 543
reopening databases; 485
selection, summary description; 486
starting a session; 447
summary description; 485
system files listed in Systabls file; 493
tables, summary description; 486
why use it,
  at all; 445
  with dBASE IV, 446
SQLCODE system variable,
  testing SQL operation results with; 521
START DATABASE command,
  reopening an SQL database with; 485
statisical,
  programs; 117
status bar,
  counting records with; 28
  screen display environment; 98
STD function,
  CALCULATE command use of; 119
STORE command,
  assigning values to more than one variable with; 144
  initializing array variables with; 246
STR function,
  converting numbers into strings; 157
strategy concept,
  summary description; 88
strings,
  See Also text;
  converting numbers into; 157
  handling, using $ operator for; 64
  trimming blank spaces in; 157
structure,
  database, See database structure;
STRUCTURE option (DEFINE POPUP command),
  creating item lists with; 298
Structured Query Language,
  See SQL;
STYLE clause (? question command),
  controling device-dependent effects with; 105
  parameters (table); 106
STYLE clause (? question command),
  purpose; 103

STYLE clause (? question command),
  summary description; 134
subqueries,
  use in SQL queries; 483
subroutines,
  concepts and use; 76
SUBSTR function,
  extracting substrings with; 351
SUM command,
  using in statistical programs; 117
SUM function,
  CALCULATE command use of; 119
  SQL; 464
  summary description; 135
system,
  functions that access the value of system variables (table); 156
  variables, obtaining the value of; 156
.T. logical field symbol,
  LIST command use of; 31
tables,
  SQL,
    equivalent to dBASE IV database, 449
    temporary, reasons for using, 505
  structure, dBASE IV characteristics and implications; 7
  view,
    changing from forms view to, 22
    displaying records with, 22
tabs,
  affect of auto-indent on; 191
tag,
  index order synonym; 79
talk,
  screen display environment; 98
terminating,
  commands in Command mode; 5
  programs with RETURN command; 52
testing,
  false values with .NOT.; 61
  programs using validity checks; 153
  search results with FOUND function; 190
text,
  centering on screen displays; 109
  converting to upper case; 104
  copying blocks of; 126
  editor; 20
    features summary description, 135
    role in deferring execution, 49
  extracting substrings, using SUBSTR for; 351
  highlighting; 126
  literal, See literals;
  moving; 126
  saving; 53
  searching and replacing; 128
strings,
  determining the length of, 110
  inserting special characters in, 108

Index ■ I-9

time,
    displaying the current; 112
TIME function,
    obtaining the current time with; 112
    summary description; 135
TO clause (@ at command),
    drawing boxes with; 148
    summary description; 184
TO PRINT (LIST command option),
    printing data with; 35
    summary description; 43
TRANSACTION command,
    summary description; 253
transactions,
    handling; 205
TRANSFORM function,
    converting numeric in character values with; 114
TRIM function,
    removing trailing blanks with; 176

undeleting,
    file changes; 205
    records using RECALL command; 29
UNIQUE clause (INDEX command),
    creating unique indexes with; 364
UPDATE SQL command,
    same as dBASE IV REPLACE command; 473
updating,
    See changing;
UPPER function,
    case sensitivity handling with; 65

USE command,
    opening database files with; 37
    summary description; 43
VALID clause (@ at command GET),
    checking program validity with; 153
validity,
    checking of programs; 153
values,
    displaying in the debugger; 270
VAR function,
    CALCULATE command use of; 119
variables,
    assigning values to more than one; 144
    character, length of; 97
    combining with literals in screen displays; 113
    date,
        creating, 95
        length of; 97
    decimal, length of; 97
    global See variables, public;
    initializing, summary description; 184
    local See variables, private;
    memory; 94
    numeric, length of; 97
    private,
        creating, 278
        summary description, 307
    public,
        compared with private, 278
        summary description, 307
    shared See variables, public;
    SQL system, summary description; 544
    system, summary description; 439
verb,
    command component; 57
VERSION function,
    meaning; 156

WAIT command,
    pausing a program with; 145
WHERE clause (SELECT SQL command),
    summary description; 486
    using; 466
WHERE CURRENT OF clause (DECLARE SQL command),
    updating records with; 515
width,
    field, syntax and use; 10
wildcards,
    use in SQL; 467
work areas,
    summary description; 372

YEAR function,
    purpose; 63

ZAP command,
    deleting all records with; 457